SIMON & SCHUSTER
HANDBOOK
FOR WRITERS

Fourth Canadian Edition

D0014686

SIMON & SCHUSTER
HANDBOOK
FOR WRITERS

Fourth Canadian Edition

LYNN QUITMAN TROYKA
DOUGLAS HESSE

With the assistance of Cy Strom

Toronto

Library and Archives Canada Cataloguing in Publication

Troyka, Lynn Quitman, 1938–
   Simon & Schuster handbook for writers / Lynn Quitman Troyka, Douglas Hesse; with the assistance of Cy Strom.—4th Canadian ed.

Includes index.
ISBN 0-13-127255-1

1. English language—Rhetoric—Handbooks, manuals, etc. 2. English language—Grammar—Handbooks, manuals, etc.
I. Hesse, Douglas II. Strom, Cy, 1954– III. Title. IV. Title: Simon and Schuster handbook for writers.

PE1408.T76 2006   808'.042   C2004-904293-9

Copyright © 2006, 2002, 1999, 1996 by Lynn Quitman Troyka. Published by Pearson Education Canada, a division of Pearson Canada Inc., Toronto, Ontario

Original edition published by Pearson Education Inc., Upper Saddle River, New Jersey 07458, USA. Copyright © 2005 by Lynn Quitman Troyka.
This edition is authorized for sale in Canada only.

Pearson Prentice Hall. All Rights Reserved. This publication is protected by copyright, and permission should be obtained from the publisher prior to any prohibited reproduction, storage in a retrieval system, or transmission in any form or by any means, electronic, mechanical, photocopying, recording, or likewise. For information regarding permission, write to the Permissions Department.

For permission to use copyrighted material, grateful acknowledgment is made to the copyright holders on pages xv–xx, which are considered an extension of this copyright page.

ISBN 0-13-127255-1

Vice President, Editorial Director: Michael J. Young
Acquisitions Editor: Patty Riediger
Sponsoring Editor: Carolin Sweig
Marketing Manager: Toivo Pajo
Supervising Developmental Editor: Suzanne Schaan
Production Editor: Avivah Wargon
Copy Editor: Cy Strom
Proofreaders: Stephanie Fysh, Lesley Mann
Senior Production Coordinator: Peggy Brown
Permissions Research: Amanda McCormick
Art Direction: Julia Hall
Cover Design: Gillian Tsintziras
Cover Image: *Wheat Field with a Lark* by Vincent Van Gogh,
   Van Gogh Museum, Amsterdam/Superstock
Page Layout: Jansom

3 4 5   10 09 08 07 06

Printed and bound in Canada.

Personal message to students from Lynn Troyka and Doug Hesse

As writers, many of you have much in common with both of us. Sure, we've been at it longer, so we've had more practice, and most rules have become cemented in our heads. However, you share a common bond with us: our experiences during writing. All of us want to put ideas into words worthy of someone else's reading time.

When we write, we're often unsure of how to begin. Lynn likes to start in the middle and then work ahead and back. Doug likes to make long lists of ideas and then throw most of them away. Sometimes, we're stuck for examples sufficiently effective to get our points across, and we jump-start our ideas by talking with friends, either in person or by e-mail. Frequently, the precise expression we're looking for eludes us as we rummage through the clutter of words in our minds.

We offer this book to you as our partners in the process of writing, hoping that its pages suggest strategies that enhance your ability to give voice to your thoughts. You're always welcome to write us at LQTBook@aol.com to share your reactions to this book and your experiences as writers. We promise to answer.

Each of us would like to end this message with a personal story.

From Doug: I first glimpsed the power of writing in high school, when I wrote sappy—but apparently successful—love poems. Still, when I went to college, I was surprised to discover all I didn't know about writing, especially for college courses. Fortunately, I had good teachers and developed lots of patience. I needed it. I continue to learn, including from Lynn, who graciously invited me to join her in writing this edition of her handbook.

From Lynn: When I was an undergraduate, writing handbooks weren't around. Questions about writing nagged at me. One day, browsing in the library, I found an incorrectly shelved, dust-covered book whose title included the words *handbook* and *writing*. I read it hungrily and kept checking it out from the library. Back then, I could never have imagined that someday I might write such a book myself. Now that I've completed the *Simon & Schuster Handbook for Writers*, Seventh Edition, I'm amazed that I ever had the nerve to begin. This proves to me— and I hope to you—that anyone can write. Students don't always believe that. I hope you will.

With cordial regards,

Lynn Quitman Troyka   Doug Hesse

Preface

Welcome to the fourth Canadian edition of the *Simon & Schuster Handbook for Writers*, a book whose U.S. counterpart is now in its seventh edition. I have written this handbook to fulfil three purposes: to serve students as a classroom text, as a self-instruction manual, and as a reference book. My greatest wish is for students to succeed and achieve their potential in writing for academic, personal, workplace, and public audiences. I hope that my pages in this book reflect my conviction that students are empowered by knowledge and that they deserve their instructors' unwavering respect as emerging academic writers.

The *Simon & Schuster Handbook for Writers* gives students comprehensive information about processes for writing college- and university-level essays, source-based arguments, and research papers; thinking and reading critically; using documentation style correctly; designing documents; writing for the Web; writing about literature; writing for business; taking essay tests; and using grammar, punctuation, and mechanics correctly.

As in prior editions, I consciously include people of diverse backgrounds. You'll find no stereotyping of race, ethnicity, gender, or religion here. My language is gender neutral: *man* or *he* is never used generically to stand for the human race. In examples, I draw equally from male and female writers, both students and professionals, and from a variety of cultures.

With this edition, I'm honoured to welcome my new writing associate, with whom I share a high esteem for students and a research-based orientation to the teaching of writing: Doug Hesse, Director of the Center for the Advancement of Teaching (CAT) and Professor of English at Illinois State University. Many of you know his excellent scholarship as well as his major leadership roles in our profession. Doug has served as president of the Council of Writing Program Administrators and, when this handbook is published, he will be the new Chair of the Conference on College Composition and Communication (CCCC). He brings extraordinary expertise to the present edition's assumptions that most students today use computers, that research sources reside online as well as in libraries, and that the research process has become more complex and more exciting than ever. Together, we look forward to many years of cordial collaboration.

As the following material shows, this new edition of the *Simon & Schuster Handbook for Writers* includes extensive updates while retaining the core features of the best-selling earlier editions.

Lynn Quitman Troyka

NEW FEATURES OF THE FOURTH CANADIAN EDITION

- Writing Research (Part V) has been expanded to seven chapters. The process of online research, with a focus on its special possibilities and challenges, has been integrated thoroughly into every chapter. The updated and reorganized chapters cover research writing, finding and evaluating sources, and using sources well to avoid plagiarism, including a specific discussion of plagiarism and the Internet.

- A new separate chapter on MLA-style documentation (Chapter 34), based on the sixth edition of the *MLA Handbook* (2003), provides expanded coverage of online and electronic sources coupled with an updated student MLA sample paper.

- A new separate chapter on APA-style documentation (Chapter 35), based on the fifth edition of the APA *Publication Manual* (2001), gives expanded coverage of online and electronic sources and an updated student APA sample paper.

- A new chapter on document design in print and Web media (Chapter 37), covers page layout and incorporating visuals, and includes information on writing for the Web and maintaining a Web site.

- A new chapter on oral presentations (Chapter 43), outlines the steps for writing and delivering effective presentations.

- Expanded guidelines on public writing, in and outside of the formal business environment, include letters, reports, proposals, and e-mail messages, as well as an introduction to the targeted résumé (Chapter 41).

- The chapter on writing paragraphs (Chapter 4) has been revised to reflect the natural progression followed in composing, from introductory paragraph to body paragraphs to concluding paragraph.

- The revised chapter on pronouns (Chapter 9) incorporates the discussions of pronoun case and pronoun reference into one chapter.

- The chapters on sentence fragments (Chapter 12) and on comma splices and run-on sentences (Chapter 13) have been revised, with an emphasis on the questions that students ask themselves about these topics. (This edition replaces the term *run-together sentences,* used in earlier editions, with the commonly used expression *run-on sentences.*)

- Two separate chapters, "Misplaced and Dangling Modifiers" and "Shifting and Mixed Sentences" (Chapters 14 and 15), divide the contents of former Chapter 15 to adjust the pace for covering these concepts.

- The chapter on writing in the social and natural sciences (Chapter 40) now includes a sample student report.

- The Usage Glossary has been moved from the end of the book to its own chapter (Chapter 20). This positions the glossary near related material on language and provides a more logical reference point for students.
- Main headings in each chapter are worded as FAQs (frequently asked questions), informed by research into how students phrase questions to themselves.
- Additional ESL Notes and Alerts throughout the text assist students for whom English is a second language and highlight interactions between grammatical and rhetorical issues.
- Over 20 percent of the exercise content is new for this edition, with many exercises featuring options for both individual and collaborative work.

RAPID LOCATOR GUIDE

The Overview of Contents, which begins inside the front cover, gives you a brief list of contents. To find a more specific subtopic, use the Index.

This handbook has seven parts, each divided into chapters and then sections. On each part's opening page, you'll find a detailed list of chapters. Within chapters, sections contain uncomplicated discussions in small "chunks" of information. Each chunk carries a chapter number plus a letter in alphabetical order within the chapter. I encourage you to personalize your book by placing a sticky note, with a useful label on both sides, to overhang each page that you consult frequently.

Rapid locator for every page's information

The title of each section in every chapter resembles an FAQ (frequently asked question) to match the questions you might ask as you consult the *Simon & Schuster Handbook for Writers*. Look for the same question at the top of each right-hand page, so that you can flip through a chapter to find what you're looking for.

Rapid locator for documentation styles

On the front of the opening page for Part Five, you'll see where to find each documentation style—MLA, APA, CM, CSE, COS.

Rapid locator for special elements throughout

Each numbered box in this handbook provides a thumbnail sketch of key information. An icon in each box carries a message: ⊚ means the box is a summary; ▥ says the box shows a pattern; and ☑ tells that the box is a checklist. Alerts ☜ announce special information about the current topic and reference additional information elsewhere in the handbook. Notes for students for whom English isn't a first language are indicated by ⊕. Also, SMALL CAPITAL LETTERS signal that a term is defined in the Terms Glossary, located immediately before the Index at the back of this handbook. This feature allows you to concentrate on the material you're reading, with the assurance that a definition you might need is always at hand.

Rapid locator for grammar help

In Parts Two through Four, whether English is your native language or you're bilingual or multilingual, you'll find quick answers to your questions about Standard Canadian English grammar, sentence correctness, and style and punctuation. Part Seven addresses questions of special concern to multilingual students.

SUPPLEMENTS FOR THE FOURTH CANADIAN EDITION

Pearson Education Canada offers a wider choice of student supplements and instructor supplements to help faculty augment and customize their courses.

For Students

Simon & Schuster Workbook for Writers, Fourth Canadian Edition (0-13-127254-3)—This workbook contains hundreds of additional exercises and activities to help improve writing skills.

Companion Website—Visit the Troyka site at <www.pearsoned.ca/troyka> to access lots of great resources, including an e-book version of the entire text, a diagnostic test, extra exercises, and research help. The Access Code Card is included with every new copy of the *Simon & Schuster Handbook for Writers*, Fourth Canadian Edition.

Understanding Plagiarism—Hailed by instructors as the best information available on understanding and avoiding plagiarism, this self-paced tutorial teaches students how to avoid committing plagiarism and how to properly quote, summarize, paraphrase, cite, and attribute information. Access the tutorial at <www.prenhall.com/understanding>.

For Instructors

Instructor's Manual—This supplement offers many resources to new and experienced instructors in the composition classroom. This manual is offered on the Instructor's Resource CD-ROM and can also be downloaded by instructors from a password-protected section of Pearson Education Canada's online catalogue at <http://vig.pearsoned.ca>.

Diagnostic and Competency Tests—Offered in TestGen software, these tests can be used to assess students' strengths and weaknesses or to provide additional practice exercises. This supplement is offered on the Instructor's Resource CD-ROM and can also be downloaded by instructors from a password-protected section of Pearson Education Canada's online catalogue at <http://vig.pearsoned.ca>.

Instructor's Resource CD-ROM (0-13-196738-X)—This CD includes both the Instructor's Manual and the Diagnostic Tests listed above.

ACKNOWLEDGMENTS

Students, past and present, have inspired me to compose this *Simon & Schuster Handbook for Writers*. Thank you for being my audience. I hope my discussions and explanations help you excel as writers. Thank you, also, for granting me official permission to publish your fine writing and for speaking with me through e-mail or in person about your experiences with, and suggestions for, my handbooks. Please feel welcome to e-mail me directly at LQTBook@aol.com. I always answer personally.

Doug Hesse, Director of the Center for the Advancement of Teaching (CAT) and Professor of English at Illinois State University, becomes with this edition my new collaborator and writing colleague. His vast experience as writer, teacher, and leader in our profession has greatly enriched my pages and my enjoyment of the creative process. Doug warmly seconds all the thanks I extend here to students, contributors, and reviewers.

Other outstanding colleagues have contributed significantly to this *Simon & Schuster Handbook for Writers*. Esther DiMarzio of Kishwaukee College served indispensably as overall consultant. Carolyn Calhoun-Dillahunt, Director of the Writing Center and Professor of English at Yakima Valley Community College, lent her extraordinary talent to the chapter on argument and Kip Strasma, Professor of English at Illinois Central College, enhanced the chapter on Web-based writing. Cy Strom of Colborne Communications in Toronto, Ontario, continues his critically important role as adapter of my Canadian editions and adviser to my overall work on handbooks.

Many thanks are due to all those instructors who have provided valuable comments over the various editions of this book, including the reviewers of the fourth Canadian edition: Tim Acton, Capilano College; Kathy Cocchio, Northern Alberta Institute of Technology; Arlene Davies-Fuhr, Grant MacEwan College; Karen Inglis, Kwantlen University College; Kathleen Wall, University of Regina; and Jeanie Warnock, University of Ottawa. In addition to her astute review comments, Kathy Cocchio provided detailed material on targeted résumés, which is provided in full on the Companion Website and summarized in Chapter 41 of the text.

At Prentice Hall, a highly professional team facilitated Doug's and my work on the latest U.S. edition of the *Simon & Schuster Handbook for Writers*. For the Canadian edition, Cy Strom was supported by Carolin Sweig (Sponsoring Editor), Suzanne Schaan (Supervising Developmental Editor), Avivah Wargon (Supervising Production Editor), and Peggy Brown (Senior Production Coordinator).

Doug Hesse appreciates the support of Lori Ostergaard and Beth Welch in completing this project; the professional friendships of Kathi Yancey, Jeanne Gunner, Chris Anson, and John Lovas, among many others; and the continued vitality of his students at Illinois State University. He further states, "My children, Monica, Andrew, and Paige, amaze me with their creativity, as does the very best writer I know: Becky Bradway, my wife. Finally, I value the extraordinary trust Lynn showed by inviting me to join in her amazing work. She's a generous teacher."

Lynn Quitman Troyka thanks family and friends who nourish her spirit as a writer and participant in the larger world. She says, "For ten superb years, Ida Morea, my Administrative Assistant and dear friend, has kept me organized and sane with her warmth, outstanding talents, and incredible patience. Doug Hesse, my new handbook partner, made our collaboration stimulating and grand fun. Kristen Black, beloved child of my heart if not of my womb, along with her wonderful family, Dan, Lindsey, and Ryan, sustains me with her indomitable spirit, vision, and brilliance. My treasured companions in life's journey include Susan Bartlestone; Florence Bolden; Carol Carter; Rita and Hy Cohen; Elaine Gilden Dushoff; Alan, Lynne, Adam, and Joshua Furman; Elliott Goldhush; Warren Herendeen; Edith Klausner, my sister, a true friend who generously bestows her wisdom, experience, and calming presence upon my life; my niece, Randi Klausner Friedman, and nephews Michael and Steven Klausner along with their marvelous children; Jo Ann Lavery, my much-loved 'sister' and buddy through thick and thin, and her husband, Tom Lavery; Cynthia Lester, my amazing spiritual inspiration and newest 'sister'; Edie and Alan Lipp; Brenda and John Lovas; Lois Powers; Betty Renshaw; Magdalena Rogalskaja; Avery Ryan, my cherished 'niece' and great friend, along with her delightful Jimmy,

Gavin, and Ian Ryan; Shirley and Don Stearns; Ernest Sternglass and his wife, the late Marilyn Sternglass, one of my most treasured friends, generous mentors, and admired scholars; Joseph Wayne Thweatt; Douglas and Anna Young; Lisa Wallace, my other cherished 'niece' and prized friend, along with her delightful husband, Nathaniel Wallace; Muriel Wolfe; and Tzila Zwas. I'm grateful for the support of my long-standing mentors and pals at Prentice Hall, J. Phillip Miller, Publisher of Modern Languages, and Bud Therien, Publisher for Art. Above all, I thank David Troyka, my beloved husband, discerning reader, and the love of my life."

Credits

James L. Kinneavy, adapted from *Theory of Discourse.* New York: W. W. Norton & Company, 1971. Reprinted by permission of The Center for American History. (Page 4)

Daniel Casey, student. (Page 4)

Carol Grant Gould, "Out of the Mouths of Beasts" from *Science* 83 (April), p. 69. (Page 5)

Sheila Tobias, *Overcoming Math Anxiety.* New York: W. W. Norton & Company, 1978. (Page 6)

Joseph D'Agnese, "Brothers with Heart" from *Discover* 22, no. 7 (July 2001). Copyright © The Walt Disney Company. (Pages 6–7, Exercise 1-1A)

T. Berry Brazelton, "Issues for Working Parents" from *American Journal of Orthopsychiatry* 56, pp. 14–25. Used with permission. (Page 7, Exercise 1-1B)

Sharon Butala, excerpt from "Rural Saskatchewan: Creating the Garden," from *Voices: Essays on Canadian Families,* edited by Marian Lynn. Toronto: Nelson Canada. © 1995 Sharon Butala. With permission of the author. (Page 7, Exercise 1-1C)

Microsoft Word for Windows Screen. Copyright © Microsoft Corporation. All rights reserved. (Page 18)

FirstSearch Web Screen. Used with permission of OCLC. FirstSearch and World Cat are registered trademarks of OCLC Online Computer Library Center, Inc.; the screen capture is copyrighted by OCLC and/or its third-party database providers. (Page 20)

Google screen shots reproduced with permission of Google.com. (Pages 37 and 38)

Carol Moreno, student. (Pages 63–74)

Daniel Goleman, "Researchers Trace Empathy's Roots to Infancy" from *Working with Emotional Intelligence.* New York: Bantam Books, 1998. (Pages 76–77)

Tara Foster, student. (Page 77)

Gerald Secor Couzens, "If Lightning Strikes" from *House Calls/How Doctors Treat Themselves and Their Own Families for Common Illnesses and Injuries: The Most Effective At-Home Remedies for Everything.* New York: Simon & Schuster, 1993. (Page 77)

Jane Goldman, "What's Bugging You?" (Page 78)

Witold Rybczynski, excerpt from *Home*. Copyright © Witold Rbyczynski. (Pages 79–80)

George Woodcock, excerpt from "The Tyranny of the Clock" from *The Rejection of Politics and Other Essays on Canada, Canadians, Anarchism and the World*. Copyright © 1972. (Page 80).

Bradley Howard, student. (Pages 80–81)

Harry Bruce, excerpt from "The Softball Was Always Hard," © Harry Bruce. Reprinted by arrangement with Bella Pomer Agency. (Page 81)

Dan Cody, "Puppet Poetry." (Page 81)

Frank T. Rhodes, "Let the Student Decide." (Page 82, Exercise 4-2A)

Wendy Thomas, excerpt from *Getting Started on a Great Canadian Garden*, by Wendy Thomas. Copyright © 2001 Bookmark Publishing Group. Reprinted with permission of Colborne Communications. (Page 82, Exercise 4-2B)

Mark Kingwell, "The Intellectual Possibilities of Television," excerpt from *Marginalia: A Cultural Reader*, by Mark Kingwell. Toronto: Penguin Canada, 1999. Copyright © 1999 Mark Kingwell. With permission of the author. (Page 82, Exercise 4-2C)

Terry Bullick, excerpt from "When Is a Grizzly Not a Grizzly?" *Equinox*, December 1993. (Page 83)

Michael Clugston, "Twice Struck." Oxford University Press Southern Africa. (Page 84)

Geoff Pevere and Greig Dymond, excerpt from *Mondo Canuck*. Toronto: Prentice Hall Canada, 1996. By permission of Prentice Hall Canada. (Page 86)

Roger Rosenblatt, "What Brand of Laughter Do You Use?" from *The New York Times* (November 17, 1991), p. 86. (Page 86)

Carol Carter and Lynn Quitman Troyka, *Majoring in the Rest of Your Life*. Englewood Cliffs, NJ: Prentice Hall, 1999. (Page 87)

Margaret Mead and Rhoda Metraux, "New Superstitions for Old." (Page 87)

Richard Gwyn, excerpt from *The 49ᵗʰ Paradox* by Richard Gwyn. Used by permission of McClelland & Stewart Ltd., *The Canadian Publishers*.

Claire Burke, student. (Page 88, Exercise 4-4A)

Randolph H. Manning, "Fighting Racism with Inclusion." (Page 88, Exercise 4-4B)

Robert Harris, excerpt from *What to Listen for in Mozart*. © Simon & Schuster. (Page 89)

Allan Moult, "Volcanic Peaks, Tropical Rainforest, and Mangrove Swamps" adapted from *Australia the Beautiful: Wilderness*. Australia in Print, 1998. (Page 90)

William Least Heat-Moon, excerpt from *Blue Highway: A Journey into America*. Little, Brown and Company, 1982. (Page 91)

Wayne Grady, excerpt from *Chasing the Chinook* by Wayne Grady. Copyright © Wayne Grady 1998. Reprinted by permission of Penguin Group (Canada), A division of Pearson Penguin Canada, Inc. (Page 91)

Danny Witt, student. (Pages 91–92)

Arthur Andrew, excerpt from *The Rise and Fall of a Middle Power* by Arthur Andrew, published by James Lorimer & Company Ltd., Publishers. (Page 92)

Adapted from Linda Weltner, "Stripping Down to Bare Happiness." (Page 92)

Edwin Bliss, *Getting Things Done: The ABC's of Time Management*. New York: Charles Scribner's Sons, 1976. Copyright © 1976. galeord@gale.com (Page 93, Exercise 4-6A)

Heather Martin, student. (Page 93, Exercise 4-6B)

Lise Bernard, student. (Page 93, Exercise 4-6C)

Deborah Harris, student. (Page 94, Exercise 4-7A)

Carol Tavris, "Old Age Isn't What It Used to Be." (Page 94, Exercise 4-7B)

Jim Doherty, "The Hobby That Challenges You to Think Like a Bee." (Page 94, Exercise 4-7C)

Douglas Goold and Andrew Willis, excerpt from *The Bre-X Fraud* by Douglas Goold and Andrew Willis. Used by permission of McClelland & Stewart Ltd., *The Canadian Publishers*. (Pages 95–96)

Gretel Ehrlich, "Other Lives" from *The Solace of Open Spaces*. New York: Penguin Books, 1986. Copyright © 1985. (Page 96)

Ruth Mehrtens Galvin, "Sybaritic to Some, Sinful to Others." Used by permission of Smith College. (Page 96)

John Warde, "Safe Lifting Techniques" from *the New York Times* (March 11, 1990). (Page 96)

Sivan Chand, student. (Page 97)

Banesh Hoffman, "My Friend, Albert Einstein," pp. 139–144. (Page 97)

John Arrend Timm, *General Chemistry*, Editions McGraw-Hill Book Company Inc., 3rd edition, 1956. (Page 97)

Bill Siuru and John D. Busick, *Future Flight: The Next Generation of Aircraft Technology* from TAB Books, 1987. Copyright © The McGraw-Hill Companies, Inc. (Page 98)

Terence Dickinson, excerpt from "Galactic Encounters," *Equinox*, November/December 1986. (Page 98)

Rosanne Labonte, student. (Page 99)

Warren Bennis, "Time to Hang Up the Old Sports Clichés." (Pages 99–100)

Alison Lurie, *The Language of Clothes* (nonfiction). New York: Random House, 1981. Copyright © 1981 by Alison Lurie. Reprinted by permission of Melanie Jackson Agency, L.L.C. (Page 100)

Marie Winn, *The Plug-In Drug*. New York: Penguin Books, 2002. (Page 100)

Deborah Tannen, *You Just Don't Understand*. Copyright © 1990 by Deborah Tannen. Reprinted by permission of HarperCollins Publishers Inc./William Morrow. (Page 101, Exercise 4-9A)

Michael Ignatieff, excerpt from *Blood and Belonging*. Copyright © 1993 by Michael Ignatieff. (Page 101, Exercise 4-9B)

James Gorman, "Gadgets." (Page 101, Exercise 4-9C)

Wayne Grady, excerpt from *Chasing the Chinook* by Wayne Grady. Copyright © Wayne Grady 1998. Reprinted by permission of Penguin Group (Canada), A division of Pearson Penguin Canada, Inc. (Pages 101–102, Exercise 4-9D)

Jane Brody, "A Hoarder's Life: Filling the Cache—and Finding It" from *The New York Times* (November 19, 1991). (Pages 101–102, Exercise 4-9E)

Jean Rosenbaum, M.D., *Is Your Volkswagen a Sex Symbol?* New York: Bantam Books, Random House Inc., 1973. (Page 102)

Lisa Pratt, "A Slice of History" from *Newsday* (April 29, 1990), combined editions, p. 19. (Page 104)

Ovide Mercredi, excerpt from *In the Rapids: Navigating the Future of First Nations* by Ovide Mercredi and Mary Ellen Turpel. Copyright © 1993 by Ovide Mercredi and Mary Ellen Turpel. Reprinted by permission of Penguin Group (Canada), a Division of Pearson Penguin Canada, Inc. (Page 104)

Jean Vanier, excerpt from *Becoming Human*, by Jean Vanier. Copyright © 1998, Paulist Press, Inc., New York/Mahwah, NJ. Used with permission of Paulist Press. (Pages 112–13, Exercise 5-2A)

Ora Gygi, "Things Are Seldom What They Seem." (Pages 108–109)

Sydney J. Harris, "Sports Only Exercise Our Eyes" from *The Best of Sydney J. Harris*. Copyright © 1975 by Sydney J. Harris. Reprinted by permission of Houghton Mifflin Company. All rights reserved. (Pages 116–117, Exercise 5-3)

Robert Lipsyte, excerpts from "The Emasculation of Sports" from *The New York Times Sunday Magazine* (May 2, 1995). (Page 118; Pages 119–20, Exercise 5-4)

Anna Lozanov, student. (Pages 121–122)

Jo Goodwin Parker, "What's Poverty?" from George Henderson, *America's Other Children*, 1998. Used by permission of the University of Oklahoma Press. (Page 124)

Carl Sagan, *Cosmos*. New York: Random House, 1980. Copyright © 1980 the Estate of Carl Sagan. (Page 125)

William S. Ellis, "Brazil's Imperiled Rain Forest." (Page 126, Exercise 5-5A)

Steve Olson, "Computing Climate." (Page 126, Exercise 5-5B)

Lacie Juris, student. (Pages 151–155)

Northrop Frye, excerpt from "Commission to the Graduating Class of 1988" in *Vic Report* 1991, edited by Alexandra Johnston. Published by permission of the Board of Regents, Victoria University, Toronto. (Page 224)

Alice Munro, excerpt from "Royal Beatings," from *Who Do You Think You Are?* Copyright © 1977 by Alice Munro. Reprinted by permission of William Morris Agency, Inc. on behalf of the Author. (Page 420)

Home page of University of Alberta Library reproduced with permission of University of Alberta Library, <http://www.library.ualberta.ca>. (Page 487)

Google Directory page reproduced with permission of Google.com. (Page 489)

Guided keyword search page reproduced with permission of University of Alberta Library, <http://www.library.ualberta.ca> (Page 491)

Yahoo Directory pages reproduced with permission of Yahoo! Inc. Yahoo! and the Yahoo! Logo are trademarks of Yahoo! Inc. (Page 495)

PsycINFO Web Screens. Reprinted with permission of the American Psychological Association, publisher of the PsycINFO® Database. Copyright © 1872–present, APA. All rights reserved. For more information, contact PsycINFO@apa.org. (Page 501)

Kenneth McRoberts, excerpt from *Misconceiving Canada: The Struggle for National Unity* by Kenneth McRoberts, Copyright © 1997 by Oxford University Press Canada. Reprinted by permission of the publisher. (Page 526)

Mark Kingwell, excerpt from *Marginalia: A Cultural Reader* by Mark Kingwell. Copyright © 1999 by Mark Kingwell. Reprinted by permission of Penguin Group (Canada), A division of Pearson Penguin Canada, Inc. (Page 527)

Paul Fussell, *Uniforms: Why We Are What We Wear*. Boston: Houghton Mifflin, 2002. Copyright © 2002 by Paul Fussell. Excerpted and reprinted by permission of Houghton Mifflin Company. All rights reserved. (Page 530, Exercise 33-3)

Susan Sontag. *Regarding the Pain of Others*. New York: Farrar, Straus and Giroux, 2003. Copyright © 2003 Susan Sontag. Reprinted by permission of Farrar, Straus and Giroux, LLC. (Page 531, Exercise 33-4)

Northrop Frye, excerpt from *Anatomy of Criticism: Essays* by Northrop Frye, Copyright © 1957 by Princeton University Press. (Page 532)

Credits

Naomi Klein, extracted from *No Logo: Taking Aim at the Brand Bullies* by Naomi Klein. Copyright © 2000 by Naomi Klein. Reprinted by permission of Alfred A. Knopf Canada. (Pages 533–534)

Michele Landsberg, excerpt from *Michele Landsberg's Guide to Children's Books* by Michele Landsberg. © 1985 by Michele Landsberg. Reprinted with permission of the author. (Pages 534–535)

Edwin Jahiel, screen shot of Movie Reviews by Edwin Jaheel. With permission of Edwin Jahiel, Professor of French, Comparative Literature and Cinema; Film Critic; Founder and Director, Unit of Cinema Studies at the University of Illinois. (Page 658)

Valerie Cuneo, "The Sound of a Murderous Heart." (Pages 697–700, Student essay)

Adam Furman, "The Effectiveness of Common Antibiotics." (Pages 719–721, Sample student paper)

About the Authors

LYNN QUITMAN TROYKA, Professor of Writing at the City University of New York (CUNY), has taught at Queensborough Community College and in the graduate Language and Literacy program at City College. She is a former editor of the *Journal of Basic Writing* and her writing and research appear in major journals and various scholarly collections. She conducts workshops in the teaching of writing nationally and internationally. Author of the *Simon & Schuster Quick Access Reference for Writers*, Fourth Edition, Prentice Hall (2003), and Canadian editions of her *Simon & Schuster Handbook for Writers* and *Quick Access Reference for Writers*, she is also co-author of *Structured Reading*, Sixth Edition, Prentice Hall (2003), and *Steps in Composition*, Eighth Edition, Prentice Hall (2004).

Dr. Troyka received the 2001 CCCC Exemplar Award, the highest CCCC (Conference on College Composition and Communication) award for scholarship, teaching, and service; the Rhetorician of the Year Award; and the TYCA (Two-Year College Association) Pickett Award for Service. She is a past chair of the Conference on College Composition and Communication of the National Council of Teachers of English (NCTE); the Two-Year College Association (TYCA) of NCTE; the College Section of NCTE; and the Writing Division of the Modern Language Association.

"This information," says Dr. Troyka, "tells what I've done, not who I am. I am a teacher. Teaching is my life's work, and I love it."

DOUG HESSE is Professor of English and Director of the Center for the Advancement of Teaching at Illinois State University. There he served as director of writing programs and won both outstanding teaching and research awards. Current Chair of the Conference on College Composition and Communication and Past President of the Council of Writing Program Administrators, Dr. Hesse was editor of *WPA: Writing Program Administration.* He has published over forty articles and book chapters, mainly on writing and on creative nonfiction, and he has also taught at Findlay College, Michigan Tech University, and Miami University (Ohio). Married to a well-published essayist and fiction writer, Dr. Hesse has three children, one in high school, one in college, and one a college graduate who is herself a writer.

xxi

To David,
my husband and sweetheart

Lynn Quitman Troyka

To Coral Krukow Hesse

Doug Hesse

Part One

Writing an Essay

Visit the Troyka Web site at
http://www.pearsoned.ca/troyka for

- a writing workshop

- chapter exercises

- other resources, including an e-book version of this text

Chapter 1

Thinking About Purposes, Audiences, and Technologies

1a   Why bother to write?

In this age of cell phones, video conferencing, and the Internet, why do you need the ability to write well? Surprisingly, today's fast-paced, digital world demands more, not less, writing. Whether for an entry-level job, for later advancement, or for a professional career, your success potential in workplaces of the twenty-first century relies heavily on how well you write documents. Recent surveys of people working in a variety of jobs and professional fields say that each day they spend an average of thirty percent of the time writing. They write letters, memos, product evaluations, technical manuals, business-trip reports, feasibility reports, lab reports, proposals, minutes, Web pages, newsletters, and brochures (the first four are most common).

Your success in college or university is another reason to have solid writing ability. Throughout your education, you need to write essays, research papers, lab reports, and other assignments. The better your skills and fluency as a writer, the more smoothly your course work will go.

Yet another benefit of writing skill comes from the physical activity of writing. In the act of writing, studies show, people significantly increase their insights, understanding, and ability to remember the subject they're writing about. Here's how this phenomenon operates.

Writing is a way of discovering and learning

The act of writing triggers brain processes that lead you to make new connections among ideas. Pleasant shocks of recognition occur as your mind starts from what you already know and leaps to what you did not "see" before. One of my favourite statements comes from the world-famous writer E. M. Forster: "How can I know what I mean until I've seen what I said?" Writing activates unique mental pathways that enable you to pursue knowledge and think through complex concepts.

Writing is a way of thinking and reflecting

Only humans can think about thinking. They reflect on what they know and have experienced, a process greatly accelerated and enhanced during the act of writing. For you as a student, this means that writing forces you to clarify your thinking as you use words to convey your thoughts. And when you revise a draft, you push yourself further so that your writing represents as closely as possible what you're thinking.

Writing is a way of owning and sharing knowledge

Few educated people remember specific classroom sessions or chapters from textbooks, but nearly everyone recalls the topics of their research papers. By writing intensively about a topic that you have thought about deeply, you become an authority on that topic. As this happens, others begin to identify you as a disciplined, educated person.

Writing is a way of participating in our democracy

Our society can thrive only when people are educated to assess information, raise important questions, evaluate the answers, and exercise their rights and responsibilities as informed citizens. The ability to write helps you influence decisions and policies, from student government issues to outcomes of national elections.

1b How is "writing" defined?

Writing communicates a message for a purpose to readers. The four key terms in the prior sentence are important. **Written communication** involves sending a message to a destination. The **message** of writing is its content. The **purpose** (1c) of each writing task strongly influences decisions writers make as they put their ideas into words. **Readers,** usually referred to as the **audience** (1d), are the destination that a writer wishes to reach.

1c What are the major purposes for writing?

A writer's **purpose** for writing motivates what and how he or she writes. Some students think their purpose is to fulfil an assignment, but that's only the beginning. The concept of purpose relates to your reason for writing. Every writer, whether student or professional, needs to get under way by choosing which of the four major purposes of writing, listed in Box 1, they want to pursue.

   In this handbook, I concentrate on the two major purposes of most **academic writing,** the writing you do for your courses and in other scholarly endeavours: to inform and to persuade. I've chosen these two because they're the most practical and helpful for students. The two remaining purposes listed in Box 1 are important for contributing to human thought and culture, but they relate less to what most academic writing involves.

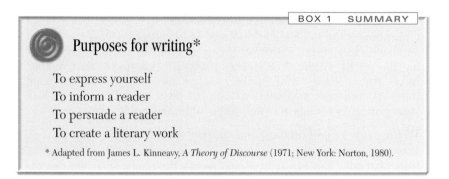

BOX 1   SUMMARY

Purposes for writing*

To express yourself
To inform a reader
To persuade a reader
To create a literary work

* Adapted from James L. Kinneavy, *A Theory of Discourse* (1971; New York: Norton, 1980).

1c.1   What is expressive writing?

Expressive writing is writing to express your personal thoughts and feelings. Much expressive writing is for the writer's eyes only, such as that in diaries, personal journals, or exploratory drafts. When expressive writing is for public reading, it usually falls into the category of literary writing. The excerpt here comes from a student's memoir.

> When we lived in Manitoba, the fall and winter holidays were my touchstones—the calendar moved along in comforting sequence. I wrapped the snow and foods and celebrations around me like a soft blanket. I burrowed in. Now that we live in Victoria, I don't need that blanket. But I surely do miss it.
>
> —Daniel Casey, student

1c.2   What is informative writing?

Informative writing seeks to give information to readers and usually to explain it. Another name for this type of writing is *expository writing* because it expounds on—sets forth in detail—observations, ideas, and facts. You can find informative writing in textbooks, encyclopedias, technical and business reports, nonfiction books, newspapers, and many magazines.

The essential goal of informative academic writing is to educate your readers about something. Like all good educators, therefore, you want to present your information clearly, accurately, completely, and fairly. In section 4i of this handbook, I show you many strategies that writers use for informative writing. These strategies can help you deliver your message, but above all, your success depends on whether your readers can verify your information as accurate. Box 2 gives you a checklist to assess your informative writing. But first, here's a paragraph written to inform.

> In 1914 in what is now Addo Park in South Africa, a hunter by the name of Pretorius was asked to exterminate a herd of 140 elephants. He killed all but 20, and those survivors became so cunning at evading him

that he was forced to abandon the hunt. The area became a preserve in 1930, and the elephants have been protected ever since. Nevertheless, elephants now four generations removed from those Pretorius hunted remain shy and strangely nocturnal. Young elephants evidently learn from the adults' trumpeting alarm calls to avoid humans.

—Carol Grant Gould, "Out of the Mouths of Beasts"

As informative writing, this paragraph works because it focuses clearly on its TOPIC* (elephant behaviour), presents facts that can be verified (who, what, when, where), and is written in a reasonable TONE.

BOX 2   CHECKLIST

☑ Informative writing

- Is its information clear?
- Does it present facts, ideas, and observations that can be verified?
- Does its information seem complete and accurate?
- Is the writer's tone reasonable and free of distortions? (1e)

1c.3 What is persuasive writing?

Persuasive writing, also called *argument writing,* seeks to persuade readers about a matter of opinion. When you write to persuade, you deal with debatable topics, those that people can consider from more than one point of view. Your goal is to change your readers' minds about the topic—or at least to bring your readers' opinions closer to your point of view. To succeed, you want to evoke a reaction in your audience so that they think beyond their present position or take action. Examples of persuasive writing include newspaper editorials, letters to the editor, opinion essays in newspapers and magazines, reviews, sermons, books that argue a point of view, and business proposals that advocate certain approaches over others.

In Chapter 4 of this handbook, I show you strategies of paragraph development that effective writers use in their persuasive writing. Chapter 6 discusses ways to write effective arguments.

In general terms, persuasive writing means you need to move beyond merely stating your opinion. You need to give the basis for that opinion. You support your opinion by using specific, illustrative details to back up your **generalizations,** which are usually very broad statements. The first sentences of sections 1c.1, 1c.2, and 1c.3 in this chapter are examples of generalizations.

---

* Find the definition of all words in small capital letters (such as TOPIC) in the Terms Glossary at the back of this book directly before the Index.

Box 3 gives you a checklist to assess your persuasive writing. But first, here's a paragraph written to persuade.

The search for some biological basis for math ability or disability is fraught with logical and experimental difficulties. Since not all math under-achievers are women, and not all women are mathematics-avoidant, poor performance in math is unlikely to be due to some genetic or hormonal difference between the sexes. Moreover, no amount of research so far has unearthed a "mathematical competency" in some tangible, measurable substance in the body. Since "masculinity" can't be injected into women to test whether or not it improves their mathematics, the theories that attribute such ability to genes or hormones must depend for their proof on circumstantial evidence. So long as about seven percent of the PhD's in mathematics are earned by women, we have to conclude either that these women have genes, hormones, and brain organization different from those of the rest of us, or that certain positive experiences in their lives have largely undone the negative fact that they're female, or both.

—Sheila Tobias, *Overcoming Math Anxiety*

As persuasive writing, this passage works because it provides undistorted information on math ability; it expresses a point of view that resides in sound reasoning (math ability isn't based on gender); it offers evidence (a logical line of reasoning); and it tries to get the reader to agree with the point of view.

BOX 3 CHECKLIST

✓ Persuasive writing

- Does it present a point of view about which opinions vary?
- Does it support its point of view with specifics?
- Does it base its point of view on sound reasoning and logic?
- Are the parts of its argument clear?
- Does it intend to evoke a reaction from the reader?

EXERCISE 1-1

For each paragraph, decide if the dominant purpose is informative or persuasive. Then apply the questions in Box 2 or Box 3 to the paragraph, and explain your answers.

A. The number one challenge in tissue engineering is to get the specimen cells to grow at all. Freshly plucked from a human, a batch of cells hasn't got long to live. They need oxygen, a temperature of about 98 degrees Fahrenheit, and nutrients. So, a tissue engineer doesn't waste time. He places the cells in a petri dish with liquid nutrients—carbohydrates and amino acids do nicely—then tucks them away in an incubator. With a little luck, they multiply and in a few days produce enough cells to be considered tissue. As amazing as the process is up to this point, it's relatively useless, because clumps of tissue are of little use to a patient. The tissue engineer must convince cells to morph from a meaningless jumble of flesh into a functioning organ.

—Joseph D'Agnese, "Brothers with Heart"

B. Efforts to involve the father in the birth process, to enhance his sense of paternity and empowerment as he adjusts to his new role, should be increased. Having the father involved in labor and delivery can significantly increase his sense of himself as a person who is important to his child and to his mate. Several investigators have shown that increased participation of fathers in the care of their babies, increased sensitivity to their baby's cues at one month, and significantly increased support of their wives can result from the rather simple maneuver of sharing the newborn baby's behavior with the new father at three days, using the Neonatal Behavioral Assessment Scale (NBAS). In light of these apparent gains, we would do well to consider a period of paid paternity leave, which might serve both symbolically and in reality as a means of stamping the father's role as critical to his family. Ensuring the father's active participation is likely to enhance his image of himself as a nurturing person and to assist him toward a more mature adjustment in his life as a whole.

—T. Berry Brazelton, "Issues for Working Parents"

C. Much of how the people live in rural Saskatchewan today continues to stem from the value system and the exigencies of pioneer life. The first settlers here almost immediately had to become self-sufficient, since the governmental system of land division ensured large distances between families at a time when transportation was always slow and uncertain, and in a climate where the weather was frequently too severe to allow travel. (That this system also ensured loneliness for the women who were always less mobile than the men is an underlying, but not fully articulated, theme in western Canadian life.) In most respects farm life at least has changed a great deal since those early days, and these changes have left the society in a general way still operating within a value system that does not always make sense in the new conditions.

—Sharon Butala, "Rural Saskatchewan: Creating the Garden"

EXERCISE 1-2

Using each topic listed here, work individually or with your peer-response group to think through two different essays: one informative, the second persuasive. Be ready to discuss in detail how the two essays would differ. For help, consult section 1c.

1. fast food	4. road rage
2. tastes in music	5. body piercing
3. required academic courses	

1d What does "audience" mean for writing?

Your **audience** consists of everyone who will read your writing. After you graduate, your audiences will be readers of your business, professional, and public writing (Chapter 41). In college or university, you address a mix of audience types, each of which expects to read ACADEMIC WRITING. Here's a list of categories of audiences for academic writing.

- Your peers (1d.1)
- A general audience (1d.2)
- A specialist audience (1d.3)
- Your instructor (who represents either general or specialized readers) (1d.4)

The more specifics you can assume about your audience for your academic writing, the better your chances of reaching it successfully. The questions in Box 4 can serve as a guide.

BOX 4   SUMMARY

Characteristics of reading audiences

What Setting Are They Reading In?

- Academic setting?
- Workplace setting?
- Public setting?

Who Are They?

- Age, gender
- Ethnic or linguistic backgrounds, political philosophies, religious beliefs
- Roles (student, parent, voter, wage earner, property owner, and others)
- Interests, hobbies

What Do They Know?

- Level of education
- Amount of general or specialized knowledge about the topic
- Probable preconceptions and prejudices brought to the topic

When you know or can reasonably assume who will be in your reading audience for each assignment, your chances of reaching it improve. For example, if you're writing a sales report for your supervisor, you can use terms such as *product life cycle, break-even quantity, competition,* and *markup.* In contrast, if general readers were the audience for the same information, you would want to avoid specialized, technical vocabulary—or if you had to use specialized terms, you would define them in a nontechnical way.

ESL NOTE: If you come from outside North America, you may be surprised by the directness with which people speak and write in Canada. If so, I hope you'll read my open letter to multilingual students about honouring one's own culture. (It introduces Part Seven of this handbook.) Your own tradition may expect elaborate or ceremonial written language that does not introduce the central point immediately, preferring tactful, indirect discussion. In contrast, Canadian writing contains language and style that are direct, straightforward, and without digressive embellishments. Instructors here expect academic writing to contain a thesis statement (usually at the end of the introductory paragraph); to demonstrate a tightly organized presentation of information from one paragraph to the next; to back up generalizations with supporting details; and to end with a logical concluding paragraph. In addition, you are expected to use standard English grammar that follows the rules used by educated speakers.

1d.1 What is a peer audience?

Your *peers* are other writers like you. In some writing classes, instructors divide students into **peer-response groups.** Participating in a peer-response group makes you part of a respected tradition of colleagues helping colleagues. Professional writers often seek comments from other writers to improve their rough drafts. As a member of a peer-response group, you're not expected to be a writing expert. Rather, you're expected to offer responses as a practised reader and as a fellow student writer who understands what writers go through.

The role of members of a peer-response group is to react and discuss, not to do the work for someone. Hearing or reading comments from your peers might be your first experience with seeing how others read your writing. This can be informative, surprising, and helpful. When peers share their writing with the group, each member gets the added advantage of learning about other students' writing for the same assignment.

Peer-response groups are set up in different ways. One arrangement calls for students to pass around and read each other's drafts silently, writing down reactions or questions in the margins or on a response form. In another arrangement, students read their drafts aloud, and then each peer responds either orally or in writing on a response form. Yet another arrangement asks for focused responses to only one or two features of each draft (perhaps the thesis statement, or topic sentences and supporting details, or use of transitional words). Still another method is for the group to BRAINSTORM a topic together before writing, to discuss various sides of a debatable topic, or to share reactions to an essay or piece of literature the class has read, and so on.

Whatever the arrangement of your group, be clear about exactly what you are expected to do, both as a peer-responder and as a writer. If your instructor gives you guidelines for working in a peer-response group, follow them carefully. If you've never before participated in a peer-response group, or in the particular kind of group that your instructor forms, here are ways to get started: Consult the guidelines in Box 5 at the end of this section; watch what experienced peers do; and ask your instructor. Otherwise, just dive in knowing that you will learn as you go.

Now to the sometimes sticky issue of how to take criticism of your writing: Here's my personal advice as a writer for being able (or at least appearing able) to take constructive criticism gracefully. First, know that most students don't like to criticize their peers. They worry about being impolite or inaccurate, or losing someone's friendship. Try, therefore, to cultivate an attitude that encourages your peers to respond as freely and as helpfully as possible. Show that you can listen without getting angry or feeling intruded upon.

Second, realize that most people tend to be defensive about even well-intentioned and tactful criticism. Of course, if a comment is purposely mean or sarcastic, you and all others in your peer-response group have every right to say so and not tolerate it. Third, if you don't understand a comment fully, ask for clarification.

Finally, no matter what anyone says about your writing, it remains yours alone. You retain "ownership" of your writing always, and you don't have to make every suggested change. Use only the comments that you think can move you closer to reaching your intended audience. Of course, if a comment from your instructor points out a definite problem and you choose to ignore it, it could have an impact on your grade—though many instructors are open to an explanation of your rationale for deciding to ignore what they said.

👁 **ALERT:** Some instructors and students use the terms *peer-response group* and *collaborative writing* to mean the same thing. In this handbook, I assign the terms to two different situations. I use peer-response group (1d.1) for students getting together in small groups to help each other write and revise, as shown in Box 5. I use collaborative writing (3f) for students writing a group essay, research paper, or report. 👁

BOX 5 SUMMARY

Guidelines for participating in peer-response groups

One major principle needs to guide your participation in a peer-response group: Always take an upbeat, constructive attitude, whether you're responding to someone else's writing or receiving responses from others.

As a Responder

- Think of yourself in the role of a coach, not a judge.
- Consider all writing by your peers as "works in progress."
- After hearing or reading a peer's writing, briefly summarize it to check that you and your peer are clear about what the peer said or meant to say.
- Start with what you think is well done. No one likes to hear only negative comments.
- Be honest in your suggestions for improvements.
- Base your responses on an understanding of the writing process, and remember that you're reading drafts, not finished products. All writing can be revised.
- Give concrete and specific responses. General comments such as "This is good" or "This is weak" aren't much help. Say specifically what is good or weak.
- Follow your instructor's system for putting your comments in writing so that your fellow writer can recall what you said. If one member of your group is supposed to take notes, speak clearly so that the person can take accurate notes. If you're the note taker, SUMMARIZE accurately, and ask the speaker to repeat what he or she said if it went by too quickly.

As a Writer

- Adopt an attitude that encourages your peers to respond freely. Listen and try to resist any urge to interrupt during a comment or to jump in to react.
- Remain open-minded. Your peers' comments can help you see your writing in a fresh way, which, in turn, can help you produce a better-revised draft.
- Ask for clarification if a comment isn't clear. If a comment is too general, ask for specifics.
- As much as you encourage your peers to be honest, remember that the writing is yours. You "own" it, and you decide which comments to use or not use.

⊕ **ESL NOTE:** Students from cultures other than those in Canada and the United States might feel uncomfortable in the role of critic or questioner of other people's writing. Please know, however, that peer-response groups are fairly common in schools and at jobs because people usually think that "two heads are better than one." Sharing and questioning others' ideas—as well as how they are expressed in writing—is an honourable tradition in Canada and the United States. Peer-response groups help writers politely but firmly explore concepts and language, so please feel free to participate fully. In fact, some instructors grade you on your open participation in such activities. ⊕

1d.2 What is a general audience?

A **general audience** of readers is composed of educated, experienced readers. These are people who regularly read newspapers, magazines, and books. These readers, with general knowledge of many subjects, probably know something about your topic, but may not possess specialized knowledge on that particular subject (1d.3). Consequently, avoid specialized or technical terms, although you can use a few as long as you include everyday definitions.

In addition, general readers approach a piece of writing expecting to become interested in it. They hope to learn about a new topic, to add to their store of knowledge about a subject, and, often, to see a subject from a perspective other than their own. As a writer, you need to fulfil those expectations.

1d.3 What is a specialist audience?

A **specialist audience** is composed of readers who have expert knowledge of specific subjects or who are particularly committed to those subjects. Many people are experts in their occupational fields, and some become experts in areas that simply interest them. People from a particular group background (for example, religious, linguistic, geographic, or occupational) share specialized knowledge.

Specialist readers, however, share more than knowledge: They share assumptions and beliefs. You will want to take these into account and write respectfully about deeply held beliefs. Additionally, whenever you introduce a concept that's likely to be new to a specialist audience, explain the new concept thoroughly rather than assume that they'll understand it right away.

1d.4 What is my instructor's role as audience?

As your audience, your instructor functions in three ways. First, your instructor assumes the role of your target audience, either as general reader (1d.2) or specialist reader (1d.3). Second, your instructor is a coach committed to helping you improve your writing. Third, your instructor is the eventual evaluator of your final drafts.

Instructors know that few students are experienced writers or experts on the subjects they write about. Still, instructors expect your writing to reflect your having taken the time to learn something worthwhile about a topic and then to write about it clearly. Instructors are experienced readers who can recognize a minimal effort almost at once.

As important, instructors are people whose professional lives centre on intellectual endeavours. You need, therefore, to write on topics that contain intrinsic intellectual interest (2d) and to discuss them according to the expectations for academic writing.

If you're a relatively inexperienced writer, you may wrongly assume that your instructor can mentally fill in what you leave out of your writing. Instructors—indeed, all readers—can't be mind readers, so they expect students to write on a topic fully. If you think you might be saying too little, ask your peers to read your writing and tell you if you've developed your topic sufficiently.

1e What is "tone" in writing?

Tone is more than what you say; tone is *how* you say it. Your tone reveals your attitude toward your AUDIENCE as well as the topic. Tone in writing operates like tone of voice, except in writing you can't rely on facial expressions and voice intonations to communicate your message.

Your DICTION (choice of words), LEVEL OF FORMALITY, and writing style create your tone. While you can use SLANG and other highly INFORMAL LANGUAGE in a note to your roommate or a close friend, such a relaxed tone isn't appropriate for ACADEMIC WRITING or BUSINESS WRITING. As a rule, when you write for an audience about which you know little, use more formality in your tone. "More formality," by the way, doesn't mean dull and drab. Lively language in a serious discussion enhances your message.

Problems with tone result from the phrasing you choose. It's the combination and location, not the words taken separately, that create a tone. For example, you want to avoid sarcastic language in an academic or business setting that calls for a reasonable tone. If you were to write "He was a regular Albert Einstein" to describe the subject of an interview who left a poor impression, those sarcastic words would say more about you than about the person interviewed. Such a tone implies that you have an overly critical or nasty streak. In contrast, some kinds of informal writing or journalism allow you to introduce IRONY, as in the following: "The Information Department was conspicuously lacking in information that day."

In business and professions, if you write a memo to your supervisor about a safety hazard in your workplace, avoid writing a chatty message with a joke about an accident that could happen. Such a tone directed at your supervisor would be considered flippant or irresponsible. Equally important, if you include minute details of background information that your supervisor already knows, your tone may seem condescending and your supervisor might become annoyed with you.

Academic writing usually calls for a medium-to-formal tone (21b), which is a reasonable, even-handed tone. It's somewhat formal and serious but never pompous. Such a tone avoids language that attempts to manipulate your readers. Distorted facts or SLANTED LANGUAGE (21h) (for example, *the corrupt, deceitful politician*) rather than neutral words (for example, *the politician under investigation for taking bribes*) jump off the page, making your readers decide immediately that your message isn't objective or trustworthy.

Additionally, in all types of writing, GENDER-NEUTRAL LANGUAGE that represents both men and women fairly (for example, replace *policeman* with *police officer,* and replace *doctors' wives* with *doctors' spouses*) demonstrates an even-handed tone. Similarly, avoid SEXIST LANGUAGE, which involves words with sexist overtones (21g), or you'll alienate your readers because you appear to be insensitive to gender issues or crude in your understanding about the effects of language choices.

Another type of language that carries a message larger than the words themselves is pretentious language. Its use implies either that you're showing off to impress people (which always backfires) or that you're obscuring a message. Choose straightforward rather than extravagant words (use *concert,* not *orchestral event*) if you want readers to take you seriously. Also, readers usually assume that you want to conceal something unpleasant if you use EUPHEMISMS (such as *downsizing* or *rightsizing* instead of *cutting jobs*). Box 6 lists guidelines for handling tone in your writing.

BOX 6   SUMMARY

How to use tone in writing

- Reserve a highly informal tone for conversational writing.
- Use a formal tone or a medium level of formality in your academic writing and when you write for supervisors, professionals, and other people you know from a distance.
- Avoid an overly formal, ceremonial tone.
- Avoid sarcasm and other forms of nastiness.
- Choose language appropriate for your topic and your readers.
- Choose words that work with your message, not against it.
- Whatever tone you choose to use, be consistent in each document.

EXERCISE 1-3

Using the topics listed here, work individually or with your peer-response group to think through specific ways the tone of an essay would differ for the following three audiences: an academic instructor, a close friend, and a supervisor at a job. Be ready to discuss in some detail how the three essays on each topic would differ for each audience. For help, consult sections 1d and 1e.

1. Suggestions for a fair way to evaluate each person's work
2. Benefits of having greater access to one's own evaluations or personnel records
3. An explanation of why you were absent from class or work yesterday

1f What does "sources for writing" mean?

Sources for writing consist of material that contains someone else's ideas, not yours. Sources, often called *outside sources*, include credible information on the Internet, library collections, and the spoken words of experts. Sources can add authority to what you write, especially if the topic is open to debate. But be careful: Different instructors have differing policies on students' using outside sources. Some instructors want students to draw on sources only when writing a research paper (Chapters 31–36). Other instructors encourage "source-based writing" for most assignments. Still other instructors never want students to use outside sources. Find out your instructor's stand on the use of sources so you can fulfil the requirements of your course successfully.

Some students wonder whether consulting sources for their writing might suggest that they can't come up with ideas of their own. Actually, the opposite is true. When students use sources well, they demonstrate their ability to locate relevant material, assess its credibility and usefulness, integrate it with skill, and credit the sources accurately. To achieve this, follow the guidelines in Box 7 at the end of this section.

Of course, no matter how many outside sources you refer to, you remain your own first source. Throughout your life, you've been building a fund of knowledge by reading, going to school, attending cultural and sports events, hearing speeches, watching television, and exploring the Internet. The basis for your writing is the information you have, as well as your ideas, reflections, reactions, and opinions. Sources offer support and additional information and points of view, but you are always the starting point for your writing.

When you use sources in your writing, never plagiarize. As a student, you want to become a full participant in the community of knowledge seekers and makers. The expected honourable standard for participants is always to credit thinkers who have come before you and upon whose shoulders you stand as you learn and create. You therefore never want to behave unethically by stealing someone's thinking or language.

15

PLAGIARISM occurs when you take ideas or words from a source without revealing that you used a source. Always reveal your source and credit it by using DOCUMENTATION to tell your readers the exact place where your thinking is influenced by a source. Adhering to the requirements of the DOCUMENTATION STYLE you're using (Chapters 34–36), state the name of the source and where anyone who wishes to consult it can find it.

If you forget to document your sources, you're plagiarizing (Chapter 33). Using quotation marks without naming your source is a form of plagiarizing. Leaving out quotation marks from a direct quotation that you take from a source, even if you name the source, is a form of plagiarizing. Plagiarism is a major academic offence. A student who plagiarizes can instantly fail a course or be expelled from an academic institution.

New computer technologies make plagiarism especially easy to detect today. If ethical reasons aren't enough to prevent you from plagiarizing, then the real chance of strong punishment definitely should be.

BOX 7   SUMMARY

Guidelines for using sources in writing

- Evaluate sources critically. Not all are accurate, true, or honest (5g, especially Box 34).
- Represent your sources accurately. Be sure to quote, PARAPHRASE, and summarize well so that you avoid distorting the material (Chapter 33).
- Never plagiarize (Chapter 33).
- Know the difference between writing a SUMMARY and writing a SYNTHESIS (5e). A summary simply reports the source material. That is not enough. A synthesis makes intelligent connections between the source and your ideas, or between a variety of sources, or between a variety of sources and your ideas. Synthesizing is what college and university writers are expected to do.
- Credit your sources with DOCUMENTATION that names them clearly and completely. Ask your instructor which DOCUMENTATION STYLE to use. Five widely used styles are presented in Chapters 34–36.

ESL NOTE: In many cultures other than those in Canada and the United States, original thinking and responses to reading aren't acceptable. Instead, instructors expect students to respect and copy the thoughts and exact language of scholars, without naming the people who wrote the scholarship. This practice is not acceptable in North American educational systems. You always need to use documentation to credit your source. Otherwise, you are plagiarizing—that is, "stealing" the ideas of others, which is a major offence.

1g What resources can help me with writing?

Your **personal bookshelf** needs to contain three essential volumes: a dictionary, a thesaurus, and a handbook for writers. A **dictionary** is indispensable. Most college and university bookstores offer a variety of hardback "college dictionaries." Before buying one, browse through a few to read some definitions you want to learn or to understand more clearly. Choose the book you like best. Also, a lightweight paperback abridged dictionary in your book pack can be very handy for checking unknown words on the spot. Unabridged dictionaries list all recognized words in standard use in English. The reference section of every library usually stocks one for all students to consult (21e.1).

Another valuable resource for writers is a **thesaurus,** which is a collection of synonyms. The alphabetically arranged ones are the easiest to use.

A **handbook for writers** is also vital for you to own. A handbook— such as the one you're holding as you read this—gives you detailed information about rules of grammar, punctuation, and other writing conventions. It also offers extensive advice about how to write successfully, whether for college or university, business, or the public. It shows you step by step how to write and document research papers. Some handbooks, including this one, contain guidance on how to write for a variety of courses other than English.

Finally, **college and university libraries,** sometimes called *learning resource centres,* are essential for writers. Libraries are fully stocked with all manner of reference books, circulating books, resources for online access, and more. Some of the books listed above are available online, although you'll probably need to be connected through the library's Web site. Before you actually use the library, spend some time getting to know what's available. Then you can dive right in when you need to get information. Chapter 32 provides extensive advice on using the library.

1h How do writers use technology?

For centuries, new technologies have changed how writers write. Consider, for example, the difference between writing with a quill pen, a pencil, and a manual typewriter. Today, of course, when you think of technology and writing, computers and everything associated with them usually come to mind: printers, scanners, the Internet, e-mail and instant messaging, the World Wide Web, digital still and video cameras, and thousands of software programs.

Writing for most jobs now requires at least some use of computers. Similarly, more and more academic writing assignments need to be done on computers. Some professors make allowances for students for whom this is impossible, but the clear trend is toward word-processed final drafts. If you have regular access to a computer, you enjoy some obvious conveniences. If you do not, however, you can take advantage of computer labs on most campuses, often in libraries or student centres; public libraries; Internet cafés; and printing shops (although these last two will cost you money). Computers are important tools for writers in four ways.

1h.1 Word-processing tools

A computer's word-processing software (the most popular programs are Microsoft Word and WordPerfect) offers invaluable help at various stages of the WRITING PROCESS. Word processing allows you easily to add, delete, revise, or move material, including from one document to another. You can always have a clean copy. Some writers prefer to print their drafts to revise or edit them by hand and then enter the changes in the computer; other writers do almost all their revising and editing on the screen. As you gain more experience in writing, you'll probably develop the strategies that suit you best.

Word processing also allows you to make quick format changes. You can easily shift between single-spacing and double-spacing or put a WORKS CITED page or bibliography into the correct DOCUMENTATION STYLE. In addition, word processing allows you to create clean-looking tables or graphs. The toolbar at the top of the word-processing window contains numerous formatting options. Spending some time exploring how they work can save you time in the long run.

Word-processing programs also have special aids for writers built into their software. They offer some advantages, but they also have severe limitations. In no case are such tools substitutes for your own careful editing and proofreading. Software, after all, can't "think" and make distinctions between *form* and *from* in spelling, between the way you use or misuse *deep* and *profound,* or between an unwarranted and a warranted use of a passive construction (8p).

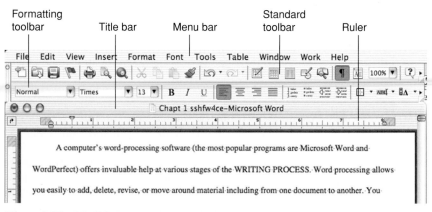

Microsoft Word for Windows toolbar and document

- **Spell-check programs** show you words that don't match the dictionary in the software. These programs are a big help for spotting a misspelling or mistyping (*typo*), but they won't call your attention to your having typed *west* when you intended to type *rest*.
- **Thesaurus programs** give you SYNONYMS for words. They can't, however, tell you which ones fit well into your particular sentences. Whenever a synonym is unfamiliar or hazy, look it up in your dictionary. You don't want to use words that strike you as attractive options but then turn out to distort your communication. For example, a synonym for *friend* is *acquaintance*, but these words have different senses.
- **Grammar- or style-check programs** check your writing against the software's strict interpretations of rules of grammar, word use, punctuation, and other conventions. They signal you about elements of your writing that differ from the program's standards. Can you always rely on those standards? No. While most signals are useful for getting you to rethink the way you've said something, the final decision about how to deliver your message is yours. You might decide to use a semicolon even when the program suggests a period, to keep the spelling of a HOMONYM (such as *it's* versus *its*), to retain a phrase even when the program says you aren't being concise, or to accept a long sentence when it precedes or follows a few very short sentences. Consult this handbook when you're not sure what a program is suggesting or whether you're justified in deviating from the program's rules.

1h.2 Computers as research tools

In addition to helping you produce and revise writing, computers help you find sources. Most library catalogues and databases are now searchable with computers. Catalogues and databases are large collections of references that experts have gathered and organized in several ways, most importantly by topic. You can search them from computers in the library itself or, often, remotely online. Chapter 32 provides extensive explanations of such catalogues and databases and how best to use them.

Computers also help you find sources on the World Wide Web (the Web), a vast collection of Web sites and pages that are accessible through the Internet. Chapter 32 explains how to use the Web—and how to avoid misusing it. As you find information on the Web, keep in mind that anyone can post anything on the Web. Some of what you find is just plain wrong, although much is accurate and useful. To help you evaluate the quality of a Web site, see Boxes 141 and 142 in Chapter 32. The example on the next page shows results from a search for sources on "animal rights" in an online database. This database, the *Humanities Index*, is a high-quality site compiled by professional bibliographers.

1h.3 Computers as tools for managing your work

Computers allow you to save different drafts of your papers as they evolve or to organize your work into various folders. For example, you might create a folder for each paper you write and also keep all notes, drafts, and ideas related to that project in the folder. Many people now take notes from sources directly into computer files. On the next page you can see how one student has started a folder for all the projects in her Writing 001 course. In the sub-folder for project 2 she has ideas,

Results of a FirstSearch of the *Humanities Index*

Name of student's work folder (in My Documents)

Location of work folder

Map of student's work
from desktop to project 2

Five documents that the student
has created for this project

Student's directory for her writing projects

notes, peer comments, and drafts. She created this folder in the "My Documents" directory in Microsoft Word.

1h.4 Computers as communication tools

You're probably familiar with e-mail and instant messaging as ways to communicate with friends and others. These and similar technologies can sometimes also help you with formal writing projects. Discussing a TOPIC online with classmates can help generate ideas for writing, and some instructors organize such discussions in Web-based programs like WebCT, Blackboard, and WebBoard.

Computers also allow you to share drafts of your work with others without physically meeting them. You can send a draft as an e-mail attachment to classmates for peer response—or even to your instructors for comments, if they invite you to do so. Some instructors post student papers on class Web pages so that other students can read and respond to the writing. Obviously, if you're working on a collaborative project, the ability to share drafts and to discuss revisions online has many advantages.

1h.5 Computers and new forms of writing

For decades, student writing in college and university has been essays and reports consisting only of words, with occasional tables and figures. These forms will always remain essential, and you need to master them. However, computers enable new kinds of writing. Instead of traditional diaries, writers can keep Web logs (or blogs), which are online journals that anyone can read through the Internet. In addition, writers can now copy and paste photographs or illustrations into documents, and they can use different fonts and graphical elements such as ruler lines or textboxes. Interestingly, certain documents today can exist only in digital form on computers because they contain audio or video files, or they connect to other documents and Web sites. Yet another development is that some instructors may ask students to develop a Web page rather than write a traditional paper.

If you, like most students, have a limited knowledge of how to produce these emerging types of documents, don't worry. Instructors who require such projects know that many of you need help to get started. On the other hand, even if you're technologically skilled, always check with your instructors before you use graphical and other elements in your papers because instructors may have important reasons for assigning traditional papers—they may want you to focus more on crafting ideas and arguments through words than on designing and manipulating images.

Chapter 2

Planning and Shaping

2a   What is the writing process?

Many people think that professional writers can sit down at their computers, think of ideas, and magically produce a finished draft, word by perfect word. Experienced writers know better. They know that writing is a process, a series of activities that starts the moment they begin thinking about a subject and ends with proofreading the final draft. Experienced writers also know that good writing is rewriting, again and yet again. Their drafts are filled with additions, deletions, rewordings, and rearrangements.

For example, see below how I revised the paragraph you just read. I didn't make all the changes at the same time, even though it looks that way on the example. I went through the paragraph four times before I was satisfied with it. Notice that I deleted and added text and changed wording throughout.

~~Chapter One discusses what writing is. This chapter explains~~

~~how writing happens.~~ Many people think that professional writers

can sit down at their computers, think of ideas, and produce a
                                                    ^magically

finished draft, word by perfect word. Experienced writers know

better. They know that writing is a process. ~~The writing process is~~

a series of activities that starts the moment thinking about a subject
                                              ^they begin

~~begins~~ and ends with the final draft. Experienced writers also know
                              ^proofreading

that good writing is rewriting, again and yet again. Their drafts

are filled with additions, deletions, rewordings, and rearrangements.

Draft and revision of Lynn Troyka's first paragraph in Chapter 2

Writing is an ongoing process of considering alternatives and making choices. The better you understand the writing process, the better you'll write; and the more you feel in control of your writing, the more you'll enjoy it.

In this chapter, I discuss each part of the writing process separately. In real life, the steps overlap. They loop back and forth, which is why writing is called a recursive process. Box 8 lists the steps.

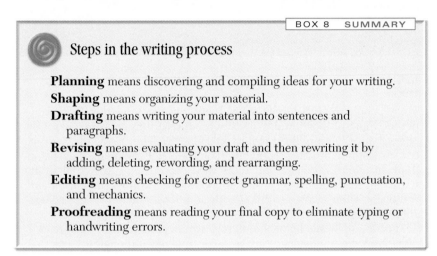

BOX 8   SUMMARY

Steps in the writing process

Planning means discovering and compiling ideas for your writing.

Shaping means organizing your material.

Drafting means writing your material into sentences and paragraphs.

Revising means evaluating your draft and then rewriting it by adding, deleting, rewording, and rearranging.

Editing means checking for correct grammar, spelling, punctuation, and mechanics.

Proofreading means reading your final copy to eliminate typing or handwriting errors.

Do you like, as I do, to visualize a process? If so, see the drawing here. The arrows show movement. You might move back before going ahead (perhaps as you revise, you realize you need to plan some more); or you might skip a step and come back to it later (perhaps in the middle of revising, you jump into editing for a few minutes because a punctuation or grammar rule affects how you express your point); and so on.

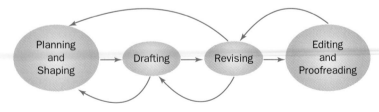

Visualizing the writing process

As you work with the writing process, allow yourself to move freely through each step to see what's involved. Notice what works best for you. As you develop a sense of your preferred writing methods, adapt the process to fit each writing situation. No single way exists for applying the writing process.

My personal advice from one writer to another is this: Most writers struggle some of the time with ideas that are difficult to express, sentences that won't take shape, and words that aren't precise. Be patient with yourself. Don't get discouraged. Writing takes time. The more you write, the easier it will become—though writing never happens magically.

2b What terms describe different kinds of writing?

Terms that describe different types of writing are often used interchangeably. Most instructors attach specific meanings to each one. Listen closely so you can sort out what terms your instructor uses. If your instructor's use of terms isn't clear, ask for clarification. For example, the words *essay, theme,* and *composition* usually—but not always—refer to writing of about 500 to 1000 words. In this handbook, I use *essay*. Similarly, the word *paper* can mean anything from a few paragraphs to a complex research project. In this handbook, I use *paper* for longer writing projects, such as research papers. Also, I sometimes use the general term *piece of writing* to refer to all types of writing.

2c What is a "writing situation"?

The writing situation of each assignment gives you the information to start thinking about your writing. Its four elements are *topic, purpose, audience,* and *special requirements.* The questions in Box 9 cover each aspect.

A **topic** is the foundation of every writing situation. As you think through a topic, you want to remain within the constraints of academic writing. Whatever your topic, stick to it, and resist any temptation to bend it in another direction.

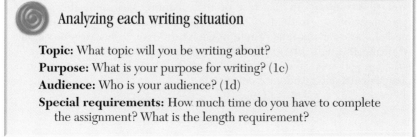

BOX 9   SUMMARY

Analyzing each writing situation

Topic: What topic will you be writing about?
Purpose: What is your purpose for writing? (1c)
Audience: Who is your audience? (1d)
Special requirements: How much time do you have to complete the assignment? What is the length requirement?

The PURPOSE of most college and university writing is to inform or persuade (1c.2 and 1c.3). Some assignments state the writing purpose; others imply it. For example, if you were asked, "Describe government restrictions on cigarette advertising," your purpose would be informative. In contrast, if you were asked to respond to the statement "Smoking should (or should not) be banned in all public places," your purpose would be persuasive.

But suppose your assignment doesn't indicate a writing purpose: for example, "Write an essay on smoking." Here, you're expected to choose a purpose and think about what you intend to write on the topic. As you plan how to develop the topic, you'll begin to see whether your purpose is informative or persuasive. It's normal to switch purposes midstream to better suit what you are saying.

Your reading AUDIENCE (1d) consists of everyone who will read what you write. Depending on your assignment and the procedures in your class, your audience includes your PEER-RESPONSE GROUP (1d.1), friends, readers who have specialized knowledge (1d.3) about your topic, and your instructor (1d.4). Think through the characteristics and expectations of your audience so that your writing will successfully deliver its intended meaning.

Special requirements are practical matters such as how much time you're given to complete the assignment and how long it should be. For example, for an assignment due in one week, your reading audience expects more than one day's work. However, if an assignment is due overnight, your readers realize your need to write in relative haste, though they never expect sloppy or careless work. Perhaps the highest expectations in a reading audience are applied to an assignment that calls for reading or other research, so be sure to build time for that into your schedule from the start.

Some instructors put each assignment in writing, either on the board or in a handout. Others give assignments orally during class, expecting you to write them down. Try to record every word. Don't hesitate to ask questions if you don't catch all the words or if something isn't clear—and be sure to write down the answers, because they often tend to slip from memory. Listen, too, to questions other students ask, and write down the answers. Such notes can serve as useful springboards when you start writing. In the rest of this chapter, I present the writing processes of two students, Carol Moreno and Lacie Juris, as they plan and shape their material. Then, in Chapter 3, you'll see Moreno's essay evolving through three separate, complete drafts. Later, in Chapter 6, you'll see how Juris's essay developed. To start, here are the written assignments each student received.

Carol Moreno received this assignment:

Write an essay of 700 to 800 words discussing a challenge you faced and tried to meet. Your writing purpose can be informative or persuasive. Expect to write three drafts. (1) Your first draft, typed double-spaced, is due two classes from today. (2) Your clean second draft, typed double-spaced, without notes or comments, is due two classes later. Clip to it your first draft showing all notes you made to yourself or took from comments your peer-response group made; you can handwrite notes and comments. I'll read your second draft as an "essay in progress" and will make comments to help you toward a third (and final) draft. (3) The third draft, typed double-spaced, is due one week after I return your second draft with my comments.

Lacie Juris was given this assignment:

Write an essay of 900 to 1000 words that argues for a particular action on an issue that interests you. Your final draft is due in two weeks.

Moreno's first step was to analyze her writing situation (Box 9). She looked at the *topic*—a challenge she had faced and tried to meet—and saw that she needed to narrow it. She tentatively decided her *purpose* would be informative, though she thought she might have to switch to a persuasive purpose as she went along. She knew that she would share her first draft with her peer-response group to help her toward her second draft. She also understood that her instructor would be her final *audience*. She was aware of the *requirements* for time and length.

Juris also read her assignment and analyzed her writing situation. Because the *topic* was very broad, she knew she would have to spend time deciding what she wanted to write about. She understood that her assigned *purpose* was persuasive. The *audience* was not specified; she knew that her instructor would be the main audience, but she also decided to address a broader public audience. She kept in mind the *requirements* for time and length.

EXERCISE 2-1

For each assignment below, work individually or with a peer-response group to list the elements in the writing situation. Consult section 2c for help.

1. *Family and Consumer Science:* Write a 500- to 700-word essay that explains important safety procedures to daycare providers. This assignment is due in one week.

2. *Journalism:* Write a 300-word editorial for the student newspaper (to be published next week) supporting or attacking your student

council's call for a boycott of a controversial speaker. Draw on your own opinions and refer to one outside source.

3. *Art:* You have twenty minutes in class to discuss the differences between a photograph and a painting of the same scene, using a specific example from the textbook or class discussions.

4. *Politics:* Write a one-paragraph description of what is meant by "freedom of the press."

5. *Computer Science:* Write a 1000-word paper that argues that computers will/will not simulate most aspects of human intelligence in the next ten years. Read and draw on sources to support your argument. Be sure to document your sources. This assignment is due in two weeks.

2d How can I think through a writing topic?

Situations vary. Some assignments are very specific. For example, here's an assignment that leaves no room for choice: "Explain how oxygen is absorbed in the lungs." Students need to do precisely what's asked. Only rarely, however, are writing-class assignments as specific as that one. Often, you'll be expected to select your own topic (2d.1), broaden a narrow topic (2d.2), or narrow a broad topic (2d.3). Regardless of the situation, keep in mind that **what separates most good writing from bad is the writer's ability to move back and forth between general statements and specific details.**

2d.1 Selecting your own topic

If you have to choose a topic, don't rush. Take time to think through your ideas. Avoid getting so deeply involved in one topic that you cannot change to a more suitable topic in the time allotted.

Not all topics are suitable for ACADEMIC WRITING. Your topic needs to have inherent intellectual interest: ideas and issues meaty enough to demonstrate your thinking and writing abilities. Think through potential topics by breaking each into its logical subsections. Then, make sure you can supply specific details to back up each general statement. Conversely, make sure you aren't bogged down in so many details you can't figure out what GENERALIZATIONS they support.

Work toward balance by finding a middle ground. Beware of topics so broad they lead to well-meaning but vague generalizations and of topics so narrow that they lead nowhere after a few sentences.

2d.2 Broadening a narrow topic

You know a topic is too narrow when you realize there's little to say after a few sentences. When faced with a too-narrow topic, think about underlying concepts. For example, suppose you want to write about Wilfrid Laurier. If you chose "Wilfrid Laurier was the first French-speaking prime minister of Canada," you would be working with a single fact rather than a topic. To expand beyond such a narrow thought, you could think about the general area that your fact fits into—Canadian political history. Although that is too broad to be a useful topic, you are headed in the right direction. Next, you might think of a topic that relates to Laurier's political impact, such as "What effect did Wilfrid Laurier's francophone origins have on the success of the Liberal Party?" Depending on your writing situation (2c), you might need to narrow your idea further by focusing on Laurier's impact in a single area such as the question of national unity or the debate over religious education.

2d.3 Narrowing a broad topic

Narrowing a broad topic calls for you to break the topic down into subtopics. Most broad subjects can be broken down in hundreds of ways, but you need not think of all of them. Settle on a topic that interests you, one narrowed enough—but not too much—from a broad topic. For example, if you're assigned "marriage" as the topic for a 1000-word essay, "What makes a successful marriage?" is too broad. "Alexandra and Gavin were married by a justice of the peace" is too narrow. You'd likely be on target with a subtopic such as "In successful marriages, husbands and wives learn to accept each other's faults." You could use 1000 words to explain and give concrete examples of typical faults and discuss why accepting them is important. Here are two more examples:

SUBJECT	*music*
WRITING SITUATION	first-year composition class
	informative purpose
	instructor as audience
	500 words; one week
POSSIBLE TOPICS	"How music affects moods"
	"The main characteristics of country music"
	"The relationships between plots of Puccini's operas"
SUBJECT	*cities*
WRITING SITUATION	sociology course
	persuasive purpose
	peers and then instructor as audience
	950 to 1000 words; ten days
POSSIBLE TOPICS	"Comforts of city living"
	"Discomforts of city living"
	"Influence of the writings of Jane Jacobs on city planning"

Carol Moreno knew her assigned topic—"a challenge you faced and tried to meet" (2c)—was too broad. To narrow it, she used the following structured techniques for discovering and compiling ideas: browsing her journal (2f), FREEWRITING (2g), and MAPPING (2j). They helped her decide to write about the challenge of increasing her strength.

Lacie Juris also needed to narrow her topic. To explore several possible topics, she used BRAINSTORMING (2h). Once she had chosen a topic (whether wild animals should be kept as pets), she used the "journalist's questions" (2i) to compile more ideas and then a subject tree (2p) to check whether she was ready to begin drafting.

2e What can I do if no ideas occur to me?

If you've ever felt you'll never think of anything to write about, don't despair. Instead, use structured techniques, sometimes called *prewriting strategies* or *invention techniques,* for discovering and compiling ideas. Professional writers use them to uncover hidden resources in their minds. For a list of the techniques, see Box 10 (the section numbers after each tell you where to find more explanation and an example).

Try out each one. Experiment to find out which techniques suit your style of thinking. Even if one technique produces good ideas, try another to see what additional possibilities might turn up.

Save all of the ideas you generate as you explore possible topics. You never know when something you have initially rejected might prove useful. Computers make it easy to keep a folder labelled, for example, "explorations," in which you can store your ideas.

BOX 10   SUMMARY

Ways to discover and compile ideas for writing

- Keep an idea log and a journal (2f).
- Freewrite (2g).
- Brainstorm (2h).
- Ask the "journalist's questions" (2i).
- Map (2j).
- Talk it over (2k).
- Do an Internet search (2l).
- Incubate (2m).

🌐 **ESL NOTE:** The structured techniques discussed here aim to let you create ideas spontaneously without judging them right away. If such techniques are unfamiliar to you or seem difficult to implement, consider doing them first in your native language and then translating the results into English when one idea seems to have potential for your writing. 🌐

2f How do I use an idea log and a journal?

As you develop the habits of mind and behaviour of a writer, your ease with writing will grow. One such habit is keeping an idea log. Professional writers are always on the lookout for ideas to write about and details to develop their ideas. They listen, watch, talk with people, and generally keep an open mind. Because they know that good ideas can evaporate as quickly as they spring to mind, they're always ready to jot down their thoughts and observations. Some carry a pocket-size notepad, while others use a PDA (personal digital assistant, such as a Palm Pilot) or a laptop. If you use an idea log throughout your college or university years, you'll see your powers of observation increase dramatically.

Additionally, many professional writers keep a **journal.** This allows you to have a conversation in writing with yourself. Your audience is you, so the content and tone can be as personal and informal as you wish. Even fifteen minutes a day can be enough. If you don't have that chunk of time, write in your journal before you go to bed, between classes, on a bus. Some people find that the feel of pen on paper is important to this kind of writing. Others keep journals in computer files. Many even put their journals online as blogs (short for Web logs). For examples of blogs (or to start one of your own), go to <http://www.blogger.com/>.

Unlike a diary, a journal isn't a record of what you do each day. A journal is for thoughts from your reading, your observations, even your dreams. You can respond to quotations, react to movies or plays, or reflect on your opinions, beliefs, and tastes. Keeping a journal can help you in three ways. First, writing every day gives you the habit of productivity; the more you write, the more you let the words flow, the more easily you'll write in all situations. Second, a journal instils the practice of close observation and discovery, habits of mind that good writers cultivate. Third, a journal is an excellent source of ideas for assignments.

Here's an excerpt of a journal entry Carol Moreno had made before she got the assignment to write about having faced a challenge (see page 27). Even though she hadn't thought of her entry as a potential essay subject, when she read through her journal for ideas, she realized that improving her physical preparedness for nursing school was indeed a challenge she had faced.

> *September 30 I got to add 5 more reps today and it's only the sixth weight lifting class. I wasn't really surprised — I can tell I'm stronger. I wonder if I'm strong enough yet to lift Gran into the wheelchair alone. I was so scared last summer when I almost dropped her. Besides being terrified of hurting her, I thought that somehow the admissions committee would find out and tell me I was too weak to be accepted into nursing school. What if I hadn't noticed the weight lifting course for P.E. credit!?! Weight lifting is the best exercise I've ever done and I'm not getting beefy looking either.*

Excerpt from Carol Moreno's journal

2g What is freewriting?

Freewriting is writing nonstop. You write down whatever comes into your mind without stopping to wonder whether the ideas are good or the spelling is correct. When you freewrite, don't do anything to interrupt the flow. Don't censor any thoughts or flashes of insight. Don't go back and review. Don't delete.

Freewriting helps get you used to the "feel" of your fingers rapidly hitting computer keys or your pen moving across paper. Freewriting works best if you set a goal—perhaps writing for fifteen minutes or filling one or two pages. Keep going until you reach that goal, even if you have to write one word repeatedly until a new word comes to mind. Some days when you read over your freewriting, it might seem mindless, but other days your interesting ideas may startle you.

In **focused freewriting,** you write from a specific starting point—a sentence from your general freewriting, an idea, a quotation, or anything else you choose. Except for this initial focal point, focused freewriting is the same as regular freewriting. Write until you meet your time or page limit, and don't censor yourself. If you go off the topic, that's fine: See where your thoughts take you. Just keep moving forward.

Like a journal, freewriting is a good source of ideas and details. When Carol Moreno thought her weight-training course might qualify for her assignment (see page 27), she explored the topic through focused freewriting on "pumping iron."

Pumping iron—what the steroid jocks call it and exactly what I DO NOT want to be—a muscle cube. Great that Prof. Moore told us women's muscles don't bulk up much unless a weight lifting program is really intense—they just get longer. No bulk for me PLEASE. Just want upper body strength—oh and the aerobic stuff from swimming, which makes me feel great. Lift sweat swim lift sweat swim lift sweat swim.

Excerpt from Carol Moreno's freewriting

2h What is brainstorming?

Brainstorming means listing everything you can think of about a topic. Let your mind range freely, generating quantities of ideas. Write words, phrases, or sentence fragments—whatever comes to you. If you run out of ideas, ask yourself exploratory questions, such as *What is it? What is it the same as? How is it different? Why or how does it happen? How is it done? What causes it or results from it? What does it look, smell, sound, feel, or taste like?*

After you've compiled a list, go to step two: Look for patterns, ways to group the ideas into categories. You'll probably find several categories. Set aside any items that don't fit into a group. If a category interests you but has only a few items, brainstorm that category alone.

You can brainstorm in one concentrated session or over several days, depending on how much time you have for an assignment. Brainstorming in a PEER-RESPONSE GROUP can be especially fruitful: One person's ideas bounce off the next person's; more ideas come to mind.

When brainstorming or FREEWRITING on a computer, try "invisible writing." Temporarily turn off your computer monitor. A blank screen can help you focus on getting the words out without the temptation to stop and criticize, but the computer will still be recording your words. When you can write no more, turn on the monitor to see what you have.

Brainstorming was a technique Lacie Juris used to find her topic about keeping wild animals as pets (6b). Brainstorming helped her think through several topics and generate some ideas about the one that most appealed to her.

- women on TV commercials: realistic?
- health care funding—don't know much on that
- holidays are too commercial
- parking situation at this college—solutions?
- protecting wild animals
- wild animals as pets—that bothers me; why?
- is it healthy for the animals? for people? is it fair?
- ~~famous people and their pets~~ nope
- laws about pets and pet owners

Lacie Juris's brainstorming

EXERCISE 2-2

Here's a list brainstormed for a writing assignment. The topic was "Ways to promote a new movie." Working individually or in a peer-response group, look over the list and group the ideas. You'll find that some ideas don't fit into a group. Then, add any other ideas you have to the list.

coming attractions	suspense
TV ads	book the movie was based on
provocative	controversy
movie reviews	rating
how movie was made	adventure
sneak previews	newspaper ads
word of mouth	stars
director	dialogue
topical subject	excitement
special effects	photography

2i What are the "journalist's questions"?

When journalists report a story, they gather and write about information by asking who did what, where it happened, when it happened, and why and how it happened. The same questions come in handy for writers exploring a topic. The **journalist's questions** are *Who? What? When? Where? Why?* and *How?*

Lacie Juris used the journalist's questions to expand her thinking on the problems of keeping wild animals as pets. Her answers, listed below, showed her that she had enough material for a good essay.

WHO?	**Who** benefits from keeping wild animals as pets?
WHAT?	**What** kinds of pets do people keep?
WHEN?	**When** did the practice of owning wild animals begin?
WHERE?	**Where** can I find evidence that wild animals make dangerous pets?
WHY?	**Why** do some people think they have a right to do this?
HOW?	**How** exactly would we stop this process?

2j   What is mapping?

Mapping, also called *clustering,* is a visual form of brainstorming. When some writers actually see ways that their ideas connect, they begin to think more creatively. Other writers like mapping to help them check the logical relationships between ideas.

Carol Moreno's mapping

To map, write your topic in the middle of a sheet of paper and draw a circle around it. Now, moving out from the centre, use lines and circles to show ideas that are subtopics of the topic in the centre circle. Continue to subdivide and add details. At any time, you can move to a blank space on your map and start a new subtopic. Try to keep going without censoring yourself.

Carol Moreno used mapping to prompt herself to discover ideas about women and weight training (see previous page). When she finished, she was satisfied that she'd have enough to say in her essay.

2k How can "talking it over" help?

Talking it over is based on the notion that two heads are better than one. The expression "bouncing ideas off each other" captures this idea. When you discuss a topic with someone interested in listening and making suggestions, you often think of new ideas. You can collaborate with others while brainstorming, asking the journalist's questions, or mapping. Ways of approaching a point of discussion include debating, questioning, analyzing (5b), evaluating (5c.3), synthesizing (5e), and assessing reasoning (5i).

People you trust can serve as "sounding boards" and tell you if your ideas are complete and reasonable. If your instructor sets up PEER-RESPONSE GROUPS in your class, you might ask the other members to serve as sounding boards. Otherwise, talk with a good friend or another adult.

2l How can an Internet search help?

Internet searches help you find topics to write about; understand your subject's categories from the most general to the most specific; and locate specific information. Internet searches scan the WORLD WIDE WEB using **search engines,** which are software programs that rapidly locate online information sources. Some instructors want students to think of ideas on their own, without searching the Web. If that's the case, don't.

Chapter 33 provides extensive guidelines for searching the Internet. Briefly, however, try <http://www.google.ca>. When you get there, click the "Directory" button to see a screen that lists broad subject areas.

Next, click on "Society" to see a number of slightly more specific topics. Note that each of them would be much too broad to write about. However, if you keep clicking on topic headings, you'll move to more and more specific subjects. Browsing through the layers of topics can help you think of several ideas for your writing. If you know a general topic area, you can type it in the search window of the program and then click on more specific subcategories.

EXERCISE 2-3

On a computer connected to the Internet, go to <http://www.google.ca>. Click on "Directory" (accessible via "more >>" above the search window) and then choose one of the headings. Continue to click on topics under that heading to create a "path" to a specific possible topic. Be ready to explain the sequence (or path) you used, what you found, and what you think the strengths and weaknesses of the topics you identified would be. Finally, go back to the opening "Directory" page and repeat the process with a different heading.

URL for Google
<http://www.google.com>   Choices within Google

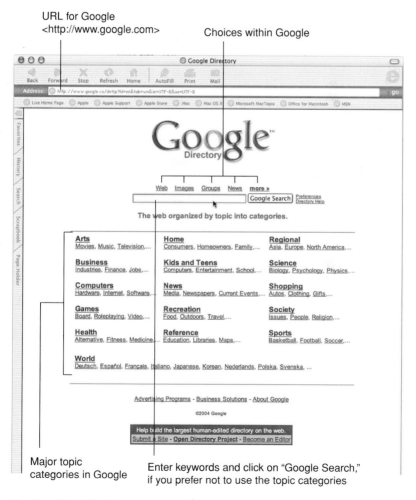

Major topic
categories in Google   Enter keywords and click on "Google Search,"
                          if you prefer not to use the topic categories

Google subject directory

EXERCISE 2-4

Explore some of the following topics by typing them into the search window of a search engine. You can use Google, as for Exercise 2-3, or you can try a different search engine. Be ready to explain the sequence of topics you discover.

1. global warming
2. intelligence
3. plagiarism
4. memory
5. disability

URL for major topic category "Society"

Enter keywords and click "Google Search" if you prefer not to use the "Society" topic categories

Topic categories within major topic "Society"

Google "Society" directory

2m How can incubation help me?

Incubation refers to giving your ideas time to grow and develop. This technique works especially well when you need to step back and evaluate what you've discovered and compiled for your writing. For example, you might not see how your material can be pulled together at first, but if you let it incubate, you might discover connections you didn't see originally. Conversely, if some parts of your essay seem too thin in content, incubation gives you distance from your material so that you can decide what works. Ideally, incubate your ideas overnight or for a couple of days; but even a few hours can help.

If you don't have the luxury of a lengthy incubation period, some strategies may help you jump-start your writing. One method is to turn your attention to something entirely unrelated. Concentrate hard on that other matter. After a while, relax and guide your mind back to your writing. Often, you'll see what you've discovered and compiled for writing in a different way. Another strategy for incubation is to allow your mind to wander without thinking about anything in particular. Relax and open your mind to random thoughts, but don't dwell on any one thought very long. After a while, guide your mind back to your writing. Often, you'll see solutions that hadn't occurred to you before.

EXERCISE 2-5

Try each structured technique for discovering and compiling ideas discussed in 2e through 2m. Use your own topics or select from the suggestions below.

1. a dream trip
2. an important personal decision
3. professional sports
4. meeting deadlines
5. what you want in a life partner

2n How can shaping help me?

Shaping writing means organizing your material. Like a story, an essay needs a beginning, a middle, and an end. The essay's introduction sets the stage; the essay's body paragraphs provide the substance of your message in a sequence that makes sense; the conclusion ends the essay logically. The major elements in an informative essay are listed in Box 11. (For the major elements in a persuasive essay using classical argument, see Box 39 in 6f.)

BOX 11   SUMMARY

Elements in an informative essay

1. **Introductory paragraph:** Leads into the topic of the essay and tries to capture the reader's interest.
2. **Thesis statement:** States the central message of the writing. The thesis statement (2q) usually appears at the end of the introductory paragraph.

→

Elements in an informative essay (*continued*)

3. **Background information:** Provides a context for understanding the points a writer wants to make. You can integrate background information into the introductory paragraph. More complex information may require a separate paragraph (as in the second paragraph in Carol Moreno's essay, in section 3g).
4. **Points of discussion:** Support the essay's thesis statement. They're the essential content of the body paragraphs in an essay. Each point of discussion consists of a general statement backed up by specific details.
5. **Concluding paragraph:** Ends the essay smoothly, flowing logically from the rest of the essay (4k).

Each paragraph's length in an informative essay needs to be in proportion to its function. Introductory and concluding paragraphs are usually shorter than body paragraphs. Body paragraphs need to be somewhat approximate to each other in length. If one body paragraph becomes overly long in relation to the others, consider breaking it into two paragraphs. (I discuss paragraph writing extensively in Chapter 4.)

2o How can looking for "levels of generality" help me?

Generality is a relative term. Concepts exist in the context of—in relationship with—other concepts. When you look for **levels of generality,** you're figuring out which ideas or concepts can be grouped. Levels of generality start with the most general and work down to the most specific. Conversely, **levels of specificity** start with the most specific and work up to the most general. Being aware of levels, particularly when writing body paragraphs, gives you a sensible sequence for presenting your material. Use whichever pattern works for you because each sequence is merely the reverse of the other. Here's an example.

LEVELS OF GENERALITY (BIG TO SMALL) ▽

MOST GENERAL: LEVEL 1	a bank
LESS GENERAL: LEVEL 2	money in the bank
LESS GENERAL: LEVEL 3	bank account
LESS GENERAL: LEVEL 4	chequing account
LEAST GENERAL: LEVEL 5	account #123456 at Bank EZCome, EZGo

LEVELS OF SPECIFICITY (SMALL TO BIG) △

MOST SPECIFIC: LEVEL 5	account #123456 at Bank EZCome, EZGo
LESS SPECIFIC: LEVEL 4	chequing account
LESS SPECIFIC: LEVEL 3	bank account
LESS SPECIFIC: LEVEL 2	money in the bank
LEAST SPECIFIC: LEVEL 1	a bank

2p How can a subject tree help me?

A **subject tree** shows you visually whether you have sufficient content, at varying levels of generality or specificity, to start a first draft of your writing. A subject tree also visually demonstrates whether you have a good balance of general ideas and specific details. If what you have are mostly general ideas—or, the other way around, mostly specific details—go back to techniques for discovering and compiling ideas (2e through 2m) so that you can come up with the sorts of materials that are missing.

Lacie Juris used a subject tree to help her shape the fifth and sixth paragraphs in her essay (6m).

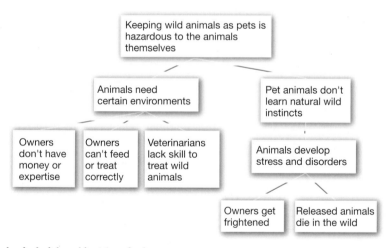

Lacie Juris's subject tree for her essay

2q What is a thesis statement?

A **thesis statement** is the central message of an essay. It's the essay's main idea. As a writer, you want to write a thesis statement with great care so that it prepares your readers for what follows in the essay. This means your thesis statement has to reflect with some accuracy the content of your essay. Box 12 lists the basic requirements for a thesis statement.

BOX 12 SUMMARY

Basic requirements for a thesis statement

- It states the essay's subject—the topic that you discuss.
- It conveys the essay's purpose—either informative or persuasive.
- It indicates your focus—the assertion that presents your point of view.
- It uses specific language, not vague words.
- It may briefly state the major subdivisions of the essay's topic.

Some instructors add to these basic requirements. You might, for example, be asked to put your thesis statement at the end of your introductory paragraph (as in the final draft of Carol Moreno's essay, in section 3g.3). Some instructors require that the thesis statement be contained in one sentence; other instructors permit two sentences if the topic is complex. All requirements, basic and additional, are designed to help you develop a thesis statement that will guide the writing of your essay and help you communicate clearly with your reader. Be sure not to confuse a thesis statement with the essay's title (3c.3).

ESL NOTE: A thesis statement, especially in the introductory paragraph, is commonly found in the ACADEMIC WRITING of North American and some other cultures. If your culture would consider such an early, blunt, and straightforward statement to be rude or crude, respect your tradition but nevertheless write one for your Canadian academic essays.

Most writers find that their thesis statement changes somewhat with each successive draft of an essay. Still, when you revise its language, be sure to stick to the essential idea you want to communicate. A thesis statement is a guide; it helps you stay on the topic and develop your ideas in an essay. To start, make an **assertion**—a sentence stating your topic and the point you want to make about it. This assertion focuses your thinking as you develop a preliminary thesis statement. Next, move toward a final thesis statement that most accurately reflects the content of your essay.

Following is the evolution of Carol Moreno's thesis statement as she moved from a simple assertion to her final version for her essay on weight training.

NO I think women can "pump iron" like men. [This assertion is a start.]

NO If she is trained well, any woman can "pump iron" well, just like a man. [This can be considered a preliminary thesis because it's more specific (it mentions training), but the word *any* is vague and inaccurate, and the word *well* appears twice.]

NO In spite of most people thinking only men can "pump iron," women can also do it successfully with the right training. [This draft is better because it's more specific, but "most people thinking only men" goes off Moreno's intended topic. Also, this draft doesn't mention Moreno's central concept of building strength.]

YES With the right training, women can "pump iron" to build strength. [This is a good thesis statement.]

Thesis statements for informative essays

Here are more examples of thesis statements for 500- to 700-word essays with an informative purpose (1c.2). The NO versions are assertions or preliminary thesis statements. The YES versions fulfil the requirements in Box 12.

TOPIC *suing for malpractice*
NO There are many kinds of malpractice suits.
YES Recent changes to legal structures are facilitating malpractice suits against lawyers, teachers, and even parents.

TOPIC *women artists*
NO Paintings by women express gender issues.
YES The series of biblical paintings by Artemisia Gentileschi highlights acts of revenge by women against men.

Thesis statements for persuasive essays

Here are examples of thesis statements written for 500- to 700-word essays with a persuasive purpose (1c.3). Again, the NO versions are assertions or preliminary thesis statements. The YES versions fulfil the requirements in Box 12.

TOPIC *urban sprawl*
NO Large North American cities and their suburbs are expanding into the countryside uncontrollably.
YES Despite their stated concerns about urban sprawl, municipal politicians actually facilitate it through zoning, transportation, and infrastructure policies.

TOPIC *deceptive advertising*
NO Deceptive advertising is not adequately prosecuted.
YES Political contributions and the nomination of ex-politicians to their boards effectively exempt large corporations from laws against deceptive advertising.

EXERCISE 2-6

Each set of sentences below offers several versions of a thesis statement. Within each set, the thesis statements progress from weak to strong. The fourth thesis statement in each set is the best. Based on the requirements listed in Box 12, work individually or with a peer-response group to explain why the first three choices in each set are weak and the last is best.

A. 1. Advertising is complex.
    2. Magazine advertisements appeal to readers.
    3. Magazine advertisements must be creative and appealing to all readers.
    4. To appeal to readers, magazine advertisements must skilfully use language, colour, and design.
B. 1. Tennis is excellent exercise.
    2. Playing tennis is fun.
    3. Tennis requires various skills.
    4. Changes in racquet technology and serving styles call for a different set of skills than the one that champion players needed in the past.
C. 1. Tom Thomson painted in Algonquin Park.
    2. The Tom Thomson "myth" portrays him as an untaught phenomenon.
    3. Tom Thomson studied art and worked in an advertising studio.
    4. The influence of Tom Thomson's art education and professional environment shows in the painting techniques he explored.
D. 1. We should pay attention to the environment.
    2. We should worry about air pollution.
    3. Automobile emissions cause air pollution.
    4. Governments should raise emissions standards for passenger cars and SUVs.
E. 1. Many people aren't interested in politics.
    2. Citizens have become increasingly dissatisfied with the political process.
    3. Many postsecondary students are cynical about the political process.
    4. Lowering the voting age would involve students constructively in the political process, harness their idealism, and increase their voting turnout.

EXERCISE 2-7

Here are writing assignments, narrowed topics, and tentative thesis statements. Alone or with a peer-response group, evaluate each thesis statement according to the basic requirements in Box 12.

1. *Marketing assignment:* 700- to 800-word persuasive report on the school's cafeteria. *Audience:* the instructor and the cafeteria's manager. *Topic:* cafeteria conditions. *Thesis:* The cafeteria could attract more students if it improved the quality of its food, its appearance, and the friendliness of its staff.
2. *Art assignment:* 300- to 500-word analysis of an Inuit print. *Audience:* the instructor and other students in the class. *Topic:* Pitseolak Ashoona's *Perils of the Sea Travellers. Thesis: Perils of the Sea Travellers* is one of the most moving images of traditional Inuit life.
3. *Chemistry assignment:* 800- to 1000-word informative report about the ozone layer. *Audience:* the instructor and visiting students and instructors attending a seminar. *Topic:* recent research on the ozone layer. *Thesis:* Canada should increase efforts to slow the destruction of the ozone layer.
4. *Journalism assignment:* 200- to 300-word article about student debt. *Audience:* the instructor, the student body, and the administration. *Topic:* indebtedness of graduates. *Thesis:* The average debt rate of four-year graduates has tripled over the past fifteen years, while student assistance has remained stable for the past five years.
5. *Nursing assignment:* 400- to 500-word persuasive report about technology changes in nursing. *Audience:* nursing students and professionals. *Topic:* using hand-held computers to track patient information. *Thesis:* More hospitals are requiring nurses to use hand-held computers to enter patient data instead of using traditional charts.

2r What is outlining?

An **outline** lays out the relationships among ideas in a piece of writing. Outlines can lead writers to see how well their writing is organized. Many instructors require that outlines be handed in either before or with an essay.

Some writers like to outline; others don't. If you don't, but you're required to write an outline, tackle the job with an open mind. You may be pleasantly surprised at what the rigour of outline writing does to your perception of your essay.

An outline can be *informal* or *formal.* Try outlining at various steps of the WRITING PROCESS: before drafting, to arrange ideas; while you draft, to keep track of your material; while you revise, to check the logical flow of thought or to reveal what information is missing, repeated, or off the topic; or in whatever other ways you find helpful.

Informal outlines

An **informal outline** is a working plan that lays out the major points of an essay. Because it's informal, it doesn't need to use the numbering and lettering conventions of a formal outline. Complete sentences aren't required; words and phrases are acceptable. Carol Moreno used an informal outline for planning her essay (3g). Here's how she roughed out her third paragraph.

CAROL MORENO'S INFORMAL OUTLINE

Thesis statement: With the right training, women can "pump iron" to build strength.

> how to use weights
> > safety is vital
> > free weights
> > > don't bend at waist
> > > align neck and back
> > > look straight ahead
> > > weight machines—safety

Formal outlines

A **formal outline** requires you to use the conventions that dictate how to display relationships among ideas. You need to adhere strictly to the numbering and lettering conventions required, as shown below. A formal outline can be either a topic outline or a sentence outline. In a topic outline, each entry is a word or phrase. In a sentence outline, each entry is a complete sentence. Never mix the two types.

Writers who use formal outlines say that a sentence outline brings them closer to drafting than a topic outline does. This makes sense because topic outlines carry less information. But you have to find out which type works better for you.

Here's a topic outline of the final draft of Carol Moreno's essay on weight lifting for women (3g.3). A sentence outline follows it so that you can compare the two types of outlines.

TOPIC OUTLINE

Thesis statement: With the right training, women can "pump iron" to build strength.

  I. Avoidance of massive muscle development
    A. Role of women's biology
      1. Not much muscle-bulking hormone
      2. Muscles get longer, not bulkier
    B. Role of combining exercise types
      1. Anaerobic (weight lifting)
      2. Aerobic (swimming)
  II. Safe use of weights
    A. Free weights
      1. Unsafe lifting techniques
      2. Safe lifting techniques
        a. Head alignment
        b. Neck and back alignment

    B. Weight machines

III. Individualized program based on physical condition
    A. Role of resistance and reps
    B. Characteristics for personalizing the program
        1. Weight
        2. Age
        3. Physical condition

IV. Individualized weight-training program
    A. Upper body strength
    B. Individual objectives
        1. Mine
        2. Car crash victim's
        3. Physical therapist's

SENTENCE OUTLINE

Thesis statement: With the right training, women can "pump iron" to build strength.

I. The right training lets women who lift weights avoid developing massive muscles.
    A. Women's biology plays a role.
        1. Women don't produce much of a specific muscle-bulking hormone.
        2. Women's muscles tend to grow longer rather than bulkier.
    B. Combining different kinds of exercise also plays a role.
        1. Anaerobic exercise, like weight lifting, builds muscle.
        2. Aerobic exercise, like swimming, builds endurance and stamina.

II. The right training shows women how to use weights safely to prevent injury.
    A. Free weights require special precautions.
        1. Bending at the waist and jerking a barbell up are unsafe.
        2. Squatting and using leg and back muscles to straighten up are safe.
            a. The head is held erect and faces forward.
            b. The neck and back are aligned and held straight.
    B. Weight machines make it easier to lift safely because they force proper body alignment.

III. The right training includes individualized programs based on a woman's physical condition.
    A. Progress comes from resistance and from repetitions tailored to individual capabilities.
    B. Programs consider a woman's physical characteristics.
        1. Her weight is a factor.
        2. Her age is a factor.
        3. Her physical conditioning is a factor.

IV. The right training includes individualized programs based on a woman's personal goals.
   A. Certain muscle groups are targeted to increase women's upper body strength.
   B. Other muscle groups are targeted based on individual objectives.
      1. I wanted to strengthen muscles needed for lifting patients.
      2. An accident victim wanted to strengthen her neck muscles.
      3. A physical therapist wanted to strengthen her fingers and hands.

EXERCISE 2-8

Here is a sentence outline. Individually or with your peer-response group, revise it into a topic outline. Then, be ready to explain why you prefer using a topic outline or a sentence outline as a guide to writing. For help, consult 2r.

Thesis statement: Common noise pollution, although it causes many problems in our society, can be reduced.

I. Noise pollution comes from many sources.
   A. Noise pollution occurs in many large cities.
      1. Traffic rumbles and screeches.
      2. Construction work blasts.
      3. Airplanes roar overhead.
   B. Noise pollution occurs in the workplace.
      1. Machines in factories boom.
      2. Office machines beep, buzz, hum, and even speak.
   C. Noise pollution occurs during leisure-time activities.
      1. Stereo headphones blare directly into eardrums.
      2. Film soundtracks bombard the ears.
      3. Music in clubs assaults the ears.
II. Noise pollution causes many problems.
   A. Excessive noise damages hearing.
   B. Excessive noise alters mood.
   C. Constant exposure to noise limits learning ability.
III. Reduction in noise pollution is possible.
   A. Pressure from community groups can support efforts to control excessive noise.
   B. Traffic regulations can help alleviate congestion and noise.
   C. Pressure from workers can force management to reduce noise.
   D. People can wear earplugs to avoid excessive noise.
   E. Reasonable sound levels for headphones, soundtracks, and clubs can be required.

Chapter 3

Drafting and Revising

In the WRITING PROCESS, drafting and revising come after PLANNING and SHAPING (Chapter 2). **Drafting** means you get ideas onto paper or into a computer file in sentences and paragraphs. In everyday conversation, people use the word *writing* to talk about drafting, but writing is too broad a term here. The word *drafting* more accurately describes what you do when you write your first attempt—your first *draft*—to generate words. **Revising** means you look over your first draft, analyze and evaluate it for yourself, and then rewrite it by composing a number of subsequent versions, or drafts, to get closer to what you want to say. Revising involves adding, cutting, moving material, and after that, EDITING and PROOFREADING.

3a What can help me write a first draft?

A **first draft** is the initial version of a piece of writing. Before you begin a first draft, seek out places and times of the day that encourage you to write. You might write best in a quiet corner of the library, or at 4:30 a.m. at the kitchen table before anyone else is awake, or outside alone with nature, or with a steady flow of people walking by. Most experienced writers, myself among them, find they concentrate best when they're alone and where they won't be interrupted. But individuals differ, and you may prefer background noise—a crowded cafeteria with the low hum of conversation, for example.

A caution: Don't mislead yourself. You can't produce a useful first draft while talking to friends and stopping only now and then to jot down a sentence. You won't draft smoothly while watching television or being constantly interrupted.

Some writers do all their planning, shaping, drafting, revising, and editing on the computer. Other writers create first drafts by hand and reserve the computer for revising and editing. Experiment to see which steps are easier for you to do by hand, and which by computer.

Finally, resist delaying tactics. While you certainly need a computer or a pad of paper and a pen or pencil, you don't need fifteen perfectly sharpened pencils neatly lined up on your desk.

Box 13 offers suggestions for the transition from PLANNING and SHAPING into drafting. Experiment to see what works best for you. Be ready to adjust what works according to each WRITING SITUATION.

BOX 13   SUMMARY

Ways to start drafting

- **Write a discovery draft.** Put aside all your notes from planning and shaping, and write a discovery draft. This means using FOCUSED FREEWRITING to get ideas on paper or onto your computer screen so that you can make connections that spring to mind as you write. Your discovery draft can serve as a first draft or as notes for a more structured first draft.

- **Work from your notes.** Sort your notes from planning and shaping into groups of subtopics. When you start writing, you can systematically concentrate on each subtopic without having to search repeatedly through your pile of notes. Arrange the subtopics in what seems to be a sensible sequence, knowing you can always go back later and re-sequence the subtopics. Now write a first draft by working through your notes on each subtopic. Draft either the entire essay or chunks of a few paragraphs at one time.

- **Use a combination of approaches.** When you know the shape of your material, write according to that structure. When you feel "stuck" and don't know what to say next, switch to writing as you would for a discovery draft.

Now, dive in. Based on the planning and shaping you've done (Chapter 2), start writing. The direction of drafting is forward: Keep pressing ahead. If you wonder about the spelling of a word or a point in grammar, don't stop. Use a symbol or other signal to alert you to revisit later. Use whatever you like: boldface, underlining, a question mark before and after, an asterisk, or all capital letters. If the exact word you want escapes you while you're drafting, substitute an easy synonym and mark it to go back to later. If you question your sentence style or the order in which you present supporting details, boldface or underline it, or insert a symbol or the word *Style?* or *Order?* nearby so that you can return to it later. If you begin to run out of ideas, reread what you have written—not to start revising prematurely, but only to propel yourself to keep moving ahead with your first draft. Once you finish your draft, search for the boldfaces, underlines, symbols, or words that you've used to alert you to reconsider something. If it's a word, you can use the "Edit>Find" function on your word-processing program toolbar.

When drafting on the computer, use the "Save" function often to protect your work, at least every ten minutes. This prevents your losing what you've written. Also, print your work regularly—very definitely at the end of each work session—so that you always have a hard copy in case your computer develops problems (a not unusual occurrence).

A first draft is a preliminary or rough draft. Its purpose is to get your ideas onto disk or into computer memory or on paper. Never are first drafts meant to be perfect.

3b How can I overcome writer's block?

If you're afraid or otherwise feel unable to start writing, perhaps you're being stopped by **writer's block.** You want to get started but somehow can't. Often, writer's block occurs because the writer harbours a fear of being wrong. To overcome that fear, or any other cause of your block, first admit it to yourself. Face it honestly so that you can understand whatever is holding you back. Writer's block can strike professional as well as student writers, and a variety of techniques to overcome it have become popular.

The most common cause of writer's block involves a writer's belief in myths about writing.

MYTH   Writers are born, not made.

TRUTH   Everyone can write. Writers don't expect to "get it right" the first time. Being a good writer means being a patient rewriter.

MYTH   Writers have to be "in the mood" to write.

TRUTH   If writers always waited for "the mood" to occur, few would write at all. News reporters and other professional writers have deadlines to meet.

MYTH   Writers have to be really good at grammar and spelling.

TRUTH   Writers don't let spelling and grammar block them. They write, and when they suspect that a word or sentence isn't quite right, they mark the spot with a symbol or word in all capitals. After they're finished drafting, they return to these, perhaps using this handbook or a dictionary or thesaurus to check themselves.

MYTH   Writers don't have to revise.

TRUTH   Writers expect to revise—several times. Once words are on paper, writers can see what readers will see. This "re-vision" helps writers revise.

MYTH   Writing can be done at the last minute.

TRUTH   Drafting and revising take time. Ideas don't leap onto paper in final, polished form.

Box 14 lists reliable strategies writers have developed to overcome writer's block. If you feel blocked, experiment to discover which works best for you. Add your own ideas. As you use the list in Box 14, suspend judgment of your writing. Let things flow. Don't find fault with what you're writing. You can evaluate and improve your writing when you're revising it. According to research, premature revision stops many writers cold—and leads to writer's block. Your reward for waiting to revise until after you finish your first draft is the comfort of having a springboard for your revising in front of you.

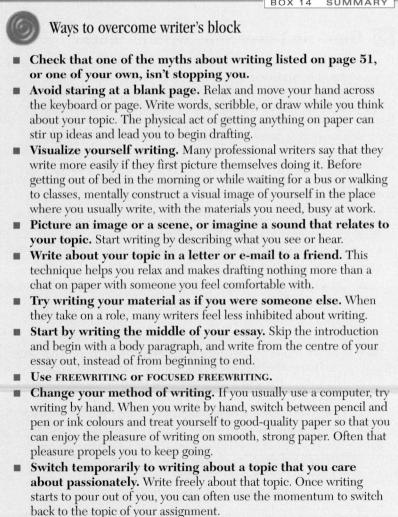

BOX 14   SUMMARY

Ways to overcome writer's block

- **Check that one of the myths about writing listed on page 51, or one of your own, isn't stopping you.**
- **Avoid staring at a blank page.** Relax and move your hand across the keyboard or page. Write words, scribble, or draw while you think about your topic. The physical act of getting anything on paper can stir up ideas and lead you to begin drafting.
- **Visualize yourself writing.** Many professional writers say that they write more easily if they first picture themselves doing it. Before getting out of bed in the morning or while waiting for a bus or walking to classes, mentally construct a visual image of yourself in the place where you usually write, with the materials you need, busy at work.
- **Picture an image or a scene, or imagine a sound that relates to your topic.** Start writing by describing what you see or hear.
- **Write about your topic in a letter or e-mail to a friend.** This technique helps you relax and makes drafting nothing more than a chat on paper with someone you feel comfortable with.
- **Try writing your material as if you were someone else.** When they take on a role, many writers feel less inhibited about writing.
- **Start by writing the middle of your essay.** Skip the introduction and begin with a body paragraph, and write from the centre of your essay out, instead of from beginning to end.
- **Use FREEWRITING or FOCUSED FREEWRITING.**
- **Change your method of writing.** If you usually use a computer, try writing by hand. When you write by hand, switch between pencil and pen or ink colours and treat yourself to good-quality paper so that you can enjoy the pleasure of writing on smooth, strong paper. Often that pleasure propels you to keep going.
- **Switch temporarily to writing about a topic that you care about passionately.** Write freely about that topic. Once writing starts to pour out of you, you can often use the momentum to switch back to the topic of your assignment.

3c How do I revise?

Revising is rewriting. When you see the word *revision,* break it down to *re-vision,* which means "to see again with fresh eyes." To revise, evaluate, change, and re-evaluate your draft to figure out ways to improve it. To do this, you need to read your writing honestly, without losing confidence or becoming defensive. After all, what's on the page is ink, not ego. As you work, look at whatever you change and evaluate the revision first on its own and then in the context of the surrounding material. Continue until you're satisfied that your essay is the best you can make it, in light of your specific WRITING SITUATION.

Whenever possible within your time frame, distance yourself from each draft. The best way is to leave a chunk of time between finishing a first draft and starting to revise. Doing so helps you develop an objective sense of your work. Student writers often want to hold on to their every word, especially if they had trouble getting started on a first draft. Resist such a feeling vigorously. Put away your draft, and allow the rosy glow of authorial pride to dim a bit. The Roman writer Horace recommended waiting nine years before revising! You might try to wait a few hours or even thirty minutes. Better yet, take a day or two before going back to look at your work with fresh eyes.

Also, as you're revising, don't start EDITING too soon. Editing comes after revising. Research shows that premature editing distracts writers from dealing with the larger issues that revision involves.

3c.1 Goals and activities during revision

Your goal during revision is to improve your draft at two levels: the *global level,* which involves the whole essay and paragraphs, and the *local level,* which involves sentences and words.

To revise successfully, you need first to expect to revise. The myth that good writers never have to revise is nonsense. Only the opposite is true: Writing is revising. Final drafts evolve from first drafts. Here's how to prepare your mind for revising:

- Shift mentally from suspending judgment (during idea gathering and drafting) to making judgments. Read your draft objectively with "a cold eye" to evaluate it.

- Decide whether to write an entirely new draft or to revise the one you have. Be critical as you evaluate your first draft, but don't be overly harsh. Many early drafts provide sufficient raw material for revision to get under way.

- Be systematic. Don't evaluate at random. Most writers work best when they concentrate on each element sequentially. Start with your draft's overall organization; next, move to its paragraphs, then to its sentences, and finally to its word choice. If you need practice in being systematic, try using a revision checklist, either one supplied by your instructor or the ones in this handbook in Box 17.

You can engage in the activities of revision, listed in Box 15, by using a computer or revising by hand. Computers have removed much of the tedious work of copying and recopying material, allowing you to make both large and small changes easily. For example, moving text is easy on a computer. First, print a copy of your original draft to have at hand in case you later decide that you prefer your original version of a sentence or a section. Then "Cut" and "Paste" to reorder sentences or rearrange paragraphs.

BOX 15   SUMMARY

Major activities during revision

Add: Insert needed words, sentences, and paragraphs. If your additions require new content, return to the structured techniques shown in Chapter 2.

Cut: Get rid of whatever goes off the topic or repeats what has already been said.

Replace: As needed, substitute new words, sentences, and paragraphs for what you have cut.

Move: Change the sequence of paragraphs if the material isn't presented in logical order. Move sentences within paragraphs or to other paragraphs when your PARAGRAPH ARRANGEMENT does not allow the material to flow.

Beware of two temptations when writing with the computer. Because you can rearrange and otherwise revise endlessly, you may need to set limits, or you'll never finish the assignment. The opposite seduction is also possible: A neatly printed page may look like a final draft, but it definitely isn't one.

3c.2 The role of a thesis statement in revision

The THESIS STATEMENT of your essay has great organizing power because it controls and limits what your essay can cover. The thesis statement presents the TOPIC of your essay, your particular focus on that topic, and your PURPOSE for writing about that topic. Your first draft of a thesis statement is usually only an estimate of what you plan to cover in your essay. Therefore, as you revise, keep checking the accuracy of your thesis statement. Use the thesis statement's controlling power to bring it and your essay into line with each other. When your essay is finished, the thesis statement and what you say in your essay should match. If they don't, you need to revise either the thesis statement or the essay— or sometimes both.

Every writer's experience with revising a thesis statement varies from essay to essay. Carol Moreno, the student you met in Chapter 2 as she did her planning and shaping, wrote several versions of her thesis statement (shown in 2q) before she started to draft. After writing her first draft, she checked her last draft of her thesis statement, "With the right training, women can 'pump iron' to build strength," and decided that it communicated what she wanted to say. But that wasn't the end of it: Moreno had to change parts of her essay to conform more closely to her thesis statement. You can read Moreno's three complete drafts, along with comments, at the end of this chapter (3g).

3c.3 The role of an essay title in revision

Your essay **title** can also show you what needs revising because it clarifies the overall point of the essay. An effective title sets you on your course and tells your readers what to expect. Some writers like to begin their first drafts with a title at the top of the page to focus their thinking. Then, as they revise drafts, they revise the title. If, however, no title springs to mind, don't be concerned. Often, a good title doesn't surface until after drafting, revising, and even editing. Whatever you do, never tack on a title as an afterthought right before handing in your essay. A suitable title is essential for readers to think about as they begin focusing on your essay.

Titles can be direct or indirect. A **direct title** tells exactly what your essay is about. A direct title contains key words under which the essay could be catalogued in a library or an online database.

A direct title shouldn't be too broad. For example, Moreno's first title was "Pumping Iron." By her final draft (3g.3), Moreno realized her early title was too broad, so she revised it to "Women Can Pump Iron, Too." Conversely, a direct title should not be too narrow. "Avoiding Injury When Pumping Iron" is too narrow a title for Moreno's essay, given what she discusses in it.

An **indirect title** only hints at the essay's topic. It tries to catch the reader's interest by presenting a puzzle that can be solved by reading the essay. When writing an indirect title, avoid titles that are obscure or cute. A satisfactory indirect title for Moreno's final draft might be "On Goals." In contrast, the indirect title "Equal Play" wouldn't work because it's only remotely related to the point of the essay.

👁 **ALERT:** When you write the title at the top of the page or on a title page, never enclose it in quotation marks or underline it. Let your title stand on its own, without decoration, on your title page or at the top centre of the first page of your essay. 👁

Whether direct or indirect, your essay title stands on its own. It's never the opening sentence of your essay. For example, Moreno's essay,

BOX 16 SUMMARY

Guidelines for writing essay titles

■ Don't wait until the last minute to tack a title on your essay. Try writing a title before you begin drafting or while you're revising. Then double-check as you prepare your final draft to confirm that the title clearly relates to your essay's content.

■ For a direct title, use key words that relate to your topic, but don't get overly specific and try to reveal your entire essay.

■ For an indirect title, be sure that its meaning will become very clear when your readers have finished your essay. Be sure, also, that it isn't too cute.

■ Don't use quotation marks with the title or underline it (unless your title includes another title; see pages 556, 612, 643).

■ Don't consider your essay title as the first sentence of your essay.

titled "Women Can Pump Iron, Too," would suffer a major blow if the first sentence were "Women certainly can" or "I am the proof." Similarly, never does the first sentence of an essay refer to the essay's title. Rather, the first sentence starts the flow of the essay's content. Box 16 offers you guidelines for writing effective essay titles.

3c.4 The role of unity and coherence in an essay

Chapter 4 in this handbook shows you many techniques for achieving unity and coherence in an essay, but here I need to preview the concepts because they're central concerns as you revise.

An essay has **unity** (4d) when all of its parts relate to the THESIS STATEMENT and to each other. Use two criteria to judge this. First, does the thesis statement clearly tie in to all TOPIC SENTENCES? Second, does each paragraph—especially the body paragraphs—contain examples, reasons, facts, and details that relate directly to its topic sentence and, in turn, to the thesis statement? In a nutshell, as you revise make sure that nothing in the essay is off the topic.

An essay achieves **coherence** (4g) through closely built relationships among ideas and details that are built on word choice, use of TRANSITIONAL EXPRESSIONS, clear use of PRONOUNS, and effective PARALLELISM.

3c.5 Using a revision checklist

A revision checklist can focus your attention as you evaluate and revise your writing. Use such a checklist, either one provided by your instructor or one that you compile on your own, based on Box 17.

BOX 17 CHECKLIST

✓ Revision

Your goal is to answer yes to each question. If you answer no, you need to revise. The section numbers in parentheses tell you where to look in this handbook for help.

The Global View: Whole Essay and Paragraphs

1. Is your essay topic suitable and sufficiently narrow? (Chapter 2)
2. Does your thesis statement communicate your topic, focus, and purpose? (2q, Box 12)
3. Does your essay show that you are aware of your audience? (1d, Box 4)
4. Is your essay arranged effectively? (4i)
5. Have you checked for material that strays off the topic? (4d)
6. Does your introduction prepare your reader for the rest of the essay? (4b)
7. Do your body paragraphs express main ideas in topic sentences as needed? (4c) Are your main ideas clearly related to your thesis statement? (4d)
8. Do your body paragraphs provide specific, concrete support for each main idea? (4c, 4f)
9. Do you use transitions and other techniques to connect ideas within and between paragraphs? (4j)
10. Does your conclusion give your essay a sense of completion? (4k)

The Local View: Sentences and Words

1. Are your sentences concise? (Chapter 16)
2. Do your sentences show clear relationships among ideas? (Chapter 17)
3. Do you use parallelism, variety, and emphasis correctly and to increase the impact of your writing? (Chapters 18 and 19)
4. Have you eliminated sentence fragments? (Chapter 12) Have you eliminated comma splices and fused sentences? (Chapter 13)
5. Have you eliminated confusing shifts? (Chapter 15)
6. Have you eliminated disjointed sentences? (Chapter 15)
7. Have you eliminated misplaced and dangling modifiers? (Chapter 14)
8. Have you used exact words? (21e, 21f)
9. Is your usage correct and your language appropriate? (Chapters 20 and 21)
10. Have you avoided sexist language? (21g)

⊕ **ESL NOTE:** If you'd like information about issues of English grammar that often affect ESL students, consult Part Seven in this handbook. Topics covered include ARTICLES (Chapter 45); word order (Chapter 46); VERB–PREPOSITION combinations (Chapter 47); VERBALS (Chapter 48); and MODAL AUXILIARIES (Chapter 49). ⊕

3d How do I edit?

Editing means checking the technical correctness of your writing. You carefully examine your writing for correct grammar, spelling, punctuation, capitalization, and use of numbers, italics, and abbreviations. Some people use the terms *editing* and *revising* interchangeably, but they're very different steps in the writing process. In contrast to revising, editing means looking at each word for its technical correctness. By editing, you fine-tune the surface features of your writing.

Editing is crucial in writing. No matter how much attention you've paid to planning, shaping, drafting, and revising, you need to edit carefully. Slapdash editing distracts and annoys your reader; lowers that reader's opinion of you and what you say in your essay; and, in a course assignment, usually earns a lower grade.

My best advice to you about editing is this: Don't rush. Editing takes time. Be systematic and patient. Checking grammar and punctuation takes your full concentration, along with time to look up and apply the rules in this handbook.

When do you know you've finished revising and are ready to edit? Ask yourself, "Is there anything else I can do to improve the content, organization, development, and sentence structure of this draft?" If the answer is no, you're ready to edit.

Many word-processing programs include editing tools such as a spell-checker, style-checker, thesaurus, and readability analyzer. As I explained in Chapter 1, each tool has shortcomings serious enough to create new errors. Yet, if you use the tools intelligently with their shortcomings in mind, they can be useful.

Whenever possible, edit on a paper copy of your writing. It's much easier to spot editing errors on a printed page than on a computer screen. Double-space your paper before printing it for revising or editing. The extra space gives you room to write in your changes clearly so that you can read them easily later. After you finish editing, you can transfer your corrections to the computer. If you must edit onscreen, highlight every two or three sentences, and read each slowly. By working in small segments, you reduce the tendency to read too quickly and miss errors.

An editing checklist helps you find errors. Using an editing checklist, either one provided by your instructor or one based on Box 18, can help you move through editing systematically.

BOX 18   CHECKLIST

✓ Editing

Your goal is to answer yes to each question below. If you answer no, you need to edit. The numbers in parentheses tell you which chapters in this handbook to go to for more information.

1. Is your grammar correct? (Chapters 7–15)
2. Is your spelling, including hyphenation, correct? (Chapter 22)
3. Have you used commas correctly? (Chapter 24)
4. Have you used all other punctuation correctly? (Chapters 23 and 25–29)
5. Have you used capital letters, italics, abbreviations, and numbers correctly? (Chapter 30)

A timesaving method for editing is to create a personal file of editing errors you tend to make repeatedly. For example, if the difference between *its* and *it's* always escapes you, or if you tend to misuse the colon, your personal file of editing errors can remind you to look over your draft for those problems.

3e How do I proofread?

To **proofread,** check your final draft for accuracy and neatness before handing it in. In contrast to editing, which is a check for technical correctness, proofreading is typographical. This is your last chance to catch typing (or handwriting) errors and to make sure what you hand in is a clean transcription of your final draft. No matter how hard you worked on earlier parts of the writing process, your final copy needs to be free of proofreading oversights. Shoddy proofreading distracts and annoys your reader; lowers that reader's opinion of you and your work; and, if you're writing for college or university, usually earns a lower grade.

When proofreading, read your work carefully line by line, looking for typing errors, such as letters or words accidentally omitted, words typed twice in a row, wrong indents to start each paragraph, and similar typos or slips. Whenever a page has more than one error, consider printing (or rewriting) a new page. Never expect your instructor to make allowances for crude typing (or handwriting). If you can't type well (or write legibly), arrange to have your paper typed properly.

Unless your instructor gives different directions, proofreading calls also for you to type, at the top right of each page, your last name and the page number. Unless you use a title page (34e.2), on the first page at the left margin, type your full name, your professor's name (initial for first name, only if needed), your course title, your class and section number, and the date. For an example, see 3g.3.

Some techniques for proofreading include (1) using a ruler under each line as you read it to prevent yourself from looking beyond that line; (2) reading backwards, sentence by sentence, to prevent yourself from being distracted by the content of the paper; and (3) proofreading your final draft aloud, to yourself or to a friend, so that you can hear errors that have slipped past your eyes. As with revising and editing, whenever possible print and proofread a double-spaced paper copy of your writing. Again, it's much easier to spot errors on a printed page than onscreen.

3f What is collaborative writing?

Some instructors use the term **collaborative writing** interchangeably with the term *peer-group writing*. In this handbook, the term *collaborate* refers to "students working together to write a paper." The underlying idea is that two (or more) heads are better than one.

Writing collaboratively enhances confidence, as writers support one another. Also important, the benefits of acquiring experience in collaborative writing extend beyond your college or university years. Many professions require participation in writing committees; members of the group must reach general agreement on how to proceed and contribute equally to a written report. Marketing managers, for example, head up teams who conduct consumer research, and then—as a group—write up their findings. Box 19 provides guidelines for collaborative writing.

BOX 19 SUMMARY

Guidelines for collaborative writing

Starting

1. Learn each other's names. If the group wishes, exchange e-mail addresses and/or phone numbers so that you can be in touch outside of class.

2. Participate actively in the group process. During discussions, help set a tone that encourages everyone to participate, including people who don't like to interrupt, who want time to think before they talk, or who are shy. Conversely, help the group set limits if someone dominates the discussions or makes all the decisions. If you lack experience contributing in a group setting, plan personal ways you'll take an active role.

→

Guidelines for collaborative writing (*continued*)

3. As a group, assign work to be done between meetings. Distribute the responsibilities as fairly as possible. Also, decide whether to choose one discussion leader or to rotate leadership, unless your instructor assigns a particular procedure.

4. Make decisions regarding the technology you'll use. If everyone can use the same word-processing program, for example, that will make sharing drafts or parts of drafts much easier. If not, you can use the "Save As" function or an equivalent to save in a common format. Decide if you'll share materials via a floppy disk or as an e-mail attachment. If any group members are unfamiliar with these processes, others need to help them learn. (Different areas and levels of expertise are an advantage of working in groups.)

5. Set a timeline and deadlines for the project. Agree on what to do in the event that someone misses a deadline.

Planning the Writing

6. After discussing the project, BRAINSTORM as a group or use structured techniques for discovering and compiling ideas.

7. Together agree on the ideas that seem best and allow for a period of INCUBATION, if time permits. Then, discuss your group choices again.

8. As a group, divide the project into parts and distribute assignments fairly. For example, if the project requires research, decide who will do it and how they'll share findings with others. If one person is going to be responsible for preparing drafts from pieces that others have written, make sure his or her other responsibilities are balanced.

9. As you work on your part of the project, take notes in preparation for giving your group a progress report.

10. As a group, OUTLINE or otherwise sketch an overview of the paper to get a preliminary idea of how best to use material contributed by individuals.

Drafting the Writing

11. Draft a THESIS STATEMENT. The thesis statement sets the direction for the rest of the paper. Each member of the group can draft a thesis statement and the group can discuss the advantages of each, but the group needs to agree on one version before getting too far into the rest of the draft. Your group might revise the thesis statement after the whole paper has been drafted, but using a preliminary version gets everyone started in the same direction.

→

Guidelines for collaborative writing (*continued*)

12. Draft the rest of the paper. Decide whether each member of the group should write a complete draft or one part of the whole. For example, each group member might take one main idea and be responsible for drafting that section. Share draft materials using disks or e-mail attachments (see step 4). If this is impossible, make photocopies. For most group meetings it will be important to have a paper copy of group materials, so print (or photocopy) copies for everyone.

Revising the Writing

13. Read over the drafts. Are all the important points included?
14. Use the revision checklist (Box 17 in 3c.5), and work either as a group or by assigning portions to subgroups. If different people have drafted different sections, COHERENCE and UNITY should receive special attention in revision, as should your introduction and conclusion.
15. Agree on a final version. Assign someone to prepare the final draft and make sure every group member has a copy.

Editing and Proofreading the Writing

16. As a group, review printouts or photocopies of the final draft. Don't leave the last stages to a subgroup. Draw on everyone's knowledge of grammar, spelling, and punctuation. Use everyone's eyes for proofreading.
17. Use the editing checklist (Box 18 in 3d) to double-check for errors. If you find more than one or two errors per page, correct and print out the page again. No matter how well the group has worked collaboratively, or how well the group has written the paper, a sloppy final version reflects negatively on the entire group.
18. If your instructor asks, be prepared to describe your personal contribution to the project and/or to describe or evaluate the contributions of others.

3g A student essay in three drafts

The following sections observe Carol Moreno, a student, planning to write on the topic of weight lifting for women. In Chapter 2, you'll find her writing assignment (2c), how she used an entry in her journal (2f), mapped her ideas (see 2j), wrote her THESIS STATEMENT (2q), and outlined (2r). During these activities, Moreno chose an informative writing purpose (1c.2).

3g.1 The first draft of a student essay

Here's Moreno's first draft showing her own notes to herself about revisions to make in the second draft. The notes resulted from comments of her PEER-RESPONSE GROUP and from her personal rereading of her draft.

Carol Moreno's first draft, with notes

What do I mean here?

Pumping Iron

I should say why she needed lifting

It all began when my grandmother broke her hip. I

She does not weigh much, but she was too much for me.

couldn't lift her alone when I was helping take care of her. I

I need to clarify the connection

I have to check when I revise whether this thesis statement fits the rest of my essay

needed strength, and I'm planning to be a nurse. Then I

found out I could satisfy a phys ed requirement in college

with a weight-lifting course for women. I thought only

Lots of I's — is this only about me?

big, macho men lift weights. But if she is trained well, any

woman can "pump iron" well, just like a man.

Hoping for strength and endurance

The first day of class we did not exercise. We talked

about who we are and why we wanted to take the course.

MOVE. This should be my third ¶.

can lead to *unless lifters*

We heard about how to avoid injury by learning the safe

and weight machines. Free weights are barbells.

use of free weights (barbells). To be safe, no matter how

my second ¶ should give background

little the weight, lifters must never raise a barbell by

grasp

bending at the waist. Instead, they should squat, grab the

barbell, and then straighten up into a standing position.

To avoid a *that* *serious*

I need to go into more detail here

Twists can lead to injury, so lifters must keep head erect,

facing forward, back and neck aligned. Lifters use weight

machines sitting down, which is a big advantage of the

Nautilus and Universal.

→

happy

I was relieved that I won't develop overly masculine

move up to be #2 (background)

muscle mass. We learned that we can rely on women's

I have to bring in more than myself to say who we are

biology. Our bodies produce only very small amounts of

With normal training,

the hormones that enlarge muscles in men. ~~Normally,~~

I need to tie these together (check 4d)

muscles

women's grow longer rather than bulkier. Weight lifting is a

form of anareobic *(sp)* exercise. It does not make people breathe

harder or their hearts beat faster. Arobic *(sp)* exercise like

am I too informal here?

my topic sentence needs work

running, walking, and

swimming builds endurance, so I took up swimming.

After safety comes our needs for physical strength. A

well-planned, progressive weight training program. ~~You~~ *It*

a person

begin with whatever weight ~~you~~ can lift comfortably and

to the base weight as one gets stronger.

then gradually add. What builds muscle strength is the

the lifter does;

number of "reps", ~~we do,~~ not necessarily an increase in the

resistance from adding

amount of ~~added~~ weight. In my class, we ranged from 18 to

pudgy couch potato

43, scrawny to ~~fat,~~ and ~~lazy~~ to superstar, and we each

I'm not trying here

developed a program that was OK for us. Some women

try

Start sentence here? Not sure

didn't listen to our instructor who urged us not to ~~do~~ more

our first workouts

reps or weight than our programs called for, even if ~~it~~

seemed too easy. This turned out to be good advice because

the next morning

those of us who didn't listen woke up feeling as though our

bodies had been twisted by evil forces.

→

In addition to
fitting to ~~After meeting her~~ physical capabilities, a weight

lifter needs to design her personal goals. Most students in

I need specific examples of students my group wanted to improve their upper body strength.

(Each) student learned to use specific exercises to isolate

certain muscle groups, for example we might work on our

sp? arms and (abdomen) one day and our shoulders and chest

the next day. ~~My goal is nursing, which I want to pursue. I~~

I'm off the topic ~~want to help others, but I'm also very interested in the~~

~~science I'll learn. I hear there is a lot of memorization,~~

~~which I'm pretty good at. I also will have "clinical"~~

~~assignments to give us hands on experience in hospitals.~~

Because I had had such trouble lifting my grandmother, I

added exercises to strengthen my legs and back. Another

student added neck strengthening exercises. Someone else

added finger and hand exercises.

I forget to talk about my swimming At the end of the course, we had to evaluate our

over my head for 3 reps.
progress. When I started, I could lift 10 pounds, ~~but~~ By the

over my head
end, I could lift 10 pounds for 20 reps and 18 pounds for 3

still
I need a stronger ending reps. I am so proud of my accomplishments that I work out

three or four times a week. I am proof that any woman can

become stronger and have more stamina.

3g.2 The second draft of a student essay

For her second draft, Moreno revised by working systematically through the notes she had written on the draft. The notes came from her own thinking as well as from the comments of the PEER-RESPONSE GROUP with which she had shared her paper.

From the assignment (2c), Moreno knew that her instructor would consider this second draft an "essay in progress." Her instructor's responses would help her write a final draft. She expected two types of comments: questions to help her clarify and expand on some of her ideas, and references to some of this handbook's section codes (number-letter combinations) to point out errors. Here is her second draft.

Carol Moreno's second draft, with her instructor's responses

> *This title is very broad. Try again?* ⟶ Pumping Iron   *I like this sentence— good balance.*
>
> When my grandmother fell and broke her hip last
>
> summer, I wanted to help take care of her. She was   *Interesting reaction— can you be more descriptive?*
>
> bedridden, but I couldn't lift her and I was shocked. My
>
> grandmother doesn't weigh much, but she was too much for
>
> me. I'm planning to be a nurse, so I need my strength. When I   *Can you explain why to help your readers understand your concerns?*
>
> *(see 30i)*
>
> realized that I could satisfy one of my (phys ed) requirements
>
> *This thesis state-ment says you'll* ⟵ by taking a weight-lifting course, I decided to try it. In spite
>
> of most people thinking that only men can "pump iron,"
>
> *discuss what most people think, but do you? (see 2q)* ⟵ women can also do it successfully with the right training.
>
> Women who lift weights, I was happy to learn from
>
> *To do what?* ⟶ my course, can easily avoid overly masculine muscle mass.
>
> Women can rely on their biology. Women's bodies produce   *Good for you! This information is instructive.*
>
> only very small amounts of the hormone ₅ that enlarge
>
> muscles in men. With normal weight training, women's
>
> ⟶

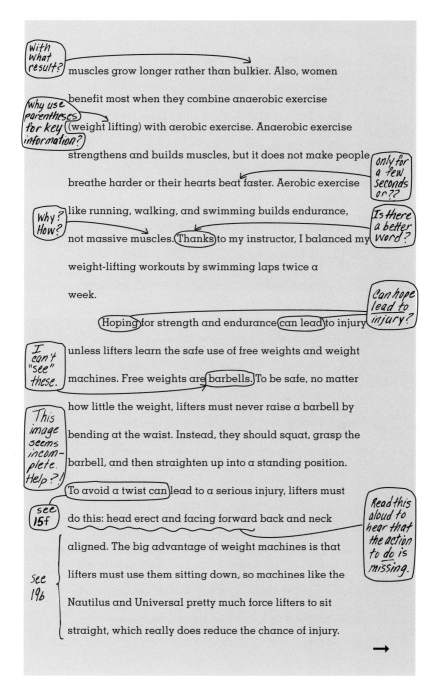

With what result? muscles grow longer rather than bulkier. Also, women

Why use parentheses for key information? benefit most when they combine anaerobic exercise (weight lifting) with aerobic exercise. Anaerobic exercise

strengthens and builds muscles, but it does not make people

only for a few seconds or?? breathe harder or their hearts beat faster. Aerobic exercise

Why? How? like running, walking, and swimming builds endurance, *Is there a better word?*

not massive muscles. Thanks to my instructor, I balanced my

weight-lifting workouts by swimming laps twice a

week.

Can hope lead to injury? Hoping for strength and endurance can lead to injury

I can't "see" these. unless lifters learn the safe use of free weights and weight

machines. Free weights are barbells. To be safe, no matter

This image seems incomplete. Help?! how little the weight, lifters must never raise a barbell by

bending at the waist. Instead, they should squat, grasp the

barbell, and then straighten up into a standing position.

see 15f To avoid a twist can lead to a serious injury, lifters must

do this: head erect and facing forward back and neck

Read this aloud to hear that the action to do is missing. aligned. The big advantage of weight machines is that

see 19b lifters must use them sitting down, so machines like the

Nautilus and Universal pretty much force lifters to sit

straight, which really does reduce the chance of injury.

→

Do you want to use one word so much?

Once a weight lifter understands how to lift safely,

she (needs) to meet her personal (needs) No one (needs) to

be strong to get started. A well-planned progressive

See 12b.2

weight training program. It begins with whatever weight

a person can lift comfortably and gradually adds to the

base weight as she gets stronger. What builds strength

is the number of ("reps") the lifter does, not necessarily an *meaning?*

increase in the amount of (resistance) from adding weight.

Our instructor helped the women in our class, who rang-

These adjectives are fun.

ed from 18 to 43, scrawny to pudgy, couch potato to

superstar, to develop a program that suited us. Our

instructor urged us not to try more reps or weight than our

programs called for, even if our first workouts seemed too

easy. This turned out to be good advice because those *Fun again.*
Your voice
of us who did not listen woke up the next morning *(personality)*
comes
feeling as though our bodies had been twisted by evil *through.*

forces.

In addition to fitting a program to her physical *Does*
one
design
capabilities, a weight lifter needs to design her personal *a goal?*

goals. Most students in my group wanted to improve their

upper body strength, so we focused on exercises to

→

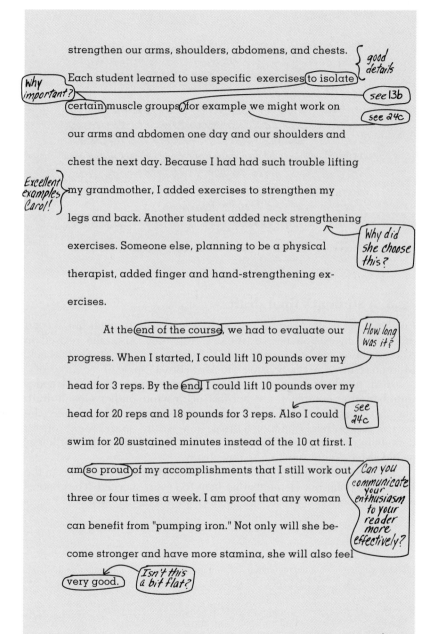

strengthen our arms, shoulders, abdomens, and chests. *good details*

Each student learned to use specific exercises to isolate *Why important?* *see 13b*

certain muscle groups, for example we might work on *see 24c*

our arms and abdomen one day and our shoulders and

chest the next day. Because I had had such trouble lifting

Excellent examples Carol! my grandmother, I added exercises to strengthen my

legs and back. Another student added neck strengthening

exercises. Someone else, planning to be a physical *Why did she choose this?*

therapist, added finger and hand-strengthening ex-

ercises.

At the end of the course, we had to evaluate our *How long was it?*

progress. When I started, I could lift 10 pounds over my

head for 3 reps. By the end, I could lift 10 pounds over my

head for 20 reps and 18 pounds for 3 reps. Also I could *see 24c*

swim for 20 sustained minutes instead of the 10 at first. I

am so proud of my accomplishments that I still work out *Can you communicate your enthusiasm to your reader more effectively?*

three or four times a week. I am proof that any woman

can benefit from "pumping iron." Not only will she be-

come stronger and have more stamina, she will also feel

very good. *Isn't this a bit flat?*

→

Dear Carol,
    You have truly earned the right to feel proud of yourself. You've also inspired me to consider weight training myself!
    As you revise for your final draft, I'd urge you to get more _voice_ (your personality) into the essay. To do this, you don't have to become too informal; instead, think about how you _felt_ about what you were doing and try to put that into words. Also, think about my questions and the codes that refer you to sections of the Troyka handbook.
    I will enjoy reading your final draft, I'm sure.

3g.3 A student's final draft

For her final draft, Moreno worked systematically through her second draft with an eye on her instructor's responses. Also, she revised in places where her instructor hadn't commented. As another check, Moreno referred to the revision checklist (Box 17 in 3c.5).

Next, to edit her final draft, Moreno looked up the handbook codes (number-letter combinations) her instructor wrote on her second draft. She also consulted the editing checklist (Box 18 in 3d). Then, before she started to proofread, she took a break from writing so she could refresh her ability to see typing errors. Distance from her work, she knew, would also help her see it more objectively.

Moreno's final draft appears on the following pages with notes in the margins to point out elements that help the essay succeed. These notes are for you only; don't write any notes on your final drafts.

Carol Moreno's final draft

Moreno 1

Carol Moreno

Professor K. Norris

English Composition 101, Section LR

4 December 2003

TITLE — Women Can Pump Iron, Too

INTRODUCTION: Gets reader's attention with personal anecdote — When my grandmother fell and broke her hip last summer, I wanted to help take care of her. Because she was bedridden, she needed to be lifted at times, but I was shocked to discover that I could not lift her without my mother's or brother's help. My grandmother does not weigh much, but she was too much for me. My pride was hurt, and even more important, I began to worry

Question to add sentence variety — about my plans to be a nurse specializing in the care of elderly people. What if I were too weak to help my patients get around? When I realized that I could satisfy one of my Physical Education requirements by taking a weight-lifting course for women, I decided to try it. Many people picture only big, macho men

THESIS STATEMENT: Focus of essay — wanting to lift weights, but times have changed. With the right training, women can also "pump iron" to build strength.

BODY PARAGRAPH ONE: Gives background information — Women who lift weights, I was happy to learn from my course, can easily avoid developing overly masculine muscle mass. Women can rely on their biology to protect them. Women's bodies produce only very small amounts of the hormones that

Refutes possible objection — enlarge muscles in men. With normal weight training, women's muscles grow longer rather than bulkier. The result is smoother,

Transition to signal additional point — firmer muscles, not massive bulges. Also, women benefit most when they combine weight lifting, which is a form of anaerobic exercise, with aerobic exercise. Anaerobic exercise strengthens

→

(Proportions shown in this paper are adjusted to fit space limitations of this book. Follow actual dimensions discussed in this book and your instructor's directions.)

and builds muscles, but it does not make people breathe harder

Specific details of two types of conditioning

or their hearts beat faster for sustained periods. In contrast, aerobic exercises like running, walking, and swimming build endurance, but not massive muscles, because they force a person to take in more oxygen, which increases lung capacity, improves circulatory health, and tones the entire body. Encouraged by my instructor, I balanced my weight-lifting workouts by swimming laps twice a week.

BODY PARAGRAPH TWO: Describes safe use of equipment and lifting techniques

Striving for strength can end in injury unless weight lifters learn the safe use of free weights and weight machines. Free weights are barbells, the metal bars that round metal weights can be attached to at each end. To be safe, no matter how little the weight, lifters must never raise a barbell by bending at the waist, grabbing the barbell, and then

Transition to show contrast

straightening up. Instead, they should squat, grasp the barbell, and then use their leg muscles to straighten into a standing position. To avoid a twist that can lead to serious injury, lifters must use this posture: head erect and facing forward, back and neck aligned. The big advantage of weight machines, which use weighted handles and bars hooked to wires and pulleys, is that lifters must use them sitting down. Therefore, machines like the Nautilus and Universal actually force lifters to keep their bodies properly aligned, which drastically reduces the chance of injury.

BODY PARAGRAPH THREE: Describes and explains the design and purpose of weight-training programs

Once a weight lifter understands how to lift safely, she needs a weight-lifting regimen personalized to her specific physical needs. Because benefits come from "resistance," which is the stress that lifting any amount of weight puts on a muscle, no one has to be strong to get started. A well-planned,

$\longrightarrow$

Moreno 3

progressive weight-training program begins with whatever
weight a person can lift comfortably and gradually adds to the
base weight as she gets stronger. What builds muscle strength
is the number of repetitions, or "reps," the lifter does, not
necessarily an increase in resistance from adding weight. Our
instructor helped the women in the class, who ranged from 18 to
43, scrawny to pudgy, and couch potato to superstar, to develop
a program that was right for our individual weight, age, and
overall level of conditioning. Everyone's program differed in
how much weight to start out with and how many reps to do for
each exercise. Our instructor urged us not to try more weight or
reps than our programs called for, even if our first workouts
seemed too easy. This turned out to be good advice because
those of us who did not listen woke up the next day feeling as
though evil forces had twisted our bodies.

Specific details for reader to visualize a class

In addition to fitting a program to her physical
capabilities, a weight lifter needs to design an individual
routine to fit her personal goals. Most students in my group
wanted to improve their upper body strength, so we focused on
exercises to strengthen arms, shoulders, abdomens, and chests.
Each student learned to use specific exercises to isolate certain
muscle groups. Because muscles strengthen and grow when
they're rested after a workout, our instructor taught us to work
alternate muscle groups on different days. For example, a
woman might work on her arms and abdomen one day and then
her shoulders and chest the next day. Because I had had such
trouble lifting my grandmother, I added exercises to strengthen
my legs and back. Another student, who had hurt her neck in
a car crash, added neck-strengthening exercises. Someone

BODY PARAGRAPH FOUR: Explains the need for developing a program to fit individual needs

Specific examples to add interest

→

else, planning to be a physical therapist, added finger- and

hand-strengthening exercises.

CONCLUSION:
Reports
writer's
personal
progress

At the end of our 10 weeks of weight training, we had to

evaluate our progress. Was I impressed! I felt ready to lift the

world. When I started, I could lift only 10 pounds over my head

for 3 reps. By the end of the course, I could lift 10 pounds over my

head for 20 reps, and I could lift 18 pounds for 3 reps. Also, I

could swim laps for 20 sustained minutes instead of the 10 I had

barely managed at first. I am so proud of my weight-training

accomplishments that I still work out three or four times a week.

I am proof that any woman can benefit from "pumping iron." Not

only will she become stronger and have more stamina, but she

will also feel energetic and confident. After all, there isn't a

thing to lose--except maybe some flab.

Chapter 4
Writing Paragraphs

4a What is a paragraph?

A **paragraph** is a group of sentences that work together to develop a unit of thought. Paragraphing permits writers to divide material into manageable parts. When a group of paragraphs works together in logical sequence, the result is a complete essay or other whole piece of writing.

To signal the start of a new paragraph, indent the first line one-half inch, or about 1.25 cm. Skip no extra lines between paragraphs. Business writing (Chapter 41) is an exception: It calls for *block format* for paragraphs, which means you do not indent the first line but rather leave a double space between paragraphs. If you're already double-spacing, then leave two double lines for a total of four lines.

I explain later in this chapter the rich variety of paragraph arrangements (4h) and rhetorical strategies (4i) at your disposal for writing paragraphs. But first, let's look at characteristics of paragraphs in general. I start by discussing introductory paragraphs (4b); then, body paragraphs (4c through 4j); and last, concluding paragraphs (4k).

4b How can I write effective introductory paragraphs?

An **introductory paragraph** leads the reader to sense what's ahead. It sets the stage. It also attempts to arouse a reader's interest in the topic.

A THESIS STATEMENT can be an important component in an introduction. Many instructors require students to place their thesis statement at the end of the opening paragraph. Doing so disciplines students to state early the central point of the essay. If an introduction points in one direction, and the rest of the essay goes off in another, the essay isn't communicating a clear message. Professional writers don't necessarily include a thesis statement in their introductory paragraphs. Most have the skill to maintain a line of thought without overtly stating a main idea.

Introductory paragraphs, as well as concluding paragraphs (4k), are usually shorter than body paragraphs (4c).

Be careful not to tack on a sloppy introduction at the last minute. The introductory paragraph plays too important a role to be tossed off with merely a few shallow lines. While many writers prefer to write only a thesis statement as an introduction in an early draft, they always return to write a complete introductory paragraph after the main part of the writing is finished. For a list of specific strategies to use—and pitfalls to avoid for introductory paragraphs—see Box 20.

BOX 20   SUMMARY

Introductory paragraphs

Strategies to Use

- Providing relevant background information
- Relating briefly an interesting story or anecdote
- Giving one or more pertinent—perhaps surprising—statistics
- Asking one or more provocative questions
- Using an appropriate quotation
- Defining a KEY TERM (6e)
- Presenting one or more brief examples (4i)
- Drawing an ANALOGY (4i)

Strategies to Avoid

- Don't write statements about your purpose, such as "I am going to discuss the causes of falling oil prices."
- Don't apologize, as in "I am not sure this is right, but this is my opinion."
- Don't use overworked expressions, such as "Haste makes waste, as I recently discovered" or "Love is grand."

Always integrate an introductory device into the paragraph so that it leads smoothly into the thesis statement. Some examples follow. In this chapter, each example paragraph has a number to its left for your easy reference. Here's an introductory paragraph that uses two brief examples to lead into the thesis statement at the end of the paragraph.

1   On seeing another child fall and hurt himself, Hope, just nine months old, stared, tears welling up in her eyes, and crawled to her mother to be comforted—as though she had been hurt, not her friend. When 15-month-old Michael saw his friend Paul crying, Michael fetched his own teddy bear and offered it to Paul; when that didn't stop Paul's tears, Michael brought Paul's security blanket from another room. Such small acts of sympathy and caring, observed in scientific studies, are leading researchers to trace the roots of empathy—the ability to

share another's emotions—to infancy, contradicting a long-standing assumption that infants and toddlers were incapable of these feelings.

—Daniel Goleman, "Researchers Trace Empathy's Roots to Infancy"

In paragraph 2, the opening quotation sets up a dramatic contrast with the thesis statement.

> 2 "Alone one is never lonely," says May Sarton in her essay "The Rewards of Living a Solitary Life." Most people, however, don't share Sarton's opinion: They're terrified of living alone. They're used to living with others—children with parents, roommates with roommates, friends with friends, spouses with spouses. When the statistics catch up with them, therefore, they're rarely prepared. Chances are high that most adult men and women will need to know how to live alone, briefly or longer, at some time in their lives.
>
> —Tara Foster, student

In paragraph 3, the writer asks a direct question, and next puts the reader in a dramatic situation to arouse interest in the topic.

> 3 What should you do? You're out riding your bike, playing golf, or in the middle of a long run when you look up and suddenly see a jagged streak of light shoot across the sky, followed by a deafening clap of thunder. Unfortunately, most outdoor exercisers don't know whether to stay put or make a dash for shelter when a thunderstorm approaches, and sometimes the consequences are tragic.
>
> —Gerald Secor Couzens, "If Lightning Strikes"

EXERCISE 4-1

Write an introduction for the three essays informally outlined here. Then, for more practice, write one alternative introduction for each. If you have a peer-response group, share the various written introductions and decide which are most effective. For help, see 4b.

1. Surfing the Web
   Thesis statement: The contents of the World Wide Web reveal people's obsessions at the start of the twenty-first century.
   Body paragraph 1: sites with offensive content
   Body paragraph 2: chat rooms and hobbies
   Body paragraph 3: financial investments and auctions
2. Cell phones
   Thesis statement: Cell phones have changed how some people behave in public.
   Body paragraph 1: driving
   Body paragraph 2: restaurants
   Body paragraph 3: movies and concerts
   Body paragraph 4: sidewalks, parks, and other casual spaces

3. Using credit cards

   Thesis statement: Although credit cards can help people manage their finances wisely, they also offer too much temptation.

   Body paragraph 1: convenience and safety

   Body paragraph 2: tracking of purchases

   Body paragraph 3: overspending dangers

4c What are body paragraphs?

Each **body paragraph,** which belongs between an introductory paragraph (4b) and a concluding paragraph (4k), consists of a main idea and support for that idea. To be effective, a body paragraph needs three characteristics: unity (4d and 4e), development (4f), and coherence (4g). Box 21 gives an overview of all three characteristics.

BOX 21   SUMMARY

Characteristics of effective body paragraphs

Unity: Have you made a clear connection between the main idea of the paragraph and the sentences that support the main idea (4d and 4e)?

Development: Have you included detailed and sufficient support for the main idea of the paragraph (4f)?

Coherence: Have you progressed from one sentence to the next in the paragraph smoothly and logically (4g)?

Paragraph 4 is an example of an effective body paragraph. It's from an essay called "What's Bugging You?"

4   The cockroach lore that has been daunting us for years is mostly true. Roaches can live for twenty days without food, fourteen days without water; they can flatten their bodies and crawl through a crack thinner than a dime; they can eat huge doses of carcinogens and still die of old age. They can even survive "as much radiation as an oak tree can," says William Bell, the University of Kansas entomologist whose cockroaches appeared in the movie *The Day After.* They will eat almost anything—regular food, leather, glue, hair, paper, even the starch in book bindings. (The New York Public Library has quite a cockroach problem.) They sense the slightest breeze, and they can react and start running in .05 second; they can also remain motionless for days. And if all this isn't creepy enough, they can fly too.

—Jane Goldman, "What's Bugging You?"

Paragraph 4 has UNITY (4d) in that the main idea (stories we've heard about cockroaches are true), stated in the TOPIC SENTENCE (4e), which is the first sentence, is supported by detailed examples. It has COHERENCE (4g) in that the content of every sentence ties into the content of the other sentences. Also, the paragraph *coheres*—sticks together—through word choices (repeating *they can* each time to put the emphasis on the interesting facts) and with consistent grammar (a different ACTIVE VERB [see VOICE, 8n through 8p] for each example). It has PARAGRAPH DEVELOPMENT (4c and 4i) in that the details provide support for the main idea.

4d How can I create unity in paragraphs?

A paragraph has **unity** when the connection between the main idea and its supporting sentences is clear. Paragraph 4 in section 4c is a good example.

Unity is ruined when any sentence in a paragraph "goes off the topic," which means its content doesn't relate to the main idea or to the other sentences in the paragraph. Here is a paragraph about the novelist Jane Austen. To show you broken unity, in the version shown as paragraph 5 I've deliberately inserted two sentences (the second and the last) that go off the topic. Paragraph 6 is the original version as written by an award-winning author at McGill University. It is unified: All its sentences relate to the central subject.

NO 　5　An Austen novel is a *tour de force,* at least by modern standards. Of course, Jane Austen did not feel the need to sprinkle her text with foreign phrases. Nothing extraordinary happens—no murders, escapades, or disasters. Instead of adventure or melodrama we read about the prosaic daily comedy of family life. There is little complexity to the plots (compared to Dickens, say), and the suspense, such as it is, arises chiefly out of questions of love and marriage. Jane Austen single-handedly invented, and brought to perfection, what could be called the domestic genre of novel-writing, the literary equivalent to the seventeenth-century Dutch school of interior painting. In contrast, Rembrandt, the pre-eminent Dutch painter of that era, avoided domesticity for its own sake.

YES 　6　An Austen novel is a *tour de force,* at least by modern standards. Nothing extraordinary happens—no murders, escapades, or disasters. Instead of adventure or melodrama we read about the prosaic daily comedy of family life. There is little complexity to the plots (compared to Dickens, say), and the suspense, such as it is, arises chiefly out of questions of love and marriage. Jane Austen single-handedly invented, and brought to perfection, what could be called the domestic genre of novel-writing, the literary equivalent to the seventeenth-century Dutch school of interior painting. Her books are, of course, much more than a faithful representation of the period, just as Vermeer's paintings were more than illustrations of young Dutch women at home. Like Vermeer, de Witte, and the other Dutch domestic painters, Austen chose to stay strictly within the limits of the everyday, not because her talent was small, but because her imagination did not require a broader canvas.

—Witold Rybczynski, *Home*

4e How can topic sentences create paragraph unity?

A **topic sentence** contains the main idea of a paragraph and controls its content. Often, the topic sentence comes at the beginning of a paragraph, though not always. Professional essay writers, because they have the skill to carry the reader along without explicit signposts, sometimes decide not to use topic sentences. However, instructors often require students to use topic sentences. As apprentice writers, students might have more difficulty writing unified paragraphs.

Topic sentence starting a paragraph

In ACADEMIC WRITING, most paragraphs begin with a topic sentence so that readers know immediately what to expect. Paragraph 7 is an example.

7   The clock, Lewis Mumford has pointed out, is the key machine of the machine age, both for its influence on technics and for its influence on the habits of men. Technically, the clock was the first really automatic machine that attained any importance in the life of men. Previous to its invention, the common machines were of such nature that their operation depended on some external and unreliable force, such as human or animal muscles, water, or wind. It is true that the Greeks had invented a number of primitive automatic machines, but these were used, like Hero's steam engine, either for obtaining "supernatural" effects in the temples or for amusing the tyrants of Levantine cities. But the clock was the first automatic machine that attained public importance and a social function. Clock-making began the industry from which men learnt the elements of machine-making and gained the technical skill that was to produce the complicated machinery of the Industrial Revolution.

—George Woodcock, "The Tyranny of the Clock"

Sometimes, a topic sentence both starts a paragraph and, in different wording, ends the paragraph. Paragraph 8 is an example.

8   Burnout is a potential problem for hardworking and persevering students to fight. A preliminary step for preventing student burnout is for students to work in moderation. Students can concentrate on school every day, if they don't overtax themselves. One method students can use is to avoid concentrating on a single project for an extended period.

For example, if students have to read two books for a midterm history test, they should do other assignments at intervals so that the two books will not get boring. Another means to moderate a workload is to regulate how many extracurricular projects to take on. When a workload is manageable, a student's immunity to burnout is strengthened.

—Bradley Howard, student

Topic sentence ending a paragraph

Some paragraphs give supporting details first and wait to state the topic sentence at the paragraph's end. This approach is particularly effective for building suspense or for creating a bit of drama. Paragraph 9 is an example.

9   When I tell young softball players I played the game bare-handed, they regard me warily. Am I one of these geezers who's forever jawing about the fact that, in his day, you had to walk through six miles of snowdrifts just to get to school? Will I tediously lament the passing of the standing broad jump, and the glorious old days when the only football in the Maritimes was English rugger, and when hockey was an outdoor art rather than indoor mayhem, and at decent yacht clubs men were gentlemen and women were *personae non grata*? No, but I will tell today's softball players that—with their fancy uniforms, batters' helmets and, above all, gloves for every fielder—the game they play is more tarted-up and sissy than the one I knew.

—Harry Bruce, "The Softball Was Always Hard"

Topic sentence implied, not stated

Some paragraphs are a unified whole even without a single sentence that readers can point to as the topic sentence. They are constructed so that most readers can catch the main idea. Paragraph 10 is an example. What do you think might be a straightforward topic sentence for it?

10   The Romans were entertained by puppets, as were the rulers of the Ottoman Empire with their favorite shadow puppet, Karaghoiz, teller of a thousand tales. In the Middle Ages, puppets were cast as devil and angel in religious mystery and morality plays until cast out entirely by the church. For centuries, a rich puppetry heritage in India has matched that country's multilayered culture. The grace of Bali is reflected in its stylized, ceremonial rod and shadow puppets. The Bunraku puppets of Japan, unequaled for technique anywhere in the world, require a puppet master and two assistants to create one dramatic character on stage.

—Dan Cody, "Puppet Poetry"

EXERCISE 4-2

Working individually or with a peer-response group, identify the topic sentences in the following paragraphs. If the topic sentence is implied, write the point the paragraph conveys. For help, consult section 4e.

A.   A good college program should stress the development of high-level reading, writing, and mathematical skills and should provide you with a broad historical, social, and cultural perspective, no matter what subject you choose as your major. The program should teach you not only the most current knowledge in your field but also—just as important— prepare you to keep learning throughout your life. After all, you'll probably change jobs, and possibly even careers, at least six times, and you'll have other responsibilities, too—perhaps as a spouse and as a parent and certainly as a member of a community whose bounds extend beyond the workplace.

11

—Frank T. Rhodes, "Let the Student Decide"

B.   You've already assessed your site and been introduced to soil composition. You know that light and shade are important. All these conditions and more are important. There's another I haven't discussed yet: hardiness. Hardiness refers to the ability of a plant to withstand cold temperatures, the kind of cold we get in a Canadian winter. Beginning gardeners—just as anyone starting out in a chosen field—need positive reinforcement. Although our friends and relations will laud our efforts, the true critics will be the plants and their feedback can be ruthless: "I'm dying! You failed me!" So if you're starting out, make life easy and happy for yourself. Choose plants for *your* conditions to ensure success.

12

—Wendy Thomas, *Getting Starting on a Great Canadian Garden*

C.   Can you draw intricate distinctions on television? No. Can you say everything there is to be said, even everything you have to say, about a given topic? No. Can you back your way into the subject the way you might write the opening pages of a journal article? Also no. These are irritants to people trained in academic discourse, but they are not, in themselves, barriers to thought. On the contrary, I think it is the very sharpness of television discourse that dismays many intellectuals. It forces them to be direct. There is no time to gratify your ego by holding the floor, no opportunity to set the terms of the debate in your own favour, no licence for exclusive and proprietary language.

13

—Mark Kingwell, "The Intellectual Possibilities of Television"

4f   How can I develop body paragraphs?

You develop a **body paragraph** by supplying detailed support for the main idea of the paragraph communicated by your TOPIC SENTENCE (4e), whether stated or implied. **Paragraph development** is not merely a repetition, using other words, of the main idea. I've deliberately created paragraph 14 to show you a bad example of development. It goes nowhere because all that happens is that one idea is restated three times in different words. Compare it with the well-developed paragraph 4 that appears in section 4c.

NO	The cockroach lore that has been daunting us for years is
14	mostly true. Almost every tale we have heard about cockroaches is correct. The stories about cockroaches have frightened people for generations.

What separates most good writing from bad is the writer's ability to move back and forth between main ideas and specific details. To check whether you are providing sufficient detail in a body paragraph, use the RENNS test. Each letter in this acronym cues you to remember a different kind of supporting detail at your disposal, as listed in Box 22.

BOX 22   SUMMARY

The RENNS test: Checking for supporting details

R = **Reasons**
E = **Examples**
N = **Names**
N = **Numbers**
S = **Senses**—sight, sound, smell, taste, touch

Use the RENNS test to check the quality of your paragraph development. Of course, not every paragraph needs all five kinds of RENNS details. Paragraph 15 contains three of the five types of RENNS details. Identify the topic sentence and as many RENNS as you can before reading the analysis that follows the paragraph.

15   A dramatic increase in the grizzly bear sightings in Alberta has touched off a heated dispute among wildlife experts that centres on a seemingly simple issue: Are there really more grizzlies or merely more observers? More than 400 sightings were reported in Alberta in 1992, almost 10 times the number reported 10 years ago. The province's Department of Environmental Protection now estimates that 800 to 850 grizzly bears live in Alberta and that their number will reach 1000 by the turn of the century. Wildlife-conservation groups say the jump in sightings is mainly fuelled by greater activity by recreational users in the remote backcountry where grizzlies live. "My guess is, there are only 300 to 400 bears, and more likely, it's closer to the lower end," says Brian Horejsi, a conservation biologist with the group Speak Up For Wildlife.
        —Terry Bullick, "When Is a Grizzly Not a Grizzly?"

Paragraph 15 succeeds because it does more than merely repeat its topic sentence, which is its first sentence. It develops the topic sentence to support the claim that grizzlies have not actually increased in number. It uses numbers to document the apparent increase in sightings of grizzlies, but it uses reasons to discount the claim that the rise in numbers means more actual bears. It has names, such as Speak Up For Wildlife and the Department of Environmental Protection, that serve to support the claim.

Paragraph 16 contains four of the five types of RENNS. Identify the topic sentence and as many RENNS as you can before you read the analysis that follows the paragraph.

16 Tennyson called it a "flying flame," Benjamin Franklin termed it a "sudden and terrible mischief." In Roman mythology, the god Jupiter used spiky thunderbolts as letters to the editor when he chose to show displeasure to the poor mortals below. By whatever name, lightning is a spectacular natural event. Captured in photographs, its grandeur and beauty are safely petrified in static portraits of primal energy. In reality, at 24,000 to 28,000 degrees C, it is four times hotter than the surface of the sun. It can vaporize steel, plough up fields, shatter giant trees, and scatter live incendiary sparks over vast forests. Each day it kills 20 people.

—Michael Clugston, "Twice Struck"

In paragraph 16, the third sentence is the topic sentence. Supporting details for the main idea include examples (vaporize steel, plough up fields, shatter giant trees); the writer also uses names and numbers. Sensory details, given in images, provide more support (flying flame, sudden and terrible mischief).

EXERCISE 4-3

Working individually or with a peer-response group, look again at the paragraphs in Exercise 4-2. Identify the RENNS in each paragraph. For help, consult 4f.

4g How can I write coherent paragraphs?

A paragraph has **coherence** when its sentences relate to each other, not only in content but also in choice of words and grammatical structures. A coherent paragraph conveys continuity because the sentences follow naturally from one to the next. Techniques for achieving coherence are listed in Box 23, with the section that offers a complete explanation shown in parentheses.

BOX 23   SUMMARY

Techniques for achieving coherence

- Using appropriate transitional expressions (4g.1)
- Using pronouns when possible (4g.2)
- Using deliberate repetition of a key word (4g.3)
- Using parallel structures (4g.4)
- Using coherence techniques to create connections between paragraphs (4g.5)

4g.1 Using transitional expressions for coherence

Transitional expressions are words and phrases that signal connections among ideas. **Transitions** are bridges that lead your reader along your line of thought. They offer cues about what follows. Commonly used transitional expressions are listed in Box 24.

BOX 24   SUMMARY

Transitional expressions and the relationships they signal

ADDITION	also, in addition, too, moreover, and, besides, furthermore, equally important, then, finally
EXAMPLE	for example, for instance, thus, as an illustration, namely, specifically
CONTRAST	but, yet, however, nevertheless, nonetheless, conversely, in contrast, still, at the same time, on the one hand, on the other hand
COMPARISON	similarly, likewise, in the same way
CONCESSION	of course, to be sure, certainly, granted
RESULT	therefore, thus, as a result, so, accordingly
SUMMARY	hence, in short, in brief, in summary, in conclusion, finally
TIME	first, second, third, next, then, finally, afterward, before, soon, later, meanwhile, subsequently, immediately, eventually, currently
PLACE	in the front, in the foreground, in the back, in the background, at the side, adjacent, nearby, in the distance, here, there

---

👁 **ALERT:** In ACADEMIC WRITING, set off a transitional expression with a comma, unless the expression is one short word. 👁

Vary your choices of transitional words. Also, when choosing a transitional word, make sure it correctly says what you mean. The three brief examples below demonstrate how to use transitional expressions for each context.

COHERENCE BY ADDITION

Woodpeckers use their beaks to find food and to chisel out nests. In addition, they claim their territory and signal their desire to mate by using their beaks to drum on trees.

COHERENCE BY CONTRAST

Most birds communicate by singing. Woodpeckers, however, communicate by the duration and rhythm of the drumming of their beaks.

COHERENCE BY RESULT

The woodpecker's strong beak enables it to communicate by drumming on dry branches and tree trunks. As a result, woodpeckers can communicate across greater distances than songbirds can.

Paragraph 17 demonstrates how transitional expressions (shown in bold) enhance a paragraph's COHERENCE.

17 Certain aspects of Canadian cultural activity bear the stamp of this nation's rough, windswept, wilderness origins: ice hockey, wildlife prints, Farley Mowat, cottage-going, curling, toques. **To this list** we propose adding cuisine. **How else to account for** the enduring Canadian fondness for heavy, bland and non-nutritious fare than by noting that decades after there was any compelling reason to do so, Canadians still seem to eat purely for ballast: to bulk up to keep from being blown away. **Indeed,** it must be considered a providential accident of history that no less a pioneer of high-calorie, comfort-and-convenience cuisine than James Lewis Kraft, founding father of processed cheese and namesake of the unstoppable Kraft Dinner, was born in 1875 in Stevensville, Ontario. **Moreover,** a Canuck invented that handy, fattening favourite—the chocolate bar. **Yes,** in 1910, Arthur Ganong, a St. Stephen, New Brunswick, mogul with a sweet tooth, decided he'd had enough of messing up his pockets with sticky, individual chocolates. **Within months,** the world's first bars of chocolate (conveniently wrapped in tin foil) were rolling off Ganong's factory's line.

—Geoff Pevere and Greig Dymond, *Mondo Canuck*

4g.2 Using pronouns for coherence

Pronouns—words that refer to nouns or other pronouns—allow readers to follow your train of thought from one sentence to the next without boring repetition. Paragraph 18 illustrates how pronouns (shown in bold) contribute to COHERENCE.

18 The funniest people I know are often unaware of just how ticked off **they** are about things until **they** start to kid around about **them.** Nature did not build **these** people to sputter or preach; instead, in response to the world's irritations, **they** create little plays in **their** minds—parodies, cartoons, fantasies. When **they** see how funny **their** creations are, **they** also understand how really sore **they** were at **their** sources. **Their** anger is a revelation, one that works backward in the minds of an audience: the audience starts out laughing and winds up fuming.

—Roger Rosenblatt, "What Brand of Laughter Do You Use?"

4g.3 Using deliberate repetition for coherence

A key word is a strong word that's central to the main idea of the paragraph. **Repetition** of a key word is a useful way to achieve COHERENCE in a paragraph. The word usually appears first in the paragraph's TOPIC SENTENCE (4e) and then again throughout the paragraph. The idea of key-word repetition is to keep a concept in front of the reader.

Use this technique sparingly to avoid being monotonous. Also, limit your selection of a key word to one or at the most two words. The shorter a paragraph, the more likely a repeated key word will seem repetitious, and the less likely it'll be effective. In a longer paragraph, however, the repetition of a key word can be effective. Paragraph 19 contains repeated words (shown in bold) closely tied to the concept of emotions, contributing to the paragraph's coherence.

> **19** **Emotions** are, technically speaking, chemical impulses to act. The root of the word **emotion** is *movere,* the Latin verb meaning "to move," plus the prefix *e* which means "away," suggesting a tendency to act is implicit in every **emotion.** One of the primary functions of **emotion** is to warn us of danger. Goleman refers to this warning process as an "**emotional** alarm." When you experience an **emotional** alarm, like an unexpectedly loud noise, the **emotional** part of your brain takes over the analytical part of your brain, and you react.
>
> —Carol Carter and Lynn Quitman Troyka,
> *Majoring in the Rest of Your Life*

4g.4 Using parallel structures for coherence

Parallel structures are created when grammatically equivalent forms are used in series, usually of three or more items, but sometimes only two (see PARALLELISM, Chapter 18). Using parallel structures helps to give a paragraph coherence. The repeated parallel structures reinforce connections among ideas, and they add both tempo and sound to the sentence.

In paragraph 20, the authors use several parallel structures (shown in bold): a parallel series of words (*the sacred, the secular, the scientific*); parallel phrases (*sometimes smiled at, sometimes frowned upon*); and six parallel clauses (the first being *banish danger with a gesture*).

> **20** Superstitions are **sometimes smiled at** and **sometimes frowned upon** as observances characteristic of **the old-fashioned, the unenlightened,** children, peasants, servants, immigrants, foreigners, or backwoods people. Nevertheless, they give all of us ways of moving back and forth among the different worlds in which we live—**the sacred, the secular,** and **the scientific.** They allow us to keep a private world also, where, smiling a little, we can **banish danger with a gesture** and **summon luck with a rhyme, make the sun shine in spite of storm clouds, force the stranger to do our bidding, keep an enemy at bay,** and **straighten the paths of those we love.**
>
> —Margaret Mead and Rhoda Metraux, "New Superstitions for Old"

4g.5 Creating coherence among paragraphs

The same techniques for achieving COHERENCE in a paragraph apply to showing connections among paragraphs in a piece of writing. All four techniques help: transitional expressions (4g.1), pronouns (4g.2), deliberate repetition (4g.3), and parallel structures (4g.4). To see them in action, look over this handbook's student essays (one in 3g, two in 39g), research papers (6m, 34e.2, and 35h.2), and science report (40h.1).

Passage 21 shows two paragraphs and the start of a third. Repeated words connecting these paragraphs include *nation, nationalism, history, historical,* and *Canadian(s).* The "From that year on" sentence tightly links the first and second paragraphs: A reader does not know what year is meant or what important events made it a turning point without reading the first paragraph. The opening sentence of the third paragraph creates another strong link by repeating the term *nationalism,* the word that concludes the second paragraph. This concept, introduced in the first two paragraphs, is qualified and nuanced in the final paragraph.

21

> As a nation, Canada was born again in 1957. The year lies across our history like a fault-line: Diefenbaker won his first election; Pearson won his Nobel Peace Prize; Walter Gordon brought down his report on foreign ownership; and the Canada Council was established. These events, along with Quebec's Quiet Revolution, which began three years later, created the Canada of today, a society that seems to contain only a few trace elements of what Earle Birney called in the 1940s "a highschool land/deadset in adolescence."
>
> From that year on, Canadian-American relations were redefined by a force for which there was no historical antecedent. This was the force, at first tentative and apologetic, then increasingly vocal, then rancorous, then celebratory, of Canadian nationalism.
>
> This nationalism was always firmly rooted in pragmatism. Whenever times got tough or the price of flag-waving seemed likely to be too high, Canadians lowered their banners. This was predictable. Far more interesting was the way the minimum acceptable low-water mark of nationalist expression demanded by Canadians of their governments kept getting raised.
>
> —Richard Gwyn, *The 49th Paradox*

EXERCISE 4-4

Working individually or with a peer-response group, locate the coherence techniques in each paragraph. Look for transitional expressions, pronouns, deliberate repetition, and parallel structures. For help, consult 4g.

A.   Kathy sat with her legs dangling over the edge of the side of the hood. The band of her earphones held back strands of straight copper

22 hair that had come loose from two thick braids that hung down her back. She swayed with the music that only she could hear. Her shoulders raised, making circles in the warm air. Her arms reached out to her side; her open hands reached for the air; her closed hands brought the air back to her. Her arms reached over her head; her opened hands reached for a cloud; her closed hands brought the cloud back to her. Her head moved from side to side; her eyes opened and closed to the tempo of the tunes. Kathy was motion.

—Claire Burke, student

B. Newton's law may have wider application than just the physical world. In the social world, racism, once set into motion, will remain in motion unless acted upon by an outside force. The collective "we" must be the outside force. We must fight racism through education.

23 We must make sure every school has the resources to do its job. We must present to our children a culturally diverse curriculum that reflects our pluralistic society. This can help students understand that prejudice is learned through contact with prejudiced people, rather than with the people toward whom the prejudice is directed.

—Randolph H. Manning, "Fighting Racism with Inclusion"

C. The Classical period—Mozart's era—coincided with the political upheavals of the French Revolution, and the two were closely linked.

24 As polished and restrained as Classical music might seem today, it is important to remember that it was revolutionary in its own time. It created a revolution for simplicity, for direct communication, for common humanity against aristocratic exclusiveness in music.

—Robert Harris, *What to Listen for in Mozart*

EXERCISE 4-5

Working individually or with a peer-response group, use RENNS (4f) and techniques for achieving coherence (4g) to develop three of the following topic sentences into paragraphs. When finished, list the RENNS and the coherence techniques you used in each paragraph.

1. It is important to read the newspaper with a critical, and even skeptical, eye.
2. Marshall McLuhan's "global village" has come true with the World Wide Web.
3. Part-time jobs can be very unappealing.
4. Learning to cook involves more than just learning to follow recipes.
5. The friends we make at college (or university) will remain important in our later lives and careers.

4h How can I arrange a paragraph?

When you choose a **paragraph arrangement** during DRAFTING, you order its sentences to communicate the paragraph's message clearly and effectively. Later, during REVISION, experiment with other arrangements to see how else your sentences might be arranged for greatest impact. You may find sometimes that only one possible arrangement can work, but at other times, you may find more than one possible arrangement. Box 25 lists the most common ways to arrange a paragraph. More about each arrangement appears below in this section.

> BOX 25   SUMMARY
>
> ### Ways to arrange sentences in a paragraph
>
> - By time
> - By location
> - From general to specific
> - From specific to general
> - From least to most important
> - From problem to solution

Arranging by time

In a paragraph arranged according to time, or **chronological order,** events are presented in whatever order they took place. Narratives often follow this arrangement. Using a time sequence is a very natural and easy way to organize a paragraph. Paragraph 25 is an example.

25 | Other visitors include schools of dolphin swimming with synchronized precision and the occasional humpback whale. Before 1950, these 14-meter marine mammals were a common sight in the waters of the Great Barrier Reef as they passed on their annual migration between Antarctic waters and the tropics, where their calves were born. Then in the 1950s, whaling stations were set up on the New South Wales and Queensland coasts, and together with the long-established Antarctic hunts by the Soviet Union and America, whales were slaughtered in the thousands. By the time the whaling stations on the eastern Australian coast closed in the early 1960s, it was estimated that only two hundred remained in these waters. Today, their numbers are slowly increasing, but sightings are still rare.

—Allan Moult, "Volcanic Peaks, Tropical Rainforest, and Mangrove Swamps"

Arranging by location

A paragraph arranged according to location, or **spatial order,** leads the reader's attention from one place to another. The movement can be in any direction—from top to bottom, left to right, inside to outside, and so on. Paragraph 26 moves the reader through an interior.

> 26 The old store, lighted only by three fifty-watt bulbs, smelled of coal oil and baking bread. In the middle of the rectangular room, where the oak floor sagged a little, stood an iron stove. To the right was a wooden table with an unfinished game of checkers and a stool made from an apple-tree stump. On shelves around the walls sat earthen jugs with corncob stoppers, a few canned goods, and some of the two thousand old clocks and clockworks Thurmond Watts owned. Only one was ticking; the others he just looked at.
>
> —William Least Heat-Moon, *Blue Highways*

Arranging from general to specific

The most common pattern for arranging information is from **general to specific.** Typically, the general statement is the TOPIC SENTENCE, and the supporting details (see RENNS, 4f) explain the specifics. Paragraph 27 is an example.

> 27 The problem with vitamin D in Canada is one of geography and climate. Because the sun is low on the horizon during winter, it passes through more of the Earth's atmosphere; the atmosphere acts as a filter and shuts out most of the low-wavelength UV rays that we need to make vitamin D. That, plus shorter day length and our tendency to cover our bodies with clothing, means that from October to April we don't get nearly enough sunlight to produce natural vitamin D. If we don't take large doses of artificial vitamin D, in the form of fish oils (halibut and cod livers are best, but there are no more cod, and any fatty fish will do) and egg yolk, then we get poor bone development and repair. Dark or tanned skin is also a poorer producer of vitamin D than fair or untanned skin.
>
> —Wayne Grady, *Chasing the Chinook*

Arranging from specific to general

A less common paragraph arrangement moves from **specific to general.** Paragraph 28 is an example. To achieve greatest impact, the paragraph starts with details that support the topic sentence, which ends the paragraph.

> 28 Replacing the spark plugs is probably the first thing most home auto mechanics do. But too often, the problem lies elsewhere. In the ignition system, the plug wires, distributor unit, coil, and ignition control unit play just as vital a role as the spark plugs. Moreover, performance problems are by no means limited to the ignition system. The fuel system and emissions control system also contain several components that equal the spark plug in importance. The do-it-yourself mechanic who

wants to provide basic care for a car must be able to do more than change the spark plugs.

—Danny Witt, student

Arranging from least to most important

A paragraph arranged from **least to most important** uses **climactic order,** which means that the high point—the climax—comes at the end. The last item always packs the greatest impact and is the most memorable. Paragraph 29 is an example. ("The Department" in the paragraph is Canada's Department of External Affairs.)

29 The significance of General de Gaulle's famous *"Vive le Québec libre"* spoken from a balcony in Montreal in 1967 was debated in the Department as it was throughout the country. Mr. Pearson declared the general's utterance to be unacceptable, and de Gaulle promptly left the country without completing his visit. Although there were some dissenting voices, particularly to the effect that the government had overreacted, there was general agreement that the General's statement was not a slip of the tongue. After General de Gaulle's visitation, the government could no longer assume that the influence of France would always be benign so far as Canada was concerned. Now one thing had become clear: Canada's relations with France had become a matter of prime concern not just within the Department, but at all its diplomatic posts.

—Arthur Andrew, *The Rise and Fall of a Middle Power* (James Lorimer & Company Ltd.)

Arranging from problem to solution

In some cases, an effective arrangement for a paragraph is **problem to solution.** Usually, the topic sentence presents the problem. The very next sentence presents the main idea of the solution. Then, the rest of the paragraph covers the specifics of the solution. Paragraph 30 is an example.

30 When I first met them, Sara and Michael were a two-career couple with a home of their own, and a large boat bought with a large loan. What interested them in a concept called voluntary simplicity was the birth of their daughter and a powerful desire to raise her themselves. Neither one of them, it turned out, was willing to restrict what they considered their "real life" into the brief time before work and the tired hours afterward. "A lot of people think that as they have children and things get more expensive, the only answer is to work harder in order to earn more money. It's not the only answer," insists Michael. The couple's decision was to trade two full-time careers for two half-time careers, and to curtail consumption. They decided to spend their money only on things that contributed to their major goal, the construction of a world where family and friendship, work and play, were all of a piece, a world, moreover, which did not make wasteful use of the earth's resources.

—Linda Weltner, "Stripping Down to Bare Happiness"

EXERCISE 4-6

Working individually or with a peer-response group, rearrange the sentences in each paragraph below so that it flows logically. To begin, identify the topic sentence, use it as the paragraph's first sentence, and continue from there. For help, consult 4h.

PARAGRAPH A

1. Remember, many people who worry about offending others wind up living according to other people's priorities.
2. Learn to decline, tactfully but firmly, every request that doesn't contribute to your goals.
3. Of all the timesaving techniques ever developed, perhaps the most effective is the frequent use of the word *no.*
4. If you point out that your motivation isn't to get out of work but to save your time to do a better job on the really important things, you'll have a good chance of avoiding unproductive tasks.

—Edwin Bliss, "Getting Things Done: The ABC's of Time Management"

PARAGRAPH B

1. After a busy day, lens wearers often don't feel like taking time out to clean and disinfect their lenses, and many wearers skip the chore.
2. When buying a pair of glasses, a person deals with just the expense of the glasses themselves.
3. Although contact lenses make the wearer more attractive, glasses are easier and less expensive to care for.
4. However, in addition to the cost of the lenses themselves, contact lens wearers must shoulder the extra expense of cleaning supplies.
5. This inattention creates a danger of infection.
6. In contrast, contact lenses require daily cleaning and weekly enzyming that inconvenience lens wearers.
7. Glasses can be cleaned quickly with water and tissue at the wearer's convenience.

—Heather Martin, student

PARAGRAPH C

1. Significantly, scientists have found that radiated light activates a different part of the brain than reflected light.
2. Many people believe that reading a page on a computer screen is no different than reading a printed page.
3. The result is that reading with radiated light causes both the reader's eye and the reader's mind to wander.
4. This belief is inaccurate, however, because a computer screen *radiates* light, while a paper page *reflects* light at the reader's eye.

—Lise Bernard, student

93

EXERCISE 4-7

Working individually or with a peer-response group, determine the arrangements in these paragraphs. Choose from time, location, general to specific, specific to general, least to most important, and problem to solution. For help, consult 4h.

A.   A combination of cries from exotic animals and laughter and gasps from children fills the air along with the aroma of popcorn and peanuts. A hungry lion bellows for dinner, his roar breaking through the confusing chatter of other animals. Birds of all kinds chirp endlessly at curious children. Monkeys swing from limb to limb, 31 performing gymnastics for gawking onlookers. A comedy routine by orangutans employing old shoes and garments incites squeals of amusement. Reptiles sleep peacefully behind glass windows, yet they send shivers down the spines of those who remember the quick death many of these reptiles can induce. The sights and sounds and smells of the zoo inform and entertain children of all ages.
—Deborah Harris, student

B.   No one even agrees anymore on what "old" is. Not long ago, 30 was middle-aged and 60 was old. Now, more and more people are 32 living into their 70s, 80s and beyond—and many of them are living well, without any incapacitating mental or physical decline. Today, old age is defined not simply by chronological years, but by degree of health and well-being.
—Carol Tavris, "Old Age Isn't What It Used to Be"

C.   Lately, bee researchers have been distracted by a new challenge from abroad. It's, of course, the so-called "killer bee" that was imported into Brazil from Africa in the mid-1950s and has been heading our way ever since. The Africanized bee looks like the Italian bee but is more 33 defensive and more inclined to attack in force. It consumes much of the honey that it produces, leaving relatively little for anyone who attempts to work with it. It travels fast, competes with local bees and, worse, mates with them. It has ruined the honey industry in Venezuela and now the big question is: Will the same thing happen here?
—Jim Doherty, "The Hobby That Challenges You
to Think Like a Bee"

EXERCISE 4-8

Working individually or with a peer-response group, decide what would be the best arrangement for a paragraph on each topic listed here. Choose from one or a combination of time, location, general to specific, specific to general, least to most important, and problem to solution. For help, consult 4h.

1. ways to make friends
2. automobile accidents

3. how to combine work and studies
4. teaching children table manners

4i How can rhetorical strategies help me write paragraphs?

Rhetorical strategies are techniques for presenting ideas clearly and effectively. You choose a specific rhetorical strategy according to what you want to accomplish. Box 26 lists the common rhetorical strategies at your disposal.

Sometimes, you need to use a combination of rhetorical strategies. For example, in a paragraph on types of colour blindness, you might use a combination of definition and classification. A paragraph explaining why one brand of house paint is superior to another might call for comparison and contrast combined with description—and, perhaps, also definition and examples. Often, your TOPIC SENTENCE will steer you toward a particular pattern.

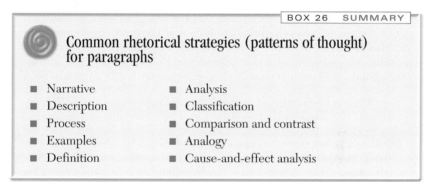

BOX 26   SUMMARY

Common rhetorical strategies (patterns of thought) for paragraphs

- Narrative
- Description
- Process
- Examples
- Definition

- Analysis
- Classification
- Comparison and contrast
- Analogy
- Cause-and-effect analysis

Writing a narrative

Narrative writing is a rhetorical strategy that tells a story. A *narration* relates what is happening or what has happened. Paragraph 34 is an example.

34
There were ten major gold company analysts waching Bre-X stock in October 1995, when the price blew through $30 on October 20, a level that meant investors valued the company at more than $700 million. Normally, analysts move up their target price for a $30 stock by a few dollars at a time. Not with Bre-X. Targets rose in leaps and bounds. By October 23, 1995, Bre-X was changing hands at $43 and Lévesque's Fowler, still enthralled by his "visual inspection," set out a one-year target of $62, which would rank Bre-X as one of the five largest gold companies in Canada. In Indonesia, the geologists stayed true to form. Rather than verifying the existing deposit, Felderhof and de Guzman

continued to do step-out drilling. Three new holes were drilled that extended the size of the deposit to a strip 2.75 kilometres long. All three found gold. The stock soared on the news.

—Douglas Goold and Andrew Willis, *The Bre-X Fraud*

Writing a description

Writing a **description** is a rhetorical strategy that appeals to a reader's senses—sight, sound, smell, taste, and touch. *Descriptive writing* paints a picture in words. Paragraph 35 is an example.

35 Walking to the ranch house from the shed, we saw the Northern Lights. They looked like talcum powder fallen from a woman's face. Rouge and blue eye shadow streaked the spires of a white light which exploded, then pulsated, shaking the colors down—like lives—until they faded from sight.

—Gretel Ehrlich, "Other Lives"

Writing about a process

Writing about a **process** is a rhetorical strategy that reports a sequence of actions by which something is done or made. A process usually proceeds chronologically—first do this, then do that. A process's complexity dictates the level of detail in the writing. For example, paragraph 36 provides an overview of a complicated process. Paragraph 37, on the other hand, gives explicit step-by-step directions.

36 Making chocolate isn't as simple as grinding a bag of beans. The machinery in a chocolate factory towers over you, rumbling and whirring. A huge cleaner first blows the beans away from their accompanying debris—sticks and stones, coins and even bullets can fall among cocoa beans being bagged. Then they go into another machine for roasting. Next comes separation in a winnower, shells sliding out one side, beans falling from the other. Grinding follows, resulting in chocolate liquor. Fermentation, roasting, and "conching" all influence the flavor of chocolate. Chocolate is "conched"—rolled over and over against itself like pebbles in the sea—in enormous circular machines named conches for the shells they once resembled. Climbing a flight of steps to peer into this huge, slow-moving glacier, I was expecting something like molten mud but found myself forced to conclude it resembled nothing so much as chocolate.

—Ruth Mehrtens Galvin, "Sybaritic to Some, Sinful to Others"

37 Carrying loads of equal weight like paint cans and toolboxes is easier if you carry one in each hand. Keep your shoulders back and down so that the weight is balanced on each side of your body, not suspended in front. With this method, you'll be able to lift heavier loads and also to walk and stand erect. Your back will not be strained by being pulled to one side.

—John Warde, "Safe Lifting Techniques"

Writing using examples

A paragraph developed by **examples** presents particular instances of a larger category. For instance, examples of the category "endangered animals" could include the black rhinoceros, South China tiger, Bulmer's fruit bat, and silvery gibbon. Paragraph 38 is an example of this strategy. On the other hand, sometimes one **extended example,** often called an *illustration,* is useful. Paragraph 39 is an example of this technique.

38 What meaning can we give to the symbols chosen to represent different countries? Ever since the Middle Ages, England has had its regal lion, whose image needs no explanation. France still uses "Marianne," a beautiful woman symbolizing the French Revolution, and the American revolutionaries chose for their country's totem the fierce, independent bald eagle. Canadians used to display the beaver, an animal that was seen as an industrious lumberjack—maybe early Canadians recognized themselves in that image. Now we prefer the maple leaf, to which we can give whatever meaning we want.

—Sivan Chand, student

39 He was one of the greatest scientists the world has ever known, yet if I had to convey the essence of Albert Einstein in a single word, I would choose *simplicity.* Perhaps an anecdote will help. Once, caught in a downpour, he took off his hat and held it under his coat. Asked why, he explained, with admirable logic, that the rain would damage the hat, but his hair would be none the worse for its wetting. This knack of going instinctively to the heart of the matter was the secret of his major scientific discoveries—this and his extraordinary feeling for beauty.

—Banesh Hoffman, "My Friend, Albert Einstein"

Writing using definition

When you define something, you give its meaning. **Definition** is often used together with other rhetorical strategies. If, for example, you were explaining how to organize a seashell collection, you'd probably want to define the two main types of shells: bivalve and univalve. You can also develop an entire paragraph by definition, called an **extended definition.** An extended definition discusses the meaning of a word or concept in more detail than a dictionary definition. If the topic is very abstract, the writer tries to put the definition in concrete terms. Sometimes a definition tells what something is not, as well as what it is, as in paragraph 40.

40 Chemistry is that branch of science that has the task of investigating the materials out of which the universe is made. It is not concerned with the forms into which they may be fashioned. Such objects as chairs, tables, vases, bottles, or wires are of no significance in chemistry; but such substances as glass, wool, iron, sulfur, and clay, as the materials out of which they are made, are what it studies. Chemistry is concerned not only with the composition of such substances, but also with their inner structure.

—John Arrend Timm, *General Chemistry*

Writing using analysis

Analysis, sometimes called *division,* divides things up into their parts. It usually starts, often in its topic sentence, by identifying one subject and continues by explaining the subject's distinct parts. Paragraph 41 discusses the parts of the wing of a supersonic aircraft.

41   A wing design is a compromise. For example, if a designer wants a wing for an aircraft that will cruise at supersonic speeds, he must also design the wing to fly at subsonic speeds as well as for takeoffs and landings. Thus, the optimum cruise configuration is compromised to gain other necessary characteristics. Granted, devices such as ailerons, flaps, spoilers, and slats can partially compensate for deficiencies, but these still do not give the optimum performance of a wing designed for a particular flight regime.

—Bill Siuru and John D. Busick, *Future Flight:*
The Next Generation of Aircraft Technology

Writing using classification

Classification groups items according to an underlying, shared characteristic. Paragraph 42 groups—classifies—galaxies into three different types.

42   There are three basic types of galaxies: spiral galaxies, like the Milky Way; spherical swarms of stars called elliptical galaxies; and loose collections of stars with no distinct structural form, called irregular galaxies. The Large and Small Magellanic Clouds, the Milky Way satellite galaxies, are irregulars. Two nearby ellipticals are companions of the Andromeda Galaxy and are easily seen in photographs. The smallest elliptical galaxies, called dwarf spheroidal systems, have only a few thousand stars. But giant ellipticals are the titans of the cosmos, with populations of up to 50 trillion stars. Spiral galaxies have a comparatively small size range. The upper limit is marked by NGC 6872 and UGC 2885, both roughly 10 times the number of the Milky Way, while NGC 3928 is only about one-quarter of our galaxy's diameter. Although spiral galaxies are outnumbered by ellipticals, they *appear* to be most common because a typical spiral is larger and brighter than an average elliptical. Irregular galaxies are less numerous than spirals or ellipticals, and most are quite small.

—Terence Dickinson, "Galactic Encounters"

Writing using comparison and contrast

A paragraph developed by *comparison* deals with similarities; a paragraph developed by *contrast* deals with differences. **Comparison and contrast** writing is usually organized in one of two ways: You can use *point-by-point organization,* which moves back and forth between the items being compared; or you can use *block organization,* which discusses one item completely before discussing the other. Box 27 lays out the two patterns visually.

BOX 27   PATTERN

Comparison and contrast

Point-by-Point Structure
Student body: college A, university B
Curriculum: college A, university B
Location: college A, university B

Block Structure
College A: student body, curriculum, location
University B: student body, curriculum, location

Paragraph 43 is structured point by point, going back and forth between the two children (whose names are in boldface) being compared.

43   My husband and I constantly marvel at the fact that our two sons, born of the same parents and only two years apart in age, are such completely different human beings. The most obvious differences became apparent at their births. Our firstborn, **Mark,** was big and bold—his intense, already wise eyes, broad shoulders, huge and heavy hands, and powerful, chunky legs gave us the impression he could have walked out of the delivery room on his own. Our second son, **Wayne,** was delightfully different. Rather than having the football physique that **Mark** was born with, **Wayne** came into the world with a long, slim, wiry body more suited to running, jumping, and contorting. **Wayne's** eyes, rather than being intense like **Mark's,** were impish and innocent. When **Mark** was delivered, he cried only momentarily, and then seemed to settle into a state of intense concentration, as if trying to absorb everything he could about the strange, new environment he found himself in. Conversely, **Wayne** screamed from the moment he first appeared. There was nothing helpless or pathetic about his cry either—he was darn angry!

—Rosanne Labonte, student

Paragraph 44 uses the block pattern for comparison and contrast. The writer first discusses games and then business (each key word is in boldface).

44   **Games** are of limited duration, take place on or in fixed and finite sites, and are governed by openly promulgated rules that are enforced on the spot by neutral professionals. Moreover, they're performed by relatively evenly matched teams that are counseled and led through every move by seasoned hands. Scores are kept, and at the end of the game, a winner is declared. **Business** is usually a little different. In fact, if there is anyone out there who can say that the business is of limited duration, takes

place on a fixed site, is governed by openly promulgated rules that are enforced on the spot by neutral professionals, competes only on relatively even terms, and performs in a way that can be measured in runs or points, then that person is either extraordinarily lucky or seriously deluded.

—Warren Bennis, "Time to Hang Up the Old Sports Clichés"

Writing using analogy

An **analogy** is an extended comparison between objects or ideas from different classes—things not normally associated. Analogy is particularly effective in explaining unfamiliar or abstract concepts because it allows a comparison to be drawn between what is familiar and what is not. An analogy often begins with a SIMILE or METAPHOR (21d), as in paragraph 45.

45 Casual dress, like casual speech, tends to be loose, relaxed, and colorful. It often contains what might be called "slang words": blue jeans, sneakers, baseball caps, aprons, flowered cotton housedresses, and the like. These garments could not be worn on a formal occasion without causing disapproval, but in ordinary circumstances, they pass without remark. "Vulgar words" in dress, on the other hand, give emphasis and get immediate attention in almost any circumstances, just as they do in speech. Only the skillful can employ them without some loss of face, and even then, they must be used in the right way. A torn, unbuttoned shirt or wildly uncombed hair can signify strong emotions: passion, grief, rage, despair. They're most effective if people already think of you as being neatly dressed, just as the curses of well-spoken persons count for more than those of the customarily foul-mouthed do.

—Alison Lurie, *The Language of Clothes*

Writing using cause-and-effect analysis

Cause-and-effect analysis examines outcomes and the reasons for those outcomes. Causes lead to an event or an effect, and effects result from causes. (For a discussion of correct logic for assessing CAUSE AND EFFECT, see 5h.) Paragraph 46 discusses how television (the cause) becomes indispensable (the effect) to parents of young children.

46 Because television is so wonderfully available as child amuser and child defuser, capable of rendering a volatile three-year-old harmless at the flick of a switch, parents grow to depend upon it in the course of their daily lives. And as they continue to utilize television day after day, its importance in their children's lives increases. From a simple source of entertainment provided by parents when they need a break from childcare, television gradually changes into a powerful and disruptive presence in family life. But despite their increasing resentment of television's intrusions into their family life, and despite their considerable guilt at not being able to control their children's viewing, parents don't take steps to extricate themselves from television's domination. They can no longer cope without it.

—Marie Winn, *The Plug-In Drug*

EXERCISE 4-9

Working individually or with a peer-response group, decide what rhetorical strategies are used in each paragraph. Choose any one or a combination of narrative, description, process, examples, definition, analysis, classification, comparison and contrast, analogy, and cause and effect. For help, consult 4i.

A.   Another way to think about metamessages is that they frame a conversation, much as a picture frame provides a context for the images in the picture. Metamessages let you know how to interpret
47 what someone is saying by identifying the activity that is going on. Is this an argument or a chat? Is it helping, advising, or scolding? At the same time, they let you know what position the speaker is assuming in the activity, and what position you are being assigned.
　　　　　　　　　　　　　—Deborah Tannen, *You Just Don't Understand*

B.   The contrast between English Canadian and Quebecois attitudes to the United States is striking. In English Canada there has been an anguished debate for generations as to whether Canadian culture can preserve its distinctiveness amid the nightly electronic deluge of up to sixty cable TV stations in most Canadian homes. At Videotron, Que-
48 bec's largest cable TV company, they beam all the American soaps into Quebec homes, but they know that the most popular shows—the ones that get up to 80 percent of the Quebec population staying home at night—are the ones written and acted in Quebec. As long as they can see what they want in their own language, Quebecois believe their culture will be secure.
　　　　　　　　　　　　　—Michael Ignatieff, *Blood and Belonging*

C.   In the case of wool, very hot water can actually cause some structural changes within the fiber, but the resulting shrinkage is minor. The fundamental cause of shrinkage in wool is felting, in which the
49 fibers scrunch together in a tighter bunch, and the yarn, fabric, and garment follow suit. Wool fibers are curly and rough-surfaced, and when squished together under the lubricating influence of water, the fibers wind around each other, like two springs interlocking. Because of their rough surfaces, they stick together and can't be pulled apart.
　　　　　　　　　　　　　—James Gorman, "Gadgets"

D.   Buctouche is a small town at the mouth of the Buctouche River in New Brunswick. It is also the summer home of Antonine Maillet. I had just translated Maillet's short novel *Christophe Cartier de la noisette, dit Nounours,* and was about to embark on her monumental allegory
50 *Le huitième jour,* and I wanted to get the lay of the Acadian landscape. I had a literary sense of the Buctouche area, but I wanted to see it and hear it for myself. I stopped outside a low brick building, one of those five-and-dime stores that sell cheap clothes and expensive souvenirs,

including small Acadian flags—the French *tricolore* with a yellow *Stella maris* in one corner. When I went up to the cash, I asked, in my best French, which house belonged to Antonine and received a long, friendly reply. To my complete astonishment I could not understand a word of it. I had entered a private realm, a kind of hidden valley that had its own customs, its own flag and its own language. Some call this place the Republic of Madawaska, but for more than 350 years it has been known as the land of Acadia.

—Wayne Grady, *Chasing the Chinook*

E.   Lacking access to a year-round supermarket, the many species—from ants to wolves—that in the course of evolution have learned the advantages of hoarding must devote a lot of energy and ingenuity to protecting their stashes from marauders. Creatures like beavers and honeybees, for example, hoard food to get them through cold winters. Others, like
51   desert rodents that face food scarcities throughout the year, must take advantage of the short-lived harvests that follow occasional rains. For animals like burying beetles that dine on mice hundreds of times their size, a habit of biting off more than they can chew at the moment forces them to store their leftovers. Still others, like the male MacGregor's bowerbird, stockpile goodies during mating season so they can concentrate on wooing females and defending their arena d'amour.

—Jane Brody, "A Hoarder's Life: Filling the Cache—and Finding It"

EXERCISE 4-10

Working individually or with a peer-response group, reread the paragraphs in Exercise 4-7 and determine the rhetorical strategy (or strategies) being used in each.

4j   What is a transitional paragraph?

Transitional paragraphs are found in long essays. These paragraphs form a bridge between one long discussion on a single topic that requires a number of paragraphs and another discussion, usually lengthy, of another topic. Paragraph 52 is an example of a transitional paragraph that allows the writer to move from a long discussion of people's gestures to a long discussion of people's eating habits.

52   Like gestures, eating habits are personality indicators, and even food preferences and attitudes toward food reveal the inner self. Food plays an important role in the lives of most people beyond its obvious one as a necessity.

—Jean Rosenbaum, M.D., *Is Your Volkswagen a Sex Symbol?*

4k What are effective concluding paragraphs?

A **concluding paragraph** ends the discussion smoothly by following logically from the essay's introductory paragraph (4b) and the essay's body paragraphs (4c). Always integrate a concluding device into the final paragraph so that the discussion does not end abruptly. A conclusion that is hurriedly tacked on is a missed opportunity to provide a sense of completion and a finishing touch that adds to the whole essay. Box 28 lists strategies for concluding your essay as well as strategies to avoid.

The same writers who wait to write their introductory paragraph until they've drafted their body paragraphs often also wait to write their concluding paragraph until they've drafted their introduction. They do this to coordinate the beginning and end so that they can make sure they don't repeat the same strategy in both places.

BOX 28   SUMMARY

Strategies for concluding paragraphs

Strategies to Try

■ A strategy adapted from those used for introductory paragraphs (4b)—but be careful to choose a different strategy for your introduction and conclusion:
  • Relating a brief concluding interesting story or anecdote
  • Giving pertinent—perhaps surprising—concluding statistics
  • Asking one or more provocative questions for further thought
  • Using an appropriate quotation to sum up the THESIS STATEMENT
  • Redefining a key term for emphasis
■ An ANALOGY that summarizes the thesis statement
■ A SUMMARY of the main points, but only if the piece of writing is longer than three to four pages
■ A statement that urges awareness on the part of readers
■ A statement that looks ahead to the future
■ A call to readers

Strategies to Avoid

■ Introducing new ideas or facts that belong in the body of the essay
■ Rewording your introduction
■ Announcing what you've discussed, as in "In this paper, I have explained why oil prices have dropped."
■ Making absolute claims, as in "I have proved that oil prices don't always affect gasoline prices."
■ Apologizing, as in "Even though I'm not an expert, I feel my position is correct."

Paragraph 53, a concluding paragraph from an essay on the history of pizza and its modern appeal, summarizes the main points of the essay.

53 For a food that is traced to Neolithic beginnings, like Mexico's tortillas, Armenia's lahmejoun, Scottish oatcakes, and even matzos, pizza has remained fresh and vibrant. Whether it's galettes, the latest thin-crusted invasion from France with bacon and onion toppings, or a plain slice of a cheese pie, the varieties of pizza are clearly limited only by one's imagination.

—Lisa Pratt, "A Slice of History"

Paragraph 54 concludes an essay that argues for the recognition of First Nations governments in Canada. It reinforces the essay's message with a call for justice and cooperation.

54 What we are looking for is not just power to deal with the social problems we face but reconciliation with Canada. We are trying to find a way of creating harmony in the country. The way you achieve that is to produce justice; our people have to feel justice, not just think about it. We have to experience it before we can believe it. There is absolutely no way that First Nations governments can meet the needs of the First Nations peoples without the help of the provinces or the federal government. What we are asking is to become partners working towards the same future.

—Ovide Mercredi, "Self-Government as a Way to Heal"

EXERCISE 4-11

Working individually or in a peer-response group, return to Exercise 4-1, in which you wrote introductory paragraphs for three informally outlined essays. Now, write a concluding paragraph for each.

Chapter 5

Critical Thinking, Reading, and Writing

Getting a college or university education and living a reflective life mean participating in a world of ideas and opinions. Your success with these activities depends largely on your level of comfort with critical thinking as a concept (5a) and as an activity (5b); critical reading as a concept (5c) and as an activity (5d and 5e); critical writing (5f); and critical reasoning (5g through 5j). The word *critical* here has a neutral meaning. It doesn't mean taking a negative view or finding fault, as when someone criticizes another person for doing something wrong. Rather, *critical* here applies to a mental stance of examining ideas thoroughly and deeply, refusing to accept ideas merely because they seem sensible at first thought, and tolerating questions that often lack definitive answers.

5a What is critical thinking?

Thinking isn't something you choose to do, any more than a fish chooses to live in water. To be human is to think. But while thinking may come naturally, awareness of how you think doesn't. Thinking about thinking is the key to critical thinking.

Critical thinking means taking control of your conscious thought processes. If you don't take control of those processes, you risk being controlled by the ideas of others. In fact, critical thinking is an attitude as much as an activity. If you face life with curiosity and a desire to dig beneath the surface, you're a critical thinker. The essence of critical thinking is thinking beyond the obvious—beyond the flash of visual images on a television screen, the alluring promises of glossy advertisements, the evasive statements by some people in the news, the half-truths of propaganda, the manipulations of SLANTED LANGUAGE, and faulty reasoning. Its skills are both an aim of your program of study and a means of getting the most out of your education.

5b How do I engage in critical thinking?

To engage in CRITICAL THINKING, you become fully aware of an idea or an action, reflect on it, and ultimately react to it. You already engage in this process numerous times every day. For example, you're thinking critically when you meet someone new and decide whether you like the person; when you read a book and form an opinion of it based on reasonable analysis; or when you interview for a job and then evaluate its requirements and your ability to fulfil them.

Box 29 describes the general process of critical thinking in academic settings. This same process applies as well to reading critically (5c and 5d) and writing critically (5f).

The steps in the critical thinking process are somewhat fluid, just as are the steps in the WRITING PROCESS. Expect sometimes to combine steps, reverse their order, and return to parts of the process you thought you had completed. As you do so, remember that synthesis and evaluation are two different mental activities: *Synthesis* calls for making connections; *evaluation* calls for making judgments.

BOX 29   SUMMARY

Steps in the critical thinking process

1. **Summarize.** Extract and restate the material's main message or central point. Use only what you see on the page. Add nothing.

2. **Analyze.** Examine the material by breaking it into its component parts. By seeing each part of the whole as a distinct unit, you discover how the parts interrelate. Consider the line of reasoning as shown by the EVIDENCE offered (5g) and logic used (5j). Read "between the lines" to draw INFERENCES (5c.2), gaining information that's implied but not stated. When reading or listening, notice how the reading or speaking style and the choice of words work together to create a TONE (1e).

3. **Synthesize.** Pull together what you've summarized and analyzed by connecting it to your own experiences, such as reading, talking with others, watching television and films, using the Internet, and so on. In this way, you create a new whole that reflects your newly acquired knowledge and insights combined with your prior knowledge.

4. **Evaluate.** Judge the quality of the material now that you've become informed through the activities of SUMMARY, ANALYSIS, and SYNTHESIS. Resist the very common urge to evaluate before you summarize, analyze, and synthesize.

5c What is the reading process?

Reading is an active process—a dynamic, meaning-making interaction between the page and your brain. Understanding the **reading process** helps people become critical thinkers.

Making **predictions** is a major activity in the reading process. Your mind is constantly guessing what's coming next. When it sees what comes next, it either confirms or revises its prediction and moves on. For example, suppose you're glancing through a magazine and come upon the title "The Heartbeat." Your mind begins guessing: Is this a love story? Is this about how the heart pumps blood? Maybe, you say to yourself, it's a story about someone who had a heart attack. Then, as you read the first few sentences, your mind confirms which guess was correct. If you see words like *electrical impulse, muscle fibres,* and *contraction,* you know instantly that you're in the realm of physiology. In a few more sentences, you narrow your prediction to either "the heart as pump" or "the heart suffering an attack."

To make predictions efficiently, consciously decide your purpose for reading. People generally read for two reasons—for relaxation or for learning. Reading a popular novel helps you relax. Reading for college or university courses calls for you to understand material and remember it. When you read to learn, you usually have to reread. One encounter with new material is rarely enough to understand it fully.

The speed at which you read depends on your purpose for reading. When you're hunting for a particular fact, you can skim the page until you come to what you want. When you read about a subject you know well, you might read somewhat rapidly, slowing down when you come to new material. When you're unfamiliar with the subject, you need to work slowly because your mind needs time to absorb the new material.

The reading process involves your thinking on three levels, which is another reason your academic work calls for much rereading, as described in Box 30.

BOX 30   SUMMARY

Steps in the reading process

1. **Reading for literal meaning:** Read "on the lines" to see what's stated (5c.1).
2. **Reading to draw inferences:** Read "between the lines" to see what's not stated but implied (5c.2).
3. **Reading to evaluate:** Read "beyond the lines" to form your own opinion about the material (5c.3).

5c.1 Reading for literal meaning

Reading for **literal meaning** is reading for comprehension. Your goal is to discover the main ideas, the supporting details, or, in a work of fiction, the central details of plot and character.

Reading for literal meaning is not as easy as it might sound. When you come across a new concept, think it through. Rushing through material to "cover" it rather than to understand it takes more time in the end. If the author's writing style is complex, "unpack" the sentences: Break them into smaller units or reword them in a simpler style. See Box 31 for suggestions about ways to improve your reading comprehension.

5c.2 Reading to draw inferences

When you read for **inferences,** you're reading to understand what's suggested or implied but not stated. This is similar to the kind of critical thinking discussed in 5b. Often, you need to infer the author's PURPOSE. Here's an example.

How to tell the difference between modern art and junk puzzles many people, although few are willing to admit it. The owner of an art

---

BOX 31 SUMMARY

Ways to help your reading comprehension

- **Make associations.** Link new material to what you already know, especially when you're reading about an unfamiliar subject. You may even find it helpful to read an easier book on the subject first in order to build your knowledge base.

- **Make it easy to focus.** If your mind wanders, be fiercely determined to concentrate. Do whatever it takes: Arrange for silence or music, for being alone or in the library with others who are studying. Try to read at your best time of day (some people concentrate better in the morning, others in the evening).

- **Allot the time you need.** To comprehend new material, you must allow sufficient time to read, reflect, reread, and study. Discipline yourself to balance classes, working, socializing, and family activities. Reading and studying take time. Nothing prevents success as much as poor time management.

- **Master the vocabulary.** If you don't understand the key terms in your reading, you can't fully understand the concepts. As you encounter new words, first try to figure out their meanings from context clues (21e). Also, many textbooks list key terms and their definitions (called a *glossary*) at the end of each chapter or the book. Of course, nothing replaces having a good dictionary at hand.

gallery in Chicago had a prospective buyer for two sculptures made of discarded metal and put them outside his warehouse to clean them up. Unfortunately, some junk dealers, who apparently didn't recognize abstract expressionism when they saw it, hauled the two 300-pound pieces away.
—Ora Gygi, "Things Are Seldom What They Seem"

The literal meaning of the Gygi paragraph is that some people can't tell the difference between art and junk. A good summary would say that two abstract metal sculptures were carted away as junk when an art dealer set them outside a warehouse to clean them. However, looking at the inferential meaning reveals that the paragraph explains that few people will admit it when they don't know the difference between art and junk. Further, the paragraph implies that people often don't want to appear uneducated or show themselves lacking in good taste because something called "art" looks like "junk" to them. The word *apparently*— a good word for writing inferences—uses IRONY (21d) to seem tactful but is just the opposite. Readers may dispute whether the target of the irony is the art dealer, his client, or the junk dealers—although the ultimate laugh is on the whole art world.

Drawing inferences takes practice. Box 32 lists questions to help you read "between the lines." A discussion of each point follows the box.

BOX 32   CHECKLIST

✓ Drawing inferences during reading

- Is the **tone** of the material appropriate?
- Can I detect **prejudice** or **bias** in the material?
- Is the separation of **fact** and **opinion** clear or muddy?
- What is the writer's **position,** even if he or she doesn't come out and state it?

Tone

Tone in writing emerges from many aspects of what you write, but mostly from your word choice. Tone in writing is like tone in speaking: it can be formal, informal, pompous, sarcastic, and so on. If you read exclusively for literal meaning (5c.1), you'll be likely to miss the tone and possibly the point of the whole piece.

For example, as a critical reader, be suspicious of a highly emotional tone in writing. If you find it, chances are the writer is trying to manipulate the audience. Resist this. As a writer, if you find your tone growing emotional, step back and rethink the situation. No matter what point you want to make, your chance of communicating successfully to an audience depends on your using a moderate, reasonable tone. For instance, the exaggerations below in the NO example (*robbing treasures, politicians are murderers*) might hint at the truth of a few cases, but they're too extreme to be taken seriously. The language of the YES version is far more likely to deliver its intended message.

> **NO**   Urban renewal must be stopped. Urban redevelopment is ruining this country, and money-hungry capitalists are robbing treasures from law-abiding citizens. Corrupt politicians are murderers, caring nothing about people being thrown out of their homes into the streets.

> **YES**   Urban renewal is revitalizing our cities, but it has caused some serious problems. While investors are trying to replace slums with decent housing, they must also remember that they're displacing people who don't want to leave their familiar neighbourhoods. Surely, a cooperative effort between government and the private sector can lead to creative solutions.

Prejudice or bias

For inferential reading, you want to detect **prejudice** or **bias.** These concepts go further than the attempt by most writers to influence readers to accept their points of view. When writing is distorted by hatred or dislike of individuals, groups of people, or ideas, you as a critical reader should suspect its accuracy and fairness. Prejudice and bias can be worded in positive language, but critical readers aren't deceived by such tactics. Similarly, writers can merely imply their prejudices and bias rather than state them outright. Suppose you read, "Poor people like living in crowded conditions because they're used to such surroundings" or "Women are so wonderfully nurturing that they can't succeed in business." As a critical reader, you will immediately detect the prejudice and bias. Always, therefore, question material that rests on a weak foundation of discrimination and narrow-mindedness.

Fact versus opinion

Another skill in reading inferentially is the ability to differentiate **fact** from **opinion.** *Facts* are statements that can be verified. *Opinions* are statements of personal beliefs. Facts can be verified by observation, research, or experimentation, but opinions are open to debate. A problem arises when a writer intentionally blurs the distinction between fact and opinion. Critical readers will know the difference.

For example, here are two statements, one a fact and one an opinion.

1. Women can never make good mathematicians.
2. Although fear of math isn't purely a female phenomenon, girls tend to drop out of math classes sooner than boys, and some adult women have an aversion to math and math-related activity that is akin to anxiety.

Reading inferentially, you can see that statement 1 is clearly an opinion. Is it worthy of consideration? Perhaps it could be open to debate, but the word *never* implies that the writer is unwilling to allow for even one exception. Conversely, statement 2 at least seems to be factual, though research would be necessary to confirm or deny the position.

As a reader, when you can consider the source—that is, find out who exactly made a statement—you hold an advantage in trying to distinguish between fact and opinion. To illustrate, statement 1 above is from a male Russian mathematician, as reported by David K. Shipler, a well-respected veteran reporter on Russian affairs for the *New York Times*. Statement 2 is from the book *Overcoming Math Anxiety* by Sheila Tobias, a university professor who has extensively studied why many people dislike math. Her credentials can help readers accept her statement as true. If, however, someone known for belittling women had made statement 2, a critical reader's reaction would be quite different.

To differentiate between fact and opinion, reflect on the material and think beyond the obvious. For example, is the statement "Strenuous exercise is good for your health" a fact? It has the ring of truth, but it definitely isn't a fact. Some people with severe arthritis or heart trouble should avoid some forms of exercise. Also, what does *strenuous* mean— a dozen push-ups, jogging, aerobics for an hour?

EXERCISE 5-1

Working individually or with a peer-response group, decide which statements are facts and which are opinions. When the author and source are provided, explain how that information influenced your judgment. For help, consult 5c.2.

1. Our cities tend to be functional but nondescript, anchored against the wind, with nothing to please the eye. Quebec City is an exception.
   —Mordecai Richler, *Oh Canada! Oh Quebec!*

2. Advertisements for synthetic sports clothing frequently claim that it insulates better and dries more quickly than cotton.

3. Every journey into the past is complicated by delusions, false memories, false naming of real events.
   —Adrienne Rich, poet, *Of Woman Born*

4. The vested interests of acquired knowledge and conventional wisdom have always been by-passed and engulfed by new media.
   —Marshall McLuhan, *Understanding Media*

5. History is the branch of knowledge that deals systematically with the past.
   —*Webster's New World College Dictionary,* Fourth Edition

6. In 1927, F. E. Tylcote, an English physician, reported in the medical journal *Lancet* that in almost every case of lung cancer he had seen or known about, the patient smoked.
   —William Ecenbarger, "The Strange History of Tobacco"

7. At present, carbon emissions are about 6.5 billion metric tons each year worldwide—that works out to 22 billion tons of CO_2, which is created when carbon is burned. . . . Now, with climate worries on the rise, many scientists believe these emissions are doing damage to the planet.

—"Surviving the Greenhouse,"
<http://www.msnbc.com/news/291336.asp>

8. David Suzuki and Naomi Klein are essential reading for anyone who wants to gain an understanding of globalization.

9. Since the mid-1960s, hepatitis—meaning, simply, the inflammation of the liver—has become a major health problem. As many as 500 million people carry hepatitis B or C, the most serious forms. Up to 500,000 of them live in Canada.

—Anita Elash, *Maclean's*

10. A critical task for all of the world's religions and spiritual traditions is to enrich the vision—and the reality—of the sense of community among us.

—Joel D. Beversluis, *A Sourcebook for Earth's Community of Religions*

EXERCISE 5-2

Read the following passages, then (1) list all literal information, (2) list all implied information, and (3) list the opinions stated. Refer to sections 5c.1 and 5c.2 for help.

EXAMPLE   The study found many complaints against the lawyers were not investigated, seemingly out of a "desire to avoid difficult cases."
—Norman F. Dacey

Literal information: Few complaints against lawyers are investigated.
Implied information: The words *difficult cases* imply a cover-up: Lawyers, or others in power, hesitate to criticize lawyers for fear of being sued or for fear of a public outcry if the truth about abuses and errors were revealed.
Opinions: No opinions. It reports on a study.

A.   I remember a weekend in Ottawa in the 1970s, when I helped to organize a meeting with men in prison; a group of ex-inmates and offenders, prison guards, policemen, prison chaplains, prison directors, and psychologists. We shared together, ate together, slept in dormitories. Nobody carried any label or sign showing to which group they belonged. We were together as persons, not as representatives of a group. It was, if you like, an image for me of how we actually behave towards each other

when we have no "markers" to tell us what we are supposed to feel towards someone. It was also a small indication of what society might look like, and how it might function, if we could overcome our prejudices.
—Jean Vanier, *Becoming Human*

B.   The kind of constitution and government Gandhi envisaged for an independent India was spelled out at the forty-fifth convention of the All-India Congress, which began at Karachi on March 27, 1931. It was a party political convention the like of which I had not seen before—nor seen since—with its ringing revolutionary proclamations acclaimed by some 350 leaders, men and women, just out of jail, squatting in the heat under a tent in a semicircle at Gandhi's feet, all of them, like Gandhi, spinning away like children playing with toys as they talked. They made up the so-called Subjects Committee, selected from the five thousand delegates to do the real work of the convention, though in reality, it was Gandhi alone who dominated the proceedings, writing most of the resolutions and moving their adoption with his customary eloquence and surprising firmness.
—William L. Shirer, *Gandhi: A Memoir*

5c.3 Reading to evaluate

When you read to evaluate, you're judging the writer's work. **Evaluative reading** comes after you've summarized, analyzed, and synthesized the material (Box 29). Reading "between the lines" is usually concerned with recognizing tone, detecting prejudice, and differentiating fact from opinion. Reading to evaluate, "beyond the lines," requires an overall assessment of the soundness of the writer's reasoning, evidence, or observations and the fairness and perceptiveness the writer shows, from accuracy of word choice and tone to the writer's respect for the reader.

5d How do I engage in critical reading?

Critical reading is a process parallel to CRITICAL THINKING (5a and 5b). To read critically is to think about what you're reading while you're reading it. This means that words don't merely drift by as your eyes scan the lines. To prevent that from happening, use approaches such as reading systematically (5d.1) and reading closely and actively (5d.2).

5d.1 Reading systematically

To **read systematically** is to use a structured plan: **P**review, **R**ead, and **R**eview. Reading systematically closely parallels the writing process. Like PLANNING in writing, *previewing* gets you ready and keeps you from reading inefficiently. Like DRAFTING in writing, *reading* means moving through the material so that you come to understand and remember it. Like REVISION in writing, *reviewing* takes you back over the material to clarify, fine-tune, and make it thoroughly your own. Here are techniques for reading systematically.

1. **Preview:** Before you begin reading, look ahead. Glance at the pages you intend to read so that your mind can start making predictions (5c). As you look over the material, ask yourself questions. Don't expect to answer all the questions at this point; their purpose is to focus your thoughts.

   ■ To preview a chapter in a textbook, first look at the table of contents. How does this chapter fit into the whole book? What topics come before? Which come after? Now turn to the chapter you're assigned and read all the headings, large and small. Note the boldfaced words (in darker print), and all visuals and their captions, including photographs, drawings, figures, tables, and boxes. If there's a glossary at the end of the chapter, scan it for words you do and do not know.

   ■ To preview a book or material in a book that has few or no headings, again, begin with the table of contents and ask questions about the chapter titles. If the book has a preface or introduction, skim it. Check for introductory notes about the author and head notes, which often precede individual works in collections of essays or short stories. Read pivotal paragraphs, such as the opening paragraphs and (unless you're reading for suspense) the last few paragraphs.

2. **Read:** Read the material closely and actively (5d.2). Seek the full meaning at all three levels of reading: *literal, inferential,* and *evaluative* (5c). Most of all, expect to reread. Rarely can anyone fully understand and absorb college- and university-level material in one reading. When you read, always set aside time to allow for more than one rereading.

3. **Review:** Go back to the spots you looked at when you previewed the material. Also, go back to other important places you discovered as you were reading. Ask yourself the same sorts of questions as when you previewed, this time answering as fully as possible. If you can't come up with answers, reread. For best success, review in *chunks*—small sections that you can capture comfortably. Don't try to cover too much material at one time.

   ■ To help you concentrate as you read, keep in mind that you intend to review—and then do it: Review immediately after you read. Review again the next day and again about a week later. Each time you review, add new knowledge to refine your understanding of the material. As much as time permits, review at intervals during a course. The more reinforcement, the better.

   ■ Collaborative learning can reinforce what you learn from reading. Ask a friend or classmate to discuss the material with you and quiz you. Conversely, offer to teach the material to someone; you'll quickly discover whether you've mastered it well enough to communicate it.

5d.2 Reading closely and actively

The secret to **reading closely** and **actively** is to annotate as you read. Annotating means writing notes to yourself in a book's margins and using asterisks and other codes to alert you to special material. Some readers start annotating right away, while others wait to annotate after they've previewed the material and read it once. Experiment to find what works best for you. I recommend your using two different ink colours, one for close reading (green in the following example) and one for active reading (black in the following example).

Close reading means annotating for content. You might, for example, number and briefly list the steps in a process or summarize major points in the margin. When you review, your marginal notes help you glance over the material and quickly recall what it's about.

Doesn't matter who wins, but tactics and prowess can be admired. Although I like to play, and sometimes like to watch, I cannot see what possible difference it makes which team beats which. The tactics are sometimes *Sports talk is boring.* interesting, and certainly the prowess of the players deserves applause—but most men seem to use commercial sports as a kind of (narcotic,) shutting out reality, rather than heightening it.

There is nothing more boring, in my view, than a prolonged discussion by laymen of yesterday's *Other examples include soap operas and sitcoms.* game. These dreary conversations are a form of social alcoholism, enabling them to achieve a *When my son and husband watch together, the rapport is very real.* (dubious rapport) without ever once having to come to grips with a subject worthy of a grown man's concern.

It is easy to see the (opiate) quality of sports in our society when tens of millions of men will spend a splendid Saturday or Sunday fall afternoon sitting *Instead of watching men should exercise.* (stupefied) in front of the TV, watching a "big game," when they might be out exercising their own flaccid muscles and stimulating their lethargic corpuscles.

Annotations of an excerpt from the essay shown in Exercise 5-3, using green for content (close reading) and black for synthesis (active reading).

Active reading means annotating to make connections between the material and what you already know or have experienced. This is your chance to converse on paper with the writer. Consider yourself a partner in the making of meaning, a full participant in the exchange of ideas.

If you feel uncomfortable writing in a book—even though the practice of annotating texts dates back to the Middle Ages—create a *double-entry notebook*. Draw a line down the middle of your notebook page. On one side, write content notes (close reading). On the other, write synthesis notes (active reading). Be sure to identify the passages you're referring to. Illustrated on page 117 is a short example from a double-entry notebook (the symbol ¶ stands for "paragraph").

EXERCISE 5-3

The following essay was published as a newspaper column. Annotate the entire essay, using one colour of ink for your notes about content and another for your notes that synthesize as you connect the material to your knowledge and experience.

Sports Only Exercise Our Eyes
By Sydney J. Harris

Before I proceed a line further, let me make it clear that I enjoy physical exercise and sport as much as any man. I like to bat a baseball, dribble a basketball, kick a soccer ball and, most of all, swat a tennis ball. A man who scorned physical activity would hardly build a tennis court on his summerhouse grounds, or use it every day.

Having made this obeisance, let me now confess that I am puzzled and upset—and have been for many years—by the almost obsessive interest in sports taken by the average American male.

Athletics is one strand in life, and even the ancient Greek philosophers recognized its importance. But it is by no means the whole web, as it seems to be in our society. If American men are not talking business, they're talking sports, or they're not talking at all.

This strikes me as an enormously adolescent, not to say retarded, attitude on the part of presumed adults. Especially when most of the passion and enthusiasm center on professional teams, which bear no indigenous relation to the city they play for, and consist of mercenaries who will wear any town's insignia if the price is right.

Although I like to play, and sometimes like to watch, I cannot see what possible difference it makes which team beats which. The tactics are sometimes interesting, and certainly the prowess of the players deserves applause—but most men seem to use commercial sports as a kind of narcotic, shutting out reality, rather than heightening it.

There is nothing more boring, in my view, than a prolonged discussion by laymen of yesterday's game. These dreary conversations are a form of social alcoholism, enabling them to achieve a dubious rapport without ever once having to come to grips with a subject worthy of a grown man's concern.

S. Harris essay, "Sports Only"

content	connections I make
#1 H. likes sports and exercise. He even built a tennis court for his summer home.	H. isn't "everyman." It takes big bucks to build one's own tennis court.
#2 H. thinks the average American male is obsessed with sports.	That "average" (if there is such a thing) male sounds a lot like my husband.
#3 Athletics/Sports are one strand, not the web, of society.	It's worth thinking why sports have such a major hold on men. And why not women, on "average"? (This might be a topic for a paper someday.)

Double-entry notebook excerpt, based on the first three paragraphs of the essay in Exercise 5-3. The left column deals with content (close reading), and the right covers synthesis (active reading).

It is easy to see the opiate quality of sports in our society when tens of millions of men will spend a splendid Saturday or Sunday fall afternoon sitting stupefied in front of the TV, watching a "big game," when they might be out exercising their own flaccid muscles and stimulating their lethargic corpuscles.

Ironically, our obsession with professional athletics not only makes us mentally limited and conversationally dull, it also keeps us physically inert—thus violating the very reason men began engaging in athletic competitions. Isn't it tempting to call this national malaise of "spectatoritis" childish? Except children have more sense, and would rather run out and play themselves.

5e How do I tell the difference between summary and synthesis?

Distinguishing between summary and synthesis is crucial in critical thinking, critical reading, and critical writing. **Summary** comes before synthesis (Box 29 in 5b) in the critical thinking process. To summarize is to extract the main message or central point and restate it in a sentence or

117

two. A summary doesn't include supporting evidence or details. It is the gist, the hub, the seed of what the author is saying. Also, it isn't your personal reaction to what the author says. (For help in writing a summary, see Box 149, section 33j.)

Synthesis comes after summary in the critical thinking process (Box 29 in 5b). To *synthesize* is to weave together material from several sources, including your personal prior knowledge, to create a new whole. Unsynthesized ideas and information are like separate spools of thread, neatly lined up, possibly coordinated but not integrated. Synthesized ideas and information are threads woven into a tapestry—a new whole that shows relationships.

People synthesize unconsciously all the time—interpreting and combining ideas from various sources to create new patterns. These thought processes are mirrored in the RHETORICAL STRATEGIES used in writing (4i). To synthesize, consciously apply those strategies. For instance, compare ideas in sources, contrast ideas in sources, create definitions that combine and extend definitions in individual sources, apply examples or descriptions from one source to illustrate ideas in another, and find causes and effects described in one source that explain another.

Now, let's examine two different examples of synthesis. Their sources are the essay by Sydney J. Harris in Exercise 5-3 above and the following excerpt from a long essay by Robert Lipsyte. (Lipsyte, a sports columnist for the *New York Times,* is writing in the spring of 1995, at the end of a nine-month major-league baseball strike. Lipsyte argues that commercial interests have invaded sports and, therefore, that sports no longer inspire loyalty, teach good sportsmanship, or provide young people with admirable role models.)

> Baseball has done us a favor. It's about time we understood that staged competitive sports events—and baseball can stand for all the games—are no longer the testing ground of our country's manhood and the theater of its once seemingly limitless energy and power.
>
> As a mirror of our culture, sports now show us spoiled fools as role models, cities and colleges held hostage and games that exist only to hawk products.
>
> The pathetic posturing of in-your-face macho has replaced a once self-confident masculinity.
>
> —Robert Lipsyte, "The Emasculation of Sports"

SYNTHESIS BY COMPARISON AND CONTRAST

Both Harris and Lipsyte criticize professional sports, but for different reasons. In part, Harris thinks that people who passively watch sports on TV and rarely exercise are ruining their health. Lipsyte sees a less obvious but potentially more sinister effect of sports: the destruction of traditional values and transformation of athletes into puppets of "big business."

SYNTHESIS BY DEFINITION

The omission of women from each writer's discussion seems a very loud silence. Considered together, these essays define sports only in terms of males. Harris criticizes men for their inability to think and talk beyond sports and business, an insulting and exaggerated description made even less valid by the absence of women. Lipsyte, despite the numbers of women excelling both in team and individual sports, claims that sports have lost a "once self-confident masculinity." An extended definition would include women, even though they might prefer to avoid the negative portraits of Harris and Lipsyte.

Each synthesis belongs to the person who made the connections. Another person might make entirely different connections.

Here are techniques to help you recall prior knowledge and synthesize several sources. (The CRITICAL RESPONSE essay by a student, Anna Lozanov, in section 5f, is an excellent example of making connections between reading and personal experience.)

- Use MAPPING to discover relationships between sources and your prior knowledge.
- Use your powers of play. Mentally toss ideas around, even if you make connections that seem outrageous. Try opposites (for example, read about athletes and think about the most non-athletic person you know). Try turning an idea upside down (for example, list the benefits of being a bad sport). Try visualizing what you're reading about, and then tinker with the mental picture (for example, picture two people playing tennis and substitute dogs playing Frisbee or seals playing table tennis). The possibilities are endless— make word associations, think up song lyrics, draft a TV advertisement. The goal is to jump-start your thinking so that you can see ideas in new ways.
- Discuss your reading with someone else. Summarize its content, and elicit the other person's opinions and ideas. Deliberately debate that opinion or challenge those ideas. Discussions and debates are good ways to get your mind moving.

EXERCISE 5-4

Here is another excerpt from the essay by Robert Lipsyte quoted earlier. First, summarize the excerpt. Then, annotate it for its content and for the connections you make between Lipsyte's ideas and your prior knowledge. Finally, write a synthesis of this excerpt and the Sydney J. Harris essay in Exercise 5-3. Words in brackets supply background information some readers might need.

We have come to see that [basketball star] Michael Jordan, [football star] Troy Aikman and [baseball star] Ken Griffey have nothing to offer us beyond the gorgeous, breathtaking mechanics of what they do. And it's not enough, now that there's no longer a dependable emotional return

beyond the sensation of the moment itself. The changes in sports—the moving of franchises, free agency—have made it impossible to count on a player, a team, and an entire league still being around for next year's comeback. The connection between player and fan has been irrevocably destabilized, for love and loyalty demand a future. Along the way, those many virtues of self-discipline, responsibility, altruism, and dedication seem to have been deleted from the athletic contract with America.
—Robert Lipsyte, "The Emasculation of Sports"

5f How do I write a critical response?

A **critical response** essay has two missions: to SUMMARIZE a source's main idea and to respond to the main idea based on your SYNTHESIS (5b and 5e).

A well-written critical response accomplishes these two missions with style and grace. That is, it doesn't say, "My summary is . . ." or "Now, here's what I think. . . ." Instead, you want the two missions to blend together as seamlessly as possible. A critical response essay may be short or somewhat long, depending on whether you're asked to respond to a single passage or to an entire work. Box 33 gives general guidelines for writing a critical response.

BOX 33   SUMMARY

Guidelines for writing a critical response

1. Write a SUMMARY of the main idea or central point of the material you're responding to.
2. Write a smooth TRANSITION between that summary and what comes next: your response. This transitional statement, which bridges the two parts, need not be a formal THESIS STATEMENT (2q), but it needs to signal clearly the beginning of your response.
3. Respond to the source based on your prior knowledge and experience.
4. Fulfil all DOCUMENTATION requirements. See Chapters 34–36 for coverage of five DOCUMENTATION STYLES (MLA, APA, CM, CSE, and COS). Ask your instructor which to use.

Here's a student essay written as a critical response. The assignment was to read and respond to "Sports Only Exercise Our Eyes" by Sydney J. Harris, shown in Exercise 5-3. Anna Lozanov's transition from summary to response comes at the beginning of her third paragraph.

Anna Lozanov

Professor Dawson

English 102

24 September 2003

Critical Response to "Sports Only Exercise

Our Eyes" by Sydney J. Harris

Except for a brief period in high school when I was wild about a certain basketball player, I never gave sports much thought. I went to games because my friends went, not because I cared about football or baseball or track. I certainly never expected to defend sports, and when I first read Sydney Harris's essay "Sports Only Exercise Our Eyes," I thoroughly agreed with him. Like Harris, I believed that men who live and breathe sports are "mentally limited and conversationally dull" (111).

For the entire thirteen years of my marriage, I have complained about the amount of time my husband, John, spends watching televised sports. Of course, I've tried to get him to take an interest in something else. There was the time as a newlywed when I flamboyantly interrupted the sixth game of the World Series--wearing only a transparent nightie. Then, one year, I had the further audacity to go into labour with our first child--right in the middle of the Grey Cup game.

Even the child tried to help me cure my husband of what Harris calls an "obsession" (111). Nearly a year after the fateful football game, the kid thoroughly soaked his father, who was concentrating so intently on the struggle for the American League pennant that he didn't even notice! Only a commercial brought the dazed sports fan back into the living room from the baseball stadium.

Just this weekend, however, I had an occasion to reconsider the value of sports. Having just read the Harris essay, I found myself paying closer attention to my husband and sons' weekend afternoon

→

television routine. I was surprised to discover that they didn't just "vegetate" in front of the TV; during the course of the afternoon, they actually discussed ethics, priorities, commitments, and the consequences of abusing one's body. When one of the commentators raised issues like point shaving and using steroids, John and the kids talked about cheating and using steroids. When another commentator brought up the issue of skipping one's final year to go straight to the pros, John explained the importance of a university education and discussed the short career of most professional football players.

Then, I started to think about all the times I've gone to the basement and found my husband and sons performing exercise routines as they watched a game on TV. Even our seven-year-old, who loathes exercise, pedals vigorously on the exercise bike while the others do sit-ups and curls. Believe it or not, there are times when they're all exercising more than just their eyes.

I still agree with Harris that many people spend too much time watching televised sports, but after this weekend, I certainly can't say that all of that time is wasted--at least not at my house. Anything that can turn my couch potatoes into thinking, talking, active human beings can't be all bad. Next weekend, instead of putting on a nightie, I think I'll join my family on the couch.

Work Cited

Harris, Sydney J. "Sports Only Exercise Our Eyes." The Best of Sydney J. Harris. Boston: Houghton, 1975. 111-12.

5g How do I assess evidence critically?

The cornerstone of all reasoning is evidence. **Evidence** consists of facts, statistical information, examples, and opinions of experts. As a reader, you expect writers to provide solid evidence for any claim made or conclusion reached. As a writer, you want to use evidence well to support your claims and conclusions. To assess evidence, you want to know how to evaluate it (5g.1) and how to tell the differences between primary and secondary sources (5g.2).

5g.1 Evaluating evidence

You can evaluate evidence by asking the following questions to guide your judgment.

- **Is the evidence sufficient?** As a rule, the more evidence, the better. Readers have more confidence in the results of a survey that draws on a hundred respondents rather than on ten. As a writer, you may convince your reader that violence is a serious problem in high schools based on only two examples, but you'll be more convincing with additional examples.

- **Is the evidence representative?** Evidence is representative if it is typical. As a reader, assess the objectivity and fairness of evidence. Don't trust a claim or conclusion about a group based on only a few members rather than on a truly typical sample. A pollster surveying national political views would not get representative evidence by interviewing people only in Calgary, because that group doesn't represent the regional, racial, political, and ethnic makeup of the entire electorate. As a writer, the evidence you offer should represent your claim fairly; don't base your point on an exception.

- **Is the evidence relevant?** Relevant evidence is directly related to the conclusion you're drawing. Determining relevance often demands subtle thinking. Suppose you read that one hundred students who had watched television for more than two hours a day throughout high school earned significantly lower scores on a college entrance exam than one hundred students who had not. Can you conclude that students who watch less television perform better on college entrance exams? Not necessarily. Other differences between the two groups could account for the different scores: geographical region, family background, socioeconomic group, or the quality of schools attended.

- **Is the evidence accurate?** Accurate evidence is correct and complete. Inaccurate evidence is useless. Evidence must come from a reliable source, whether it is primary or secondary (5g.2). Equally important, evidence must be presented honestly, not misrepresented or distorted.

- **Is the evidence qualified?** Reasonable evidence doesn't make extreme claims. Claims that use words such as *all, always, never,* and *certainly* are disqualified if even one exception is found. Conclusions are more sensible and believable when qualified with words such as *some, many, may, possibly, often,* and *usually.* Remember that today's "facts" may be revised as time passes and knowledge grows.

5g.2 Recognizing primary versus secondary sources as evidence

Primary sources are firsthand evidence. They're based on your own or someone else's original work or direct observation. Because there's no one to distort the meaning of the original work, firsthand evidence has the greatest impact on a reader. Consider this eyewitness account:

> Poverty is dirt. . . . Let me explain about housekeeping with no money. For breakfast, I give my children grits with no oleo or cornbread without eggs and oleo. This doesn't use up many dishes. What dishes there are, I wash in cold water and with no soap. Even the cheapest soap has to be saved for the baby's diapers. Look at my hands, so cracked and red. Once I saved for two months to buy a jar of Vaseline for my hands and the baby's diaper rash. When I had saved enough, I went to buy it and the price had gone up two cents. The baby and I suffered on.
> —Jo Goodwin Parker, "What's Poverty?"

What in Parker's account makes the reader trust what she says? She is specific, and she is authoritative. She is therefore reliable.

Of course, not all eyewitnesses are reliable, so you must judge which ones to believe. Few people will ever see the top of Mount Everest. People rely, therefore, on the firsthand observation of mountain climbers who've been there. Indeed, much of what we learn of history depends on letters, diaries, and journals—the reports of eyewitnesses who have seen events unfold.

Surveys, polls, and experiments—if the data are carefully controlled and measured—extend everyone's powers of observation. The outcomes of such work are considered primary sources. What can one individual know about the attitude of the public toward marriage, or a candidate for office, or inflation? For evidence on such matters, polls or surveys constitute primary evidence.

Secondary sources report, describe, comment on, or analyze the experiences or work of others. As evidence, a secondary source is at least once removed from the primary source. It reports on the original work, the direct observation, or the firsthand experience. Still, secondary evidence can have great value and impact if it meets the evaluation criteria listed in 5g.1. Here's a secondhand report of an observation:

> The immediate causes of death from nuclear attack are the blast wave, which can flatten heavily reinforced buildings many kilometers away, the firestorm, the gamma rays, and the neutrons, which effectively fry the insides of passersby. A schoolgirl who survived the American nu-

clear attack on Hiroshima, the event that ended the Second World War, wrote this firsthand account:

> Through a darkness like the bottom of hell, I could hear the voices of the other students calling for their mothers. And at the base of the bridge, inside a big cistern that had been dug out there, was a mother weeping, holding above her head a naked baby that was burned bright red all over its body. . . . But every single person who passed was wounded, all of them, and there was no one, there was no one to turn to for help. And the singed hair on the heads of the people was frizzled and whitish and covered with dust. They did not appear to be human, not creatures of this world.
>
> —Carl Sagan, *Cosmos*

The value of a secondhand account hinges on the reliability of the reporter. And that reliability comes from how specific, accurate, and authoritative the observations are. An expert's reputation comes from some special experience (the parents of children) or special training (an accountant could be an expert on taxes). Carl Sagan, the author of the sample paragraph above, was a respected scientist, scholar, and writer; therefore, readers can be quite confident that he has fully and fairly represented what the schoolgirl said. Still, of course, no one can be sure of that without seeing her original account. Box 34 gives guidelines for evaluating a secondary source.

BOX 34   CHECKLIST

 ## Evaluating a secondary source

- **Is the source authoritative?** Did an expert or a person you can expect to write credibly on the subject write it?
- **Is the source reliable?** Does the material appear in a reputable publication—a book published by an established publisher, a respected journal or magazine—or on a reliable Internet site?
- **Is the source well known?** Is the source cited elsewhere as you read about the subject? (If so, the authority of the source is probably widely accepted.)
- **Is the information well supported?** Is the source based on primary evidence? If the source is based on secondary evidence, is the evidence authoritative and reliable?
- **Is the tone balanced?** Is the language relatively objective (and therefore more likely reliable), or is it slanted (probably not reliable)?
- **Is the source current?** Is the material up to date and therefore more likely reliable, or has later authoritative and reliable research made it outdated? ("Old" isn't necessarily unreliable. In many fields, classic works of research remain authoritative for decades or even centuries.)

EXERCISE 5-5

Indicate for each passage whether it constitutes primary or secondary evidence. Then, decide whether the evidence is reliable or not, and explain why or why not. Refer to section 5g for help.

A. I went one morning to a place along the banks of the Madeira River where the railroad ran, alongside rapids impassable to river traffic, and I searched for any marks it may have left on the land. But there was nothing except a clearing where swarms of insects hovered over the dead black hen and other items spread out on a red cloth as an offering to the gods of macumba, or black magic. This strain of African origins in Brazil's ethnic character is strong in the Northwest Region.
—William S. Ellis, "Brazil's Imperiled Rain Forest"

B. Most climatologists believe that the world will eventually slip back into an ice age in 10,000 to 20,000 years. The Earth has been unusually cold for the last two to three million years, and we are just lucky to be living during one of the warm spells. But the concern of most weather watchers looking at the next century is with fire rather than ice. By burning fossil fuels and chopping down forests, humans have measurably increased the amount of carbon dioxide in the atmosphere. From somewhere around 300 parts per million at the turn of the century, this level has risen to 340 parts per million today. If the use of fossil fuels continues to increase, carbon dioxide could reach 600 parts per million during the next century.
—Steve Olson, "Computing Climate"

EXERCISE 5-6

Individually or with a peer-response group, choose one of the following thesis statements and list the kinds of primary and secondary sources you might consult to support the thesis (you can guess intelligently, rather than being sure that the sources exist). Then, decide which sources in your list would be primary and which secondary.

Thesis statement 1: The federal government should intervene to help Canada's cities.

Thesis statement 2: The federal government has no business intervening in urban affairs.

5h How do I assess cause and effect critically?

Some evidence has to rely on the accuracy of a cause-and-effect relationship. **Cause and effect** describes the relationship between one event (cause) and another, resulting event (effect). The relationship also works in reverse: One event (effect) *results from* another event (cause). Whether you begin with a cause or with an effect, you're using the same basic pattern.

Cause A ⟶ produces ⟶ effect B

You may seek to understand the effects of a known cause:

More studying ⟶ produces ⟶ ?

Or you may seek to determine the cause or causes of a known effect:

? ⟶ produces ⟶ recurrent headaches

    Be careful not to take cause-and-effect statements at face value. Think through the relationship between cause A and effect B. Sometimes, the relationship is exactly the opposite of what's being claimed. Consult the guidelines in Box 35.

BOX 35   CHECKLIST

 ## Assessing cause and effect

■ **Is there a clear relationship between events?** Related causes and effects happen in sequence: A cause occurs before an effect. First the wind blows; then a door slams; then a pane of glass in the door breaks. But CHRONOLOGICAL ORDER merely *implies* a cause-and-effect relationship. Perhaps someone slammed the door shut. Perhaps someone threw a baseball through the glass pane. A cause-and-effect relationship must be linked by more than chronological sequence. The fact that B happens after A doesn't prove that A causes B.

■ **Is there a pattern of repetition?** Scientific proof depends on a pattern of repetition. To establish that A causes B, every time A is present B must occur. Or, put another way, B never occurs unless A is present. The need for repetition explains why Health Canada sponsors or runs many clinical trials before approving a new medicine.

■ **Are there multiple causes and/or effects?** Avoid oversimplification. The basic pattern of cause and effect—single cause, single effect (A causes B)—rarely represents the full picture. Multiple causes and/or effects are more typical of real life. For example, it would be oversimplification to assume that a lower crime rate is strictly due to high employment rates. Similarly, one cause can produce multiple effects. For example, advertisements for a liquid diet drink focus on the drink's most appealing effect, rapid weight loss, ignoring less desirable effects such as lost nutrients and a tendency to regain the weight.

5i How do I assess reasoning processes critically?

To think, read, and write critically, you need to distinguish *sound reasoning* from *faulty reasoning*. **Induction** and **deduction** are the two basic reasoning processes. They're natural thought patterns people use every day to help them think through ideas and make decisions. The two processes are summarized in Box 36.

BOX 36   SUMMARY

Comparison of inductive and deductive reasoning

	Inductive Reasoning	Deductive Reasoning
Argument begins	with specific evidence	with a general claim
Argument concludes	with a general statement	with a specific statement
Conclusion is	reliable or unreliable	true or false
Purpose is	to discover something new	to apply what's known

Recognizing and using inductive reasoning

Inductive reasoning moves from particular facts or instances to general principles. Suppose you go to the Motor Vehicle Licence Agency to renew your driver's licence and have to stand in line for two hours. A few months later you return to get new licence plates, and once again you have to stand in line for two hours. You mention your annoyance to a couple of friends who say they had exactly the same experience. You conclude that the agency is inefficient and indifferent to the needs of its patrons. You've arrived at this conclusion by means of induction. Box 37 shows the features of inductive reasoning.

Recognizing and using deductive reasoning

Deductive reasoning is the process of reasoning from general claims to a specific instance. Suppose you know that students who don't study for Professor Sanchez's history tests tend to do poorly. If your friend tells you she didn't study, you can make a reasonable conclusion about her grade. Your reasoning might go something like this:

PREMISE 1	Students who don't study do poorly on Professor Sanchez's exams.
PREMISE 2	My friend didn't study.
CONCLUSION	Therefore, my friend probably did poorly on the exam.

BOX 37 SUMMARY

Inductive reasoning

- **Inductive reasoning moves from the specific to the general.** It begins with specific evidence—facts, observations, or experiences— and moves to a general conclusion.
- **Inductive conclusions are considered reliable or unreliable, not true or false.** Because inductive thinking is based on a sampling of facts, an inductive conclusion indicates probability—the degree to which the conclusion is likely to be true—not certainty.
- **An inductive conclusion is held to be reliable or unreliable in relation to the quantity and quality of the evidence** (5g) on which it's based.
- **Induction leads to new "truths."** It can support statements about the unknown based on what's known.

Deductive arguments have three parts: two **premises** and a conclusion. This three-part structure is known as a **syllogism.** The first and second premises of a deductive argument may be statements of fact or assumptions. They lead to a conclusion, which is the point at which you want to think as precisely as possible because you're into the realm of *validity.*

Whether or not an argument is **valid** has to do with its form or structure. Here the word *valid* isn't the general term people use in conversation to mean "acceptable" or "well grounded." In the context of reading and writing logical arguments, the word *valid* has a very specific meaning. A deductive argument is *valid* when the conclusion logically follows from the premises; otherwise, it is *invalid.* For example:

VALID DEDUCTIVE ARGUMENT

PREMISE 1   When it snows, the streets get wet. [fact]
PREMISE 2   It is snowing. [fact]
CONCLUSION   Therefore, the streets are getting wet.

INVALID DEDUCTIVE ARGUMENT

PREMISE 1   When it snows, the streets get wet. [fact]
PREMISE 2   The streets are getting wet. [fact]
CONCLUSION   Therefore, it is snowing.

Here's the problem with the invalid deductive argument: It has acceptable premises because they are facts. However, the argument's conclusion is wrong because it ignores other reasons why the streets might be wet. For example, the street could be wet from rain, from street-cleaning trucks that spray water, or from people washing their cars. Therefore, because the conclusion doesn't follow logically from the premises, the argument is invalid.

Another problem in a deductive argument can occur when the premises are implied but not stated—called **unstated assumptions.** Remember that an argument can be logically valid even though it is based on wrong assumptions. To show that such an argument is invalid, you need to attack the assumptions, not the conclusion, as wrong. For example, suppose a corporation argues that it can't install pollution-control devices because the cost would cut deeply into its profits. This argument rests on the unstated assumption that no corporation should do something that would lower its profits. That assumption is wrong, and so is the argument. To show that both are wrong, you need to challenge the assumptions.

Similarly, if a person says that certain information is correct because it's written in the newspaper, the reasoning is flawed. The unstated assumption is that everything in a newspaper is correct—which isn't true. Whenever there's an unstated assumption, you need to state it outright and then check that it's true. Box 38 summarizes deductive reasoning.

BOX 38   SUMMARY

Deductive reasoning

- **Deductive reasoning moves from the general to the specific.** The three-part structure that makes up a deductive argument, or SYLLOGISM, includes two premises and a conclusion drawn from them.
- **A deductive argument is valid if the conclusion logically follows from the premises.**
- **A deductive conclusion may be judged true or false.** If both premises are true, the conclusion is true. If the argument contains an assumption, the writer must prove the truth of the assumption to establish the truth of the argument.
- **Deductive reasoning applies what the writer already knows.** Though it doesn't yield new information, it builds stronger arguments than inductive reasoning because it offers the certainty that a conclusion is either true or false.

EXERCISE 5-7

Working individually or with a peer-response group, determine whether each conclusion here is valid or invalid. Be ready to explain your answers. For help, consult 5i.

1. All required reading for my course is accessible on the Internet.
   My professor assigned her thesis as required reading.
   My professor's thesis is accessible on the Internet.

2. You should not believe everything you read on the Internet.
   Your professor's thesis is posted on the Internet.
   You should not believe your professor's thesis.

3. The Prairies produced politicians who were charismatic speakers.
   John Diefenbaker and Tommy Douglas were Prairie politicians.
   Therefore, John Diefenbaker and Tommy Douglas were charismatic speakers.

4. Mosquitoes are a problem in tropical climates.
   Mosquitoes are a problem in Winnipeg.
   Therefore, Winnipeg has a tropical climate.

5. All great chefs are men.
   Madame Benoît was a great chef.
   Madame Benoît was a man.

5j How can I recognize and avoid logical fallacies?

Logical fallacies are flaws in reasoning that lead to illogical statements. Though logical fallacies tend to occur when ideas are argued, they can be found in all types of writing. Interestingly, most logical fallacies masquerade as reasonable statements, but in fact, they're attempts to manipulate readers by appealing to their emotions instead of their intellects, their hearts rather than their heads. The name for each logical fallacy indicates the way that thinking has gone wrong.

Hasty generalization
A hasty generalization draws conclusions from inadequate evidence. If someone says, "My hometown is the best place in the province to live," and gives only two examples to support the opinion, that's not enough. The person who makes such a statement is indulging in a hasty generalization. **Stereotyping** is another kind of hasty generalization. It happens, for example, when someone says, "Everyone from country X is dishonest." Such a sweeping claim about all members of a particular ethnic, religious, racial, or political group relies on an unjustifiable stereotype. Yet another kind of stereotyping is **sexism,** which occurs when someone discriminates against another person based on GENDER.

False analogy
A false analogy draws a comparison in which the differences outweigh the similarities or the similarities are irrelevant. For exam-

ple, "Old Joe Smith would never make a good prime minister because an old dog can't learn new tricks" is a false analogy. Joe Smith doesn't learn political skills the way a dog learns tricks. Homespun analogies like this have an air of wisdom about them, but they tend to fall apart when examined closely.

Begging the question

Begging the question, also called *circular reasoning*, tries to offer proof by simply using another version of the argument itself. For example, the statement "Wrestling is a dangerous sport because it is unsafe" begs the question. Because *unsafe* is a synonym for *dangerous*, the statement goes around in a circle, getting nowhere. Rather, it returns to (it "begs") the question that was being asked in the first place. Here's another example of circular reasoning but with a different twist: "Wrestling is a dangerous sport; otherwise, those powerful wrestlers would not get injured." Here, the support for the second part of the statement is the argument made in the first part of the statement.

Irrelevant argument

An irrelevant argument reaches a conclusion that doesn't follow from the premises. Irrelevant argument is also called *non sequitur* (Latin for "it does not follow"). An argument is irrelevant when a conclusion doesn't follow from the premises. Here's an example: "Marie Trudel is a forceful speaker, so she'll make a good mayor." You'd be on target if you asked, "What does speaking ability have to do with being a good mayor?"

False cause

A false cause assumes that because two events are related in time, the first caused the second. False cause is also known as *post hoc, ergo propter hoc* (Latin for "after this, therefore because of this"). For example, if someone claims that a new weather satellite launched last week has caused the rain that's been falling ever since, that person is connecting two events that, while related in time, have no causal relationship to each other. The launching didn't cause the rain.

Self-contradiction

Self-contradiction uses two premises that can't both be true at the same time. Here's an example: "Only when nuclear weapons have finally destroyed us will we be convinced of the need to control them." This is self-contradictory because no one would be around to be convinced if everyone has been destroyed.

Red herring

A red herring, also called *ignoring the question*, tries to distract attention from one issue by introducing a second that's unrelated

to the first. Here's an example: "Why worry about pandas becoming extinct when we haven't solved the plight of the homeless?" You'd be on target if you asked, "What do homeless people have to do with pandas?" If the argument were to focus on proposing that the money spent to prevent the extinction of pandas should go instead to the homeless, the argument would be logical; however, the original statement is a fallacy. By using an irrelevant issue, a person hopes to distract the audience, just as putting a herring in the path of a bloodhound would distract it from the scent it's been following.

Argument to the person

An argument to the person means attacking the person making the argument rather than the argument itself. It's also known as the *ad hominem* attack (Latin for "to the man"). When someone criticizes a person's appearance, habits, or character instead of the merits of that person's argument, the attack is a fallacy. Here's an example: "We'd take her position on child abuse seriously if she were not so nasty to her husband." You'd be on target if you were to ask, "What does nastiness to an adult, though not at all nice, have to do with child abuse?"

Guilt by association

Guilt by association means that a person's arguments, ideas, or opinions lack merit because of that person's activities, interests, or companions. Here's an example: "Jack belongs to the International Hill Climbers Association, which declared bankruptcy last month. This makes him unfit to be mayor of our city." That Jack is a member of a group that declared bankruptcy has nothing to do with Jack's ability to be mayor.

Jumping on the bandwagon

Jumping on the bandwagon means something is right or permissible because "everyone does it." It's also called *ad populum* (Latin for "to the people"). This fallacy operates in a statement such as "How could bungee jumping be unhealthy if thousands of people have done it?" Following the crowd doesn't work where research and careful reasoning indicate otherwise.

False or irrelevant authority

Using false or irrelevant authority means citing the opinion of someone who has no expertise in the subject at hand. This fallacy attempts to transfer prestige from one area to another. Many television commercials rely on this tactic—a famous golf player praising a brand of motor oil or a popular movie star lauding a brand of cheese.

Card-stacking

Card-stacking, also known as *special pleading*, ignores evidence on the other side of a question. From all available facts, people choose only those facts that show the best (or worst) possible case. Many television commercials use this strategy. When three slim, happy consumers praise a diet plan, only at the very end of the ad does the announcer say—in a very low and speedy voice—that results vary. Indeed, even that statement is vague and uninformative.

The either-or fallacy

The either-or fallacy, also called *false dilemma*, offers only two alternatives when more exist. Such fallacies tend to touch on emotional issues, so many people accept them until they analyze the statement. Here's an example: "Either go to college or forget about getting a job." Obviously, this rigid, two-sided statement ignores the truth that many jobs don't require a college education.

Taking something out of context

Taking something out of context deliberately distorts an idea or a fact by removing it from its original setting. Here's an example: Suppose that a newspaper movie critic writes, "The plot was predictable and boring, but the music was sparkling." The next day, an advertisement for the movie claims "critics call it 'sparkling.'" Clearly, the ad has taken the critic's words out of context (only the music was called "sparkling") and thereby distorts the original.

Appeal to ignorance

Appeal to ignorance tries to make an incorrect argument based on something never having been shown to be false—or, the reverse, never having been shown to be true. Here's an example: "Because it hasn't been proven that eating food X doesn't cause cancer, we can assume that it does." The statement is a fallacy because the absence of opposing evidence proves nothing. Such appeals can be very persuasive because they prey on people's superstitions or lack of knowledge. Often, they're stated in the fuzzy language of DOUBLE NEGATIVES.

Ambiguity and equivocation

Ambiguity and equivocation describe statements open to more than one interpretation, thus concealing the truth. "Because of the Opposition's rowdy and impertinent behaviour during Question Period, Prime Minister Chrétien had no duty to give pertinent answers." The argument contains a fallacy because it takes "pertinent," meaning "relevant to the question," as the counterpart of "impertinent," which in this sentence means "ill-mannered."

EXERCISE 5-8

Following are letters to the editor of a newspaper. Working alone or with a group, do a critical analysis of each, paying special attention to logical fallacies.

slippery slope ~ one event happens and then one thing!

1. To the Editor:

I am writing to oppose the plan to convert the abandoned railroad tracks into a bicycle trail. Everyone knows that the only reason the mayor wants to do this is so that she and her wealthy friends can have a new place to play. No one I know likes this plan, and if they did, it would probably be because they're part of the wine and cheese set, too. The next thing you know, the mayor will be proposing that we turn the schools into art museums or the park into a golf course. If you're working hard to support a family, you don't have time for this bike trail nonsense. And if you're not working hard, I don't have time for you.

Jan Gonesh

Hasty generalizations
Stereotyping

Slippery slope

Either or

2. To the Editor:

I encourage everyone to support the bicycle trail project. Good recreation facilities are the key to the success of any community. Since the bike trail will add more recreation opportunities, it will guarantee the success of our town. Remember that several years ago our neighbours over in Douglas Lake decided not to build a new park, and look what happened to their economy, especially that city's high unemployment rate. We can't afford to let the same thing happen to us. People who oppose this plan are narrow-minded, selfish, and unmindful of Canada's multicultural mosaic and the "Just Society" that Pierre Trudeau fought for.

Susan Thompson

Hasty generalization

False or irrelevant authority

Ad hominum

Taking something out of context

3. To the Editor:

I'm tired of all this nonsense about pollution and global warming. We had plenty of cold days last winter, and as my dentist said, "If this is global warming, then I'd sure hate to see global cooling." Plus, there were lots of days this summer when I haven't had to turn on my air conditioner. I know there are statistics that some people say show the climate is changing, but you can't trust numbers, especially when they come from overpaid scientists. These people just aren't happy unless they're giving us something to feel guilty about, whether it's smoking, drinking, or driving SUVs. Maybe if they stopped wasting their time worrying about pollution they could do something useful, like find a cure for cancer.

Mario Dubé

False analogy

Hasty generalization

irrelivant argument

more of a Red herring

Chapter 6

Writing Arguments

6a What is a written argument?

When you write an **argument,** you attempt to convince a reader to agree with you on a topic open to debate. You support your position, proposal, or interpretation with evidence, reasons, and examples—factual, logical data, not opinions. Some people use the terms *argument* and *persuasive writing* interchangeably. When people distinguish between them, *persuasive writing* is the broader term. It includes advertisements, letters to editors, emotionally charged speeches and writing, and formal written arguments. This chapter focuses on the kind of formal written argument usually assigned in college and university courses.

Taking and defending a position in a written argument is an engaging intellectual process, especially when it involves a topic of substance. For ACADEMIC WRITING, arguments are ways of demonstrating CRITICAL THINKING. In fact, before you choose a position and convincingly defend it, you want to examine all sides of the issue critically. This means considering your intended audience's likely feelings and beliefs about your topic. Your audience's viewpoints and values need to influence your decisions about content, organization, and style.

Written arguments are completely different from the arguing people do in everyday life. Verbal arguments often originate in anger and involve bursts of temper or unpleasant emotional confrontations. Written argument, in contrast, is constructive, setting forth a debatable position calmly and respectfully. The passion that underlies a writer's position comes not from angry words but from the force of a balanced, well-developed, clearly written presentation.

The ability to argue reasonably and effectively is an important skill not only in your studies but also throughout life—in family relationships, with friends, and in the business world. And as you become experienced with written arguments, you can apply the same techniques to oral arguments.

In this chapter, you'll examine three approaches to writing about argument: the classical pattern, the Toulmin model, and the Rogerian approach. In addition, you'll find information about how to analyze and refute opposing arguments. As you read this chapter, I suggest that you keep your eye on what I discuss in Chapters 1 through 5 of this handbook. If you take a few minutes to review those chapters, you'll have a richer context for understanding this chapter.

6b How do I choose a topic for an argument?

When you choose a topic for written argument, be sure that it's open to debate. Don't confuse matters of information (facts) with matters of debate. An essay becomes an argument when it makes a claim—that is, *takes a position*—about a debatable topic.

FACT	Students at this college must take an English credit.
DEBATABLE QUESTION	Should this college require students to take an English credit?
ONE SIDE	This college should not require students to take an English credit.
OPPOSING SIDE	This college should require students to take an English credit.

For your essay, you select only one side of a debatable question to defend, always keeping the opposing side(s) in mind. The bulk of your essay systematically presents and discusses the position you're defending, but some space remains for you to state and counter the opposing viewpoint. If multiple alternative viewpoints exist, choose the major opposing one, unless otherwise directed by your instructor. If you neglect to mention opposing views, your readers could justifiably assume you're not well informed, fair-minded, or disciplined as a thinker.

Instructors sometimes assign students the argument topic and the position to take about it. In such cases, you need to fulfil the assignment even if you disagree with the point of view. Readers expect you to reason logically about the assigned position.

If you choose your own topic and position, think of one that has sufficient substance for academic writing. Readers expect you to take an intelligent, defensible position on your chosen topic and to support it reasonably and convincingly. For example, "book censorship in public libraries" is worthy of a college or university essay; "the best way to eat apples" is not.

If you think that all sides of a debatable topic have merit, you need to choose one of them anyway. Don't become paralyzed from indecision. You're not making a lifetime commitment. Beware, also, of switching sides at the last minute; you'll be wasting valuable time. Concentrate on the merits of one position and argue that position as effectively as possible. Once you decide on the assertion you want to argue, don't stop there. The more thoroughly you think through all sides of the topic, the broader the perspective you'll bring to your writing, and the more likely it will be effective.

6c How do I develop an assertion and a thesis statement for my argument?

An **assertion** is a statement that expresses a point of view on a debatable topic. It can be supported by evidence, reasons, and examples (including facts, statistics, names, experiences, and experts). The exact wording of the assertion rarely finds its way into the essay, but the assertion serves as a focus for your thinking. Later, it serves as the basis for developing your thesis statement.

TOPIC	Wild animals as domestic pets.
ASSERTION	People should not be allowed to own wild animals.
ASSERTION	People should be allowed to own wild animals.

Before you decide on an assertion—the position you want to argue—explore the topic. Don't rush. Consider all sides. **Remember that what mainly separates most good writing from bad is the writer's ability to move back and forth between general statements and specific details.** Therefore, before you start drafting, use the RENNS test (4f) to check whether you can marshal sufficient details to support your generalizations.

Keep your argument in mind as you develop your thesis statement (2q). You want your essay, and the points you argue, to be interesting to academic readers—your instructor and your peers. In this context, *interesting* has more than its familiar meaning. An interesting argument grabs readers' attention and stimulates their curiosity. Equally important, though, an interesting argument is one that argues an assertion deserving of the attention you're going to give it, and shows your readers a thoughtful, critical mind at work. For most university-level essays, and for research essays (6d) in particular, use your thesis statement to point out the path you intend your argument to take.

The two draft thesis statements below were written for the same essay. The first makes its point clearly and concisely but gives little evidence of the complexity of the essay's argument. The second thesis statement, although less concise, takes the argument into account. It identifies a controversy that the essay will evaluate and forecasts the kinds of evidence presented.

THESIS STATEMENT 1	Scientific studies show that both overfishing and climate change are endangering the existence of North Atlantic cod stocks.
THESIS STATEMENT 2	Although quantitative analysis of catches gives direct evidence of the effects of overfishing on North Atlantic cod stocks, the statistical models that link changes in water temperature to the disappearance of the plankton that young cod feed upon are still controversial.

To stimulate your thinking about the topic and the assertion of your position, work with the PLANNING techniques discussed in Chapter 2. Another well-favoured strategy is to create a two-column list, labelling one column *pro* or *for,* the other *con* or *against.* If there are more than two opposing sides, label the columns accordingly. The columned list displays the quantity and quality of your material so that you can decide whether you're ready to start DRAFTING.

6d **How does source-based writing work for arguments?**

Source-based writing, or *research writing,* means that writers conduct research about a topic and draw on their findings to support their position. If your instructor assigns such writing, use the library and the Internet to research your topic so that your essay has additional depth. Chapters 31 through 36 in this handbook guide you in writing research.

Lacie Juris, the student who wrote the argument essay that appears in section 6m, chose her own topic. Juris was thinking about a career as a zookeeper, which in turn led her to become interested in issues concerning wild animals. In her career research, especially when she looked for the latest information on the Web, she discovered a major controversy: the problem of private ownership of wild animals. Her curiosity aroused, Juris read a number of sources and discovered a topic appropriate for her assignment. She worked on developing a position about that topic and then extended it into the thesis statement for her essay. Here's how Juris progressed from the topic to the first draft of her thesis statement and then its final draft.

TOPIC	Private ownership of wild animals
MY POSITION	I think private ownership of wild animals should not be allowed.
THESIS STATEMENT (FIRST DRAFT)	It is bad for private citizens to own wild animals as pets. [This is a preliminary thesis statement. It clearly states the writer's position, but the word *bad* is vague, and the writer doesn't address how to stop private ownership of wild animals.]
THESIS STATEMENT (SECOND DRAFT)	To eliminate what few people realize are increasingly dangerous situations for people and animals alike, ownership of wild animals as pets by ordinary people needs to be made completely illegal. [This revised thesis statement is better, but it suffers from lack of conciseness and from the unnecessary passive construction *needs to be made.*]
THESIS STATEMENT (FINAL DRAFT)	To eliminate dangerous situations for both people and animals alike, legislatures need to ban private ownership of wild animals as pets. [This final version

works well because it states the writer's claim clearly and its language is concise, with verbs all in the active voice. The writer now has a thesis statement suitable for the time and length given in her assignment. It meets the requirements for a thesis statement given in Box 12 in 2q.]

EXERCISE 6-1

Working individually or with a peer-response group, develop an assertion and a thesis statement for each of the topics listed in this exercise. You may choose any defensible position. For help, consult 6a through 6d.

EXAMPLE **Topic:** Book censorship in high school

Assertion: Books should not be censored in high school.

Thesis statement: When books are taken off high school library shelves or are dropped from high school curricula, students are denied an open exchange of ideas.

1. the relationship of reason to belief
2. the conflict between equality and freedom
3. taking body-building supplements
4. grading on a pass/fail system

6e Why might I need to define key terms?

Key terms in an essay are the words central to its topic and message. While the meaning of some key terms might be readily evident in your writing, others may be open to interpretation. For example, abstract words such as *love, freedom,* and *democracy* have different meanings in different contexts. Therefore, if you want to argue the position "Justice demands that sixteen-year-olds be given the vote," the definition of *justice* would be crucial to your argument.

Many students ask whether they can use dictionary definitions in an essay. While you always want to look up words in a dictionary to understand their precise meanings, you should avoid quoting directly from a dictionary, which is often seen as lacking in grace or SYNTHESIS. Avoid also the unappealing, inexact expression "according to Webster's" to introduce a definition. However, if the meaning of a word is complex, highly unfamiliar to most readers, or easily misinterpreted, you can indeed decide that a quoted dictionary definition would serve well. If you do, include the complete title of the dictionary you're citing: for example, the *Canadian Oxford Dictionary* or the *Gage Canadian Dictionary*.

6f What is the structure of a classical argument?

No single method is best for organizing all arguments, but a frequently used structure is the **classical argument.** The ancient Greeks and Romans developed the six-part structure described in Box 39.

BOX 39   SUMMARY

The structure of a classical argument

1. **Introductory paragraph:** Sets the stage for the position argued in the essay. It gains the reader's interest and respect (4b).

2. **Thesis statement:** States the topic and position you want to argue (2q).

3. **Background information:** Gives readers the basic information they need for understanding your thesis and its support. As appropriate, you might include definitions of key terms (6e), historical or social context, prior scholarship, and other related material. You can include this as part of your introductory paragraph, or it can appear in its own paragraph placed immediately after the introduction.

4. **Evidence and reasons:** Supports the position you are arguing on the topic. This is the core of the essay. Each reason or piece of evidence usually consists of a general statement backed up with specific details, including examples and other RENNS (4f). Evidence needs to meet the standards for critical thinking (5g) and reasoning (5h through 5j). Depending on the length of the essay, you might devote one or two paragraphs to each reason or type of evidence. For organization, you might choose to present the most familiar reasons and evidence first, saving the most unfamiliar for last. Alternatively, you might proceed from the least important to the most important point so that your essay builds to a climax. (For alternative ways to arrange paragraphs, consult 4h and 4i.)

5. **Response to opposing position:** Sometimes referred to as the *rebuttal* or *refutation*. This material mentions and defends against an opposite point of view. Often this refutation, which can be lengthy or brief according to the overall length of the essay, appears in its own paragraph or paragraphs, usually immediately before the concluding paragraph or immediately following the introductory paragraph, as a bridge to the rest of the essay. If you use the latter structure, you can choose to place your thesis statement either at the end of the introductory paragraph or at the end of the rebuttal paragraph. Yet another choice for structure consists of each paragraph's presenting one type of evidence or reason and then immediately stating and responding to the opposing position. (See 6k for advice on handling opposing arguments.)

6. **Concluding paragraph:** Ends the essay logically and gracefully—never abruptly. It often summarizes the argument, elaborates its significance, or calls readers to action (4k).

6g What is the Toulmin model for argument?

One powerful method of analyzing arguments is the **Toulmin model.** This model defines three essential elements in an effective argument: the claim, the support, and the warrants. They describe concepts that you've encountered before, as Box 40 explains.

BOX 40   SUMMARY

The Toulmin model of argument

Toulmin's Term	More Familiar Terms
claim	the main point or central message, usually expressed in the thesis statement
support	data or other evidence, from broad reasons to specific details
warrants	underlying assumptions, usually not stated but clearly implied; readers infer assumptions

Analyzed in Toulmin's terms, here's the argument in the student essay written by Lacie Juris, the final draft of which appears in section 6m.

- **Claim:** Legislatures need to ban private ownership of wild animals as pets.
- **Support:** (1) Wild animals are dangerous to humans. (2) Domestication is hazardous to the animals themselves.
- **Warrants:** (1) We should outlaw situations that are dangerous to people. (2) We should outlaw situations that are dangerous to animals.

The concept of *warrant* is similar to the concept of *inferences,* a key component of reading critically (5d). Inferences are not stated outright but are implied "between the lines" of the writing. Similarly, warrants are unspoken underlying assumptions in an argument. Consider the following simple argument: "Johnson should not be elected mayor. She was recently divorced." The claim is that Johnson shouldn't be elected. The support is that Johnson has been divorced. The unstated warrant is "divorced people are not qualified to be mayor." Before they can accept the claim that Johnson shouldn't be elected, readers have to accept this warrant. Of course, a majority of readers would reject the warrant. Thus, this argument is weak. To identify the warrants in an argument, ask "What do I need to assume so that the support is sufficient for establishing each claim?"

The concepts in the Toulmin model can help you write arguments with a critical eye. They can be quite useful on their own as well as applied to the CLASSICAL ARGUMENT structure (Box 39 in 6f). As you read and revise your own arguments, identify the claim, support, and warrants. If you don't have a clear claim or support, you will probably have to assume that your argument is weak. Furthermore, make sure that each of your warrants will be convincing to readers. If you can't assume that a warrant will be instantly accepted as reasonable, you need to support it with logical reasons.

EXERCISE 6-2

Individually or with a peer-response group, discuss these simple arguments. Identify the claim, support, and warrants for each.

EXAMPLE   This department should establish an honour code. Last year over fifty students were caught cheating on exams.

> **Claim:** The department should establish an honour code.
>
> **Support:** Last year, over fifty students were caught cheating on exams.
>
> **Warrants:** Enough students cheat on exams that the department should address the problem.
>
> Cheating should be prevented.
>
> Students would not have cheated if there had been an honour code.

1. The student council should raise student activity fees. It is planning an expensive campaign to lobby the education minister.
2. Vote against raising our taxes. In the past two years, we have already had a 2 percent tax increase.
3. The university should require all students to own laptop computers. Most students will have to use computers in their jobs after graduation.

6h What part does audience play in my argument?

The PURPOSE of written argument is to convince your readers—your AUDIENCE—either to agree with you or to be open to your position. In writing an argument, consider the degree of agreement you can expect from your readers. Will the audience be hostile or open-minded to your position? Will it resist or adopt your point of view?

The more emotionally charged a topic, the greater the chance that any position argued will elicit either strong agreement or strong disagreement. For example, abortion and censorship are emotionally loaded topics because they touch on matters of personal belief. Topics such as the best responses to air pollution or bans on loud radios in recreation areas are usually not so emotionally loaded. Even less emotionally loaded, yet

still open to debate, would be whether computer X is better than computer Y. The degree to which you can expect your readers to be friendly
or firmly opposed will influence your choice of strategies.

Rogerian argument, an approach that seeks common ground
between points of view, might be an effective context for reaching readers
when you're quite certain they'll disagree with you. The Rogerian
approach is based on the principles of communication developed by the
psychologist Carl Rogers. According to Rogers, communication is eased
when people find common ground in their points of view. Box 41 explains
the structure of a Rogerian argument.

BOX 41   SUMMARY

The structure of a Rogerian argument

1. **Introduction:** Sets the stage for the position that is argued in the
   essay. It gains the reader's interest and respect (4b).

2. **Thesis statement:** States the topic and position you want to argue
   (2q and 6c).

3. **Common ground:** Explains the issue, acknowledging that your
   readers probably don't agree with you. Respectfully gives attention
   to the points of agreement you and your readers are likely to share
   concerning the underlying problem or issue. As appropriate, you
   might include definitions of key terms (6e), historical or social
   context, prior scholarship, and other related material. This may take
   one paragraph or several, depending on the complexity of the issue.

4. **Discussion of your position:** Gives evidence and reasons for your
   stand on the topic, elaborated similarly to the parallel material in
   classical argument (Box 39 in 6f).

5. **Concluding paragraph:** Summarizes why your position is
   preferable to your opponent's (4k).

In many instances, of course, you can't expect to change your reader's
mind, though you can seek to convince your reader that your point of
view has merit. People often "agree to disagree" in the best spirit of intellectual exchange. As you write a Rogerian argument, remember that your
audience wants to see how effectively you've reasoned and presented
your position. This stance approaches that of a formal oral debate in
which all sides are explored with similar intellectual rigour.

6i How do I appeal to my audience by reasoning effectively in an argument?

A sound argument relies on three types of appeals to reason: logical, emotional, and ethical. Box 42 summarizes how to use the three appeals.

BOX 42   SUMMARY

Guidelines for reasoning effectively in written argument

- **Be logical**: Use sound reasoning.
- **Enlist the emotions of the reader**: Appeal to the values and beliefs of the reader by arousing the reader's "better self."
- **Establish credibility**: Show that you as the writer can be relied on as a knowledgeable person with good sense.

The **logical appeal,** called *logos* by the ancient Greeks, is the most widely used appeal in arguments. The logic relies on evidence provided for claims and on sound reasoning (5g–j). When Lacie Juris argues that owning wild animals as pets is dangerous, for example, she provides facts about deaths, injuries, and property damage. Logical writers analyze CAUSE AND EFFECT correctly. Also, they use appropriate patterns of INDUCTIVE REASONING and DEDUCTIVE REASONING, and they distinguish clearly between fact and opinion. Finally, sound reasoning means avoiding LOGICAL FALLACIES.

Emotional appeals, called *pathos* by the ancient Greeks, can be effective when used in conjunction with logical appeals. The word *emotional* has a specific meaning in this context: "arousing and enlisting the emotions of the reader." Used honestly and with restraint, emotional appeals arouse the audience's "better self" by eliciting sympathy, civic pride, or similar feelings based on values and beliefs. Effective emotional appeals use description and examples to stir emotions; they do not rely on sentimentality or biased, SLANTED LANGUAGE designed to exploit human feelings and thereby manipulate them.

In her essay, Juris uses an emotional appeal well in her sixth paragraph. By referring to baby wild animals whose "capture robs [them] of the chance to learn skills necessary for survival," Juris invokes the image of young and helpless creatures, but she shows restraint in her choice of language. Suppose she had written instead, "Picture these poor, innocent, forlorn animal babies racked with life-threatening hunger and viciously stalked by cruel beasts of the wild." Such words would be excessively dramatic, and the audience would resent being manipulated.

Ethical appeals, called *ethos* by the ancient Greeks, establish the credibility of the writer. Audiences don't trust a writer who states opinions as fact, distorts evidence, or makes claims that can't be supported. They do trust a writer who comes across as honest, knowledgeable, and fair. Ethical appeals can't take the place of logical appeals, but the two work well together. One effective way to make an ethical appeal is to draw on your personal experience. (Some college and university instructors don't want students to write in the first person, so check with your instructor before you try this technique.) Be sure that any personal experience you cite relates directly to the generalization you're supporting.

6j   What is a reasonable tone in an argument?

A reasonable TONE tells your audience that you're being fair-minded. When you anticipate opposing positions and refute them with balanced language and emphasis, you demonstrate that you respect the other side. No matter how strongly you disagree with opposing arguments, never insult the other side. Name-calling reflects poor judgment and a lack of self-control. Avoid exaggerating, and never show anger. The more emotionally loaded a topic (for example, abortion or capital punishment), the more tempted you might be to use careless, harsh words. For instance, calling the opposing position "stupid" would say more about you as the writer than it would about the issue.

Experienced writers know that using either a formal tone or a medium level of formality (1e) promotes a reasonable and calm style of argument. An academic AUDIENCE, or anyone with an interest in the sophisticated treatment of a serious subject, normally expects to be addressed in one or the other of these tones. The thesis statement in section 6d is written in a medium level of formality. It is meant to strike readers as fair criticism expressed in neutral language.

> To eliminate dangerous situations for both people and animals alike, legislatures need to ban private ownership of wild animals as pets.

The following is a more formal restatement of the same thesis statement. Some readers may consider this level of formality to be out of place in a North American student essay on such a topic. In certain contexts, or when handled with little skill, a highly formal tone may convey awkwardness and even insincerity.

> To eliminate dangerous situations to which both people and animals alike may be subjected, it is incumbent upon legislatures to ban private ownership of wild animals as pets.

Irony, as in the following version, has an important place in literature and essay writing, but instructors usually do not expect to find it in student essays. An ironic tone puts readers on their guard, so a reader who encounters it in an argument may not respect the seriousness of the writer's intentions. Even in the proper context, to achieve its intended effect irony needs to be employed with subtlety, taste, and skill.

> If the people who write our laws can't see the need to ban private ownership of a pet like a purebred wolf, they should try taking Old White Fang out for a walk in the park some day, among the chihuahuas and the chows.

This final variation on the thesis statement may not at first glance seem to differ in an important way from the original. Like the original, it is written in a medium level of formality. Yet it fails the test of neutrality and fair-mindedness—it insinuates that those who have not met the writer's expectations are acting out of a dishonourable motive (see 5j). Its tone is sarcastic, even though it is disguised as a reasonable argument.

> If legislators were concerned with eliminating dangerous situations for people and animals, they would quickly ban private ownership of wild animals as pets.

EXERCISE 6-3

Here is the text of a notorious e-mail fraud that has been sent to many people. Hundreds of variations of this e-mail exist, but usually the writer claims to have a large amount of money that he or she wants to transfer to a Canadian or American bank. The writer wants the recipient's help in making the transfer. This is a complete lie. The writer has no money and is trying to trick people into revealing their bank account numbers in order to steal their money.

Either alone or in a small group, examine the ways this writer tries to establish emotional and ethical appeals. *Note:* I have reproduced the e-mail with the often incorrect original wording, grammar, and punctuation.

> Good day,
>   It is my humble pleasure to write this letter irrespective of the fact that you do not know me. However, I came to know of you in my private search for a reliable and trustworthy person that can handle a confidential transaction of this nature in respect of this, I got your contact through an uprooted search on the internet. Though I know that a transaction of this magnitude will make any one apprehensive and worried, but I am assuring you that all will be well at the end of the day.
>   I am Ruth Malcasa, daughter of late Mr James Malcasa, who was killed by rebel forces on the 24th of December, 1999 in my country. When he was still alive, he deposited one trunk box containing the sum of USD$10 million dollars in cash (Ten Million dollars). with a private security and safe deposit company here. This money was made from the sell of Gold and Diamond by my mother and she has already decided to use this money for future investment of the family.
>   My father instructed me that in the case of his death, that I should look for a trusted foreigner who can assist me to move out this money from my country immediately for investment. Based on this, I solicit for your assistance to transfer this fund into your Account, but I will

147

demand for the following requirement: (1) Could you provide for me a safe Bank Account where this fund will be transferred to in your country after retrieving the box containing the money from the custody of the security company. (2) Could you be able to introduce me to a profitable business venture that would not require much technical expertise in your country where part of this fund will be invested?

I am a Christian and I want you to handle this transaction based on the trust I have established on you. For your assistance in this transaction, I have decided to compensate you with 10 percent of the total amount at the end of this business. The security of this business is very important to me and as such, I would like you to keep this business very confidential. I shall expect an early response from you. Thank you and God bless. Yours sincerely, Ruth Malcasa.

6k How do I handle opposing arguments?

Dealing with opposing positions is crucial to writing an effective argument. If you don't acknowledge arguments that your opponents might raise and explain why they are faulty or inferior, you create doubts that you have thoroughly explored the issue. You risk looking narrow-minded.

The next-to-last paragraph in Juris's paper (6m), which summarizes opposing arguments, strengthens both her ethos and her logic. She is so confident in her own position that she can state the possible opponents' argument that owners will be able to control their wild pets. Then she provides reasons why that argument is wrong. Juris had encountered this counterargument while doing her research. While you do research for your own arguments, you need to look for essays, articles, and opinions that oppose your position, not only ones that agree with yours.

If your research doesn't generate opposing arguments, develop them yourself. Imagine that you're debating someone who disagrees with you; what positions would they take and why? Note that you can ask a classmate or friend to perform this role. Another strategy is to take the opposite side of the argument and try to develop the best reasons you can for that position. (In some formal debating situations, people are expected to prepare both sides of an issue and only learn immediately before the debate which position they are to argue.)

Once you have formulated opposing arguments, you need to refute them, which means to show why they are weak or undesirable. Imagine that you're writing about national security and individual rights. You believe that the government should not be allowed to monitor a private citizen's e-mail without a court order, and you have developed a number of reasons for your position. To strengthen your paper, you consider the opposing arguments "People will be safer from terrorism if police can monitor e-mail" and "Only people who have something to hide have anything to fear." How might you refute these claims? Following are some suggestions.

- **Examine the evidence for each opposing argument** (5g). Look especially for missing or contradictory facts (5j). In the given example, you might question the evidence that people would be safer from terrorism if police could monitor e-mail.

- **Use the Toulmin model to analyze the opposing argument** (6g). What are the claims, support, and warrants? Often it's possible to show that the warrants are questionable or weak. For example, a warrant in the counter-arguments above is that the promise of increased safety is worth the price of privacy or individual rights. You might show why this warrant is undesirable.

- **Demonstrate that an opposing argument depends on emotion rather than reasoning.** An argument that relies on fear of terrorism may be open to the charge that it manipulates emotions.

- **Redefine key terms.** The expression *something to hide* is intended to make readers think of criminal activities, but it may also extend to our own innocent secrets.

- **Explain the negative consequences of the opposing position.** Imagine that the opposing position actually won out, and explain how the results would be damaging. For example, if everyone knew that government officials might monitor their computer use, consider how this might affect free speech. Would people hesitate to browse Web sites about Islam?

- **Concede an opposing point, but explain that doing so doesn't destroy your own argument.** For example, you might decide to concede that monitoring of e-mail by the police may be more efficient than monitoring governed by the courts. However, you could argue that police procedures are carried out more conscientiously and thus with more real effectiveness when subject to court scrutiny.

- **Explain that the costs of the other position are not worth the benefits.** You might argue that the increase in safety (if any) resulting from police monitoring is not worth the threat to privacy and personal freedom.

EXERCISE 6-4

Individually or with a peer-response group, practise developing objections to specific arguments and responses to those objections. To do this, choose a debatable topic and brainstorm a list of points on that topic, some on one side of the topic, some on another. Following are some arguments to get you started. If you're part of a group, work together to assign the different positions for each topic to different sets of students. Then, conduct a brief debate on which side has more merit, with each side taking turns. At the end, your group can vote for the side that is more convincing.

1. It should be legal/illegal to ride motorcycles without a helmet.
2. Women should/should not expect pay equal to men's for the same work.
3. Students should/should not be required to take certain courses in order to graduate.

6l How did one student draft and revise her argument essay?

Lacie Juris chose the topic of the essay shown in section 6m because of her career interest in being a zookeeper. Her preliminary reading on the Internet about keeping wild animals as pets led her to develop a thesis statement (see 6d). In a discovery draft, Juris focused on why it was unfair to wild animals to be kept as pets, but she realized that she would need to be more precise. That led to her argument that being kept as a pet could be harmful to the animal. In a second draft, she realized that harm to animals might not by itself be convincing to members of her audience. She then developed a second main point, that pet wild animals could be dangerous to people. Knowing that this claim required evidence, Juris did further research in databases and on the Internet to find the support she needed.

In a third draft, Juris considered some opposing arguments to her position. She also looked carefully at her use of pathos and ethos. At one point she realized that she was relying on excessively emotional language, which she knew could turn off some readers, so she revised several sentences. Also, she consulted the revision checklist (Box 17 in 3c). Finally, she referred to the special checklist for revising written arguments in Box 43.

BOX 43 CHECKLIST

☑ Revising written arguments

- Is the thesis statement about a debatable topic? (6b and 6c)
- Do the reasons or evidence support the thesis statement? Are the generalizations supported by specific details? (6f)
- Does the argument take the reader into account? (6h)
- Does the argument appeal chiefly to reason? Is it supported by an ethical appeal? If it uses an emotional appeal, is the appeal restrained? (6i)
- Is the tone reasonable? (6j)
- Is the opposing position stated and refuted? (6k)

EXERCISE 6-5

Working individually or with a peer-response group, choose a topic from this list. Then plan an essay that argues a debatable position on the topic. Apply all the principles you've learned in this chapter.

1. animal experimentation
2. luxury taxes for sport utility vehicles
3. cloning of human beings
4. genetically modified foods
5. value of space exploration
6. French immersion

Final draft of a student's argument essay in MLA style

HEADING Lacie Juris

Professor Calhoon-Dillahunt

English 101

16 June 2004

TITLE   Exotic Pets: Not at Home in Your Home

INTRODUCTION: Tiger cubs look and behave like kittens. Baby chimps look
Captures
reader's   almost human and sometimes act like precocious human
attention
infants. For many Canadians, owning one of these as a pet, to

play with and show off to neighbours, sounds like a childhood

fantasy come true. Yet for many, it is no fantasy: Tigers can cost

as little as $200 in Canada (Nikolovsky A18). Animal-rights

advocates estimate that as many tigers are kept as pets in the

United States as exist in the wild worldwide (Boehm B1).

Unfortunately, these exotic dreams can turn deadly at any

moment. Because wild animal ownership comes under a

confusion of federal, provincial, and local laws, there is little

effective regulation (Nikolovsky A18). To eliminate dangerous
THESIS
STATEMENT situations for both people and animals alike, legislatures need

to ban private ownership of wild animals as pets.

BODY: Logical   Wild animals are dangerous to humans, both owners and
appeal—first
main point nearby residents. Wild animals have inborn behaviour patterns

and instincts, such as stalking prey, attacking when threatened,

and self-defence. Such patterns remain no matter where or how

the animals grow up, no matter how well the owners train them

for domesticated living. This is what makes the animals truly

wild. Humans cannot influence, change, or even predict an

animal's wild behaviours. An attack can occur at any time when

→

151

an animal's wild instincts take over without warning ("Wild Animals Are Not Pets"). In addition, wild pets can cause tremendous property damage, as illustrated by the case of Stoli, a tiger who caused $20 000 worth of damage to his owner's Mercedes in less than five minutes ("Stoli and Lil" 1). Zoocheck Canada, an advocacy group for animals in captivity, realistically puts emphasis both on the humane treatment of animals and on the dangers that some exotic pets can pose ("About Zoocheck Canada").

Anecdote to support thesis and bolster logical appeal

Many animal owners teach their young exotic pets little games and tricks. Owners do not realize, however, that when the wild animals have grown to three or four times the strength of most people, the "pets" still expect to take part in the same games and tricks. Take, for example, the story of a pet African serval named Kenya. Servals are known as "leaping cats," able to jump four metres straight up and run 70 kilometres an hour. The woman who purchased Kenya believed that the tiny cub would make the perfect "exotic pet." However, no one told the woman about servals' amazing jumping abilities--or about their becoming extremely territorial as adults. At home, the woman taught the cub to leap onto her shoulder, without realizing that she was actually teaching him to leap onto people in general. In addition, as he grew, he became so territorial that he attacked anyone who would come to her house ("Kenya").

Additional logical appeal

Transition to signal additional point

Another little-realized fact is that wild animals greatly endanger owners and people in the surrounding areas by transmitting diseases. Few purchasers of exotic animals know if their animals are carrying diseases. Wild animals can host internal parasites and other pathogenic organisms that can be debilitating or even fatal to their human caretakers--especially small children (Laidlaw).

→

ogical appeal—
second main
point

Transition to
show contrast

While the risk to humans of exotic pet ownership is very high, domestication is hazardous to the animals themselves. After all, wild animals need specific and natural environments to survive. Such settings do not include humans, houses, or backyard kennels. Owners of wild animals usually lack the knowledge and funds to recreate the animal's environment or to provide proper nutrition, let alone care for the animals if they were to become sick or injured (Boehm B1). Very few professional veterinarians are trained or willing to work on wild animals.

Emotional
appeal

Usually, infant wild animals are stolen from their parents at only a few weeks, or even days, of life. Their capture robs the babies of the chance to learn skills necessary for survival if they are ever abandoned or re-released into the wild. These animals often develop stress and behaviour disorders, because they have never experienced social interaction with their own species ("Wild Animals Are Not Pets"). Eventually, many owners become frightened or confused by sudden behaviour problems with their "little babies," and they decide to leave the animals in remote places to fend for themselves. These animals that never learned how to survive on their own often starve to death. Some seek out food near rural homes or suburbs, which frequently ends in their death at the hands of frightened people ("Wild Animals Do Not Make Good Pets" 2).

Summary of
opposing
arguments

Transition to
show contrast

Some people may argue for the benefits of personal ownership of wild animals. It allows ordinary people to enjoy exotic pets in their own homes. These people insist that they can safely restrict their wild animals' movements to their own property. Further, defenders of the private possession of wild animals argue that owners can help preserve endangered species. Increasingly, however, exotic pet owners' fantasies turn

→

into nightmares as the wild animals become adults increasingly controlled by their basic instincts and inbred behaviours. Owners often expect local animal control agencies or animal sanctuaries to deal with their problems, even though such facilities are already over capacity or are staffed by people unequipped to deal with undomesticated animals (Milloy A19).

CONCLUSION:
Call to action and
emotional appeal

Keeping wild animals as pets must be outlawed. Though exotic creatures may look like Simba or Tigger, they are still completely wild, and it is in the wild that they belong. As pointed out in "Wild Animals Are Not Pets," "The only ones who benefit from the practice of sales of exotic animals as pets are the breeders and sellers. These people make an enormous amount of money by exploiting these animals once they are sold" (1). Poachers also profit when they capture baby wild animals from their native habitats and sell them as pets to the highest bidder. The best way for humans to see and experience wild animals in safe environments is to visit and support zoos and wildlife parks that specialize in providing professionally constructed natural habitats for animals. In such settings, people can enjoy the beauty and behaviours of wild animals without putting humans and the animals at risk.

→

Juris 5

Works Cited

MLA style "About Zoocheck Canada." <u>Zoocheck Canada</u>. 2004. 19 Apr. 2004
<http://www.zoocheck.com/about/>.

Boehm, Ted. "A New Local Worry: Exotic Cats--Lion and Tiger
Prices Fall, and Once Rare Pets Become a Costly
Menace." <u>Wall Street Journal</u> 30 June 2000: B1.

"Kenya." <u>Cat Tales Zoological Park</u>. 1999. 19 Apr. 2004
<http://cattales.org/kenya.html>.

Laidlaw, Rob. "Salmonella, Captivity-Related Stress and the
Human Health Implications of Pet Reptiles." 2002.
25 Apr. 2004 <http://www.wspa.ca/reptiles/reports/
zoonoses/report.html>.

Milloy, Ross E. "Banning Lions and Other Large Pets." <u>New York
Times</u> 10 Dec. 2001: A19.

Nikolovsky, Boris. "Critics Growl over Keeping of Exotic Pets:
Zoo Animals Live in Basements and Backyards." <u>Toronto
Star</u> 11 Aug. 1994: A18.

"Stoli and Lil." <u>Cat Tales Zoological Park</u>. 1999. 19 Apr. 2004
<http://cattales.org/stolilil.html>.

"Wild Animals Are Not Pets." <u>The Wild Animal Orphanage</u>. 2001. 19
Apr. 2004 <http://www. wildanimalorphanage.org/wild.html>.

"Wild Animals Do Not Make Good Pets." <u>Cat Tales Zoological
Park</u>. 1999. 19 Apr. 2004 <http://cattales.org/notapet.html>.

Part Two

Understanding Grammar and Writing Correct Sentences

Visit the Troyka Web site at
http://www.pearsoned.ca/troyka for

- diagnostic test
- chapter exercises
- other resources, including an e-book version of this text

Chapter 7

Parts of Speech and Sentence Structures

PARTS OF SPEECH

7a Why learn the parts of speech?

Knowing the names and definitions of parts of speech gives you a vocabulary for identifying words and understanding how language works to create meaning. No part of speech exists in a vacuum. To identify a word's part of speech correctly, you need to see how the word functions in a sentence. Sometimes the same word functions differently in different sentences, so check the part of speech used in each instance.

> We ate **fish.** [*Fish* is a noun. It names a thing.]
> We **fish** on weekends. [*Fish* is a verb. It names an action.]

7b What is a noun?

A **noun** names a person, place, thing, or idea: *student, college, textbook, education.* Box 44 lists different kinds of nouns.

 ESL NOTES: Here are some useful tips for working with nouns.

- Nouns often appear with words that tell how much or how many, whose, which one, and similar information. These words include ARTICLES* (*a, an, the*), see Chapter 45, and other determiners or limiting adjectives, see 7f.

- Nouns sometimes serve as ADJECTIVES. For example, in the term *police officer,* the word *police* serves as an adjective to describe *officer.*

- Words with these suffixes (word endings) are usually nouns: *-ness, -ence, -ance, -ty,* and *-ment.*

---

* Find the definition of all words in small capital letters (such as ARTICLES) in the Terms Glossary at the back of this book directly before the Index.

BOX 44 SUMMARY

Nouns

PROPER	name specific people, places, or things (first letter is always capitalized)	*Céline Dion, Paris, Buick*
COMMON	name general groups, places, people, or things	*singer, city, automobile*
CONCRETE	name things experienced through the senses: sight, hearing, taste, smell, and touch	*landscape, pizza, thunder*
ABSTRACT	name things not knowable through the senses	*freedom, shyness*
COLLECTIVE	name groups	*family, team*
NONCOUNT OR MASS	name "uncountable" things	*water, time*
COUNT	name countable items	*lake, minute*

7c What is a pronoun?

A **pronoun** takes the place of a NOUN. The words or word that a pronoun replaces is called the pronoun's ANTECEDENT. See Box 45 on the next page for a list of different kinds of pronouns. For information on how to use pronouns correctly, see Chapters 9 and 10.

> **David** is an accountant. [noun]
> **He** is an accountant. [pronoun]
> The finance committee needs to consult **him**. [The pronoun *him* refers to its antecedent *David*.]

EXERCISE 7-1

Underline and label all nouns (N) and pronouns (P). Refer to 7a through 7c for help.

> EXAMPLE Treadmills help people achieve fitness and rehabilitation.

1. Not only humans use them.
2. Scientists conduct experiments by placing lobsters on treadmills.
3. Scientists can study a lobster when it is fitted with a small mask.
4. The mask allows researchers to monitor the crustacean's heartbeat.
5. The lobster may reach speeds up to one kilometre an hour.

BOX 45   SUMMARY

 Pronouns

PERSONAL *I, you, its, her,* *they, ours,* and others	refer to people or things	*I saw **her** take a book to **them.***
RELATIVE *who, which, that*	introduce certain NOUN CLAUSES and ADJECTIVE CLAUSES	*The book **that** I lost was valuable.*
INTERROGATIVE *what, which, who,* *whose,* and others	introduce a question	***Who** called?*
DEMONSTRATIVE *this, that, these,* *those*	point out the ANTECEDENT	*Whose books are **these**?*
REFLEXIVE **OR INTENSIVE** *myself, themselves,* and other *-self* or *-selves* words	reflect back to the antecedent; intensify the antecedent	*They claim to support **themselves.** I **myself** doubt it.*
RECIPROCAL *each other, one* *another*	refer to individual parts of a plural antecedent	*We respect **each other.***
INDEFINITE *all, anyone, each,* and others	refer to nonspecific persons or things	***Everyone** is welcome here.*

7d What is a verb?

Main verbs express action, occurrence, or state of being. For information on how to use verbs correctly, see Chapter 8.

> I **dance.** [action]
> The audience **became** silent. [occurrence]
> Your dancing **was** excellent. [state of being]

👁 **ALERT:** If you're not sure whether a word is a verb, try changing the TENSE of the word. If the sentence still makes sense, the word is a verb.

> **NO**   He is a **changed** man. He is a **will change** man. [*Changed* isn't a verb because the sentence doesn't make sense when *will change* is substituted.]

| YES | The man **changed** his profession. The man **will change** his profession. [*Changed* is a verb because the sentence makes sense when the verb *will change* is substituted.] 👁 |

EXERCISE 7-2

Underline all verbs. Refer to 7d for help.

EXAMPLE A distinctive group of self-published magazines <u>is called</u> simply "zines."

1. Many young writers found regular mass-market magazines boring and irrelevant.
2. Some of them created their own small magazines, or "zines," for readers with the same interests and tastes.
3. Most zines contain cartoons, short stories, and personal essays.
4. Typically, zines are given odd names like *Ottawa's Plague* and *I Hate My Generation*.
5. Their creators shock their small group of readers with satire, bizarre fantasies, and wild rumours about popular rock bands.

7e What is a verbal?

Verbals are verb parts functioning as NOUNS, ADJECTIVES, or ADVERBS. Box 46 lists the three different kinds of verbals.

🌐 **ESL NOTE:** For information about correctly using the verbals called infinitives and gerunds as objects, see Chapter 48. 🌐

BOX 46   SUMMARY

Verbals and their functions

INFINITIVE *to* + verb	1. noun 2. adjective or adverb	***To eat** now is inconvenient.* *Still, we have far **to go**.*
PAST PARTICIPLE *-ed* form of REGULAR VERB or equivalent in IRREGULAR VERB	adjective	***Boiled, filtered** water is safe.*
PRESENT PARTICIPLE *-ing* form of verb	1. noun (called a GERUND) 2. adjective	***Eating** in diners on the road is an adventure.* ***Running** water may not be safe.*

7f What is an adjective?

Adjectives modify—that is, they describe or limit—NOUNS, PRONOUNS, and word groups that function as nouns. For information on how to use adjectives correctly, see Chapter 11.

> I saw a **green** tree. [*Green* modifies the noun *tree*.]
> It was **leafy.** [*Leafy* modifies the pronoun *it*.]
> The flowering trees were **beautiful.** [*Beautiful* modifies the noun phrase *the flowering trees*.]

ESL NOTE: You can identify some kinds of adjectives by looking at their endings. Usually, words with the SUFFIXES *-ful, -ish, -less,* and *-like* are adjectives.

Determiners, frequently called **limiting adjectives,** tell whether a noun is general (*a* tree) or specific (*the* tree). Determiners also tell which one (*this* tree), how many (*twelve* trees), whose (*our* tree), and similar information.

The determiners *a, an,* and *the* are almost always called **articles.** *The* is a **definite article.** Before a noun, *the* conveys that the noun refers to a specific item (*the* plan). *A* and *an* are **indefinite articles.** They indicate that a noun refers to an item in a nonspecific or general way (*a* plan).

ALERT: Use *a* when the word following it starts with a consonant: *a carrot, a broken egg.* Also, use *a* when the word following starts with an *h* that is sounded: *a hip, a home.* Use *an* when the word following starts with a vowel sound: *an honour, an old bag, an egg.*

ESL NOTE: For information about using articles with COUNT and NONCOUNT NOUNS, and about articles with PROPER NOUNS and GERUNDS, see Chapter 45.

Box 47 lists kinds of determiners. Notice, however, that some words in Box 47 function also as PRONOUNS. To identify a word's part of speech, always check to see how it functions in each particular sentence.

> **That** car belongs to Harold. [*That* is a demonstrative adjective.]
> **That** is Harold's car. [*That* is a demonstrative pronoun.]

BOX 47   SUMMARY

Determiners (or limiting adjectives)

ARTICLES
a, an, the

The *news reporter used **a** cell phone to report **an** assignment.*

DEMONSTRATIVE
this, these, that, those

Those *students rent **that** house.*

INDEFINITE
any, each, few, other,
some, and others

Few *films today have complex plots.*

INTERROGATIVE
what, which, whose

What *answer did you give?*

NUMERICAL
one, first, two, second,
and others

*The **fifth** question was tricky.*

POSSESSIVE
my, your, their, and others

My *violin is older than **your** cello.*

RELATIVE
what, which, whose,
whatever, and others

*We do not know **which** road to take.*

7g What is an adverb?

Adverbs modify—that is, adverbs describe or limit—VERBS, ADJECTIVES, other adverbs, and CLAUSES. For information on how to use adverbs correctly, see Chapter 11.

Chefs plan meals **carefully.** [*Carefully* modifies the verb *plan*.]
Vegetables provide **very** important vitamins. [*Very* modifies the adjective *important*.]
Those potato chips are **too** heavily salted. [*Too* modifies the adverb *heavily*.]
Fortunately, people are learning that overuse of salt is harmful.
[*Fortunately* modifies the rest of the sentence, an independent clause.]

Descriptive adverbs show levels of intensity, usually by adding *more* (or *less*) and *most* (or *least*): *more* happily, *least* clearly (see section 11e). Many descriptive adverbs are formed by adding *-ly* to adjectives: *sadly, loudly, normally.* But many adverbs do not end in *-ly: very, always, not, yesterday,* and *well* are a few. Some adjectives look like adverbs but are not: *brotherly, lonely, lovely.*

Relative adverbs are words such as *where, why,* and *when.* They are used to introduce ADJECTIVE CLAUSES.

Conjunctive adverbs modify by creating logical connections to give words meaning. Conjunctive adverbs can appear anywhere in a sentence: at the start, in the middle, or at the end.

However, we consider Isaac Newton an even more important scientist.
We consider Isaac Newton, **however,** an even more important scientist.
We consider Isaac Newton an even more important scientist, **however.**

Box 48 lists the kinds of relationships that conjunctive adverbs can show.

BOX 48   SUMMARY

Conjunctive adverbs and relationships they express

Relationship	Words
ADDITION	*also, furthermore, moreover, besides*
CONTRAST	*however, still, nevertheless, conversely, nonetheless, instead, otherwise*
COMPARISON	*similarly, likewise*
RESULT OR SUMMARY	*therefore, thus, consequently, accordingly, hence, then*
TIME	*next, then, meanwhile, finally, subsequently*
EMPHASIS	*indeed, certainly*

EXERCISE 7-3

Underline and label all adjectives (ADJ) and adverbs (ADV). For help, consult 7e through 7g.

               ADJ   ADJ

EXAMPLE   <u>Scientific</u> evidence shows that <u>massage</u> therapy can

           ADV   ADJ

       <u>dramatically</u> improve <u>human</u> health.

1. Premature babies who are gently massaged gain 47 percent more weight than babies who do not receive touch treatment.
2. Frequently, massaged premature babies go home from the hospital sooner, saving medical expense and parental concern.
3. Also, daily massage helps many people with stomach problems digest their food easily because important hormones are released during the rubdown.
4. People with the HIV virus find their weakened immune system significantly improved by targeted massage.
5. In addition, massage treatments have helped people with asthma breathe more freely.

7h What is a preposition?

Prepositions are words that convey relationships, usually in time or space. Common prepositions include *in, under, by, after, to, on, over,* and *since.* A PREPOSITIONAL PHRASE consists of a preposition and the words it modifies. For information about prepositions and commas, see 24k.2.

> **In the fall,** we will hear a concert **by our favourite tenor.**
> **After the concert,** he will fly **to San Francisco.**

🌐 **ESL NOTE:** For a list of prepositions and the IDIOMS they create, see Chapter 47. 🌐

7i What is a conjunction?

A **conjunction** connects words, PHRASES, or CLAUSES. **Coordinating conjunctions** join two or more grammatically equal words, phrases, or clauses. Box 49 lists the coordinating conjunctions and the relationships they express.

> We hike **and** camp every summer. [*And* joins two words.]
> We hike along scenic trails **or** in the wilderness. [*Or* joins two phrases.]
> I love the outdoors, **but** my family does not. [*But* joins two independent clauses.]

BOX 49   SUMMARY

Coordinating conjunctions and relationships they express

Relationship	Words
ADDITION	*and*
CONTRAST	*but, yet*
RESULT OR EFFECT	*so*
REASON OR CAUSE	*for*
CHOICE	*or*
NEGATIVE CHOICE	*nor*

Correlative conjunctions are two conjunctions that work as a pair: *both . . . and; either . . . or; neither . . . nor; not only . . . but (also); whether . . . or;* and *not . . . so much as.*

> **Both** English **and** French are spoken in many homes in Canada.
> **Not only** students **but also** business people should study a second language.

Subordinating conjunctions introduce DEPENDENT CLAUSES and express relationships making the dependent clause in a sentence grammatically less important than the INDEPENDENT CLAUSE in the sentence. Box 50 lists the most common subordinating conjunctions. For information about how to use them correctly, see 17e through 17h.

Because it snowed, school was cancelled.
Many people were happy **after** they heard the news.

BOX 50　SUMMARY

Subordinating conjunctions and relationships they express

Relationship	Words
TIME	after, before, once, since, until, when, whenever, while
REASON OR CAUSE	as, because, since
RESULT OR EFFECT	in order that, so, so that, that
CONDITION	if, even if, provided that, unless
CONTRAST	although, even though, though, whereas
LOCATION	where, wherever
CHOICE	than, whether

7j What is an interjection?

An **interjection** is a word or expression that conveys surprise or a strong emotion. Alone, an interjection is usually punctuated with an exclamation point (*!*). As part of a sentence, an interjection is usually set off by one or more commas.

Hooray! I won the race.
Oh, my friends missed seeing the finish.

EXERCISE 7-4

Identify the part of speech of each numbered and underlined word. Choose from noun, pronoun, verb, adjective, adverb, preposition, coordinating conjunction, correlative conjunction, and subordinating conjunction. For help, consult 7b through 7i.

1
The geneticist Barbara McClintock was a nonconformist. She
2   3   4
preferred the company of the corn plants that she eagerly studied
5
to the companionship of many of the people she knew. When she won
6
the Nobel Prize in 1983, she learned of it over the radio because she

had no telephone.

7
McClintock worked alone throughout her fifty-year career at the
8   9
Cold Spring Harbor Laboratory in New York. In the 1940s and
10
1950s, McClintock discovered that parts of chromosomes break off
11   12   13
and recombine with neighbouring chromosomes to create unique genetic
14
combinations. This process, known as crossing over, amazed scientists

and demonstrated that chromosomes formed the basis of genetics.

Still, scientists resisted McClintock's findings and did not recognize the
15   16   17   18
importance of her research for many years. Only after geneticists found
19
crossing over genes in both plants and animals was the great value of
20
McClintock's discovery acknowledged. Years later, she won the Nobel

Prize for her groundbreaking achievement.

21   22
Overall, McClintock's life was lonely, but her career was very
23
productive. By the time of her death in 1992, her colleagues had finally
24   25
come to realize that Barbara McClintock was one of the towering

giants of genetics.

SENTENCE STRUCTURES

7k How is a sentence defined?

A **sentence** is defined in several ways: On a strictly mechanical level, a sentence starts with a capital letter and finishes with a period, question mark, or exclamation point. Grammatically, a sentence consists of an INDEPENDENT CLAUSE: *Skydiving is dangerous.* You might hear a sentence described as a "complete thought," but that definition is too vague to help much. From the perspective of its purpose, a sentence is defined as listed in Box 51.

BOX 51   SUMMARY

Sentences and their purposes

- A **declarative sentence**
  makes a statement: Skydiving is dangerous.
- An **interrogative sentence**
  asks a question: Is skydiving dangerous?
- An **imperative sentence**
  gives a command: Be careful when you skydive.
- An **exclamatory sentence**
  expresses strong feeling: How I love skydiving!

7l What are a subject and a predicate in a sentence?

The **subject** and **predicate** of a sentence are its two essential parts. Without both, a group of words isn't a sentence. Box 52 shows the sentence pattern with both. Terms used in the box are defined after it.

The **simple subject** is the word or group of words that acts, is described, or is acted upon.

> The **telephone** rang. [Simple subject, *telephone*, acts.]
> The **telephone** is red. [Simple subject, *telephone*, is described.]
> The **telephone** was being connected. [Simple subject, *telephone*, is acted upon.]

The **complete subject** is the simple subject and its MODIFIERS.

> **The red telephone** rang.

A **compound subject** consists of two or more NOUNS or PRONOUNS and their modifiers.

> **The telephone and the doorbell** rang.

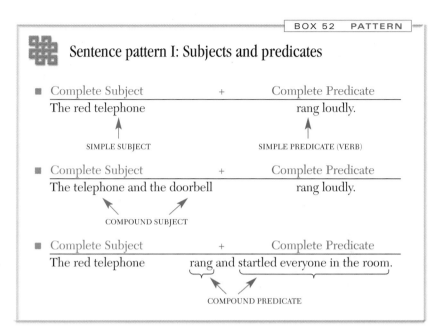

The **predicate** contains the VERB in the sentence. The predicate tells what the subject is doing or experiencing or what is being done to the subject.

> The telephone **rang.** [*Rang* tells what the subject, *telephone*, did.]
> The telephone **is** red. [*Is* tells what the subject, *telephone*, experiences.]
> The telephone **was being connected.** [*Was being connected* tells what was being done to the subject, *telephone*.]

A **simple predicate** contains only the verb.

> The lawyer **listened.**

A **complete predicate** contains the verb and its modifiers.

> The lawyer **listened carefully.**

A **compound predicate** contains two or more verbs.

> The lawyer **listened and waited.**

 ESL NOTES: (1) The subject of a declarative sentence usually comes before the predicate, but there are exceptions (19f). In sentences that ask a question, part of the predicate usually comes before the subject. For more information about word order in English sentences, see Chapter 46. (2) In English, don't add a PERSONAL PRONOUN to repeat the stated noun.

NO My **grandfather he** lived to be eighty-seven. [The personal pronoun, *he*, repeats the stated noun, *grandfather.*]

YES My **grandfather** lived to be eighty-seven.

NO **Winter storms** that bring ice, sleet, and snow **they** can cause traffic problems. [The personal pronoun, *they*, repeats the stated noun, *winter storms.*]

YES **Winter storms** that bring ice, sleet, and snow can cause traffic problems. ⊕

EXERCISE 7-5

Use a slash to separate the complete subject from the complete predicate. For help, consult 7I.

EXAMPLE   A scientific project in Manitoba / is studying the gas emitted by livestock as they digest their food.

1. Greenhouse-gas emissions have been linked to climate change and are limited by international treaties.
2. Greenhouse gases include industrial gases such as carbon dioxide, nitrous oxide, and methane.
3. This last gas, methane, is also produced in huge quantities in the stomachs of pigs, cattle, and sheep.
4. Methane emitted by livestock probably amounts to less than five percent of Canada's total greenhouse-gas emissions.
5. Nevertheless, the need to meet our international obligations means that scientists will be sniffing around cattle barns and recommending dietary changes for Canadian cows.

7m   What are direct and indirect objects?

A **direct object** is a noun, pronoun, or group of words acting as a noun that receives the action of a TRANSITIVE VERB. To check for a direct object, make up a *whom?* or *what?* question about the verb.

An **indirect object** is a noun, pronoun, or group of words acting as a noun that tells *to whom* or *for whom* the action expressed by a transitive verb was done. To check for an indirect object, make up a *to whom? for whom? to what?* or *for what?* question about the verb.

Direct and indirect objects always fall in the PREDICATE of a sentence. Box 53 shows how direct and indirect objects function in sentences.

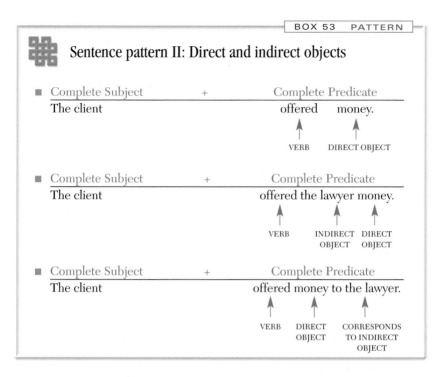

BOX 53   PATTERN

Sentence pattern II: Direct and indirect objects

■ Complete Subject   +   Complete Predicate
The client   offered   money.
                                    ↑   ↑
                                    VERB   DIRECT OBJECT

■ Complete Subject   +   Complete Predicate
The client   offered the lawyer money.
                                    ↑   ↑   ↑
                                    VERB   INDIRECT   DIRECT
                                               OBJECT   OBJECT

■ Complete Subject   +   Complete Predicate
The client   offered money to the lawyer.
                                    ↑   ↑   ↑
                                    VERB   DIRECT   CORRESPONDS
                                               OBJECT   TO INDIRECT
                                                          OBJECT

 ESL NOTES: (1) In sentences where the object of the preposition *to* or *for* acts as indirect object, always put the direct object before the preposition and its object.

> NO   Will you please give **to John** this letter?
> YES   Will you please give this letter **to John?**

(2) When a PRONOUN would normally be used as an indirect object, some verbs require *to* or *for* before the pronoun, and others do not.

> NO   Please explain **me** the rule. [*Explain* requires *to* before an indirect object.]
> YES   Please explain the rule **to me.**
> YES   Please give **me** that book. Please give that book **to me.** [*Give* uses both patterns.]

(3) When both the direct object and the indirect object are pronouns, put the direct object first and replace the indirect object with a phrase beginning with *to*.

> NO   He gave **me it.**
> YES   He gave **it to me.**

(4) An indirect object can be replaced with a phrase beginning with *to.* If you do use *to,* be sure to put the direct object before the indirect object.

> **YES**   Please hand **me the letter.**
> **YES**   Please hand **the letter to me.**

EXERCISE 7-6

Draw a single line under all direct objects and a double line under all indirect objects. For help, consult 7m.

> **EXAMPLE**   Toni Morrison's award-winning novels give <u>readers</u> the <u>gifts</u> of wisdom, inspiration, and pleasure.

1. Literary critics gave high praise to Toni Morrison for her first novel, *The Bluest Eye,* but the general public showed little interest.

2. *Song of Solomon* won Morrison the U.S. National Book Critics Circle Award in 1977, and *Beloved* won her the Pulitzer Prize in 1988.

3. A literary panel awarded Toni Morrison the 1993 Nobel Prize in Literature, the highest honour a writer can receive.

4. Her 1998 novel, *Paradise,* traces for readers the tragic lives of a rejected group of former slaves.

5. Twenty-five years after *The Bluest Eye* was published, Oprah Winfrey selected it for her book club, and it immediately became a bestseller.

7n What are complements, modifiers, and appositives?

Complements

A **complement** renames or describes a SUBJECT or an OBJECT. It appears in the PREDICATE of a sentence.

A **subject complement** is a NOUN, PRONOUN, or ADJECTIVE that follows a LINKING VERB. **Predicate nominative** is another term for a noun used as a subject complement, and **predicate adjective** is another term for an adjective used as a subject complement.

An **object complement** follows a DIRECT OBJECT and either describes or renames the direct object. Box 54 shows how subject and object complements function in a sentence.

BOX 54   PATTERN

Sentence pattern III: Complements

- Complete Subject   +   Complete Predicate
  The caller   was a student.

                                                  LINKING   SUBJECT
                                                  VERB   COMPLEMENT

- Complete Subject   +   Complete Predicate
  The student   called himself a victim.

                                                  VERB   DIRECT   OBJECT
                                                          OBJECT   COMPLEMENT

EXERCISE 7-7

Underline all complements and identify each as a subject complement (SUB) or an object complement (OB).

> **EXAMPLE**   Architect Frank Gehry's buildings have been called bizarre.   **SUB**

1. Frank Gehry's colleagues consider him brilliant for his work in designing remarkable structures.

2. In 1989, he was awarded the Pritzker Architecture Prize, which is said to be equivalent to winning a Nobel.

3. From a distance, his Guggenheim Museum in Bilbao, Spain, seems poised over the city like a huge, splashing silver whale.

4. Gehry was born Canadian, but he made his career in California.

5. For years he wondered why no Canadian individuals or institutions ever found him appropriate to design their projects.

Modifiers

A **modifier** is a word or group of words that describes or limits other words. Modifiers appear in the SUBJECT or the PREDICATE of a sentence.

The **large red** telephone rang. [The adjectives *large* and *red* modify the noun *telephone*.]

The lawyer answered **quickly.** [The adverb *quickly* modifies the verb *answered*.]

The person **on the telephone** was **extremely** upset. [The prepositional phrase *on the telephone* modifies the noun *person*; the adverb *extremely* modifies the adjective *upset*.]

173

Therefore, the lawyer spoke **gently.** [The adverb *therefore* modifies the independent clause *the lawyer spoke gently;* the adverb *gently* modifies the verb *spoke.*]

Because the lawyer's voice was calm, the caller felt reassured. [The adverb clause *because the lawyer's voice was calm* modifies the independent clause *the caller felt reassured.*]

Appositives

An **appositive** is a word or group of words that renames the NOUN or PRONOUN preceding it.

The student's story, **a tale of broken promises,** was complicated. [The appositive *a tale of broken promises* renames the noun *story.*]

The lawyer consulted an expert, **her law professor.** [The appositive *her law professor* renames the noun *expert.*]

The student, **Jamil Amin,** asked to speak to his lawyer. [The appositive *Jamil Amin* renames the noun *student.*]

👁 **ALERT:** When an appositive is not essential for identifying what it renames (that is, when it is NONRESTRICTIVE), use a comma or commas to set off the appositive from the rest of the sentence; see section 24f. 👁

7o What is a phrase?

A **phrase** is a group of words that does not contain both a SUBJECT and a PREDICATE and therefore cannot stand alone as an independent unit.

Noun phrase

A **noun phrase** functions as a NOUN in a sentence.

The modern census dates back to the seventeenth century.

Verb phrase

A **verb phrase** functions as a VERB in a sentence.

Two military censuses **are mentioned** in the Bible.

Prepositional phrase

A **prepositional phrase** always starts with a PREPOSITION and functions as a MODIFIER.

William the Conqueror conducted a census **of landowners in newly conquered England in 1086.** [three prepositional phrases in a row, beginning with *of, in, in*]

Absolute phrase

An **absolute phrase** usually contains a noun or PRONOUN and a PRESENT or PAST PARTICIPLE. An absolute phrase modifies its entire sentence.

Censuses being the fashion, Quebec and Nova Scotia took sixteen counts between 1665 and 1754.

Eighteenth-century Sweden and Denmark had complete records of their populations, **each adult and child having been counted.**

Verbal phrase

A **verbal phrase** contains a verbal—a verb part that functions not as a verb, but as a noun or an ADJECTIVE. Verbals are INFINITIVES, present participles, and past participles.

In 1624, Virginia began **to count its citizens** in a census. [*To count its citizens* is an infinitive phrase.]

Going from door to door, census takers interview millions of people. [*Going from door to door* is a present participial phrase.]

Amazed by some people's answers, census takers always listen carefully. [*Amazed by some people's answers* is a past participial phrase.]

Gerund phrase

A **gerund phrase** functions as a noun. Telling the difference between a gerund phrase and a present participial phrase can be tricky because both use the -*ing* verb form. The key is to determine how the phrase functions in the sentence: A gerund phrase functions only as a noun, and a participial phrase functions only as a modifier.

Including each person in the census was important. [This is a gerund phrase because it functions as a noun and is the subject of the sentence.]

Including each person in the census, Abby spent many hours on the crowded city block. [This is a present participial phrase because it functions as a modifier, namely, an adjective describing Abby.]

EXERCISE 7-8

Combine each set of sentences into a single sentence by converting one sentence into a phrase—either a noun phrase, verb phrase, prepositional phrase, absolute phrase, verbal phrase, or gerund phrase. You can omit, add, or change words. Identify which type of phrase you created.

You can combine most sets in several correct ways, but make sure the meaning of your finished sentence is clear. For help, consult 7o.

EXAMPLE Large chain stores often pose threats to local independent retailers. Smaller store owners must find innovative ways to stay in business.

With large chains posing threats to local independent retailers, smaller store owners must find innovative ways to stay in business. (prepositional phrase)

1. Independent stores develop creative marketing strategies to compete with chain stores. Independent stores figure out ways to offer special features.

2. One independent children's bookstore attracted new customers. It did that by bringing live animals into the store.

3. Animals are popular with children. The store purchased two pet chickens, plus tarantulas, rats, cats, and fish.

4. This children's bookstore did not need to lower prices to draw customers. The store could survive by owning animals that appeal to youngsters.

5. Other sorts of independent stores sometimes take a slightly different approach. They compete by offering better service than the large chain stores can.

6. For example, independent hardware and housewares stores can be service-oriented and customer friendly. They sometimes can thrive financially doing this.

7. Many independent hardware and housewares store owners have begun to offer home-repair and decorating advice and to recommend house calls from staff members. They do this to attract and hold customers.

8. These store owners also feature high-end items that chains do not carry. They feature in-store displays and advertise their high-end items.

9. Independent hardware and housewares stores often stock fine items such as expensive lawn ornaments, costly brand-name paints, and rare Italian tiles. These stores tend to attract wealthier customers.

10. Some independent stores struggle for survival. They cannot always compete with the lower prices at impersonal chain stores.

7p What is a clause?

A **clause** is a group of words with both a SUBJECT and a PREDICATE. Clauses can be either *independent clauses,* also called *main clauses,* or *dependent clauses,* also called *subordinate clauses.*

Independent clauses

An **independent clause** contains a subject and a predicate and can stand alone as a sentence. Box 55 shows the basic pattern.

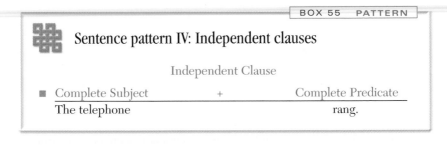

BOX 55 PATTERN

Sentence pattern IV: Independent clauses

Independent Clause

Complete Subject	+	Complete Predicate
The telephone		rang.

Dependent clauses

A **dependent clause,** also called a *subordinate clause,* contains a subject and a predicate but cannot stand alone as a sentence. To be part of a complete sentence, a dependent clause must be joined to an independent clause. Dependent clauses may be *adverb clauses, adjective clauses,* or certain *noun clauses.*

An **adverb clause** starts with a SUBORDINATING CONJUNCTION, such as *although, because, when,* or *until.* A subordinating conjunction expresses a relationship between a dependent clause and an independent clause; see Box 50 in section 7i. Adverb clauses usually answer some question about the independent clause: *How? Why? When? Under what circumstances?*

> **If the vote passes,** the city will install sewers. [The adverb clause modifies the verb *install;* it explains under what circumstances.]
>
> They are drawing up plans **as quickly as they can.** [The adverb clause modifies the verb *drawing up;* it explains how.]
>
> The homeowners feel happier **because they know the flooding will soon be better controlled.** [The adverb clause modifies the entire independent clause; it explains why.]

👁 **ALERT:** When you write an adverb clause before an independent clause, separate the clauses with a comma; see section 24b. 👁

An **adjective clause,** also called a *relative clause,* is a dependent clause that starts with a RELATIVE PRONOUN, such as *who, which,* or *that,* or with a RELATIVE ADVERB, such as *when* or *where.* An adjective clause modifies the NOUN or PRONOUN that it follows. Box 56 shows how adverb and adjective clauses function in sentences. See also Box 71 in section 9s.

> The car **that Jack bought** is practical. [The adjective clause describes the noun *car; that* is a relative pronoun referring to *car.*]
>
> The day **when I can buy my own car** is getting closer. [The adjective clause modifies the noun *day; when* is a relative adverb referring to *day.*]

Use *who, whom, whoever, whomever,* and *whose* when an adjective clause refers to a person or to an animal with a name.

> The di Pietros, **who collect cars,** are wealthy.
>
> Their dog Bowser, **who is large and loud,** has been spoiled.

Use *which* or *that* when an adjective clause refers to a thing or to an animal that isn't a pet. Sometimes, writers omit *that* from an adjective clause. For grammatical analysis, however, consider the omitted *that* to be implied and, therefore, present.

For help in deciding whether to use *that* or *which,* see Box 71 in section 9s.

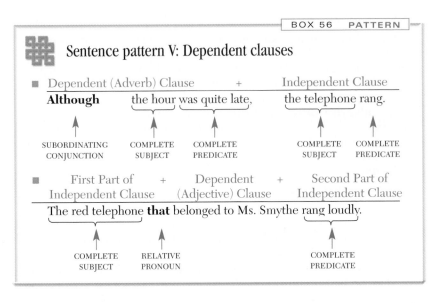

BOX 56 PATTERN

Sentence pattern V: Dependent clauses

■ Dependent (Adverb) Clause + Independent Clause

Although the hour was quite late, the telephone rang.

SUBORDINATING CONJUNCTION | COMPLETE SUBJECT | COMPLETE PREDICATE | COMPLETE SUBJECT | COMPLETE PREDICATE

■ First Part of Independent Clause + Dependent (Adjective) Clause + Second Part of Independent Clause

The red telephone **that** belonged to Ms. Smythe rang loudly.

COMPLETE SUBJECT | RELATIVE PRONOUN | COMPLETE PREDICATE

👁 **ALERT:** When an adjective clause is NONRESTRICTIVE, use *which* and set it off from the independent clause with commas. Don't use commas with *that* in a RESTRICTIVE CLAUSE.

My car, **which** I bought used, needs major repairs. [The adjective clause is nonrestrictive, so it begins with *which* and is set off with commas.]

The car **that** I want to buy has a CD player. [The adjective clause uses *that* and is restrictive, so it is not set off with commas.] 👁

EXERCISE 7-9

Underline the dependent clause in each sentence, and label it an ADJ or an ADV clause. For help, consult 7p.

                            ADV

EXAMPLE   When umbrellas were invented, people used them for sun protection.

1. Eighteenth-century ladies carried fancy umbrellas as a fashion statement while strolling down the street.

2. Although today umbrellas are mostly used in the rain, they have many other uses.

3. Gentlemen in England carry sturdy umbrellas, which make convenient walking sticks.

4. One company makes a "sporting umbrella" that unfolds into a seat.

5. Marketing consultants, who receive requests for moveable advertising, suggest umbrellas can be mini-billboards when they are decorated with a company's name and logo.

Noun clauses function as nouns. Depending on their function in a sentence, they may be either independent or dependent clauses. They can begin with many of the same words that begin adjective clauses: *that, who, which,* and their derivatives, as well as *when, where, whether, why,* and *how.*

> **Promises** are not always dependable. [noun]
> **What politicians promise** is not always dependable. [independent noun clause]
> The electorate often cannot figure out the **truth.** [noun]
> The electorate often cannot know **that the truth is being manipulated.** [dependent noun clause]

Because they start with similar words, noun clauses and adjective clauses are sometimes confused with each other. The way to tell them apart is that the word starting an adjective clause has an ANTECEDENT, while the word starting a noun clause doesn't.

> Good politicians understand **whom they must please.** [Noun clause; *whom* does not have an antecedent.]
> Good politicians **who make promises** know to keep the important ones. [Adjective clause modifies *politicians*, which is the antecedent of *who*.]

🌐 **ESL NOTE:** Noun clauses in INDIRECT QUESTIONS are phrased as statements, not questions: *Kara asked why we needed the purple dye.* Don't phrase a noun clause this way: *Kara asked why **did** [or **do**] we need the purple dye?* If you prefer to change to a DIRECT QUESTION, usually VERB TENSE, PRONOUN, and other changes are necessary; see section 15e. 🌐

Elliptical clauses

In an **elliptical clause,** one or more words are deliberately left out for CONCISENESS. For an elliptical clause to be correct, the context must reveal what the missing words are. In a comparison and when using PARALLELISM, the words you leave out need to be identical to those already appearing in the clause.

> Engineering is one of the majors [**that**] **she considered.** [*that*, functioning as a relative pronoun, omitted from adjective clause]
> She decided [**that**] **she would rather major in management.** [*that*, functioning as a conjunction, omitted from the noun clause]
> After [**he takes**] **a refresher course,** he will be eligible for a raise. [subject and verb omitted from adverb clause]
> Broiled fish tastes better **than boiled fish** [**tastes**]. [second half of the comparison omitted]
> Lucie attended graduate school **with the aid of a big scholarship** and [**with the aid of**] **a huge student loan**. [part of the parallel structure omitted]

EXERCISE 7-10

Use subordinate conjunctions and relative pronouns from the list below to combine each pair of sentences. You may use words more than once, but try to use as many different ones as possible. Some sentence pairs may be combined in several ways. Create at least one elliptical construction.

since which if after when as that although so that unless

EXAMPLE Reports of flying snakes have been around for hundreds of years. Scientists have never believed them.

Even though reports of flying snakes have been around for hundreds of years, scientists have never believed them.

1. The idea that snakes can fly or even glide from treetops seems impossible. They lack wings, feathers, or any kind of flying or gliding apparatus.
2. Yet, what seems impossible is not so for the paradise tree snake. This snake possesses many adaptations to allow it to soar long distances through the air.
3. The paradise tree snake has evolved into an animal of amazing agility. This allows it both to escape from predators and to catch its prey.
4. The paradise tree snake can land as far as 21 metres from its launch point. People who visit the jungles of Southeast Asia can see this.
5. The snake jumps by dangling like the letter J from a tree branch. Then it throws itself upward and away from the branch, giving the impression of leaping in midair.
6. Immediately, it begins to fall at a steep angle. It then takes on an S-shape, ripples through the air, and appears to be crawling.
7. The snake changes to an S-shape. Its fall becomes much less steep. The snake then soars outward from its launch point.
8. A special characteristic permits the snake to change its shape and begin to glide. This characteristic permits the snake to flatten its body.
9. Most snakes cannot glide through the air. The paradise tree snake most certainly can.
10. The paradise tree snake must maintain its ability to glide effortlessly through the treetops. Otherwise, birds and mammals may eat it into extinction.

7q What are the four sentence types?

English uses four **sentence types:** simple, compound, complex, and compound-complex. A **simple sentence** is composed of a single INDEPENDENT CLAUSE and no DEPENDENT CLAUSES.

Charlie Chaplin was born in London on April 16, 1889.

A **compound sentence** is composed of two or more independent clauses. These clauses may be connected by a COORDINATING CONJUNCTION (*and, but, for, or, nor, yet, so*), a semicolon alone, or a semicolon and a CONJUNCTIVE ADVERB.

His father died early, **and** his mother spent time in psychiatric hospitals.

Many people enjoy Chaplin films; others do not.

Many people enjoy Chaplin films; **however,** others do not.

A **complex sentence** is composed of one independent clause and one or more dependent clauses.

When times were bad, Chaplin lived in the streets. [dependent clause starting *when;* independent clause starting *Chaplin*]

When Chaplin was performing with a troupe that was touring the United States, he was hired by Mack Sennett, **who owned the Keystone Company.** [dependent clause starting *when;* dependent clause starting *that;* independent clause starting *he;* dependent clause starting *who*]

A **compound-complex sentence** integrates a compound sentence and a complex sentence. It contains two or more independent clauses and one or more dependent clauses.

Chaplin's comedies were immediately successful, and he became rich **because he was enormously popular for playing the Little Tramp, who was loved for his tiny moustache, baggy trousers, big shoes, and trick derby.** [independent clause starting *Chaplin's;* independent clause starting *he;* dependent clause starting *because;* dependent clause starting *who*]

When studios could no longer afford him, Chaplin cofounded United Artists, **and** then he produced and distributed his own films. [dependent clause starting *when;* independent clause starting *Chaplin;* independent clause starting *then*]

👁 **ALERTS:** (1) Use a comma before a coordinating conjunction connecting two independent clauses; see 24b. (2) When independent clauses are long or contain commas, use a subordinating conjunction— or use a semicolon to connect the clauses; see 25d. 👁

EXERCISE 7-11

Decide whether each of the following sentences is simple, compound, complex, or compound-complex. For help, consult 7q.

EXAMPLE   Many people would love to eat a healthy meal at a fast-food restaurant or a food concession at the movies. (*simple*)

1. Fast-food restaurants and healthy meals rarely go together.

2. A fried-chicken sandwich packs an enormous number of calories and fat, and a fried-fish sandwich is no better.

3. A double cheeseburger with bacon at a fast-food restaurant can contain over 1000 calories and 80 grams of fat, but a plain burger reduces the unhealthy overload considerably.

4. You can purchase other relatively healthy meals at a fast-food restaurant, if you first do some research.

5. Even though governments and medical associations release vast amounts of reliable advice, consumers often ignore the information, and they choose main meals and side dishes with the most flavour, calories, and fat.

6. A healthy meal available at many fast-food restaurants is a salad with low-fat dressing, along with bottled water.

7. The temptations of high fat and calories also entice people at the food concessions in movie theatres.

8. Because calories from sugar have zero nutritional value, health experts use the expression "empty calories" for all sugar products, yet sales of sugar-laden soft drinks at the movies continue to increase yearly.

9. The silent ingredient in a serving of chips with melted cheese, or nachos, is artery-clogging fat, and the culprits in extra-large candy bars are not only fat but also "empty calories."

10. In truth, many people need to stay away from fast-food restaurants and food concessions at the movies and thereby avoid the tasty temptations of high-calorie foods.

Chapter 8

Verbs

8a What do verbs do?

A **verb** expresses an action, an occurrence, or a state of being. Verbs also reveal when something occurs—in the present, the past, or the future. Verbs convey other information as well; see Box 57. For types of verbs, see Box 58.

Many people **overeat** on Thanksgiving. [action]

Mother's Day **fell** early this year. [occurrence]

New Year's Day **is** tomorrow. [state of being]

BOX 57   SUMMARY

Information that verbs convey

PERSON	First person (the speaker: *I* dance), second person (the one spoken to: *you* dance), or third person (the one spoken about: *the dog* dances).
NUMBER	Singular (one) or plural (more than one).
TENSE	Past (*we* **danced**), present (*we* **dance**), or future (*we* **will dance**); see 8g through 8k.
MOOD	Indicative (*we* **dance**), imperative (commands and direct requests: ***Dance***), or subjunctive (speculation, wishes: *if we* **were dancing** . . .); see 8l and 8m.
VOICE	Active voice or passive; see 8n through 8p.

BOX 58 SUMMARY

Types of verbs

MAIN VERB	The word in a PREDICATE that says something about the SUBJECT: *She **danced** for the group.*
AUXILIARY VERB	A verb that combines with a main verb to convey information about TENSE, MOOD, or VOICE (8e). The verbs *be, do,* and *have* can be auxiliary verbs or main verbs. The verbs *can, could, may, might, should, would, must,* and others are MODAL AUXILIARY VERBS. They add shades of meaning such as ability or possibility to verbs: *She **might dance** again.*
LINKING VERB	The verb that links a subject to a COMPLEMENT, a word or words that rename or describe the subject: *She **was** happy dancing. Be* is the most common linking verb; sometimes sense verbs (*smell, taste*) or verbs of perception (*seem, feel*) function as linking verbs. See also Box 59.
TRANSITIVE VERB	The verb followed by a DIRECT OBJECT that completes the verb's message: *They **sent** her a fan letter.*
INTRANSITIVE VERB	A verb that does not require a direct object: *Yesterday she **danced.***

Linking verbs

Linking verbs are main verbs that indicate a state of being or a condition. They link a SUBJECT with one or more words that rename or describe the subject: a SUBJECT COMPLEMENT. A linking verb works like an equal sign between a subject and its complement. Box 59 shows how linking verbs function in sentences.

BOX 59 SUMMARY

Linking verbs

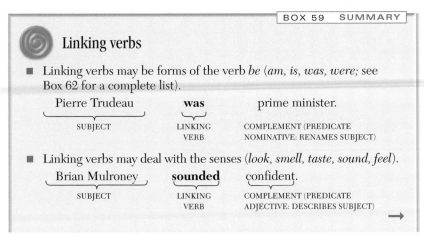

■ Linking verbs may be forms of the verb *be* (*am, is, was, were;* see Box 62 for a complete list).

Pierre Trudeau	**was**	prime minister.
SUBJECT	LINKING VERB	COMPLEMENT (PREDICATE NOMINATIVE: RENAMES SUBJECT)

■ Linking verbs may deal with the senses (*look, smell, taste, sound, feel*).

Brian Mulroney	**sounded**	confident.
SUBJECT	LINKING VERB	COMPLEMENT (PREDICATE ADJECTIVE: DESCRIBES SUBJECT)

Linking verbs (*continued*)

- Linking verbs can be verbs that convey a sense of existing or becoming—*appear, seem, become, get, grow, turn, remain, stay,* and *prove,* for example.

Lester Pearson	**grew**	old.
SUBJECT	LINKING VERB	COMPLEMENT (PREDICATE ADJECTIVE DESCRIBES SUBJECT)

- To test whether a verb other than a form of *be* is functioning as a linking verb, substitute *was* (for a singular subject) or *were* (for a plural subject) for the original verb. If the sentence makes sense, the original verb is functioning as a linking verb.

> **NO**　Pierre Trudeau **grew** a beard ⟶ Pierre Trudeau **was** a beard. [*Grew* is not functioning as a linking verb.]

> **YES**　Lester Pearson **grew** old ⟶ Lester Pearson **was** old. [*Grew* is functioning as a linking verb.]

VERB FORMS

8b　What are the forms of main verbs?

A **main verb** names an action (*People **dance***), an occurrence (*Christmas **comes** once a year*), or a state of being (*It **will be** warm tomorrow*). Every main verb has five forms.

- The **simple form** conveys an action, occurrence, or state of being taking place in the present (*I **laugh***) or, with an AUXILIARY VERB, in the future (*I **will laugh***).

- The **past-tense form** conveys an action, occurrence, or state completed in the past (*I **laughed***). REGULAR VERBS add *-ed* or *-d* to the simple form. IRREGULAR VERBS vary (see Box 60).

- The **past-participle form** in regular verbs uses the same form as the past tense. Irregular verbs vary; see Box 60. To function as a verb, a past participle must combine with a SUBJECT and one or more auxiliary verbs (*I **have laughed***). Otherwise, past participles function as ADJECTIVES (***crumbled** cookies*).

- The **present-participle form** adds *-ing* to the simple form (***laughing***). To function as a verb, a present participle combines with a subject and one or more auxiliary verbs (*I **was laughing***). Otherwise, present participles function as adjectives (*my **laughing** friends*) or as NOUNS (***Laughing** is healthy*).

- The **infinitive** usually consists of *to* and the simple form following *to* (*I started **to laugh** at his joke*); see 9i. The infinitive functions as a noun or an adjective, not a verb.

🌐 **ESL NOTE:** When verbs function as other parts of speech, they're called VERBALS: INFINITIVES, PRESENT PARTICIPLES, PAST PARTICIPLES. When present participles function as nouns, they're called GERUNDS. For information about using gerunds and infinitives as OBJECTS after certain verbs, see Chapter 48. 🌐

8c What is the -s form of a verb?

The **-s form of a verb** is the third-person singular in the PRESENT TENSE. The ending -s (or -es) is added to the verb's SIMPLE FORM (*smell* becomes *smells*, as in *The bread **smells** delicious*).

Be and *have* are irregular verbs. For the third-person singular, present tense, *be* uses *is* and *have* uses *has*.

The cheesecake **is** popular.
The éclair **has** chocolate icing.

If you tend to drop the -s or -es ending when you speak, always use it when you write. Proofread carefully to make sure you've not omitted any -s forms.

EXERCISE 8-1

Rewrite each sentence, changing the subjects to the word or words given in parentheses. Change the form of the verbs shown in italics to match the new subject. Keep all sentences in the present tense. For help, consult 8c.

> EXAMPLE   The song of a bird *represents* different things to different listeners. (the songs of birds)
>
> *The songs of birds represent* different things to different listeners.

1. The poet Keats *imagines* a songbird as a fellow poet creating beautiful art. (The poets Keats and Shelley)
2. To a biologist, however, singing birds *communicate* practical information. (a singing bird)
3. A male sparrow that *whistles* one melody to attract a mate *sings* a different tune to warn off other male sparrows. (Male sparrows)
4. Female redwing blackbirds usually *distinguish* a male redwing's song from a mockingbird's imitation, but a male redwing almost never *hears* the difference. (A female redwing blackbird) (male redwings)
5. Nevertheless, in experiments, female birds *are* sometimes fooled by a carved wooden male and a recorded mating song. (the female bird)

8d What is the difference between regular and irregular verbs?

A **regular verb** forms its PAST TENSE and PAST PARTICIPLE by adding *-ed* or *-d* to the SIMPLE FORM: *type, typed; cook, cooked; work, worked.* Most verbs in English are regular.

In informal speech, some people skip over the *-ed* sound, pronouncing it softly or not at all. In ACADEMIC WRITING, however, you're required to use it. If you're not used to hearing or pronouncing this sound, proofread carefully to see that you have written all the needed *-ed* endings.

> **NO** The cake was **suppose** to be tasty.
> **YES** The cake was **supposed** to be tasty.

Irregular verbs, in contrast, don't consistently add *-ed* or *-d* to form the past tense and past participle. Some irregular verbs change an internal vowel to make past tense and past participle: *sing, sang, sung.* Some change an internal vowel and add an ending other than *-ed* or *-d*: *grow, grew, grown.* Some use the simple form throughout: *cost, cost, cost.* Unfortunately, a verb's simple form doesn't indicate with certainty whether the verb is irregular or regular.

Although you can always look up the principal parts of any verb, memorizing any you don't know is much more efficient in the long run. About two hundred verbs in English are irregular. Box 60 lists the most frequently used irregular verbs.

👁 **ALERT:** For information about changing *y* to *i*, or doubling a final consonant before adding the *-ed* ending, see 22d. 👁

BOX 60   SUMMARY

 Common irregular verbs

SIMPLE FORM	PAST TENSE	PAST PARTICIPLE
arise	arose	arisen
awake	awoke *or* awaked	awaked *or* awoken
be (am, is, are)	was, were	been
bear	bore	borne *or* born
beat	beat	beaten
become	became	become
begin	began	begun
bend	bent	bent
bet	bet	bet
bid ("to offer")	bid	bid
bid ("to command")	bade	bidden

→

Common irregular verbs (*continued*)

SIMPLE FORM	PAST TENSE	PAST PARTICIPLE
bind	bound	bound
bite	bit	bitten *or* bit
blow	blew	blown
break	broke	broken
bring	brought	brought
build	built	built
burst	burst	burst
buy	bought	bought
cast	cast	cast
catch	caught	caught
choose	chose	chosen
cling	clung	clung
come	came	come
cost	cost	cost
creep	crept	crept
cut	cut	cut
deal	dealt	dealt
dig	dug	dug
dive	dived *or* dove	dived
do	did	done
draw	drew	drawn
drink	drank	drunk
drive	drove	driven
eat	ate	eaten
fall	fell	fallen
feed	fed	fed
feel	felt	felt
fight	fought	fought
find	found	found
flee	fled	fled
fling	flung	flung
fly	flew	flown
forbid	forbade *or* forbad	forbidden
forget	forgot	forgotten *or* forgot
forgive	forgave	forgiven
forsake	forsook	forsaken
freeze	froze	frozen
get	got	got *or* gotten
give	gave	given
go	went	gone
grow	grew	grown

→

Common irregular verbs (*continued*)

SIMPLE FORM	PAST TENSE	PAST PARTICIPLE
hang ("to suspend")*	hung	hung
have	had	had
hear	heard	heard
hide	hid	hidden
hit	hit	hit
hurt	hurt	hurt
keep	kept	kept
know	knew	known
lay	laid	laid
lead	led	led
leave	left	left
lend	lent	lent
let	let	let
lie	lay	lain
light	lighted *or* lit	lighted *or* lit
lose	lost	lost
make	made	made
mean	meant	meant
pay	paid	paid
prove	proved	proved *or* proven
quit	quit	quit
read	read	read
rid	rid	rid
ride	rode	ridden
ring	rang	rung
rise	rose	risen
run	ran	run
say	said	said
see	saw	seen
seek	sought	sought
send	sent	sent
set	set	set
shake	shook	shaken
shine ("to glow")†	shone	shone
shoot	shot	shot
show	showed	shown *or* showed
shrink	shrank	shrunk
sing	sang	sung

* When it means "to execute by hanging," *hang* is a regular verb: *In wartime, some armies routinely **hanged** deserters.*

† When it means "to polish," *shine* is a regular verb: *We **shined** our shoes.*

$\longrightarrow$

Common irregular verbs (*continued*)

SIMPLE FORM	PAST TENSE	PAST PARTICIPLE
sink	sank *or* sunk	sunk
sit	sat	sat
slay	slew	slain
sleep	slept	slept
sling	slung	slung
speak	spoke	spoken
spend	spent	spent
spin	spun	spun
spring	sprang *or* sprung	sprung
stand	stood	stood
steal	stole	stolen
sting	stung	stung
stink	stank *or* stunk	stunk
stride	strode	stridden
strike	struck	struck
strive	strove	striven
swear	swore	sworn
sweep	swept	swept
swim	swam	swum
swing	swung	swung
take	took	taken
teach	taught	taught
tear	tore	torn
tell	told	told
think	thought	thought
throw	threw	thrown
understand	understood	understood
wake	woke *or* waked	waked *or* woken
wear	wore	worn
wring	wrung	wrung
write	wrote	written

EXERCISE 8-2

Write the correct past-tense form of the regular verbs given in parentheses. For help, consult 8d.

EXAMPLE   The football team at one American university (uses) <u>used</u> an innovative system to cool down after workouts.

(1) Many athletes (need) _____ a way to lower their body temperatures quickly. (2) They normally just (dump) _____ ice on

themselves, but this method (lack) _____ efficiency and sometimes even (cause) _____ collapse. (3) To solve the problem, scientists (develop) _____ the Rapid Thermal Exchange system, which (cools) _____ an athlete from inside. (4) To test the new device, a football player (places) _____ his hand on a cool metal plate inside an airtight chamber, where a mild vacuum pressure (increases) _____ blood flow. (5) This (results) _____ in lowered body temperature as the cooled-down blood (flows) _____ throughout the body and (reduces) _____ the discomfort of being overly hot.

EXERCISE 8-3

Write the correct past-tense form of the irregular verbs given in parentheses. For help, consult Box 60 in 8d.

> EXAMPLE   In the mid-1990s, the new information economy (lead) led big corporations to imitate smaller ones.

(1) Economic and social changes (teach) _____ older companies to copy new ones, as they (seek) _____ to swim with the dot-com sharks. (2) Those that (do) _____ not adapt soon (fall) _____ far behind. (3) Smart corporations (throw) _____ out their dress codes. (4) They (shrink) _____ their managerial staffs. (5) They (make) _____ themselves less hierarchical and more informal, as they (go) _____ after the most intelligent and creative graduates. (6) The visionaries who (understand) _____ these things (know) _____ from the start that the wired world (be) _____ the domain of teenagers and twenty-somethings. (7) Now, from Microsoft down to the smallest dot-com, the workers' skills counted, not the years they (spend) _____ in the organization. (8) In big high-tech firms, older managers (begin) _____ to learn from their younger subordinates. (9) The word (come) _____ down from the very top: Senior employees who once (wear) _____ business suits (put) _____ on blue jeans and (sling) _____ a knapsack over their shoulders. (10) Predictably, the managerial staff (take) _____ the directive to be informal more seriously than anyone else. (11) One visitor (say) _____ that she (know) _____ who the managers (be) _____ at IBM because they were the people wearing blue jeans!

8e What are auxiliary verbs?

Auxiliary verbs, also called *helping verbs,* combine with MAIN VERBS to make VERB PHRASES. Box 61 shows how auxiliary verbs work.

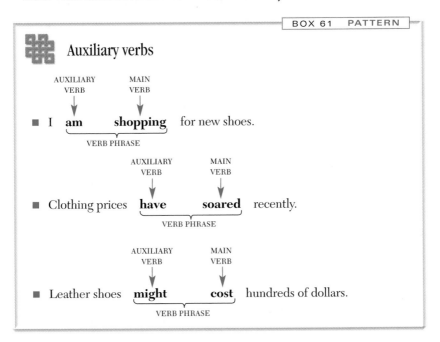

BOX 61   PATTERN

Auxiliary verbs

AUXILIARY   MAIN
VERB   VERB

■ I   **am**   **shopping**   for new shoes.

VERB PHRASE

AUXILIARY   MAIN
VERB   VERB

■ Clothing prices   **have**   **soared**   recently.

VERB PHRASE

AUXILIARY   MAIN
VERB   VERB

■ Leather shoes   **might**   **cost**   hundreds of dollars.

VERB PHRASE

Using be, do, have

The three most common auxiliary verbs are *be, do,* and *have.* These three verbs can also be main verbs. Their forms vary more than most irregular verbs, as Boxes 62 and 63 show.

BOX 62   SUMMARY

Forms of the verb *be*

SIMPLE FORM	be
-S FORM	is
PAST TENSE	was, were
PRESENT PARTICIPLE	being
PAST PARTICIPLE	been

→

Forms of the verb *be* (*continued*)

Person	Present Tense	Past Tense
I	am	was
you (singular)	are	were
he, she, it	is	was
we	are	were
you (plural)	are	were
they	are	were

BOX 63   SUMMARY

Forms of the verbs *do* and *have*

SIMPLE FORM	do	have
-*S* FORM	does	has
PAST TENSE	did	had
PRESENT PARTICIPLE	doing	having
PAST PARTICIPLE	done	had

ESL NOTE: When *be, do,* and *have* function as auxiliary verbs, change their form to agree with a third-person singular subject—and don't add -*s* to the main verb.

NO	**Does** the library **closes** at 6:00?
YES	**Does** the library **close** at 6:00?

Modal auxiliary verbs

Can, could, shall, should, will, would, may, might, and *must* are modal auxiliary verbs. **Modal auxiliary verbs** communicate ability, permission, obligation, advisability, necessity, or possibility. They never change form.

Exercise **can lengthen** lives. [possibility]
She **can jog** for ten kilometres. [ability]
The exercise **must occur** regularly. [necessity, obligation]
People **should protect** their bodies. [advisability]
May I exercise? [permission]

ESL NOTE: For more about modal auxiliary verbs and the meanings they communicate, see Chapter 49.

193

EXERCISE 8-4

Using the auxiliary verbs in the list below, fill in the blanks in the following passage. Use each auxiliary word only once, even if a listed word can fit into more than one blank. For help, consult section 8e.

> are   have   may   will   might   can   has

EXAMPLE   Psychologists have discovered that most personal memories focus on recent events.

(1) Most adults _____ recall recent events more readily than distant ones when they _____ presented with a standard test of memory. (2) However, an important exception _____ been found among older adults, those age fifty and above. (3) People in this older age group _____ most readily recall events that happened in their late teens and early adulthood. (4) Researchers _____ concluded that because many significant life events, such as getting married and choosing a career, occur during this period, older adults _____ prefer to look back on this highly memorable period. (5) Similarly, younger adults _____ tend to focus on those same memorable events, which means that they summon more recent memories.

8f What are intransitive and transitive verbs?

A verb is **intransitive** when an OBJECT isn't required to complete the verb's meaning: *I **sing**.* A verb is **transitive** when an object is necessary to complete the verb's meaning: *I **need** a guitar.* Many verbs have both transitive and intransitive meanings. Some verbs are only transitive: *need, have, like, owe.* Only transitive verbs function in the PASSIVE VOICE. Dictionaries label verbs as transitive (*vt*) or intransitive (*vi*). Box 64 shows how transitive and intransitive verbs operate in sentences.

BOX 64   SUMMARY

Comparing intransitive and transitive verbs

INTRANSITIVE (OBJECT NOT NEEDED)

They **sat** together quietly. [*Together* and *quietly* are not direct objects; they are modifiers.]

The cat **sees** in the dark. [*In the dark* is not a direct object; it is a modifier.]

I can **hear** well. [*Well* is not a direct object; it is a modifier.]

TRANSITIVE (OBJECT NEEDED)

They **sent** a birthday card to me. [*Birthday card* is a direct object.]

The cat **sees** the dog. [*Dog* is a direct object.]

I can **hear** you. [*You* is a direct object.]

The verbs *lie* and *lay* are particularly confusing. *Lie* means "to recline, to place oneself down, or to remain." *Lie* is intransitive (it cannot be followed by an object). *Lay* means "to put something down." *Lay* is transitive (it must be followed by an object). As you can see in Box 65, the word *lay* is both the past tense of *lie* and the present-tense simple form of *lay*. That makes things difficult. My best advice is to memorize these two verbs.

BOX 65   SUMMARY

Using *lie* and *lay*

	lie	lay
SIMPLE FORM	lie	lay
-S FORM	lies	lays
PAST TENSE	lay	laid
PRESENT PARTICIPLE	lying	laying
PAST PARTICIPLE	lain	laid

Intransitive Forms

PRESENT TENSE	The hikers **lie** down to rest.
PAST TENSE	The hikers **lay** down to rest.

Transitive Forms

PRESENT TENSE	The hikers **lay** their backpacks on a rock. [*Backpacks* is a direct object.]
PAST TENSE	The hikers **laid** their backpacks on a rock. [*Backpacks* is a direct object.]

Two other verb pairs tend to confuse people because of their intransitive and transitive forms: *raise* and *rise* and *set* and *sit*.

Raise and *set* are transitive (they must be followed by an object). *Rise* and *sit* are intransitive (they cannot be followed by an object). Fortunately, unlike *lie* and *lay*, *raise* and *rise* and *set* and *sit* do not share any forms: *raise, raised, raised; rise, rose, risen;* and *set, set, set; sit, sat, sat.*

EXERCISE 8-5

Underline the correct word of each pair in parentheses. For help, consult 8f.

EXAMPLE   Whenever I come home, I always check to see where my cat is (laying, <u>lying</u>).

(1) Coming home from jogging one morning, I (laid, lay) my keys on the counter and saw my cat, Andy, (laying, lying) in a patch of sunlight on the living room floor. (2) When I (sat, set) down beside him, he (raised, rose) up on his toes, stretched, and then (laid, lay) down a few feet away. (3) (Sitting, Setting) there, I reached out to Andy, and my contrary cat jumped up onto the couch. As he landed, I heard a clinking noise. (4) I (raised, rose) the bottom of the slipcover, and there (laid, lay) my favourite earrings, the ones I thought I had lost last week. Deciding he had earned a special privilege, Andy curled up on a red silk pillow in the corner of the couch. (5) Since the earrings now (laid, lay) safely in my pocket, I let him (lay, lie) there undisturbed.

VERB TENSE

8g What is verb tense?

Verb tense conveys time. Verbs show tense (time) by changing form. English has six verb tenses, divided into simple and perfect groups. The three **simple tenses** divide time into present, past, and future. The simple **present tense** describes what happens regularly, what takes place in the present, and what is consistently or generally true. The simple **past tense** tells of an action completed or a condition ended. The simple **future tense** indicates action yet to be taken or a condition not yet experienced.

Rick **wants** to speak Spanish fluently. [simple present tense]
Rick **wanted** to improve rapidly. [simple past tense]
Rick **will want** to progress even further next year. [simple future tense]

The three **perfect tenses** also divide time into present, past, and future. They show more complex time relationships than the simple tenses. For information on using the perfect tenses, see section 8i.

The three simple tenses and the three perfect tenses also have **progressive forms.** These forms indicate that the verb describes what is ongoing or continuing. For information on using progressive forms, see section 8j. Box 66 summarizes verb tenses and progressive forms.

⊕ **ESL NOTE:** Box 66 shows that most verb tenses are formed by combining one or more AUXILIARY VERBS with the SIMPLE FORM, the PRESENT PARTICIPLE, or the PAST PARTICIPLE of a MAIN VERB. Auxiliary verbs are necessary in the formation of most tenses, so never omit them.

NO   I **talking** to you.
YES   I **am talking** to you. ⊕

BOX 66   SUMMARY

Simple and perfect tenses with their progressive forms

Simple Tenses

	REGULAR VERB	IRREGULAR VERB	PROGRESSIVE FORM
PRESENT	I talk	I eat	I am talking; I am eating
PAST	I talked	I ate	I was talking; I was eating
FUTURE	I will talk	I will eat	I will be talking; I will be eating

Perfect Tenses

	REGULAR VERB	IRREGULAR VERB	PROGRESSIVE FORM
PRESENT PERFECT	I have talked	I have eaten	I have been talking; I have been eating
PAST PERFECT	I had talked	I had eaten	I had been talking; I had been eating
FUTURE PERFECT	I will have talked	I will have eaten	I will have been talking; I will have been eating

8h How do I use the simple present tense?

The **simple present tense** uses the SIMPLE FORM of the verb (see 8b). It describes what happens regularly, what takes place in the present, and what is generally or consistently true. Also, it can convey a future occurrence with verbs like *start, stop, begin, end, arrive,* and *depart.*

> Calculus class **meets** every morning. [regularly occurring action]
> Mastering calculus **takes** time. [general truth]
> The course **ends** in eight weeks. [specific, time-limited future event]

👁 **ALERT:** For a work of literature, always describe or discuss the action in the present tense. This holds true no matter how old the work.

> In Shakespeare's *Romeo and Juliet,* Juliet's father **wants** her to marry Paris, but Juliet **loves** Romeo. 👁

8i How do I form and use the perfect tenses?

The **perfect tenses** generally describe actions or occurrences that are still having an effect at the present time or are having an effect until a specified time. The perfect tenses are composed of an AUXILIARY VERB and a main verb's PAST PARTICIPLE (see 8b).

For the **present perfect tense** (see Box 66), use *has* only for the THIRD-PERSON SINGULAR subjects and *have* for all other subjects. For the **past perfect,** use *had* with the past participle. For the **future perfect,** use *will have* with the past participle.

PRESENT PERFECT	Our government **has offered** to help. [having effect now]
PRESENT PERFECT	The drought **has created** terrible hardship. [having effect until a specified time—when the rains come]
PAST PERFECT	As soon as the tornado **had passed,** the heavy rain started. [Both events occurred in the past; the tornado occurred before the rain, so the earlier event uses *had.*]
FUTURE PERFECT	Our chickens' egg production **will have reached** five hundred per day by next year. [The event will occur before a specified time.]

8j How do I form and use progressive forms?

Progressive forms describe an ongoing action or condition. They also express habitual or recurring actions or conditions. The **present progressive** uses the present-tense form of *be* that agrees with the subject in PERSON and NUMBER, plus the PRESENT PARTICIPLE (the *-ing* form) of the main verb. The **past progressive** uses *was* or *were* to agree with the subject in person and number, plus the present participle. The **future progressive** uses *will be* and the present participle. The **present perfect progressive** uses *have been* or *has been* to agree with the subject, plus the present participle. The **past perfect progressive** uses *had been* and the present participle. The **future perfect progressive** uses *will have been* plus the present participle.

PRESENT PROGRESSIVE	The smog **is stinging** everyone's eyes. [event taking place now]
PAST PROGRESSIVE	Eye drops **were selling** well last week. [event ongoing in the past within stated limits]
FUTURE PROGRESSIVE	We **will be ordering** more eye drops than usual this month. [recurring event that will take place in the future]

PRESENT PERFECT PROGRESSIVE	Scientists **have been warning** us about air pollution for years. [recurring event that took place in the past and may still take place]
PAST PERFECT PROGRESSIVE	We **had been ordering** three cases of eye drops a month until the smog worsened. [recurring past event that has now ended]
FUTURE PERFECT PROGRESSIVE	By May, we **will have been selling** eye drops by the barrel for eight months. [ongoing condition to be completed at a specific time in the future]

EXERCISE 8-6

Underline the correct verb in each pair of parentheses. If more than one answer is possible, be prepared to explain the differences in meaning between the choices. For help, consult 8g through 8j.

EXAMPLE   Before 1999, no head of state still holding office (has been charged, <u>had been charged</u>) with war crimes by an international court.

1. In May 1999, Judge Louise Arbour (accused, was accusing) the then president of Yugoslavia of committing crimes against humanity.
2. The crimes with which he was charged (have occurred, occurred) during the conflicts following the breakup of Yugoslavia in the early 1990s.
3. Arbour (was acting, has been acting) in her role as chief prosecutor of the United Nations International Criminal Tribunal for the former Yugoslavia.
4. This court (is known, is being known) also as the Hague Tribunal, after the Dutch city where it (has been, is) based since its establishment.
5. Its mission (is, has been) to prosecute crimes committed by all sides in the former Yugoslavia.
6. The last time such a court (existed, was existing) was after World War II, when the Nuremberg and Tokyo war crimes tribunals (have judged, judged) the defeated side.
7. Until her appointment to the Hague Tribunal in 1996, Arbour (was serving, has been serving) on the Ontario Court of Appeal. Before that, she (has been, had been) a leader of the Canadian Civil Liberties Association and a law professor at York University.
8. Arbour (is, was) a native of Quebec, however, and (is speaking, has spoken) English only since her early twenties.
9. In late 1999, Louise Arbour (has been appointed, was appointed) to the Supreme Court of Canada.
10. Arbour regularly (is taking on, takes on) new challenges; time (will tell, will be telling) how well she handles her 2004 appointment as UN High Commissioner for Human Rights.

8k How do I use tense sequences accurately?

Verb **tense sequences** communicate time relationships. They help deliver messages about actions, occurrences, or states that take place at different times. Box 67 shows how tenses in the same sentence can vary depending on when actions (or occurrences or states) occur.

BOX 67   SUMMARY

Tense sequences

- If your independent clause contains a simple-present-tense verb, then in your dependent clause you can
  - Use PRESENT TENSE to show same-time action:
    I **avoid** shellfish because I **am** allergic to it.
  - Use PAST TENSE to show earlier action:
    I **am** sure that I **deposited** the cheque.
  - Use the PRESENT PERFECT TENSE to show (1) a period of time extending from some point in the past to the present or (2) an indefinite past time:
    They **claim** that they **have visited** the planet Venus.
    I **believe** that I **have seen** that movie before.
  - Use the FUTURE TENSE for action to come:
    The book **is** open because I **will be reading** it later.

- If your independent clause contains a past-tense verb, then in your dependent clause you can
  - Use the past tense to show another completed past action:
    I **closed** the door because you **told** me to.
  - Use the PAST PERFECT TENSE to show earlier action:
    The sprinter **knew** that she **had broken** the record.
  - Use the present tense to state a general truth:
    Christopher Columbus **determined** that the world **is** round.

- If your independent clause contains a present-perfect-tense or past-perfect-tense verb, then in your dependent clause you can
  - Use the past tense:
    The bread **has become** mouldy since I **purchased** it.
    Sugar prices **had** already **declined** when artificial sweeteners first **appeared.**

→

Tense sequences (*continued*)

■ If your independent clause contains a future-tense verb, then in your dependent clause you can

- Use the present tense to show action happening at the same time:

  You **will be** rich if you **win** the prize.

- Use the past tense to show earlier action:

  You **will** surely **win** the prize if you **remembered** to mail the entry form.

- Use the present perfect tense to show future action earlier than the action of the independent-clause verb:

  The river **will flood** again next year unless we **have built** a better dam by then.

■ If your independent clause contains a future-perfect-tense verb, then in your dependent clause you can

- Use either the present tense or the present perfect tense:

  Dr. Chang **will have delivered** five thousand babies by the time she **retires.**

  Dr. Chang **will have delivered** five thousand babies by the time she **has retired.**

 ALERT: Never use a future-tense verb in a dependent clause when the verb in the independent clause is in the future tense. Instead, use a present-tense verb in the independent clause.

> NO   The river **will flood** us unless we **will prepare** our defence.
>
> YES   The river **will flood** us unless we **prepare** our defence.
> [*Prepare* is a present-tense verb.]
>
> YES   The river **will flood** us unless we **have prepared** our defence.
> [*Have prepared* is a present-perfect-tense verb.] ◉

Tense sequences may include INFINITIVES and PARTICIPLES. To name or describe an activity or occurrence coming either at the same time or after the time expressed in the MAIN VERB, use the **present infinitive.**

> I **hope to buy** a used car. [*To buy* comes at a future time. *Hope* is the main verb, and its action is now.]
>
> I **hoped to buy** a used car. [*Hoped* is the main verb, and its action is over.]
>
> I **had hoped to buy** a used car. [*Had hoped* is the main verb, and its action is over.]

The PRESENT PARTICIPLE (a verb's -*ing* form) can describe action happening at the same time.

> **Driving** his new car, the man **smiled.** [The driving and the smiling happened at the same time.]

To describe an action that occurs before the action in the main verb, use the **perfect infinitive** (*to have gone, to have smiled*), the PAST PARTICIPLE, or the **present perfect participle** (*having gone, having smiled*).

> Candida **claimed to have written** fifty short stories in college. [*Claimed* is the main verb, and *to have written* happened first.]
>
> **Pleased** with the short story, Candida **mailed** it to several magazines. [*Mailed* is the main verb, and *pleased* happened first.]
>
> **Having sold** one short story, Candida **invested** in a laptop. [*Invested* is the main verb, and *having sold* happened first.]

EXERCISE 8-7

Underline the correct verb in each pair of parentheses that best suits the sequence of tenses. Be ready to explain your choices. For help, consult 8k.

> EXAMPLE   When he (is, was) seven years old, Yo-Yo Ma, possibly the world's greatest living cellist, (moves, moved) to the United States with his family.

1. Yo-Yo Ma, who (had been born, was born) in France to Chinese parents, (lived, lives) in Boston, Massachusetts, today and (toured, tours) as one of the world's greatest cellists.

2. Years from now, after Mr. Ma has given his last concert, music lovers still (treasure, will treasure) his many fine recordings.

3. Mr. Ma's older sister, Dr. Yeou-Cheng Ma, was nearly the person with the concert career. She had been training to become a concert violinist until her brother's musical genius (began, had begun) to be noticed.

4. Even though Dr. Ma eventually (becomes, became) a physician, she still (had been playing, plays) the violin.

5. The family interest in music (continues, was continuing), for Mr. Ma's children (take, had taken) piano lessons.

6. Although most people today (knew, know) Mr. Ma as a brilliant cellist, he (was making, has made) films as well.

7. One year, while he (had been travelling, was travelling) in the Kalahari Desert, he (films, filmed) dances of southern Africa's Bush people.

8. Mr. Ma first (becomes, became) interested in the Kalahari people when he (had studied, studied) anthropology as an undergraduate at Harvard University.

9. When he shows visitors around Boston now, Mr. Ma has been known to point out the Harvard University library where, he claims, he (fell asleep, was falling asleep) in the stacks when he (had been, was) a student.

10. Indicating another building, Mr. Ma admits that in one of its classrooms he almost (failed, had failed) German.

MOOD

8l What is "mood" in verbs?

Mood in verbs conveys an attitude toward the action in a sentence. English has the *indicative, imperative,* and *subjunctive* moods. Use the **indicative mood** to make statements about real things, about highly likely things, and for questions about fact.

INDICATIVE   The door to the tutoring centre opened. [real]

She seemed to be looking for someone. [highly likely]

Do you want to see a tutor? [question about a fact]

The **imperative mood** expresses commands and direct requests. Often the subject is omitted in an imperative sentence, but nevertheless the subject is implied to be either *you* or one of the indefinite pronouns such as *anybody, somebody,* or *everybody.*

👁 **ALERT:** Use an exclamation point after a strong command; use a period after a mild command or a request (23e, 23a).

IMPERATIVE   Please shut the door.

Watch out! That screw is loose. 👁

The **subjunctive mood** expresses speculation, other unreal conditions, conjectures, wishes, recommendations, indirect requests, and demands. Often, the words that signal the subjunctive mood are *if, as if, as though,* and *unless.* Subjunctive verb forms were once used frequently in spoken English, but they're heard far less today. Nevertheless, in ACADEMIC WRITING, you need to use the subjunctive mood.

SUBJUNCTIVE   If I **were** you, I would ask for a tutor.

8m What are subjunctive forms?

For the **present subjunctive,** always use the SIMPLE FORM of the verb for all PERSONS and NUMBERS.

The prosecutor asks that she **testify** [not *testifies*] again.

It is important that they **be** [not *are*] allowed to testify.

For the **past subjunctive,** use the simple past tense: *I wish that I had a car.* The one exception is for the past subjunctive of *be:* Use *were* for all forms.

> I wish that I **were** [not *was*] leaving on vacation today.
> They asked if she **were** [not *was*] leaving on vacation today.

Using the subjunctive in *if,* as if, as though, *and* unless *clauses*

In dependent clauses introduced by *if* and sometimes by *unless,* the subjunctive expresses speculations or conditions contrary to fact.

> If it **were** [not *was*] to rain, attendance at the race would be disappointing. [speculation]
> The runner looked as if he **were** [not *was*] winded, but he said he wasn't. [a condition contrary to fact]

In an *unless* clause, the subjunctive signals that what the clause says is highly unlikely.

> Unless rain **were** [not *was*] to create floods, the race will be held this Sunday. [Floods are highly unlikely.]

Not every clause introduced by *if, unless, as if,* or *as though* requires the subjunctive. Use the subjunctive only when the dependent clause expresses speculation or a condition contrary to fact.

> **INDICATIVE**   If she **is** going to leave late, I will drive her to the race. [Her leaving late is highly likely.]
>
> **SUBJUNCTIVE**   If she **were** going to leave late, I would drive her to the race. [Her leaving late is a speculation.]

Using the subjunctive in *that clauses*

When *that* clauses express wishes, requests, demands, or recommendations, the subjunctive can convey the message.

> I wish that this race **were** [not *was*] over. [a wish about something happening now]
> He wishes that he **had seen** [not *saw*] the race. [a wish about something that is past]
> The judges are demanding that the doctor **examine** [not *examines*] the runners. [a demand for something to happen in the future]

Also, MODAL AUXILIARY VERBS *would, could, might,* and *should* can convey speculations and conditions contrary to fact.

> If the runner **were** [not *was*] faster, we **would** see a better race. [*Would* is a modal auxiliary verb.]

When an INDEPENDENT CLAUSE expresses a conditional statement using a modal auxiliary verb, be sure that in the DEPENDENT CLAUSE you don't use another modal auxiliary verb.

> **NO**   If I **would have trained** for the race, I **might have** won.
> **YES**   If I **had trained** for the race, I **might have** won.

EXERCISE 8-8

Fill in each blank with the correct form of the verb given in parentheses. For help, consult 8l and 8m.

> **EXAMPLE**   Imagining the possibility of brain transplants requires that we (to be) <u>be</u> open-minded.

(1) If almost any organ other than the brain (to be) _____ the candidate for a swap, we would probably give our consent. (2) If the brain (to be) _____ to hold whatever impulses form our personalities, few people would want to risk a transplant. (3) Many popular movies have asked that we (to suspend) _____ disbelief and imagine the consequences should a personality actually (to be) _____ transferred to another body. (4) In real life, however, the complexities of a successful brain transplant require that not-yet-developed surgical techniques (to be) _____ used. (5) For example, it would be essential that during the actual transplant each one of the 500 trillion nerve connections within the brain (to continue) _____ to function as though the brain (to be) _____ lying undisturbed in a living human body.

VOICE

 What is "voice" in verbs?

Voice in a verb tells whether a SUBJECT acts or is acted upon. English has two voices, *active* and *passive*. A subject in the **active voice** performs the action.

> Most clams **live** in salt water. [The subject *clams* does the acting: Clams *live*.]
> They **burrow** into the sandy bottoms of shallow waters. [The subject *they* does the acting: They *burrow*.]

A subject in the **passive voice** is acted upon. The person or thing doing the acting often appears in a PHRASE that starts with *by*. Verbs in the passive voice use forms of *be, have,* and *will* as AUXILIARY VERBS with the PAST PARTICIPLE of the MAIN VERB.

Clams **are considered** a delicacy by many people. [The subject *clams* is acted upon *by many people.*]

Some types of clams **are** highly **valued** by seashell collectors. [The subject *types* is acted upon *by seashell collectors.*]

8o How do I write in the active, not passive, voice?

Because the ACTIVE VOICE emphasizes the doer of an action, active constructions are direct and dramatic. They usually require fewer words than passive constructions, which makes for greater conciseness (see 16c). Most sentences in the PASSIVE VOICE can be converted to active voice.

> PASSIVE African tribal masks are often imitated by Western sculptors.
>
> ACTIVE Western sculptors often imitate African tribal masks.

8p What are proper uses of the passive voice?

Although the active voice is usually best, in special circumstances you need to use the passive voice.

When no one knows who or what did something, or when the doer of an action isn't important, writers use the passive voice.

> The lock **was broken** sometime after four o'clock. [Who broke the lock is unknown.]
>
> In 1899, the year I was born, a peace conference **was held** at The Hague. [The doers of the action—holders of the conference—aren't important.]
>
> —E. B. White, "Unity"

Sometimes the action in the sentence is more important than the doer of the action. For example, if you want to focus on historical discoveries in a narrative, use the passive voice. Conversely, if you want to emphasize the people making the discoveries, use the active voice.

> ACTIVE **Joseph Priestley discovered** oxygen in 1774. [*Joseph Priestley* is the subject.]
>
> PASSIVE **Oxygen was discovered** in 1774 by Joseph Priestley. [*Oxygen* is the subject.]
>
> ACTIVE **The postal clerk sent** the unsigned letter before I could retrieve it from the mailroom. [The emphasis is on the person, *the postal clerk*, rather than the action, *sent*.]
>
> PASSIVE The unsigned letter **was sent** before it **could be retrieved** from the postal clerk. [The emphasis is on the events, *was sent* and *could be retrieved*, not on the doer of the action, the unknown sender and *the postal clerk*.]

In former years, the social sciences and natural sciences preferred the passive voice. Recently, style manuals for these disciplines have been advising writers to use the active voice whenever possible. "Verbs are vigorous, direct communicators," point out the editors of the *Publication Manual of the American Psychological Association.* "Use the active rather than the passive voice."*

EXERCISE 8-9

First, determine which sentences are in the active voice and which the passive voice. Second, rewrite the sentence in the other voice, and then decide which voice better suits the meaning. Be ready to explain your choice. For help, consult 8n through 8p.

> EXAMPLE   In the West African country of Ghana, a few woodcarvers are creating coffins that reflect their occupants' special interests. (*active; change to passive*)
>
> In the West African country of Ghana, *coffins that reflect their occupants' special interests are being created by a few woodcarvers.*

1. A coffin in the shape of a green onion was chosen by a farmer.
2. A hunter's family buried him in a wooden coffin shaped like a leopard.
3. A dead chief was carried through his fishing village by friends and relatives bearing his body in a large pink wooden replica of a fish.
4. The family of a wealthy man who greatly admired cars buried him in a coffin shaped like a Mercedes car.
5. Although a few of these fantasy coffins have been displayed in museums, most of them end up buried in the ground.

*American Psychological Association, *Publication Manual of the American Psychological Association,* 5th ed. (Washington: APA, 2001) 41.

Chapter 9

Pronouns: Case and Reference

PRONOUN CASE

9a What does "case" mean?

Case applies in different ways to PRONOUNS and to NOUNS. For pronouns, case refers to three pronoun forms: the **subjective** (pronoun as a SUBJECT), the **objective** (pronoun as an OBJECT), and the **possessive** (pronouns used in possessive constructions). For nouns, case refers to only one noun form: the possessive. (For help in using apostrophes in the possessive case, see Chapter 27.)

9b What are personal pronouns?

Personal pronouns refer to persons or things. Box 68 shows the case forms of personal pronouns (subjective, objective, and possessive), in both the singular and the plural.

Many of the most difficult questions about pronoun case concern *who/whom* and *whoever/whomever.* For a full discussion of how to choose between them, see 9g.

BOX 68   SUMMARY

Case forms of personal pronouns

	SUBJECTIVE	OBJECTIVE	POSSESSIVE
SINGULAR	I, you, he, she, it	me, you, him, her, it	my/mine, your/yours, his, her/hers, its
PLURAL	we, you, they	us, you, them	our/ours, your/yours, their/theirs

---

9c How do pronouns work in case?

In the subjective case, pronouns function as SUBJECTS.

> **We** were going to get married. [*We* is the subject.]
>
> John and **I** wanted an inexpensive band for our wedding. [*I* is part of the compound subject *John and I*.]
>
> **He and I** found an affordable one-person band. [*He and I* is the compound subject.]

In the objective case, pronouns function as OBJECTS.

> We saw **him** perform in a public park. [*Him* is the direct object.]
>
> We showed **him** our budget. [*Him* is the indirect object.]
>
> He wrote down what we wanted and shook hands with **us.** [*Us* is the object of the preposition *with*.]

In the possessive case, nouns and pronouns usually indicate ownership.

> The **musician's contract** was very fair. [The possessive noun *musician's* implies a type of ownership.]
>
> **His contract** was very fair. [The possessive pronoun *his* implies a type of ownership.]
>
> The **musicians' problems** stem from playing cheap instruments. [The possessive noun *musicians'* implies a type of relationship.]
>
> **Their problems** stem from playing with cheap instruments. [The possessive pronoun *their* implies a type of relationship.]

Sometimes, however, the possessive case indicates not a notion of ownership but rather an abstract relationship.

> The **musician's arrival** was eagerly anticipated.

👁 **ALERT:** Never use an apostrophe in personal pronouns: *ours, yours, its, his, hers, theirs* (27c). 👁

9d Which case is correct when *and* connects pronouns?

When *and* connects pronouns, or nouns and pronouns, the result is a **compound construction.** Compounding has no effect on case. Always use pronouns in the subjective case when they serve as the subjects of a sentence, and use pronouns in the objective case when they serve as objects in a sentence. Never mix cases.

COMPOUND PRONOUN SUBJECT	**He and I** saw the solar eclipse. [*He and I* is a compound subject.]
COMPOUND PRONOUN OBJECT	That eclipse astonished **him and me.** [*Him and me* is a compound object.]

209

When you're unsure of the case of a pronoun, use the "Troyka test for case" in Box 69. In this four-step test, you drop some of the words from your sentence so that you can tell which case sounds correct.

When pronouns are in a PREPOSITIONAL PHRASE, they are always in the objective case. (That is, a pronoun is always the OBJECT of the preposition.) This rule holds whether the pronouns are singular or plural. You can also use the test in Box 69 to check what is correct.

BOX 69 SUMMARY

Troyka test for case

Subjective Case

STEP 1: Write the sentence twice, once using the subjective case, and once using the objective case.

STEP 2: Cross out enough words to isolate the element you are questioning.

~~Janet and~~ **me**

learned about the moon.

~~Janet and~~ **I**

STEP 3: Omit the crossed-out words and read each sentence aloud to determine which one sounds right.

   NO   **Me** learned about the moon. [This doesn't sound right.]

   YES   **I** learned about the moon. [This sounds right, so the subjective case is correct.]

STEP 4: Select the correct version and restore the words you crossed out.

   Janet and I learned about the moon.

Objective Case

STEP 1: Write the sentence twice, once using the subjective case, and once using the objective case.

STEP 2: Cross out enough words to isolate the element you are questioning.

The astronomer taught ~~Janet and~~ **I**

about the moon.

The astronomer taught ~~Janet and~~ **me**

→

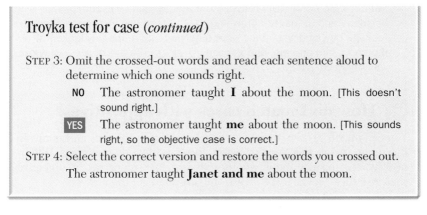

Troyka test for case (*continued*)

STEP 3: Omit the crossed-out words and read each sentence aloud to determine which one sounds right.

NO The astronomer taught **I** about the moon. [This doesn't sound right.]

YES The astronomer taught **me** about the moon. [This sounds right, so the objective case is correct.]

STEP 4: Select the correct version and restore the words you crossed out.

The astronomer taught **Janet and me** about the moon.

NO Ms. Lester gave an assignment **to Sam and I.** [The prepositional phrase, which starts with the preposition *to,* cannot use the subjective-case pronoun *I.*]

YES Ms. Lester gave an assignment **to Sam and me.**

Be especially careful when one or more pronouns follow the preposition *between.*

NO The dispute is **between Thomas and I.** [The prepositional phrase, which starts with the preposition *between,* cannot use the subjective-case pronoun *I.*]

YES The dispute is **between Thomas and me.**

EXERCISE 9-1

Underline the correct pronoun from each pair in parentheses. For help, consult 9c and 9d.

EXAMPLE Mario and (I, me) noticed two young swimmers being pulled out to sea.

(1) The two teenagers caught in the rip current waved and hollered at Mario and (I, me). (2) The harder (they, them) both swam toward shore, the further away the undercurrent pulled them from the beach. (3) The yellow banners had warned Mario and (I, me) that a dangerous rip current ran beneath the water. (4) I yelled at Mario, "Between you and (I, me), (we, us) have to save them!" (5) (He and I, Him and me) both ran and leapt into the crashing waves. (6) As former lifeguards, Mario and (I, me) knew what to do. (7) (We, Us) two remembered the rule for surviving a rip current is to swim across the current. (8) Only when swimmers are safely away from the current should (they, them)

211

swim toward shore. (9) I reached the teenage girl, who cried, "My boyfriend and (I, me) are drowning." (10) Mario rescued the frightened teenage boy, and when they were safely on shore, the boy looked at (he and I, him and me) and gasped, "Thanks. The two of (we, us) know you saved our lives."

9e How do I match cases with appositives?

You can match cases with APPOSITIVES by putting pronouns and nouns in the same case as the word or words the appositive is renaming. Whenever you're unsure about whether to use the subjective or objective case, use the "Troyka test for case" in Box 69 to get the answer.

- **We** (not *Us*) tennis players practise hard. [Here, the subjective-case pronoun *we* renames the noun *tennis players,* which is the subject of this sentence.]
- The winners, **she and I** (not *her and me*), advanced to the finals. [The subjective-case pronouns *she and I* rename the noun *winners,* which is the subject of this sentence.]
- The coach tells **us** (not *we*) tennis players to practise hard. [The objective-case pronoun *us* renames the noun *tennis players,* which is the object in this sentence.]
- The crowd cheered the winners, **her and me** (not *she and I*). [The objective-case pronouns *her and me* rename the noun *winners,* which is the object in this sentence.]

9f How does case work after linking verbs?

A pronoun that comes after a LINKING VERB either renames the SUBJECT or shows possession. In both constructions, always use a pronoun in the subjective case. If you're unsure about how to identify a pronoun's case, use the "Troyka test for case" in Box 69.

- The contest winner was **I** (not *me*). [*Was* is a linking verb. *I* renames the subject, the noun *contest winner,* so the subjective-case pronoun *I* is correct.]
- The prize is **mine.** [*Is* is a linking verb. *Mine* shows possession, so the possessive-case pronoun *mine* is correct.]

EXERCISE 9-2

Underline the correct pronoun of each pair in parentheses. For help, consult 9c through 9f.

EXAMPLE   Dad, because your wedding anniversary is next week, (we, us) sisters decided to get you and Mother a memorable gift.

(1) Anne and (me, I) have given this a great deal of thought, especially in light of the conversations you and Mom have had with us about stress at work. (2) You and Mom have always insisted that (we, us) children save money for special occasions, and Anne asked (me, I) if she and I could use our savings for a weekend getaway for you as the perfect anniversary gift. (3) It is (she and I, she and me) who most worry about how (you and her, you and she) are doing, so Anne and (I, me) think this trip will benefit everyone. (4) In fact, Dad, Mom mentioned to Anne last week how much she'd love for you and (she, her) to spend more time together. (5) It would make Anne and (me, I) feel great to do something nice for you two. (6) So, Dad, you and Mom start packing for a weekend at your favourite bed and breakfast, which you and (her, she) desperately need and deserve. (7) Anne and (I, me) will be waiting when you two come home rested and free of stress.

9g When should I use *who, whoever, whom,* and *whomever*?

The pronouns *who* and *whoever* are in the SUBJECTIVE CASE. The pronouns *whom* and *whomever* are in the OBJECTIVE CASE.

Informal spoken English tends to blur distinctions between *who* and *whom,* so with these words some people can't rely entirely on what "sounds right." Whenever you're unsure of whether to use *who* or *whoever* or to use *whom* or *whomever,* apply a variation of the "Troyka test for case." If you see *who* or *whoever,* test by temporarily substituting *he, she,* or *they.* If you see *whom* or *whomever,* test by temporarily substituting *him, her,* or *them.*

- My father tells the same story to **whoever/whomever** is willing to listen.
- **She/~~Her~~** is willing to listen. [By substituting the subjective-case *she* and the objective-case *her* for *whoever/whomever,* you see that *she* is correct. Therefore, the subjective-case *whoever* is correct.]
- My father tells the same story to **whoever** is willing to listen.

The most reliable variation of the test for *who, whom, whoever, whomever* calls for you to add a word before the substituted word set. In this example, the word *if* is added:

- I wondered **who/whom** would vote for Ms. Wallace.
- I wondered ***if* he/~~*if* him~~** would vote for Ms. Wallace. [The subjective case *who* is correct because the sentence works only when you substitute *if he* for *who/whom.*]
- I wondered **who** would vote for Ms. Wallace.

Another variation of the test for *who, whom, whoever, whomever* calls for you to invert the word order in the test sentence.

- Babies **who/whom** mothers cuddle grow faster and feel happier.
- Mothers cuddle ~~they/them~~. [When substituting, stop at *they/them*. By inverting the word order in the sentence—using *mothers* as the subject—and substituting *they/them* for *who/whom,* you see that *them* is correct. Therefore, the objective case *whom* is correct.]
- Babies **whom** mothers cuddle grow faster and feel happier.

At the beginning or end of a question, use *who* if the question is about the subject and *whom* if the question is about the object. To determine which case to use, recast the question into a statement, substituting *he* or *him* (or *she* or *her*).

- **Who** watched the space shuttle liftoff? [*He* (not *Him*) *watched the space shuttle liftoff* uses the subjective case, so w*ho* is correct.]
- Ted admires **whom?** [*Ted admires him* (not *he*) uses the objective case, so *whom* is correct.]
- **Whom** does Ted admire? [*Ted admires him* (not *he*) uses the objective case, so *whom* is correct.]
- To **whom** does Ted speak about becoming an astronaut? [*Ted speaks to them* (not *they*) uses the objective case, so *whom* is correct.]

EXERCISE 9-3

Underline the correct pronoun of each pair in parentheses. For help, consult 9g.

> **EXAMPLE**   Women (<u>who</u>, whom) both hold jobs outside the home and are mothers work a "double shift."

(1) Women (who, whom) raise a family do as much work at home as at their jobs. (2) In North American society, it is still women (who, whom) cook dinner, clean the house, check the children's homework, read to them, and put them to bed. (3) Nevertheless, self-esteem runs high, some researchers have found, in many women on (who, whom) a family depends for both wage earning and child rearing. (4) Compared with women (who, whom) pursue careers but have no children, those (who, whom) handle a double shift experience less anxiety and depression, according to the research. (5) Perhaps the reason for this finding is that those for (who, whom) the extra paycheque helps pay the bills feel pride and accomplishment when they rise to the challenge. (6) However, other studies note that women (who, whom) have both jobs and children experience tremendous stress. (7) Those (who, whom) feel unable both to support and to nurture their children despite their maximum efforts are the women for (who, whom) the dual responsibility is an almost unbearable burden.

9h What pronoun case comes after *than* or *as*?

When *than* or *as* is used in a comparison, the sentence sometimes omits the words that complete the comparison. For example, *My two-month-old Saint Bernard is larger **than** most full-grown dogs [are]* doesn't need the final word *are*.

When a pronoun follows *than* or *as*, the meaning of the sentence depends entirely on whether the pronoun is in the subjective case or the objective case. Here are two sentences that convey two very different messages, depending on whether the subjective case (*I*) or the objective case (*me*) is used.

1. My sister loved that dog more **than I.**
2. My sister loved that dog more **than me.**

In sentence 1, because *I* is in the subjective case, the sentence means *My sister loved that dog more than **I** [loved it].* In sentence 2, because *me* is in the objective case, the sentence means *My sister loved that dog more than [she loved] **me.*** In both situations, you can check whether you're using the correct case by supplying the implied words to see if they make sense.

9i How do pronouns work before infinitives?

Most INFINITIVES consist of the SIMPLE FORMS of verbs that follow *to:* for example, *to laugh, to sing, to jump, to dance.* (A few exceptions occur when the *to* is optional: *My aunt helped the elderly man [to] cross the street;* and when the *to* is awkward: *My aunt watched the elderly man [to] get on the bus.*) For both the SUBJECTS of infinitives and the OBJECTS of infinitives, use the objective case.

> Our tennis coach expects **me *to serve.*** [Because the word *me* is the subject of the infinitive *to serve,* the objective-case pronoun is correct.]
>
> Our tennis coach expects **him *to beat*** me. [Because the word *him* is the subject of the infinitive *to beat,* and *me* is the object of the infinitive, the objective-case pronoun is correct for both.]

9j How do pronouns work with gerunds?

A GERUND is a verb's -*ing* form functioning as a NOUN: *Brisk **walking** is excellent exercise.* When a noun or PRONOUN comes before a gerund, the POSSESSIVE CASE is required: ***His** brisk **walking** built up his stamina.* In contrast, a PRESENT PARTICIPLE, a verb's -*ing* form functioning as a MODIFIER, requires the subjective case for the pronoun: ***He**, **walking** briskly, caught up to me.*

Here are two sentences that convey different messages, depending entirely on whether a possessive comes before the -*ing* word.

1. The detective noticed the **man *staggering.***
2. The detective noticed the **man's *staggering.***

Sentence 1 means that the detective noticed the *man;* sentence 2 means that the detective noticed the *staggering.* The same distinction applies to pronouns: When *the man* is replaced by either *him* or *his,* the meaning is the same as in sentences 1 and 2.

1. The detective noticed **him *staggering.***
2. The detective noticed **his *staggering.***

In conversation, such distinctions are often ignored, but use them in ACADEMIC WRITING.

EXERCISE 9-4

Underline the correct pronoun of each pair in parentheses. For help, consult 9h through 9j.

> **EXAMPLE** The two inventors of the Quebec dish known as poutine say that no one is more surprised than (<u>they</u>, them) at its huge popularity.

> (1) Poutine was invented in 1957 when a truck driver named Eddy Lainesse pulled into Fernand Lachance's roadside diner and asked Lachance to serve (he, him) an order of french fries with melted cheese curds. (2) The diner was located in Quebec's dairy country, which accounts for (its, it) having fresh cheese curds for sale. (3) Although Lachance found (them, their) appearing on a plate with french fries a strange idea, Lainesse was able to persuade (him, he) to give it a try. The new dish was a triumph. (4) Popular demand at Lachance's diner for an even more filling snack soon had (his, him) adding gravy, the way it is served today throughout Quebec. (5) Poutine's success—it is now on the menu of a nationwide hamburger chain and has been seen as far away as Florida—can be traced to (it, its) being a classic fast food: heavy, high in cholesterol, and gooey. (6) As far as Lainesse and Lachance are concerned, no one could be happier than (them, they) that Quebec is now known for this humble dish, even if Quebeckers who value their province's reputation for fine dining are annoyed at (it, its) winning such fame. (7) What explains (their, them) calling their invention "poutine," a slang word meaning a "mess"? (8) When Lainesse first asked for the dish, Lachance was not nearly as sure as (him, he) that it would work, and predicted, "If you do that, you'll get a real *poutine.*"

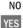 What case should I use for *-self* pronouns?

Two types of pronouns end in *-self:* reflexive pronouns and intensive pronouns.

A **reflexive pronoun** reflects back on the subject. Without a subject, the reflexive pronoun cannot operate correctly.

> The **detective** disguised ***himself.*** [The reflexive pronoun *himself* reflects back on the subject *detective.*]

Never use a reflexive pronoun to replace a personal pronoun in the subjective case.

> **NO**　My teammates and **myself** will vote for a team captain.
>
> **YES**　My teammates and **I** will vote for a team captain.

Also, never use a reflexive pronoun to replace a personal pronoun in the objective case. The only exception is when the object restates the subject.

> **NO**　That decision is up to my teammates and **myself.**
>
> **YES**　That decision is up to my teammates and **me.**

Intensive pronouns, which reflect back in the same way as reflexive pronouns, provide emphasis by making the message of the sentence more intense in meaning.

> The detective felt that **his career *itself*** was at risk. [*Itself* intensifies the idea that the detective's career was at risk.]

PRONOUN REFERENCE

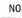 What is pronoun reference?

The word or group of words that a pronoun replaces is called its **antecedent.** In order for your writing to communicate its message clearly, each pronoun must relate precisely to an antecedent.

> I knew a **woman,** lovely in **her** bones / When small **birds** sighed, **she** would sigh back at **them.**
>
> —Theodore Roethke, "I Knew a Woman"

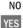 What makes pronoun reference clear?

Pronoun reference is clear when your readers know immediately to whom or what each pronoun refers. Box 70 lists guidelines for using pronouns clearly, and the section in parentheses where each is explained.

BOX 70   SUMMARY

Guidelines for clear pronoun reference

- Place pronouns close to their ANTECEDENTS (9n).
- Make a pronoun refer to a specific antecedent (9n).
- Do not overuse *it* (see 9q).
- Reserve *you* only for DIRECT ADDRESS (9r).
- Use *that*, *which*, and *who* correctly (9s).

9n How can I avoid unclear pronoun reference?

Every pronoun needs to refer to a specific, nearby ANTECEDENT. If the same pronoun in your writing has to refer to more than one antecedent, replace some pronouns with nouns.

> **NO** In 1911, **Roald Amundsen** reached the South Pole just thirty-five days before **Robert F. Scott** arrived. **He** [who? Amundsen or Scott?] had told people that **he** [who? Amundsen or Scott?] was going to sail for the Arctic, but **he** [who? Amundsen or Scott?] was concealing **his** [whose? Amundsen's or Scott's?] plan. Soon, **he** [who? Amundsen or Scott?] turned south for the Antarctic. Meanwhile, on the journey home, **he** [who? Amundsen or Scott?] and **his** [whose? Amundsen's or Scott's?] party froze to death just a few kilometres from safety.

> **YES** In 1911, **Roald Amundsen** reached the South Pole just thirty-five days before **Robert F. Scott** arrived. **Amundsen** had told people that **he** was going to sail for the Arctic, but **he** was concealing **his** plan. Soon, **Amundsen** turned south for the Antarctic. Meanwhile, on **their** journey home, **Scott** and **his party** froze to death just a few kilometres from safety.

👁 **ALERT:** Be careful with the VERBS *said* and *told* in sentences that contain pronoun reference. To maintain clarity, use quotation marks and slightly reword each sentence.

> **NO** **Her** mother told **her she** was going to visit **her** grandmother.
>
> **YES** **Her** mother told **her,** "**You** are going to visit your grandmother."
>
> **YES** **Her** mother told **her,** "**I** am going to visit your grandmother." 👁

Further, if too much material comes between a pronoun and its antecedent, readers can lose track of the meaning.

Alfred Wegener, a German meteorologist and professor of geophysics at the University of Graz in Austria, was the first to suggest that all the continents on earth were originally part of one large landmass. According to this theory, the supercontinent broke up long ago and the fragments drifted apart. ~~He~~ *Wegener* named this supercontinent Pangaea.

[*He* can refer only to Wegener, but material about Wegener's theory intervenes, so using *Wegener* again instead of *he* jogs the reader's memory and makes reading easier.]

When you start a new paragraph, be cautious about beginning it with a pronoun whose antecedent is in a prior paragraph. You're better off repeating the word.

ESL NOTE: Many languages omit a pronoun as a subject because the verb delivers the needed information. English requires the pronoun subject. For example, never omit *it* in the following: *Political science is an important academic subject.* **It** *is studied all over the world.*

EXERCISE 9-5

Revise so that each pronoun refers clearly to its antecedent. Either replace pronouns with nouns or restructure the material to clarify pronoun reference. For help, consult 9n.

EXAMPLE   Pierre Trudeau became prime minister of Canada the year after Expo 67, the world's fair that presented it as youthful, exciting, and self-confident. These were the qualities that he embodied, too.

Here is one acceptable revision: *Pierre Trudeau became prime minister of Canada the year after Expo 67, the world's fair that presented Canada as youthful, exciting, and self-confident. These were the qualities that Trudeau embodied, too.*

Trudeau exploded onto the scene as a sportscar-driving intellectual who—Canadians instantly recognized—was not like other politicians. He fascinated them, so they tolerated things from him that they would never accept from them: his dismissive shrugs, his arrogance, his insults. They were merely politicians; Trudeau was a star. Moreover, he combined them with an engaging playfulness. Most of them were delighted when he did an exaggerated pirouette behind the Queen's back at a royal reception.

Once, Trudeau had said "Just watch me." Journalists knew that Canada's "philosopher-king" was both spectacle and symbol to Canadians. They saw in him an idealized mirror of themselves. Significantly, when he retired, the critic Larry Zolf called the aging leader "our permanent Expo"—as though he were pure image.

Trudeau emerged again in the 1990s to launch his thunderbolts at Canada's new leaders, calling them "weaklings." When his son Michel died in 1998, he appeared frail and aged at his funeral. Then, when he died in late September 2000, Canadians acted much as Americans and British had at the deaths of Kennedy family members and of Princess Diana. They felt Trudeau's death as personally as they had felt their deaths. Mourning became a public spectacle.

Now they must ask themselves if this reaction represents their coming of age or is rather a sign of political immaturity. Perhaps when they say that he somehow touched them personally they are substituting emotions and wishes for political realism. Or perhaps Canadians have finally accepted their own identity and given it a necessary symbolic expression.

9o   How do pronouns work with *it, that, this,* and *which*?

When you use *it, that, this,* and *which,* be sure that your readers can easily understand what each word refers to.

> **NO**   Comets usually fly by the earth at 160 000 km/h, whereas asteroids sometimes collide with the earth. **This** interests scientists. [Does *this* refer to the speed of the comets, to comets flying by the earth, or to asteroids colliding with the earth?]

> **YES**   Comets usually fly by the earth at 160 000 km/h, whereas asteroids sometimes collide with the earth. **This difference** interests scientists. [Adding a noun after *this* or *that* clarifies the meaning.]

> **NO**   I told my friends that I was going to major in geology, **which** made my parents happy. [Does *which* refer to telling your friends or to majoring in geology?]

> **YES**   My parents were happy **because I discussed my major with my friends.**

> **YES**   My parents were happy **because I chose to major in geology.**

Also, the title of any piece of writing stands on its own. Therefore, in your introductory paragraph, never refer to your title with *this* or *that.*

For example, if an essay's title is "Geophysics as a Major," the following holds for the first sentence:

> **NO** **This subject** unites the sciences of physics, biology, and paleontology.
>
> **Geophysics** unites the sciences of physics, biology, and paleontology.

9p How do I use *they* and *it* precisely?

The expression *they say* can't take the place of stating precisely who is doing the saying. Your credibility as a writer depends on your mentioning a source precisely.

> **NO** In Alberta **they say** that Eastern politicians have never understood the West. [*They* doesn't identify who has made the statement.]
>
> **Many Albertans say** that Eastern politicians have never understood the West.

The expressions *it said* and *it is said that* reflect imprecise thinking. Also, they're wordy. Revising such expressions improves your writing.

> **NO** **It said** in the newspaper that ranchers have demanded assistance in exporting their cattle. [*It said in the newspaper that* is awkward and wordy.]
>
> 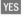 **The newspaper reported** that ranchers have demanded assistance in exporting their cattle.

9q How do I use *it* to suit the situation?

The word *it* has three different uses in English. Here are examples of correct uses of *it*.

1. PERSONAL PRONOUN: Kumar wants to visit the Canadian observatory where a supernova was discovered, but **it** is located in Chile.
2. EXPLETIVE (sometimes called a *subject filler,* it delays the subject): **It** is interesting to observe the stars.
3. IDIOMATIC EXPRESSION (pertaining to weather, time, distance, and environmental conditions): **It** is sunny. **It** is midnight. **It** is not far to the hotel. **It** is very hilly.

All three uses listed above are correct, but avoid combining them in the same sentence. The result can be an unclear and confusing sentence.

NO	Because our car was overheating, **it** came as no surprise that **it** broke down just as **it** began to rain. [*It* is overused here, even though all three uses—2, 1, and 3 above, respectively—are acceptable.]
YES	**It** came as no surprise that our overheating car broke down just as the rain began. [The word order is revised so that *it* is used once.]

⊕ **ESL NOTE:** In some languages, *it* is not used in an expletive. In English, it is. ⊕

NO	Is a lovely day.
YES	**It** is a lovely day.

9r When should I use *you* for direct address?

Reserve *you* for **direct address,** writing that addresses the reader directly. For example, I use *you* in this handbook to address you, the student. *You* is not a suitable substitute for specific words that refer to people, situations, or occurrences.

NO	Prison uprisings often happen **when you allow** overcrowding. [The reader, *you,* did not allow the overcrowding.]
YES	Prison uprisings often happen **when prisons are** overcrowded.
NO	When **you** are crowned Queen of England, **you** automatically become Head of the Commonwealth. [Are *you*, the reader, planning to become Queen of England?]
YES	**Queen Elizabeth, when she was crowned** Queen of England, automatically became Head of the Commonwealth.

EXERCISE 9-6

Revise these sentences so that all pronoun references are clear. If a sentence is correct, circle its number. For help, consult 9q and 9r.

EXAMPLE	By collecting data on animal species around the world, you gain insight into the ways animals communicate.
	By collecting data on animal species around the world, researchers gain insight into the ways animals communicate. [Revision changes person from *you*, used incorrectly, to third person, the noun *researchers*.]

1. Researchers find that animal communication is more complex and more varied than you might expect.
2. Throughout the animal kingdom, they use low-pitched noises to convey aggression and high-pitched noises to convey fear.
3. They say that dogs bark for many reasons: to ask for food, to alert a family to danger, to convey excitement.

4. Elephants send messages to herds five kilometres away using sounds too low for you to hear.

5. In the water, damselfish emit squeaks and dolphins send out clicks and whistles. This interests marine biologists.

6. Elk males have rutting contests to prove which male is stronger, with the one that ruts louder and longer proving his dominance.

7. They do not communicate only by using sounds: lobsters use chemical signals, lizards use head bobs, fireflies use light signals.

8. You can teach chimps to use sign language to communicate in simple sentences, such as "Give JoJo banana."

9s When should I use *that, which,* and *who*?

To use the pronouns *that* and *which* correctly, check the context of the sentence you're writing. *Which* and *that* refer to animals and things. Only sometimes do they refer to anonymous or collective groups of people. Box 71 shows how to choose between *that* and *which*. For information about the role of commas with *that* and *which*, see 24f.

Who refers to people and to animals mentioned by name.

BOX 71   SUMMARY

 ### Choosing between *that* and *which*

Choice: Some instructors and style guides use either *that* or *which* to introduce a RESTRICTIVE CLAUSE (a DEPENDENT CLAUSE that is essential to the meaning of the sentence or part of the sentence). Others may advise you to use only *that* so that your writing distinguishes clearly between restrictive and NONRESTRICTIVE CLAUSES. Whichever style you use, be consistent in each piece of writing:

■ The zoos **that** (or **which**) **most children like** display newborn and baby animals. [The point in this sentence concerns children's preferences. Therefore, the words *most children like* are essential for delivering the meaning and make up a restrictive clause.]

No choice: You are required to use *which* to introduce a nonrestrictive clause (a dependent clause that isn't essential to the meaning of the sentence or part of the sentence).

■ Zoos, **which most children like,** attract more visitors if they display newborn and baby animals. [The point in this sentence concerns attracting more visitors to zoos. Therefore, the words *most children like* are not essential to the meaning of the sentence and make up a nonrestrictive clause.]

John Polanyi, who was awarded the Nobel Prize in chemistry, speaks passionately in favour of nuclear disarmament. [*John Polanyi* is a person.]

Lassie, who was known for her intelligence and courage, was actually played by a series of male collies. [*Lassie* is the name of an animal.]

Many professional writers reserve *which* for nonrestrictive clauses and *that* for restrictive clauses. Other writers use *that* and *which* interchangeably for restrictive clauses. Current practice allows the use of either as long as you're consistent in each piece of writing. However, for ACADEMIC WRITING, your instructor might expect you to maintain the distinction.

👁 **ALERT:** Use commas before and after a nonrestrictive clause. Don't use commas before and after a restrictive clause; see 24k.4. 👁

EXERCISE 9-7

Fill in the blanks with *that, which,* or *who.* For help, consult 9s.

> EXAMPLE   For years, consumers <u>who</u> want the very latest electronic gadgets have had to travel to Japan to buy them.

1. In Japan, consumers can buy a set of tiny clip-on headphones _____ have enough memory for an hour's worth of music.

2. These headphones, _____ are a popular item in Japan, are unlikely to reach foreign markets, because manufacturers don't export them.

3. People from outside Japan _____ crave innovative Japanese products now have an alternative way of buying them _____ is less expensive than travelling to Japan.

4. Web-based businesses, _____ are springing up every day, now specialize in exporting products _____ are trend-setting in Japan.

5. These companies, _____ offer extra advantages such as English-language warranties and manuals, are finding a ready market among English-speaking technophiles.

Chapter 10

Agreement

10a What is agreement?

In everyday speech, agreement indicates that people hold the same ideas. Grammatical **agreement** is also based on sameness. Specifically, you need to match SUBJECTS and VERBS; see 10b through 10n. You also need to match PRONOUNS and ANTECEDENTS; see 10o through 10t.

SUBJECT–VERB AGREEMENT

10b What is subject–verb agreement?

Subject–verb agreement means that a SUBJECT and its VERB match in NUMBER (singular or plural) and PERSON (first, second, or third person). Box 72 presents these major concepts in grammatical agreement.

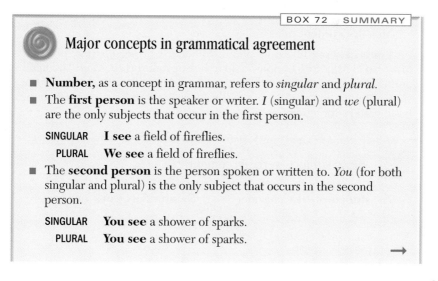

BOX 72   SUMMARY

Major concepts in grammatical agreement

- **Number,** as a concept in grammar, refers to *singular* and *plural.*
- The **first person** is the speaker or writer. *I* (singular) and *we* (plural) are the only subjects that occur in the first person.

SINGULAR	**I see** a field of fireflies.
PLURAL	**We see** a field of fireflies.

- The **second person** is the person spoken or written to. *You* (for both singular and plural) is the only subject that occurs in the second person.

SINGULAR	**You see** a shower of sparks.
PLURAL	**You see** a shower of sparks.

  →

> ## Major concepts in grammatical agreement (*continued*)
>
> ■ The **third person** is the person or thing being spoken or written about. *He, she, it* (singular), and *they* (plural) are the third-person subject forms. Most rules for subject–verb agreement involve the third person.
>
> **SINGULAR**   The **scientist sees** a cloud of cosmic dust.
> **PLURAL**   The **scientists see** a cloud of cosmic dust.

The **firefly glows.** [*Firefly* is a singular subject in the third person; *glows* is a singular verb in the third person.]

Fireflies glow. [*Fireflies* is a plural subject in the third person; *glow* is a plural verb in the third person.]

10c Why is a final *-s* or *-es* in a subject or verb so important?

SUBJECT–VERB AGREEMENT often involves one letter: *s* (or *es* for words that end in *-s*). For verbs in the present tense, you form the SIMPLE FORM of third-person singular by adding *-s* or *-es: laugh, laugh***s;*** *kiss, kiss***es.*** Major exceptions are the verbs *be (is), have (has)* and *do (does);* see 8c.

That **student agrees** that **young teenagers watch** too much television.
Those **young teenagers are** taking valuable time away from studying.
That **student has** a part-time job for ten or twenty hours a week.
Still, that **student does** well in college.

For a subject to become plural, you add *-s* or *-es: lip, lip***s;*** *princess, princess***es.*** Major exceptions include most pronouns (*it, they*) and a few nouns that for singular and plural either don't change (*deer, deer*) or change internally (*mouse, mice*). Box 73 shows you how to visualize the basic pattern for agreement using *-s* or *-es*.

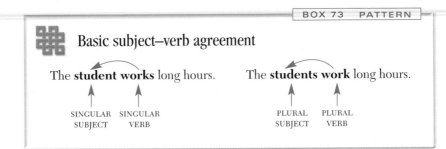

┤ BOX 73   PATTERN ├

Basic subject–verb agreement

The **student works** long hours.   The **students work** long hours.

⬆   ⬆   ⬆   ⬆
SINGULAR   SINGULAR   PLURAL   PLURAL
SUBJECT   VERB   SUBJECT   VERB

Here's a device for remembering how agreement works for most subject–verb agreement. Note that the final -*s* or -*es* can take only one path at a time—to the end of the verb or to the end of the subject.

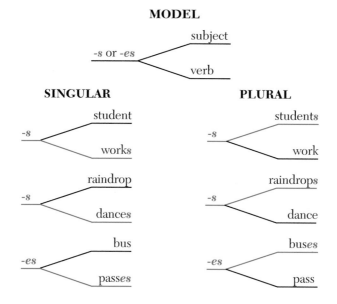

MODEL

ESL NOTE: When you use an AUXILIARY VERB with a main verb, never add -*s* or -*es* to the main verb: *The coach **can walk*** [not *can walks*] *to campus. The coach **does like*** [not *does likes*] *his job.*

EXERCISE 10-1

Use the subject and verb in each set to write two complete sentences—one with a singular subject and one with a plural subject. Keep all verbs in the present tense. For help, consult 10c.

EXAMPLE   climber, increase

Singular subject: Without proper equipment, a mountain *climber increases* the risk of falling.

Plural subject: Without proper equipment, mountain *climbers increase* the risk of falling.

1. dog, bark
2. flower, bloom
3. team, compete
4. planet, rotate
5. author, write
6. tornado, demolish
7. jet, depart
8. professor, might quiz

10d Can I ignore words between a subject and its verb?

For purposes of subject–verb agreement, ignore all words between a subject and its verb. Focus strictly on the subject and its verb. Box 74 shows you this pattern.

NO   **Winners** of the regional contest **goes** to the national finals.
[*Winners* is the subject; the verb must agree with it. Ignore the words *of the regional contest.*]

YES   **Winners** of the regional contest **go** to the national finals.

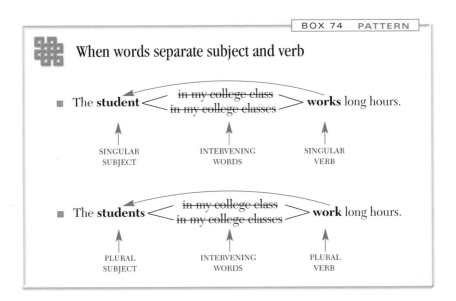

BOX 74   PATTERN

When words separate subject and verb

■ The **student** *in my college class* / *in my college classes* **works** long hours.

SINGULAR SUBJECT   INTERVENING WORDS   SINGULAR VERB

■ The **students** *in my college class* / *in my college classes* **work** long hours.

PLURAL SUBJECT   INTERVENING WORDS   PLURAL VERB

The words *one of the* . . . often require a second look. Use a singular verb to agree with the word *one*. Don't be distracted by the plural noun that comes after *of the*. (For information on the phrase *one of the . . . who,* see 10l.)

NO   **One** of the problems **are** the funds needed for travelling to the national finals.

YES   **One** of the problems **is** the funds needed for travelling to the national finals.

Similarly, eliminate all word groups between the subject and the verb, starting with *including, together with, along with, accompanied by, in addition to, except,* and *as well as.*

NO The **moon,** *as well as* the planet Venus, **are** visible in the night sky. [*Moon* is the subject. The verb must agree with it. Ignore the words *as well as the planet Venus.*]

YES The **moon,** as well as the planet Venus, **is** visible in the night sky.

10e How do verbs work when subjects are connected by *and?*

When two SUBJECTS are connected by *and,* they create a single COMPOUND SUBJECT. A compound subject calls for a plural verb. Box 75 shows you this pattern. (For related material on PRONOUNS and ANTECEDENTS, see 10p.)

The Cascade Diner *and* **the Wayside Diner** *have* [not *has*] fried halibut today. [These are two different diners.]

┌─ BOX 75 PATTERN ─┐

 When subjects are joined by *and*

The student and the instructor work long hours.

COMPOUND SUBJECT (uses *and*)

PLURAL VERB

One exception occurs when *and* joins subjects that refer to a single thing or person.

My friend *and* **neighbour** *makes* [not *make*] excellent chili. [In this sentence, the friend is the same person as the neighbour. If they were two different people, *makes* would become *make.*]

Macaroni *and* **cheese** *contains* [not *contain*] carbohydrates, protein, and many calories. [*Macaroni and cheese* is one dish, not two separate dishes, so it requires a singular verb.]

10f How do verbs work with *each* and *every?*

The words *each* and *every* are singular even if they refer to a compound subject. Therefore, they take a singular verb.

Each **human hand and foot** *makes* [not *make*] a distinctive print.

To identify lawbreakers, ***every*** **police chief, detective, and RCMP officer** *depends* [not *depend*] on such prints.

👁 **ALERT:** Use one word, either *each* or *every,* not both at the same time: **Each** (not *Each and every*) *robber has been caught.* (For more information about pronoun agreement for *each* and *every,* see 10i, 10p, and 10r.) 👁

10g How do verbs work when subjects are connected by *or*?

As Box 76 shows, when SUBJECTS are joined by *or,* or the sets *either . . . or, neither . . . nor, not only . . . but (also),* the verb agrees with the subject closest to it. Ignore everything before the last-mentioned noun or pronoun. The box shows this pattern with *either . . . or.* (For related material on pronouns and antecedents, see 10q.)

~~*Neither* spiders *nor*~~ **flies upset** me.

~~*Not only* spiders *but also* all other~~ **arachnids have** four pairs of legs.

~~A dinner of six clam fritters, four blue crabs, *or* one steamed~~ **lobster sounds** good.

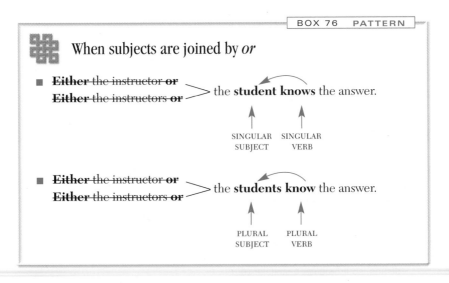

BOX 76   PATTERN

When subjects are joined by *or*

■ **Either** ~~the instructor~~ **or**
Either ~~the instructors~~ **or** ⟩ the **student knows** the answer.

SINGULAR SUBJECT   SINGULAR VERB

■ **Either** ~~the instructor~~ **or**
Either ~~the instructors~~ **or** ⟩ the **students know** the answer.

PLURAL SUBJECT   PLURAL VERB

10h How do verbs work with inverted word order?

In English sentences, the SUBJECT normally comes before its VERB: **Astronomy is** *interesting.* **Inverted word order** reverses the typical pattern by putting the verb first. Most questions use inverted word order: **Is astronomy** *interesting?* In inverted word order, find the subject first and then check whether the verb agrees with it.

Into deep space **shoot** probing **satellites.** [The plural verb *shoot* agrees with the inverted plural subject *satellites*.]

On the television screen **appears** an **image** of Saturn. [The singular verb *appears* agrees with the inverted singular subject *image*.]

👁 **ALERT:** When you start a sentence with *there*, check whether the subject is singular or plural, and then choose the right form of *be* to agree with the subject. If your sentence begins with *it*, always use the singular form of *be* (*is*, *was*) no matter whether the subject is singular or plural.

> **There *are*** nine **planets** in our solar system. [The verb *are* agrees with the subject *planets*.]
>
> **There *is*** probably no **life** on eight of them. [The verb *is* agrees with the subject *life*.]
>
> **It *is*** the life forms on the ninth planet that have been making so much trouble lately. [The verb *is* agrees with *it*, not with *life forms*.] 👁

EXERCISE 10-2

Supply the correct present-tense form of the verb in parentheses. For help, consult 10c through 10h.

> **EXAMPLE** Detectives and teachers (to know) <u>know</u> experienced liars can fool almost anybody, but a new computer can tell who is telling the truth.

1. Police officers and teachers often (to wish) _____ they could "read" people's facial expressions.
2. Trained police officers or a smart teacher (to know) _____ facial tics and nervous mannerisms (to show) _____ someone is lying.
3. However, a truly gifted liar, along with well-coached eyewitnesses, (to reveal) _____ very little through expressions or behaviour.
4. There (to be) _____ forty-six muscle movements in the human face that create all facial expressions.
5. Neuroscientist Terrence Seinowski, accompanied by a team of researchers, (to be) _____ developing a computer program to recognize even slight facial movements made by the most expert liars.

10i How do verbs work with indefinite pronouns?

Indefinite pronouns usually refer to nonspecific persons, things, quantities, or ideas—thus the label "indefinite." As part of a sentence, however, the indefinite pronoun usually takes on a clear meaning.

Most indefinite pronouns are singular and require a singular verb for agreement. Others are always plural, and a few can be singular *or* plural. Box 77 lists indefinite pronouns according to the verb form they require. (For related material on pronouns and antecedents, see 10r.)

BOX 77　SUMMARY

Common indefinite pronouns

Always Plural

both	many

Always Singular

another	every	no one
anybody	everybody	nothing
anyone	everyone	one
anything	everything	somebody
each	neither	someone
either	nobody	something

Singular *or* Plural, Depending on Context

all	more	none
any	most	some

Here are sample sentences:

SINGULAR INDEFINITE PRONOUNS

Everything about that intersection **is** dangerous.

But whenever **anyone says** anything, **nothing is** done.

Each of us **has** [not *have*] to shovel snow; **each is** [not *are*] expected to help.

Every snowstorm of the past two years **has** [not *have*] been severe.

Every one of them **has** [not *have*] caused massive traffic jams.

SINGULAR OR PLURAL INDEFINITE PRONOUNS (DEPENDING ON MEANING)

Some of our streams **are** polluted. [*Some* refers to the plural noun *streams*, so the plural verb *are* is correct.]

Some pollution **is** reversible, but **all** pollution **threatens** the balance of nature. [*Some* and *all* refer to the singular noun *pollution*, so the singular verbs *is* and *threatens* are correct.]

All that environmentalists ask **is** to give nature a chance. [*All* has the meaning here of "everything" or "the only thing," so the singular verb *is* is correct.]

Winter has driven the birds south; **all have** left. [*All* refers to the plural noun *birds,* so the plural verb *have* is correct.]

👁 **ALERTS:** (1) Don't mix singular and plural with *this, that, these,* and *those* used with *kind* and *type. This* and *that* are singular, as are *kind* and *type; these* and *those* are plural, as are *kinds* and *types:* **This** [not These] **kind** of rainwear is waterproof. **These** [not This] **kinds** of sweaters keep me warm. (2) The rules for indefinite pronouns collide with one strategy for avoiding SEXIST LANGUAGE. For suggestions, see 10s and 21g. 👁

10j How do verbs work with collective nouns?

A **collective noun** names a group of people or things: *family, audience, class, number, committee, team, group,* and the like. When the group of people or things is acting as one unit, use a singular verb. When members of the group are acting individually, use a plural verb. As you're writing, be careful not to shift back and forth between a singular and a plural verb for the same noun.

The graduating **class** nervously *awaits* final exams. [The *class* is acting as a single unit, so the verb is singular.]
The graduating **class** *were fitted* for their graduation robes today. [The members (of the class) were fitted as individuals, so the verb is plural.]

👁 **ALERT:** Although British usage allows plural verbs and pronouns with collective nouns and with proper names that act as collective nouns (*the government are considering their options; Sainsbury's are proud to present this award*), this practice is rare in North America and is usually considered wrong (see also 10n). 👁

10k Does a linking verb agree with the subject or the subject complement?

A LINKING VERB, which connects a sentence's SUBJECT to its SUBJECT COMPLEMENT, agrees with the subject. It does not agree with the subject complement.

NO   The worst **part** of owning a car *are* the bills. [The subject is the singular *part,* so the plural verb *are* is wrong. The subject complement is the plural *bills* and doesn't affect agreement.]

> YES   The worst **part** of owning a car *is* the bills. [The singular subject *part* agrees with the singular verb *is*. The subject complement doesn't affect agreement.]

10l   What verbs agree with *who, which, and that*?

If the ANTECEDENT of *who, which,* or *that* is singular, use a singular verb. If the antecedent is plural, use a plural verb.

> The scientist will share the prize with the **researchers *who* work** with her. [*Who* refers to *researchers,* so the plural verb *work* is used.]
>
> George Jones is the **student *who* works** in the science lab. [*Who* refers to *student,* so the singular verb *works* is used.]

If you use phrases including *one of the* or *the only one of the* immediately before *who, which,* or *that* in a sentence, be careful about the verb you use. *Who, which,* or *that* always refers to the plural word immediately following *one of the,* so the verb must be plural. Although *the only one of* is also always followed by a plural word, *who, which,* or *that* must be singular to agree with the singular *one.*

> Tracy is *one of the* students *who* **talk** in class. [*Who* refers to *students,* so the verb *talk* is plural. *Tracy* is pointed out, but the talking is still done by all the students.]
>
> Jim is *the only one of the* students *who* **talks** in class. [*Who* refers to *one,* so the verb *talks* is singular. *Jim* is the single person who is talking.]

EXERCISE 10-3

Supply the correct present-tense form of the verb in parentheses. For help, consult 10i through 10l.

> EXAMPLE   Everybody on a class trip to the coastal waters of the Pacific Ocean (to enjoy) <u>enjoys</u> an opportunity to study dolphins in their natural habitat.

1. A class of students in marine biology (to take) _____ notes individually while watching dolphins feed off the British Columbia coast.
2. Everyone in the class (to listen) _____ as a team of dolphin experts (to explain) _____ some of the mammals' characteristics.
3. A group of dolphins, called a pod, usually (to consist) _____ of 10 000 to 30 000 members.
4. One unique characteristic of dolphins' brains (to be) _____ the sleep patterns that (to keep) _____ one-half of the brain awake at all times.
5. All (to need) _____ to stay awake to breathe or else they would drown.

10m How do verbs work with amounts, fields of study, and other special nouns?

Amounts

SUBJECTS that refer to time, sums of money, distance, or measurement are singular. They take singular verbs.

Two hours *is* not enough time to finish. [time]
Three hundred dollars *is* what we must pay. [sum of money]
Five kilometres *is* a short sprint for some serious joggers. [distance]
Three-quarters of an inch *is* needed for a perfect fit. [measurement]

Fields of study

A field of study is singular in meaning, even though it appears to be plural: *economics, mathematics, physics, statistics.*

***Statistics* is required** of science majors. [*Statistics* is a course of study, so the singular verb *is* is correct.]
***Statistics* show** that a teacher shortage is coming. [*Statistics* isn't used here as a field of study, so the plural verb *show* is correct.]

Special nouns

Athletics, news, ethics, and *measles* are singular despite their plural appearance. Also, names such as *United States of America* and *United Nations* are singular. However, *politics* and *sports* take singular or plural verbs depending on the meaning of the sentence.

The ***news* gets** better each day. [*News* is a singular noun, so the singular verb *gets* is correct.]
***Sports* is** a good way to build physical stamina. [*Sports* is one general activity, so the singular verb *is* is correct.]
Three ***sports* are offered** at the recreation centre. [*Sports* are separate activities, so the plural verb *are offered* is correct.]

Jeans, pants, scissors, clippers, tweezers, eyeglasses, thanks, and *riches* are some of the words that require a plural verb, even though they refer to one thing. However, if you use *pair* with *jeans, pants, scissors, clippers, tweezers,* or *eyeglasses,* use a singular verb for agreement.

Those ***slacks* need** pressing. [plural]
That ***pair*** of slacks **needs** pressing. [singular]

Series and *means* can be singular or plural, according to the meaning you intend.

Two new TV ***series* are** big hits. [*Series* refers to individual items (two different series), so the plural verb *are* is correct.]
A ***series*** of disasters **is** plaguing our production. [*Series* refers to a whole group (the whole series of disasters), so the singular verb *is* is correct.]

235

10n How do verbs work with titles, company names, and words as themselves?

Titles

A title itself refers to one work or entity (even when plural and compound NOUNS are in the title), so a singular verb is correct.

> ***Fugitive Pieces*** by Anne Michaels **is** a prize-winning novel.

Company Names

Many companies have plural words in their names. However, North American usage treats a company as a singular unit requiring a singular verb.

> ***Cohn Brothers* boxes** and **delivers** fine art.

Words as Themselves

Whenever you write about words as themselves to call attention to those words, use a singular verb, even if more than one word is involved.

> ***We* implies** that everyone is included.
> ***Protective reaction strikes* is** a euphemism for *bombing.*

EXERCISE 10-4

Supply the correct present-tense form of the verb in parentheses. For help, consult 10j through 10n.

> **EXAMPLE**   Is it true that shoppers who (to pay) <u>pay</u> attention to marketing science (to walk) <u>walk</u> out of stores wiser, if not richer?

1. Hardly anyone (to doubt) _____ any longer that for years, shoppers have been buying carefully constructed lifestyles, not simply products.
2. Roots (to provide) _____ one of the best examples of applied marketing psychology.
3. A flood of sensations (to hit) _____ customers who (to step) _____ into a Roots clothing store.
4. The key to the marketing strategy (to be) _____ the elements that (to create) _____ the store's environment, including sensuous piles of bulky sweaters and glossy leather goods whose scent fills the store.
5. One of the most prominent elements (to be) _____ the company brand, which has been worn by our Olympic athletes and (to mark) _____ every Roots product as an object of desire.

EXERCISE 10-5

This is an exercise covering all of subject–verb agreement (10b through 10n). Supply the correct form of the verb in parentheses.

> EXAMPLE   Of the thirty thousand plant species on earth, the rose (to be) <u>is</u> the most universally known.

1. Each plant species (to invite) _____ discussion about origins and meanings; when talk turns to flowers, the rose is usually the first mentioned.

2. More fragrant and colourful (to be) _____ other types of flowers, yet roses (to remain) _____ the most popular worldwide.

3. Each of the types of roses (to symbolize) _____ beauty, love, romance, and secrecy.

4. There (to be) _____ over two hundred pure species of roses and thousands of mixed species, thirty-five of which (to flourish) _____ in the soil of North America.

5. It's impossible to determine exactly where or when the first rose (to be) _____ domesticated, because roses have existed for so many centuries; one of the earliest references dates back to 3000 BC.

6. One myth from Greek mythology (to suggest) _____ that the rose first appeared with the birth of the goddess Aphrodite.

7. Another myth, which focuses on the rose's thorns, (to say) _____ that an angry god shot arrows into the stem to curse the rose forever with arrow-shaped thorns.

8. While theories of this kind (to explain) _____ the significance and evolution of the rose, few people can explain the flower's enduring popularity.

9. Even today, a couple (to demonstrate) _____ love by exchanging red roses.

10. Of all flowers, the bestseller (to remain) _____ the rose.

PRONOUN–ANTECEDENT AGREEMENT

10o   What is pronoun–antecedent agreement?

Pronoun–antecedent agreement means that a PRONOUN matches its ANTECEDENT in NUMBER (singular or plural) and PERSON (first, second, or third person). Box 78 shows you how to visualize this pattern of grammatical agreement. You might also want to consult Box 72 in 10b for explanations and examples of the concepts *number* and *person*.

> The **firefly** glows when **it** emerges from **its** nest at night. [The singular pronouns *it* and *its* match their singular antecedent, *firefly*.]
> **Fireflies** glow when **they** emerge from **their** nests at night. [The plural pronouns *they* and *their* match their plural antecedent, *fireflies*.]

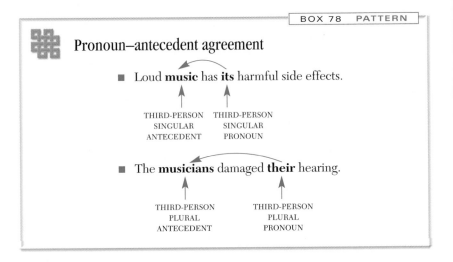

BOX 78   PATTERN

Pronoun–antecedent agreement

■ Loud **music** has **its** harmful side effects.

THIRD-PERSON
SINGULAR
ANTECEDENT

THIRD-PERSON
SINGULAR
PRONOUN

■ The **musicians** damaged **their** hearing.

THIRD-PERSON
PLURAL
ANTECEDENT

THIRD-PERSON
PLURAL
PRONOUN

10p How do pronouns work when *and* connects antecedents?

When *and* connects two or more ANTECEDENTS, they require a plural pronoun. This rule applies even if each separate antecedent is singular. (For related material on subjects and verbs, see 10e.)

> **The Cascade Diner *and* the Wayside Diner** closed for New Year's Eve to give **their** [not *its*] employees the night off. [Two separate diners require a plural pronoun.]

When *and* joins singular nouns that nevertheless refer to a single person or thing, use a singular pronoun.

> **My friend *and* neighbour** makes **his** [not *their*] excellent chili every Saturday. [The friend is the same person as the neighbour, so the singular *his* (or *her*) is correct. If two different people were involved, the correct pronoun would be *their*, and *make* would be the correct verb.]

each, every

The words *each* and *every* are singular, even when they refer to two or more antecedents joined by *and*. The same rule applies when *each* or *every* is used alone (10i). (For related material on subjects and verbs, see 10f.)

> ***Each* human hand *and* foot** leaves **its** [not *their*] distinctive print.

The rule still applies when the construction *one of the* follows *each* or *every*.

> ***Each one of the* robbers** left **his** [not *their*] fingerprints at the scene.

10q How do pronouns work when *or* connects antecedents?

When ANTECEDENTS are joined by *or* or by CORRELATIVE CONJUNCTIONS such as *either . . . or, neither . . . nor,* or *not only . . . but (also),* the antecedents might mix singulars and plurals. For the purposes of agreement, ignore everything before the final antecedent. Box 79 shows you how to visualize this pattern. (For related material on subjects and verbs, see 10g.)

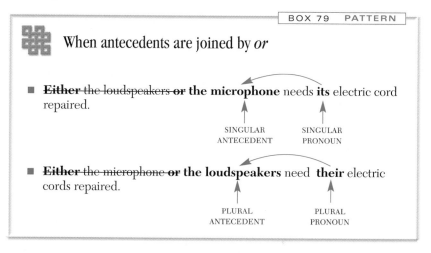

BOX 79   PATTERN

When antecedents are joined by *or*

■ **Either** the loudspeakers **or** the microphone needs **its** electric cord repaired.

SINGULAR ANTECEDENT   SINGULAR PRONOUN

■ **Either** the microphone **or** the loudspeakers need **their** electric cords repaired.

PLURAL ANTECEDENT   PLURAL PRONOUN

After the restaurant closes, **either** the resident mice **or** the owner's **cat** gets **itself** a meal.

After the restaurant closes, **either** the owner's cat **or** the resident **mice** get **themselves** a meal.

10r How do pronouns work when antecedents are indefinite pronouns?

INDEFINITE PRONOUNS usually refer to nonspecific persons, things, quantities, or ideas. In a sentence, context gives an indefinite pronoun a clear meaning, even if the pronoun doesn't have a specific antecedent. Most indefinite pronouns are singular. Two indefinite pronouns, *both* and *many,* are plural. A few can be singular or plural, depending on the meaning of the sentence.

For a list of indefinite pronouns, grouped as singular or plural, see Box 77 in 10i. For more information about avoiding sexist language, especially when using indefinite pronouns, see 10s and 21g. (For related material on subjects and verbs, see 10i.)

239

SINGULAR INDEFINITE PRONOUNS

Everyone taking this course hopes to get **his or her** [not *their*] degree within a year.

Anybody wanting to wear a cap and gown at graduation must have **his or her** [not *their*] measurements taken.

Each of the students handed in **his or her** [not *their*] final term paper.

SINGULAR *OR* PLURAL INDEFINITE PRONOUNS

When winter break arrives for students, **most** leave **their** dormitories for home. [*Most* refers to *students,* so the plural pronoun *their* is correct.]

As for the luggage, **most** is already on **its** way to the airport. [*Most* refers to *luggage,* so the singular pronoun *its* is correct.]

None thinks that **he or she** will miss graduation. [*None* is singular as used in this sentence, so the singular pronoun *he or she* is correct.]

None of the students has paid **his or her** [not *their*] graduation fee yet. [*None* is singular as used in this sentence, so the singular pronoun *his or her* is correct.]

None are so proud as **they** who graduate. [*None* is plural as used in this sentence, so the plural pronoun *they* is correct.]

10s How do I use nonsexist pronouns?

A word is **sexist** when it assigns male or female gender unfairly or inappropriately. Each PRONOUN in English carries one of three genders: male (*he, him, his*); female (*she, her, hers*); or neutral (*you, your, yours, we, our, ours, them, they, their, theirs, it, its*). Usage today favours **nonsexist** terms in all word choices. Use gender-free pronouns whenever possible. In the past, it was conventional to use only masculine pronouns to refer to INDEFINITE PRONOUNS: "*Everyone open his book.*" Today, however, people know that the pronouns *he, his, him,* and *himself* exclude women, who make up over half the population. Box 80 shows three ways to avoid using masculine pronouns when referring to males and females together. For more information on gender-neutral language, see 21g.

BOX 80   SUMMARY

Avoiding the masculine pronoun when referring to males and females together

- **Solution 1:** Use a pair of pronouns—*he or she.* However, avoid using a pair more than once in a sentence or in many sentences in a row. A *he or she* construction acts as a singular pronoun.

  Everyone hopes that **he or she** will win a scholarship.

  A **doctor** usually has time to keep up to date only in **his or her** specialty.

→

> ### Avoiding the masculine pronoun when referring to males and females together (*continued*)
>
> - **Solution 2:** Revise into the plural.
>   **Many students** hope that **they** will win a scholarship.
>   **Most doctors** have time to keep up to date only in **their** specialties.
>
> - **Solution 3:** Recast the sentence.
>   Everyone hopes to win a scholarship.
>   Few specialists have time for general reading.

Questions often arise concerning the use of *he or she* and *his or her.* In general, writers find these gender-free pronoun constructions awkward. To avoid them, many writers make the antecedents plural. This becomes problematic when the subject is best stated as a SINGULAR INDEFINITE PRONOUN (Box 77 in section 10i). In the popular press (such as newspapers and magazines), the use of the plural pronoun *they* or *them* with a singular antecedent has been gaining favour. Indeed, some experts find that the history of English supports this use. In ACADEMIC WRITING, however, it is better for you not to follow the practice of the popular press. Language practice changes, however; what I say here is my best advice as I write this book.

10t How do pronouns work when antecedents are collective nouns?

A COLLECTIVE NOUN names a group of people or things, such as *family, group, audience, class, number, committee,* and *team.* When the group acts as one unit, use a singular pronoun to refer to it. When the members of the group act individually, use a plural pronoun. In the latter case, if the sentence is awkward, substitute a plural noun for the collective noun. (For related material on subjects and verbs, see 10j.)

The **audience** was cheering as **it** stood to applaud the performers. [The audience was acting as one unit, so the singular pronoun *it* is correct.]

The **audience** put on **their** coats and walked out. [The members of the audience were acting as individuals, so all actions become plural; therefore, the plural pronoun *their* is correct.]

The **family** is spending **its** vacation in the Laurentians. [All the family members went to one place together.]

The parallel sentence to the last example above would be *The **family** are spending **their** vacations in the Laurentians, the Rockies, and Rome,* which might mean that each family member is going to a different place. But such a sentence is awkward. Therefore, revise the sentence.

The **family members** are spending **their** vacations in the Laurentians, the Rockies, and Rome. [Substituting a plural noun *family members* for the collective noun *family* sounds more natural.]

EXERCISE 10-6

Underline the correct pronoun in parentheses. For help, consult 10o through 10t.

> **EXAMPLE** Many people wonder what gives certain leaders (his or her, their) spark and magnetic personal appeal.

1. The cluster of personal traits that produces star quality is called *charisma,* a state that bestows special power on (its, their) bearers.

2. Charisma is the quality that allows an individual to empower (himself, herself, himself or herself, themselves) and others.

3. Power and authority alone don't guarantee charisma; (it, they) must be combined with passion and strong purpose.

4. A charismatic leader has the ability to draw other people into (his, her, his or her, their) dream or vision.

5. (He, She, He or she, They) can inspire followers to believe that the leader's goals are the same as (his, her, his or her, their) own.

6. Not all leaders who possess charisma enjoy having this ability to attract and influence (his, his or her, their) followers.

7. Charismatic leaders are often creative, especially in (his, her, his or her, their) capacity for solving problems in original ways.

8. Today, a number of major corporations offer (its, their) employees charisma-training courses to enhance leadership qualities.

9. Usually, it's not the quiet, low-profile manager but rather the charismatic manager with strong leadership qualities who convinces others that (his, her, his or her, their) best interests are served by the course of action (he, she, he or she, they) is/are proposing.

10. Charisma trainers advise would-be leaders to start by bringing order to (his, her, his or her, their) activities; in stressful times, anyone who appears to have some part of (his, her, his or her, their) life under control makes others relax and discharge (his, her, his or her, their) responsibilities better.

Chapter 11

Adjectives and Adverbs

11a What are the differences between adjectives and adverbs?

Both adjectives and adverbs are MODIFIERS—that is, words or groups of words that describe other words. **Adjectives** modify NOUNS and PRONOUNS. **Adverbs** modify VERBS, adjectives, and other adverbs. Box 81 compares adjectives and adverbs in action.

ADJECTIVE   The **brisk** *wind* blew. [Adjective *brisk* modifies noun *wind*.]

ADVERB   The wind *blew* **briskly.** [Adverb *briskly* modifies verb *blew*.]

BOX 81   SUMMARY

Differences between adjectives and adverbs

WHAT ADJECTIVES MODIFY	EXAMPLES
nouns	The **busy** *lawyer* took a **quick** *look* at her schedule.
pronouns	*She* felt **triumphant,** for *they* were **attentive.**

WHAT ADVERBS MODIFY	EXAMPLES
verbs	The lawyer *spoke* **quickly** and **well.**
adverbs	The lawyer spoke **very** *quickly*.
adjectives	The lawyer was **extremely** *busy*.
independent clauses	**Therefore,** *the lawyer rested.*

Not all adverbs end in *-ly*. While many adverbs do end in *-ly* (eat *swiftly*, eat *frequently*, eat *hungrily*), some common adverbs do not (eat *fast*, eat *often*, eat *seldom*). To complicate matters further, some adjectives end in *-ly* (*lovely* flower, *friendly* dog). Use meaning, not an *-ly* ending, to identify adverbs.

ESL NOTES: (1) In English, the adjective is always singular, even if its noun is plural: *The **hot*** [not *hots*] *drinks warmed us up.* (2) Word order in English calls for special attention to the placement of adjectives and adverbs. Here is an example using the adverb *carefully: Thomas closed* [don't place *carefully* here] *the window **carefully*** (see 46b and 46c).

EXERCISE 11-1

Underline and label all adjectives (ADJ) and adverbs (ADV). Then, draw an arrow from each adjective and adverb to the word or words it modifies. For help, consult 11a.

1. While shopping for new faucets and drills, today's singles also carefully look for possible mates at discount home improvement stores.
2. Understandably, many people find these stores a healthy alternative to dark bars and blind dates.
3. Recently, an employee in the flooring department quietly confided that the best nights for singles are Wednesdays and Thursdays, while weekends generally attract families.
4. A young single mom returns home excitedly because a quick trip to the lumber department for a new door resulted in a date for Saturday night.
5. A lonely widower in his fifties jokingly says he wishes he had developed earlier an interest in wallpapering and gardening.

11b When should I use adverbs—not adjectives—as modifiers?

Adverbs MODIFY verbs, adjectives, and other adverbs. Don't use adjectives as adverbs.

> **NO** The candidate inspired us **great.** [Adjective *great* cannot modify verb *inspired*.]
>
> **YES** The candidate inspired us **greatly.** [Adverb *greatly* can modify verb *inspired*.]

NO   The candidate felt **unusual** energetic. [Adjective *unusual* cannot modify adjective *energetic*.]

 YES   The candidate felt **unusually** energetic. [Adverb *unusually* can modify adjective *energetic*.]

NO   The candidate spoke **exceptional** forcefully. [Adjective *exceptional* cannot modify adverb *forcefully*.]

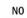 **YES**   The candidate spoke **exceptionally** forcefully. [Adverb *exceptionally* modifies adverb *forcefully*.]

11c   What is wrong with double negatives?

A **double negative** is a nonstandard form. It is a statement with two negative MODIFIERS, the second of which repeats the message of the first. Negative modifiers include *no, never, not, none, nothing, hardly, scarcely,* and *barely.*

NO   The factory workers will **never** vote for **no** strike.

 YES   The factory workers will **never** vote for **a** strike.

NO   The union members did **not** have **no** money in reserve.

YES   The union members did **not** have **any** money in reserve.

YES   The union members had **no** money in reserve.

Take special care to avoid double negatives with contractions of *not: isn't, don't, didn't, haven't,* and the like (27d). The contraction containing *not* serves as the only negative in a sentence.

NO   He **didn't** hear **nothing.**

 YES   He **didn't** hear **anything.**

NO   They **haven't** had **no** meetings.

YES   They **haven't** had **any** meetings.

Similarly, be careful to avoid double negatives when you use *nor.* The word *nor* is correct only after *neither* (7i). Use the word *or* after any other negative.

NO   Stewart **didn't** eat dinner **nor** watch television last night.

 YES   Stewart **didn't** eat dinner **or** watch television last night.

YES   Stewart **neither** ate dinner **nor** watched television last night.

11d Do adjectives or adverbs come after linking verbs?

LINKING VERBS connect a SUBJECT to a COMPLEMENT. Always use an adjective, not an adverb, as the complement.

The *guests looked* **happy.** [Verb *looked* links subject *guests* to adjective *happy.*]

The words *look, feel, smell, taste, sound,* and *grow* are usually linking verbs, but sometimes they're simply verbs. Check how any of these verbs is functioning in a sentence.

Zora *looks* **happy.** [*Looks* functions as a linking verb, so the adjective *happy* is correct.]

Zora *looks* **happily** at the sunset. [*Looks* doesn't function as a linking verb, so the adverb *happily* is correct.]

bad, badly

The words *bad* (adjective) and *badly* (adverb) are particularly prone to misuse with linking verbs.

NO   The students felt **badly.** [This means the students used their fingers badly.]

YES   The student felt **bad.** [This means the student had a bad feeling about something.]

NO   The food smelled **badly.** [This means the food had a bad ability to smell.]

YES   The food smelled **bad.** [This means the food had a bad smell to it.]

good, well

When the word *well* refers to health, it is an adjective; at all other times, *well* is an adverb. The word *good* is always an adjective, but is not used after a linking verb to refer to health.

Evander looks **well.** [This means that Evander seems to be in good health, so the adjective *well* is correct.]

Evander writes **well.** [This means that Evander writes skilfully, so the adverb *well* is correct.]

Use *good* as an adjective, never as an adverb. *Well* is its corresponding adverb.

NO   She sings **good.** [*Sings* isn't a linking verb, so it calls for an adverb, not the adjective *good.*]

YES   She sings **well.** [*Sings* isn't a linking verb, so the adverb *well* is correct.]

EXERCISE 11-2

Underline the correct uses of negatives, adjectives, and adverbs by selecting between the choices in parentheses. For help, consult 11a through 11d.

EXAMPLE Online translation programs are one of the (undoubtedly, <u>undoubted</u>) triumphs of the information age.

(1) From what I have read, computer translation programs were (original, originally) (secretly, secret) developed during the Cold War to translate masses of sensitive documents (quick, quickly) from Russian into English. (2) By the late 1980s, (commercially, commercial) developers began to bring out their products, proving that automatic computer-based translation was (practically, practical) and reliable. (3) I was intrigued to discover that today, (free, freely) available online translation programs work with (nearly, near) twenty languages. (4) Such programs (apparently, apparent) can bring (linguistically, linguistic) competence within reach of any Internet user. (5) This is some of the latest technology from the region where a (high, highly) sophisticated analysis of human language meets advanced software development. (6) I decided that one way to verify just how (well, good) this cutting-edge technology actually is would be to have an online program translate a sentence into French and then back into English. (7) I felt (eager, eagerly) to test my theory, so I (expectantly, expectant) typed the following into the on-screen translation box: "It was raining cats and dogs, so I spent the day cooped up at home." (8) No one (could, could not) have been more shocked than I was to see this result: "It rained of the cats and from the dogs, thus I spent the day locked to the top of the house."

11e What are comparative and superlative forms?

When you state comparisons, ADJECTIVES and ADVERBS often carry the message, communicating degrees of intensity. When a comparison is made between two things, a **comparative** form is used. When a comparison is made about three or more things, a **superlative** form is used.

Regular forms of comparison

Most adjectives and adverbs are regular. They communicate degrees of intensity in one of two ways: either by adding *-er* and *-est* endings or by adding the words *more, most, less,* and *least* (see Box 82).

BOX 82 SUMMARY

Regular forms of comparison for adjectives and adverbs

POSITIVE	Use when nothing is being compared.
COMPARATIVE	Use when two things are being compared. Add the ending *-er* or the word *more* or *less*.
SUPERLATIVE	Use to compare three or more things. Add the ending *-est* or the word *most* or *least*.

POSITIVE [1]	COMPARATIVE [2]	SUPERLATIVE [3+]
green	greener	greenest
happy	happier	happiest
selfish	less selfish	least selfish
beautiful	more beautiful	most beautiful

That tree is **green.**
That tree is **greener** than this tree.
That tree is the **greenest** tree on the block.

The number of syllables in the adjective or adverb usually determines whether to use *-er, -est* or *more, most* and *less, least*.

- **One-syllable words** usually take *-er* and *-est* endings: *large, larger, largest* (adjectives); *far, farther, farthest* (adverbs).
- **Adjectives of two syllables** vary. If the word ends in *-y*, change the *y* to *i* and add *-er, -est* endings: *pretty, prettier, prettiest*. Otherwise, some two-syllable adjectives take *-er, -est* endings: *yellow, yellower, yellowest*. Others take *more, most* and *less, least*: *tangled, more tangled, most tangled; less tangled, least tangled*.
- **Adverbs of two syllables** take *more, most* and *less, least*: *easily, more easily, most easily; less easily, least easily*.
- **Three-syllable words** take *more, most* and *less, least*: *dignified, more/most dignified, less/least dignified* (adjective); *carefully, more/most carefully, less/least carefully* (adverb).

◉ **ALERT:** Be careful not to use a double comparative or double superlative. Use either the *-er* and *-est* endings or *more, most* or *less, least*.

He was **younger** [not *more younger*] than his brother.
Her music was the **loudest** [not *most loudest*] on the stereo.
Children are **more easily** [not *more easier*] influenced than adults. ◉

Irregular forms of comparison

A few comparative and superlative forms are irregular. Box 83 gives you the list. I suggest that you memorize them so they come to mind easily.

BOX 83   SUMMARY

Irregular forms of comparison for adjectives and adverbs

POSITIVE [1]	COMPARATIVE [2]	SUPERLATIVE [3+]
good (*adjective*)	better	best
well (*adjective* and *adverb*)	better	best
bad (*adjective*)	worse	worst
badly (*adverb*)	worse	worst
many	more	most
much	more	most
some	more	most
little*	less	least

The Wallaces saw a **good** movie.
The Wallaces saw a **better** movie than the Pascals did.
The Wallaces saw the **best** movie they had ever seen.
The Changs had **little** trouble finding jobs.
The Changs had **less** trouble finding jobs than the Smiths did.
The Changs had the **least** trouble finding jobs of everyone.

*When you're using *little* for items that can be counted (e.g., pickles), you may use the regular forms *little, littler, littlest.*

👁 **ALERTS:** (1) Be aware of the difference between *less* and *fewer.* They aren't interchangeable. Use *less* with NONCOUNT NOUNS, either items or values: *The sugar substitute has less* **aftertaste.** Use *fewer* with numbers or COUNT NOUNS: *The sugar substitute has fewer* **calories.** (2) Don't use *more, most* or *less, least* with **absolute adjectives,** that is, adjectives that communicate a noncomparable quality or state, such as *unique* or *perfect.* Something either *is,* or *is not,* one of a kind. No degrees of intensity are involved: *This teapot is* **unique** [not the most unique]; *The artisanship is* **perfect** [not the most perfect]. 👁

EXERCISE 11-3

Complete the chart on the next page. Then, write a sentence for each word in the completed chart. For help, consult 11e.

249

EXAMPLE *funny, funnier, funniest:* My brother has a *funny* laugh; he thinks Mom has a *funnier* laugh; the person who has the *funniest* laugh in our family is Uncle Dominic.

POSITIVE	COMPARATIVE	SUPERLATIVE
small	_____	_____
_____	greedier	_____
_____	_____	most complete
gladly	_____	_____
_____	_____	fewest
_____	thicker	_____
some	_____	_____

11f Why avoid a long string of nouns as modifiers?

NOUNS sometimes MODIFY other nouns: *truck driver, train track, security system.* Usually, these terms create no problems. However, avoid using several nouns in a row as modifiers. A string of too many nouns makes it difficult for your reader to figure out which nouns are being modified and which are doing the modifying. You can revise such sentences in several ways.

REWRITE THE SENTENCE

NO I asked my adviser to write **two college recommendation letters** for me.

YES I asked my adviser to write *letters of recommendation to two colleges* for me.

CHANGE ONE NOUN TO A POSSESSIVE AND ANOTHER TO AN ADJECTIVE

NO Advanced students may use the **university psychology lab facilities** for **cognition research projects.**

YES Advanced students may use the *university's* psychology lab facilities for **cognitive** research projects.

CHANGE ONE NOUN TO A PREPOSITIONAL PHRASE

NO Our **student adviser training program** has won many awards.

YES Our *training program for student advisers* has won many awards. [This change requires a change from the singular *adviser* to the plural *advisers.*]

EXERCISE 11-4

Underline the better choice in parentheses. For help, consult this entire chapter.

EXAMPLE   A modern sculpture by Haida artist Bill Reid, done in a style that seems (traditionally, <u>traditional</u>), depicts his people's legend of the creation of mankind.

1. According to the Haida people of the Queen Charlotte Islands, before the (most early, earliest) humans appeared the world was the home of powerful beings.

2. One of these beings was the Raven, a playful bird who created the moon and the stars and did many other important deeds—but seldom out of the desire to do (good, well) at his tasks.

3. (Fewer, Less) of the Raven's creations were the product of his (well, good) intentions than of his sense of mischief.

4. While flying over a (more remote, remote) part of the islands, the Raven saw a clam shell lying on the beach and heard tiny creatures scrambling around inside it.

5. Although none of us (cannot, can) hear it today, the Raven had a beautiful voice, which he could use for magical purposes, in addition to his hoarse cawing sound.

6. The (curious, curiously) Raven used this beautiful voice to coax the creatures out of the shell, and so brought the first naked, helpless humans crawling (fearful, fearfully) into the world.

Chapter 12

Sentence Fragments

12a What is a sentence fragment?

A **sentence fragment** looks like a sentence, but it's actually only part of a sentence. That is, even though a sentence fragment begins with a capital letter and ends with a period (or question mark or exclamation point), it doesn't contain an INDEPENDENT CLAUSE. Fragments are merely unattached PHRASES or DEPENDENT CLAUSES.

FRAGMENT	The telephone with redial capacity. [no verb]
CORRECT	The telephone has redial capacity.
FRAGMENT	Rang loudly for ten minutes. [no subject]
CORRECT	The telephone rang loudly for ten minutes.
FRAGMENT	At midnight. [a phrase without a verb or subject]
CORRECT	The telephone rang at midnight.
FRAGMENT	Because the telephone rang loudly. [dependent clause starting with subordinating conjunction *because*]
CORRECT	Because the telephone rang loudly, the family was awakened in the middle of the night.
FRAGMENT	Which really annoyed me. [dependent clause with relative pronoun *which*]
CORRECT	The telephone call was a wrong number, which really annoyed me.

Sentence fragments can ruin the clarity of your writing. Moreover, in ACADEMIC WRITING and BUSINESS WRITING, sentence fragments imply that you don't know basic sentence structure or that you're a careless proofreader.

NO The lawyer was angry. When she returned from court. She found the key witness waiting in her office. [Was the lawyer angry when she returned from court, or when she found the witness in her office?]

YES The lawyer was angry when she returned from court. She found the key witness waiting in her office.

YES The lawyer was angry. When she returned from court, she found the key witness waiting in her office.

Let's go beyond the grammatical terms to a more practical approach to recognizing SENTENCE FRAGMENTS, so that you avoid them in your writing. (Remember that any words in small capital letters in this handbook are defined, usually with examples, in the Terms Glossary at the back of this book.) To learn to recognize sentence fragments, see 12b; to learn several ways to correct sentence fragments, see 12c and 12d.

Many writers wait until the REVISING and EDITING stages of the WRITING PROCESS to check for sentence fragments. During DRAFTING, the goal is to get ideas down on paper or disk. As you draft, if you suspect that you've written a sentence fragment, simply underline or highlight it in boldface or italics and move on. Later, you can easily find it to check and correct.

12b How can I recognize a sentence fragment?

If you tend to write SENTENCE FRAGMENTS, you want a system for recognizing them. Box 84 shows you a Sentence Test for checking that you haven't written a sentence fragment. Following Box 84, I discuss each question in more detail in 12b.1 through 12b.3.

BOX 84   SUMMARY

Sentence Test to identify sentence fragments

Question 1: Is the word group a dependent clause?

A DEPENDENT CLAUSE is a word group that has a subject and a verb but starts with a subordinating word—either a SUBORDINATING CONJUNCTION or a RELATIVE PRONOUN.

FRAGMENT **When** winter comes early. [starts with *when*, a subordinating conjunction]

CORRECT **When** winter comes early, **ships often rescue the stranded whales.** [adds an independent clause to create a sentence]

→

Sentence Test to identify sentence fragments (*continued*)

FRAGMENT **Which** can happen quickly. [starts with *which,* a relative pronoun]

CORRECT **Whales cannot breathe through the ice and will drown, which** can happen quickly. [adds an independent clause to create a sentence]

Question 2: Is there a verb?

FRAGMENT Thousands of whales in the Arctic Ocean. [Because a verb is missing, it's a phrase, not a sentence.]

CORRECT Thousands of whales **live** in the Arctic Ocean. [adds a verb to create a sentence]

Question 3: Is there a subject?

FRAGMENT Stranded in the Arctic Ocean. [Because a subject is missing, this is a phrase, not a sentence.]

CORRECT **Many whales *were*** stranded in the Arctic Ocean [adds a subject (and the verb *were* to *stranded*) to create a sentence]

12b.1 Question 1: Is the word group a dependent clause?

If you answer yes to question 1, you're looking at a sentence fragment. A DEPENDENT CLAUSE is a word group that has a subject and a verb but starts with a subordinating word—either a SUBORDINATING CONJUNCTION or a RELATIVE PRONOUN. Such a word before an INDEPENDENT CLAUSE creates a dependent clause, which can't stand alone as a sentence and is therefore a sentence fragment. To become a complete sentence, the fragment needs either to be joined to an independent clause or to be rewritten.

Fragments with subordinating conjunctions

A complete list of subordinating conjunctions appears in Box 50 in 7i. Some frequently used ones are *after, although, because, before, if, unless,* and *when.*

FRAGMENT **Because** she returned my books. [*Because,* a subordinating conjunction, creates a dependent clause.]

CORRECT **Because** she returned my books, ***I can study.*** [The independent clause *I can study* is added, following a comma, and the sentence becomes complete.]

FRAGMENT   **Unless** I study. [*Unless,* a subordinating conjunction, creates a dependent clause.]

CORRECT   *I won't pass the test* **unless** I study. [The independent clause *I won't pass the test* is added, and the sentence becomes complete.]

👁 **ALERT:** When a dependent clause starts with a subordinating conjunction and comes before its independent clause, use a comma to separate the clauses (24c). 👁

Fragments with relative pronouns

Relative pronouns are *that, which, who, whom,* and *whose.*

FRAGMENT   **That** we had studied for all week. [*That,* a relative pronoun, creates a dependent clause.]

CORRECT   *We passed the midterm exam* **that** we had studied for all week. [The independent clause *We passed the midterm exam* is added, and the sentence becomes complete.]

When *which, who,* and *whose* begin questions, they function as INTERROGATIVE PRONOUNS, not relative pronouns. Questions are complete sentences, not fragments: *Which* class are you taking? *Who* is your professor? *Whose* book is that?

12b.2 Question 2: Is there a verb?

If you answer no to question 2, you're looking at a sentence fragment. When a VERB is missing from a word group, the result is a PHRASE, not a sentence. You can figure out if a word is a verb by seeing if it can change in TENSE.

Now the telephone **rings.** [present tense]
Yesterday, the telephone **rang.** [past tense]

When you check for verbs, remember that VERBALS are not verbs. Verbals might look like verbs, but they don't function as verbs (see 7e).

FRAGMENT   Yesterday, the students **registering** for classes. [*Registering* is a verbal called a present participle.]

CORRECT   Yesterday, the students **were registering** for classes. [Adding the auxiliary verb *were* to the present participle *registering* creates a verb.]

FRAGMENT   They **informed** that the course was not being offered. [*Informed* is a verbal called a past participle.]

CORRECT   They **had been informed** that the course was not being offered. [Adding the auxiliary verbs *had been* to the past participle *informed* creates a verb.]

FRAGMENT	Now the students **to register** for classes. [*To register* is a verbal called an infinitive.]
CORRECT	Now the students **want to register** for classes. [Adding the verb *want* to the infinitive *to register* creates a verb.]

12b.3 Question 3: Is there a subject?

If you answer no to question 3, you're looking at a sentence fragment. When a SUBJECT is missing from a word group, the result is a PHRASE, not a sentence. To see if a word is a subject, ask, "Who (or What) performs the action?"

FRAGMENT	Studied hard for class. [*Who* studied hard for class? unknown]
CORRECT	The students studied hard for class. [*Who* studied hard for class? *The students* is the answer, so a subject makes the sentence complete.]

FRAGMENT	Contained some difficult questions. [*What* contained some difficult questions? unknown]
CORRECT	The test contained some difficult questions. [*What* contained some difficult questions? *The test* is the answer, so a subject makes the sentence complete.]

Be especially careful with COMPOUND PREDICATES—for example, *We **took** the bus to the movie **and walked** home.* If you were to place a period after *movie,* the second part of the compound predicate would be a sentence fragment. Every sentence needs its own subject. To check for this kind of sentence fragment, ask the question "Who?" or "What?" of each verb.

NO	A few students organized a study group to prepare for midterm exams. **Decided to study together for the rest of the course.** [*Who* decided to study together? The answer is *The students* (who formed the group), but this subject is missing.]
YES	A few students organized a study group to prepare for midterm exams. ***The students* decided to study together for the rest of the course.**

IMPERATIVE SENTENCES—commands and some requests—may appear at first glance to be fragments caused by missing subjects. They're not fragments, however. Imperative sentences are complete sentences because their subjects are implied. An implied subject can be *you, anybody, somebody,* or *everybody,* and other INDEFINITE PRONOUNS.

Run! [This sentence implies the pronoun *you.*]

Return all library books to the front desk. [This sentence implies the indefinite pronoun *everyone.*]

EXERCISE 12-1

Identify each word group as either a complete sentence or a fragment. If the word group is a sentence, circle its number. If it's a fragment, tell why it's incomplete. For help, see Box 84 in 12b and sections 12b.1 through 12b.3.

> **EXAMPLE** Because gold is shiny, flexible, and scarce. [Starts with a subordinating conjunction (*because*) and lacks an independent clause to complete the thought; see Box 84 and section 12c.1]

1. Making gold ideal for a variety of uses.
2. Since gold does not easily tarnish, corrode, or rust.
3. Provides brilliance to coins, jewellery, and artwork.
4. Because gold combines easily with the harder metals copper and silver.
5. Weighs twice as much as the equivalent volume of lead.
6. Ten grams of gold can cover a surface nearly 10 metres square.
7. Or can be pulled into a 65-kilometre-long wire.
8. The melting point of gold is 1060°C.
9. Although tonnes of gold lie under the oceans.
10. The value of gold being less than the cost of mining gold from the ocean floor.

12c What are major ways of correcting fragments?

Once you've identified a SENTENCE FRAGMENT (12b), you're ready to correct it. You can do this in one of two ways: by joining it to an independent clause (12c.1) or by rewriting it (12c.2).

12c.1 Correcting a sentence fragment by joining it to an independent clause

One way to correct a sentence fragment is by joining it to an INDEPENDENT CLAUSE—that is, a complete sentence. The first two examples below deal with dependent-clause fragments; the examples following the ALERT examine fragments with missing subjects and/or verbs.

> **FRAGMENT** **Because** the ice was thick. [Although this word group has a subject (*ice*) and verb (*was*), it starts with the subordinating conjunction *because*.]
>
> **CORRECT** **Because** the ice was thick, ***icebreakers were required to serve as rescue ships.*** [By adding a comma and joining the fragment to the independent clause *icebreakers were required to serve as rescue ships,* a complete sentence is created.]

CORRECT	*Icebreakers were required to serve as rescue ships* **because** the ice was thick. [By joining the fragment to the independent clause *Icebreakers were required to serve as rescue ships,* a complete sentence is created.]
FRAGMENT	**Who** feared the whales would panic. [This fragment starts with the relative pronoun *who.*]
CORRECT	*The noisy motors of the ships worried the crews,* **who** feared the whales would panic. [By joining the fragment to the independent clause *The noisy motors of the ships worried the crews,* a complete sentence is created.]

👁 **ALERT:** Be careful with all words that indicate time, such as *after, before, since,* and *until.* They aren't always subordinating conjunctions. Sometimes they function as ADVERBS—especially if they begin a complete sentence. At other times, they function as PREPOSITIONS. When you see one of these words that indicate time, realize that you aren't necessarily looking at a dependent-clause fragment.

Before, the whales responded to classical music. [This is a complete sentence in which *Before* is an adverb that modifies the independent clause *the whales responded to classical music.*]

Before the whales responded to classical music, some crew members had tried rock and roll music. [If the word group before the comma stood on its own, it would be a sentence fragment because it starts with *Before* functioning as a subordinating conjunction.] 👁

FRAGMENT	**To announce new programs for crime prevention.** [*To announce* starts an infinitive phrase, not a sentence.]
CORRECT	*The mayor called a news conference last week* **to announce** new programs for crime prevention. [The infinitive phrase starting with *to announce* is joined to an independent clause.]
FRAGMENT	**Hoping for strong public support.** [*Hoping* starts a present-participle phrase, not a sentence.]
CORRECT	**Hoping** for strong public support, *she gave examples of problems throughout the city.* [The present-participle phrase starting with *Hoping* is joined to an independent clause.]
FRAGMENT	**Introduced by her assistant.** [*Introduced* starts a past-participle phrase, not a sentence.]
CORRECT	**Introduced** by her assistant, *the mayor began with an opening statement.* [The past-participle phrase starting with *Introduced* is joined to an independent clause.]

258

FRAGMENT   **During the long news conference.** [*During* functions as a preposition—starting a prepositional phrase, not a sentence.]

CORRECT   *Cigarette smoke made the conference room seem airless* **during** the long news conference. [The prepositional phrase starting to *during* is joined to an independent clause.]

FRAGMENT   **A politician with fresh ideas.** [*A politician* starts an appositive phrase, not a sentence.]

CORRECT   *Most people respected the mayor,* **a politician** with fresh ideas. [The appositive phrase starting with *a politician* is joined to an independent clause.]

EXERCISE 12-2

Find and correct any sentence fragments. If a sentence is correct, circle its number. For help, consult 12a through 12c.

EXAMPLE   Many communities prohibit the building of cell-phone transmission towers. Which they consider to be unsightly.

Many communities prohibit the building of cell-phone transmission towers, which they consider to be unsightly.

1. Although telephone companies always need to build more towers to fulfil the increasing demand for cell-phone service.
2. The companies are hard-pressed to find suitable locations, especially in densely populated areas.
3. Because cell-phone use is expanding rapidly. One telecommunications analyst predicts that the number of cell-phone towers will triple over five years.
4. Companies have built the towers inside tall structures such as flagpoles, silos, water towers, and even smokestacks. To disguise the ugly structures.
5. The best hiding places of all are church steeples. Which are often the tallest structures in a community.
6. While the equipment that runs the towers usually fits out of sight in the church basement. The tall antenna is concealed inside the steeple.
7. Strapped for funds. Churches are often eager to rent space to telecommunications companies.
8. In one case, a church whose steeple had burned down was unable to rebuild it without payments provided by a telecommunications company.
9. Even though the steeple is a historic structure that appears on the town's seal.
10. The reconstruction preserved the historic architecture, hid the tower, and even left room for the bats and pigeons. That inhabited the original steeple.

12c.2 Correcting a sentence fragment by rewriting it

A second way to correct a sentence fragment is by rewriting it as an INDEPENDENT CLAUSE—that is, a complete sentence. The first two examples below deal with dependent-clause fragments; the others examine fragments with missing subjects and/or verbs.

FRAGMENT   **Because** the ice was thick. [Although this word group has a subject (*ice*) and verb (*was*), it starts with the subordinating conjunction *because*.]

CORRECT   The ice was thick. [The fragment is rewritten to become a complete sentence.]

FRAGMENT   **Who** feared the whales would panic. [This fragment starts with the relative pronoun *who*.]

CORRECT   *The crew* feared the whales would panic. [The fragment starting with *Who* is rewritten to become a complete sentence.]

FRAGMENT   **To announce** new programs for crime prevention. [*To announce* starts an infinitive phrase, not a sentence.]

CORRECT   *The mayor called a news conference last week because she wanted* to announce new programs for crime prevention. [The infinitive phrase is rewritten to become a complete sentence.]

FRAGMENT   **Hoping** for strong public support. [*Hoping* starts a present-participle phrase, not a sentence.]

CORRECT   *She was* hoping for strong public support. [The present-participle phrase is rewritten to become a complete sentence.]

FRAGMENT   **Introduced** by her assistant. [*Introduced* starts a past-participle phrase, not a sentence.]

CORRECT   **Introduced** by her assistant, *the mayor began with an opening statement.* [The past-participle phrase is rewritten to become a complete sentence.]

FRAGMENT   **During** the long news conference. [*During* functions as a preposition that starts a prepositional phrase, not a sentence.]

CORRECT   *It was hard to breathe* during the long news conference. [The prepositional phrase is rewritten to become a complete sentence.]

FRAGMENT   **A politician** with fresh ideas. [*A politician* starts an appositive phrase, not a sentence.]

CORRECT   *She seemed to be* a politician with fresh ideas. [The appositive phrase is rewritten to become a complete sentence.]

12d How can I fix a fragment that is part of a compound predicate?

A COMPOUND PREDICATE contains two or more VERBS. When the second half of a compound predicate is punctuated as a separate sentence, it becomes a sentence fragment.

FRAGMENT	The reporters asked the mayor many questions about the new program. **And then discussed her answers among themselves.** [*And then discussed* starts a compound predicate fragment, not a sentence.]
CORRECT	The reporters asked the mayor many questions about the new program and then discussed her answers among themselves. [The compound predicate fragment starting with *and then discussed* is joined to the independent clause.]
CORRECT	The reporters asked the mayor many questions about the new program. ***Then the reporters* discussed** her answers among themselves. [The compound predicate fragment starting with *And then discussed* is rewritten as a complete sentence.]

EXERCISE 12-3

Go back to Exercise 12-1 and revise the sentence fragments into complete sentences. In some cases, you may be able to combine two fragments into one complete sentence.

12e What are the two special fragment problems?

Two special fragment problems sometimes involve lists and examples. Lists and examples must be part of a complete sentence, unless they are formatted as a column.

You can correct a list fragment by attaching it to the preceding independent clause using a colon or a dash. You can attach an example fragment to an independent clause (with or without punctuation, depending on the meaning) or rewrite it as a complete sentence.

FRAGMENT	You have a choice of desserts. **Carrot cake, butter tarts, apple pie, or peppermint ice cream.** [The list cannot stand on its own as a sentence.]
CORRECT	You have a choice of desserts: carrot cake, butter tarts, apple pie, or peppermint ice cream. [A colon joins the sentence and the list.]
CORRECT	You have a choice of desserts—carrot cake, butter tarts, apple pie, or peppermint ice cream. [A dash joins the sentence and the list.]

FRAGMENT	Several good places offer brunch. **For example, the Bluenose Inn and Peggy's Retreat.** [Examples can't stand on their own as a sentence.]
CORRECT	Several good places offer brunch—**for example,** the Bluenose Inn and Peggy's Retreat.
CORRECT	Several good places offer brunch. **For example, *there are*** the Bluenose Inn and Peggy's Retreat.

12f How can I recognize intentional fragments?

Professional writers sometimes intentionally use fragments for emphasis and effect.

> But in the main, I feel like a brown bag of miscellany propped against a wall. Pour out the contents, and there is discovered a jumble of small things priceless and worthless. **A first-water diamond, an empty spool, bits of broken glass, lengths of string, a key to a door long since crumbled away, a rusty knife-blade, old shoes saved for a road that never was and never will be, a nail bent under the weight of things too heavy for any nail, a dried flower or two still a little fragrant.**
>
> —Zora Neale Hurston, *How It Feels to Be Colored Me*

The ability to judge the difference between an acceptable and an unacceptable sentence fragment comes from years of reading the work of skilled writers. Most instructors don't accept sentence fragments in student writing until a student demonstrates a consistent ability to write well-constructed, complete sentences. As a rule, avoid sentence fragments in ACADEMIC WRITING.

EXERCISE 12-4

Revise this paragraph to eliminate all sentence fragments. In some cases, you can combine word groups to create complete sentences; in other cases, you may have to supply missing elements to rewrite. Some sentences may not require revision. In your final version, check not only the individual sentences but also the clarity of the whole paragraph. For help, consult 12a through 12f.

EXAMPLE	Mordecai Richler was a novelist and essayist. Who was born in Montreal in 1931.
	Mordecai Richler was a novelist and essayist who was born in Montreal in 1931.

(1) Richler made his reputation with the satirical novel *The Apprenticeship of Duddy Kravitz*. A hard-edged portrait of a young entrepreneur and hustler from Montreal's Jewish quarter. (2) Still, Richler must have

had warm feelings for his old St. Urbain neighbourhood and the remarkable characters who inhabited it. Because mingled with the satire are sympathy and even nostalgia. (3) Unless people can be convinced otherwise. They will continue to believe that there is much of Richler himself in his funny, pathetic, yet engaging anti-heroes. Who try to make their way in an unsympathetic world. (4) The writer was sensitive to this inference. And attached a preface to his second novel expressly to deny it. (5) Even though much of Richler's wit is aimed at people striving to escape their modest backgrounds. Satires like *Solomon Gursky Was Here* have not spared the Canadian elite, whom Richler shows with feet of clay and closets full of embarrassing secrets. (6) These satires may support Richler's contention that as a serious writer, he was obliged to serve a moral purpose. As well as act as the "loser's advocate." (7) In a series of essays, Richler turned his pen against nationalist intellectuals in Quebec. If Richler insisted. That his essay *Oh Canada! Oh Quebec!* with its sad subtitle *Requiem for a Divided Country* was serious political analysis. Why did his publisher catalogue it as "humour"?

EXERCISE 12-5

Revise this paragraph to eliminate all sentence fragments. In some cases, you can combine word groups to create complete sentences; in other cases, you must supply missing elements to revise word groups. Some sentences may not require revision. In your final version, check not only the individual sentences but also the clarity of the whole paragraph. Refer to sections 12a through 12f for help.

(1) Some teenagers and young adults. (2) Are on instant messaging almost every moment that they are using their computers. (3) Which are rarely turned off. (4) According to America Online (AOL), the most popular instant-messaging service. (5) 195 million people use its instant-messaging service. (6) Creating more than 1.6 billion messages per day. (7) Becoming an integral part of the social fabric of our world. (8) Instant messaging has replaced the telephone, and even some e-mail. (9) For millions of young adults. (10) As a result, AOL and its main rivals, Microsoft and Yahoo! (11) Continue to add new features to their instant-messaging services. (12) Such as tiny video images embedded in messages or interface between messaging and cell phones. (13) All these companies acknowledge, however. (14) That instant messaging, while a wildly popular communications tool, does not make money for them. (15) Now provided as a free service. (16) Instant messaging may eventually become a way for these companies to increase their income. (17) Perhaps the companies could sell the software that manages multitudes of instant messages. (18) That are sent within large corporations for the business-related use of their employees.

Chapter 13

Comma Splices and Run-on Sentences

13a What are comma splices and run-on sentences?

Comma splices and run-on sentences are somewhat similar errors: One has a comma by itself between two complete sentences, and one has no punctuation at all between two complete sentences.

A **comma splice,** also called a *comma fault,* occurs when a comma, rather than a period, is used incorrectly between complete sentences. The word *splice* means "to fasten ends together," which is a handy procedure, except when splicing has anything to do with sentences.

A **run-on sentence,** also called a *fused sentence* and a *run-together sentence,* occurs when two complete sentences run into each other without any punctuation. Comma splices and run-on sentences create confusion—readers can't tell where one thought ends and another begins.

COMMA SPLICE	The icebergs broke off from the **glacier, they** drifted into the sea.
RUN-ON SENTENCE	The icebergs broke off from the **glacier they** drifted into the sea.
CORRECT	The icebergs broke off from the **glacier. They** drifted into the sea.

There is one exception. You can use a comma between two independent clauses, but only if the comma is followed by one of the seven coordinating conjunctions: *and, but, for, or, nor, yet, so.* A comma in such a construction is correct; see 24b.

CORRECT	The icebergs broke off from the glacier, **and** they drifted into the sea.

👁 **ALERT:** Occasionally, when your meaning allows it, you can use a colon or a dash to join two independent clauses. 👁

Many writers wait until the REVISING and EDITING stages of the WRITING PROCESS to check for comma splices and/or run-on sentences. During DRAFTING, the goal is to put ideas down on paper or disk. As you draft, if you suspect that you've written a comma splice or a run-on sentence, simply underline or highlight it in boldface or italics, and move on. Later, you can easily find it to check and correct.

13b How can I recognize comma splices and run-on sentences?

When you know how to recognize an INDEPENDENT CLAUSE, you'll know how to recognize COMMA SPLICES and RUN-ON SENTENCES. An independent clause can stand alone as a complete sentence. An independent clause contains a SUBJECT and a PREDICATE. Also, an independent clause doesn't begin with a subordinating word—a SUBORDINATING CONJUNCTION or a RELATIVE PRONOUN.

Interestingly, almost all comma splices and run-on sentences are caused by only four patterns. If you become familiar with these four patterns, listed in Box 85, you'll more easily locate them in your writing.

BOX 85   PATTERN

 Detecting comma splices and run-on sentences

- Watch out for a PRONOUN starting the second independent clause.

    NO   Grey Owl was an author and **conservationist, he** lived in northern Ontario and the Prairies.

    YES   Grey Owl was an author and **conservationist. He** lived in northern Ontario and the Prairies.

- Watch out for a CONJUNCTIVE ADVERB (such as *furthermore, however, similarly, therefore,* and *then*) starting the second independent clause; see Box 48, section 7g, for a complete list.

    NO   He passed himself off as a North American **Indian, however,** he was born Archibald Belaney in England.

    YES   He passed himself off as a North American **Indian. However,** he was born Archibald Belaney in England.

- Watch out for a TRANSITIONAL EXPRESSION (such as *in addition, for example, in contrast, of course,* and *meanwhile*) starting the second independent clause; see Box 24, section 4g.1, for a reference list.

    NO   Grey Owl served as a conservation **officer, in addition,** he lectured and wrote bestselling books.

    YES   Grey Owl served as a conservation **officer; in addition,** he lectured and wrote bestselling books.

    ⟶

265

Detecting comma splices and run-on sentences (*continued*)

■ Watch out for a second independent clause that explains, says more about, contrasts with, or gives an example of what's said in the first independent clause.

NO   Belaney appeared to be expert in First Nations **traditional lore, most of the traditions** he knew he learned from his Iroquois wife and his Ojibway friends.

YES   Belaney appeared to be expert in First Nations **traditional lore. Most of the traditions** he knew he learned from his Iroquois wife and his Ojibway friends.

ALERT: To proofread for comma splices, cover all words on one side of the comma and see if the words remaining form an independent clause. If they do, next cover all the words on the other side of the comma. If the second side of the comma is also an independent clause, you're looking at a comma splice. (This technique doesn't work for run-on sentences because a comma isn't present.)

Experienced writers sometimes use a comma to join very short independent clauses, especially if one independent clause is negative and the other is positive: *Mosquitoes don't **bite, they** stab.* In ACADEMIC WRITING, however, many instructors consider this an error, so you'll be safe if you use a period. (Another option is a semicolon, if the two independent clauses are closely related in meaning: *Mosquitoes don't **bite; they** stab.*)

13c   How can I correct comma splices and run-on sentences?

Once you have identified a COMMA SPLICE or a RUN-ON SENTENCE, you're ready to correct it. You can do this in one of four ways, as shown in Box 86 and discussed further in the sections given in parentheses.

BOX 86   SUMMARY

Ways to correct comma splices and run-on sentences

■ Use a period between the INDEPENDENT CLAUSES (13c.1).
■ Use a semicolon between the independent clauses (13c.2).
■ Use a comma together with a COORDINATING CONJUNCTION (13c.3).
■ Revise one independent clause into a DEPENDENT CLAUSE (13c.4).

13c.1 Using a period to correct comma splices and run-on sentences

You can use a period to separate the independent clauses in comma splices and run-on sentences. For the sake of sentence variety and emphasis (see Chapter 19), however, you want to choose other options as well, such as those shown in 13c.3 and 13c.4. Strings of short sentences rarely establish relationships and levels of importance among ideas.

COMMA SPLICE	A shark is all **cartilage, it** doesn't have a bone in its body.
RUN-ON SENTENCE	A shark is all **cartilage it** doesn't have a bone in its body.
CORRECT	A shark is all **cartilage. It** doesn't have a bone in its body. [A period separates the independent clauses.]
COMMA SPLICE	Sharks can smell blood from 400 metres **away, they** then swim toward the source like a guided missile.
RUN-ON SENTENCE	Sharks can smell blood from 400 metres **away they** then swim toward the source like a guided missile.
CORRECT	Sharks can smell blood from 400 metres **away. They** then swim toward the source like a guided missile. [A period separates the independent clauses.]

13c.2 Using a semicolon to correct comma splices and run-on sentences

You can use a semicolon to separate the independent clauses in comma splices and run-on sentences. Use a semicolon only when the separate sentences are closely related in meaning. For the sake of sentence variety and emphasis, however, you'll want to choose other options, such as those shown in 13c.1, 13c.3, and 13c.4; for correct semicolon use, see Chapter 25.

COMMA SPLICE	The great white shark supposedly eats **humans, research** shows that most white sharks spit them out after the first bite.
RUN-ON SENTENCE	The great white shark supposedly eats **humans research** shows that most white sharks spit them out after the first bite.
CORRECT	The great white shark supposedly eats **humans; research** shows that most white sharks spit them out after the first bite. [A semicolon separates two independent clauses that are close in meaning.]

13c.3 Using a comma together with a coordinating conjunction to correct comma splices and run-on sentences

You can connect independent clauses by inserting a coordinating conjunction (*and, but, for, or, nor, yet, so*) following a comma to correct a comma splice or a run-on sentence.

👁 **ALERT:** Use a comma before a coordinating conjunction that links independent clauses (24b). 👁

When you use a coordinating conjunction, be sure that your choice fits the meaning of the material. *And* signals addition; *but* and *yet* signal contrast; *for* and *so* signal cause; and *or* and *nor* signal alternatives.

COMMA SPLICE	Every living creature gives off a weak electrical charge in the **water, special** pores on a shark's skin can detect these signals.
RUN-ON SENTENCE	Every living creature gives off a weak electrical charge in the **water special** pores on a shark's skin can detect these signals.
CORRECT	Every living creature gives off a weak electrical charge in the **water, *and* special** pores on a shark's skin can detect these signals.

EXERCISE 13-1

Revise the comma splices and run-on sentences by using a period, a semicolon, or a comma and coordinating conjunction. For help, consult 13c.1 through 13c.3.

EXAMPLE	Emily Carr was born in Victoria, British Columbia, in 1871, she died there in 1945.
	Emily Carr was born in Victoria, British Columbia, *in 1871;* *she* died there in 1945.

1. Carr grew up in a disciplined, conventional household in a small and conservative city, however she went off to study art in San Francisco in 1891, after the death of her parents.
2. When she came home two years later, Carr set up a studio of her own, she roamed the beaches and forests of British Columbia sketching Indian totem poles and longhouses in their natural setting.
3. In 1910, Carr began her most important voyage she travelled to France where she developed the vivid postimpressionist style of painting for which she became known.

4. After Carr's return to Canada, her work showed new vigour clearly, her French experience had taught her how to interpret the powerful rhythms of Northwest Coast Indian art and the majesty of the region's mountains and forests.

5. Carr worked in obscurity until she was fifty-seven, she displayed her work that year in a national exhibition and, with the help of Lawren Harris and other members of the Group of Seven, she began to win wider recognition.

13c.4 Revising one independent clause into a dependent clause to correct comma splices and run-on sentences

You can revise a comma splice or run-on sentence by rewriting one of the two independent clauses into a dependent clause. This method is suitable only when one idea can logically be subordinated (17e) to the other. Also, be careful never to end the dependent clause with a semicolon, or, if it precedes the independent clause, with a period. If you do, you've created the error of a SENTENCE FRAGMENT.

Create dependent clauses with subordinating conjunctions

One way to create a dependent clause is to insert a SUBORDINATING CONJUNCTION (such as *because, although, when,* and *if*—see Box 50, section 7i, for a complete list). Always choose a subordinating conjunction that fits the meaning of each particular sentence: *because* and *since* signal cause; *although* signals contrast; *when* signals time; and *if* signals condition. Dependent clauses that begin with a subordinating conjunction are called ADVERB CLAUSES.

COMMA SPLICE	Homer and Langley Collyer had packed their house from top to bottom with **junk, police** could not open the front door to investigate a reported smell.
RUN-ON SENTENCE	Homer and Langley Collyer had packed their house from top to bottom with **junk police** could not open the front door to investigate a reported smell.
CORRECT	**Because** Homer and Langley Collyer had packed their house from top to bottom with **junk, police** could not open the front door to investigate a reported smell. [*Because* starts a dependent clause that is joined by a comma with the independent clause starting with *police*.]

COMMA SPLICE	Old newspapers and car parts filled every room to the **ceiling, enough** space remained for fourteen pianos.
RUN-ON SENTENCE	Old newspapers and car parts filled every room to the **ceiling enough** space remained for fourteen pianos.
CORRECT	**Although** old newspapers and car parts filled every room to the **ceiling, enough** space remained for fourteen pianos. [The subordinating conjunction *although* starts a dependent clause that is joined by a comma with the independent clause starting with *enough*.]

👁 **ALERT:** Place a comma between an introductory dependent clause and the independent clause that follows (24c). 👁

Create dependent clauses with relative pronouns

You can create a dependent ADJECTIVE CLAUSE with a RELATIVE PRONOUN (*who, whom, whose, which, that*).

COMMA SPLICE	The Collyers had been crushed under a pile of **newspapers, the newspapers** had toppled onto the brothers.
RUN-ON SENTENCE	The Collyers had been crushed under a pile of **newspapers the newspapers** had toppled onto the brothers.
CORRECT	The Collyers had been crushed under a pile of **newspapers *that* had toppled** onto the brothers. [The relative pronoun *that* starts a dependent clause and is joined with the independent clause starting with *The Collyers* after deletion of *the newspapers*.]

👁 **ALERT:** Sometimes you need commas to set off an adjective clause from the rest of the sentence. This happens only when the adjective is NONRESTRICTIVE (nonessential), so check carefully (see 24f). 👁

EXERCISE 13-2

Identify and then revise the comma splices and run-on sentences. Circle the numbers of correct sentences. For help, consult 13b through 13c.

(1) Grey Owl's true identity was revealed after his death in 1938, the scandal that arose when his admirers discovered him to be an English writer stemmed from their anger at having been deceived. (2) At that time, few people asked Canadian Indians whether they were scandalized at having their identity taken by a stranger, few people probably cared. (3) Today, however, the concept of "cultural appropriation" provides a way to examine issues like this. (4) Actions like Grey Owl's, even when undertaken with respectful intent, lead to accusations that the minority group is being misrepresented perhaps its identity and culture are being

appropriated—that is, taken over—unjustly. (5) Modern literary criticism is interested in this question it relates to the authenticity and "ownership" of stories and traditions. (6) Many writers commented on the accusation of cultural appropriation, this was brought against Robert Bringhurst in 1999, after he published his poetic retelling of Haida myths in *A Story As Sharp As a Knife*. (7) Questions like this can have one meaning for some minority groups at the same time they can have a very different meaning for members of the comfortable majority.

13d How can I correctly use a conjunctive adverb or other transitional expression between independent clauses?

CONJUNCTIVE ADVERBS and other TRANSITIONAL EXPRESSIONS link ideas between sentences. When these words fall between sentences, a period or semicolon must immediately precede them—and a comma usually immediately follows them.

Conjunctive adverbs include such words as *however, therefore, also, next, then, thus, furthermore,* and *nevertheless* (see Box 48, section 7g, for a complete list). Be careful to remember that conjunctive adverbs are not COORDINATING CONJUNCTIONS (*and, but,* and so on; see 13c.3).

COMMA SPLICE	Buying or leasing a car is a matter of individual preference**, however,** it's wise to consider several points before making a decision.
RUN-ON SENTENCE	Buying or leasing a car is a matter of individual preference **however** it's wise to consider several points before making a decision.
CORRECT	Buying or leasing a car is a matter of individual preference. **However,** it's wise to consider several points before making a decision.
CORRECT	Buying or leasing a car is a matter of individual preference**; however,** it's wise to consider several points before making a decision.

Transitional expressions include *for example, for instance, in addition, in fact, of course,* and *on the one hand/on the other hand* (see Box 24, section 4g.1, for a complete list).

COMMA SPLICE	Car leasing requires a smaller down payment**, for example,** in many cases, you need only $1000 or $2000 and the first monthly payment.
RUN-ON SENTENCE	Car leasing requires a smaller down payment **for example** in many cases, you need only $1000 or $2000 and the first monthly payment.

CORRECT	Car leasing requires a smaller down payment. **For example,** in many cases, you need only $1000 or $2000 and the first monthly payment.
CORRECT	Car leasing requires a smaller down payment**; for example,** in many cases, you need only $1000 or $2000 and the first monthly payment.

👁 **ALERT:** A conjunctive adverb or a transitional expression is usually followed by a comma when it starts a sentence (24c). 👁

EXERCISE 13-3

Consulting all sections in this chapter, revise all comma splices and run-on sentences, using as many different methods of correction as you can. If a sentence is correct, circle its number.

(1) Shortly after midnight on August 21, 1853, the bow of the H.M.S. *Breadalbane* was pierced by a huge shard of ice. (2) The wooden hull's copper sheathing was no protection against a summer storm in Canada's Arctic thus, within fifteen minutes the crew was standing on the pack ice, watching the last of their ship's three masts slip below the surface. (3) The *Breadalbane* was a sturdy Scottish-built merchant ship it had been pressed into service by the Royal Navy to help in the search for the missing Franklin Expedition. (4) Sir John Franklin's two ships and their crews had not returned from their attempt eight years earlier to navigate the Northwest Passage, they were never again seen alive by Europeans.

(5) The twenty-one sailors and officers of the *Breadalbane* were more fortunate they were plucked off the ice by their sister ship, the *Phoenix*. (6) They returned safely to England, however, their ship remained on the ocean floor, almost miraculously preserved by the freezing temperature. (7) Only in 1980 was the wreck located by Dr. Joseph MacInnis he had spent three years searching the southern coast of Beechey Island. (8) The following summer saw MacInnis return to continue studying the most northerly shipwreck ever discovered, it was also the best preserved wooden wreck. (9) MacInnis's team were forced to develop new diving and photographic techniques to use beneath the ice then in 1983 they employed an advanced arctic diving suit and miniature submersible vehicle to complete their exploration. (10) The underwater searchers found a ship that looks almost ready to set sail it still contains the crew's tools and personal effects, and above the deck hangs the signal lamp, forever dark.

Chapter 14

Misplaced and Dangling Modifiers

MISPLACED MODIFIERS

What is a misplaced modifier?

A **modifier** is a word or group of words that describes or limits another word or group of words. A **misplaced modifier** is positioned incorrectly in a sentence, which means, therefore, that it describes the wrong word and changes the writer's meaning. Always place a modifier as close as possible to what it describes.

Avoiding squinting modifiers

A **squinting modifier** is misplaced because it modifies both the word that comes before it and the word that follows it. Check that your modifiers are placed so that they communicate the meaning you intend.

> **NO** The football player being recruited **eagerly** believed each successive offer would be better. [What was *eager*? The recruitment or the player's belief?]
>
> **YES** The football player being recruited believed **eagerly** that each successive offer would be better.
>
> **YES** The football player being **eagerly** recruited believed that each successive offer would be better.

Placing limiting words carefully

Words such as *only, not only, just, not just, almost, hardly, nearly, even, exactly, merely, scarcely,* and *simply* serve to limit the meaning of a word according to where they are placed. When you use such words, position them precisely. Consider how moving the placement of the word *only* changes the meaning of this sentence: *Professional coaches say that high salaries motivate players.*

Only professional coaches say that high salaries motivate players.
[No one else says this.]

Professional coaches **only** say that high salaries motivate players.
[The coaches probably do not mean what they say.]

Professional coaches say **only** that high salaries motivate players.
[The coaches say nothing else.]

Professional coaches say that **only** high salaries motivate players.
[Nothing except high salaries motivates players.]

Professional coaches say that high salaries **only** motivate players.
[High salaries do nothing other than motivate players.]

Professional coaches say that high salaries motivate **only** players.
[High salaries do motivate the players but not the coaches and managers.]

14b How can I avoid split infinitives?

An INFINITIVE is a VERB form that starts with *to: to motivate, to convince, to create* are examples (see 7e). A **split infinitive** occurs when words are placed between the word *to* and its verb. The effect is awkward.

> NO   Orson Welles's radio drama "War of the Worlds" managed ***to, in October 1938, convince*** listeners that they were hearing an invasion by Martians. [*In October 1938* is misplaced because the words come between *to* and *convince.*]

> YES   **In October 1938,** Orson Welles's radio drama "War of the Worlds" managed ***to convince*** listeners that they were hearing an invasion by Martians.

Often, the word that splits an infinitive is an ADVERB ending in *-ly.* In general, place adverbs either before or after the infinitive.

> NO   People feared that they would no longer be able **to *happily* live** in peace.

> YES   People feared that they would no longer be able **to live *happily*** in peace.

The rule about split infinitives has changed recently. Current usage says that when the best placement for a single adverb is between *to* and the verb, use that structure freely.

> Welles wanted **to *realistically* portray** a Martian invasion for the radio audience.

If you want to avoid splitting infinitives in your ACADEMIC WRITING, revise to avoid the split:

> Welles wanted his "Martian invasion" **to sound *realistic*** for the radio audience. [The adverb *realistically* was changed to the adjective *realistic.*]

14c How can I avoid other splits in my sentences?

When too many words split a SUBJECT and its VERB or a verb and its OBJECT, the result is a sentence that lurches rather than flows from beginning to end.

NO The **announcer,** because the script, which Welles himself wrote, called for perfect imitations of emergency announcements, **opened** with a warning that included a description of the "invasion." [The subject *announcer* is placed too far away from the verb *opened,* so this split is too large.]

YES Because the script, which Welles himself wrote, called for perfect imitations of emergency announcements, the **announcer opened** with a warning that included a description of the "invasion." [The subject and verb, *announcer opened,* aren't split.]

NO Many churches **held** for their frightened communities **"end of the world" prayer services.** [The verb *held* is placed too far away from the object *"end of the world" prayer services,* so this split is too large.]

YES Many churches **held "end of the world" prayer services** for their frightened communities. [The verb and object, *held "end of the world" prayer services,* aren't split.]

EXERCISE 14-1

Revise these sentences to correct misplaced modifiers, split infinitives, and other splits. If a sentence is correct, circle its number. For help, consult 14a through 14c.

EXAMPLE When futurologists make predictions, probably, if their guesses turn out to be correct, they are relying on the science of demographics.

When futurologists make predictions, if their guesses turn out to be correct, *they are probably relying* on the science of demographics.

1. Demographics, according to one researcher, David K. Foot, in this field, is capable of explaining "two-thirds of everything."

2. What Foot means is that most of the trends observed, from mortgage rate fluctuations to fast-food sales, in our society, can be traced to the study of human populations, and particularly their age structures.

3. When some futurologists speak of foreseeing changes in the "spirit of the times," these people only are obscuring the science that lies behind thoughtful trend-spotting.

4. Foot writes with amusement of popular authors who claim to with scientific accuracy predict "value shifts."

275

5. Demographers, because they can demonstrate that social values evolve as people's social and economic situations change, insist that social values cannot be treated as independent factors.

6. Young adults tend to move into downtown neighbourhoods or onto university campuses for the first time where they are free from parental control.

7. When this age group explores its new freedom and consumes, limited by the relatively low income at its disposal, the "alternative" products aimed at the youth market, its behaviour appears to express the values of the youth culture.

8. Briefly, this is a description of the ten-million-strong Canadian Baby Boom generation, who were believed to have at one time permanently introduced a shift in values.

9. As young parents in the 1980s and 90s, these same "boomers" invested in suburban houses and minivans, took on mortgages, complained about dirty downtowns and unruly youth, and, while "cocooning" at home, set the tone for the so-called family values movement.

10. Foot observes that in countries that have had no comparable Baby Boom along with its related economic movements, such as Italy, there has been no parallel cycle of cultural trends and "value shifts."

EXERCISE 14-2
Using each list of words and phrases, create all the possible logical sentences. Insert commas as needed. Explain differences in meaning among the alternatives you create. For help, consult 14a through 14c.

EXAMPLE   exchange students
               learned to speak French
               while in Paris
               last summer

A. Last summer, / exchange students / learned to speak French / while in Paris.

B. While in Paris, / exchange students / learned to speak French / last summer.

C. Exchange students / learned to speak French / while in Paris / last summer.

D. Exchange students / learned to speak French / last summer / while in Paris.

1. chicken soup
   according to folklore
   helps
   cure colds

2. tadpoles
   instinctively
   swim
   toward
   their genetic relatives

3. the young driver
   while driving
   in the snow
   skidded
   carelessly

4. climbed
   the limber teenager
   a tall palm tree
   to pick a ripe coconut
   quickly

5. and cause mini-avalanches
   ski patrollers
   set explosives
   often
   to prevent big avalanches

DANGLING MODIFIERS

14d How can I avoid dangling modifiers?

A **dangling modifier** describes or limits a word or words that never actually appear in the sentence. Aware of the intended meaning, the writer unconsciously supplies the missing words, but the reader gets confused. To correct a dangling modifier, state clearly your intended SUBJECT in the sentence.

> **NO** While participating in a revolution in the Caribbean, terrible events overtook the novel's heroine. [The *terrible events* did not participate in the revolution.]
>
> **YES** **While the novel's heroine was participating** in a revolution in the Caribbean, terrible events overtook her.
>
> **YES** While **she** was participating in a revolution in the Caribbean, **the novel's heroine was overtaken** by terrible events.
>
> **NO** Reading Margaret Atwood's novel *Bodily Harm,* the ending was shocking. [The *ending* did not read the novel.]
>
> **YES** Reading Margaret Atwood's novel *Bodily Harm,* **I was shocked** by the ending.
>
> **YES** **I read** Margaret Atwood's novel *Bodily Harm* and was shocked by the ending.

A major cause of dangling modifiers is the unnecessary use of the PASSIVE VOICE. Whenever possible, use the ACTIVE VOICE.

> **NO** **Writing with a grim moral vision, the trap that fate prepares for foolish innocence** is explored by Atwood. [*The trap that fate prepares for foolish innocence* cannot write with a grim moral vision.]
>
> **YES** **Writing with a grim moral vision, Atwood explores** the trap that fate prepares for foolish innocence.

EXERCISE 14-3

Identify and correct any dangling modifiers in these sentences. For help, consult 14d.

EXAMPLE   Showing initiative and originality, the Nobel Peace Prize that was won by Lester Pearson in 1956 rewarded him for creating the first United Nations peacekeeping force.

                Showing initiative and originality, *Lester Pearson won the Nobel Peace Prize in 1956 for creating* the first United Nations peacekeeping force.

1. Stationed in the Sinai Desert, the task given to the first UN peacekeeping force was to observe the ceasefire between the armies of Egypt and Israel.

2. Emissaries of hope, the list of peacekeeping operations where UN troops have since served is a long one, including missions to the Congo, Cyprus, and Bosnia.

3. To accomplish the latest role demanded of them, the intervention in vicious wars against civilians, both physical danger and psychological trauma are risked by peacekeepers.

4. Having increased greatly in danger and complexity the soldiers wearing the UN forces' blue beret are sometimes overwhelmed by their job.

5. Unable to stop the killing with the tiny UN force he was given, the world will not be allowed by General Roméo Dallaire to forget its indifference to the Rwandan genocide of 1994.

14e How can I proofread successfully for misplaced and dangling modifiers?

Sentence errors like MISPLACED MODIFIERS and DANGLING MODIFIERS are hard to spot because of the way the human brain works. Writers know what they mean to say when they write. When they PROOFREAD, therefore, they often misread what they've written for what they intended to write. The mind unconsciously adjusts for the error. In contrast, readers see only what's on the paper or screen. I suggest that you, or someone else while you're listening, read your writing aloud to proofread it for these kinds of problems.

Chapter 15

Shifting and Mixed Sentences

SHIFTING SENTENCES

15a What is a shifting sentence?

A **shift** within a sentence is an unnecessary abrupt change in PERSON, NUMBER, SUBJECT, VOICE, TENSE, MOOD, or DIRECT or INDIRECT DISCOURSE. These shifts blur meaning. Sometimes a shift occurs between two or more sentences in a paragraph. If you set out on one track (writing in FIRST PERSON, for example), your readers expect you to stay on that same track (don't unnecessarily shift to THIRD PERSON, for example). When you go off track, you have written a shifting sentence or paragraph.

15b How can I avoid shifts in person and number?

Who or what performs or receives an action is defined by the term *person*. FIRST PERSON (*I, we*) is the speaker or writer; SECOND PERSON (*you*) is the one being spoken or written *to;* and THIRD PERSON (*he, she, it, they*) is the person or thing being spoken or written *about.*

The essential point is that SHIFTS are incorrect unless the meaning in a particular context makes them necessary.

> **NO**   **I** enjoy reading financial forecasts of the future, but **you** wonder which will turn out to be correct. [The first person *I* shifts to the second person *you*.]

> **YES**   **I** enjoy reading financial forecasts of the future, but **I** wonder which will turn out to be correct.

NUMBER refers to whether words are *singular* (one) or *plural* (more than one) in meaning. Do not start to write in one number and then shift for no reason to the other number.

> **NO**   Because **people** are living longer, **an employee** now retires later. [The plural *people* shifts to the singular *employee*.]

> **YES**   Because **people** are living longer, **employees** now retire later.

279

In ACADEMIC WRITING, reserve *you* for addressing the reader directly. Use the third person for general statements.

> **NO** **I** like my job in customer service because **you** get to solve people's problems. [*I* is in the first person, so a shift to the second person *you* is incorrect.]
>
> **YES** **I** like my job in customer service because **I** get to solve people's problems.

> **NO** **People** enjoy feeling productive, so when a job is unsatisfying, **you** usually become depressed. [*People* is in the third person, so a shift to the second person *you* is incorrect.]
>
> **YES** **People** enjoy feeling productive, so when a job is unsatisfying, **they** usually become depressed.

Be careful with words in the singular (usually NOUNS) used in a general sense, such as *employee, student, consumer, neighbour,* and *someone.* These words are always third-person singular and take the third-person singular pronouns *he, she,* and *it.* Remember that *they* is plural, so the word *they* can't be used with singular nouns.

> **NO** When **an employee** is treated with respect, **they** are more motivated to do a good job. [*Employee* is third-person singular, so the shift to the third-person plural *they* is incorrect.]
>
> **YES** When **an employee** is treated with respect, **he or she** is more motivated to do a good job.
>
> **YES** When **employees** are treated with respect, **they** are more motivated to do a good job.
>
> **YES** **An employee** who is treated with respect is more motivated to do a good job.
>
> **YES** **Employees** who are treated with respect are more motivated to do a good job.

👁 **ALERT:** When you use INDEFINITE PRONOUNS (such as *someone, everyone,* or *anyone*), use GENDER-NEUTRAL LANGUAGE. For advice, see 10s and 21g. 👁

EXERCISE 15-1

Eliminate shifts in person and number between, as well as within, sentences. Some sentences may not need revision. For help, consult 15b.

(1) In Agra, India, millions of visitors to the Taj Mahal see a glorious white-marble building that serves as a tribute to undying love, but you also see pollution and serious deterioration of the property. (2) The tourist arrives in horse-drawn carts or electric cars because they may not travel in vehicles that burn fossil fuel in the vicinity of the monu-

ment. (3) Government officials have closed down polluting factories in the immediate area, but it allows a petrochemical plant owned by people who have political connections to remain open, darkening the air and the monument. (4) Huge crowds arrive daily to see the gorgeous Taj Mahal, which is perfect in its architectural proportions and is accented by beautiful minarets. (5) But he or she also sees terrible neglect, such as huge beehives hanging from archways, litter on the lawns and in the gardens, and canals choked with trash. (6) The whole place smells of pigeon droppings, decorative panels are faded and destroyed, and many sections are off limits to sightseers. (7) However, recently a new corporation has begun managing the monument, and they are starting to make improvements. (8) Soon visitors will enter through a new, clean tourist centre, complete with a cafe and computerized ticketing, and you will find a tour of the cleansed, restored monument to eternal love a very pleasant experience.

15c How can I avoid shifts in subject and voice?

Some SUBJECT shifts are justified by the meaning of a passage: for example, *People look forward to the future, but the future holds many secrets.* Subject shift usually combine awkwardly, however, with shifts in VOICE. The voice of a sentence is either *active* (*People expect changes*) or *passive* (*Changes are expected*).

NO Most **people expect** major improvements in the future, but some **hardships are** also **anticipated.** [The subject shifts from *people* to *hardships,* and the voice shifts from active to passive.]

YES Most **people expect** major improvements in the future, but **they** also **anticipate** some hardships.

YES Most **people expect** major improvements in the future but also **anticipate** some hardships.

15d How can I avoid shifts in tense and mood?

TENSE refers to the time in which the action of a VERB takes place—past, present, or future: *We **will go** to the movies after we **finish** dinner.* An unnecessary tense SHIFT within or between sentences can make the statement confusing or illogical.

NO Canada **gave** its music industry a boost in the 1970s when government regulations **require** AM radio stations to play a minimum of 30 percent Canadian content. [The tense shifts from past to present, even though the action of both verbs occurred in the past.]

YES Canada **gave** its music industry a boost in the 1970s when government regulations **required** AM radio stations to play a minimum of 30 percent Canadian content.

> **NO** Pop music **was** the greatest beneficiary of the new Canadian content regulations. However, the artists rushing into production with their recordings in the 1970s **include** a large number of failures as well as many well-known stars. [The illogical tense shift here occurs between sentences.]
>
> **YES** Pop music **was** the greatest beneficiary of the new Canadian content regulations. However, the artists rushing into production with their recordings in the 1970s **included** a large number of failures as well as many well-known stars.

MOOD indicates whether a sentence is a statement or a question (INDICATIVE MOOD), a command or request (IMPERATIVE MOOD), or a wish or other-than-real statement (SUBJUNCTIVE MOOD). A shift in mood creates an awkward construction and can cause confusion.

> **NO** The government issued a set of rules defining Canadian content: **Include** songs with music or lyrics composed or performed by a Canadian, and production details **are also to be taken** into account. [The verbs shift from the imperative mood to the indicative mood.]
>
> **YES** The government issued a set of rules defining Canadian content: **Include** songs with music or lyrics composed or performed by a Canadian, and also **take** production details into account.
>
> **YES** The government issued a set of rules defining Canadian content: Songs with music or lyrics composed or performed by a Canadian **are included,** and production details **are also to be taken** into account.

15e How can I avoid shifts between indirect and direct discourse?

Indirect discourse is not enclosed in quotation marks because it reports, rather than quotes, something that someone said. In contrast, **direct discourse** is enclosed in quotation marks because it quotes exactly the words that someone said. It's incorrect to write direct discourse and omit the quotation marks. Also, it's incorrect to write sentences that mix indirect and direct discourse. Such SHIFT errors confuse readers who can't tell what was said and what is being merely reported.

> **NO** Some record companies said that the Canadian content rules were too complicated and **these rules are excluding genuine Canadian music.** [*Said that* sets up indirect discourse, but *these rules are excluding genuine Canadian music* is direct discourse, although lacking quotation marks.]
>
> **YES** Some record companies said that the Canadian content rules were too complicated and **that the rules were excluding genuine Canadian music.** [This revision uses indirect discourse consistently.]

YES   Some record companies said that the Canadian content rules were too complicated and claimed, **"These rules are excluding genuine Canadian music."** [This revision distinguishes between indirect and direct discourse.]

Whenever you change your writing from direct discourse to indirect discourse (when you decide to paraphrase rather than quote someone directly, for example), you need to make changes in VERB TENSE and other grammatical features for your writing to make sense. Simply removing the quotation marks is not enough.

NO   He asked **did we buy that CD?** [This version has the verb form needed for direct discourse, but the pronoun *we* is wrong and quotation punctuation is missing.]

YES   He asked **whether we bought that CD.** [This version is entirely indirect discourse, and the verb has changed from *buy* to *bought*.]

YES   He asked, **"Did you buy that CD?"** [This version is direct discourse. It repeats the original speech exactly, with correct quotation punctuation.]

EXERCISE 15-2

Revise these sentences to eliminate incorrect shifts within sentences. Some sentences can be revised in several ways. For help, consult 15b through 15e.

EXAMPLE   Novelists such as Timothy Findley and Rohinton Mistry have won the Governor General's Literary Award, and more recently, translators such as Patricia Claxton and Linda Gaboriau won as well.

Novelists such as Timothy Findley and Rohinton Mistry have won the Governor General's Literary Award, and more recently, translators such as Patricia Claxton and Linda Gaboriau *have won* as well.

1. Although some winners of the Governor General's Award have sunk into obscurity, fame has been won beyond Canada's borders by many others.
2. Examine the list of winners for proof of the award's prestige, and one can take a look at the stories surrounding the award for a glimpse at Canada's literary scene.
3. Leonard Cohen sparked a controversial episode when he announced that he was refusing the award for his *Selected Poems, 1956–1968*, explaining that much in me strives for this honour, but the poems themselves forbid it absolutely.
4. About the same time, a less enigmatic explanation for refusing the award was given by several nationalistic Quebec writers who announced they were rejecting them for political reasons.

5. However, in 1992 Cohen said that he will accept the newly instituted Governor General's Performing Arts Award, so apparently his songs, unlike his poems, did permit that honour.

EXERCISE 15-3

Revise this paragraph to eliminate incorrect shifts between sentences and within sentences. For help, consult 15b through 15e.

(1) According to sociologists, people experience role conflict when we find ourselves trying to juggle too many different social roles. (2) When people reach overload, he or she decided, "to cut back somewhere." (3) For example, a well-known politician might decide not to run for re-election because family life would be interfered with by the demands of the campaign. (4) In other cases, you may delay having children so they can achieve early career success. (5) A person might say to themselves that I can't do this right now and focus instead on career goals. (6) In yet another example, a plant manager might enjoy social interaction with employees but consequently find themselves unable to evaluate him or her objectively. (7) In short, sociologists find that although not all role conflicts cause problems, great hardships are suffered by some individuals faced with handling difficult balancing acts. (8) People can minimize role conflicts, however, if we learn to compartmentalize our lives. (9) A good example of this is people saying that I'm going to stop thinking about my job before I head home to my family.

MIXED SENTENCES

15f   What is a mixed sentence?

A mixed sentence has two or more parts, with the first part starting in one direction and the rest of the parts going off in another. This mixing of sentence parts leads to unclear meaning. To avoid this error, as you write each sentence, remember how you started it and make sure that whatever comes next in the sentence relates grammatically and logically to that beginning.

> NO   Because our side lost the contest eventually motivated us to do better. [*Because our side lost the contest* starts the sentence in one direction, but *eventually motivated us to do better* goes off in another direction.]

> YES   Because our side lost the contest, **we** eventually became motivated to do better.

> YES   Our side lost the contest, **which** eventually motivated us to do better.

NO   Because television's first large-scale transmissions included news programs quickly became popular with the public. [The opening dependent clause starts off on one track (and is not correctly punctuated), but the independent clause goes off in another direction. What does the writer want to emphasize, the first transmissions or the popularity of news programs?]

YES   Because television's first large-scale transmissions included news, programs became popular with the public. [The revision helps but is partial: the dependent clause talks about the news, but the independent clause goes off in another direction by talking about the popularity of the programs in general.]

YES   Television's first large-scale transmissions included news programs, **which were** popular with the public. [Dropping *because* and adding *which were* solves the problem by keeping the focus on news programs throughout.]

NO   By increasing the time for network news to thirty minutes increased the prestige of network news programs. [A prepositional phrase, such as *by increasing,* can't be the subject of a sentence.]

YES   Increasing the time for network news to thirty minutes increased the prestige of network news programs. [Dropping the preposition *by* clears up the problem.]

YES   By increasing the time for network news to thirty minutes, **the network executives** increased the prestige of network news programs. [Inserting a logical subject, *the network executives,* clears up the problem.]

The phrase *the fact that* lacks CONCISENESS, and it also tends to cause a mixed sentence.

NO   The fact that quiz show scandals in the 1950s prompted the networks to produce even more news shows.

YES   The fact **is** that quiz show scandals in the 1950s prompted the networks to produce even more news shows. [Adding *is* clarifies the meaning.]

YES   Quiz show scandals in the 1950s prompted the networks to produce even more news shows. [Dropping *the fact that* clarifies the meaning.]

How can I correct a mixed sentence resulting from faulty predication?

Faulty predication, sometimes called *illogical predication,* occurs when a SUBJECT and its PREDICATE don't make sense together.

> **NO** The purpose of television was invented to entertain.
> [A *purpose* cannot be *invented.*]
>
> **YES** The purpose of television was to entertain.
> **YES** Television was invented to entertain.

Faulty predication often results from a lost connection between a subject and its SUBJECT COMPLEMENT.

> **NO** Lloyd Robertson's outstanding **characteristic** as a newscaster **is credible.** [The subject complement *credible* could logically describe *Lloyd Robertson,* but *Lloyd Robertson* is not the sentence's subject. Rather, the sentence's subject is his *characteristic.* Therefore, the sentence lacks a subject complement that would name a *characteristic* of Lloyd Robertson as *a newscaster.*]
>
> **YES** Lloyd Robertson's outstanding **characteristic** as a newscaster **is credibility.** [When *credibility* is substituted for *credible,* the sentence is correct.]
>
> **YES** Lloyd Robertson is credible as a newscaster. [When *Lloyd Robertson* becomes the sentence's subject, *credible* is correct.]

In ACADEMIC WRITING, avoid nonstandard constructions such as *is when* and *is where.* They should be avoided not only because they are nonstandard, but also because they usually lead to faulty predication.

> **NO** A disaster **is when** TV news shows get some of their highest ratings.
>
> **YES** TV news shows get some of their highest ratings during a disaster.

In academic writing, avoid constructions such as *the reason . . . is because.* By using both *reason* and *because,* the construction is redundant (it says the same thing twice). Instead, use either *the reason . . . is that* or *because* alone.

> **NO** One **reason** that TV news captured widespread attention in the 1960s **is because** it covered the Vietnam War thoroughly.
>
> **YES** One **reason** TV news captured widespread attention in the 1960s **is that** it covered the Vietnam War thoroughly.
>
> **YES** TV news captured widespread attention in the 1960s **because** it covered the Vietnam War thoroughly.

EXERCISE 15-4

Revise the mixed sentences so that the beginning of each sentence fits logically with its end. If a sentence is correct, circle its number. For help, consult 15f and 15g.

EXAMPLE The reason women and men sometimes behave differently is because their brains operate differently.

Women and men sometimes behave differently because their brains operate differently.

1. By studying brain scans has provided researchers with pictures of neuron activity in the human brain.

2. The reason that a man's brain is 10 to 15 percent larger than a woman's brain is because men's bodies are generally 10 to 15 percent larger than women's.

3. The fact that women use both sides of the brain and more readily see relationships among objects or ideas.

4. One theory focuses on whether women have more brain neurons that control difficult intellectual functions such as language is being studied.

5. Whether walking or doing complicated math, women activate neurons in several areas of the brain at the same time.

6. The reason most men are able to focus more intently on an activity is because their neural action stays only in one area of the brain.

7. Because of a woman's ability to think simultaneously about a variety of topics enables her to read or sew while watching television.

8. While reading a map is usually when differences in brain activity show up on the scans.

9. Neurologists are interested in men's ability to look at maps and mentally rotate positions on them.

10. Even though women perform better on a memory test are three times as likely as men to develop Alzheimer's disease.

15h What are correct elliptical constructions?

An **elliptical construction** deliberately leaves out one or more words in a sentence for CONCISENESS.

Victor has his book and Joan's. [This means *Victor has his book and Joan's book*. The second *book* is left out deliberately.]

For an elliptical construction to be correct, the one or more words you leave out need to be identical to those already appearing in the sentence. For instance, the sample sentence above about Victor and Joan would have an incorrect elliptical construction if the writer's intended meaning were *Victor has his book and Joan has her own book.*

NO   In the 1980s, software expertise and communications equipment **were becoming** two major Canadian exports, and comedy talent a third. [The plural verb *were becoming* cannot take the place of *was becoming,* which the singular subject *comedy talent* requires.]

YES   In the 1980s, software expertise and communications equipment **were becoming** two major Canadian exports, and comedy talent **was becoming** a third.

YES   In the 1980s, software expertise and communications equipment **became** two major Canadian exports, and comedy talent a third. [*Became* works because it goes with both singular and plural subjects.]

15i   What are correct comparisons?

When you write comparisons, make sure that no important words are omitted.

NO   Individuals driven to achieve make **better** business executives. [*Better* is a word of comparison (11e), but no comparison is stated.]

YES   Individuals driven to achieve make **better** business executives **than do people not interested in personal accomplishments.**

NO   Most personnel officers value high achievers **more than risk takers.** [*More* is a word of comparison, but it's unclear whether the sentence says *personnel officers value high achievers over risk takers* or *personnel officers value high achievers more than risk takers value them.*]

YES   Most personnel officers value high achievers **more than they value** risk takers.

YES   Most personnel officers value high achievers **more than** risk takers **do.**

15j   How can I proofread successfully for little words I forget to use?

If you're rushing or distracted as you write, you might unintentionally omit little words, such as ARTICLES, PRONOUNS, CONJUNCTIONS, and PREPOSITIONS. I do, unfortunately. I solve this by reading my writing aloud, word by word; or, better still, I ask someone else to read it aloud because I tend to fill in any missing words in my own work.

NO   On May 2, 1808, citizens Madrid rioted against French soldiers and were shot.

YES   On May 2, 1808, citizens **of** Madrid rioted against French soldiers and were shot.

NO   The Spanish painter Francisco Goya recorded both the riot the execution in a pair of pictures painted 1814.

YES   The Spanish painter Francisco Goya recorded both the riot **and** the execution in a pair of pictures painted **in** 1814.

EXERCISE 15-5

Revise this paragraph to create correct elliptical constructions, to complete comparisons, and to insert any missing words. For help, see 15h through 15j.

(1) A giant tsunami is as destructive and even larger than a tidal wave. (2) The word *tsunami* is Japanese for "harbour wave," for this kind wave appears suddenly in harbour or bay. (3) A tsunami begins with rapid shift in ocean floor caused by an undersea earthquake or volcano. (4) The wave this produces in the open sea is less than one metre high, but it can grow to a height of thirty metres as it rushes and strikes against the shore. (5) For this reason, tsunamis are much more dangerous to seaside towns than ships on the open sea. (6) In 1960, a huge tsunami that struck coasts of Chile, Hawaii, and Japan killed total of 590 people.

Part Three

Writing Effectively

Visit the Troyka Web site at
http://www.pearsoned.ca/troyka for

- a writing workshop
- chapter exercises
- other resources, including an e-book version of this text

Chapter 16

Conciseness

16a What is conciseness?

Conciseness requires you to craft sentences that are direct and to the point. Its opposite, **wordiness,** means you are filling sentences with empty words and phrases that increase the word count but contribute nothing to meaning. Wordy writing is padded with deadwood, forcing readers to clear away the branches and overgrowth—an annoying waste of time that implies the writer isn't skilled. Usually, the best time to work on making your writing more concise is while you're REVISING.*

> T local
>
> **WORDY** ~~As a matter of fact,~~ ᴛhe ∧ television station ~~which is situated~~
>
> ~~in the local area~~ wins ~~a great~~ many awards ~~in the final~~
>
> ~~analysis~~ because of its ~~type of~~ coverage of ~~all kinds of~~
>
> controversial issues.

> **CONCISE** The local television station wins many awards for its coverage of controversial issues.

16b What common expressions are not concise?

Many common expressions we use in informal speech are not concise. Box 87 lists some and shows you how to eliminate them.

---

* Find the definition of all words in small capital letters (such as REVISING) in the Terms Glossary at the back of this book directly before the Index.

BOX 87   SUMMARY

Cutting unnecessary words and phrases

EMPTY WORD OR PHRASE	WORDY EXAMPLE REVISED
as a matter of fact	Many marriages, ~~as a matter of fact,~~ end in divorce.
at the present time	The revised proposal for outdoor lighting angers many villagers ^*now.* ~~at the present time.~~
because of the fact that, in light of the fact that, due to the fact that	Because ~~of the fact that~~ the museum has a special exhibit, it stays open late.
by means of	We travelled by ~~means of a~~ car.
factor	The project's final cost was the essential factor ~~to consider.~~
for the purpose of	Work crews arrived ~~for the purpose of~~ ^*to* fixing the potholes.
have a tendency to	The team ~~has a tendency~~ ^*tends* to lose home games.
in a very real sense	~~In a very real sense,~~ *A* all firefighters are heroes.
in the case of	~~In the case of~~ *The* the election, ~~the results~~ will be close.
in the event that	~~In the event that~~ ^*If* you're late, I will buy our tickets.
in the final analysis	~~In the final analysis,~~ *N* no two eyewitnesses agreed on what they saw.
in the process of	We are ~~in the process of~~ reviewing the proposal.
it seems that	~~It seems that~~ *T* the union went on strike over health benefits.

→

Cutting unnecessary words and phrases (*continued*)

EMPTY WORD OR PHRASE	WORDY EXAMPLE REVISED
manner	*reluctantly.* The child spoke ∧ ~~in a reluctant manner.~~
nature	The movie review was ~~of~~ a sarcastic~~, nature.~~
that exists	The crime rate ~~that exists~~ is unacceptable.
the point I am trying to make	~~The point I am trying to make is~~ *T*elevision reporters invade our privacy.
type of, kind of	Gordon took a relaxing ~~type of~~ vacation.
What I mean to say is	~~What I mean to say is~~ I love you.

EXERCISE 16-1

Working individually or with a group, revise this paragraph in two steps. First, underline all words that interfere with conciseness. Second, revise each sentence to make it more concise. (You'll need to drop words and replace or rearrange others.)

EXAMPLE   It seems that most North Americans think of motor scooters as vehicles that exist only in European countries.

It seems that most North Americans think of motor scooters as vehicles that exist only in European countries.

Most North Americans think of motor scooters as only European vehicles.

1. As a matter of fact, in the popular imagination, motor scooters are the very essence of European style.
2. Today, over one million scooters are purchased by people in Europe each year, compared with a number that amounts to only a few thousand buyers in Canada.
3. In fact, Europeans have long used fuel-efficient, clean-running scooters for the purpose of getting around in a manner that is relatively easy in congested cities.
4. The use of these brightly coloured, manoeuvrable scooters allows city dwellers to zip through traffic jams and thereby to save time as well as to save gas.

5. However, sales of scooters, it might interest you to know, are in the process of increasing in North America.

6. What I am trying to say is that motor scooters use much less gasoline than cars, and that as a matter of fact the cost factor is about one-fourth that of an inexpensive new car.

7. In addition, some motor scooters, it is pleasing to note, now run on electricity, which in fact makes them noise and emission free.

8. A scooter running by means of electrical power amounts to a cost in the neighbourhood of 50 cents to travel 80 kilometres at 50 km/h.

9. Members of many different population groups, from students to retired persons, have begun to be finding this type of vehicle to be of a useful nature in a very real sense.

10. Travelling by means of an agile, snappy scooter makes getting around campus or doing errands in a city neighbourhood quick and easy.

16c What sentence structures usually work against conciseness?

Two sentence structures, although appropriate in some contexts, often work against CONCISENESS because they can lead to WORDINESS: EXPLETIVE constructions and the PASSIVE VOICE.

Avoiding expletive constructions

An expletive construction starts with *it* or *there* followed by a form of the VERB *be*. When you cut the expletive construction and revise, the sentence becomes more direct.

~~It is necessary for~~ $\overset{S}{students}$ ~~to~~ $\overset{must}{\wedge}$ fill in both questionnaires.

~~There are~~ $\overset{E}{eight}$ instructors ~~who~~ teach in the Computer Science Department.

⊕ **ESL NOTES:** (1) *It* in an expletive construction is not a PRONOUN referring to a specific ANTECEDENT. *It* is an "empty" word that fills the SUBJECT position in the sentence but does not function as the subject. The actual subject appears after the expletive construction: ***It was the teacher*** *who answered the question.* If put concisely, the sentence would be *The teacher answered the question.* (2) *There* in an expletive construction does not indicate a place. Rather, *there* is an "empty" word that fills the subject position in the sentence but does not function as the subject. The actual subject appears after the expletive construction: ***There are many teachers*** *who can answer the question.* If put concisely, the sentence would be *Many teachers can answer the question.* ⊕

Avoiding the passive voice

In general, the passive voice is less concise—as well as less lively—than the ACTIVE VOICE. In the active voice, the subject of a sentence does the action named by the verb.

> **ACTIVE** Professor Higgins teaches public speaking. [*Professor Higgins* is the subject, and he does the action: He *teaches*.]

In the passive voice, the subject of a sentence receives the action named by the verb.

> **PASSIVE** Public speaking is taught by Professor Higgins. [*Public speaking* is the subject, and it receives the action *taught*.]

Unless your meaning justifies using the passive voice, choose the active voice. (For more information, see 8n through 8p.)

> **PASSIVE** Volunteer work was done by students for credit in sociology. [The passive phrase *was done by students* is unnecessary for the intended meaning. *Students* are doing the action and should be the subject of the sentence.]
>
> **ACTIVE** **The students did** volunteer work for credit in sociology.
>
> **ACTIVE** **Volunteer work earned** students credit in sociology. [Since the verb has changed to *earned, volunteer work* performs the action of the verb.]

In mistakenly believing the passive voice sounds "mature" or "academic," student writers sometimes deliberately use it. The result is wordy, overblown sentences that suggest a writer's lack of careful revision.

> **NO** One very important quality developed by individuals during their first job is self-reliance. This strength was gained when I was allowed by my supervisor to set up and conduct a survey project on my own.
>
> **YES** Many individuals develop the important quality of self-reliance during their first job. I gained this strength when my supervisor allowed me to set up and conduct my own survey project.
>
> **YES** During their first job, many people develop self-reliance, as I did when my supervisor let me set up and conduct my own survey project.

16d How else can I revise for conciseness?

Four other techniques can help you achieve CONCISENESS: eliminating unplanned repetition (16d.1); combining sentences (16d.2); shortening CLAUSES (16d.3); and shortening PHRASES and cutting words (16d.4). These techniques involve matters of judgment.

16d.1 Eliminating unplanned repetition

Unplanned repetition lacks conciseness because it delivers the same message more than once, usually in slightly different words. Unplanned repetition, or redundancy, implies that the writer lacks focus and judgment. The opposite, planned repetition, creates a powerful rhythmic effect; see 19e. As you revise, check that every word is necessary for delivering your message.

> **NO** Bringing **the project** to **final completion** three weeks early, the supervisor of **the project** earned our **respectful regard.**
> [*Completion* implies *bringing to final; project* is used twice in one sentence; and *regard* implies *respect.*]

> **YES** Completing the project three weeks early, the supervisor earned our respect. [eighteen words reduced to eleven by cutting all redundancies]

> **NO** The package, **rectangular in shape,** lay on the counter.
> [*Rectangular* is a shape, so *shape* is redundant.]

> **YES** The **rectangular** package lay on the counter.

> **NO** **Astonished,** the architect **circled around** the building **in amazement.**

> **YES** **Astonished,** the architect **circled** the building.
> **YES** The architect **circled** the building **in amazement.**

ESL NOTE: In all languages, words often carry an unspoken message that is assumed by native speakers of the language. In English, some implied meanings can cause redundancy in writing. For example, *I sent an e-mail by computer* is redundant. *To send an e-mail* implies *by computer* for native speakers of English.

16d.2 Combining sentences

Look at sets of sentences in your writing to see if you can combine their information into a single sentence. (For more about combining sentences, see Chapter 17, particularly section 17i.)

> **TWO SENTENCES** The *Titanic* hit an iceberg and sank. Seventy-three years later, a team of French and American scientists located the ship's resting site.

> **SENTENCES COMBINED** Seventy-three years after the *Titanic* hit an iceberg and sank, a team of French and American scientists located the ship's resting site.

TWO SENTENCES	Cameras revealed that the stern of the ship was missing and showed external damage to the ship's hull. Otherwise, the *Titanic* was in excellent condition.
SENTENCES COMBINED	Cameras revealed that, aside from a missing stern and external damage to the hull, the *Titanic* was in excellent condition.

16d.3 Shortening clauses

Look at clauses in your writing to see if you can state them more concisely. For example, sometimes you can cut a RELATIVE PRONOUN and its verb:

WORDY	The *Titanic,* **which was** a huge ocean liner, sank in 1912.
CONCISE	The *Titanic,* a huge ocean liner, sank in 1912.

Sometimes you can reduce a clause to a word.

WORDY	The scientists held a memorial service for the passengers and crew **who had drowned.**
CONCISE	The scientists held a memorial service for the **drowned** passengers and crew.

Sometimes a ELLIPTICAL CONSTRUCTION (7p and 15h) can shorten a clause. If you use this technique, be sure that any omitted word is implied clearly.

WORDY	**When they were** confronted with disaster, some passengers behaved heroically, **while** others **behaved** selfishly.
CONCISE	Confronted with disaster, some passengers behaved heroically, others selfishly.

16d.4 Shortening phrases and cutting words

Sometimes you can reduce a phrase or redundant word pair to a single word. Redundant word pairs include *each and every, one and only, forever and ever, final and conclusive, perfectly clear, few* (or *many*) *in number, consensus of opinion,* and *reason . . . is because.*

NO	**Each and every** person was hungry after the movie.
YES	**Every** person was hungry after the movie.
YES	**Each** person was hungry after the movie.

NO	The **consensus of opinion** was that the movie was disappointing.
YES	The **consensus** was that the movie was disappointing.
YES	**Everyone agreed** that the movie was disappointing.

WORDY	More than fifteen hundred **travellers on that voyage** died in the shipwreck.
CONCISE	More than fifteen hundred **passengers** died in the shipwreck.

Sometimes you can rearrange words so that others can be deleted.

WORDY	**Objects** found inside the ship included **unbroken** bottles of wine and expensive **undamaged** china.
CONCISE	Found **undamaged** inside the ship were bottles of wine and expensive china.

16e How do verbs affect conciseness?

ACTION VERBS are strong verbs. *Be* and *have* are weak verbs that often lead to wordy sentences. When you revise weak verbs to strong ones, you can both increase the impact of your writing and reduce the number of words in your sentences. Strong verbs come into play when you revise your writing to reduce PHRASES and to change NOUNS to verbs.

WEAK VERB	The plan before the city council **has to do with** tax rebates.
STRONG VERB	The plan before the city council **proposes** tax rebates.

WEAK VERB	The board members **were of the opinion** that the changes in the rules **were changes they would not accept.**
STRONG VERB	The board members **said** that **they would not accept** the changes in the rules.

Replacing a phrase with a verb
Phrases such as *be aware of, be capable of, be supportive of* can often be replaced with one-word verbs.

I **envy** [not *am envious of*] your mathematical ability.
I **appreciate** [not *am appreciative of*] your modesty.
Your skill **illustrates** [not *is illustrative of*] how hard you studied.

Revising nouns into verbs
Many nouns are derived from verbs, including nouns that end in *-ance,* *-ment,* and *-tion* (*toler**ance,** enforce**ment,** narra**tion***). When you turn such nouns back into verbs, your writing becomes more concise.

NO	The **accumulation of** paper lasted thirty years.
YES	The paper **accumulated** for thirty years.

NO	We **arranged for the establishment of** a student advisory committee.
YES	We **established** a student advisory committee.

> NO   The building **had the appearance of** having been neglected.
>
> YES   The building **appeared** to have been neglected.

EXERCISE 16-2

Working individually or with a group, combine each set of sentences to eliminate wordy constructions. For help, consult 16c through 16e.

EXAMPLE   In recent years, ranchers have tried to raise and market many exotic meats. These meats have included emu, ostrich, and bison. These attempts have failed.

In recent years, ranchers have tried and failed to raise and market many exotic meats, such as emu, ostrich, and bison.

1. Each new attempt of ranchers to raise exotic animals like emu, ostrich, and bison for the commercial value of their meat follows a pattern. There is a similar pattern to each new attempt. Each new attempt begins when a few people make the claim that some exotic animal tastes better than beef and is more nutritious.

2. Emus were discovered by ranchers. Emus are birds with undeveloped wings that look like small ostriches. Emus quickly became unprofitable to raise. Only a few consumers found emu meat tasty.

3. It was found by ostrich ranchers that there was an early, strong demand for the meat of ostriches. That strong demand soon fizzled out quite a bit, the ranchers found.

4. There is the American Ostrich Association. The membership of the American Ostrich Association once used to be 3000. Today, the membership of the American Ostrich Association now has only 500 people belonging to it.

5. Bison, also known as buffalo, was a longer-lasting craze. Ranchers had a strong desire to own the mighty animals; however, the price of bison was increased greatly by the demand. It became uneconomical for ranchers to purchase young animals.

6. Also, bison are difficult to raise. They tend to need strong fences to hold them in. They cannot find enough food to eat. They eat by grazing. The land of some buffalo ranches consists of poor pasture land or is in mountainous terrain.

7. Recently, the yak has been discovered by ranchers. The yak is an animal from Central Asia. It is from rugged mountainous areas. For centuries, the yak has supported the people of the Himalayan region.

8. Yaks have the ability to forage more efficiently compared to bison or cows. Yaks are easier to care for than bison or cows. Yaks possess a better resistance to many diseases.

9. Chefs in a few gourmet restaurants are beginning to serve yak meat. They are devising fancy recipes for it. They are featuring it on their menus. The meat is mild-tasting and succulent. The meat is also low in fat.

10. Even though yaks are easy to raise and even are environmentally friendly, there is a problem. The ranchers must overcome that problem before they can raise yaks profitably. That problem is the fact that consumers lack familiarity with yaks. Consumers have a reluctance to try yak meat.

EXERCISE 16-3

Working individually or with a group, revise this paragraph in two steps. First, underline all words that interfere with conciseness. Second, revise the paragraph to make it more concise. (You'll need to drop words and replace or rearrange others.)

EXAMPLE   Within a matter of minutes after the completion of a championship game, the winning team's players are enabled to put on caps that have been embroidered with their team's name, the year, as well as the word "champions."

Within a matter of minutes after the completion of a championship game, the winning team's players are enabled to put on caps that have been embroidered with their team's name, the year, as well as the word "champions."

Minutes after the completion of a championship game, the winning team's players receive caps embroidered with their team's name, the year, and the word "champions."

(1) At the present time, caps for sports teams are manufactured in factories located primarily in Asian countries such as China, Korea, and Taiwan. (2) Championship caps are quickly produced and shipped by factories wherever they are needed for both of the two teams playing in a final game or series. (3) The very moment the game ends, a trucking company delivers the caps to the winning team's locker room, and it then immediately and instantly burns the losing team's caps so as to avoid embarrassing anyone. (4) Companies that produce all types of sports apparel know that in most cases there is only a short period of time available for making and earning high profits from merchandise connected to a winning team. (5) Within barely a day or two, they flood the market with all sorts of every kind of t-shirts, jackets, caps, coffee mugs, in addition to banners showing and presenting the winning team's championship information.

Chapter 17

Coordination and Subordination

Used well, **coordination** and **subordination** in sentences enhance writing style. These structuring methods reflect the relationships between ideas that a writer seeks to express. Some writers enlist coordination and subordination while they DRAFT, but often writers wait until they REVISE to check for good opportunities to use these two techniques.

TWO SENTENCES	The sky turned dark grey. The wind died down.
USING COORDINATION	The sky turned dark grey, **and** the wind died down.
USING SUBORDINATION 1	**As** the sky turned dark grey, the wind died down. [Here, the wind is the focus.]
USING SUBORDINATION 2	**As** the wind died down, the sky turned dark grey. [Here, the sky is the focus.]

COORDINATION

17a What is coordination of sentences?

Coordination of sentences is a grammatical strategy to communicate that the ideas in two or more INDEPENDENT CLAUSES are equivalent or balanced. Coordination can produce harmony by bringing related elements together. Whenever you use the technique of coordination of sentences, make sure that it works well with the meaning you want to communicate.

The sky turned **brighter, and** people emerged happily from buildings.
The sky turned **brighter;** people emerged happily from buildings.

17b What is the structure of a coordinate sentence?

A **coordinate sentence,** also known as a *compound sentence,* consists of two or more INDEPENDENT CLAUSES joined either by a semicolon or by a comma working in concert with a COORDINATING CONJUNCTION (*and, but, for, or, nor, yet, so*). Box 88 shows the pattern for coordination of sentences.

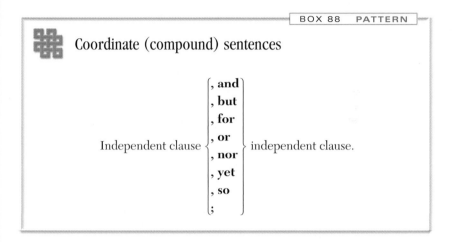

BOX 88   PATTERN

Coordinate (compound) sentences

Independent clause $\left\{ \begin{array}{l} \text{, and} \\ \text{, but} \\ \text{, for} \\ \text{, or} \\ \text{, nor} \\ \text{, yet} \\ \text{, so} \\ ; \end{array} \right\}$ independent clause.

17c What meaning does each coordinating conjunction convey?

Each COORDINATING CONJUNCTION has its own meaning. When you choose one, be sure that its meaning accurately expresses the relationship between the equivalent ideas that you want to convey.

- **and** means addition
- **but** and **yet** mean contrast
- **for** means reason or choice
- **or** means choice
- **nor** means negative choice
- **so** means result or effect

ALERT: Always use a comma before a coordinating conjunction that joins two INDEPENDENT CLAUSES (24b).

17d How can I avoid misusing coordination?

One major misuse of COORDINATION occurs when unrelated or nonequiv-
alent ideas, each in its own INDEPENDENT CLAUSE, are coordinated. The
result looks like a coordinated sentence, but the ideas are unrelated.

> **NO** Computers came into common use in the 1970s, and they
> sometimes make costly errors. [The statement in each independent
> clause is true, but the ideas are not related or equivalent.]
>
> **YES** Computers came into common use in the 1970s, and now they
> are indispensable business tools.

A second major misuse of coordination occurs when it's overused.
Simply stringing sentences together with COORDINATING CONJUNCTIONS
makes relationships among ideas unclear—and it lacks style.

> **NO** Dinosaurs could have disappeared for many reasons, **and** one
> theory holds that a sudden shower of meteors and asteroids hit
> the earth, **so** the impact created a huge dust cloud that caused a
> false winter. The winter lasted for years, **and** the dinosaurs died.
>
> **YES** Dinosaurs could have disappeared for many reasons. One theory
> holds that a sudden shower of meteors and asteroids hit the
> earth. The impact created a huge dust cloud that caused a false
> winter. The winter lasted for years, killing the dinosaurs.

EXERCISE 17-1

Working individually or with a group, revise these sentences to eliminate
illogical or overused coordination. If you think a sentence needs no revision, explain why. For help, consult 17a through 17d.

> **EXAMPLE** Fencing, once a form of combat, has become a competitive
> sport worldwide, and today's fencers disapprove of those who
> identify fencing with fighting.
>
> Fencing, once a form of combat, has become a competitive
> sport worldwide, but today's fencers disapprove of those who
> identify fencing with fighting.

1. As depicted in movies, fencing sometimes appears to be reckless
   swordplay, and fencing requires precision, coordination, and
   strategy.
2. In the 1800s, fencing became very popular, and it was one of the few
   sports included in the first modern Olympic Games in 1896, and
   fencing has been part of the Olympics ever since.

3. Fencing equipment includes a mask, a padded jacket, a glove, and one of three weapons—a foil, épée, or sabre—and a fencer's technique and targets differ depending on the weapon used and the fencer's experience.

4. Generally, a fencer specializes in one of the three weapons, but some competitors are equally skilled with all three.

5. The object of fencing is to be the first to touch the opponent five times, and a "president," who is sometimes assisted by a number of judges, officiates at competitions.

SUBORDINATION

17e What is subordination in sentences?

Subordination is a grammatical strategy to communicate that one idea in a sentence is more important than another idea in the same sentence. To use subordination, place the more important idea in an INDEPENDENT CLAUSE and the less important—the subordinate—idea in a DEPENDENT CLAUSE. The information you choose to subordinate depends on the meaning you want to deliver.

INDEPENDENT CLAUSE	DEPENDENT

Two ranchers fought a dangerous Alberta snowstorm **while they**

CLAUSE	DEPENDENT CLAUSE

were looking for cattle. When they came to a canyon,

INDEPENDENT CLAUSE

they saw outlines of buildings through the blizzard.

To illustrate the difference in writing style when you use subordination, here's a passage with the same message as the example above, but without subordination.

Two ranchers fought a dangerous Alberta snowstorm. They were looking for cattle. They came to a canyon. They saw outlines of buildings through the blizzard.

17f What is the structure of a subordinate sentence?

A subordinate sentence starts the DEPENDENT CLAUSE with either a SUB-ORDINATING CONJUNCTION (see Box 90 in 17g) or a RELATIVE PRONOUN.

If they are very lucky, the passengers may glimpse dolphins breaking water playfully near the ship.

—Elizabeth Gray, student

Pandas are solitary animals, **which** means they are difficult to protect from extinction.

—Jose Santos, student

For patterns of subordination with dependent clauses, see Box 89. Two types of dependent clauses are ADVERB CLAUSES and ADJECTIVE CLAUSES. An adverb clause starts with a subordinating conjunction. An adjective clause starts with a relative pronoun.

BOX 89 PATTERN

Subordination

Sentences with Adverb Clauses

- **Adverb clause,** independent clause.
  - **After the sky grew dark,** the wind died suddenly.
- Independent clause, **adverb clause.**
  - Birds stopped singing, **as they do during an eclipse.**
- Independent clause **adverb clause.**
  - The stores closed **before the storm began.**

Sentences with Adjective Clauses

- Independent clause, **restrictive (essential)** * **adjective clause.**
  - Weather forecasts warned of a storm **that might bring a 45-centimetre snowfall.**
- Independent clause, **nonrestrictive (nonessential)** * **adjective clause.**
  - Spring is the season for tornadoes, **which may have wind speeds over 350 km/h.**
- Beginning of independent clause, **restrictive (essential)** * **adjective clause,** end of independent clause.
  - Anyone **who lives through a tornado** remembers its power.
- Beginning of independent clause, **nonrestrictive (nonessential)** * **adjective clause,** end of independent clause.
  - The sky, **which had been clear,** turned greenish black.

* For an explanation of RESTRICTIVE and NONRESTRICTIVE ELEMENTS, see 24f.

17g What meaning does each subordinating conjunction convey?

Each SUBORDINATING CONJUNCTION has its own meaning. When you choose one, be sure that its meaning accurately expresses the relationship between the ideas that you want to convey. Box 90 lists subordinating conjunctions according to their different meanings.

BOX 90   SUMMARY

Subordinating conjunctions and their meanings

Time

after, before, once, since, until, when, whenever, while

- **After** you have handed in your report, you cannot revise it.

Reason or Cause

as, because, since

- **Because** you have handed in your report, you cannot revise it.

Purpose or Result

in order that, so, so that, that

- I want to read your report **so that** I can evaluate it.

Condition

if, even if, provided that, unless

- **Unless** you have handed in your report, you can revise it.

Contrast

although, even though, though, whereas, while

- **Although** you have handed in your report, you can ask to revise it.

Choice or Comparison

than, whether

- You took more time to revise **than** I did before the lab report deadline.

Place or Location

where, wherever

- **Wherever** you say, I'll come to hand in my report.

307

EXERCISE 17-2

Working individually or with a group, combine each pair of sentences, using an adverb clause to subordinate one idea. Then, revise each sentence so that the adverb clause becomes the independent clause. For help, see 17e through 17g, especially Box 89.

EXAMPLE   Some people think of their bodies as a blank canvas. They feel free to transform themselves into strange and unique works of art.

    a. Because some people think of their bodies as a blank canvas, they feel free to transform themselves into strange and unique works of art.

    b. Some people feel free to transform themselves into strange and unique works of art, for they think of their bodies as a blank canvas.

1. Body modification has become astonishingly popular. No one can walk the streets of a Canadian city without seeing a parade of piercings and tattoos.

2. Unusual trends and rituals emerge in the urban subculture. Scholars rush in with their theories.

3. One theory sees body decorations and mutilations as an initiation into a symbolic community. A sociologist named David Le Breton focuses instead on their ability to promote individual self-expression.

4. Le Breton thinks that people use nose rings and tongue piercings, implants, and vivid tattoos to construct their own identity in a consumer society. Some people ask if our society is developing a whole new approach to the human body.

5. Not long ago, a man with a simple earring was considered outré. Our perceptions must have changed along with our customs.

EXERCISE 17-3

Working individually or with a group, combine each pair of sentences, using an adjective clause to subordinate one idea to the other. Then, revise each sentence so that the adjective clause becomes the independent clause. Use the relative pronoun given in parentheses. For help, consult 17e through 17g, especially Box 89.

EXAMPLE   Aristides was an ancient Greek politician famous for his honesty and judgment. He was known as Aristides the Just. (who)

    a. Aristides, who was an ancient Greek politician famous for his honesty and judgment, was known as Aristides the Just.

    b. Aristides, who was known as Aristides the Just, was an ancient Greek politician famous for his honesty and judgment.

1. An ancient Athenian law allowed voters to banish politicians from the city. It asked citizens to write the name of an unpopular politician on their ballots. (that)
2. A voter was filling out a ballot when Aristides the Just walked by. The voter needed help in spelling *Aristides.* (who)
3. Aristides knew the voter did not recognize him. He asked why the voter wanted to banish that particular politician. (who)
4. The voter said he resented hearing someone called "the Just" all the time. He handed Aristides his ballot. (who)
5. Aristides' reaction demonstrated that the nickname "the Just" was well deserved. His reaction was to write his own name on the voter's ballot even though that person's vote helped banish Aristides. (which)

17h How can I avoid misusing subordination?

One major misuse of SUBORDINATION occurs when a SUBORDINATING CONJUNCTION doesn't communicate a sensible relationship between the INDEPENDENT CLAUSE and the DEPENDENT CLAUSE. See Box 90 in 17g for a list of subordinating conjunctions and their different meanings.

> **NO** Because Beethoven was deaf when he wrote them, his final symphonies were masterpieces. [*Because* is illogical here; it says the masterpieces resulted from the deafness.]
>
> **YES** Although Beethoven was deaf when he wrote them, his final symphonies were masterpieces. [*Although* is logical here; it says Beethoven wrote masterpieces in spite of his being deaf.]

A second major misuse of subordination occurs when it's overused, resulting in too many images or ideas crowded together in one sentence. This causes readers to lose track of the message. Whenever you write a sentence with two or more dependent clauses, check that your message is clear. If it isn't, you've likely overused subordination.

> **NO** A new technique for eye surgery, **which is supposed to correct nearsightedness, which previously could be corrected only by glasses,** has been developed, **although many eye doctors do not approve of the new technique because it can create unstable vision, which includes intense glare from headlights on cars and many other light sources.** [The base sentence *A new technique for eye surgery has been developed* is crowded with five dependent clauses attached to it.]
>
> **YES** A new technique for eye surgery, **which is supposed to correct nearsightedness,** has been developed. Previously, only glasses could correct nearsightedness. Many doctors do not approve of the new technique **because it can create unstable**

vision. The problems include intense glare from car headlights and many other sources of light. [In this revision, one long sentence has been broken into four sentences, making the material easier to read and the relationships among ideas clearer. Two dependent clauses remain, which balance well with the other sentence constructions. Some words have been moved to new positions.]

🌐 **ESL NOTE:** If you're told that your sentences are too long and complex, limit the number of words in each sentence. The advice of many ESL teachers is to revise any sentence you write that contains more than three independent and dependent clauses in any combination. 🌐

EXERCISE 17-4

Working individually or with a group, correct illogical or excessive subordination in this paragraph. As you revise according to the message you want to deliver, use some dependent clauses as well as some short sentences. (Also, if you wish, apply the principles of coordination discussed in sections 17a through 17d.) For help, consult 17h.

Although people in North America think of hot dogs as their traditional food, this local favourite originated in Germany in 1852 when butchers in Frankfurt stuffed meat into a long casing, which in honour of the town, they called their creation a "frankfurter." Because one butcher noticed that the frankfurter resembled the shape of his dog, a dachshund, he decided to name the meat roll a "dachshund sausage," a name which caught on in Germany. When Germans brought dachshund sausages to the United States, peddlers sold them on the street, although the dachshund sausages were so hot that people often burned their fingers because they had trouble holding the meat. When one clever peddler put the sausage in a bun, a *New York Times* cartoonist decided to draw a picture of hot dachshund sausages in buns, although he called them "hot dogs" because he didn't know how to spell *dachshund.*

17i How can I effectively use coordination and subordination together?

Your writing style improves when you use a logical and pleasing variety of SENTENCE TYPES, utilizing COORDINATION and SUBORDINATION to improve the flow of ideas. Here's a paragraph that demonstrates a good balance in the use of coordination and subordination.

When I was growing up, I lived on a farm just across the field from my grandmother. My parents were busy trying to raise six children and to establish their struggling dairy farm. It was nice to have Grandma so close. While my parents were providing the necessities of life, my patient grandmother gave her time to her shy, young granddaughter. I always enjoyed going with Grandma and collecting the eggs that her chickens had just laid. Usually, she knew which chickens would peck, and she was careful to let me gather the eggs from the less hostile ones.

—Patricia Mapes, student

When you use both coordination and subordination, never use both a COORDINATE CONJUNCTION and a SUBORDINATE CONJUNCTION to express one relationship in one sentence.

NO **Although** the story was well written, **but** it was too illogical.
[The subordinating conjunction *although* expresses the contrast, so also using *but* is incorrect.]

YES **Although** the story was well written, it was too illogical.

YES The story was well written, **but** it was too illogical.

EXERCISE 17-5

Working individually or in a group, use subordination and coordination to combine these sets of short, choppy sentences. For help, consult all sections of this chapter.

EXAMPLE Owls cannot digest the bones and fur of the mice and birds they eat. They cough up a furry pellet every day.

Because owls cannot digest the bones and fur of the mice and birds they eat, they cough up a furry pellet every day.

1. Owl pellets are the latest teaching tool in biology classrooms. The pellets provide an alternative to dissecting frogs and other animals.
2. Inside the pellet are the remains of the owl's nightly meal. They include beautifully cleaned hummingbird skulls, rat skeletons, and lots of bird feathers.
3. The owl-pellet market has been cornered by companies in the United States. These companies distribute pellets to thousands of biology classrooms all over the world.
4. Company workers scour barns and the ground under trees where owls nest to pick up the pellets. The pellets sell for $1 each.
5. The owl-pellet business may have a short future. The rural areas of the United States are vanishing. Old barns are being bulldozed. All the barns are torn down. The owls will be gone, too.

EXERCISE 17-6

Working individually or with a group, revise this paragraph to make it more effective by using coordination and subordination. For help, consult all sections of this chapter.

Thirst is the body's way of surviving. Every cell in the body needs water. People can die by losing as little as 15 to 20 percent of their water requirements. Blood contains 83 percent water. Blood provides indispensable nutrients for the cells. Blood carries water to the cells. Blood carries waste away from the cells. Insufficient water means cells cannot be fuelled or cleaned. The body becomes sluggish. The body can survive eleven days without water. Bodily functions are seriously disrupted by a lack of water for more than one day. The body loses water. The blood thickens. The heart must pump harder. Thickened blood is harder to pump through the heart. Some drinks replace the body's need for fluids. Alcohol or caffeine in drinks leads to dehydration. People know they should drink water often. They can become moderately dehydrated before they even begin to develop a thirst.

Chapter 18
Parallelism

18a What is parallelism?

When you write words, PHRASES, or CLAUSES within a sentence to match in their grammatical forms, the result is **parallelism.** Parallelism serves to emphasize information or ideas in writing. The technique relates to the concept of parallel lines in geometry, lines that run alongside each other and never meet. Parallelism delivers grace, rhythm, and impact.

> They come like foxes through the woods. They attack like lions. They take flight like birds, disappearing before they really appear.
> —Jérôme Lalemant, *The Jesuit Relations*

The Jesuit missionary and martyr conveys the sense of stealth, courage, and speed of the Iroquois by using parallel sets of similes from the natural world. The images gather force relentlessly.

You gain several advantages by using parallel structures:

■ You can express ideas of equal weight in your writing.

■ You can emphasize important information or ideas.

■ You can add rhythm and grace to your writing style.

Many writers attend to parallelism when they are REVISING. If you think while you're DRAFTING that your parallelism is faulty or that you can enhance your writing style by using parallelism, underline or highlight the material and keep moving forward. When you revise, you can return to the places you've marked.

18b What is a balanced sentence?

A **balanced sentence** is a type of parallelism in which contrasting content is delivered. The two parallel structures are usually, but not always, INDEPENDENT CLAUSES. A balanced sentence uses COORDINATION. The two coordinate structures are characterized by opposites in meaning, sometimes with one structure cast in the negative.

By night, the litter and desperation disappeared as the city's glittering lights came on; by day, the filth and despair reappeared as the sun rose.

—Jennifer Kirk, student

ALERT: Authorities differ about using a comma, a semicolon, or nothing between the parts of a short balanced sentence. In ACADEMIC WRITING, to avoid appearing to make the error of a COMMA SPLICE, use a semicolon (or revise in some other way), as in the following sentence.

Mosquitoes don't bite; they stab. ◉

18c How do words, phrases, and clauses work in parallel form?

When you put words, PHRASES, and CLAUSES into parallel form, you enhance your writing style with balance and grace.

PARALLEL WORDS
Recommended exercise includes running, swimming, and cycling.

PARALLEL PHRASES
Exercise helps people maintain healthy bodies and handle mental pressures.

PARALLEL CLAUSES
Many people exercise because they want to look healthy, because they need to increase stamina, and because they hope to live longer.

18d How does parallelism deliver impact?

Parallel structures emphasize the meaning that sentences deliver. Deliberate, rhythmic repetition of parallel forms creates an effect of balance, reinforcing the impact of a message.

Travel a thousand miles by train and you are a brute; pedal five hundred on a bicycle and you remain basically a bourgeois; paddle a hundred in a canoe and you are already a child of nature.

—Pierre Elliott Trudeau, "The Ascetic in a Canoe"

Here's a longer passage in which parallel structures, concepts, and rhythms operate. Together, they echo the intensity of the writer's message.

> **It is a good country for** the honest, industrious artisan. **It is a fine country for the** poor labourer who, after a few years of hard toil, can sit down in his own log-house and look abroad on his own land and see his children well settled in life as independent freeholders. **It is a good country for** the rich speculator who can afford to lay out a large sum in purchasing land in eligible situations; for if he has any judgement he will make a hundred per cent as interest for his money after waiting a few years. But **it is a hard country for** the poor gentleman whose habits have rendered him unfit for manual labour.
>
> —Catherine Parr Traill, *The Backwoods of Canada*

EXERCISE 18-1

Working individually or with a group, highlight all parallel elements of the Catherine Parr Traill passage above in addition to those shown in boldface.

How can I avoid faulty parallelism?

Faulty parallelism usually results when you join nonmatching grammatical forms.

Parallelism with coordinating conjunctions

The coordinating conjunctions are *and, but, for, or, nor, yet,* and *so.* To avoid faulty parallelism, write the words that accompany coordinating conjunctions in matching grammatical forms.

> NO   **Love *and* being married** go together.
> YES   **Love *and* marriage** go together.
> YES   **Being in love *and* being married** go together.

Parallelism with correlative conjunctions

Correlative conjunctions are paired words such as *not only . . . but (also), either . . . or,* and *both . . . and.* To avoid faulty parallelism, write the words joined by correlative conjunctions in matching grammatical forms.

> NO   Differing expectations for marriage *not only* **can lead to** disappointment *but also* **make the couple angry.**
> YES   Differing expectations for marriage *not only* **can lead to** disappointment *but also* **can make the couple angry.**

Parallelism with than *and* as

To avoid faulty parallelism when you use *than* and *as* for comparisons, write the elements of comparison in matching grammatical forms.

> **NO** **Having a solid marriage** can be more satisfying *than* **the acquisition of wealth.**

> **YES** **Having a solid marriage** can be more satisfying *than* **acquiring wealth.**

> **YES** **A solid marriage** can be more satisfying *than* **wealth.**

Parallelism with function words

Function words include ARTICLES (*the, a, an*); the *to* of the INFINITIVE (*to* love); PREPOSITIONS (for example, *of, in, about*); and sometimes RELATIVE PRONOUNS. When you write a series of parallel structures, be consistent in the second and successive structures about either repeating or omitting a function word. Generally, repeat function words only if you think that the repetition clarifies your meaning or highlights the parallelism that you intend.

> **NO** **To assign** unanswered letters their proper weight, **free** us from the expectations of others, **to give** us back to ourselves—here lies the great, singular power of self-respect.

> **YES** **To assign** unanswered letters their proper weight, **to free** us from the expectations of others, **to give** us back to ourselves— here lies **the great, the singular** power of self-respect.
> —Joan Didion, "On Self-Respect"

I have in my own life a precious friend, a woman of 65 **who has** lived very hard, **who is** wise, **who listens** well, **who has been** where I am and can help me understand it, and **who represents** not only an ultimate ideal mother to me but also the person I'd like to be when I grow up.
> —Judith Viorst, "Friends, Good Friends— and Such Good Friends"

We looked into the bus, which **was** painted blue with orange daisies, **had** picnic benches instead of seats, and **showed** yellow curtains billowing out its windows.
> —Kerrie Falk, student

EXERCISE 18-2

Working individually or with a group, revise these sentences by putting appropriate information in parallel structures. For help, consult 18a through 18e.

EXAMPLE   Difficult bosses affect not only their employees' performances but their private lives are affected as well.

Difficult bosses affect not only their employees' performances *but their private lives as well.*

1. According to the psychologist Harry Levinson, the five main types of bad boss are the workaholic, the kind of person you would describe as bullying, a person who communicates badly, the jellyfish type, and someone who insists on perfection.

2. As a way of getting ahead, to keep their self-respect, and for simple survival, wise employees handle problem bosses with a variety of strategies.

3. To cope with a bad-tempered employer, workers can both stand up for themselves and reasoning with a bullying boss.

4. Often, bad bosses communicate poorly or fail to calculate the impact of their personality on others; being a careful listener and sensitivity to others' responses are qualities that good bosses possess.

5. Employees who take the trouble to understand what makes their boss tick, engage in some self-analysis, and staying flexible are better prepared to cope with a difficult job environment than suffering in silence like some employees.

EXERCISE 18-3

Working individually or with a group, combine the sentences in each numbered item, using techniques of parallelism. For help, consult 18a through 18e.

EXAMPLE   A few years ago Canadians witnessed a renaissance of skateboarding. Skateboarding inspired its own clothing styles. In fact, a skateboard culture also was developed.

A few years ago Canadians witnessed a renaissance of skateboarding, *which not only inspired its own clothing styles but also developed its own culture.*

1. Cities became filled with whirling skateboarders; they flew on their skateboards. These skateboarders hopped curbs and would leap boldly up and down stairs. They also careened unsteadily down railings.

2. Not long afterward began the reign of in-line skates. They were built for speed. Young adults adopted them to commute and also in order to show off their style.

3. Skateboarders, who had a preference for gymnastic feats, were unlike the people who used in-line skates. These people favoured a graceful, undulating style marked by sweeping strides.

4. Late in the 1990s, small-wheeled scooters became popular. Adults liked them. They also became popular with young children.

5. Any town that has a sidewalk has certainly seen children wobbling on these scooters. If a town is big enough to have a rush hour, people there probably have seen businesspeople on motorized versions, trying to beat the traffic.

EXERCISE 18-4

Working individually or with a group, find the parallel elements in these three passages. Next, imitate the parallelism in the examples, using a different topic of your choice for each.

1. The time will come when that national spirit which has been spoken of will be truly felt among us, when we shall realize that we are four million Britons who are not free, when we shall be ready to take up that freedom, and to ask what the late prime minister of England assured us we should not be denied—our share of national rights.
   —Edward Blake, *A National Sentiment!*

2. It was the 18th of October, 1830, in the morning, when my feet first touched the Canadian shore. I threw myself on the ground, rolled in the sand, seized handfuls of it and kissed them, and danced around, till, in the eyes of several who were present, I passed for a madman.
   —Josiah Henson (an escaped slave and the model for Harriet Beecher Stowe's Uncle Tom), *An Autobiography*

3. It was Sunday morning at 11 o'clock and David Suzuki was on the radio, warning of the environmental catastrophe looming around his listeners. A generation ago most of us would have been in church at this time; and here we were in church again. Dr. Suzuki's programme, with its visions of Armageddon and its call to repentance and conversion, was surely a sermon.
   —David Cayley, "The Beer Can or the Highway?"

18f How does parallelism work in outlines and lists?

All items in formal OUTLINES and lists must be parallel in grammar and structure. (For more about outline format and outline development, see 2r.)

Outlines

NO   Reducing Traffic Fatalities
   I. Stricter laws
      A. Top speed should be 80 km/h on highways.
      B. Higher fines
      C. Requiring jail sentences for repeat offenders
   II. The use of safety devices should be mandated by law.

YES   Reducing Traffic Fatalities

    I. Passing stricter speed laws
        A. Making 80 km/h the top speed on highways
        B. Raising fines for speeding
        C. Requiring jail sentences for repeat offenders
   II. Mandating by law the use of safety devices

Lists

NO   Workaholics share these characteristics:
      1. They are intense and driven.
      2. Strong self-doubters
      3. Labour is preferred to leisure by workaholics.

YES   Workaholics share these characteristics:
      1. They are intense and driven.
      2. They have strong self-doubts.
      3. They prefer labour to leisure.

EXERCISE 18-5

Working individually or with a group, revise this outline so that all lines are complete sentences in parallel form. For help, consult 2r and 18f.

Planning for Your First Paycheque

  I. How to live within your means

      A. You should keep track of current expenses
      B. Working out a sensible breakdown of your paycheque among savings and expenses
      C. Credit cards and their uses

  II. Investing for your future

      A. Awareness of your company pension plan
      B. Learn about stocks, bonds, and other investments
      C. A long-term investment portfolio: first steps

Chapter 19
Variety and Emphasis

19a What are variety and emphasis in writing?

When you write sentences of various lengths and structures within a paragraph or longer piece of writing, you create **sentence variety.** Working in concert with sentence variety, **emphasis** allows you to add weight to ideas of special importance.

Using techniques of variety and emphasis adds style and clarity to your writing. Usually, the best time to apply the principles of variety and emphasis is while you are REVISING.

19b How do different sentence lengths create variety and emphasis?

To emphasize one idea among many others, you can express it in a sentence noticeably different in length from the sentences surrounding it. In the following example, a four-word sentence between two longer sentences carries the key message of the passage.

> Today is one of those excellent January partly cloudies in which light chooses an unexpected landscape to trick out in gilt, and then shadow sweeps it away. **You know you're alive.** You take huge steps, trying to feel the planet's roundness arc between your feet.
>
> —Annie Dillard, *Pilgrim at Tinker Creek*

Sometimes a string of short sentences creates impact and emphasis. Yet, at other times, a string of short sentences can be dull to read.

NO There is a problem. It is widely known as sick-building syndrome. It comes from indoor air pollution. It causes office workers to suffer. They have trouble breathing. They have painful rashes. Their heads ache. Their eyes burn.

YES　Widely known as sick-building syndrome, indoor air pollution causes office workers to suffer. They have trouble breathing. They have painful rashes. Their heads ache. Their eyes burn. [Many revisions are possible. This uses a long sentence to mention indoor air pollution and its victims; next, this retains the series of short sentences to emphasize each problem. Also, the conciseness of the revised version reduces 37 words to 27.]

Similarly, a string of COMPOUND SENTENCES can be monotonous to read and may fail to communicate relationships among ideas.

NO　Science fiction writers are often thinkers, **and** they are often dreamers, **and** they let their imaginations wander. Jules Verne was such a writer, **and** he predicted spaceships, **and** he forecast atomic submarines, **but** most people did not believe airplanes were possible.

YES　Science fiction writers are often thinkers and dreamers who let their imaginations wander. Jules Verne was one such writer. He predicted spaceships and atomic submarines before most people believed airplanes were possible.

EXERCISE 19-1

Working individually or with a group, revise these sets of sentences to vary the sentence lengths effectively. For help, consult 19a and 19b.

1.　Biometeorology is a science. It examines the study of weather's unseen power over living things. The science concentrates on the effects of weather patterns on human behaviour and health. Many researchers study these effects. One researcher is William Ferdinand Peterson. He has spent the past twenty years collecting statistics and anecdotes. He wrote the book *The Patient and the Weather.* His research focuses on the invisible elements of air. These elements include passing fronts. These elements include falling barometric pressure. The elements include shifting wind directions.

2.　Feared winds and all their variations—from katabatic to chinook to Santa Ana—are frequently considered the cause of every illness that can be imagined by many people in every country. In Russia, high winds and the frequency of strokes seem related, and in Italy, southern winds and heart attacks seem connected, and in Japan, researchers have noticed an increase in asthma attacks whenever the wind changes direction.

19c How do occasional questions, commands, or exclamations create variety and emphasis?

The majority of sentences in English are DECLARATIVE—they declare something by making a statement. Declarative sentences offer an almost infinite variety of structures and patterns. For variety and emphasis, you might want to use three alternative types of sentences occasionally.

A sentence that asks a question is called INTERROGATIVE. Occasional questions, placed appropriately, tend to involve readers. A sentence that issues a mild or strong command is called IMPERATIVE. Occasional mild commands urge a reader to think along with you. A sentence that makes an exclamation is called EXCLAMATORY. An occasional exclamatory sentence can enliven writing, but this sentence type is rarely appropriate in ACADEMIC WRITING.

ALERT: A declarative statement ends with a period (Chapter 23)—or semicolon (Chapter 25) or colon (Chapter 26). A mild command ends with a period. A strong command and an exclamation end with an exclamation point (Chapter 23).

Here's a paragraph with declarative, interrogative, and imperative sentences.

> Imagine what people ate during the winter as little as seventy-five years ago. They ate food that was local, long-lasting, and dull, like acorn squash, turnips, and cabbage. Walk into an American supermarket in February and the world lies before you: grapes, melons, artichokes, fennel, lettuce, peppers, pistachios, dates, even strawberries, to say nothing of ice cream. Have you ever considered what a triumph of civilization it is to be able to buy a pound of chicken livers? If you lived on a farm and had to kill a chicken when you wanted to eat one, you wouldn't ever accumulate a pound of chicken livers.
>
> —Phyllis Rose, "Shopping and Other Spiritual Adventures in America Today"

EXERCISE 19-2

Working individually or with a group, write an imitation of the following paragraph. This paragraph varies sentence lengths and uses a question and a command effectively. The result emphasizes the key points. Choose your own topic, but follow the style of the paragraph closely. For help, consult 19c.

> Why are some animal species easily pushed to the verge of extinction while others thrive in almost every type of environment? Consider the humble cottontail rabbit. Equally at home in city parks, suburban backyards, or wilderness areas, this species thrives everywhere it can

find a little greenery. It is not choosy about diet, either. It survives by eating woody stems in winter and gorging on the lush growth of summer. And what about shelter? The cottontail rabbit builds a nest and raises its young wherever it locates bits of dried grass to hide its babies. Other small mammals, such as woodchucks, weasels, and beaver, have more exacting needs for food or shelter that limit their adaptability. The cottontail survives by remaining flexible, refusing to specialize.

19d How can modifiers create variety and emphasis?

MODIFIERS can expand sentences to add richness to your writing and create a pleasing mixture of variety and emphasis. Your choice of where to place modifiers to expand your sentences depends on the focus you want each sentence to communicate, either on its own or in concert with its surrounding sentences. Be careful where you place modifiers because you don't want to introduce the error known as a MISPLACED MODIFIER (see 14a).

BASIC SENTENCE	The river rose.
ADJECTIVE	The **swollen** river rose.
ADVERB	The river rose **dangerously.**
PREPOSITIONAL PHRASE	The river rose **above its banks.**
PARTICIPIAL PHRASE	**Swelled by melting snow,** the river rose.
ABSOLUTE PHRASE	**Uprooted trees swirling away in the current,** the river rose.
ADVERB CLAUSE	**Because the snows had been heavy that winter,** the river rose.
ADJECTIVE CLAUSE	The river, **which runs through vital farmland,** rose.

EXERCISE 19-3

Working individually or with a group, expand each sentence by adding each kind of modifier illustrated in 19d.

1. We bought a house.
2. The roof leaked.
3. I remodelled the kitchen.
4. Neighbours brought food.
5. Everyone enjoyed the barbecue.

19e How does repetition affect variety and emphasis?

You can repeat one or more words that express a main idea when your message is suitable. This technique creates a rhythm that focuses attention on the main idea. Here's an example that uses deliberate repetition.

> The **knowledge** that you can have is inexhaustible, and what is inexhaustible is benevolent. The **knowledge** that you cannot have is of the riddles of birth and death, of our future destiny and the purposes of God. Here there is no **knowledge,** but illusions that restrict freedom and limit hope. Accept the mystery behind **knowledge.** It is not darkness but shadow.
>
> —Northrop Frye, Convocation Address, 1988

Frye repeats the word *knowledge* in different contexts to distinguish between the kinds of knowledge available to humans and to show the importance of respecting the limits of our knowledge. His repetition of *inexhaustible,* his use of the parallel phrases *The knowledge that you can have . . . The knowledge that you cannot have,* and his linking of important concepts with the conjunctions *and* and *but* set up a series of rhythms that give this passage an almost prophetic power, in keeping with its subject matter.

At the same time, don't confuse deliberate repetition with a lack of vocabulary variety.

> **NO** An insurance agent can be an excellent adviser when you want to buy a car. An insurance agent has complete records on most cars. An insurance agent knows which car models are prone to have accidents. An insurance agent can tell you which car models are the most expensive to repair if they are in a collision. An insurance agent can tell you which models are most likely to be stolen.

> **YES** If you are thinking of buying a new car, an insurance agent, who usually has complete records on most cars, can be an excellent adviser. Any professional insurance broker knows which automobile models are prone to have accidents. Did you know that some cars suffer more damage than others in a collision? If you want to know which vehicles crumple more than others and which are least expensive to repair, ask an insurance agent. Similarly, some car models are more likely to be stolen, so find out from the person who specializes in dealing with car insurance claims.

19f How else can I create variety and emphasis?

Changing word order

Standard word order in English places the SUBJECT before the VERB.

> The **mayor *walked*** into the room. [*Mayor* is the subject, which comes before the verb *walked*.]

Any variation from standard word order creates emphasis. For example, **inverted word order** places the verb before the subject.

> Into the room ***walked*** the **mayor.** [*Mayor* is the subject, which comes after the verb *walked*.]

Changing a sentence's subject

The subject of a sentence establishes the focus for that sentence. To create the emphasis you want, you can vary each sentence's subject. All the sample sentences below express the same information, but the focus changes in each according to the subject (and its corresponding verb).

> **Our study *showed*** that 25 percent of undergraduates' time is spent eating or sleeping. [Focus is on the study.]
>
> **Undergraduates *eat or sleep*** 25 percent of the time, according to our study. [Focus is on the undergraduates.]
>
> **Eating or sleeping *occupies*** 25 percent of undergraduates' time, according to our study. [Focus is on eating and sleeping.]
>
> **Twenty-five percent of undergraduates' time *is spent*** eating or sleeping, according to our study. [Focus is on the percentage of time.]

Using a periodic sentence among cumulative sentences

The **cumulative sentence** is the most common sentence structure in English. Its name reflects the way information accumulates in the sentence until it reaches a period. Its structure starts with a SUBJECT and VERB and continues with modifiers. Another term for a cumulative sentence is *loose sentence* because it lacks a tightly planned structure.

For greater impact, you might occasionally use a **periodic sentence,** also called a *climactic sentence,* which reserves the main idea for the end of the sentence. This structure tends to draw in the reader as it moves toward the period. If overused, however, periodic sentences lose their punch.

CUMULATIVE	We expect them all to thank us for it after we have frightened our own people, disregarded our friends, and intimidated those we should be trying to win over to our side.
PERIODIC	We have frightened our own people, disregarded our friends, and intimidated those we should be trying to win over to our side, and now we expect them all to thank us for it.

Chapter 20

Usage Glossary

A usage glossary presents the customary manner of using particular words and phrases. "Customary manner," however, is not as firm in practice as the term implies. Usage standards change. If you think a word's usage might differ from what you read here, consult a dictionary published more recently than the current edition of this handbook.

The meaning of *informal* or *colloquial* in the definition of a word or phrase is that it's found in everyday or conversational speech, but it needs to be avoided in ACADEMIC WRITING. Another term, *nonstandard*, indicates that the word or phrase, although widely understood in speech and dialect writing, isn't suitable in standard spoken or written English.

All terms of grammar and writing in this Usage Glossary are defined in the Terms Glossary, which begins directly before the Index.

a, an Use *a* before words that begin with a consonant (*a dog, a grade, a hole*) or a consonant sound (*a one-day sale, a European*). Use *an* before words or acronyms that begin with a vowel sound or a silent *h* (*an owl; an hour; an MRI*). Most writers of North American English use *a*, not *an*, before words starting with a pronounced *h*: *a* (not *an*) *historical event*.

accept, except The verb *accept* means "agree to; receive." As a preposition, *except* means "excluding." As a verb, *except* means "exclude; leave out."

- The workers wanted to **accept** [verb] management's offer **except** [preposition] for one detail: They wanted the limit on overtime **excepted** [verb] from the contract.

advice, advise *Advice*, a noun, means "recommendation." *Advise*, a verb, means "recommend; give advice."

- I **advise** [verb] you to follow your car mechanic's **advice** [noun].

affect, effect As a verb, *affect* means "cause a change in; influence." (*Affect* is a noun in psychology.) As a noun, *effect* means "result or conclusion"; as a verb, *effect* means "bring about."

■ Loud music **affects** people's hearing for life, so some bands have **effected** changes to lower the volume. Many fans, however, don't care about the harmful **effects** of high decibel levels.

aggravate, irritate *Aggravate* is used colloquially to mean "irritate." In academic writing, use *aggravate* only to mean "intensify; make worse." Use *irritate* to mean "annoy; make impatient."

■ The coach was **irritated** by reduced time for practice, which **aggravated** the team's difficulties with concentration.

ain't *Ain't* is a nonstandard contraction. Use *am not, is not,* or *are not* for standard spoken and written English.

all ready, already *All ready* means "completely prepared." *Already* means "before; by this time."

■ The team was **all ready** to play, but the coach was **already** in a bad mood.

all right *All right* is always written as two words, never one (never *alright*).

all together, altogether *All together* means "in a group; in unison." *Altogether* means "entirely; thoroughly."

■ The three cousins and six nephews said that it was **altogether** absurd for them to stay **all together** in a single hotel room.

allude, elude *Allude* means "refer to indirectly." *Elude* means "escape notice."

■ The detectives **alluded** to budget cuts by saying, "Conditions beyond our control allowed the suspect to **elude** us."

allusion, illusion An *allusion* is an indirect reference to something. An *illusion* is a false impression or idea.

■ The couple's casual **allusions** to European tourist sites created the **illusion** that they had visited them.

a lot *A lot* is informal for *a great deal* or *a great many.* Avoid using it in academic writing. If you must use it, write it as two words (never *alot*).

a.m., p.m. Use these abbreviations only with numbers, not as substitutes for the words *morning, afternoon,* and *evening.* Capital letters are used for these abbreviations by many editors and dictionaries. Whichever style you choose, be consistent in each piece of writing.

■ We will arrive in the **evening** [not *p.m.*], and we must leave by **8:00 a.m.**

among, amongst, between Use *among* for three or more items. Use *between* for two items. North American English prefers *among* to *amongst.*

- My three housemates discussed **among** [not *between*] themselves the choice **between** staying in school and getting full-time jobs.

amoral, immoral *Amoral* means "neither moral nor immoral." *Amoral* also means "without any sense of what's moral or immoral." *Immoral* means "morally wrong."

- Although many people consider birth control an **amoral** issue, the Catholic Church considers the practice **immoral.**

amount, number Use *amount* for noncountable things (wealth, work, happiness). Use *number* for countable items.

- The **amount** of rice to cook depends on the **number** of guests.

an See *a, an.*

and/or This term is appropriate in business and legal writing when either or both of the two items can apply: *Sending documents is quicker by e-mail **and/or** fax.* In the humanities, writers usually express the alternatives in words: *Sending documents is quicker by e-mail, fax, or both.*

anymore Use *anymore* with the meaning "now, any longer" only in negations or questions. In positive statements, instead of *anymore,* use an adverb such as *now.*

- No one wants to live without air conditioning **anymore.** Summers are so hot **now** [not *anymore*] that more people than ever suffer from heatstroke.

anyone, any one *Anyone* is a singular indefinite pronoun meaning "any person at all." *Any one* (two words), an adjective that modifies a pronoun, means "a member of a group."

- **Anyone** could test-drive **any one** of the display vehicles.

anyplace *Anyplace* is informal. Use *any place* or *anywhere* instead.

anyways, anywheres *Anyways* and *anywheres* are nonstandard for *anyway* and *anywhere.*

apt, likely, liable *Apt* and *likely* are often used interchangeably. Strictly, *apt* indicates a tendency or inclination. *Likely* indicates a reasonable expectation or greater certainty than *apt* does. *Liable* usually denotes legal responsibility or implies unpleasant consequences but usage today allows it to mean *likely.*

- Evander is **apt** to run stop signs, so he'll **likely** get a ticket. [Some authorities in Canada do not allow this use of *likely* as an adverb and prefer *probably* here.] That means he's **liable** for any consequences.

as, as if, as though, like   Use *as, as if,* or *as though,* but not *like,* to introduce a clause.

- This hamburger tastes good, **as** [not *like*] a hamburger should. It tastes **as if** [or *as though,* not *like*] it were barbecued over charcoal, not gas.

Both *as* and *like* can function as prepositions in comparisons. However, use *as* to indicate equivalence between two nouns or pronouns, and use *like* to indicate similarity but not equivalence.

- My friend Roger served **as** [not *like*] mediator in a dispute about my neighbour's tree that dripped sap on my driveway **like** [not *as*] a leaky tap.

assure, ensure, insure   *Assure* means "promise; convince." *Ensure* and *insure* both mean "make certain or secure," but *insure* is reserved for financial or legal matters.

- The insurance agent **assured** me that he could **insure** my car, but only I could **ensure** that I would drive safely.

as to   *As to* is nonstandard for *about.*

awful, awfully   *Awful* is an adjective meaning "inspiring awe" and "creating fear." *Awfully* is an adverb meaning "in a way to inspire awe" and "terrifying." Only colloquially are *awful* and *awfully* used to mean "very" or "extremely."

- I was **extremely** [not *awfully*] tired yesterday.

a while, awhile   As two words, *a while* (an article and a noun) can function as a subject or object. As one word, *awhile* is an adverb. In a prepositional phrase, the correct form is *for a while, in a while,* or *after a while.*

- It took **a while** [article and noun] to drive to the zoo, where we saw the seals bask **awhile** [adverb modifying verb *bask*] in the sun after romping **for a while** [prepositional phrase] in the water.

backup, back up   As a noun, *backup* means "a replacement, fill-in, surrogate; a copy of computer files." As an adjective, *backup* means "alternative." As a verb, *back up* (two words) means "to serve as a substitute or support"; "to accumulate, as from a stoppage"; and "to make a backup copy of a computer disk or hard drive."

- I'll need a **backup** [noun] of your hard drive if I'm going to serve as your **backup** [adjective] computer consultant. I **back up** [verb] all computer disks and drives when I work with them.

bad, badly   *Bad* is an adjective; use it and not *badly* after linking verbs (*look, feel, smell, taste, sound*; these verbs can function as either linking verbs or action verbs depending on the context). *Badly* is an adverb.

- Farmers feel **bad** [*feel* is a linking verb, so *bad* is the adjective] because a **bad** [adjective] drought is **badly** [adverb] damaging their crops.

been, being   *Been* (a past participle) and *being* (a present participle) cannot stand alone as main verbs. They work only with auxiliary verbs.

- You **are being** [not *being*] honest to admit that you **have been** [not *been*] tempted to eat the whole pie.

being as, being that   *Being as* and *being that* are nonstandard for *because* or *since.*

- We had to forfeit the game **because** [not *being as* or *being that*] our goalie was badly injured.

beside, besides   As prepositions, *beside* means "next to, by the side of," and *besides* means "other than, in addition to." As an adverb, *besides* means "also, moreover."

- She stood **beside** the new car, insisting that she would drive. No one **besides** her had a driver's licence. **Besides,** she owned the car.

better, had better   *Better* is informal for *had better.*

- We **had better** [not *better* alone] be careful of the ice.

between   See *among, amongst, between.*

bias, biased   As a noun, *bias* means "a mental leaning for or against something or someone." As an adjective, *biased* means "prejudiced." As a verb, *bias* means "to be prejudiced." The past tense of this verb is *biased.*

- Horace's **bias** [noun] against some politicians grew from his disapproval of their **biased** [adjective] attitudes toward the unemployed. Beverly was **biased** [verb] against all politicians, no matter what they believed.

breath, breathe   *Breath* is a noun; *breathe* is a verb.

- Take a deep **breath** [noun] before you start so that you can **breathe** [verb] normally afterward.

bring, take   *Bring* indicates movement from a distant place to a near place. *Take* indicates movement from a near to a distant place.

- If you **bring** over sandwiches, we'll have time to **take** [not *bring*] the dog to the vet.

but, however, yet   Use *but, however,* or *yet* alone, not in combination with each other.

- The economy is strong, **but** [not *but yet* or *but however*] unemployment is high.

calculate, figure   These are colloquial terms for *estimate, imagine, expect, think,* and the like.

can, may   *Can* signifies ability or capacity. *May* requests or grants permission. In negative expressions, *can* is acceptable for *may.*

- When you **can** [not *may*] get here on time, you **may** [not *can*] be excused early. However, if you are **not** on time, you **cannot** [or *may not*] expect privileges.

can't hardly, can't scarcely   These double negatives are nonstandard for *can hardly* and *can scarcely.*

capital, capitol   *Capital* means a city in which a national or regional government sits (Winnipeg, the *capital* of Manitoba), wealth, or "most important." *Capitol,* in the United States, means "a building in which legislators meet."

- If our group raises enough **capital,** we will send a delegation to Oregon's state **capitol** to lobby against softwood tariffs.

censor, censure   The verb *censor* means "delete objectionable material; judge." The verb *censure* means "condemn or reprimand officially."

- The town council **censured** the mayor for trying to **censor** a report.

chairman, chairperson, chair   Many writers and speakers prefer the gender-neutral terms *chairperson* and *chair* to *chairman.* In general, *chair* is used more than *chairperson.*

choose, chose   *Choose* is the simple form of the verb. *Chose* is the past-tense form of the verb.

- I **chose** a movie last week, so you **choose** one tonight.

cite, site, sight   The verb *cite* means "quote by way of example, authority, or proof." The noun *site* means "a particular place or location" and is not to be confused with *sight.*

- The private investigator **cited** evidence from the crime **site** and the defendant's Web **site.**
- We are planning a visit to the historic **sites** near Quebec City, and then we will rent a car to see the **sights** of the Gaspé.

cloth, clothe   *Cloth* is a noun meaning "fabric." *Clothe* is a verb meaning "dress with garments or fabric."

- "**Clothe** me in red velvet," proclaimed the king, and the royal tailors ran to gather samples of **cloth** to show him.

complement, compliment   As a noun, *complement* means "something that goes well with or completes." As a noun, *compliment* means "praise, flattery." As a verb, *complement* means "bring to perfection; go well with, complete." As a verb, *compliment* means "praise, flatter."

- The dean's **compliment** was a perfect **complement** to the thrill of my graduating. My parents felt proud when she **complimented** me publicly, an honour that **complemented** their joy.

comprise, include   See *include, comprise.*

conscience, conscious   The noun *conscience* means "a sense of right and wrong." The adjective *conscious* means "being aware or awake."

- Always be **conscious** of what your **conscience** is telling you.

consensus of opinion   This phrase is redundant; use *consensus* only.

- Parliament reached **consensus** on the issue of campaign reform.

continual(ly), continuous(ly)   *Continual* means "occurring repeatedly." *Continuous* means "going on without interruption."

- Larry needed intravenous fluids **continuously** for days, so the nurses **continually** monitored him.

could care less   *Could care less* is nonstandard for *could not care less.*

could of   *Could of* is nonstandard for *could have.*

couple, a couple of   These terms are nonstandard for *a few* or *several.*

- Rest here for **a few** [not *a couple* or *a couple of*] minutes.

criteria, criterion   A *criterion* is "a standard of judgment." *Criteria* is the plural of *criterion.*

- A sense of history is an important **criterion** for judging political candidates, but voters must consider other **criteria** as well.

data   *Data* is the plural of *datum*, a word rarely used today. Informally, *data* is used as a singular noun that takes a singular verb. In academic or professional writing, *data* is considered plural and takes a plural verb (although this usage is currently viewed as overly formal by some).

- The **data** suggest [not *suggests*] some people are addicted to e-mail.

different from, different than   Some authorities prefer *different from* to *different than* in all circumstances, although *different than* is usually considered acceptable to introduce a clause.

- Please advise us if your research yields data **different from** past results; your last report was far **different than** we expected it to be.

disinterested, uninterested   *Disinterested* means "impartial, unbiased." *Uninterested* is used for "not interested, indifferent."

- Jurors need to be **disinterested** in hearing evidence, but never **uninterested.**

don't   *Don't* is a contraction for *do not,* never for *does not* (whose contraction is *doesn't*).

- She **doesn't** [not *don't*] like crowds.

effect   See *affect, effect.*

elicit, illicit   The verb *elicit* means "draw forth or bring out." The adjective *illicit* means "illegal."

- The MP's **illicit** conduct **elicited** a mass outcry from her constituents.

elude   See *allude, elude.*

emigrate (from), immigrate (to)   *Emigrate* means "leave one country to live in another." *Immigrate* means "enter a country to live there."

- My great-grandmother **emigrated** from Kiev to London in 1890. Then, she **immigrated** to Toronto in 1892.

enclose, inclose; enclosure, inclosure   In North American English, *enclose* and *enclosure* are the preferred spellings.

ensure   See *assure, ensure, insure.*

enthused   *Enthused* is nonstandard for *enthusiastic.*

- Adam was **enthusiastic** [not *enthused*] about the courses he chose.

etc.   *Etc.* is the abbreviation for the Latin *et cetera,* meaning "and the rest." For writing in the humanities, avoid using *etc.* Acceptable substitutes are *and the like, and so on,* or *and so forth.*

everyday, every day   The adjective *everyday* means "daily." *Every day* (two words) is an adjective with a noun that can function as a subject or an object.

- Being late for work has become an **everyday** [adjective] occurrence for me. **Every day** [subject] brings me closer to being fired. I worry about it **every day** [object].

everyone, every one   *Everyone* is a singular, indefinite pronoun. *Every one* (two words) is an adjective and a pronoun, meaning "each member in a group."

- **Everyone** enjoyed **every one** of the comedy skits.

everywheres   *Everywheres* is nonstandard for *everywhere*.

except   See *accept, except*.

explicit, implicit   *Explicit* means "directly stated or expressed." *Implicit* means "implied, suggested."

- The warning on cigarette packs is **explicit:** "Smoking can kill you." The **implicit** message is, "Don't smoke."

farther, further   Many writers reserve *farther* for geographical distances and *further* for all other cases.

fewer, less   Use *fewer* for anything that can be counted (that is, with count nouns): *fewer* dollars, *fewer* fleas, *fewer* haircuts. Use *less* with collective (or other noncount) nouns: *less* money, *less* scratching, *less* hair.

former, latter   When two items are referred to, *former* signifies the first item and *latter* signifies the second item. Never use *former* and *latter* when referring to more than two items.

- Brazil and Ecuador are South American countries. Portuguese is the official language in the **former,** Spanish in the **latter.**

go, say   All forms of *go* are nonstandard when used in place of all forms of *say.*

- While stepping on my hand, Frank **says** [not *goes*], "Your hand is in my way."

gone, went   *Gone* is the past participle of *go; went* is the past tense of *go.*

- They **went** [not *gone*] to the concert after Ira **had gone** [not *had went*] home.

good, well   *Good* is an adjective. As an adverb, *good* is nonstandard. Instead, use *well.*

- **Good** [adjective] maintenance helps cars run **well** [adverb; not *good*].

good and   *Good and* is a nonstandard intensifier. Instead, use more precise words.

- They were **exhausted** [not *good and tired*].

got, have   *Got* is nonstandard for *have.*

- What do we **have** [not *got*] for supper?

hardly   Use *hardly* with *can*, never with *can't.*

have, of   Use *have*, not *of*, after such verbs as *could, should, would, might,* and *must.*

- You *should* **have** [not *should of*] called first.

have got, have to, have got to   In formal usage, avoid using *have got* when *have* alone delivers your meaning. Also, avoid using *have to* or *have got to* for *must.*

- I **have** [not *have got*] several more sources to read. I **must** [not *have got to*] finish my reading today.

he/she, s/he, his/her   When using gender-neutral language, write out *he or she* or *his or her* instead of using and/or constructions. To be more concise, switch to plural pronouns and antecedents. (For more about gender-neutral language, see 21g.)

- **Everyone** bowed *his or her* head. [**Everyone** bowed **his** head is considered sexist language if women were present when the heads were bowed.]
- The **people** bowed **their** heads.

historic, historical   The adjective *historic* means "important in history" or "highly memorable." The adjective *historical* means "relating to history." Most writers in North America use *a,* not *an,* before these words.

hopefully   *Hopefully* is an adverb meaning "with hope, in a hopeful manner," so as an adverb, it can modify a verb, an adjective, or another adverb. However, *hopefully* is often considered nonstandard as a sentence modifier meaning "we hope"; therefore, in academic writing, avoid this usage.

- They waited **hopefully** [adverb] for the crippled airplane to land. **We hope** [not *Hopefully,*] it will land safely.

humanity, humankind, humans, mankind   To use gender-neutral language, choose *humanity, humankind,* or *humans* instead of *mankind.*

- Some think that the computer has helped **humanity** more than any other twentieth-century invention.

i.e.   This abbreviation refers to the Latin term *id est.* In academic writing, use the English translation, *that is.*

if, whether   At the start of a noun clause that expresses speculation or unknown conditions, you can use either *if* or *whether*. However, in such conditional clauses use only *whether* (or *whether or not*) when alternatives are expressed or implied. In a conditional clause that does not express or imply alternatives, use only *if*.

- **If** [not *whether*] you promise not to step on my feet, I might dance with you. Still, I'm not sure **if** [or *whether*] I want to dance with you. Once I decide, I'll dance with you **whether** [not *if*] I like the music or **whether** [not *if*] the next song is fast or slow.

illicit   See *elicit, illicit.*

illusion   See *allusion, illusion.*

immigrate   See *emigrate, immigrate.*

immoral   See *amoral, immoral.*

imply, infer   *Imply* means "hint at or suggest." *Infer* means "draw a conclusion." A writer or speaker *implies;* a reader or listener *infers.*

- When the cabinet minister **implied** that she would be taking French lessons, reporters **inferred** that she was planning to run for her party's leadership.

include, comprise   The verb *include* means "contain or regard as part of a whole." The verb *comprise* means "consist of or be composed of."

incredible, incredulous   *Incredible* means "extraordinary; not believable." *Incredulous* means "unable or unwilling to believe."

- Listeners were **incredulous** as the freed hostages described the **incredible** hardships they had experienced.

in regard to, with regard to, as regards, regarding   Use *about, concerning,* and *for* in place of these wordy phrases. Also, avoid the nonstandard *as regards to.*

- **Concerning** [not *in regard to, with regard to, as regards,* or *regarding*] your question, we can now confirm that your payment was received.

inside of, outside of   These phrases are nonstandard when used to mean *inside* or *outside*. When writing about time, never use *inside of* to mean "in less than."

- She waited **outside** [not *outside of*] the apartment house. He changed to clothes that were more informal in **less than** [not *inside of*] ten minutes.

insure   See *assure, ensure, insure.*

irregardless   *Irregardless* is nonstandard for *regardless.*

is when, is where   Never use these constructions when you define something. Instead, use active verbs.

■ Defensive driving **involves staying** [not *is when you stay*] alert.

its, it's   *Its* is a personal pronoun in the possessive case. *It's* is a contraction of *it is* or *it has.*

■ The dog buried **its** bone today. **It's** hot today, which makes the dog restless. **It's** been hotter the usual this week.

kind, sort   Combine *kind* and *sort* with *this* or *that* when referring to singular nouns. Combine *kinds* and *sorts* with *these* or *those* when referring to plural nouns. Also, never use *a* or *an* after *kind of* or *sort of.*

■ To stay cool, drink **these kinds** of fluids [not *this kind*] for **this sort of** day [not *this sort of a*].

kind of, sort of   These phrases are colloquial adverbs. In academic writing, use *somewhat.*

■ The campers were **somewhat** [not *kind of*] dehydrated after the hike.

later, latter   *Later* means "after some time; subsequently." *Latter* refers to the second of two items.

■ The college library stays open **later** than the town library; also, the **latter** is closed on weekends.

lay, lie   The verb *lay* (**lay,** *laid, laid, laying*) means "place or put something, usually on something else" and needs a direct object. The verb *lie* (**lie,** *lay, lain, lying*), meaning "recline," doesn't need a direct object. Substituting *lay* for *lie,* or the opposite, is nonstandard.

■ **Lay** [not *lie*] down the blanket [direct object], and then place the baby to **lie** [not *lay*] in the shade.

leave, let   *Leave* means "depart." *Leave* is nonstandard for *let. Let* means "allow, permit."

■ Could you **let** [not *leave*] me use your car tonight?

less   See *fewer, less.*

lie   See *lay, lie.*

like   See *as, as if, as though, like.*

likely   See *apt, likely, liable.*

lots, lots of, a lot of   These are colloquial constructions. Instead, use *many, much,* or *a great deal.*

mankind   See *humanity, humankind, humans, mankind.*

may   See *can, may.*

maybe, may be   *Maybe* is an adverb; *may be* (two words) is a verb phrase.
- **Maybe** [adverb] we can win, but our team **may be** [verb phrase] too tired.

may of, might of   *May of* and *might of* are nonstandard for *may have* and *might have.*

media   *Media* is the plural of *medium,* yet colloquial usage now pairs it with a singular verb: *The media saturates us with information about every fire.*

morale, moral   *Morale* is a noun meaning "a mental state relating to courage, confidence, or enthusiasm." As a noun, *moral* means an "ethical lesson implied or taught by a story or event." As an adjective, *moral* means "ethical."
- One **moral** [noun] of the story is that many people who suffer from low **morale** [noun] still abide by high **moral** [adjective] standards.

most   *Most* is nonstandard for *almost.* Also, *most* is the superlative form of an adjective (*some* words, *more* words, *most* words) and of adverbs (*most* suddenly).
- **Almost** [not *Most*] all writers agree that Shakespeare penned the **most** [adjective] brilliant plays ever written.

Ms.   *Ms.* is a woman's title free of reference to marital status, equivalent to *Mr.* for men. Generally, use *Ms.* unless a woman requests *Miss* or *Mrs.*

must of   *Must of* is nonstandard for *must have.*

nowheres   *Nowheres* is nonstandard for *nowhere.*

number   See *amount, number.*

of   Use *have,* not *of,* after modal auxiliary verbs (*could, may, might, must, should, would*). See also *could of; may of, might of; must of; should of; would of.*

off of   *Off of* is nonstandard for *off.*
- Don't fall **off** [not *off of*] the stage.

OK, O.K., okay   These three forms are informal. In academic writing, choose words that express more specific meanings. If you must use the term, choose the full word *okay.*
- The weather was **suitable** [not *okay*] for a picnic.

on account of, owing to the fact that   Use *because* or *because of* in place of these wordy phrases.
- **Because of the rain** [not *On account of the rain* or *Owing to the fact that it rained*], the picnic was cancelled.

oral, verbal   The adjective *oral* means "spoken or being done by the mouth." The adjective *verbal* means "relating to language" (*verbal* skill) or to words rather than actions, facts, or ideas.

outside of   See *inside of, outside of.*

percent, percentage   Use *percent* with specific numbers: two *percent,* 95 *percent.* Use *percentage* to refer to portions of a whole in general terms.
- Less than **6 percent** of Canada's land is legally protected as wilderness, a smaller **percentage** [not *percent*] than is commonly believed.

pixel, pixellation, pixillated   *Pixel,* a relatively new word created from "picture/pix" and "element," is the name for a small dot on a video screen. *Pixellation* (with an *e,* as in *pixel*) is a noun meaning "a film technique that makes people appear to move faster than they are." *Pixillated* (with an *i*), a verb unrelated to *pixels,* derives from *pixie,* meaning "a mischievous elf," and now describes someone who is slightly drunk.

plus   *Plus* is nonstandard for *and, also, in addition,* and *moreover.*
- The band booked three concerts in Hungary, **and** [not *plus*] it will tour Poland for a month. **In addition,** [not *Plus,*] it may perform once in Austria.

practice, practise   In Canada, *practice* is the noun; *practise* is the verb.

precede, proceed   *Precede* is a verb that means "go before." *Proceed* is a verb that means "to advance, go on, undertake, carry on."
- **Preceded** by elephants and music, the ringmaster **proceeded** into the main tent.

pretty   *Pretty* is informal for *rather, quite, somewhat,* or *very.*
- The flu epidemic was **quite** [not *pretty*] severe.

principal, principle   As a noun, *principal* means "chief person; main or original amount." As an adjective, *principal* means "most important." *Principle* is a noun that means "a basic truth or rule."

- During the assembly, the **principal** [noun] said, "A **principal** [adjective] value in our democracy is the **principle** [noun] of free speech."

proceed   See *precede, proceed.*

quotation, quote   *Quotation* is a noun, and *quote* is a verb. Don't use *quote* as a noun.

- One newspaper reporter **quoted** [verb] the candidate, and soon the **quotations** [noun—not *quotes,* which is a verb] were widely broadcast.

raise, rise   *Raise* is a verb (**raise,** *raised, raising*) that means "lift" or "construct" and needs a direct object. *Rise* (**rise,** *rose, risen, rising*) means "get up," "go upward," or "revolt," and doesn't need a direct object. Substituting *rise* for *raise,* or the opposite, is nonstandard.

- If the citizens **rise** [not *raise*], they will **raise** [not *rise* or *rise up*] the flag of liberty.

real, really   These words are nonstandard for *very* and *extremely.*

reason is because   This phrase is redundant. To be concise and correct, use *reason is that.*

- One **reason** we moved **is that** [not *is because*] our factory was relocated.

reason why   This phrase is redundant. To be concise and correct, use *reason* or *why.*

- I don't know **why** [not *the reason why*] they left home.

regarding   See *in regard to, with regard to, as regards, regarding.*

regardless   See *irregardless.*

respectful, respectfully   As an adjective, *respectful* means "showing regard or honour; marked by respect." *Respectfully* is the adverb form of *respectful.* Be careful not to confuse these words with *respective* and *respectively* (see next entry).

- The child listened **respectfully** [adverb] to the lecture about **respectful** [adjective] behaviour.

respective, respectively   *Respective,* a noun, refers to two or more individual persons or things. *Respectively,* an adverb, refers back to two or more individuals or things in the same sequence that they were originally mentioned.

- After the fire drill, Dr. Daniel Eagle and Dr. Jessica Chess returned to their **respective** offices [that is, he returned to his office, and she returned to her office] on the second and third floors, **respectively** [his office is on the second floor, and her office is on the third floor].

rise   See *raise, rise.*

scarcely   Use *scarcely* with *can*, never with *can't.*

seen   *Seen* is the past participle of the verb *see* (*see, saw,* **seen,** *seeing*). *Seen* is nonstandard for *saw*, a verb in the past tense. Always use *seen* with an auxiliary verb.

- Last night, I **saw** [not *seen*] the movie that you **had seen** [not *seen*] last week.

set, sit   The verb *set* (**set,** *setting*) means "put in place, position, put down" and needs a direct object. The verb *sit* (**sit,** *sat, sitting*) means "be seated" and doesn't need a direct object. Substituting *set* for *sit,* and the opposite, is nonstandard.

- Susan **set** [not *sat*] the sandwiches beside the salad, made Spot **sit** [not *set*] down, and then **sat** [not *set*] on the sofa.

shall, will, should   *Shall* was once used with *I* and *we* for future-tense verbs, and *will* was used for all other persons. Today, *shall* is considered formal, and *will* is more widely used. In questions, *should* and *shall* are often used synonymously.

- We **will** [or *shall*] depart on Monday, but he **will** wait until Thursday to depart. **Should** [or *Shall*] I telephone ahead to reserve a suite at the hotel?

should of   *Should of* is nonstandard for *should have.*

sit   See *set, sit.*

site   See *cite, site, sight.*

sometime, sometimes, some time   The adverb *sometime* means "at an unspecified time." The adverb *sometimes* means "now and then." *Some time* (two words) is an adjective with a noun that means "an amount or span of time."

- **Sometime** [adverb for "at an unspecified time"] next year, I must take my qualifying exams. I **sometimes** [adverb for "now and then"] worry whether I'll find **some time** [adjective with a noun] to study for them.

sort of   See *kind of, sort of.*

stationary, stationery   *Stationary* means "not moving; unchanging." *Stationery* refers to paper and related writing products.

■ Using our firm's **stationery,** I wrote to city officials about a **stationary** light pole that had been knocked over in a car accident.

such   *Such* is informal for intensifiers such as *very* and *extremely.* The standard meaning of *such* is "of the same or similar kind; to the same degree."

■ The play got **very** [not *such*] bad reviews. The playwright was embarrassed by **such** strong criticism.

supposed to, used to   The final *-d* is essential in both phrases.

■ We were **supposed** to [not *suppose to*] leave early. I **used to** [not *use to*] wake up before the alarm rang.

sure   *Sure* is nonstandard for *surely* or *certainly.*

■ I was **certainly** [not *sure*] surprised at the results.

sure and, try and   Both phrases are nonstandard for *sure to* and *try to.*

■ Please **try to** [not *try and*] reach my doctor.

than, then   *Than* indicates comparison; *then* relates to time.

■ Please put on your coat, and **then** take your hat. It's colder outside **than** you think.

that, which   Use *that* with restrictive (essential) clauses only. You can use *which* with both restrictive and nonrestrictive (nonessential) clauses; however, many people reserve *which* to use only with nonrestrictive clauses.

■ The house **that** [or *which*] Jack built is on Beanstalk Street, **which** [not *that*] runs past the reservoir.

their, there, they're   *Their* is a possessive pronoun. *There* means "in that place" or is part of an expletive construction. *They're* is a contraction of *they are.*

■ **They're** going to **their** accounting class in the building over **there** near the library. Do you know that **there** are twelve sections of Accounting 101?

theirself, theirselves, themself   These words are nonstandard for *themselves.*

them   Use *them* as an object pronoun only. Do not use *them* in place of the adjectives *these* and *those.*

■ Let's buy **those** [not *them*] delicious-looking strawberries.

then   See *than, then.*

thusly   *Thusly* is nonstandard for *thus.*

till, until   Both are acceptable, although *until* is preferred for academic writing.

to, too, two   *To* is a preposition, and may introduce an infinitive. *Too* is an adverb meaning "also; more than enough." *Two* is a number.

■ When you go **to** Prince Edward Island, visit Green Gables. Try **to** find a seaside restaurant for dinner, **too.** It won't be **too** expensive because **two** people can share a lobster.

toward, towards   Although both are acceptable, *toward* is somewhat more common in North America.

try and, sure and   See *sure and, try and.*

type   *Type* is nonstandard when used to mean *type of.*

■ I recommend that you use only that **type of** [not *type*] glue on plastic.

unique   Never combine *unique* with *more, most,* or other qualifiers.

■ A **unique** [not *very unique*] heating system in one Quebec home uses hydrogen for fuel.

uninterested   See *disinterested, uninterested.*

used to   See *supposed to, used to.*

utilize   *Utilize* is considered an overblown word for *use.*

■ The team **used** [not *utilized*] all its players to win the game.

verbal, oral   See *oral, verbal.*

wait on   *Wait on* is an informal substitute for *wait for. Wait on* is appropriate only when people give service to others.

■ I had to **wait for** [not *wait on*] the hotel desk clerk for half an hour before someone came to **wait on** me.

way, ways   When referring to distance, use *way* rather than *ways*.

- He is a long **way** [not *ways*] from home.

Web site, website   Usage at the time of this book's publication calls for two words and a capital *W*. Increasingly, the informal *website* is being used.

well   See *good, well*.

where   *Where* is nonstandard for *that* when *where* is used as a subordinating conjunction.

- I read **that** [not *where*] Wayne Gretzky is the greatest hockey player ever.

where . . . at   This phrase is redundant; use only *where*.

- **Where** is your house? [not *Where is your house at?*]

whether   See *if, whether*.

which   See *that, which*.

who, whom   Use *who* as a subject or a subject complement; use *whom* as an object (see 9g).

who's, whose   *Who's* is the contraction of *who is* or, sometimes, *who has*. *Whose* is a possessive pronoun.

- **Who's** willing to drive? **Whose** truck should we take? **Who's** seen my car keys?

will   See *shall, will*.

-wise   The suffix *-wise* means "in a manner, direction, or position." Never attach *-wise* indiscriminately to create new words. When in doubt, consult a dictionary to see if the *-wise* word you have in mind is acceptable.

World Wide Web   Written out, the three words start with a capital *W*. Its abbreviation only in URLs is *www*. When you use only the word *Web*, start it with a capital *W*.

would of   *Would of* is nonstandard for *would have*.

your, you're   *Your* is a possessive. *You're* is the contraction of *you are*.

- **You're** kind to volunteer **your** time at the seniors' centre.

Chapter 21
The Impact of Words

21a What is Canadian English?

North American English, evolving over centuries into a rich language, reflects the contributions of many cultures. Food names, for example, show how other languages and cultures loaned words to English. Africans brought the word *okra;* Spanish and Latin American peoples contributed *tortilla* and *taco.* From German we got *hamburger;* Italian supplied *spaghetti* and *antipasto;* Yiddish is responsible for *bagel;* and Japanese gave us *sushi.*

French language and culture have especially influenced the Canadian variety of North American English. This influence perhaps is felt less in the language of cuisine (itself a loan word from French) than in terms dealing with the environment, outdoor activities, and political or social institutions. Many English-speaking Canadians are familiar with French-Canadian dishes such as *poutine* and *tourtière,* and the expressions *café au lait* and *crêpes* have been adopted into English in Canada and elsewhere. Nevertheless, the most characteristic borrowings from French used in Canadian English are words such as *portage, voyageur, lacrosse, francophone, Métis,* and *concession* road. The languages of the Aboriginal peoples of Canada have also enriched the English spoken here with words such as *kayak, pemmican, chinook,* and *caribou.*

Etymology is the study of the origins and historical development of words. In all languages, the meanings of some words change with time. For example, W. Nelson Francis points out in *The English Language* (New York: Norton, 1965) that the word *nice* "has been used at one time or another in its 700-year history to mean . . . foolish, wanton, strange, lazy, coy, modest, fastidious, refined, precise, subtle, slender, critical, attentive, minutely accurate, dainty, appetizing, agreeable."

21b What are levels of formality in language?

Levels of formality in DICTION and SENTENCE VARIETY can be divided into three levels: highly informal (an e-mail or a letter to a friend); highly formal (the language of ceremony, written and often spoken); and

345

medium or semiformal (ACADEMIC WRITING). A medium or semiformal level is expected in academic writing because its TONE is reasonable and evenhanded, its writing style clear and efficient, and its word choice appropriate for an academic audience.

INFORMAL	Stars? Wow! They're, like, made of gas!
MEDIUM OR SEMIFORMAL	Gas clouds slowly transformed into stars.
FORMAL	The condensations of gas spun their slow gravitational pirouettes, slowly transmogrifying gas cloud into star.

—Carl Sagan, "Starfolk: A Fable"

In the informal example, the writer's attitude toward the subject is playful and humorous, so it's appropriate when writing to a close friend or in a journal. In the medium or semiformal example, which is appropriate for most academic and professional situations, the writer's attitude toward the subject is straightforward. In the formal example, the writer's words are appropriate for readers who know about scientific phenomena and understand FIGURATIVE LANGUAGE.

21c What is edited Canadian English?

ACADEMIC WRITING in Canada uses **edited Canadian English**, a medium or formal level of language that conforms to established standards of grammar, sentence structure, punctuation, and spelling. The same standards apply in textbooks (including this one), serious magazines and newspapers, and most nonfiction books. Edited Canadian English is one of the varieties of STANDARD ENGLISH, which is spoken and written in a number of countries and used by educated people to standardize communication throughout the world.

Nonstandard English is legitimately spoken in some regions and by some groups. As well, different forms of colloquial language and slang are used among friends or in specific social settings. With their own grammar and usage, these forms of speech (and, sometimes, writing) communicate clearly to other speakers of the same varieties of English. Yet employment and academic situations normally require the ability to write in one of the forms of standard English, at a medium or formal level (21b).

Advertising language and other popular forms have their own uses and their own appeal, but are not models of the standard English that academic writing uses to treat sophisticated subject matter in a clear and balanced manner.

21d What is figurative language?

Figurative language uses words for more than their literal meanings. Such words aren't merely decorative or pretentious (21h). Figurative language greatly enhances meaning. It makes comparisons and connections that draw on one idea or image to explain another. Box 91 explains the different types of figurative language and describes one type you should avoid, the **mixed metaphor.**

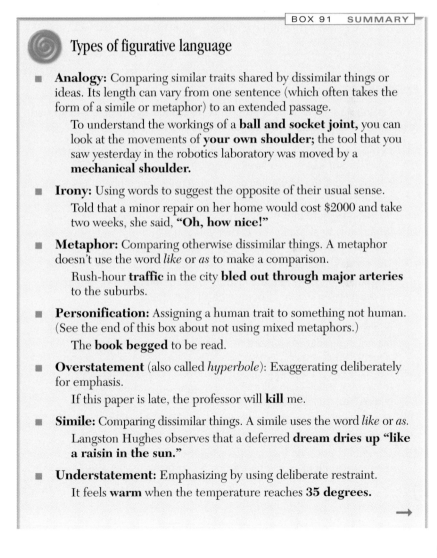

BOX 91   SUMMARY

Types of figurative language

- **Analogy:** Comparing similar traits shared by dissimilar things or ideas. Its length can vary from one sentence (which often takes the form of a simile or metaphor) to an extended passage.

    To understand the workings of a **ball and socket joint,** you can look at the movements of **your own shoulder;** the tool that you saw yesterday in the robotics laboratory was moved by a **mechanical shoulder.**

- **Irony:** Using words to suggest the opposite of their usual sense.

    Told that a minor repair on her home would cost $2000 and take two weeks, she said, **"Oh, how nice!"**

- **Metaphor:** Comparing otherwise dissimilar things. A metaphor doesn't use the word *like* or *as* to make a comparison.

    Rush-hour **traffic** in the city **bled out through major arteries** to the suburbs.

- **Personification:** Assigning a human trait to something not human. (See the end of this box about not using mixed metaphors.)

    The **book begged** to be read.

- **Overstatement** (also called *hyperbole*): Exaggerating deliberately for emphasis.

    If this paper is late, the professor will **kill** me.

- **Simile:** Comparing dissimilar things. A simile uses the word *like* or *as.*

    Langston Hughes observes that a deferred **dream dries up "like a raisin in the sun."**

- **Understatement:** Emphasizing by using deliberate restraint.

    It feels **warm** when the temperature reaches **35 degrees.**

→

Types of figurative language (*continued*)

■ **Mixed metaphor:** Combining two or more inconsistent images in one sentence or expression. Never use a mixed metaphor.

NO Quick-witted John Crosbie was skilled at stickhandling his way through the shoals of Question Period. [*Stickhandling* is a hockey manoeuvre; *shoals* are submerged sandbanks and rocks that endanger ships.]

YES Quick-witted John Crosbie was skilled at stickhandling his way through the challenges of Question Period.

EXERCISE 21-1

Working individually or with a group, identify each figure of speech. Also, revise any mixed metaphors. For help, consult 21d.

1. In the year 2000, we stood with one foot in the twentieth century while we set sail on the sea of a new era in the twenty-first.

2. Having spent the whole day on the beach, he came home as red as a lobster.

3. If I eat one more bite of that chocolate cake, I'll explode.

4. What I love best about you is that you use all the hot water every time you take a shower.

5. The daisies nodded their heads in the hot sun.

6. Beginning to testify in the courtroom, the defendant was as nervous as a long-tailed cat in a roomful of rocking chairs.

7. Think of the environment as a human body, where small problems in one part do not much affect other parts, any more than a paper cut causes most of us more than an instant's pain and a heartfelt "Ouch!" Problems throughout a system like the air or the oceans, however—say, pollution building up beyond the system's ability to cleanse itself—can kill the entire organism just as surely as cholesterol building up in arteries can kill you or me.

8. The actor displayed the entire range of human emotions from A to B.

9. My heart stopped when I opened the gift my parents gave me.

10. Our supervisor said that reorganizing the department according to our recommendations would be trading a headache for an upset stomach.

21e How can using exact diction enhance my writing?

Diction, the term for choice of words, affects the clarity and impact of any writing you do. Your best chance of delivering your intended message to your readers is to choose words that fit exactly with each piece of writing. To choose words correctly you need to understand the concepts of *denotation* and *connotation*.

21e.1 What is denotation?

The **denotation** of a word is its exact, literal meaning. It's the meaning you find when you look up the word in a dictionary. Readers expect you to use words according to their established meanings for their established functions.

Using dictionaries

A dictionary is your ultimate authority for a word's denotation—that is, its definition. The reference section in most college and university libraries includes one or more kinds of dictionaries for general use and for specialized areas.

- An **unabridged dictionary** contains the most extensive, complete, and scholarly entries. Such dictionaries include all infrequently used words that abridged dictionaries often omit. The most comprehensive, authoritative unabridged dictionary of English is the *Oxford English Dictionary (OED)*, which traces each word's history and gives quotations to illustrate changes in meaning and spelling over the life of the word.

- An **abridged dictionary** contains most commonly used words. Many of these dictionaries are referred to as "college editions." Two dictionaries intended for Canadian users are the *Gage Canadian Dictionary* (revised and expanded, 2000), and the *Canadian Oxford Dictionary* (second edition, 2004). For British style, Canadians usually consult the *Concise Oxford Dictionary;* some prefer an American dictionary such as *Merriam-Webster's Collegiate Dictionary* (also online at <http://www.m-w.com>).

- A **specialized dictionary** focuses on a single area of language. You can find dictionaries of slang (for example, *Dictionary of Slang and Unconventional English,* ed. Eric Partridge); word origins (for example, *Dictionary of Word and Phrase Origins,* ed. William Morris and Mary Morris); synonyms (for example, *Gage Canadian Thesaurus; Roget's 21st Century Thesaurus*); usage (for example, *Guide to Canadian English Usage,* by Margery Fee and Janice McAlpine); idioms (for example, *Dictionary of Canadianisms on Historical Principles,* ed. Walter S. Avis et al.; *Longman Dictionary of English Idioms*); regionalisms (for example, *Dictionary of Newfoundland English,* ed. G. M. Story et al.; *Dictionary of American Regional English,* ed. Frederic Cassidy); and many others.

⊕ **ESL NOTE:** The *Longman Dictionary of Contemporary English* and the *Longman Web Dictionary* <http://www.longmanwebdict.com> are useful for students who speak English as a second language. ⊕

21e.2 What is connotation?

Connotation refers to ideas implied by a word. Connotations are never completely fixed, for they can vary according to contexts. Connotations involve associations and emotional overtones that go beyond a word's definition. For example, *home* usually evokes more emotion than its denotation "a dwelling place" or its synonym *house. Home* carries the connotation, for some, of the pleasures of warmth, security, and love of family. For others, however, *home* may carry unpleasant connotations, such as abusive experiences or the impersonal atmosphere of an institution to house the elderly.

Using a thesaurus

Sometimes a good college dictionary explains the differences among synonyms; a thesaurus is devoted entirely to providing synonyms. In distinguishing among **synonyms**—the other words close in meaning to a word—a thesaurus demonstrates connotation in operation. As you use a thesaurus, remain very alert to the subtle shades of meaning that create distinctions among words. For instance, using *notorious* to describe a person famous for praiseworthy achievements in public life is wrong. Although *notorious* means "well-known" and "publicly discussed"—which is true of famous people—the connotation of the word is "unfavourably known or talked about." Wilfrid Laurier, Prime Minister from 1896 to 1911, is famous, not notorious. Murderer Paul Bernardo, by contrast, is notorious.

Here's another example with the word *obdurate,* which means "not easily moved to pity or sympathy." Its synonyms include *inflexible, obstinate, stubborn,* and *hardened.*

NO	Footprints showed in the **obdurate** concrete.
YES	The supervisor remained **obdurate** in refusing to accept excuses.
YES	My **obdurate** roommates won't let my pet boa constrictor live in the bathtub.

👁 **ALERT:** Most word-processing programs include a thesaurus. But be cautious in using it. Unless you know the exact meaning of an offered synonym, as well as its part of speech, you may choose a wrong word or introduce a grammatical error into your writing. For example, one word-processing program's thesaurus offers these synonyms for *deep* in the sense of "low (down, inside)": *low, below, beneath,* and *subterranean.*

None of these words could replace *deep* in a sentence such as *The crater is too deep* [not *too low, too below, too beneath,* or *too subterranean*] *to be filled with sand or rocks.* 👁

EXERCISE 21-2

Working individually or with a group, look at each list of words, and divide the words among three headings: "Positive" (good connotations); "Negative" (bad connotations); and "Neutral" (no connotations). If you think that a word belongs under more than one heading, you can assign it more than once, but be ready to explain your thinking. For help, consult a good dictionary and 21e.2.

EXAMPLE   grand, big, bulky, significant, oversized

> *Positive:* grand, significant; *Negative:* bulky, oversized;
> *Neutral:* big

1. harmony, sound, racket, shriek, melody, music, noise, pitch, voice
2. talkative, articulate, chattering, eloquent, vocal, verbose, gossipy, fluent, gabby
3. decorative, beautiful, modern, ornate, over-elaborate, dazzling, flashy, elegant, sparkling
4. long, lingering, enduring, continued, drawn-out, stretched, never-ending, unbreakable, incessant
5. calculating, shrewd, crafty, ingenious, keen, sensible, sly, smooth, underhanded

21f How can using specific words enhance my writing?

Specific words identify individual items in a group (*Buick, Honda*). **General words** relate to an overall group (*car*). **Concrete words** identify what can be perceived by the senses, by being seen, heard, tasted, felt, smelled (*black padded leather dashboard*), and convey specific images and details. **Abstract words** denote qualities (*kind*), concepts (*speed*), relationships (*friendship*), activities (*cooking*), conditions (*bad weather*), and ideas (*transportation*), and are more general.

Usually, specific and concrete words bring life to general and abstract words. Therefore, whenever you use general and abstract words, try to supply enough specific, concrete details and examples to illustrate them. Here are sentences with general words that come to life when revised with specific words.

GENERAL   His car gets good gas mileage.

SPECIFIC   His Slurpo uses about 7 litres per 100 kilometres on the high-way and 8 litres per 100 kilometres in the city.

GENERAL   Her car is comfortable and easy to drive.

SPECIFIC   When she drives her new Cushia on a five-hour trip, she arrives refreshed and does not need a long nap to recover, as she did when she drove her ten-year-old Upushme.

What separates most good writing from bad is the writer's ability to move back and forth between the general and abstract and the specific and concrete. Consider these sentences that effectively use a combination of general and specific words to compare cars:

GENERAL   CONCRETE   ┌──── SPECIFIC ────┐   ABSTRACT
My car, a midnight black Corvette LS1 convertible, has a powerful

┌──SPECIFIC──┐   GENERAL   SPECIFIC   GENERAL
5.7-litre, V8 engine with ride controls, the Tour for regular driving and

  SPECIFIC   ┌────CONCRETE────┐   GENERAL
the Sport for a close-to-the-road feel. In contrast, Harvey's automobile,

  CONCRETE ┌──────── SPECIFIC ────────┐   ABSTRACT
a bright red Dodge Viper SRT-10 convertible, has a mighty

┌──────────── SPECIFIC ────────────┐
8.3-litre, V10 engine with 6-speed manual transmission.

EXERCISE 21-3

Revise this paragraph by providing specific and concrete words and phrases to explain and enliven the ideas presented here in general and abstract language. You may revise the sentences to accommodate your changes in language. For help, consult 21f.

I hope to get a job as an administrative assistant in the company. At the interview, the person who would be my supervisor was pleasant. We seemed to get along well. The other assistants in the division appeared to be nice. My courses clearly have prepared me for the position. I think the job would teach me a great deal more. The salary is a bit less than I had hoped for, but the Human Resources representative promised me raises at regular intervals if my work is good. Also, my trip to work would not take too much time for me. If my interviewer calls to offer me the job, I will accept it.

21g What is gender-neutral language?

Gender-neutral language, also referred to as gender-free or *nonsexist language,* relies on terms that don't communicate whether the person is male or female (for example, in replacing *policeman* with *police officer* or *doctors' wives* with *doctors' spouses*).

Sexist language assigns roles or characteristics to people based on their sex and gender. Most women and men today feel that sexist language unfairly discriminates against both sexes. It inaccurately assumes that every nurse and homemaker is female (and therefore referred to as "she"), and that every physician and stockbroker is male (and therefore referred to as "he"). One common instance of sexist language is the use of the pronoun *he* to refer to someone whose sex is unknown or irrelevant. Although tradition holds that *he* is correct in such situations, many men and women find it offensive. Using only masculine pronouns to represent all humans excludes women and thereby distorts reality.

Gender-neutral language rejects demeaning STEREOTYPES or outdated assumptions, such as "women are bad drivers," "men can't cook," and "all children have two parents." In your writing, never describe women's looks, clothes, or age unless you do the same for men. Never use a title for one spouse and the first name for the other spouse: *Phil Miller* (not *Mr. Miller*) and *his wife, Jeannette,* travel on separate planes; or *Jeannette and Phil Miller* live in Regina. Box 92 gives you guidelines for using gender-neutral language.

BOX 92   SUMMARY

 How to avoid sexist language

- Avoid using only the masculine pronoun to refer to males and females together. The *he or she* and *his or hers* constructions act as SINGULAR PRONOUNS, and they therefore call for SINGULAR VERBS. Try to avoid using *he or she* constructions, especially more than once in a sentence or in consecutive sentences. A better solution is revising to the plural. You can also revise to omit the gender-specific pronoun.

  NO   A **doctor** has little time to read outside **his** specialty.
  YES   A **doctor** has little time to read outside **his or her** specialty.

  NO   A successful **stockbroker** knows **he** has to work long hours.
  YES   Successful **stockbrokers** know **they** have to work long hours.

  NO   **Everyone** hopes that **he or she** will win the scholarship.
  YES   **Everyone** hopes to win the scholarship.

→

How to avoid sexist language (*continued*)

■ Avoid using *man* when referring to both men and women.

NO **Man** is a social animal.
YES **People** are social animals.

NO The history of **mankind** is predominately violent.
YES **Human** history is predominately violent.

NO Dogs are **men's** best friends.
YES Dogs are **people's** best friends.

■ Avoid stereotyping jobs and roles by gender when referring to both men and women.

NO	YES
chairman	chair, chairperson
policeman	police officer
businessman	business person, business executive
statesman	statesperson, diplomat
teacher . . . she	teachers . . . they
principal . . . he	principals . . . they

■ Avoid expressions that seem to exclude one sex.

NO	YES
mankind	humanity
the common man	the average person
man-sized sandwich	huge sandwich
old wives' tale	superstition

■ Avoid using demeaning and patronizing labels.

NO	YES
male nurse	nurse
gal Friday	assistant
coed	student
My girl can help.	My secretary can help (or better still, Ida Morea can help).

EXERCISE 21-4

Working individually or with a group, revise these sentences by changing sexist language to gender-neutral language. For help, consult 21g.

1. Many of man's most important inventions are found not in scientific laboratories but in the home.

2. Among these inventions are the many home appliances that were designed in the early 1900s to simplify women's housework.

3. Every housewife should be grateful to the inventors of labour-saving appliances such as vacuum cleaners, washing machines, and water heaters.

4. Before such appliances became available, a family was fortunate if the husband could afford to hire a cleaning lady or a maid to help with the housework.

5. Otherwise, each family member had tasks to do that could include washing his clothes by hand or carrying hot water for bathing up or down the stairs.

6. Once family members were freed from these difficult duties early in the twentieth century, women had more time to spend with their children.

7. Also, now everyone in the household had more time for his favourite pastimes and hobbies.

8. None of the inventors of modern home appliances could have guessed what far-reaching effects his inventions would have on our society.

9. Every worker, from labourer to businessman, could return each day to a house where there was not nearly as much heavy housework waiting to be done.

10. Even more important, with less housework to do, women could now leave the home to take jobs as office girls and sometimes even lady doctors and lawyers.

21h What other types of language do I want to avoid?

Language that distorts or tries to manipulate a reader needs to be avoided in ACADEMIC WRITING. These and other types of language to avoid in an academic LEVEL OF FORMALITY are listed, with examples, in Box 93.

BOX 93   SUMMARY

Language to avoid in academic writing

■ Never use **slanted language,** also called *loaded language;* readers feel manipulated by the overly emotional TONE and DICTION.

| NO | Our MP is a deceitful, crooked thug. |
| YES | Our MP lies to the public and demands bribes. |

| NO | Why do labs employ Frankensteins to maim helpless kittens and puppies? |
| YES | Why do labs employ uncaring technicians who harm kittens and puppies? |

→

355

Language to avoid in academic writing (*continued*)

■ Never use **pretentious language;** readers realize you're showing off.

NO   As I alighted from my vehicle, my clothing became besmirched with filth.

YES   My coat got muddy as I got out of my car.

NO   He has a penchant for ostentatiously flaunting recently acquired haberdashery accoutrements.

YES   He tends to show off his new clothes shamelessly.

■ Never use **sarcastic language;** readers realize you're being nasty.

NO   He was a regular Albert Einstein with my questions. [This is sarcastic if you mean the opposite.]

YES   He had trouble understanding many of my questions.

■ Never use **colloquial language;** readers sense you're being overly casual and conversational.

NO   Christina flunked chemistry.

YES   Christina failed chemistry.

■ Never use **euphemisms,** also called *doublespeak;* readers realize you're hiding the truth (more in 21l).

NO   Our company will **downsize** to meet efficiency standards.

YES   Our company has to cut jobs to maintain our profits.

NO   We consider our hostages as **foreign guests** being guarded by **hosts.**

YES   We consider our hostages as enemies to be guarded closely.

■ Never use NONSTANDARD ENGLISH (more in 21c).
■ Never use MIXED METAPHORS (more in 21d).
■ Never use SEXIST LANGUAGE or STEREOTYPES (more in 21g and 5j).
■ Never use regional language (more in 21i).
■ Never use CLICHÉS (more in 21j).
■ Never use unnecessary JARGON (more in 21k).
■ Never use BUREAUCRATIC LANGUAGE (more in 21m).

21i   What is regional language?

Regional language, also called *dialectal language,* is specific to certain geographical areas. A small grocery store or corner store, for example, is called a *dépanneur* in Quebec, even by English speakers. In the Atlantic provinces, a *tickle* is a narrow sea channel. Using a dialect in writing for the general reading public tends to shut some people out of the communication. Except when dialect is the topic of the writing, ACADEMIC WRITING rarely accommodates dialect well. Avoid it in academic assignments.

21j What are clichés?

A **cliché** is a worn-out expression that has lost its capacity to communicate effectively because of overuse. Many clichés are SIMILES or METAPHORS, once clever but now flat. For example, these are clichés: *dead as a doornail, gentle as a lamb,* and *straight as an arrow.*

If you've heard certain expressions repeatedly, so has your reader. Instead of a cliché, use descriptive language that isn't worn out. If you can't think of a way to rephrase a cliché, drop the words entirely.

Interestingly, however, English is full of frequently used idioms that aren't clichés: for example, *up and down* and *from place to place.* If you're not sure of how to tell the difference between a cliché and a common idiom, remember that a cliché often—but not always—contains an image (*busy as a bee* and *strong as an ox*).

EXERCISE 21-5

Working individually or with a group, revise these clichés. Use the idea in each cliché to write a sentence of your own in plain, clear English. For help, consult 21j.

1. The bottom line is that Carl either raises his grade point average or finds himself in hot water.
2. Carl's grandfather says, "When the going gets tough, the tough get going."
3. Carl may not be the most brilliant engineering major who ever came down the pike, but he has plenty of get-up-and-go.
4. When they were handing out persistence, Carl was first in line.
5. The $64 000 question is, Will Carl make it safe and sound, or will the school drop him like a hot potato?

21k When is jargon unnecessary?

Jargon is the specialized vocabulary of a particular group. Jargon uses words that people outside that group might not understand. Specialized language exists in every field: professions, academic disciplines, business, various industries, government departments, hobbies, and so on.

Reserve jargon for a specialist AUDIENCE. As you write, keep your audience in mind as you decide whether a word is jargon in the context of your material. For example, a hockey fan easily understands a

357

sportswriter's use of words such as *offside, icing,* and *crosscheck,* but they are jargon words to people unfamiliar with the rules of hockey. Avoid using jargon unnecessarily. When you must use jargon for a non-specialist audience, be sure to explain any special meanings.

The example below shows specialized language used appropriately; it's taken from an undergraduate textbook. The authors can assume that students know the meaning of *eutrophicates, terrestrial,* and *eutrophic.*

> As the lake eutrophicates, it gradually fills until the entire lake will be converted into a terrestrial community. Eutrophic changes (or eutrophication) are the nutritional enrichment of the water, promoting the growth of aquatic plants.
>
> —Davis and Solomon, *The World of Biology*

21l What are euphemisms?

Euphemisms attempt to avoid the harsh reality of truth by using more pleasant, "tactful" words. Good manners dictate that euphemisms sometimes be used in social situations: For example, *passed away* is, in some situations, thought to be gentler than *died.* Such uses of euphemisms are acceptable.

In other situations, however, euphemisms drain meaning from truthful writing. Unnecessary euphemisms might describe socially unacceptable behaviour (for example, *Johnny has a wonderfully vivid imagination* instead of *Johnny lies*). They also might try to hide unpleasant facts (for example, *She is between assignments* instead of *She's lost her job*). Avoid unnecessary euphemisms.

21m What is bureaucratic language?

Bureaucratic language uses words that are stuffy and overblown. Bureaucratic language (or *bureaucratese,* a word created to describe the style) is marked by unnecessary complexity. This kind of language can take on a formality that complicates the message and makes readers feel left out.

NO In reference to the above captioned, you can include a page that additionally contains an Include instruction under the herein stated circumstances. The page including the Include instruction is included when you paginate the document, but the included text referred to in its Include instruction is not included. [This message is meaningless, but the writer seems to understand the message. Anyone who doesn't is clearly uninformed or unable to read intelligently.]

—From instructions for compiling a user's manual

In response to earlier editions of this handbook, I've been asked to give a YES alternative for this example. I regret that I can't understand enough of the NO example to do that. If you can, please contact me at <LQTBook@aol.com>.

EXERCISE 21-6

Working individually or with a group, revise these examples of pretentious language, jargon, euphemism, and bureaucratic language. For help, consult 21h and 21k through 21m.

1. In-house employee interaction of a nonbusiness nature is disallowed.
2. An index card posted on the bulletin board advertised a gently worn bridal gown; since I was about to tie the knot, I decided to check it out.
3. Your dearest, closest acquaintance, it has been circulated through rumour, is entering into matrimony with her current beloved.
4. My male sibling concocted a tale that was entirely fallacious.
5. An individual's cognitive and affective domains are at the centre of his or her personality.
6. When the finalization of this negotiation comes through, it will clarify our position in a positive manner.
7. The refuse has accumulated because the sanitation engineers were on strike last month.
8. Employees who are employed by the company for no less than five years in a full-time capacity fulfil the eligibility requirements for participation in the company's savings program.

Chapter 22

Spelling

22a What makes a good speller?

You might be surprised to hear that good spellers don't know how to spell and hyphenate every word they write. What they do know, however, is to check if they're not sure of a word's spelling. If your inner voice questions a spelling, do what good spellers do—consult a dictionary.

What do you do if even the first few letters of a word seem mysterious? This is a common dilemma among writers. My best advice is that you think of an easy-to-spell SYNONYM for the word you need; look up that synonym in a thesaurus; and among the synonyms, find the word you need to spell. Word-processing programs often suggest likely spellings based on sound and letter combinations.

Many people, surveys show, incorrectly believe that only naturally skilled spellers can write well. The truth is that correct spelling matters a great deal in final drafts, but not in earlier drafts. The best time to check spellings you doubt is when you're EDITING.

The various origins of words and ways that English-speaking people around the world pronounce words make it almost impossible to rely solely on pronunciation to spell a word. What you can rely on, however, are the proofreading hints and spelling rules explained in this chapter.

👁 **ALERT:** Word-processing software usually includes a spell-check program that searches for words that don't match the spellings in the software's dictionary. Such programs have one major drawback. The programs can't detect that you've spelled a wrong word if what you've typed is a legitimate spelling of a legitimate word. For example, if you mean *top* but type *too*, or if you mean *from* and type *form*, no spell-check program "sees" a mistake. In these and other similar cases, only the human eye can discover the errors. 👁

Canadian spelling, because it has been influenced by both British and American spelling conventions, contains elements of both. Some people claim to notice a drift toward American conventions because of the influence of the media and new information technologies. Both American and British spellings may appear in any given piece of writing. Here are some examples:

labor	*or*	labour	encyclopedia	*or*	encyclopaedia
theater	*or*	theatre	catalog	*or*	catalogue
check	*or*	cheque	realize	*or*	realise
defense	*or*	defence	program	*or*	programme

In both academic and business writing, your purpose for writing and the expectations of your audience often determine your choice of spelling conventions. Readers in the scientific and medical fields, and especially in information technologies, often expect American spellings to be used. Writing in other fields, including Canadian history and literature, usually uses a more British-oriented style to produce the hybrid that might be called a typically *Canadian* spelling style.

Whichever spellings you choose, aim for a logical and consistent style. If you use the spelling *labour* in a document, use *colour* as well; and if you spell *theatre*, use the spelling *centre*. Each of the Canadian dictionaries listed in section 21e has its own version of Canadian spelling that can guide you in finding a consistent spelling style.

22b How can I proofread for errors in spelling and hyphen use?

Many spelling errors are the result of illegible handwriting, slips of the pen, or typographical mistakes. Catching these "typos" requires especially careful proofreading, using the techniques in Box 94.

BOX 94   SUMMARY

Proofreading for errors in spelling

- Slow down your reading speed to allow yourself to concentrate on the individual letters of words rather than on the meaning of the words.
- Stay within your "visual span," the number of letters you can identify with a single glance (for most people, about six letters).
- Put a ruler or large index card under each line as you proofread, to focus your vision and concentration.
- Read each paragraph in reverse, from the last sentence to the first. This method can keep you from being distracted by the meaning of the material.

22c How are plurals spelled?

The most common way to form a plural is to add an -s or -es to the end of the word. The list below covers all variations of creating plurals.

■ **Words that add -s or -es:** Plurals of most words are formed by adding an s, including words that end in "hard" -ch (sounding like k): *leg, legs; shoe, shoes; stomach, stomachs.* Words ending in -s, -sh, -x, -z, or "soft" -ch (as in *beach*) are formed by adding -es to the singular: *lens, lenses; tax, taxes; beach, beaches.*

■ **Words ending in -o:** Add -s if the o is preceded by a vowel: *radio, radios; cameo, cameos.* Add -es if the o is preceded by a consonant: *potato, potatoes.* With a few words, you can choose either the -s or -es plural form, but current practice generally supports adding -es: *cargo, cargoes; tornado, tornadoes; zero, zeroes* or *zeros.*

■ **Words ending in -f or -fe:** Some -f and -fe words are made plural by adding an s: *belief, beliefs.* Others require changing -f or -fe to -ves: *life, lives; leaf, leaves.* Words ending in -ff or -ffe simply add -s: *staff, staffs; giraffe, giraffes.*

■ **Compound words:** For most compound words, add -s or -es at the end of the last word: *chequebooks, player-coaches.* In a few compounds, the first word is made plural: *sister-in-law, sisters-in-law; kilometres per hour.* (For information about hyphens in compound words, see 22g.)

■ **Internal changes and endings other than -s:** A few words change internally or add endings other than an s to become plural: *foot, feet; man, men; crisis, crises; child, children.*

■ **Foreign words:** The best advice is to check your dictionary. In general, many Latin words ending in -um form the plural by changing -um to -a: *curriculum, curricula; datum, data; medium, media.* Also, Latin words that end in -us usually form the plural by changing -us to -i: *alumnus, alumni; syllabus, syllabi.* Greek words that end in -on usually form the plural by changing -on to -a: *criterion, criteria; phenomenon, phenomena.*

■ **One-form words:** Some words have the same form in both the singular and the plural: *deer, elk, fish.* You need to use modifiers, as necessary, to indicate which form you mean: *one deer, nine deer.*

EXERCISE 22-1

Write the correct plural form of these words. For help, consult 22c.

1. yourself	6. millennium	11. echo
2. sheep	7. lamp	12. syllabus
3. photo	8. runner-up	13. wife
4. woman	9. criterion	14. get-together
5. appendix	10. lunch	15. crisis

22d How are suffixes spelled?

A **suffix** is an ending added to a word that changes the word's meaning or its grammatical function. For example, adding the suffix *-able* to the VERB *depend* creates the ADJECTIVE *dependable.*

- **-y words:** If the letter before a final *y* is a consonant, change the *y* to *i* and add the suffix: *try, tries, tried.* In the case of *trying* and similar words, the following rule applies: Keep the *y* when the suffix begins with *i* (*apply, applying*). If the letter before the final *y* is a vowel, keep the final *y: employ, employed, employing.* These rules don't apply to IRREGULAR VERBS (see Box 60 in section 8d).

- **-e words:** Drop a final *e* when the suffix begins with a vowel, unless doing this would cause confusion: for example, *be + ing* can't be written *bing,* but *require* does become *requiring; like* does become *liking.* Keep the final *e* when the suffix begins with a consonant: *require, requirement; like, likely.* Exceptions include *argue, argument; true, truly.*

- **Words that double a final letter:** If the final letter is a consonant, double it *only* if it passes these tests: (1) its last two letters are a vowel followed by a consonant; and (2) the suffix begins with a vowel: *drop, dropped; begin, beginning; forget, forgettable.* (American spelling adds a third test. The word must have one syllable or be accented on the last syllable: *begin* [accent on last syllable], *beginning;* but *travel* [accent on first syllable], *traveling.* British spelling doubles the final consonant in many words even when the accent is not on the last syllable: *travel, travelling; worship, worshipper.* A notable exception is *novelist,* which has the same form in both British and American spelling.)

- **-cede, -ceed, -sede words:** Only one word in the English language ends in *-sede: supersede.* Only three words end in *-ceed: exceed, proceed, succeed.* All other words with endings that sound like "seed" end in *-cede: concede, intercede, precede.*

- **-ally and -ly words:** The suffixes *-ally* and *-ly* turn words into adverbs. For words ending in *-ic,* add *-ally: logically, statistically.* Otherwise, add *-ly: quickly, sharply.*

- **-ance, -ence, and -ible, -able:** No consistent rules govern words with these suffixes. When in doubt, look up the word.

22e What is the *ie, ei* rule?

The famous rhymed rule for using *ie* and *ei* is usually true:

> *I* before *e* [bel**ie**ve, f**ie**ld, gr**ie**f],
>
> Except after *c* [c**ei**ling, conc**ei**t],
>
> Or when sounded like "ay"—
>
> As in n**ei**ghbour and w**ei**gh [**ei**ght, v**ei**n].

There are major exceptions (sorry!) to the *ie, ei* rule, listed here. My best advice is that you memorize them.

- **■** *ie:* consc**ie**nce, financ**ie**r, sc**ie**nce, spec**ie**s
- **■** *ei:* **ei**ther, n**ei**ther, l**ei**sure, s**ei**ze, counterf**ei**t, for**ei**gn, forf**ei**t, sl**ei**ght (as in *sleight of hand*), w**ei**rd

EXERCISE 22-2

Follow the directions for each group of words. For help, consult 22d and 22e.

1. Add *-able* or *-ible*: (a) profit; (b) reproduce; (c) control; (d) coerce; (e) recognize.
2. Add *-ance* or *-ence:* (a) luxuri_____; (b) prud_____; (c) devi_____; (d) resist_____; (e) independ_____.
3. Drop the final *e* as needed: (a) true + ly; (b) joke + ing; (c) fortunate + ly; (d) appease + ing; (e) appease + ment.
4. Change the final *y* to *i* as needed: (a) happy + ness; (b) pry + ed; (c) pry + ing; (d) dry + ly; (e) beautify + ing.
5. Double the final consonant as needed: (a) commit + ed; (b) commit + ment; (c) drop + ed; (d) occur + ed; (e) regret + ful.
6. Insert *ie* or *ei* correctly: (a) rel_____f; (b) ach_____ve; (c) w_____rd; (d) n_____ce; (e) dec_____ve.

22f How are homonyms and other frequently confused words spelled?

Homonyms are words that sound exactly like other words: *to, too, two; no, know.* The different spellings of homonyms tend to confuse many writers. The same holds for words that sound almost alike (*accept, except; conscience, conscious*).

Another reason for spelling problems is so-called swallowed pronunciation, which means one or more letters at the end of a word aren't pronounced clearly. For example, the *-d* ending in *used to* or *prejudiced* is often swallowed rather than pronounced. When writers spell as they mispronounce, spelling errors result.

For more information about word usage that affects spelling, see Chapter 20, "Usage Glossary." Box 95 lists homonyms and other words that can be confused and lead to misspellings.

BOX 95   SUMMARY

Homonyms and other frequently confused words

- ACCEPT — to receive
  EXCEPT — with the exclusion of

- ADVICE — recommendation
  ADVISE — to recommend

- AFFECT — to influence [verb]; emotion [noun]
  EFFECT — result [noun]; to bring about or cause [verb]

- AISLE — space between rows
  ISLE — island

- ALLUDE — to make indirect reference to
  ELUDE — to avoid

- ALLUSION — indirect reference
  ILLUSION — false idea, misleading appearance

- ALREADY — by this time
  ALL READY — fully prepared

- ALTAR — sacred platform or place
  ALTER — to change

- ALTOGETHER — thoroughly
  ALL TOGETHER — everyone or everything in one place

- ARE — PLURAL form of *to be*
  HOUR — sixty minutes
  OUR — plural form of *my*

- ASCENT — the act of rising or climbing
  ASSENT — consent [noun]; to consent [verb]

- ASSISTANCE — help
  ASSISTANTS — helpers

- BARE — nude, unadorned
  BEAR — to carry; an animal

- BOARD — piece of wood
  BORED — uninterested

- BRAKE — device for stopping [noun]; to stop [verb]
  BREAK — to destroy, make into pieces

- BREATH — air taken in
  BREATHE — to take in air

- BUY — to purchase
  BY — next to, through the agency of

→

Homonyms and other frequently confused words
(*continued*)

- CAPITAL · major city; money [noun]; main, major [adjective]
  CAPITOL · government building (U.S.)

- CHOOSE · to pick
  CHOSE · PAST TENSE of *choose*

- CITE · to point out
  SIGHT · vision
  SITE · a place

- CLOTHES · garments
  CLOTHS · pieces of fabric

- COARSE · rough
  COURSE · path; series of lectures

- COMPLEMENT · something that completes or goes well with
  COMPLIMENT · praise, flattery

- CONSCIENCE · sense of morality
  CONSCIOUS · awake, aware

- COUNCIL · governing body
  COUNSEL · advice [noun]; to advise [verb]

- DAIRY · place associated with milk production
  DIARY · personal journal

- DESCENT · downward movement
  DISSENT · disagreement

- DESERT · to abandon [verb]; dry, usually sandy area [noun]
  DESSERT · final, sweet course in a meal

- DEVICE · a plan; an implement
  DEVISE · to create

- DIE · to lose life (*dying*) [verb]; one of a pair of dice [noun]
  DYE · to change the colour of something (*dyeing*)

- DOMINANT · commanding, controlling
  DOMINATE · to control

- ELICIT · to draw out
  ILLICIT · illegal

- EMINENT · prominent
  IMMANENT · living within; inherent
  IMMINENT · about to happen

- ENVELOP · to surround
  ENVELOPE · container for a letter or other papers

→

Homonyms and other frequently confused words
(*continued*)

- FAIR — light-skinned; just, honest
  FARE — money for transportation; food

- FORMALLY — conventionally, with ceremony
  FORMERLY — previously

- FORTH — forward
  FOURTH — number four in a series

- GORILLA — animal in ape family
  GUERRILLA — soldier conducting unconventional combat

- HEAR — to sense sound by ear
  HERE — in this place

- HOLE — opening
  WHOLE — complete; an entire thing

- HUMAN — relating to the species *Homo sapiens*
  HUMANE — compassionate

- INSURE — buy or give insurance
  ENSURE — guarantee, protect

- ITS — POSSESSIVE form of *it*
  IT'S — CONTRACTION for *it is* or *it has*

- KNOW — to comprehend
  NO — negative

- LATER — after a time
  LATTER — second one of two things

- LEAD — heavy metal substance [noun]; to guide [verb]
  LED — past tense of *lead*

- LIGHTNING — storm-related electricity
  LIGHTENING — making lighter

- LOOSE — unbound, not tightly fastened
  LOSE — to misplace

- MAYBE — perhaps [adverb]
  MAY BE — might be [verb]

- MEAT — animal flesh
  MEET — to encounter

- MINER — a person who works in a mine
  MINOR — underage

→

Homonyms and other frequently confused words
(*continued*)

- MORAL — distinguishing right from wrong; the lesson of a fable, story, or event

  MORALE — attitude or outlook, usually of a group

- OF — PREPOSITION indicating origin

  OFF — away from; not on

- PASSED — past tense of *pass*

  PAST — at a previous time

- PATIENCE — forbearance

  PATIENTS — people under medical care

- PEACE — absence of fighting

  PIECE — part of a whole; musical arrangement

- PERSONAL — intimate

  PERSONNEL — employees

- PLAIN — simple, unadorned

  PLANE — to shave wood; aircraft

- PRECEDE — to come before

  PROCEED — to continue

- PRESENCE — being at hand; attendance at a place or in something

  PRESENTS — gifts

- PRINCIPAL — foremost [adjective]; school head [noun]

  PRINCIPLE — moral conviction, basic truth

- QUIET — silent, calm

  QUITE — very

- RAIN — water that falls to earth [noun]; to fall like rain [verb]

  REIGN — to rule

  REIN — strap to guide or control an animal [noun]; to guide or control [verb]

- RAISE — to lift up

  RAZE — to tear down

- RESPECTFULLY — with respect

  RESPECTIVELY — in that order

- RIGHT — correct; opposite of *left*

  RITE — ritual

  WRITE — to put words on paper

→

Homonyms and other frequently confused words
(*continued*)

- ROAD   path
  RODE   past tense of *ride*

- SCENE   place of an action; segment of a play
  SEEN   viewed

- SENSE   perception, understanding
  SINCE   measurement of past time; because

- STATIONARY   standing still
  STATIONERY   writing paper

- THAN   in comparison with; besides
  THEN   at that time; next; therefore

- THEIR   possessive form of *they*
  THERE   in that place
  THEY'RE   contraction of *they are*

- THROUGH   finished; into and out of
  THREW   past tense of *throw*
  THOROUGH   complete

- TO   toward
  TOO   also; indicates degree (*too much*)
  TWO   number following *one*

- WAIST   midsection of the body
  WASTE   discarded material [noun]; to squander, to fail to use up [verb]

- WEAK   not strong
  WEEK   seven days

- WEATHER   climatic condition
  WHETHER   if, when alternatives are expressed or implied

- WHERE   in which place
  WERE   past tense (plural) of *be*

- WHICH   one of a group
  WITCH   female sorcerer

- WHOSE   possessive form of *who*
  WHO'S   contraction for *who is* or *who has*

- YOUR   possessive form of *you*
  YOU'RE   contraction for *you are*
  YORE   long past

EXERCISE 22-3

Circle the correct homonym or commonly confused word of each group in parentheses.

Imagine that you (are, our) standing in the middle of a busy sidewalk, with a worried look on (your, you're, yore) face. In your hand (your, you're, yore) holding a map, (which, witch) you are puzzling over. If that happened in (real, reel) life, (its, it's) almost certain that within (to, too, two) or three minutes a passerby would ask if you (where, were) lost and would offer you (assistance, assistants). That helpful passerby, (buy, by) taking a (personal, personnel) interest in your problem, is displaying a quality known as empathy—the ability (to, too, two) put oneself in another person's place. Some researchers claim that empathy is an instinct that (human, humane) beings share with many other animals. Other scientists wonder (weather, whether) empathy is instead a (conscience, conscious) (moral, morale) choice that people make. Whatever explanation for the origin (of, off) empathy is (right, rite, write), such empathy generally has a positive (affect, effect)—especially if (your, you're, yore) a person who (maybe, may be) (to, too, two) lost to (know, no) (where, were) (to, too, two) turn.

22g What are compound words?

A **compound word** puts together two or more words to express one concept.

> **Open compound words** remain as separate words, such as *decision making, problem solving,* and *editor in chief.*
>
> **Hyphenated compound words** use a hyphen between the words, such as *trade-in, fuel-efficient,* and *tax-sheltered.* For punctuation advice about hyphens, see 29i.
>
> **Closed compound words** appear as one word, such as *proofread, understated,* and *handbook.*

Many single-word compounds begin as two words and then pass through a stage where they are written as hyphenated compounds. To check whether a compound term consists of closed, hyphenated, or open words, consult an up-to-date dictionary.

Part Four

Using Punctuation and Mechanics

Visit the Troyka Web site at
http://www.pearsoned.ca/troyka for

- diagnostic test
- chapter exercises
- other resources, including an e-book version of this text

Chapter 23

Periods, Question Marks, and Exclamation Points

Periods, question marks, and **exclamation points** are collectively called *end punctuation* because they occur at the ends of sentences.

I love you. Do you love me? I love you!

PERIODS

23a When does a period end a sentence?

A **period** ends a statement, a mild command, or an INDIRECT QUESTION.* Never use a period to end a DIRECT QUESTION, a strong command, or an emphatic declaration.

STATEMENT

A journey of a thousand leagues begins with a single step.
　　　　　　　　　　　　　　　　　　　—Lao-tsu, *The Way of Lao-tsu*

MILD COMMAND

Put a gram of boldness into everything you do.
　　　　　　　　　　　　　　　　　　　—Baltasar Gracian

INDIRECT QUESTION

I asked if they wanted to climb Mt. Everest. [As an indirect question, this sentence reports that a question was asked. If it were a direct question, it would end with a question mark: *I asked, "Do you want to climb Mt. Everest?"*]

---

* Find the definition of all words in small capital letters (such as INDIRECT QUESTION) in the Terms Glossary at the back of this book directly before the Index.

23b How do I use periods with abbreviations?

Most **abbreviations,** though not all, call for periods. Typical abbreviations with periods include *Mt., St., Dr., Mr., Ms., Mrs., Fri., Feb., R.N., a.m.,* and *p.m.* (For more about *a.m.* and *p.m.,* see Chapter 20, "Usage Glossary," and section 30j; for more about abbreviations in general, see 30i through 30l.

ALERT: Spell out the word *professor* in ACADEMIC WRITING; never abbreviate it.

Abbreviations without periods include the two-letter postal code abbreviations for the names of provinces and U.S. states and some organizations and government agencies (for example, CBC and NFB).

Ms. Yuan, who works at the **NFB,** lectured to **Dr.** Benet's film class at 9:30 **a.m.**

ALERT: When the period of an abbreviation falls at the end of a sentence that calls for a period, the period of the abbreviation serves also to end the sentence. If, however, your sentence ends in a question mark or an exclamation point, put it after the period of the abbreviation.

The phone rang at 4:00 **a.m.**
It's upsetting to answer a wrong-number call at 4:00 **a.m.!**
Who would call at 4:00 **a.m.?**

QUESTION MARKS

23c When do I use a question mark?

A **question mark** ends a **direct question,** one that quotes the exact words the speaker used. (In contrast, an **indirect question** reports a question and ends with a period.)

How many attempts have been made to climb Mt. Everest? [An indirect question would end with a period: *She wants to know how many attempts have been made to climb Mt. Everest.*]

ALERT: Never use a question mark with any other punctuation.

NO   She asked, "How are you**?.**"
YES   She asked, "How are you**?**"

Questions in a series are each followed by a question mark, whether or not each question is a complete sentence.

After the fierce storm, the mountain climbers debated what to do next. Turn back**?** Move on**?** Rest for a while**?**

👁 **ALERT:** When questions in a series are not complete sentences (as in the above example), you can choose whether to capitalize the first letter. Be consistent within each piece of writing. 👁

Sometimes a statement or mild command is phrased as a question to be polite. In such cases, a question mark is optional, but be consistent in each piece of writing.

Would you please send me a copy**.**

23d When can I use a question mark in parentheses?

The only time to use a question mark in parentheses (?) is if a date or other number is unknown or doubtful. Never use (?) to communicate that you're unsure of information.

Mary Astell, a British writer of pamphlets on women's rights, was born in 1666 **(?)** and died in 1731.

The word *about* is often a more graceful substitute for (?): *Mary Astell was born* **about** *1666.*

Also, never use (?) to communicate IRONY or sarcasm. Choose words to deliver your message.

NO	Having altitude sickness is a pleasant **(?)** experience.
YES	Having altitude sickness is **as** pleasant **as having a bad case of the flu.**

EXCLAMATION POINTS

23e When do I use an exclamation point?

An **exclamation point** ends a strong command or an emphatic declaration. A strong command is a firm and direct order: *Look out behind you!* An emphatic declaration is a shocking or surprising statement: *There's been an accident!*

👁 **ALERT:** Never combine an exclamation point with other punctuation.

NO	"There's been an accident**!,**" she shouted.
YES	"There's been an accident**!**" she shouted.
YES	"There's been an accident," she shouted. [Use this form if you prefer not to use an exclamation point.] 👁

23f What is considered overuse of exclamation points?

In ACADEMIC WRITING, words, not exclamation points, need to communicate the intensity of your message. Reserve exclamation points for an emphatic declaration within a longer passage.

> When we were in Nepal, we tried each day to see Mt. Everest. But each day we failed. **Clouds defeated us!** The summit never emerged from a heavy overcast.

Using exclamation points too frequently suggests an exaggerated sense of urgency.

NO Mountain climbing can be dangerous. You must know correct procedures! You must have the proper equipment! Otherwise, you could die!

YES Mountain climbing can be dangerous. You must know correct procedures. You must have the proper equipment. Otherwise, you could die!

Never use (!) to communicate amazement or sarcasm. Choose words to deliver your message.

NO At 8882 metres (!), Mt. Everest is the world's highest mountain. Yet, Chris (!) wants to climb it.

YES At **a majestic** 8882 metres, Mt. Everest is the world's highest mountain. Yet, Chris, **amazingly,** wants to climb it.

EXERCISE 23-1

Insert any needed periods, question marks, and exclamation points and delete any unneeded ones. For help, consult all sections of this chapter.

EXAMPLE Dr Madan Kataria, who calls himself the Giggling Guru (!), established the world's first laughter club in 1995.

> Dr. Madan Kataria, who calls himself the Giggling Guru, established the world's first laughter club in 1995.

1. More than 1000 (?) laughter clubs exist throughout the world, each seeking to promote health by reducing stress and strengthening the immune system!

2. Dr Madan Kataria, a physician in Bombay, India, developed a yoga-like (!) strategy based on group (!) laughter and then set up laughter clubs.

3. Laughter clubs say, "Yes!" when asked, "Is laughter the best medicine."

4. The clubs' activities include breathing and stretching exercises and playful (?) behaviours, such as performing the opera laugh (!), the chicken laugh (!), and the "Ho-Ho, Ha-Ha" (?) exercise.

5. According to the German psychologist Dr Michael Titze, "In the 1950s people used to laugh eighteen minutes a day (!), but today we laugh not more than six (?) minutes per day, despite huge rises in the standard of living."

EXERCISE 23-2

Insert needed periods, question marks, and exclamation points. For help, consult all sections of this chapter.

New York's Ellis Island immigration facility is famous as the place where millions of newcomers arrived in the United States How many people have heard of its Canadian counterpart It may be better to speak of its Canadian counterparts, rather Before the age of airplane travel, there were two important entry points for immigrants taking the Atlantic route to Canada Pier 21 in Halifax, which opened in 1928, was the arrival point for more than one million new Canadians Grosse Île, a small island near Quebec City on the St Lawrence River, was still receiving immigrants when Pier 21 opened, although the island facility closed a few years later What a contrast these two locations make Grosse Île was a quarantine station for severely ill arrivals When it opened in 1832, cholera was raging in the slums of Europe English and Irish immigrants brought this feared disease to Canada Thousands died of cholera in Quebec City and Montreal, despite the quarantine Then, in 1847, more than ninety thousand Irish immigrants arrived, fleeing the potato famine in their homeland Thousands were infected with typhus; the medical staff led by Dr Douglas worked heroically but were unable to save many of the ill This unhappy history may have led Canadians to ignore Grosse Île's heritage until recently In contrast, Pier 21 is celebrated as the place where refugees fleeing Nazism and war reached a safe shore

Chapter 24

Commas

24a What is the role of the comma?

Commas are the most frequently used marks of punctuation, occurring twice as often as all other punctuation marks combined. A comma must be used in certain places, it must not be used in other places, and it's optional in still other places. This chapter helps you sort through the various rules.

For quick access to most answers when you have a comma question, consult Box 96. The sections in parentheses indicate where you can find fuller explanations.

BOX 96   SUMMARY

Key uses of commas

Commas with Coordinating Conjunctions Linking Independent Clauses (24b)

■ Postcards are ideal for brief greetings, **and** they can also be miniature works of art. [*and* is a coordinating conjunction]

Commas after Introductory Elements (24c)

■ **Although most postcards cost only a dime,** one recently sold for thousands of dollars. [clause]

■ **On postcard racks,** several designs are usually available. [phrase]

■ **For example,** animals are timeless favourites. [transitional expression]

■ **However,** most cards show local landmarks. [transitional or introductory word]

Commas with Items in Series (24d)

■ **Places, paintings, and people** appear on postcards. [*and* between last two items]

→

Key uses of commas (*continued*)

- **Places, paintings, people, animals** occupy dozens of display racks.
  [no *and* between last two items]

Commas with Coordinate Adjectives (24e)

- Some postcards feature **appealing, dramatic** scenes.

No Commas with Cumulative Adjectives (24e)

- Other postcards feature **famous historical** scenes.

Commas with Nonrestrictive Elements (24f)

- **A few years after the first postcard appeared,** some governments began to issue pre-stamped postcards. [nonrestrictive element introduces independent clause]
- The Golden Age of postcards, **which lasted from about 1900 to 1929,** yielded many especially valuable cards. [nonrestrictive element interrupts independent clause]
- Collectors attend postcard shows, **which are similar to baseball-card shows.** [nonrestrictive element ends independent clause]

No Commas with Restrictive Elements (24f)

- Collectors **who attend these shows** may specialize in a particular kind of postcard. [restrictive clause]

Commas with Quoted Works (24h)

- One collector told me, "Attending a show is like digging for buried treasure." [quoted words at end of sentence]
- "I always expect to find a priceless postcard," he said. [quoted words at start of sentence]
- "Everyone there," he joked, "believes a million-dollar card is hidden in the next stack." [quoted words interrupted mid-sentence]

24b How do commas work with coordinating conjunctions?

Never use a comma when a coordinating conjunction links only two words, two PHRASES, or two DEPENDENT CLAUSES.

> **NO** Habitat for Humanity depends on volunteers for **labour, and donations** to help with its construction projects. [*Labour* and *donations* are two words; the conjunction explains their relationship. No comma is needed.]

YES   Habitat for Humanity depends on volunteers for **labour and donations** to help with its construction projects.

NO   Each language has **a beauty of its own, and forms of expression** that are duplicated nowhere else. [A *beauty of its own* and *forms of expression* are only two phrases.]

YES   Each language has **a beauty of its own and forms of expression** that are duplicated nowhere else.

—Margaret Mead, "Unispeak"

When a coordinating conjunction links two or more INDEPENDENT CLAUSES, place a comma before the coordinating conjunction. Box 97 shows this pattern.

BOX 97   PATTERN

Commas before coordinating conjunctions that link independent clauses

Independent clause, { **and / but / for / or / nor / yet / so** } independent clause.

The sky turned dark grey, **and** the wind died suddenly.
The November morning had just begun, **but** it looked like dusk.
Shopkeepers closed their stores early, **for** they wanted to get home.
Soon high winds would start, **or** thick snow would begin silently.
Farmers could not continue harvesting, **nor** could they round up their animals in distant fields.
People on the road tried to reach safety, **yet** a few unlucky ones were stranded.
The firehouse whistle blew four times, **so** everyone knew a blizzard was closing in.

Exceptions

■ When two independent clauses are very short, and they contrast with each other, you can link them with a comma without using a coordinating conjunction: *Mosquitoes don't bite, they stab.* Some instructors consider this an error, so in ACADEMIC WRITING, you'll never be wrong if you use a period or semicolon (Chapter 25) instead of a comma.

■ When one or both independent clauses linked by a coordinating conjunction happen to contain other commas, drop the coordinating conjunction and use a semicolon instead of the comma. This can help clarify meaning.

With temperatures below freezing, the snow did not melt; ~~and~~ **people** wondered, gazing at the white landscape, when they would see grass again.

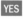 **ALERTS:** (1) Never put a comma *after* a coordinating conjunction that joins independent clauses.

NO   A house is renovated in two weeks **but,** an apartment takes a week.

YES   A house is renovated in two weeks, **but** an apartment takes a week.

(2) Never use a comma alone between independent clauses, or you'll create the error known as a COMMA SPLICE.

NO   Ten centimetres of snow fell in two hours, driving was hazardous.

YES   Ten centimetres of snow fell in two hours, **and** driving was hazardous.

24c How do commas work with introductory clauses, phrases, and words?

A comma follows any introductory element that comes before an INDEPENDENT CLAUSE. An introductory element can be a CLAUSE, PHRASE, or words. Box 98 shows this pattern.

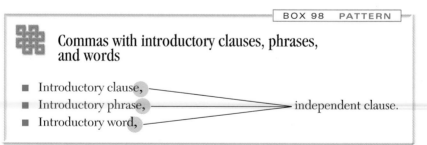

BOX 98   PATTERN

Commas with introductory clauses, phrases, and words

■ Introductory clause,
■ Introductory phrase, ──────────→ independent clause.
■ Introductory word,

When the topic is dieting, many people say sugar craving is their worst problem. [introductory dependent clause]

Between 1544 and 1689, sugar refineries appeared in London and New York. [introductory prepositional phrase]

Beginning in infancy, we develop lifelong tastes for sweet foods. [introductory participial phrase]

Sweets being a temptation for many adults, most parents avoid commercial baby foods that contain sugar. [introductory absolute phrase]

For example, fructose comes from fruit, but it's still sugar. [introductory transitional expression]

Nevertheless, many people think fructose isn't harmful. [introductory conjunctive adverb]

To satisfy a craving for ice cream, even timid people sometimes brave midnight streets. [introductory infinitive phrase]

An **interjection** is an introductory word that conveys surprise or other emotions. Use a comma after an interjection at the beginning of a sentence: ***Oh,*** *we didn't realize that you're allergic to cats.* ***Yes,*** *your sneezing worries me.*

Exception

When an introductory element is short, and the sentence can be understood easily, some writers omit the comma. However, in ACADEMIC WRITING, you'll never be wrong if you use the comma.

> YES In 1921, William Lyon Mackenzie King became prime minister for the first time. [preferred]

> YES In 1921 William Lyon Mackenzie King became prime minister for the first time.

👁 **ALERT:** Use a comma before and after a transitional expression that falls in the middle of a sentence. When the transitional expression starts a sentence, follow it with a comma. When the transitional expression ends a sentence, put a comma before it.

By the way, the parade begins at noon. [introductory transitional expression with comma after it]

The parade, **by the way,** begins at noon. [transitional expression with comma before and after it, in middle of sentence]

The parade begins at noon, **by the way.** [transitional expression with comma before it, at end of sentence]

However, our float isn't finished. [introductory conjunctive adverb with comma after it]

Our float, **however,** isn't finished. [conjunctive adverb with comma before and after it, in middle of sentence]

Our float isn't finished, **however.** [conjunctive adverb with comma before it, at end of sentence] 👁

EXERCISE 24-1

Using a comma after the introductory element, combine each set of sentences into one sentence according to the directions in parentheses. You can add, delete, and rearrange words as needed. For help, consult 24c.

381

EXAMPLE   Several magicians have revealed their secrets. They have revealed their secrets recently. (begin with *recently*)

Recently, several magicians have revealed their secrets.

1. One famous trick involves sawing a woman in half. This trick actually uses two women. (begin with *for example*)
2. The magician opens the lid to a large rectangular box. The magician shows the audience it's empty. (begin with *first*)
3. The brave female assistant lies down in the box. The opened box lid faces away from the audience. (begin with *when*)
4. The assistant puts her head outside one end of the box. She seems to put her wiggling feet out the other end. (begin with *locked inside*)
5. Observers watch in astonishment. The magician pushes a saw through the middle of the box. (begin with *in astonishment*)
6. This illusion seems impossible. This illusion is safely performed with two women participating. (begin with *although*)
7. The first assistant walks behind the box. This assistant lies down in the box and pulls her knees up to her chest. (begin with *walking*)
8. The first woman now occupies only one side. And the other woman hidden under the box's false bottom emerges to get into position on the second side. (begin with *in the closed box*)
9. The second woman folds her body by bending forward at the waist. She puts her feet out the holes at her end of the box (begin with *to create the illusion*)
10. Each woman is positioned in a different end of the box. The magician can safely make a grand show of sawing a woman in half. (begin with *because*)

24d How do commas work with items in a series?

A **series** is a group of three or more elements—words, PHRASES, or CLAUSES—that match in grammatical form and are of equal importance in a sentence. Box 99 shows this pattern.

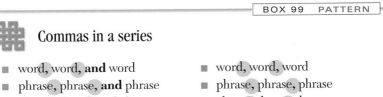

BOX 99   PATTERN

Commas in a series

- word, word, **and** word
- phrase, phrase, **and** phrase
- clause, clause, **and** clause

- word, word, word
- phrase, phrase, phrase
- clause, clause, clause

Marriage requires **sexual, financial, and emotional** discipline.
—Anne Roiphe, "Why Marriages Fail"

Culture is a way of **thinking, feeling, believing.**
—Clyde Kluckhohn, *Mirror for Man*

My love of flying goes back to those early days **of roller skates, of swings, and of bicycles.**

—Tresa Wiggins, student

We have been taught **that children develop by ages and stages, that the steps are pretty much the same for everybody, and that to grow out of the limited behavior of childhood, we must climb them all.**

—Gail Sheehy, *Passages*

Many authorities omit the comma between the next to last item of a series and the coordinating conjunction. This handbook uses the comma here for clarity (a style known as the serial comma). Check with your instructor for his or her preference.

> **NO**   Ivan wears only **natural fibres, nylon and Thinsulate.** [This appears to say that nylon and Thinsulate are natural fibres.]
>
> **YES**   Ivan wears only **natural fibres, nylon, and Thinsulate.** [This says that Ivan wears clothes made from three types of fabric.]

At all times, however, follow the "toast, juice, and ham and eggs rule." That is, when one of the items in a series contains *and*, don't use a comma in that item.

When items in a series contain commas or other punctuation, separate them with SEMICOLONS instead of commas (25e).

> If it's a bakery, they have to sell cake; if it's a photography shop, they have to develop film; and if it's a dry-goods store, they have to sell warm underwear.
>
> —Art Buchwald, "Birth Control for Banks"

Numbered or lettered lists within a sentence are considered items in a series. With three or more items, use commas (or semicolons if the items themselves contain commas) to separate them.

> To file your insurance claim, please enclose (1) a letter requesting payment, (2) a police report about the robbery, **and** (3) proof of purchase of the items you say are missing.

 ALERT: In a series, never use a comma before the first item or after the last item, unless a different rule makes it necessary.

NO   Many **artists, writers, and composers, have indulged** in daydreaming.

YES Many artists, writers, and composers have indulged in daydreaming.

NO   Such dreamers include, Miró, Debussy, Dostoevsky, and Dickinson.

YES Such dreamers include Miró, Debussy, Dostoevsky, and Dickinson.

YES Such dreamers include, **of course,** Miró, Debussy, Dostoevsky, and Dickinson. [As a transitional expression, *of course* is set off from the rest of the sentence by commas before and after it (24c).] 👁

EXERCISE 24-2

Insert commas to separate the items in a series. If a sentence needs no commas, explain why. For help, consult 24d.

EXAMPLE   Our longest serving prime minister, William Lyon Mackenzie King, left us the unemployment insurance program the first Citizenship Act and a legacy of puzzling ambiguity.

Our longest serving prime minister, William Lyon Mackenzie King, left us *the unemployment insurance program, the first Citizenship Act, and a legacy of puzzling ambiguity.*

1. During World War II, pulled by English-Canadian loyalty to the Allies pushed by French-Canadian protests against conscription and hounded by generals who needed more soldiers, King announced, "Conscription if necessary, but not necessarily conscription."

2. When he heard how severely London was being bombed in the Blitz, King asked Lester Pearson to send him pieces of damaged buildings to decorate his garden: souvenirs of a city that was being pounded burned shattered terrorized.

3. Although he was often accompanied by women on public occasions, King never married or lived with a woman friend, nor did he have children.

4. In public, King was a colourless, pragmatic politician, yet his diaries reveal a man obsessed by strange fads fears and enthusiasms.

5. Since his death in 1950, King's reputation has suffered, for his interest in attending seances communing with his dead mother and asking political advice from his dog has drawn embarrassing attention to his private life.

24e How do commas work with coordinate adjectives?

Coordinate adjectives are two or more ADJECTIVES of equal weight that modify a NOUN. In contrast, **cumulative adjectives** build meaning from word to word, as they move toward the noun. Box 100 shows the pattern for coordinate adjectives. The key to applying this rule is recognizing when adjectives are coordinate and when they aren't. Box 101 tells you how.

BOX 100 PATTERN

 Commas with coordinate adjectives

coordinate adjective, coordinate adjective noun

BOX 101 SUMMARY

 Tests for coordinate and cumulative adjectives

If either one of these tests works, the adjectives are coordinate and require a comma between them.

- Can the order of the adjectives be reversed without changing the meaning or creating nonsense? If yes, use a comma.

    NO The concert featured **new several** bands. [*New several* makes no sense.]

    YES The **huge, restless** crowd waited for the concert to begin. [*Restless, huge* still carries the same meaning, so these are coordinate adjectives.]

- Can *and* be sensibly inserted between the adjectives? If yes, use a comma.

    NO The concert featured **several and new** bands. [*Several and new* makes no sense.]

    YES The **huge and restless** crowd waited. [*Huge and restless* makes sense, so these are coordinate adjectives.]

The audience cheered when the **pulsating, rhythmic** music filled the stadium. [*Pulsating* and *rhythmic* are coordinate adjectives.]

Each band had a **distinctive musical** style. [*Distinctive* and *musical* aren't coordinate adjectives.]

👁 **ALERT:** Don't put a comma between a final coordinate adjective and the noun it modifies.

> **NO** Hundreds of **roaring, cheering, yelling, fans** filled the stadium.
>
> **YES** Hundreds of **roaring, cheering, yelling fans** filled the stadium. 👁

EXERCISE 24-3

Insert commas to separate coordinate adjectives. If a sentence needs no commas, explain why. For help, consult 24e.

EXAMPLE Only corn grown for popcorn pops consistently because all other kinds of corn lack tough enamel-like shells.

Only corn grown for popcorn pops consistently because all other kinds of corn lack *tough, enamel-like* shells.

1. The outside of an unpopped popcorn kernel is a hard plastic-like coating.
2. Inside an unpopped kernel is a soft starchy substance combined with water.
3. Applying heat causes the water molecules to expand until the pressure pops the dark yellow kernel.
4. The popped kernel turns itself inside out and absorbs air into its white pulpy matter.
5. The thinner softer shells of non-popping corn don't allow water to heat to the high popping temperature.

24f How do commas work with nonrestrictive elements?

A **restrictive element** contains information (a descriptive word, clause, or phrase) that's essential for a sentence to deliver its message; thus, it is often called an *essential element.* A **nonrestrictive element** contains information that's not essential for a sentence to deliver its meaning, and therefore, it is often called a *nonessential element.* The key is in recognizing what's essential (restrictive) and what's nonessential (nonrestrictive) in a sentence. Box 102 defines and explains the differences in the meanings of these terms.

BOX 102   SUMMARY

Restrictive and nonrestrictive defined

Restrictive

A restrictive element contains information essential for the sentence to deliver its message. By being essential, the words in the element limit—that is, "restrict"—the meaning in some way. Don't use commas with restrictive elements.

> Many provinces retest drivers **who are over sixty-five** to check their driving competency.

The information *who are over sixty-five* is essential to understanding the sentence because it limits or restricts the meaning of *drivers* to only those over the age of sixty-five. Drivers *under* sixty-five are not included. To check whether an element is essential, drop it and read the sentence. If the meaning of the sentence changes, then the information element is essential in delivering the message intended in the sentence. This means the element is restrictive (essential), and **commas are not used**.

Nonrestrictive

A nonrestrictive element contains information that's *not* essential for the sentence to deliver its message. By being nonessential, the words in the element don't limit—or "restrict"—the meaning in some way. Use commas with nonrestrictive (nonessential) elements.

> My parents, **who are both over sixty-five,** took a defensive driving course.

The information *who are both over sixty-five* is not essential because the words *my parents* carry the sentence's message so that we know who took a defensive driving course. (Information about their age is "extra" to this message, so **commas are required**.)

Box 103 shows the pattern for comma use with nonrestrictive elements. The pattern for restrictive elements calls for no commas.

BOX 103   PATTERN

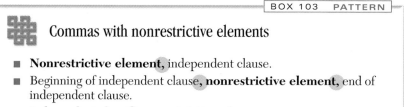

Commas with nonrestrictive elements

- **Nonrestrictive element,** independent clause.
- Beginning of independent clause, **nonrestrictive element,** end of independent clause.
- Independent clause, **nonrestrictive element.**

Restrictive and nonrestrictive elements can fall at the beginning, in the middle, or at the end of a sentence. To test whether an element is nonrestrictive, read the sentence without the element. If the meaning of the sentence does not change, the element is nonrestrictive.

MORE EXAMPLES OF RESTRICTIVE ELEMENTS

Some people **in my neighbourhood** enjoy jogging. [The reader needs the information *in my neighbourhood* to know which people enjoy jogging. The information is essential, so no commas are used.]

Some people **who are in excellent physical condition** enjoy jogging. [The reader needs the information *who are in excellent physical condition* to know which people enjoy jogging. The information is essential, so no commas are used.]

The agricultural scientist **Wendy Singh** has developed a new fertilization technique. [*Wendy Singh* is essential to identify exactly which agricultural scientist developed the new technique, so no commas are used.]

MORE EXAMPLES OF NONRESTRICTIVE ELEMENTS

An energetic person, Anna Hom enjoys jogging. [Without knowing that Anna Hom is *an energetic person,* the reader can understand that she enjoys jogging. The information is nonessential, so commas are used.]

Anna Hom, **who is in excellent physical condition,** enjoys jogging. [Without knowing Anna Hom's *physical condition,* the reader can understand that Anna Hom enjoys jogging. The information is nonessential, so commas are used.]

Anna Hom enjoys jogging, **which is also Adam's favourite pastime.** [Without knowing about *Adam's favourite pastime,* the reader can understand that Anna Hom enjoys jogging. The information is nonessential, so commas are used.]

The agricultural scientist, **a new breed of farmer,** explains how to control a farming environment. [Without knowing that the scientist is *a new breed of farmer,* the reader can understand that the agricultural scientist explains how to control a farming environment. The information is nonessential, so commas are used.]

EXERCISE 24-4

Using your knowledge of restrictive and nonrestrictive elements, insert commas as needed. If a sentence is correct, explain why. For help, consult 24f.

EXAMPLE   During the 1990s when Internet start-ups were proliferating computer science majors often received many job offers even before they graduated.

During the 1990s, *when Internet start-ups were proliferating,* computer science majors often received many job offers even before they graduated.

1. In 1998, the Ontario government which wanted to get in on the high-tech trend offered $10 000 per student to any university that doubled its computer science enrolment by the year 2000.
2. In the fall of 2000 at the height of the Internet boom over seven hundred students packed a lecture hall for an introductory computer science course at the University of California at Berkeley.
3. Students who arrived late for class had to stand around the sides and back of the room.
4. A few years later when the boom began to turn to bust the supply of students quickly dried up.
5. These students who understood the economic cycle switched to less-specialized majors.
6. A typical student might change his or her major from computer science to business information technology which offers a wider variety of commercial skills.
7. Other business-related majors such as communications and advertising are becoming more popular.
8. Because educators and computer scientists know that the decrease in the number of computer-science majors is only temporary they are not worried about the future.
9. Each time the economy gathers steam again leading to demands for advances in computer technology companies suddenly need programmers and systems analysts again.
10. Then students whose strongest interest is computer science will flock back to the courses that once more promise lucrative and interesting job possibilities.

24g How do commas set off parenthetical expressions, contrasts, words of direct address, and tag sentences?

Parenthetical expressions are "asides." They add information but aren't necessary for understanding the message of a sentence. Set them off with parentheses or commas.

> Sales of Canadian tobacco **(according to recent statistics)** have been steadily decreasing.
> Tobacco farmers, **it is clear,** must find other means of support.

Expressions of **contrast** state what is *not* the case. Set them off with commas.

> Feeding the world's population is **a serious, though not impossible,** problem.
> We must work against world hunger continuously, **not only when famines strike.**

Words of **direct address** name the person or group being spoken to (addressed). Set them off with commas.

> Join me, **brothers and sisters,** to end hunger.
> Your contribution to the Relief Fund, **Steve,** will help us greatly.

A **tag sentence** is a normal sentence that ends with a "tag," an attached phrase or question. Set off a tag with a comma. When the tag is a question, the sentence ends with a question mark.

> Canadians' response to the Manitoba flood was impressive, **wasn't it?**
> The response to future crises will be as generous, **I hope.**

EXERCISE 24-5

Add commas to set off any parenthetical or contrasting elements, words of direct address, and tag sentences. Adjust end punctuation as necessary. For help, consult 24g.

EXAMPLE   Writer's block it seems to me is a misunderstood phenomenon.

Writer's block, *it seems to me,* is a misunderstood phenomenon.

1. An inability to write some say stems from lack of discipline and a tendency to procrastinate.
2. In other words the only way to overcome writer's block is to exert more willpower.
3. But writer's block is a complex psychological event that happens to conscientious people not just procrastinators.
4. Strange as it may seem such people are often unconsciously rebelling against their own self-tyranny and rigid standards of perfection.
5. If I told you my fellow writer that all it takes to start writing again is to quit punishing yourself, you would think I was crazy wouldn't you?

24h How do commas work with quoted words?

Explanatory words are words such as *said, stated, declared,* and others that introduce DIRECT DISCOURSE. When they fall in the same sentence, quoted words are set off from explanatory words. Box 104 on the next page shows this pattern.

> Speaking of ideal love, the poet William Blake wrote, "Love seeketh not itself to please."
> "My love is a fever," said William Shakespeare about love's passion.
> "I love no love," proclaimed poet Mary Coleridge, "but thee."

> BOX 104   PATTERN
>
> ## Commas with quoted words
>
> ■ Explanatory words, "Quoted words."
> ■ "Quoted words," explanatory words.
> ■ "Quoted words begin," explanatory words, "quoted words continue."

Exception

When the quoted words are blended into the grammatical structure of your sentence, don't use commas to set them off. These are instances of INDIRECT DISCOURSE, usually occurring with *as* and *that*.

> The duke describes the duchess **as** "too soon made glad."
> The duchess insists **that** "appearing glad often is but a deception."

👁 **ALERT:** When the quoted words end with an exclamation point or a question mark, retain that original punctuation, even if explanatory words follow.

QUOTED WORDS	*"O Romeo! Romeo!"*
NO	"O Romeo! Romeo!," whispered Juliet from her window.
NO	"O Romeo! Romeo," whispered Juliet from her window.
YES	"O Romeo! Romeo!" whispered Juliet from her window.
QUOTED WORDS	*"Wherefore art thou Romeo?"*
NO	"Wherefore art thou Romeo?," continued Juliet as she thought of fate's cruel tricks.
NO	"Wherefore art thou Romeo," continued Juliet as she thought of fate's cruel tricks.
YES	"Wherefore art thou Romeo?" continued Juliet as she thought of fate's cruel tricks. 👁

EXERCISE 24-6

Punctuate the following dialogue correctly. If a sentence is correct, explain why. For help, consult 24h.

EXAMPLE	"Can you tell me just one thing?," asked the tourist.
	"Can you tell me just one thing**?**" asked the tourist.

1. "I'm happy to answer any questions you have" said the rancher to the tourist.
2. "Well, then" said the tourist "I'd like to know how you make ends meet on such a tiny ranch."
3. "Do you see that man leaning against the shed over there?" asked the rancher, pointing with a twig.
4. The rancher continued "He works for me, but I don't pay him any money. Instead, I promised him that after two years of work, he will own the ranch."
5. "Then, I'll work for him, and in two more years, the ranch will be mine again!," said the rancher with a smile.

24i   How do commas work in dates, names, addresses, correspondence, and numbers?

When you write dates, names, addresses, correspondence, and numbers, use commas according to accepted practice. Boxes 105 through 108 explain.

BOX 105   SUMMARY

Commas with dates

- Use a comma between the date and the year: *July 20, 1969*
- Use a comma between the day and the date: *Sunday, July 20.*
- Within a sentence, use a comma on either side of the year in the format month-day-year: *Everyone planned to be near a TV set on July 20, 1969, to watch the lunar landing.*
- Never use a comma when only the month and year, or the month and day, are given. Also, never use a comma between the season and year.

    YES People knew that one day in **July 1969** would change the world.

    YES News coverage was especially heavy on **July 21.**

    YES In **summer 1969** a man walked on the moon.

- Never use a comma in an inverted date (day-month-year).

    YES People stayed near their televisions on **20 July 1969** to watch the moon landing.

BOX 106 SUMMARY

Commas with names, places, and addresses

- When an abbreviated academic degree (*M.D., Ph.D.*) comes after a person's name, use a comma between the name and the title (*Angie Eng, M.D.*), and also after the title if other words follow in the sentence: *The jury listened closely to the expert testimony of **Angie Eng, M.D., last week.***
- When an indicator of birth order or succession (*Jr., Sr., III, IV*) follows a name, never use a comma: *Martin Luther **King Jr.*** or *Henry **Ford II***
- When you invert a person's name, use a comma to separate the last name from the first: ***Troyka, David***
- When city and province or territory names are written together, use a comma to separate them: ***Estevan, Saskatchewan.*** If the city and province fall within a sentence, use a comma after the province as well: *The town of **Estevan, Saskatchewan,** recorded the highest number of hours of sunshine in Canada in 1993.*
- When a complete address is part of a sentence, use a comma to separate all the items, except the postal code and province's abbreviation. The postal code follows the province after a space and is not followed by a comma: *I wrote to **Shelly Kupperman, 1001 Rule Road, Mississauga ON L5A 2Z2** for more information about the comma.*

BOX 107 SUMMARY

Commas in correspondence

- For the opening of an informal letter, use a comma: **Dear Betty,**
- For the opening of a business or formal letter, use a colon: **Dear Ms. Kiviat:**
- For the close of a letter, use a comma:
  Sincerely yours, Best regards, Love,

BOX 108 SUMMARY

Commas with numbers

SI—the international system of metric measurements used in Canada—does not use commas in numbers; it uses spaces to separate sets of three digits. Nevertheless, many people still use commas. This section explains both number systems.

→

Commas with numbers (*continued*)

Rules for Numbers in SI

■ Counting from the right, put a space after every three digits in numbers with more than four digits.

72 867   150 567 066

■ In four-digit numbers, a space is optional for money, distance, amounts, and most other measurements. Be consistent within each piece of writing.

$1867 $1 867

1867 km   1 867 km

1867 potatoes   1 867 potatoes

Never use a space in a four-digit year: **1990.** (*Note:* If the year has five digits or more, do insert a space: 25 000 BC.) Always use a space in four-digit numbers when they are aligned in columns in a table or a chart.

Rules for Numbers in Systems Using Commas

■ Counting from the right, put a comma after every three digits in numbers with more than four digits.

72,867   150,567,066

■ A comma is optional in four-digit numbers. Be consistent within each piece of writing.

$1867 $1,867

1867 km   1,867 km

1867 potatoes   1,867 potatoes

■ Never use a comma in a four-digit year: **1990** (*Note:* If the year has five digits or more, do use a comma: **25,000 BC**)

■ Never use a comma in an address of four digits or more: ***12161 Dean Drive***

■ Never use a comma in a page number of four digits or more: ***see page 1338***

■ Use a comma to separate related Imperial measurements written as words: ***five feet, four inches***

■ Use a comma to separate a scene from an act in a play: ***act II, scene iv*** (or ***act 2, scene 4***)

■ Use a comma to separate references to a page and a line: ***page 10, line 6***

EXERCISE 24-7

Insert commas (or spaces) where they are needed. For help, consult 24i.

EXAMPLE   The heaviest hailstone recorded in Canada fell on Cedoux Saskatchewan.

The heaviest hailstone recorded in Canada fell on *Cedoux,* *Saskatchewan.*

1. With a rainfall of 6655 mm, Henderson Lake British Columbia has the most annual precipitation in the country.

2. Burgeo Newfoundland has the second highest average annual precipitation with 1699.7 mm.

3. The warmest temperature in Canada—45 degrees Celsius—was recorded on July 5 1937 at Midale Saskatchewan.

4. Windsor Ontario with more than 200000 population holds the record for the highest average number of days per year with thunderstorms: 34 days.

5. Snag Yukon Territory has the record for the coldest temperature ever recorded in Canada; it was minus 63 degrees Celsius on February 3 1947.

24j How do commas clarify meaning?

A comma is sometimes needed to clarify the meaning of a sentence, even though no rule calls for one. The best solution is to revise the sentence.

NO   Of the gymnastic team's twenty five were injured.

YES   Of the gymnastic team's **twenty, five** were injured.

YES   Of **twenty on** the gymnastic team, five were injured. [preferred]

NO   Those who can practise many hours a day.

YES   **Those who can,** practise many hours a day.

YES   **They** practise many hours a day **when they can.** [preferred]

NO   George dressed and performed for the sellout crowd.

YES   **George dressed,** and performed for the sellout crowd.

YES   **After** George dressed, **he** performed for the sellout crowd. [preferred]

EXERCISE 24-8

Insert commas to prevent misreading. For help, consult, 24j.

EXAMPLE   When hunting owls use both vision and hearing.

When hunting, owls use both vision and hearing.

1. Flying at night owls consult a mental "map" of their surroundings.
2. During the day owls when they can fly over their territories and create this imaginary map.
3. A team of scientists gave owls distorting eyeglasses to make the birds relearn their mental maps.
4. The bespectacled owl scientists found wears its glasses as contentedly as humans.
5. In a short time after they have produced a new mental map using their glasses the owls once again can spot and chase small rodents across the ground.

24k How can I avoid misusing commas?

Throughout this chapter, ALERT notes remind you about comma misuses, as they relate to each comma rule. Most of these misuses are overuses—inserting a comma where one is unnecessary. This section summarizes the ALERT notes and lists other frequent misuses of the comma.

When advice against overusing a comma clashes with a rule requiring one, follow the rule that requires the comma.

> Banff, Alberta, attracts thousands of tourists each year. [Although the comma after *Alberta* separates the subject and verb, the comma is correct because it is required to set off a city–province combination within a sentence (24i).]

24k.1 Commas with coordinating conjunctions

Never use a comma after a COORDINATING CONJUNCTION that joins two INDEPENDENT CLAUSES, unless another rule makes it necessary (24b). Also, don't use a comma to separate two items joined with a coordinating conjunction—there must be at least three (see 24d).

NO The sky was dark grey **and,** it looked like dusk.
YES The sky was dark grey**, and** it looked like dusk.

NO **The moon, and the stars** were shining last night.
YES **The moon and the stars** were shining last night.

24k.2 Commas with subordinating conjunctions and prepositions

Never put a comma after a SUBORDINATING CONJUNCTION or a PREPOSITION unless another rule makes it necessary.

NO **Although,** the storm brought high winds, it did no damage.
YES **Although the storm brought high winds,** it did no damage.
[comma follows full subordinate clause, not the subordinating conjunction that begins it]

NO   The storm did no damage **although,** it brought high winds.

YES   The storm did no damage **although it brought high winds.** [no comma when subordinate clause follows the independent clause]

NO   People expected worse **from,** the high winds and the heavy downpour.

YES   People expected worse **from the high winds and the heavy downpour.** [preposition begins sentence element that needs no comma before or after]

24k.3 Commas in a series

Never use a comma before the first, or after the last, item in a series, unless another rule makes it necessary (24d).

NO   Public-spirited hardware catalogues print pictures **of, the flags, flowers, and premiers** of all the provinces and territories each Canada Day.

NO   Public-spirited hardware catalogues print **pictures of the flags, flowers, and premiers, of all the** provinces and territories each Canada Day.

YES   Public-spirited hardware catalogues print pictures of the **flags, flowers, and premiers** of all the provinces and territories each Canada Day.

Never put a comma between a final COORDINATE ADJECTIVE and the NOUN that the adjectives modify. Also, don't use a comma between adjectives that are not coordinate (24e).

NO   He wore an **old, baggy, sweater.**

YES   He wore an **old, baggy sweater.** [coordinate adjectives]

NO   He has **several, new sweaters.**

YES   He has **several new sweaters.** [noncoordinate or cumulative adjectives]

24k.4 Commas with restrictive elements

Never use a comma to set off a RESTRICTIVE (essential) element from the rest of a sentence (24f).

NO   **Vegetables, stir-fried in a wok,** are crisp and flavourful. [The words *stir-fried in a wok* are essential, so they are not set off with commas.]

YES   **Vegetables stir-fried in a wok** are crisp and flavourful.

24k.5 Commas with quotations

Never use a comma to set off INDIRECT DISCOURSE; use a comma only with DIRECT DISCOURSE (24h).

> **NO** Jon said **that, he likes** stir-fried vegetables.
>
> **YES** Jon said **that he likes** stir-fried vegetables.
>
> **YES** **Jon said, "I like** stir-fried vegetables."

24k.6 Commas that separate a subject from its verb, a verb from its object, or a preposition from its object

A comma does not make sense between these elements, though in some cases another comma rule might supersede this guideline (as in the first example in section 24k).

> **NO** **The National Aircraft Museum, attracts** enthusiasts from all over Canada. [As a rule, a comma doesn't separate a subject from its verb.]
>
> **YES** **The National Aircraft Museum attracts** enthusiasts from all over Canada.
>
> **NO** The many small airplanes developed in Canada **include, the de Havilland Otter and Dash 7.** [As a rule, a comma doesn't separate a verb from its OBJECT.]
>
> **YES** The many small airplanes developed in Canada **include the de Havilland Otter and Dash 7.**
>
> **NO** The Twin Otter did much to open up the Arctic **in, the mid-twentieth century.** [As a rule, a comma doesn't separate a preposition from its object.]
>
> **YES** The Twin Otter did much to open up the Arctic **in the mid-twentieth century.**

EXERCISE 24-9

Some deliberately misused commas have been added in these sentences. Consulting 24k and the other sections in this chapter that are referred to in 24k, delete unneeded commas. If a sentence is correct, circle its number.

EXAMPLE The "Persons Case" is the name of the court case, that finally gave women in Canada the right to serve in the Senate.

The "Persons Case" is the name of *the court case that* finally gave women in Canada the right to serve in the Senate.

1. In 1919, Judge Emily Murphy asked the prime minister to appoint a woman to the Senate, but, she received a disappointing reply.
2. Prime Minister Borden informed her that only "persons" could sit in the Senate, and, the 1867 British North America Act did not recognize women as persons.
3. Murphy, and four other women petitioned the Supreme Court of Canada to decide if the word *persons* in the BNA Act, which served as Canada's constitution, included female persons.
4. After many, long weeks of deliberation, the Court said that, the BNA Act did not count women as persons.
5. The basis of the Court's decision was, the argument that the authors of the 1867 Act, who had not given women the vote, never intended them to become senators.
6. In response, one petitioner tartly expressed the disappointment, shock, and surprise of all those women "who had not known they were not persons" until the Court told them so.
7. The five, anxious petitioners could still appeal the decision of Canada's Supreme Court to, the Privy Council in London.
8. The Privy Council ruled in 1929 that the term *persons*, must be understood in the BNA Act to include women; further, it called, the exclusion of women from politics "a relic of days more barbarous than ours."
9. Ironically, women, had already won the right to be elected to Parliament and to every provincial legislature except Quebec's.
10. To commemorate this court case, someone, who has worked to achieve justice and equality, each year, is presented with the cleverly named Persons Award.

24l | How can I avoid comma errors?

You can avoid most comma errors with these two bits of advice:

- As you write or reread what you've written, never insert a comma simply because you happen to pause to think or take a breath before moving on. Pausing isn't a reliable guide for writers, although that myth continues to thrive. People's breathing rhythms, accents, and thinking patterns vary greatly.

- As you're writing, if you're unsure about a comma, insert it and circle the spot. Later, when you're EDITING, check this handbook for the rule that applies.

Chapter 25

Semicolons

25a What are the uses of a semicolon?

While a period signals the complete separation of INDEPENDENT CLAUSES, a **semicolon** indicates only a partial ("semi") separation. Use a semicolon in only two situations. A semicolon can replace a period between sentences that are closely related in meaning (25b and 25c). Also, a semicolon belongs between sentence structures that already contain one or more commas (25d) and with certain lists (25e).

25b When can I use a semicolon, instead of a period, between independent clauses?

The choice between a period and a semicolon for separating independent clauses depends on whether your meaning is better communicated by a complete separation (period) or a partial separation (semicolon). Box 109 shows this pattern for using semicolons.

BOX 109   PATTERN

Semicolon I

- Independent clause; independent clause.

British Columbia has some of the wettest territory in Canada; it also has some of the driest.

◎ **ALERT:** Never use a comma alone between independent clauses—this rule will prevent you from creating the error known as a COMMA SPLICE. ◎

25c When else can I use a semicolon between independent clauses?

When the second of a set of independent clauses closely related in meaning starts with a CONJUNCTIVE ADVERB or with a TRANSITIONAL EXPRESSION, you can choose to separate the clauses with a semicolon instead of a period. Also, insert a comma following a conjunctive adverb or transitional expression that starts an independent clause. Although some professional writers today omit the comma after short words (*then, next, soon*), the rule remains for most ACADEMIC WRITING. Box 110 shows this pattern for using semicolons.

BOX 110   PATTERN

 Semicolon II

- Independent clause; conjunctive adverb, independent clause.
- Independent clause; transitional expression, independent clause.

The average annual rainfall in the Okanagan Valley is less than 40 cm; **nevertheless,** it lies in the shadow of the rainy Cascade Mountains.
[conjunctive adverb]

Irrigation came to the semidesert valley in the 1930s; **as a result,** it now produces much of Canada's fruit and wine. [transitional expression]

ALERT: Never use only a comma between independent clauses that are connected by a conjunctive adverb or word of transition—this rule will prevent you from creating the error known as a COMMA SPLICE.

25d How do semicolons work with coordinating conjunctions?

As a general rule, when INDEPENDENT CLAUSES are linked by a COORDIN-ATING CONJUNCTION, good practice calls for a comma, not a period or semicolon, before the coordinating conjunction (24b). However, when one or more of the independent clauses already contain a comma, link the independent clauses by substituting a semicolon for the period. This can help your reader see the relationship between the ideas more clearly. Box 111 shows the various combinations of this pattern.

BOX 111   PATTERN

Semicolon III

- Independent clause, one that contains a comma; coordinating conjunction followed by independent clause.
- Independent clause; coordinating conjunction followed by independent clause, one that contains a comma.
- Independent clause, one that contains a comma; coordinating conjunction followed by independent clause, one that contains a comma.

Summers are long, hot, and dry in the Okanagan Valley; **yet** visitors can ski down the surrounding mountains all summer long.

The Okanagan was ranching country in the nineteenth century; **and** there, in the broad, dry plain, some of Canada's oldest ranches still operate.

A tour operator in the British Columbia interior offers a package that includes skiing, either downhill or cross-country, in the morning; **but** the afternoon activities it offers are soccer, tennis, and other warm-weather sports.

25e When should I use semicolons between items in a series?

When a sentence contains a series of items that are long or that already contain one or more commas, separate the items with semicolons. Punctuating this way groups the elements so that your reader can see where one item ends and the next begins. Box 112 shows this pattern.

BOX 112   PATTERN

Semicolon IV

- Independent clause containing a series of items, any of which contain a comma; another item in the series; and another item in the series.

Alexander Mackenzie's overland voyage to the Pacific took him through grassy uplands, steep canyons, and tangled swamp; into the habitats of the grizzly bear, bald eagle, and sea otter; **and** down rivers that required running rapids, portaging, and even towing his canoe.

25f How do I avoid misusing the semicolon?

Not using a semicolon after an introductory phrase

If you use a semicolon after an introductory PHRASE, you create the error known as a SENTENCE FRAGMENT.

> **NO** **Sent by the North West Company in 1793; Mackenzie hoped to locate the great river whose mouth Captain Cook thought he had seen fifteen years earlier.**
>
> **YES** Sent by the North West Company in 1793, Mackenzie hoped to locate the great river whose mouth Captain Cook thought he had seen fifteen years earlier.

Not using a semicolon after a dependent clause

If you use a semicolon after a DEPENDENT CLAUSE, you create the error known as a sentence fragment.

> **NO** **Although the expedition was trespassing on valuable Indian trade routes; Mackenzie used negotiation, not firearms, to penetrate this well-defended territory.**
>
> **YES** Although the expedition was trespassing on valuable Indian trade routes, Mackenzie used negotiation, not firearms, to penetrate this well-defended territory.

Not using a semicolon to introduce a list

When the words that introduce a list form an independent clause, use a colon, never a semicolon (26b).

> **NO** **The Mackenzie expedition hunted and traded for fresh food; venison, trout, and especially salmon.**
>
> **YES** The Mackenzie expedition hunted and traded for fresh food: venison, trout, and especially salmon.

EXERCISE 25-1

Insert semicolons as needed in these items. Also, fix any incorrectly used semicolons. If a sentence is correct, explain why. For help, consult all sections of this chapter.

> **EXAMPLE** Bicycle racing is as popular in Europe as hockey or baseball is here, it is even more heavily commercialized.
>
> Bicycle racing is as popular in Europe as hockey or baseball is here; it is even more heavily commercialized.

1. The Tour de France is the world's best known bicycle race, the 94-year-old Giro d'Italia runs a close second.

2. Both are gruelling, three-week-long events that require cyclists to cover 4000 km of difficult, mountainous terrain, and both are eagerly anticipated, draw enormous crowds along their routes, and receive extensive media coverage.

3. That media attention leads to marketing opportunities for the events' sponsors; which place ads along each race's route, in the nearby towns, and on the cyclists themselves.

4. Martin Hvastija, a participant in the 2003 Giro d'Italia, had no chance of winning the race, nevertheless, he drew extensive media attention to his sponsors.

5. His method was simple; he managed to ride out in front of the field for a few kilometres.

6. Although he had no chance of winning the race; newscasters beamed his image around the world while at the same time; showing the world the colourful advertising logos on his jersey.

7. In addition to sponsoring individual athletes, corporations plaster ads all over the towns that the races go through, they toss samples, coupons, and gadgets to spectators from promotional vehicles that ride ahead of the cyclists, and they run TV and radio ads.

8. In 2003, the organizers of the Giro took in over $10 million in fees from advertisers and $16 million in broadcast rights from the Italian state-owned TV network, RAI, however, these figures were down a bit from the previous year.

9. An additional source of revenues for race organizers is fees from the towns where the race starts and ends each day, as a result, organizers determine the actual course according to which cities are willing to pay the $160 000 charge.

10. Media watchers think the Giro d'Italia could become even more profitable and popular, especially among young adults, but only if it took a cue from the Tour de France by encouraging; more international press coverage, more star riders, and even heavier corporate sponsorship.

EXERCISE 25-2

Combine each set of sentences into one sentence containing two independent clauses. Use a semicolon between the two clauses. You may add, omit, revise, and rearrange words. Try to use all the patterns in this chapter and explain the reasoning behind your decisions. More than one revision may be correct. For help, consult all sections of this chapter.

EXAMPLE: A Canadian-led team of archaeologists has been excavating a site. The site is on the south shore of Crete. Scholars from Greece, the United Kingdom, the United States, and other countries as well have taken part.

A Canadian-led team of archaeologists has been excavating a site on the south shore of *Crete*; *scholars* from Greece, the United Kingdom, the United States, and other countries as well have taken part.

1. Archaeologists have been excavating the site of Kommos in southern Crete for more than twenty-five years. The site has not yet yielded up all its secrets.

2. Ancient Crete was the home of the legendary King Minos. In Crete, according to Greek myth, lived the Minotaur. This was a man with the head of a terrible bull.

3. Kommos was a small seaport. Kommos was far from Knossos. Knossos was the great city at the centre of the Minoan civilization that preceded the Greeks.

4. Only a temple remained at Kommos after Crete passed to Greek rule. Phoenician merchants seem to have been the worshippers at this temple during the early Greek period.

5. The Phoenicians were a seafaring people from the Lebanese coast. They taught the Greeks to use the alphabet. Archaeologists have found few places where Phoenicians and Greeks appear to have lived side by side. Kommos may be one, though.

Chapter 26

Colons

26a   What are the uses of a colon?

A **colon** is a full stop that draws attention to the words that follow. It can be placed only at the end of an INDEPENDENT CLAUSE. A colon introduces a list, an APPOSITIVE, or a QUOTATION.

26b   When can a colon introduce a list, an appositive, or a quotation?

When a complete sentence—that is, an INDEPENDENT CLAUSE—introduces a list, an APPOSITIVE, or a QUOTATION, place a colon before the words being introduced. These words don't have to form an independent clause themselves, but a complete sentence before the colon is essential. Box 113 shows this pattern for using a colon.

BOX 113   PATTERN

Colon sentence I

- Independent clause: list.
- Independent clause: appositive.
- Independent clause: "Quoted words."

Introducing listed items

When a complete sentence introduces a list, a colon is required, as demonstrated in the example that follows.

> **If you really want to lose weight, you must do three things:**
> eat smaller portions, exercise, and drink lots of water. [An independent clause comes before the listed items, so a colon is correct.]

When the lead-in words at the end of an independent clause are *such as, including, like,* or *consists of,* never use a colon. In contrast, if the lead-in words at the end of an independent clause are *the following* or *as follows,* do use a colon.

The students demanded improvements *such as* an expanded menu in the cafeteria, improved janitorial services, and more up-to-date textbooks.

The students demanded *the following*: an expanded menu in the cafeteria, improved janitorial services, and more up-to-date textbooks.

Introducing appositives

An APPOSITIVE is a word or words that rename a NOUN or PRONOUN. When an appositive is introduced by an independent clause, use a colon.

The UBC Museum of Anthropology has one outstanding exhibit: its collection of Northwest Coast Indian artifacts. [The independent clause containing *outstanding exhibit* precedes the appositive *its collection of . . . artifacts.*]

Introducing quotations

When an independent clause introduces a quotation, use a colon after it. (If the words introducing a quotation don't form an independent clause, use a comma.)

The little boy in *E.T.* did say something neat: "How do you explain school to a higher intelligence?" [The required independent clause comes before the quotation.]

—George F. Will, "Well, I Don't Love You, E.T."

26c When can I use a colon between two independent clauses?

When a second INDEPENDENT CLAUSE explains or summarizes a first independent clause, you can use a colon to separate them. Box 114 shows this pattern for using a colon.

👁 **ALERT:** You can choose to use a capital letter or a lowercase letter for the first word of an independent clause that follows a colon. Whichever you choose, be consistent within a piece of writing. I use a capital letter in this handbook.

We will never forget the first time we made dinner together: **He** got stomach poisoning and was too sick to go to work for four days.

—Lisa Baladendrum, student 👁

BOX 114   PATTERN

Colon sentence II

■ Independent clause: Independent clause that explains or summarizes the prior independent clause.

26d What standard formats require a colon?

A variety of standard formats require a colon. Also, colons are used in many DOCUMENTATION STYLES, as shown in Chapters 34, 35, and 36.

TITLE AND SUBTITLE
A Brief History of Time: From the Big Bang to Black Holes

HOURS, MINUTES, AND SECONDS
The plane took off at 7:15 p.m.
The track star passed the halfway point at 1:23:02.

👁 **ALERT:** In the military, hours and minutes are written without colons and with four digits on a 24-hour clock: *The staff meeting originally scheduled for Tuesday at **0930** will be held Tuesday at **1430** instead.* 👁

REFERENCES TO BIBLE CHAPTERS AND VERSES
Psalms 23:1–3
Luke 3:13

👁 **ALERT:** MLA style (Chapter 34) recommends use of a period in place of the colon in biblical references, but notes that the colon is customary. 👁

MEMOS
To: Dean Kristen Olivero
From: Professor Daniel Black
Re: Student Work-Study Program

SALUTATION IN A BUSINESS LETTER
Dear Dr. Jewell:

26e When is a colon wrong?

Independent clauses

A colon can introduce a list, an APPOSITIVE, or a QUOTATION, but only when an INDEPENDENT CLAUSE does the introducing. Similarly, a colon can be used between two independent clauses when the second summarizes or explains the first. In following these rules, be sure that you're dealing with independent clauses, not other word groups.

NO   The cook bought: eggs, milk, cheese, and bread. [*The cook bought* isn't an independent clause.]

YES The cook bought eggs, milk, cheese, and bread.

Never use a colon to separate a PHRASE or DEPENDENT CLAUSE from an independent clause. Otherwise, you'll create the error known as a SENTENCE FRAGMENT.

NO   Day after day: the drought dragged on. [*Day after day* is a phrase, not an independent clause.]

YES Day after day, the drought dragged on.

NO   After the drought ended: the farmers celebrated. [*After the drought ended* is a dependent clause, not an independent clause.]

YES After the drought ended, the farmers celebrated.

Lead-in words

Never use a colon after the lead-in words *such as, including, like,* and *consists of.*

NO   The health board discussed many problems **such as:** poor water quality, aging sewage treatment systems, and the lack of alternative water supplies. [A colon is incorrect after *such as.*]

YES The health board discussed poor water quality, aging sewage treatment systems, and the lack of alternative water supplies. [*Such as* is dropped and the sentence slightly revised.]

YES The health board discussed many problems, **such as** poor water quality, an aging sewage treatment system, and the lack of alternative water supplies. [Comma before *such as* tells the reader that the list coming up is nonrestrictive (nonessential)—it illustrates *problems.*]

YES The health board discussed many problems: poor water quality, aging sewage treatment systems, and the lack of alternative water supplies. [If *such as* is dropped, a colon after the independent clause is correct.]

409

EXERCISE 26-1

Insert colons where needed and delete any not needed. If a sentence is correct, explain why. For help, consult all sections of this chapter.

EXAMPLE   The twentieth century saw a flowering of Irish literature, W. B. Yeats, G. B. Shaw, Samuel Beckett, and Seamus Heaney all won the Nobel Prize in Literature.

The twentieth century saw a flowering of Irish literature: W. B. Yeats, G. B. Shaw, Samuel Beckett, and Seamus Heaney all won the Nobel Prize in Literature.

1. People who work the night shift are typically deprived of essential sleep, an average of nine hours a week.
2. The Iroquois of the Great Lakes region lived in fortified villages and cultivated: corn, beans, and squash.
3. Five nations originally formed the Iroquois Confederacy: the Mohawk, the Oneida, the Onondaga, the Cayuga, and the Seneca.
4. Later, these five Iroquois nations were joined by: the Tuscarora.
5. Shouting: "Come back!" Adam watched the vehicle speed down the highway.
6. When a runner breaks through that unavoidable wall of exhaustion, a very different feeling sets in; an intense sense of well-being known as the "runner's high."
7. However: the "runner's high" soon disappears.
8. Two new nations were born on the same day in 1947, India and Pakistan achieved their independence from Britain at midnight on August 15.
9. To   English 101 Instructors

   From   Dean of Instruction

   Re   Classroom Assignments
10. Only a hurricane could have kept Lisa from meeting Nathaniel at 800 p.m.; unfortunately, that night a hurricane hit.
11. When he was sixteen, George's interests were the usual ones, cars, music videos, and dating.
12. Like many people who have never learned to read or write, the woman who told her life story in *Aman; The Story of a Somali Girl* was able to remember an astonishing number of events in precise detail.
13. The Greek philosopher Socrates took these words as his motto, "The unexamined life is not worth living."
14. Socrates was executed after being found guilty of: teaching young people new ideas.
15. The voice coming from the radio could belong to only one person; the great jazz singer Ella Fitzgerald.

Chapter 27

Apostrophes

27a What is the role of the apostrophe?

The **apostrophe** plays four roles in writing: It creates the POSSESSIVE CASE of NOUNS, forms the possessive case of INDEFINITE PRONOUNS, stands for one or more omitted letters in a word (a CONTRACTION), and can help form plurals of letters and numerals.

In contrast, here are two roles the apostrophe doesn't play: It doesn't belong with plurals of nouns, and it doesn't form the plural of PERSONAL PRONOUNS in the possessive case.

27b How do I use an apostrophe to show a possessive noun?

An apostrophe works with a NOUN to form the POSSESSIVE CASE, which shows ownership or a close relationship.

OWNERSHIP	The **writer's** pen ran out of ink.
CLOSE RELATIONSHIP	The **novel's** plot is complicated.

Possession in nouns can be communicated in two ways: by a PHRASE starting with *of* (comments *of* the instructor; comments *of* Professor Furman) or by an apostrophe and the letter *s* (the instructor*'s* comments; Professor Furman*'s* comments). Here's a list of specific rules governing usage of *'s*.

- **Add 's to nouns not ending in s:**

  She felt a **parent's** joy. [*Parent* is a singular noun not ending in *s*.]
  They care about their **children's** education. [*Children* is a plural noun not ending in *s*.]

■ **Add 's to singular nouns ending in s:**

You can add 's or the apostrophe alone to show possession when a singular noun ends in s. In this handbook, I use 's to clearly mark singular-noun possessives, no matter what letter ends the noun. Whichever rule variation you choose, be consistent within each piece of writing.

The **bus's** (or **bus'**) air conditioning is out of order.
Chris's (or **Chris'**) ordeal ended.

If you encounter a tongue-twisting pronunciation (*Charles **Dickens's** novel*), you may decide not to add the additional s (*Charles **Dickens'** novel*). You must, however, be consistent in each piece of writing.

■ **Add only an apostrophe to a plural noun ending in s:**

The **boys'** statements were taken seriously.
Three **months'** maternity leave is in the **workers'** contract.

■ **Add 's to the last word in compound words and phrases:**

His **mother-in-law's** corporation has bought out a competitor.
The **tennis player's** strategy was brilliant.
We want to hear the **caseworker's** recommendation.

■ **Add 's to each noun in individual possession:**

Shirley's and **Kayla's** houses are next to each other. [Shirley and Kayla each own a house; they don't own the houses jointly.]

■ **Add 's to only the last noun in joint or group possession:**

Kareem and Brina's house has a screened porch. [Kareem and Brina own one house.]
Avram and Justin's houses always have nice lawns. [Avram and Justin jointly own more than one house.]

27c How do I use an apostrophe with possessive pronouns?

When a POSSESSIVE PRONOUN ends with the letter s (*hers, his, its, ours, yours, and theirs*), never add an apostrophe. Following is a list of PERSONAL PRONOUNS and their possessive forms.

PERSONAL PRONOUNS	POSSESSIVE FORMS
I	my, mine
you	your, yours
he	his
she	her, hers

PERSONAL PRONOUNS	POSSESSIVE FORMS
it	its
we	our, ours
they	their, theirs
who	whose

27d How do I use an apostrophe with contractions?

In a **contraction,** an apostrophe takes the place of one or more omitted letters. Be careful not to confuse a contraction with a POSSESSIVE PRONOUN. Doing so is a common spelling error, one that many people—including employers—consider evidence of a poor education.

it's (contraction for *it is, it has*)   **its** (possessive pronoun)
they're (contraction for *they are*)   **their** (possessive pronoun)
who's (contraction for *who is*)   **whose** (possessive form of *who*)
you're (contraction for *you are*)   **your** (possessive pronoun)

> **NO**   The government promises to balance **it's** budget.
> **YES**   The government promises to balance **its** budget.

> **NO**   The professor **who's** class was cancelled is ill.
> **YES**   The professor **whose** class was cancelled is ill.

In choosing whether or not to use a contraction or a full form, consider that many instructors think contractions aren't appropriate in ACADEMIC WRITING. Nevertheless, the *MLA Handbook* accepts contractions, including *'90s* for *the 1990s.* In this handbook, I use contractions because I'm addressing you, the student. I suggest, however, that before you use contractions in your academic writing, check with your instructor. Here's a list of common contractions.

COMMON CONTRACTIONS

aren't = *are not*	she's = *she is, she has*
can't = *cannot*	there's = *there is, there has*
didn't = *did not*	they're = *they are*
don't = *do not*	wasn't = *was not*
he's = *he is, he has*	we're = *we are*
I'd = *I would, I had*	weren't = *were not*
I'm = *I am*	we've = *we have*
isn't = *is not*	who's = *who is, who has*
it's = *it is, it has*	won't = *will not*
let's = *let us*	you're = *you are*

👁 **ALERT:** One contraction required in all writing is *o'clock* (which stands for *of the clock*, an expression used long ago). 👁

27e How do I use an apostrophe with possessive indefinite pronouns?

An apostrophe works with an INDEFINITE PRONOUN (see list in Box 77 in 10i) to form the POSSESSIVE CASE, which shows ownership or a close relationship.

OWNERSHIP	**Everyone's** dinner is ready.
CLOSE RELATIONSHIP	**Something's** aroma is appealing.

Possession in indefinite pronouns can be communicated in two ways: by a PHRASE starting with *of* (*comments **of** everyone*) or by an apostrophe and the letter *s* (*everyone's comments*).

27f How do I form the plural of miscellaneous elements?

Some writers form the plural of elements such as letters meant as letters, words meant as words, numerals, and symbols by adding *'s*. Others add *s*. The most current MLA guidelines endorse the use of *s* only, with the exception of adding *'s* to letters meant as letters. MLA requires underlining—never italics—for two elements only: (1) letters meant as letters and (2) words meant as words. Don't underline the *s* or *'s* that creates the plural for any of the elements discussed in this section. (For published books, any underlined words in a manuscript are printed in italics, as is done in this handbook.) The examples below reflect MLA practices.

PLURAL OF LETTERS MEANT AS LETTERS	Printing **M's** and **N's** confuses young children.
	Printing **m's** and **n's** confuses young children.
PLURAL OF LETTERS MEANT AS WORDS	He was surprised to get all **Bs** in his courses.
PLURAL OF WORDS MEANT AS WORDS	Too many **ifs** in a contract make me suspicious.
PLURAL OF NUMBERS	Her e-mail address contains many **7s**.
PLURAL OF YEARS	I remember the **1990s** well.
PLURAL OF SYMBOLS	What do those **&s** mean?

27g When is an apostrophe wrong?

If you're a writer who makes the same apostrophe errors repeatedly, memorize the rules you need (you may know some almost without thought). Then, you won't be annoyed by "that crooked little mark," a nickname popular with students who wish the apostrophe would go away. Box 115 lists the major apostrophe errors.

BOX 115   SUMMARY

Leading causes of apostrophe errors

■ Never use an apostrophe with the PRESENT-TENSE VERB.

Cholesterol **plays** [not **play's**] an important role in how long we live.

■ Always use an apostrophe after the *s* in a POSSESSIVE plural of a noun.

Patients' [not **Patients**] questions seek detailed answers.

■ Never add an apostrophe at the end of a nonpossessive noun ending in *s*.

Medical **studies** [not **studies'** or **study's**] show this to be true.

■ Never use an apostrophe to form a nonpossessive plural.

Teams [not **Team's**] of doctors have studied the effects of cholesterol.

EXERCISE 27-1

Rewrite these sentences to insert *'s* or an apostrophe alone to make the words in parentheses show possession. (Delete the parentheses.) For help, consult 27b and 27e.

EXAMPLE   Every box, can, and bottle on a (supermarket) shelves is designed to appeal to (people) emotions.

Every box, can, and bottle on a *supermarket's* shelves are designed to appeal to *people's* emotions.

1. A (product) manufacturer designs packaging to appeal to (consumers) emotions through colour and design.

2. Marketing specialists know that (people) beliefs about a (product) quality are influenced by their emotional response to the design of its package.

3. Circles and ovals appearing on a (box) design supposedly increase a (product user) feelings of comfort, while bold patterns and colours attract a (shopper) attention.

415

4. Using both circles and bold designs in (Arm & Hammer) and (Tide) packaging produces both effects in consumers.

5. (Heinz) ketchup bottle and (Coca-Cola) famous logo achieve the same effects by combining a bright colour with an old-fashioned, "comfortable" design.

6. Often, a (company) marketing consultants will custom-design products to appeal to the supposedly "typical" (adult female) emotions or to (adult males), (children), or (teenagers) feelings.

7. One of the (marketing business) leading consultants, Stan Gross, tests (consumers) emotional reactions to (companies) products and their packages by asking consumers to associate products with well-known personalities.

8. Thus, (test takers) responses to (Gross) questions might reveal that a particular brand of laundry detergent has (Mark Messier) toughness, (Oprah Winfrey) determination, or (someone else) sparkling personality.

9. Manufacturing (companies) products are not the only ones relying on (Gross) and other corporate (image makers) advice.

10. (Sports teams) owners also use marketing specialists to design their (teams) images, as anyone who has seen the unforgettable angry bull logo of the Chicago Bulls basketball team will agree.

EXERCISE 27-2

Rewrite these sentences so that each contains a possessive noun. For help, consult 27b and 27e.

EXAMPLE   Strangely, the weight of the kilogram seems to be decreasing.

Strangely, the *kilogram's weight* seems to be decreasing.

1. The weight of a kilogram depends on precise measurements so that scientists of the world can assume international consistency of the mass of a kilogram in scientific reports.

2. For all measurement units except the kilogram, international standards that refer to natural phenomena such as the speed of light and electrical currents of magnetic fields are used.

3. A platinum-iridium bar created in 1889 in England became the standard of the world for the weight of a kilogram.

4. Because even the relatively stable metal of a platinum-iridium bar has been decaying slowly over time, the decrease in weight of the bar raises the possibility of imprecise results in the current research of scientists.

5. The efforts of the National Institute of Standards and Technology have captured the interest of everyone as it works to equate the weight of a kilogram to the mass of an electrical unit.

Chapter 28

Quotation Marks

28a What is the role of quotation marks?

Quotation marks are used most often to enclose **direct quotations**—the exact spoken or written words of a speaker or writer. Quotation marks also set off some titles, and quotation marks can call attention to words used in a special sense.

Double quotation marks (" ") are standard. In most computer fonts, the opening marks differ slightly in appearance from the closing marks. The opening marks look like tiny 6s, the closing marks like tiny 9s. In some computer fonts, the opening and closing marks look the same (" "). Single quotation marks (' ' or ' ') are used for quotations within quotations: *Gregory said, "I heard the man shout 'help me' but could not reach him in time."* (In materials published in Great Britain, this convention is reversed.) Quotation marks operate only in pairs: to open and to close. When you proofread your writing, check carefully that you've inserted the closing mark.

Please note, before you continue reading this chapter, that I use MLA STYLE to format the examples here and in other chapters. This affects the documentation features and the lengths of "short" and "long" quotations. These factors vary with different documentation styles. For MLA style, used in most English courses, see Chapter 34. For APA STYLE, see Chapter 35.

28b How do I use quotation marks with short direct quotations?

A DIRECT QUOTATION is any exact words from a print or nonprint source. In MLA STYLE, a quotation is considered *short* if it occupies no more than four typed lines. Use double quotation marks at the start and finish of a short quotation. Give DOCUMENTATION information after a short quotation, before the sentence's ending period.

SHORT QUOTATIONS

Gardner has suggested the possibility of a ninth intelligence: existential, "the proclivity to pose (and ponder) questions about life, death, and ultimate realities" (72).

Susana Urbina, who surveyed many studies about intelligence, found that intelligence "is such a multifaceted concept that no single quality can define it . . ." (1130).

28c Are quotation marks used with long quotations?

No. With a long DIRECT QUOTATION, don't use quotation marks. In MLA STYLE, a quotation is *long* if it occupies more than four typed lines. Instead of using quotation marks with a long quotation, indent all its lines as a block (that is, the quotation is "set off" or "displayed"). This format makes quotation marks unnecessary. Give DOCUMENTATION information after the long quotation and after the period that ends the quotation.

LONG QUOTATIONS

Gardner uses criteria by which to judge whether an ability deserves to be categorized as an "intelligence." Each must confer

> a set of skills of problem solving--enabling the individual to resolve genuine problems or difficulties [author's emphasis] that he or she encounters and, when appropriate, to create an effective product--and must also entail the potential for finding or creating problems--thereby laying the groundwork for the acquisition of new knowledge. (Frames 60-61)

In the Gardner example above, note that a capital letter is *not* used to start the quotation. The lead-in words (*Each must confer*) are an incomplete sentence, so they need the quotation to complete the sentence.

Goleman also emphasizes a close interaction of the emotional and rational states with the other intelligences that Gardner has identified:

> These two minds, the emotional and the rational, operate in tight harmony for the most part, intertwining their very different ways of knowing to guide us through the world. Ordinarily there is a balance between emotional and rational minds, with emotion feeding into and informing the operations of the rational mind, and the rational mind refining and sometimes vetoing the inputs of the emotions. (9)

In the Goleman example above, note that a capital letter starts the quotation because the lead-in words are a complete sentence. (A colon can—but isn't required to—end the lead-in sentence; see 26b.)

👁 **ALERT:** Whether a quotation is one word or occupies many lines, always DOCUMENT its SOURCE. Also, when you quote material, be very careful to record the words exactly as they appear in the original. 👁

28d How do I use quotation marks for quotations within quotations?

Practice varies between short and long quotations (see 28b and 28c) when a quotation contains internal quotation marks. In short quotations, which are themselves enclosed in double quotation marks, use single quotation marks for any internal quotation marks. In MLA STYLE, give DOCUMENTATION information after the entire quotation, before the sentence's ending period. For other documentation styles, check each style's manual.

In long quotations—those that are displayed (set off in a block) and not enclosed in quotation marks—keep the double quotation marks as they appear in the original. In MLA style, give DOCUMENTATION information after the long quotation following any closing punctuation, and before the period that ends a short quotation (see 28e).

28e How do I use quotation marks for quotations of poetry and dialogue?

Poetry (MLA Style)

A quotation of poetry is *short* if it includes three lines or fewer of the poem. As with prose quotations (28d), use double quotation marks to enclose the material and substitute single quotation marks for any internal double quotation marks. To show when a line of poetry breaks to the next line, use a slash (/) with one space on each side (see also 29e). Give DOCUMENTATION information after a short poetry quotation before the period that ends the sentence.

> As Auden wittily defined personal space, "some thirty inches from my nose / The frontier of my person goes" (*Complete*, 205).

A quotation of poetry is *long* if it includes more than three lines of the poem. As with prose quotations (28c), indent all lines as a block, without quotation marks to enclose the material. Start new lines exactly as they appear in your source. Give documentation information after the long quotation and after the period that ends the quotation.

👁 **ALERT:** When you quote lines of poetry, follow the capitalization of your source. 👁

Dialogue

Dialogue, also called DIRECT DISCOURSE, presents a speaker's exact words. Enclose direct discourse in quotation marks. In contrast, INDIRECT DISCOURSE reports what a speaker said. Don't enclose indirect discourse in quotation marks. In addition to these differences in punctuation, PRONOUN use and VERB TENSES also differ for these two types of discourse.

> **DIRECT DISCOURSE**   The mayor said, **"I intend** to oppose that bylaw."
>
> **INDIRECT DISCOURSE**   The mayor said **that he intended** to oppose that bylaw.

When you're reporting the words of a speaker, whether real of fictional, use double quotation marks at the beginning and end of a speaker's words. This tells your reader which words are the speaker's. Start a new paragraph each time the speaker changes.

> Becky Tyde climbed up on Flo's counter, made room for herself beside an open tin of crumbly jam-filled cookies.
> "Are these any good?" she said to Flo, and boldly began to eat one. "When are you going to give us a job, Flo?"
> "You could go and work in the butcher shop," said Flo innocently. "You could go and work for your brother."
> —Alice Munro, "Royal Beatings"

If two or more paragraphs present a single speaker's words, use double opening quotation marks at the start of each paragraph, but save the closing double quotation marks until the end of the last quoted paragraph.

EXERCISE 28-1

Decide whether each sentence below is direct or indirect discourse and then rewrite each sentence in the other form. Make any changes needed for grammatical correctness. With direct discourse, put the speaker's words wherever you think they belong in the sentence. For help, consult 28b through 28e.

> **EXAMPLE**   A medical doctor told some newspaper reporters that he was called into a television studio one day to treat a sick actor.
>
>   A medical doctor told some newspaper *reporters,* **"I** was called into a television studio one day to treat a sick actor."

1. The doctor was told that he would find his patient on the set of *Side Effects,* a new television series that takes place in a hospital.

2. On his arrival at the television studio, the doctor announced, "I'm Dr. Gatley, and I'm looking for *Side Effects.*"

3. The studio security guard asked him if he meant to say that he was auditioning for the part of Dr. Gatley in *Side Effects.*

4. The visitor insisted that he really was Dr. Gatley.

5. The security guard whispered, "I like your attitude. With self-confidence like that, you're sure to go far in television."

28f How do I use quotation marks with titles of short works?

When you refer to certain short works by their titles, enclose the titles in quotation marks (other works, usually longer, need to be in italics or underlined; see 30g). Short works include short stories, essays, poems, articles from periodicals, pamphlets, brochures, songs, and individual episodes of a series on television or radio.

What is the rhyme scheme of Andrew Marvell's "Delight in Disorder"? [poem]

Have you read "Insecurity" by Neil Bissoondath? [short story]

The best source I found is "The Myth of Political Consultants." [magazine article]

"Shooting an Elephant" describes George Orwell's experiences in Burma. [essay]

Titles of some other works are neither enclosed in quotation marks nor written in italics or underlined. For guidelines, see Box 119 in 30e and Box 120 in 30g.

👁 **ALERT:** When placing the title of your own piece of writing on a title page or at the top of a page, never use quotation marks. 👁

EXERCISE 28-2

Correct any misuses of quotation marks. If you think a sentence is correct, explain why. For help, consult 28f.

1. In her short story The Lady from Lucknow, Bharati Mukherjee describes a visitor from India who resents being treated as an exotic object.

2. Although his poem The Red Wheelbarrow contains only sixteen words, William Carlos Williams creates in it both a strong visual image and a sense of mystery.

3. With her soulful singing and relaxed gestures, Billie Holiday gave a bare television studio the atmosphere of a smoky jazz club in The Sound of Jazz. The program was broadcast in 1957 as part of the television series *The Seven Lively Arts*.
4. Lennie Gallant's song Pieces of You and Natalie MacMaster's Get Me Through December were nominated for the East Coast Music Awards.
5. In her essay The Imagination of Disaster, Susan Sontag writes that viewers of disaster movies like to see how these movies succeed in "making a mess"—especially if the mess includes the make-believe destruction of a big city.

28g How do I use quotation marks for words used as words?

When you refer to a word as a word, you can choose to either enclose it in quotation marks or put it in italics (or use underlining). Whichever you choose, be consistent throughout each piece of writing.

> **NO** Many people confuse affect and effect.
> **YES** Many people confuse "affect" and "effect."
> **YES** Many people confuse *affect* and *effect*.

Always put quotation marks around the English translation of a word or PHRASE. Also, use italics (or underlining) for the word or phrase in the other language.

> My grandfather usually ended arguments with *de gustibus non disputandum est* ("there is no disputing about tastes").

Many writers use quotation marks around words or phrases meant ironically or in other nonliteral ways.

> The proposed tax "reform" is actually a tax increase.

Some writers put technical terms in quotation marks and define them—but only the first time they appear. Never reuse quotation marks after a term has been introduced and defined.

> "Plagiarism"—the undocumented use of another person's words or ideas—can result in expulsion. Plagiarism is a serious offence.

Some student writers put quotation marks around words that they sense might be inappropriate for ACADEMIC WRITING, such as a SLANG term or a CLICHÉ used intentionally to make a point. However, when possible, use different language—not quotation marks. Take time to think of accurate, appropriate, and fresh words instead. If you prefer to stick with the slang or cliché, use quotation marks.

They "eat like birds" in public, but they "stuff their faces" in private.
They **eat almost nothing** in public, but they **gorge themselves** in private.

A nickname doesn't call for quotation marks, unless you use the nickname along with the full name. When a person's nickname is widely known, you don't have to give both the nickname and the full name. For example, use *Joe Clark* or *Charles Joseph Clark*, whichever is appropriate in context. Because he's well known, don't use *Charles Joseph "Joe" Clark*.

EXERCISE 28-3

Correct any misuses of quotation marks. If you think a sentence is correct, explain why. For help, consult 28g.

EXAMPLE   *Bossa nova,* Portuguese for new wave, is the name of both a dance and a musical style originating in Brazil.

             Bossa nova, Portuguese for "new wave," is the name of both a dance and a musical style originating in Brazil.

1. A "chinook" is a warm wind that blows eastward across the Rockies. "Chinooks" can transform an Alberta winter day into a brief anticipation of spring.
2. Although many people believe the old adage "Where there's a will, there's a way," psychologists say that to get results, willingness must be combined with ability and effort.
3. "Observation" and "empathy" are two of the chief qualities that mark the work of the Dutch painter Rembrandt.
4. *Casbah,* an Arabic word meaning fortress, is the name given to the oldest part of many North African cities.
5. "Flammable" and *inflammable* are a curious pair of words that once had the same meaning but today are often considered opposites.

28h How do I use quotation marks with other punctuation?

Commas and periods with quotation marks

A comma or period that is grammatically necessary is always placed inside the closing quotation mark.

Because the class enjoyed Michel Tremblay's "The Thimble," they were looking forward to his longer works. [comma before closing quotation mark]
Max said, "Don't stand so far away from me." [comma before opening quotation mark (24k.5); period before closing quotation mark]
Edward T. Hall coined the word "proxemics." [period before closing quotation mark]

Semicolons and colons with quotation marks

A semicolon or colon is placed outside the closing quotation mark, unless it is part of the quotation.

> Computers offer businesses "opportunities that never existed before"; some workers disagree. [semicolon after closing quotation mark]
>
> We have to know each culture's standard for "how close is close": No one wants to offend. [colon after closing quotation mark]

Question marks, exclamation points, and dashes with quotation marks

If the punctuation marks belong to the words enclosed in quotation marks, put them inside the quotation marks.

> "Did I Hear You Call My Name?" was the winning song.
>
> "I've won the lottery!" Arielle shouted.
>
> "Who's there? Why don't you ans—"

If a question mark, an exclamation point, or a dash doesn't belong to the material being quoted, put the punctuation outside the quotation marks.

> Have you read Al Purdy's poem "The Country North of Belleville"?
>
> If only I could write a story like Roch Carrier's "The Hockey Sweater"!
>
> Weak excuses—a classic is "I have to visit my grandparents"—change little.

If you want to know how quotation marks work with capital letters, see 30d; with brackets, 29c; with ellipsis points, 29d; and with the slash, 29e.

28i When are quotation marks wrong?

Never enclose a word in quotation marks to call attention to it, to intensify it, or to be sarcastic.

> **NO** A "massive portion" of the Quebec Bridge collapsed in 1907.
>
> **YES** A massive portion of the Quebec Bridge collapsed in 1907.

Never enclose the title of your paper in quotation marks (or underline it). However, if the title of your paper contains another title that requires quotation marks, use those marks only for the included title.

> **NO** "The Elderly in Nursing Homes: A Case Study"
>
> **YES** The Elderly in Nursing Homes: A Case Study

> **NO** Character Development in Shirley Jackson's Story The Lottery
>
> **YES** Character Development in Shirley Jackson's Story "The Lottery"

EXERCISE 28-4

Correct any errors in the use of quotation marks and other punctuation with quotation marks. If you think a sentence is correct, explain why. For help, consult 28e through 28i.

1. For reasons unknown to me, the meteorologist said, *The Canadian Encyclopedia* contains a statistical analysis of groundhog weather predictions.
2. "No", Michael Ondaatje said, describing how he invented the intricate plot of his novel *The English Patient,*" the plot wasn't there until I finished the book, probably.
3. Pierre Trudeau's claim that he used the expression fuddle-duddle, instead of a taboo four-letter word, led a member of Parliament to quip, "Mr. Trudeau wants to be obscene but not heard".
4. In his poem A Supermarket in California, Allen Ginsberg addresses the dead poet Walt Whitman, asking, Where are we going, Walt Whitman? The doors close / in an hour. Which way does your beard point tonight?
5. Gordie Howe was once asked how hockey players were coping with Canada's "language problem;" he replied, All pro athletes are bilingual. They speak English and profanity.

Chapter 29

Other Punctuation Marks

This chapter explains the uses of the **dash, parentheses, brackets, ellipsis points,** the **slash,** and the **hyphen.** These punctuation marks aren't used often, but each serves a purpose and gives you options with your writing style.

DASH

29a When can I use a dash in my writing?

The **dash,** or a pair of dashes, lets you interrupt a sentence to add information. Such interruptions can fall in the middle or at the end of a sentence. To make a dash, hit the hyphen key twice (--). Do not put a space before, between, or after the hyphens. Some word-processing programs automatically convert two hyphens into a dash; either form is correct. In print, the dash appears as an unbroken line approximately the length of two or three hyphens joined together (—). If you handwrite, make the dash at least twice as long as a hyphen.

Using dashes for special emphasis

If you want to emphasize an example, a definition, an APPOSITIVE, or a contrast, you can use a dash or dashes. Some call a dash "a pregnant pause"—that is, take note, something special is coming. Use dashes sparingly so that you don't dilute their impact.

EXAMPLE

Urban centres in Canada—Montreal, Toronto, Winnipeg, Vancouver—share problems of crime and prostitution in core areas.

—Lovus Devine, student

DEFINITION

Our aboriginal peoples—Inuit, Indian, and Métis—challenge the model of two founding peoples that excludes them.

—William Thorsell, "Let Us Compare Mythologies"

426

APPOSITIVE

And what of our national heroine—Laura Secord—our Paul Revere in drag?

—Barry Callaghan, "Canadian Wry"

CONTRAST

What could be funnier—or more offensive—than making a pun on your own friend's name?

—Matthew Pagano, student

Place what you emphasize with dashes next to or nearby the material it refers to so that what you want to accomplish with your emphasis is not lost.

NO   The current **argument is**—one that faculty, students, and coaches debate fiercely—whether to hold athletes to the same academic standards as others face.

YES   The current **argument**—one that faculty, students, and coaches debate fiercely—**is** whether to hold athletes to the same academic standards as others face.

Using dashes to emphasize an aside

An **aside** is a writer's comment, often the writer's personal views, on what's been written. Generally, this technique isn't appropriate for ACADEMIC WRITING, so before you insert an aside, carefully consider your writing PURPOSE and your AUDIENCE.

As I observed all this and felt its effects on my daily life—and received wounds from my struggle to be part of it—another part of me itched to make a record of what I was seeing.

—Sharon Butala, *Rural Saskatchewan: Creating the Garden*

ALERTS: (1) If the words within a pair of dashes require a question mark or an exclamation point, place it before the second dash.

A first date—do you remember?—stays in the memory forever.

(2) Never use commas, semicolons, or periods next to dashes. If the need for such a combination arises, revise your writing.

(3) Never enclose quotation marks in dashes, except when the meaning requires them. The following two examples show that, when required, the dash stops before or after the quotation marks; the two punctuation marks do not overlap.

Many of George Orwell's essays—"A Hanging," for example—draw on his experiences as a civil servant.

"Shooting an Elephant"—another Orwell essay—appears in many anthologies.

EXERCISE 29-1

Write a sentence about each topic shown in italics. Use dashes to set off the element asked for in each sentence. For help, consult 29a.

EXAMPLE   *science*, a definition

Ecology—the study of the interactions among animals, plants, and the physical environment—is closely related to both biology and geology.

1. *movie*, a contrast
2. *singer*, an appositive
3. *hobby*, an example
4. *a fact*, an aside
5. *career*, a definition

6. *social science*, a contrast
7. *writing*, an example
8. *teacher*, an appositive
9. *business*, a definition
10. *technology*, an aside

PARENTHESES

29b When can I use parentheses in my writing?

Parentheses let you interrupt a sentence to add various kinds of information. Parentheses are like dashes (29a) in that they set off extra or interrupting words—but unlike dashes, which emphasize material, parentheses de-emphasize what they enclose. Use parentheses sparingly, because overusing them can make your writing lurch, not flow.

Using parentheses to enclose interrupting words

EXPLANATION

After they've finished with the pantry, the medicine cabinet, and the attic, they will throw out the red geranium (too many leaves), sell the dog (too many fleas), and send the children off to boarding school (too many scuffmarks on the hardwood floors).

> —Suzanne Britt, "Neat People vs. Sloppy People"

EXAMPLE

Though other cities (Dresden, for instance) had been utterly destroyed in World War II, never before had a single weapon been responsible for such destruction.

> —Laurence Behrens and Leonard J. Rosen,
> *Writing and Reading Across the Curriculum*

ASIDE

The older girls (non-graduates, of course) were assigned the task of making refreshments for the night's festivities.

> —Maya Angelou, *I Know Why the Caged Bird Sings*

When it tastes pungent and hot (remember that the pungency will be cut by the beans) stir in a large quantity of molasses. Most people don't put in enough molasses, and yet this is the essence of all good baked bean dishes.

—Pierre Berton, "Baked Beans"

Using parentheses for listed items and alternative numbers

When you number listed items within a sentence, enclose the numbers (or letters) in parentheses. Never use closing parentheses to set off numbers in a displayed list; use periods.

Four items are on the agenda for tonight's meeting: (1) current treasury figures, (2) current membership figures, (3) the budget for renovations, and (4) the campaign for soliciting additional public contributions.

👁 **ALERTS:** For listed items that fall within a sentence, (1) use a colon before a list only if an INDEPENDENT CLAUSE introduces the list, and (2) use commas or semicolons to separate the items, being consistent within a piece of writing. If, however, any item contains internal punctuation, use a semicolon to separate the items. 👁

In legal writing and in some BUSINESS WRITING, you can use parentheses to enclose a numeral that repeats a spelled-out number.

The monthly rent is three hundred fifty dollars ($350).
Your order of fifteen (15) gross was shipped today.

In ACADEMIC WRITING, especially in subjects in which the use of figures or measurements is frequent, enclose alternative or comparative forms of the same number in parentheses: *3.2 km (2 mi)*.

Using other punctuation with parentheses

When a complete sentence enclosed in parentheses stands alone, start it with a capital letter and end it with a period. When a sentence in parentheses falls within another sentence, never start with a capital or end with a period.

NO Looking for his car keys (He had left them at my sister's house.) wasted an entire hour.

YES Looking for his car keys (he had left them at my sister's house) wasted an entire hour.

YES Looking for his car keys wasted an entire hour. (He had left them at my sister's house.)

Never put a comma before an opening parenthesis. If the material before the parenthetical material requires a comma, place that comma after the closing parenthesis.

NO   Although clearly different from my favourite film, *(The Wizard of Oz)* Kamouraska is also outstanding.

YES   Although clearly different from my favourite film *(The Wizard of Oz),* Kamouraska is also outstanding.

You can use a question mark or an exclamation point within parentheses that occur in a sentence.

Looking for clues (what did we expect to find?) wasted four days.

Never use quotation marks around parentheses that come before or after any quoted words.

NO   Alberta Hunter "(Down Hearted Blues)" is better known for her jazz singing than for her poetry.

YES   Alberta Hunter ("Down Hearted Blues") is better known for her jazz singing than for her poetry.

BRACKETS

29c When do I need to use brackets in my writing?

Brackets (also called square brackets) allow you to enclose words that you want to insert into quotations, but only in the specific cases discussed below.

Adjusting a quotation with brackets

When you use a quotation, you might need to change the form of a word (a verb's tense, for example), add a brief definition, or fit the quotation into the grammatical structure of your sentence. In such cases, enclose the material you have inserted into the quotation in brackets. (These examples use MLA STYLE for PARENTHETICAL REFERENCES; see 34b.)

ORIGINAL SOURCE

Current research shows that successful learning takes place in an active environment.

—Deborah Moore, "Facilities and Learning Styles," p. 22

QUOTATION WITH BRACKETS

Deborah Moore supports a student-centred curriculum and agrees with "current research [which] shows that successful learning takes place in an active environment" (22).

ORIGINAL SOURCE

The logic of the mind is *associative;* it takes elements that symbolize a reality, or trigger a memory of it, to be the same as that reality.

—Daniel Goleman, *Emotional Intelligence,* p. 294

QUOTATION WITH BRACKETS

The kinds of intelligence are based on the way the mind functions: "The logic of the mind is *associative* **[one idea connects with another]**; it takes elements that symbolize a reality, or trigger a memory of it, to be the same as that reality" (Goleman 294).

Using brackets to point out an error in a source or to add information within parentheses

In words you want to quote, you may find that the page-makeup technician or author has made a mistake—a wrong date, a misspelled word, or an error of fact. You fix that mistake by inserting the correct information in brackets, without changing the words you quote. This tells your readers that the error was in the original work and not made by you.

Using [sic]

Insert *sic* (without italics), enclosed in brackets, to show your readers that you've quoted an error accurately. *Sic* is a Latin word that means "so," or "thus" and expresses the thought "It is thus in the original."

USE FOR ERROR

A journalist wrote, "The judge accepted an **[sic]** plea of not guilty."

USE FOR MISSPELLING

The building inspector wrote about the consequence of doubling the apartment's floor space: "With that much extra room per person, the tennants **[sic]** would sublet."

Using brackets within parentheses

Use brackets to insert information within parentheses.

That expression **(first used in *A Fable for Critics* [1848] by James R. Lowell)** was popularized in the early twentieth century by Ella Wheeler Wilcox.

ELLIPSIS POINTS

29d How do I use ellipsis points in my writing?

The word *ellipsis* means "omission." **Ellipsis points** in writing are a series of three spaced dots (use the period key on the keyboard). You're required to use ellipsis points to indicate you've intentionally omitted words—perhaps even a sentence or more—from the source you're quoting. These rules apply to both prose and poetry.

The *MLA Handbook* no longer recommends that ellipsis points you have inserted be enclosed in brackets. See Chapter 34 for more information.

29d.1 Using ellipsis points with prose

ORIGINAL SOURCE

These two minds, the emotional and the rational, operate in tight harmony for the most part, intertwining their very different ways of knowing to guide us through the world. Ordinarily, there is a balance between emotional and rational minds, with emotion feeding into and informing the operations of the rational mind, and the rational mind refining and sometimes vetoing the inputs of the emotions. Still, the emotional and rational minds are semi-independent faculties, each, as we shall see, reflecting the operation of distinct, but interconnected, circuitry in the brain.

—Daniel Goleman, *Emotional Intelligence,* p. 9

QUOTATION OF SELECTED WORDS, NO ELLIPSIS NEEDED

Goleman explains that the "two minds, the emotional and the rational" usually provide "a balance" in our daily observations and decision making (9).

QUOTATION WITH ELLIPSIS MID-SENTENCE

Goleman emphasizes the connections between parts of the mind: "Still, the emotional and rational minds are semi-independent faculties, each . . . reflecting the operation of distinct, but interconnected, circuitry in the brain (9).

QUOTATION ENDING WITH ELLIPSIS AND PARENTHETICAL REFERENCE

Goleman emphasizes that the "two minds, the emotional and the rational, operate in tight harmony for the most part . . ." (9). [*Note:* In MLA style, place a sentence-ending period after the parenthetical reference.]

QUOTATION WITH ELLIPSIS ENDING THE SENTENCE

On page 9, Goleman states: "These two minds, the emotional and the rational, operate in tight harmony for the most part. . . ." [*Note:* In MLA style, when all needed documentation information is written into a sentence—that is, not placed in parentheses at the end of the sentence—there's no space between the sentence-ending period and an ellipsis.]

QUOTATION WITH SENTENCE OMITTED

Goleman explains: "These two minds, the emotional and the rational, operate in tight harmony for the most part, intertwining their very different ways of knowing to guide us through the world. . . . Still, the emotional and rational minds are semi-independent faculties" (9).

QUOTATION WITH WORDS OMITTED FROM THE MIDDLE OF ONE SENTENCE TO THE MIDDLE OF ANOTHER

Goleman states: "Ordinarily, there is a balance between emotional and rational minds . . . reflecting the operation of distinct, but interconnected, circuitry in the brain" (9).

QUOTATION WITH WORDS OMITTED FROM THE MIDDLE OF ONE SENTENCE TO THE BEGINNING OF ANOTHER

Goleman explains: "Ordinarily, there is a balance between emotional and rational minds. . . . Still, the emotional and rational minds are semi-independent faculties, each, as we shall see, reflecting the operation of distinct, but interconnected, circuitry in the brain" (9).

When you omit words from a quotation, you also omit punctuation related to those words, unless it's needed for the sentence to be correct.

Goleman explains: "These two minds . . . operate in tight harmony" (9). [comma in original source omitted after *minds*]

Goleman explains that the emotional and rational minds work together while, "still . . . each, as we shall see, [reflects] the operation of distinct, but interconnected, circuitry in the brain" (9). [comma kept after *still* because it's an introductory word; form of *reflecting* changed for sense of sentence]

29d.2 Using ellipsis points with poetry

When you omit one or more words from a line of poetry, follow the rules stated above for prose. However, when you omit a full line or more from poetry, use a full line of spaced dots.

ORIGINAL SOURCE

Little Boy Blue

Little boy blue, come blow your horn,
The sheep's in the meadow, the cow's in the corn
Where is the little boy who looks after the sheep?
He's under the haystack, fast asleep.

QUOTATION WITH LINES OMITTED

Little Boy Blue

Little boy blue, come blow your horn,

. . . .

Where is the little boy who looks after the sheep?

He's under the haystack, fast asleep.

SLASH

29e When can I use a slash in my writing?

The **slash** (/), also called a *virgule* or *solidus,* is a diagonal line that separates or joins words in special circumstances.

Using a slash to separate quoted lines of poetry

When you quote more than three lines of a poem, no slash is involved; you merely follow the rules in 28e. When you quote three lines or fewer, enclose them in quotation marks and run them into your sentence—and use a slash to divide one line from the next. Leave a space on each side of the slash.

> One of my mottoes comes from the beginning of Anne Sexton's poem "Words": "Be careful of words, / even the miraculous ones."

Capitalize and punctuate each line of poetry as in the original—but even if the quoted line of poetry doesn't have a period, use one to end your sentence. If your quotation ends before the line of poetry ends, use ellipsis points (29d).

Using a slash for numerical fractions in manuscripts

To type numerical fractions, use a slash (with no space before or after the slash) to separate the numerator and denominator. In mixed numbers—that is, whole numbers with fractions—leave a space between the whole number and its fraction: *1 2/3, 3 7/8.* Do not use a hyphen. (For information about using spelled-out and numerical forms of numbers, see 30o.)

Using a slash for and/or

When writing in the humanities, try not to use word combinations connected with a slash, such as *and/or.* In academic disciplines in which such combinations are acceptable, separate the words with a slash. Leave no space before or after the slash. In the humanities, listing both alternatives in normal sentence structure is usually better than separating choices with a slash.

NO   The best quality of reproduction comes from 35 mm slides/direct-positive films.

YES   The best quality of reproduction comes from 35 mm slides **or** direct-positive films.

EXERCISE 29-2

Supply needed dashes, parentheses, brackets, ellipsis points, and slashes. If a sentence is correct as written, circle its number. In some sentences, when you can use either dashes or parentheses, explain your choice. For help, consult all sections of this chapter.

EXAMPLE   In Canada, there are almost four times as many managerial and administrative nonclerical workers as there are farmers.

In Canada, there are almost four times as many managerial and administrative (nonclerical) workers as there are farmers.

1. In *The Color Purple* a successful movie as well as a novel, Alice Walker explores the relationships between women and men in traditional African American culture.

2. The three longest rivers in Canada are 1 the Mackenzie 4241 km, 2 the Yukon 3185 km, and 3 the St. Lawrence 3058 km.

3. Calgary's Saddledome, the broad roof of the arena dips like a saddle, was used in the 1988 Winter Olympic Games, several years after it first opened.

4. All the really interesting desserts ice cream, chocolate fudge cake, pumpkin pie with whipped cream are fattening, unfortunately.

5. Thunder is caused when the flash of lightning heats the air around it to temperatures up to 30 000 °C (55 000°F).

6. Christina Rossetti wonders if the end of a life also means the end of love in a poem that opens with these two lines: "When I am dead, my dearest, Sing no sad songs for me."

7. The 2001 Summit of the Americas in Quebec City was accompanied by large-scale protests, and for a few days it seemed to capture the attention of a whole generation.

8. Oscar Peterson has written, "To my way of thinking it the recording his friend Clifford Brown made in 1955 with Max Roach epitomizes the highest achievement in the world of Jazz—spontaneity."

9. Of his decision to resign as prime minister in 1984, Pierre Trudeau said, "I listened to my heart and saw if there were any signs of my destiny in the sky, and there were none there were just snowflakes."

10. Anyone in Canada who performs in public for private profit, of course a play, opera, or musical composition subject to copyright is liable to a fine of two hundred and fifty dollars $250.

11. Kim Campbell does anyone here remember Kim Campbell? seems to have found her niche.
12. Patients who pretend to have ailments are known to doctors as "Munchausens," after Baron Karl Friedrich Hieronymus von Münchhausen, he was a German army officer who had a reputation for wild and unbelievable tales.

EXERCISE 29-3

Follow the directions for each item. For help, consult all sections of this chapter.

EXAMPLE   Write a sentence about getting something right using a dash.

I tried and failed, I tried and failed again—and then I did it.

1. Write a sentence that quotes only three lines of the following sonnet by William Shakespeare:

Let me not to the marriage of true minds
Admit impediments. Love is not love
Which alters when it alteration finds,
Or bends with the remover to remove.
O, no! it is an ever-fixèd mark
That looks on tempests and is never shaken;
It is the star to every wand'ring bark,
Whose worth's unknown, although his height be taken.
Love's not Time's fool, though rosy lips and cheeks
Within his bending sickle's compass come;
Love alters not with his brief hours and weeks,
But bears it out even to the edge of doom.
    If this be error, and upon me proved,
    I never writ, nor no man ever loved.

2. Write a sentence using parentheses to enclose a brief example.
3. Write a sentence using dashes to set off a definition.
4. Write a sentence that includes four numbered items in a list.
5. Quote a few sentences from any source you choose. Omit words without losing meaning or use brackets to insert words to maintain meaning or grammatical structure. Use ellipsis points to indicate any omission, and place the parenthetical reference where it belongs.

HYPHEN

29f When do I need a hyphen in my writing?

A **hyphen** serves to divide words at the end of a line, to combine words into compounds, and to spell numbers.

29g When do I use a hyphen at the end of a line?

Generally, try not to divide a word with a hyphen at the end of a line. (In printed books, hyphens are acceptable because of the limits on line length.) If you must divide a word, try not to divide the last word on the first line of a paper, the last word in a paragraph, or the last word on a page.

When you can't avoid using a hyphen at the end of a line, break the word only between syllables. If you aren't sure about the syllables in a word, consult a dictionary. Box 116 lists guidelines for end-of-line word breaks.

BOX 116   SUMMARY

Hyphens in end-of-line word breaks

- Divide words only between syllables.

  NO   ent-ertain   proc-eed
  YES   enter-tain   pro-ceed

- Never divide words that are short, of one syllable, or pronounced as one syllable.

  NO   we-alth   en-vy   scream-ed
  YES   wealth   envy   screamed

- Never divide a word when only one or two letters would be left or carried over.

  NO   a-live   touch-y   he-licopter   helicopt-er
  YES   alive   touchy   heli-copter   helicop-ter

- Divide between two consonants according to pronunciation.

  NO   ful-lness   omitt-ing   punct-ure
  YES   full-ness   omit-ting   punc-ture

29h How do I use a hyphen with prefixes and suffixes?

Prefixes are syllables preceding a **root**—a word's core, which carries the origin or meaning—and **suffixes** follow a root. Both modify the root's meaning. Some prefixes and suffixes are attached to root words with hyphens, but others are not. Box 117 shows you how to decide.

> BOX 117 SUMMARY
>
> ## Hyphens with prefixes and suffixes
>
> - Use hyphens after the prefixes *all-*, *ex-*, *quasi-*, and *self-*.
>
>   **YES** all-inclusive self-reliant
>
> - Never use a hyphen when *self* is a root word, not a prefix.
>
>   **NO** self-ishness self-less
>   **YES** selfishness selfless
>
> - Use a hyphen to avoid a distracting string of letters.
>
>   **NO** anti**i**ntellectual be**lll**ike pr**oo**utsourcing
>   **YES** ant**i-i**ntellectual be**ll-l**ike pr**o-o**utsourcing
>
> - Use a hyphen to add a prefix or suffix to a numeral or a word that starts with a capital letter.
>
>   **NO** post1950 proAmerican Rembrandtlike
>   **YES** post-1950 pro-American Rembrandt-like
>
> - Use a hyphen before the suffix *-elect*.
>
>   **NO** presidentelect
>   **YES** president-elect
>
> - Use a hyphen to prevent confusion in meaning or pronunciation.
>
>   **YES** re-dress (means *dress again*) redress (means *set right*)
>   **YES** un-ionize (means *remove the ions*) unionize (means *form a union*)
>
> - Use a hyphen when two or more prefixes apply to one root word.
>
>   **YES** pre- and post-Renaissance

29i How do I use hyphens with compound words?

A **compound word** combines two or more words to express one concept. Compound words come in three forms: open compounds, as in *night shift;* hyphenated words, as in *tractor-trailer;* and closed compounds, as in *handbook.* Box 118 lists basic guidelines for positioning hyphens in compound words.

> BOX 118   SUMMARY
>
> ## Hyphens with compound words
>
> ■ At the end of a line, divide a compound word already containing a hyphen only after that hyphen, if possible. Also, divide a closed compound only between the two complete words, if possible.
>
> | **NO** | self-con-scious | sis-ter-in-law | mas-terpiece |
> |---|---|---|---|
> | **YES** | self-conscious | sister-in-law | master-piece |
>
> ■ Use a hyphen between a prefix and an open compound.
>
> | **NO** | antigun control [*gun control* is an open compound] |
> |---|---|
> | **YES** | anti-gun control |
>
> ■ Use a hyphen for most compound words that precede a noun but not for most compound words that follow a noun.
>
> | **YES** | well-researched report | report is well researched |
> |---|---|---|
> | **YES** | two-metre clearance | clearance of two metres |
>
> ■ Use hyphens when a compound modifier includes a series.
>
> | **YES** | two-, three-, or four-year program |
> |---|---|
>
> ■ Never use a hyphen when a compound modifier starts with an *-ly* adverb.
>
> | **NO** | happily-married couple | loosely-tied package |
> |---|---|---|
> | **YES** | happily married couple | loosely tied package |
>
> ■ Avoid using a hyphen in compounds made with the COMPARATIVE and SUPERLATIVE forms *more, less* and *most, least*. (Compounds made with other comparatives and superlatives are sometimes hyphenated for clarity or by convention.)
>
> | **NO** | more-appropriate idea [*more* is a comparative adverb] |
> |---|---|
> | **YES** | more appropriate idea |
>
> | **NO** | least-significant factors [*least* is a superlative adverb] |
> |---|---|
> | **YES** | least significant factors |
>
> ■ Never use a hyphen when a compound modifier is a foreign phrase.
>
> | **YES** | *post hoc* fallacies |
> |---|---|
>
> ■ Never use a hyphen with a possessive compound.
>
> | **NO** | a full-week's work | eight-hours' pay |
> |---|---|---|
> | **YES** | a full week's work | eight hours' pay |

EXERCISE 29-4

Provide the correct form of the words in parentheses, according to the rules in 29f through 29i. Explain your reasoning for each.

EXAMPLE   Most people lock the doors of their car when they leave it parked, but many have never thought of protecting their (all important) <u>all-important</u> computer files.

1. How do (computer users) _____ guard the privacy of their sensitive files?

2. They control access with a (pass word) _____ , often one they invent (them selves) _____ .

3. Clients of automated banking services and Internet surfers also use passwords as an (anti theft) _____ precaution.

4. Unfortunately, computer hackers are always developing new (password cracking) _____ programs.

5. Therefore, if you ever make up a password, think of one that is (hard to crack) _____ .

6. Any program that specializes in cracking passwords can break a code that follows a regular pattern, even if the code has (six hundred) _____ digits and stretches (two metres) _____ when printed out.

7. Other (easily cracked) _____ codes are based on birthdays, Social Insurance numbers, spouses' names, words, and (two word) _____ combinations.

8. You will never (out smart) _____ a determined thief with any of these.

9. Have you ever invented a password so ingenious that after a while it seemed you could not remember it (ninety nine) _____ percent of the time?

10. That kind of password is the (least useful) _____ password of all!

Chapter 30

Capitals, Italics, Abbreviations, and Numbers

CAPITALS

30a When do I capitalize a "first" word?

First word in a sentence
Always capitalize the first letter of the first word in a sentence.

Nearly two metres of snow fell last winter.

A series of questions
If questions in a series are complete sentences, start each with a capital letter. If, however, the questions aren't complete sentences, you can choose to capitalize or not. Whatever your choice, be consistent in each piece of writing. In this handbook, I use capitals for a series of questions.

What facial feature would most people like to change? Eyes? Ears? Nose?
What facial feature would most people like to change? eyes? ears? nose?

Small words in titles or headings
Capitalize small words (*the, a, an,* and short PREPOSITIONS such as *with, of, to*) in a title or heading only when they begin the title or when the source capitalizes these small words.

Always capitalize *I,* no matter where it falls in a sentence or group of words: *I love you now, although I didn't used to.* The same holds for *O,* the INTERJECTION: *You are, O my fair love, a burning fever; O my gentle love, embrace me.* In contrast, never capitalize the interjection *oh,* unless it starts a sentence or is capitalized in words you're quoting.

After a colon
When a complete sentence follows a colon, you can choose to start that sentence with either a capital or a lowercase letter, but be consistent in

441

each piece of writing. When the words after a colon are not a complete sentence, do not capitalize.

> She reacted instantly: She picked up the ice cream and pushed it back into her cone.
>
> She reacted instantly: she picked up the ice cream and pushed it back into her cone.
>
> She bought four pints of ice cream: vanilla, chocolate, strawberry, and butter pecan.

 ALERT: A colon can follow only a complete sentence (an INDEPENDENT CLAUSE; see 26a).

Formal outline

In a formal outline (2r), start each item with a capital letter. Use a period only when the item is a complete sentence.

30b When do I use capitals with listed items?

A list run into a sentence

If run-in listed items are complete sentences, start each with a capital and end each with a period (or question mark or exclamation point). If the run-in listed items are incomplete sentences, start each with a lowercase letter and end each with a comma—unless the items already contain commas, in which case use semicolons. If you list three or more items that are incomplete sentences, use *and* before the last item.

> **YES** We found three reasons for the delay: (1) **B**ad weather held up delivery of materials. (2) **P**oor scheduling created confusion. (3) **I**mproper machine maintenance caused an equipment failure.
>
> **YES** The reasons for the delay were (1) **b**ad weather, (2) **p**oor scheduling, **and** (3) **e**quipment failure.
>
> **YES** The reasons for the delay were (1) **b**ad weather, which had been predicted; (2) **p**oor scheduling, which is the airline's responsibility; **and** (3) **e**quipment failure, which no one can predict.

A displayed list

In a displayed list, each item starts on a new line. If the items are sentences, capitalize the first letter and end with a period (or question mark or exclamation point). If the items are not sentences, you can use a capital letter or not. Whichever you choose, be consistent in each piece of writing. Punctuate a displayed list as you would a run-in list.

YES   We found three reasons for the delay:
(1) **B**ad weather held up delivery of materials.
(2) **P**oor scheduling created confusion.
(3) **I**mproper machine maintenance caused an equipment failure.

YES   The reasons for the delay were
(1) **b**ad weather,
(2) **p**oor scheduling, **and**
(3) **e**quipment failure.

ALERTS: (1) If a complete sentence leads into a displayed list, you can end the sentence with a colon. However, if an incomplete sentence leads into a displayed list, use no punctuation. (2) Use PARALLELISM for items in a list. For example, if one item is a sentence, use sentences for all the items (18f); or if one item starts with a VERB, start all items with a verb in the same TENSE; and so on.

30c When do I use capitals with sentences in parentheses?

When you write a complete sentence within parentheses that falls within another sentence, don't start with a capital or end with a period—but do use a question mark or exclamation point, if needed. When you write a sentence within parentheses that doesn't fall within another sentence, capitalize the first word and end with a period (or question mark or explanation point).

You may have to line the section of river between the Mazinaw Lake Dam and Marble Lake when water levels are low. (**L**ining is guiding the canoe along from shore with ropes tied to bow and stern.) To the right, a 150-metre portage works around the worst of this shallow stretch.

After turning off Highway 38 onto Perth Road, north of Kingston, and picking up our vehicle permit at the park office trail centre (**b**ooking a reservation for this route is strongly recommended), we drove down bumpy Salmon Road to the designated launch site.
—Kevin Callan, *Up the Creek*

30d When do I use capitals with quotations?

If a quotation within your sentence is itself less than a complete sentence, never capitalize the first quoted word. If the quotation you have used in your sentence is itself a complete sentence, capitalize the first word.

> Mme Paquette says that students who are learning a new language should visit that country and "absorb a good accent with the food."
>
> Mme Paquette likes to point out that when students live in a new country, "They'll absorb a good accent with the food."

When you write DIRECT DISCOURSE—which you introduce with verbs such as *said, stated, reported,* and others (see 33k) followed by a comma—capitalize the first letter of the quoted words only if it's capitalized in the original. However, never capitalize a partial quotation, and never capitalize the continuation of a one-sentence quotation within your sentence.

> Mme Paquette said, "Students who are learning a new language should visit that country. They'll absorb a good accent with the food."
>
> Mme Paquette told me that the best way to "absorb a good accent" in a language is to visit the country and eat its food.
>
> "Of course," she continued with a smile, "the accent lasts longer than the food."

30e When do I capitalize nouns and adjectives?

Capitalize PROPER NOUNS (nouns that name specific people, places, and things): *Michael J. Fox, Mexico, World Wide Web.* Also, capitalize **proper adjectives** (adjectives formed from proper nouns): *a Mexican entrepreneur, a Web address.* Don't capitalize ARTICLES (*the, a, an*) that accompany proper nouns and proper adjectives, unless they start a sentence.

When a proper noun or adjective loses its very specific "proper" association, it also loses its capital letter: *french fries, pasteurized.* When you turn a common noun (*lake*) into a proper noun (*Lake Erie*), capitalize all words.

Expect sometimes that you'll see capitalized words that this handbook says not to capitalize. For example, a corporation's written communications usually capitalize their own entities (*our Board of Directors* or *this Company*), even though the rule calls for lowercase (*the board of directors, the company*). Similarly, the administrators of your school might write *the Faculty* and *the College* (or *the University*), even though the rule calls for a lowercase *f, c,* and *u.* How writers capitalize can depend on AUDIENCE and PURPOSE in each specific context.

Box 119 is a capitalization guide. If you don't find what you need, locate an item in it (or in Box 120) that's close to what you want, and use it as a model.

BOX 119   SUMMARY

Capitalization

	CAPITALS	LOWERCASE LETTERS
NAMES	Mother Teresa (*also,* used as names: Mother, Dad, Mom, Pa)	my mother [relationship]
	Doctor Ruth	the doctor [role]
TITLES	Prime Minister Campbell	a prime minister
	Liberal [party member]	liberal [a believer in liberal ideals]
	Member of Parliament Sarmite Bulte	a member of Parliament
	the Honourable Mr. Justice John Sopinka	the judge
	Queen Elizabeth II	the queen [*also* the Queen, referring to Canada's queen]
GROUPS OF PEOPLE	Caucasian [race]	white, black [*also* White, Black]
	Native Canadian, First Nations, South Asian [ethnic group]	
	Irish, Korean [nationality]	
	Jewish, Catholic, Protestant, Buddhist [religious affiliation]	
ORGANIZATIONS	Parliament	parliamentary
	the Supreme Court of Canada	the court [*also* the Court]
	the Conservative Party	the party
	the Canadian Broadcasting Corporation	the corporation
	Calgary Flames	hockey team
	Canadian Medical Association	professional group
	Alcoholics Anonymous	self-help group
PLACES	Whitehorse	the city
	the West [region]	turn west [direction]
	the West Coast	the western coast of Canada

→

Capitalization (*continued*)

	CAPITALS	**LOWERCASE LETTERS**
PLACES (cont.)	King Street	the street
	Atlantic Ocean	the ocean
	the Rocky Mountains	the mountains
BUILDINGS	the House of Commons	the legislature [*but* the House, the Commons]
	Pauline Johnson High School	a high school
	Front Road Café	a restaurant
	Highland Hospital	a hospital
SCIENTIFIC TERMS	Earth [as one of nine planets]	the earth [otherwise]
	the Milky Way, the Galaxy [as name]	our galaxy, the moon, the sun
	Streptococcus aureus	a streptococcal infection
	Gresham's law	the theory of relativity
LANGUAGES	Spanish, Chinese	
SCHOOL COURSES	Chemistry 342	a chemistry course
	English 111	my English class
	Introduction to Photography	a photography course
NAMES OF SPECIFIC THINGS	Black Parrot tulip	climbing rose
	Lakehead University	the university
	Heinz ketchup	ketchup, sauce
	a Toyota Camry	a car
	Twelfth Dynasty	the dynasty
	the *Calgary Herald*	a newspaper
TIMES, SEASONS, HOLIDAYS	Monday, Fri.	today
	September, February	a month
	the Roaring Twenties	the decade
	the Christmas season	spring, summer, autumn, winter, the fall semester
	New Year's Day	feast day, the holiday
	Passover, Ramadan, Kwanzaa	religious holiday or observance

→

Capitalization (*continued*)

	CAPITALS	LOWERCASE LETTERS
HISTORICAL PERIODS, EVENTS, AND DOCUMENTS	World War I Battle of Vimy Ridge the Great Depression (of the 1930s)	the war the battle the depression [any serious economic downturn]
	the Reformation Paleozoic the Quiet Revolution	the sixteenth century era or age, prehistory a sociopolitical movement
	the Charter of Rights	twentieth-century documents
RELIGIOUS TERMS	Athena, God Islam the Torah, the Koran the Bible, Scripture	a goddess, a god a religion a holy book biblical, scriptural
LETTER PARTS	Dear Ms. Schultz: Sincerely, Yours truly,	
PUBLISHED AND RELEASED MATERIAL	"The Hockey Sweater" *The Canadian Encyclopedia* *Jazz on Ice*	[Capitalize first letter of first word and all other major words] the show, a performance
	the Meech Lake Accord	a federal–provincial agreement
	Mass in B Minor	the B minor mass
ACRONYMS AND INITIALISMS	NASA, NATO, NFB, UBC, NAFTA, DNA	
COMPUTER TERMS	Microsoft Word, WordPerfect, Linux	computer software
	Netscape Navigator the Internet World Wide Web, the Web Web site, Web page	a browser a computer network www (in URLs) a home page, a link
PROPER ADJECTIVES AND THEIR COMPOUNDS	Victorian post-Victorian Indo-European pre-Confederation	

EXERCISE 30-1

Add capital letters as needed. See 30a through 30e for help.

1. When Antonine Maillet was awarded france's prix goncourt in 1979, she said of the acadian people who are the subject of her prize-winning novel, "we don't have much to say. Just that we're alive."

2. Wai-Yee turned to face west and looked out over the pacific, imagining her grandfather's journey across that wide ocean.

3. The fine art course taught by professor Sanzio accepts only students who already have credits in fine art 101 and Renaissance studies 211.

4. For years, a european travel guide written by Arthur Frommer (it advised tourists how to live on five dollars a day) could be found in the backpacks and suitcases of thousands of travellers.

5. The north pole is surrounded by an icy sea; the south pole lies in the middle of a frozen land mass, the continent known as antarctica.

6. At one point in the action, the script calls for the "assembled multi-tudes" to break into shouts of "hail, o merciful queen Tanya!"

7. How should we think of the start of the french revolution? Was it the best of times? the worst of times? a time of indecision, perhaps?

8. According to the chapter "the making of a new world," among those credited with the discovery of the Americas before Columbus are (1) the vikings, (2) various groups of european fishers and whalers, and (3) the peoples who crossed the Bering strait to Alaska in prehistoric times.

9. People who are accustomed to one of the lovely and powerful English translations of the bible sometimes forget that the bible was not originally written in English.

10. The organization of African unity (OAU) was founded in 1962, when many african nations were winning their independence.

ITALICS

30f What are italics?

Italics is the typeface that slants to the right (*hello there*). In contrast, **roman typeface** is the most common type in print (you're looking at it right now). If your word-processing program doesn't give you the option of italics, underline instead. In fact, MLA STYLE requires underlining, not italics, in all documents.

ROMAN	a novel
UNDERLINING	<u>Shampoo Planet</u>
ITALICS	*Shampoo Planet*

30g How do I choose between italics and quotation marks?

As a rule, use italics for titles of long works (*The Matrix,* a movie) or for works that contain subsections (*Masterpiece Theater,* a television show). Generally, use quotation marks for titles of shorter works ("I Wanna Hold Your Hand," a song) and for titles of subsections within longer works such as books (Chapter 1, "Loomings").

Box 120 is a guide for using italics, quotation marks, or nothing. If you don't find what you need, locate an item that is as much like what you want as possible and use it as a model.

BOX 120 SUMMARY

 Italics, quotation marks, or nothing

Titles and Names

ITALICS	QUOTATION MARKS OR NOTHING
The Englishman's Boy [a novel]	Title of Student Essay
Farther West [a play]	act 2 [part of a play]
Exotica [a film]	the epilogue [a part of a film or book]
Who Do You Think You Are? [a book]	"Royal Beatings" [a story in a book]
Simon & Schuster Handbook for Writers [a textbook]	"Agreement" [a chapter in a book]
The Prose Reader [a collection of essays]	"Putting in a Good Word for Guilt" [an essay]
Iliad [a book-length poem]	"Whatever You Do" [a short poem]
Equinox [a magazine]	"Nanook Passage" [an article in a magazine]
Symphonie Fantastique [a long musical work]	Violin Concerto No. 2 in B-flat Minor [a musical work identified by form, number, and key—neither quotation marks nor underlining]
So-Called Chaos [a CD]	"Eight Easy Steps" [a song]
The Road to Avonlea [a television series]	"After the Honeymoon" [an episode of a television series]
Kids Count [a Web site title]	Excel [a software program]
the *Brandon Sun* [a newspaper]*	

*When *The* is part of a newspaper's title, don't capitalize or italicize it in MLA-style or CM-style documentation. In APA-style documentation, capitalize and italicize *The.*

→

Italics, quotation marks, or nothing (*continued*)

Other Words

ITALICS	QUOTATION MARKS OR NOTHING
a mari usque ad mare [words in a language other than English]	burrito, chutzpah [widely understood non-English words]
What does *our* imply? [a word meant as a word]	
the *abc*'s; the letter *x* [letters meant as letters]	6s and 7s; & [numerals and symbols]

30h Can I use italics for special emphasis?

Some professional writers, especially writers of nonfiction and self-help material, occasionally use italics to clarify a meaning or stress a point. In ACADEMIC WRITING, however, you're expected to convey special emphasis through your choice of words and sentence structure, not with italics (or underlining). If your message absolutely calls for it, use italics sparingly—and only after you're sure nothing else will do.

> Many people we *think* are powerful turn out on closer examination to be merely frightened and anxious.
>
> —Michael Korda, *Power!*

EXERCISE 30-2

Edit these sentences for correct use of italics (or underlining), quotation marks, and capitals. For help, consult 30a through 30h.

1. The article on "The Canoe" in The Canadian Encyclopedia says that birchbark canoes were "perfectly adapted to summer travel" along the shallow streams and swift rivers of early Canada.

2. According to one source, *Canada*'s name is derived from the Huron-Iroquois word *kanata,* meaning a village or settlement.

3. The writer of a humour column in The Globe and Mail described an imaginary paper called The Mop and Pail, where things were just slightly more ridiculous than in real life.

4. Atom Egoyan's adaptation of the Strauss opera "Salome" had a stage full of *TV* monitors and other modern paraphernalia.

5. When a small business chooses a name beginning with the letter a repeated four times, as in AAAAbco Auto Body, we can be sure its marketing plan includes being noticed at the start of *The Telephone Directory*.

ABBREVIATIONS

30i **What are standard practices for using abbreviations?**

Some abbreviations are standard in all writing circumstances (*Mr.,* not *Mister,* in a name; *St.* Catharines, the city, not *Saint* Catharines). In some situations, you may have a choice whether to abbreviate or spell out a word. Choose what seems suited to your PURPOSE for writing and your AUDIENCE, and be consistent within each piece of writing.

NO   The great painter Vincent Van Gogh was **b.** in Holland in 1853, but he lived most of his life and died in **Fr.**

YES   The great painter Vincent Van Gogh was **born** in Holland in 1853, but he lived most of his life and died in **France.**

NO   Our hockey team left after Casey's **psych** class on **Tues., Oct.** 10, but the bus had to make an unexpected stop (in **N.B.**) before reaching **St. FXU.**

YES   Our hockey team left after Casey's **psychology** class on **Tuesday, October** 10, but the bus had to make an unexpected stop (in **New Brunswick**) before reaching **St. Francis Xavier University.**

NO   Please confirm in writing your order for one **doz.** helmets in **lg** and **x-lg.**

YES   Please confirm in writing your order for one **dozen** helmets in **large** and **extra large.**

👁 **ALERTS:** (1) Many abbreviations call for periods (*Mrs., Ms., Dr.*), but practice is changing. The trend today is to drop the periods (*PS,* not *P.S.; MD,* not *M.D.; US* and *UK,* not *U.S.* and *U.K.*), yet firm rules are still evolving.

(2) **Acronyms** (pronounceable words formed from the initials of a name) generally have no periods: *NAFTA* (North American Free Trade Agreement) and *AIDS* (*a*cquired *i*mmune *d*eficiency *s*yndrome).

(3) **Initialisms** (names spoken as separate letters) usually have no periods (*IBM, CBC, UN*).

(4) Postal abbreviations for provinces and U.S. states have no periods (see Box 122 in 30k).

(5) When the final period of an abbreviation falls at the end of a sentence, that period serves also to end the sentence. 👁

30j How do I use abbreviations with months, time, eras, and symbols?

Months

According to MLA STYLE, abbreviations for months belong only in "Works Cited" lists, tables, charts, and the like. Write out the full spelling, never the abbreviation, in your ACADEMIC WRITING. Box 121 shows month abbreviations in MLA style.

BOX 121   SUMMARY

Month abbreviations—MLA style

January	Jan.	May	(none)	September	Sept.
February	Feb.	June	(none)	October	Oct.
March	Mar.	July	(none)	November	Nov.
April	Apr.	August	Aug.	December	Dec.

Times

Use the abbreviations *a.m.* and *p.m.* only with exact times: *7:15 a.m.; 3:47 p.m.* Although some publication styles use the capitalized versions, *A.M.* and *P.M.,* MLA style calls for the use of lowercase letters.

👁 **ALERTS:** (1) Never use *a.m.* and *p.m.* in place of the words *morning, evening,* and *night.*

NO   My hardest final exam is in the **a.m.** tomorrow, but by early **p.m.,** I'll be ready to study for the rest of my finals.

YES   My hardest final exam is in the **morning** tomorrow, but by early **evening,** I'll be ready to study for the rest of my finals.

(2) Specify *12:00 noon* and *12:00 midnight*, not *12:00 a.m.* and *12:00 p.m.* (*A.m.* and *p.m.* mean, respectively, *before* noon and *after* noon.) *Noon* and *midnight* are also acceptable on their own. 👁

Eras

In MLA style, use capital letters, without periods, in abbreviations for eras. Some writers prefer using CE ("common era") in place of AD (from the Latin *anno Domini*, "in the year of our Lord") as the more inclusive term. In addition, many writers prefer use BCE ("before the common era") in place of BC ("before Christ").

When writing the abbreviations for eras, place AD before the year (*AD 476*) and all the others after the year (*29 BC; 165 BCE; 1100 CE*).

Symbols

In MLA style, decide whether to use symbols or spelled-out words based on your topic and the focus of your document (see also 30m). However, never use a freestanding symbol, such as *$, %,* or *¢* in your sentences; always use it with a numeral. Many writers abbreviate SI units (24i) in almost any context, but if you spell out a number, you should write out any unit that accompanies it (*6 km* but *six kilometres*).

Conversely, always use a numeral with the abbreviations of units of measure (both SI and Imperial) and scientific or other symbols: *6 kg; 9 lbs.; 15 cm; 6"; $18; 24 KB; 6:34 a.m.; 32°*; and numbers in addresses, dates, page references, and decimal fractions (*8.3*). In writing about money, the form *$25 million* is an acceptable combination of symbol, numeral, and spelled-out word.

When a number is more than one or two words, write it as a numeral (*345 years*, not *three hundred forty-five years*).

In confined spaces, such as charts and tables, use symbols with numerals (*20¢*). In documents that focus on technical matters, use numerals but spell out the Imperial unit of measurement (*2500 pounds*) in MLA STYLE. In other documentation styles, such as APA, CM, and CSE, the guidelines differ somewhat, so you need to check each style's manual.

30k How do I use abbreviations for other elements?

Titles

Use either a title of address before a name (***Dr.** Daniel Klausner*) or an academic degree after a name (*Daniel Klausner, **PhD***), not both. However, because *Jr., Sr., II, III,* and so forth (common designations in the United States) are part of a given name, you can use both titles of address and academic degree abbreviations: ***Dr.** Martin Luther King **Jr.**; Gavin Alexander **II, MD.***

👁 **ALERTS:** (1) Insert a comma both before and after an academic degree that follows a person's name, unless it falls at the end of a sentence: *Daljit Singh, **LLD,** is our guest speaker,* or *Our guest speaker is Daljit Singh, **LLD.*** (2) Never put a comma before an abbreviation that is part of a given name: *Steven Elliott Sr., Douglas Young III.* 👁

Names and terms

If you use a term frequently in a piece of writing, follow these guidelines: The first time you use the term, spell it out completely and then put its abbreviation in parentheses immediately after. In later references, use the abbreviation alone.

Spain voted to continue as a member of the **North Atlantic Treaty Organization** (**NATO**), to the surprise of other **NATO** members.

When referring to the *United States* or *United Kingdom,* you can use the abbreviation *U.S.* (*US*) or *U.K.* (*UK*) as a modifier before a noun (*the* **U.S.** *ski team; the* **U.K.** *skating team*). You must spell out the name when you use it as a noun.

Addresses

If you include a full address—street, city, province, and postal code—in the body of your writing, you can abbreviate the province name. Both two-letter postal abbreviations and traditional abbreviations (*Alta.*) are used in writing in Canada (see Box 122). Spell out any other combination of a city and a province, and spell out the name of a province by itself.

BOX 122   SUMMARY

Postal abbreviations

Canada

Postal Abbreviation	Traditional Abbreviation	
AB	Alta.	Alberta
BC	B.C.	British Columbia
MB	Man.	Manitoba
NB	N.B.	New Brunswick
NL	Nfld. (Nfld. and Lab.)	Newfoundland and Labrador
NS	N.S.	Nova Scotia
NT	N.W.T.	Northwest Territories
NU	—	Nunavut
ON	Ont.	Ontario
PE	P.E.I.	Prince Edward Island
QC	Que. *or* P.Q.	Quebec
SK	Sask.	Saskatchewan
YT	Y.T.	Yukon Territory

United States

AL	Alabama		**CO**	Colorado
AK	Alaska		**CT**	Connecticut
AZ	Arizona		**DE**	Delaware
AR	Arkansas		**DC**	District of Columbia
CA	California			

→

Postal abbreviations *(continued)*

FL	Florida	**NJ**	New Jersey
GA	Georgia	**NM**	New Mexico
HI	Hawaii	**NY**	New York
ID	Idaho	**NC**	North Carolina
IL	Illinois	**ND**	North Dakota
IN	Indiana	**OH**	Ohio
IA	Iowa	**OK**	Oklahoma
KS	Kansas	**OR**	Oregon
KY	Kentucky	**PA**	Pennsylvania
LA	Louisiana	**RI**	Rhode Island
ME	Maine	**SC**	South Carolina
MD	Maryland	**SD**	South Dakota
MA	Massachusetts	**TN**	Tennessee
MI	Michigan	**TX**	Texas
MN	Minnesota	**UT**	Utah
MS	Mississippi	**VT**	Vermont
MO	Missouri	**VA**	Virginia
MT	Montana	**WA**	Washington [state]
NE	Nebraska	**WV**	West Virginia
NV	Nevada	**WI**	Wisconsin
NH	New Hampshire	**WY**	Wyoming

◉ **ALERT:** When you write the names of a city and province or territory within a sentence, use a comma before and after the province or territory. Don't insert a comma before a postal code.

NO   St. John, New Brunswick is too often confused with St. John's, Newfoundland.

YES   St. John, New Brunswick, is too often confused with St. John's, Newfoundland. ◉

Scholarly writing (MLA style)

MLA style permits abbreviations for a selection of scholarly terms. These are listed in Box 123. Never use them in the body of your ACADEMIC WRITING. Reserve them for your "Works Cited" lists and for any Notes you might write in a separate list at the end of your research paper.

BOX 123   SUMMARY

Major scholarly abbreviations—MLA style

anon.	anonymous	**ms., mss.**	manuscript, manuscripts
b.	born		
c. *or* ©	copyright	**NB**	note well (*nota bene*)
c. *or* **ca.**	circa (about) [with dates]	**n.d.**	no date (of publication)
cf.	compare	**p., pp.**	page, pages
col., cols.	column, columns	**par.**	paragraph
d.	died	**pref.**	preface, preface by
ed., eds.	edition, edited by, editor(s)	**rept.**	report, reported by
		rev.	review, reviewed by; revised, revised by
e.g.	for example		
esp.	especially	**sec., secs.**	section, sections
et al.	and others	**v.** *or* **vs.**	versus [*v.* in legal cases]
ff.	following pages, following lines, folios	**vol., vols.**	volume, volumes
i.e.	that is		

30I When can I use *etc.*?

The abbreviation *etc.* comes from the Latin *et cetera,* meaning "and the rest." In ACADEMIC WRITING, don't use *etc.* Accepted substitutes include *and the like, and so on, and so forth,* among others. Even better is a more concrete description. An acceptable use of *etc.* is in tables and charts.

> **NO**   The names Baldwin and LaFontaine, Macdonald and Cartier, **etc.,** are linked in historical memory.

> **YES**   The names Baldwin and LaFontaine, Macdonald and Cartier, **and other political allies** are linked in historical memory.

 ALERT: If you do write *etc.,* always put a comma after the period if the abbreviation falls in the middle of a sentence. ◉

EXERCISE 30-3

Revise these sentences for correct use of abbreviations. For help, consult 30i through 30l.

1. Although she took her degree in a tech. field, Charlene made a point of getting as many lib. arts credits as she could.
2. The U of M in Winnipeg, Man., was the first institution of higher ed. to be established in W Canada.

3. Graham knew instantly from Lucinda's accent that she came from NS and could not possibly be a native of Alta. as she claimed.

4. Lamont gave generously to all the charities, political orgs., etc., that asked him, until the day in Nov. 2000 when he was approached by a rep of the Natural Law Party.

5. Dozens of hrs. and thousands of $$ later, the contractors finally extended the driveway to the main rd., a mere four m away.

NUMBERS

30m When do I use spelled-out numbers?

Your decision to write a number as a word or as a figure depends on what you're referring to and how often numbers occur in that piece of writing. The guidelines I give in this handbook are for MLA STYLE, which focuses on writing in the humanities. For other disciplines, follow the guidelines in their style manuals.

Reserve figures for some categories of numbers and spelled-out words for other categories. Never mix spelled-out numbers and figures for the same category.

> **NO**　In **four** days, our volunteers increased from **five** to **eight** to **17** to **233.**

> **YES**　In **four** days, our volunteers increased from **5** to **8** to **17** to **233.**
> [Numbers referring to volunteers are in numerals, while *four* is spelled out because it refers to a different category: days.]

If you use numbers infrequently in a document, spell out all numbers that call for no more than two words: *fifty-two cards, twelve hundred students.* If you use specific numbers often in a document (temperatures when writing about climate, percentages in an economics essay, or other specific measurements of time, distance, and other quantities), use figures: *11 nanoseconds.* If you give only an approximation, spell out the numbers: *About fifteen centimetres of snow fell.*

In the humanities, the names of centuries are always spelled out: *the eighteenth century.*

When you write for courses in the humanities, never start a sentence with a figure. Spell out the number—or better still, revise the sentence so that the number doesn't need to fall at the beginning. For practices in other disciplines, consult their manuals.

> **NO**　**$375 dollars** for each credit is the tuition rate for nonresidents.

> **YES**　**Three hundred seventy-five dollars** for each credit is the tuition rate for nonresidents.

> **YES**　The tuition rate for nonresidents is **$375** for each credit.

30n What are standard practices for writing numbers?

Box 124 shows standard practices for writing numbers. Consider it a basic guide, and rely on the manual of each documentation style for answers to other questions you may have.

BOX 124 SUMMARY

Specific numbers in writing

DATES	August 6, 1941
	1732–1845
	from 34 BC to AD 230 (*or* 34 BCE to 230 CE)
ADDRESSES	10 Downing Street
	237 North 8th Street
	London ON N6A 3K7
TIMES	8:09 a.m., 6:00 p.m.
	six o'clock (*not* 6 o'clock)
	four in the afternoon *or* 4 p.m. (*not* four p.m.)
DECIMALS AND FRACTIONS	0.01
	98.6
	3.1416
	7/8
	12 1/4
	a sixth
	three-quarters (*not* 3-quarters)
	one-half
CHAPTERS AND PAGES	Chapter 27, page 2
	p. 1023 *or* pp. 660–62 (MLA style)
SCORES AND STATISTICS	a 6–0 score
	29 percent (*or* 29%)
	a 5 to 1 ratio (*or* a ratio of 5:1)
	a one percent change (*and* at the 1 percent level)
IDENTIFICATION NUMBERS	94.4 FM (radio frequency)
	please call (012) 345-6789
MEASUREMENTS	100 kilometres per hour (*or* 100 km/h)
	a 700-word essay
	8-1/2-by-11-inch paper (MLA style)
	2 metres (*or* 2 m)
	1.5 litres (*or* 1.5 L)
	350 millilitres (*or* 350 mL)

→

Specific numbers in writing (*continued*)

ACT, SCENE, AND LINE	act 2, scene 2 (*or* act II, scene ii) lines 75–79
TEMPERATURES	20°C; 7.5°C; –20°C 40°F *or* –5°F
MONEY	$1.2 billion $3.41 25¢ (*or* twenty-five cents) $10 000 (*or* $10,000)

EXERCISE 30-4

Revise these sentences so that the numbers are in correct form, either spelled out or as figures. For help, consult 30m and 30n.

1. At five fifteen p.m., the nearly empty city streets filled with 1000's of commuters.

2. A tarantula spider can survive without food for about two years and 3 months.

3. By the end of act one, scene five, Romeo and Juliet are in love and at the mercy of their unhappy fate.

4. Sound travels through air at a speed of 331 metres per second, but in water it travels four hundred and fifty percent faster, at 1481 metres per second.

5. 21 years old and unhappily married, Cleopatra met middle-aged Julius Caesar in forty-eight BCE.

6. A blue whale, which can weigh one hundred tonnes—the combined weight of 30 elephants—gains over three-point-four kilograms an hour until it reaches adolescence.

7. On the morning of August thirteen, nineteen hundred thirty, 3 huge meteorites smashed into the Amazon jungle.

8. 2 out of every 5 people who have ever lived on earth are alive today, according to 1 estimate.

9. The house at six hundred and fifty-three Oak Street—the 1 that children think is haunted—has been empty for 8 years, waiting for a buyer willing to pay its price of $ six million, forty-nine thousand dollars.

10. The 1912 sinking of the *Titanic,* in which one thousand five hundred and three people drowned, is widely known, but few people remember that more than three thousand people lost their lives aboard the ferryboat *Doña Paz* when it hit an oil tanker in the Philippines in nineteen eighty-seven.

30o How do I use hyphens with spelled-out numbers?

Box 125 gives you guidelines for spelled-out numbers.

👁 **ALERT:** Use figures rather than words for a fraction written in more than two words. If your context calls for figures, use hyphens only between the words of the numerator and only between the words of the denominator—but never between the numerator and the denominator: two one-hundredths (*2/100*), thirty-three ten-thousandths (*33/10 000*). 👁

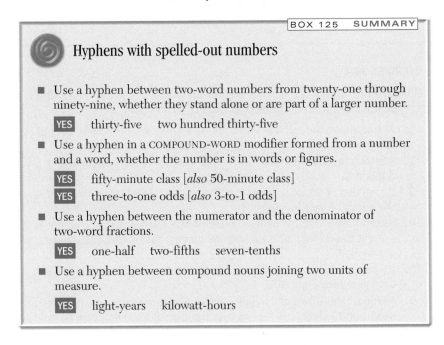

BOX 125   SUMMARY

Hyphens with spelled-out numbers

- Use a hyphen between two-word numbers from twenty-one through ninety-nine, whether they stand alone or are part of a larger number.

  YES   thirty-five   two hundred thirty-five

- Use a hyphen in a COMPOUND-WORD modifier formed from a number and a word, whether the number is in words or figures.

  YES   fifty-minute class [*also* 50-minute class]
  YES   three-to-one odds [*also* 3-to-1 odds]

- Use a hyphen between the numerator and the denominator of two-word fractions.

  YES   one-half   two-fifths   seven-tenths

- Use a hyphen between compound nouns joining two units of measure.

  YES   light-years   kilowatt-hours

Part Five

Writing Research

Visit the Troyka Web site at
http://ww.pearsoned.ca/troyka for

- help with research and documentation
- chapter exercises
- other resources, including an e-book version of this text

Chapter 31

Research Writing as a Process

31a What is research writing?

Research writing involves three steps: conducting research, understanding and evaluating the results of your research, and writing the research paper with accurate DOCUMENTATION.* Every research project requires these steps. Moreover, research writing, as is true of the WRITING PROCESS itself, often moves forward, loops back, and jumps ahead according to what unfolds as you work.

The writing process for a research paper resembles the writing process for all academic papers. Using print, electronic, and online sources adds one more level for your attention.

Some student researchers use information from **primary sources**— from direct observations, interviews, surveys, measurements, original documents and records, and so on. However, most students, especially when writing undergraduate research papers, use information from **secondary sources**—from reading, using ANALYSIS, discussing, and reviewing what people with respected credentials and authority have written. In planning the paper, you choose a suitable research TOPIC; develop that topic into a RESEARCH QUESTION; use a search strategy to locate and evaluate sources; and take notes. In DRAFTING and REVISING the paper, you present a SYNTHESIS of your findings, supported by QUOTATIONS, PARAPHRASES, and SUMMARIES of your sources.

Research is an engrossing, creative activity. By gathering information, analyzing the separate elements, and creating a synthesis of what you've learned, you come to know your subject deeply. Also, the very act of writing leads you to fresh connections and unexpected insights. All this adds up to the chance to sample the pleasures of being a self-reliant learner, an independent person with the discipline and intellectual resources to track down, absorb, synthesize, and write about your topic.

Nevertheless, many researchers—inexperienced and experienced— feel intimidated at the beginning of a research writing project. My per-

---

* Find the definition of all words in small capital letters (such as DOCUMENTATION) in the Terms Glossary at the back of this book directly before the Index.

sonal approach is to break it into manageable chunks. Those chunks construct a series of steps, each of which is explained in this chapter.

31b How do I choose and narrow a research topic?

Some instructors assign a specific TOPIC for research (for example, "the feasibility of making robots that act like humans"). Others assign a general subject area ("artificial intelligence") and expect you to narrow it to a manageable topic. Still other instructors expect you to choose a topic on your own ("Write a research paper on a topic of current importance").

A good research topic is one that your readers will perceive as significant and worthwhile. That is, the topic is important or timely, your insights are fresh, or your SYNTHESIS is clear and skilful.

On a practical level, a good research topic is narrow enough for you to research within the constraints of time and length imposed by the assignment. Also, you want to determine, before you commit too firmly to a topic, that enough print and online material exists about it to offer you a sufficient number of sources and perspectives to answer your RESEARCH QUESTION and write your paper.

The expectation that you will demonstrate CRITICAL THINKING in your research paper is another variable that needs to influence your topic decisions. You can use critical thinking in one of two broad ways, each of which is grounded in your PURPOSE for writing the paper. First, you can choose a topic on which intelligent people have differing opinions. Next, you analyze your sources to decide which position appears most reasonable. Your paper would then take the form of an ARGUMENT that shows readers you have considered the various positions and chosen a reasonable one.

Second, you can choose to write an INFORMATIVE paper in which you synthesize several sources related to a complex subject. Writing a synthesis means pulling together sometimes extensive information on a topic by finding connections that explain the essential points as you see them. For example, after you read a dozen articles on the topic of artificial intelligence, you might try to identify three or four key points and then organize information from your reading about these and closely related points. You integrate material from various sources to make each point. Your paper's goal is to clarify and create a new whole from complicated or scattered information.

Choosing a topic on your own

When your assignment allows you to select any topic that appeals to you, be sure to choose one that's worthy of research writing. You want a topic that allows you to demonstrate your ability to use critical thinking and to synthesize ideas.

Such freedom of choice pleases some students. For others, it leads to what can be called a "research-topic block." If this happens, rest assured you can overcome it by remaining calm and being proactive, using the suggestions in Box 126. Also, try using the suggestions in Box 14 in 3b.

BOX 126   SUMMARY

Finding ideas for research

- **Get ready.** Carry a pocket-size notebook and a pen, or use a PDA (such as a Palm Pilot). Ideas have a way of popping into your mind when you least expect them. Jot down your thoughts on the spot, no matter where you are, so that they don't slip away.

- **Overcome any block that prevents you from moving ahead.** First, look back at section 3b for practical ideas. Second, stop yourself from thinking about the "whole" of your research project at once. Instead, break it into chunks, according to the small steps in your research schedule (discussed in 31d).

- **Think actively.** Use the structured techniques for gathering ideas demonstrated in sections 2f through 2m.

- **Browse through textbooks.** Pick a field that interests you, and look over a textbook or two (in the bookstore, borrowed from a friend, or on reserve in the library). Read the table of contents and major headings. Scan the text for material that catches your eye. Note the names of important books and experts, often mentioned in reference lists at the end of chapters or at the back of the book. See what holds your attention and makes you want to keep reading.

- **Browse the Internet.** Many Web search engines provide topic directories, as illustrated in section 1h.2. Click on some general categories and review subcategories until you locate specific topics that interest you. Then try further subject searches or KEYWORD SEARCHES (32c.4) to see where they lead.

- **Use the *Library of Congress Subject Headings.*** This is a multi-volume reference work now in print only. In many libraries, it sits on the counter at the research librarian's station; at others, it's shelved with the other reference volumes. The *LCSH* lists every single topic (and the library call number of books on each topic) with many sublists, often coded to explain their purpose. Section 32d discusses specifically how the *LCSH* volumes can help you as a researcher.

- **Browse general encyclopedias.** These offer a wide-ranging survey of topics but give only a general, superficial sense of each subject. These reference works—available as books, CDs, or on the Internet

$\rightarrow$

Finding ideas for research (*continued*)

(often through connections to a library database)—come in handy for identifying general topics within areas that interest you. However, the content of general encyclopedias is rarely suitable for research for a university- or college-level research paper.

- **Browse specialized encyclopedias.** These volumes are considered "specialized" because each is devoted to only one specific area (for example, social science, history, philosophy, the natural sciences). Their articles and chapters treat topics in some depth, and the material is usually suitable for academic research. Most selections mention names of major figures in the field, information that comes in handy when evaluating your sources (32j).

- **Browse through books and periodicals.** These are available when your library has open stacks (fully accessible bookshelves). Browse books and academic journals, as well as popular magazines, in fields that interest you. Or you might spend some time at a public library or in a good bookstore.

Narrowing a general topic into a workable one

Whether you're working with a topic of your choice or an assigned one, check that it's sufficiently narrow for the time frame and other requirements of your research paper. Also, be sure that the narrowed topic is worthy of an academic research project. Box 127 offers guidelines.

BOX 127   SUMMARY

Deciding on a workable, worthwhile research topic

1. **Expect to consider various topics before making your final choice.** Don't rush. Give yourself time to think. Keep your mind open to flashes of insight and to alternative ideas. At the same time, be careful not to let indecision paralyze you.

2. **Choose a topic that has a sufficient number of appropriate sources available.** If you can't find useful sources—ones that relate directly to your topic and that are credible, not simply plentiful—drop the topic. Keep your RESEARCH QUESTION (31c) in mind as you look over your sources.

3. **Narrow the topic sufficiently.** Avoid topics that are too broad, such as "intelligence." Conversely, avoid topics that are so narrow that you can't present a suitable mix of GENERALIZATIONS and specific details. As you formulate your research question, you'll also be narrowing your topic.

→

> ## Deciding on a workable, worthwhile research topic (*continued*)
>
> 4. **Choose a topic worth researching.** Avoid trivial topics that prevent you from doing what instructors and others expect of a student researcher: investigating ideas, analyzing them critically, and creating a synthesis of complex concepts.
> 5. **Select a topic that interests you.** Your topic will be a companion for a while, sometimes for most of a semester. Select a topic that arouses your interest and allows you the pleasure of satisfying your intellectual curiosity.
> 6. **Confer with a professor in your field of interest, if possible.** Before the meeting, read a little about your topic so that your questions and remarks show that you've prepared for the conversation. Ask whether you've narrowed your topic sufficiently and productively. Also, ask for the titles of the major books and names of major authorities on your topic.

Case Study

"Computers" was the general subject area assigned to Chandra Johnson, the student whose research paper appears in Chapter 34. The paper was to be 1800 to 2000 words long and based on about a dozen sources. It was due in six weeks.

To get started, Johnson went to her library's online catalogue and searched for books with the word "computer" in their titles. She found 188 book titles and began browsing through them. One title caught her attention: *Computers Ltd.: What They Really Can't Do.* From what she found as she browsed the book, she started to wonder if computers can really think. That idea led her into the area of artificial intelligence.

Although this description shows each of Johnson's decisions flowing smoothly, the actual process wasn't neat and tidy. She met dead ends with a subtopic's keywords and frustration with searches for books she wanted to look over but were unavailable in her library or online searches. What looks clear-cut at the end of the research process was a more circuitous path of backing out of dead ends and making some sharp turns in searching for answers to a research question.

A more detailed narrative, including a flowchart, of Johnson's complete research process appears in 34e.1, and the final draft of her research paper appears in 34e.2.

31c What is a research question?

A **research question** controls and drives your research. Few research paper assignments are phrased as questions. Therefore, most research writing calls on you to figure out a thought-provoking underlying question and then to search for answers to it. By regarding research as a quest for an answer, you give your work a specific focus: You can't know whether you've found useful source material unless you know what you're looking for.

Research questions, whether stated or implied, and the strategies needed to answer them, vary widely. Your purpose might be to present and explain information: "How does penicillin destroy bacteria?" Or your purpose might be to argue one side of an issue: "Is Parliament still more important than the Supreme Court in setting social policy?" You can then consult various sources in an attempt to work toward an answer.

Attempt is an important word in relation to research. Some research questions lead to a final, definitive answer, but some do not. The question above about penicillin leads to a reasonably definitive answer (you describe how the antibiotic penicillin destroys the cell walls of some bacteria); this means your writing has an informative purpose. The question about social policy has no definitive answer, so you're asked to offer an informed opinion based on facts and authoritative viewpoints gathered from your research; this means your writing has a persuasive purpose.

To formulate a research question, begin by BRAINSTORMING a list of questions that comes to mind about your topic. Write your list of ideas in your research log (31e).

Suppose, for example, the topic you want to write about is "homelessness." Here are some typical questions you might ask.

- Why can't a rich country like Canada eliminate homelessness?
- Who is homeless?
- How do people become homeless?
- Is it true that many families—not just adults—are homeless?
- Is the homeless problem getting better or worse?
- What are we doing to solve the problem of homelessness?

Some questions will interest you more than others, so begin with one of those. If a question leads to a dead end, pursue another. Only when you find yourself accumulating answers—or in the case of questions without definitive answers, accumulating viewpoints—is it likely you're dealing with a usable research question. Once you have an explicitly stated research question, you can streamline your research by taking notes only from those sources that help you answer your research question.

Stay flexible as you work. The results of your research may lead you to modify the research question slightly. When you've finished researching and notetaking based on your final research question, you have a starting place for formulating the preliminary THESIS STATEMENT for your research paper.

31d How do I set up my schedule for research writing?

Dividing a research project into a series of steps makes the project far less intimidating. Research takes time, so plan ahead and budget your time intelligently. As soon as you get an assignment for a research paper, plan your schedule, using Box 128 as a model. Because no two research paper projects are alike, adapt this schedule to your needs. You might, for example, need only one day for some steps but two weeks for others. So, while you stay flexible, keep your eye on the calendar.

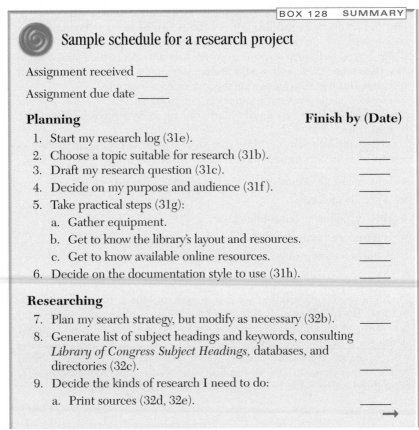

BOX 128   SUMMARY

Sample schedule for a research project

Assignment received _____

Assignment due date _____

Planning	**Finish by (Date)**
1. Start my research log (31e).	_____
2. Choose a topic suitable for research (31b).	_____
3. Draft my research question (31c).	_____
4. Decide on my purpose and audience (31f).	_____
5. Take practical steps (31g):	
a. Gather equipment.	
b. Get to know the library's layout and resources.	_____
c. Get to know available online resources.	_____
6. Decide on the documentation style to use (31h).	_____

Researching

7. Plan my search strategy, but modify as necessary (32b). _____
8. Generate list of subject headings and keywords, consulting *Library of Congress Subject Headings*, databases, and directories (32c). _____
9. Decide the kinds of research I need to do:
   a. Print sources (32d, 32e). _____

→

Sample schedule for a research project (*continued*)

Researching (*continued*)   **Finish by (Date)**

     b. Online and/or electronic sources (32c).   _____

     c. Field research? (32i) If yes, schedule tasks.   _____

 10. Locate and evaluate sources (32c, 32j).   _____

 11. Take content notes from sources I find useful (31j).   _____

Writing

 12. Draft my preliminary thesis statement (31k).   _____

 13. Outline, as required (31l).   _____

 14. Draft my paper (31m).   _____

 15. Use correct parenthetical citations (34b–34c; 35b–35c; 36a, 36c, 36e).   _____

 16. Write my final thesis statement (31k).   _____

 17. Revise my paper (31m).   _____

 18. Compile my final bibliography, using the documentation style required (Chapters 34–36).   _____

Evaluation of this schedule

Have I planned realistically for my completion date?

If I haven't, what steps should I revise in my schedule?

31e   What is a research log?

A **research log** is a diary of your research process. Start your research log as soon as you get an assignment. Use a separate notebook for the log or create a new folder or file on the computer. Whichever format you rely on, make your research schedule one of the first entries. If your instructor tells students to use Web logs, known as blogs, see section 41h.

    Although much of your research log will never find its way into your research paper, what you write in it greatly increases your efficiency. A well-kept log traces your line of reasoning as your project evolves, tells where you've ended each work session, and suggests what your next steps might be. Since college and university students take several courses at the same time, keeping this sort of record means you'll waste no time retracing a research path or reconstructing a thought. In your log, always record the date as well as the following elements:

- Your current step in your search for information; the search strategy you used to find that information; the name, location, and other details of exactly where you found the information; the main point of the information; and later on, when you have taken detailed content notes, where you saved them—for example, the exact file or folder name

- Your suggested next step for when you return to your research
- Your evolving overall thoughts and insights as you move through the research and writing processes
- Your awareness that you're becoming ready to move away from gathering material to organizing it; from organizing it to writing about it; and from drafting to revising

> October 16: Got online to find sources for "artificial intelligence" and was overwhelmed by the number of hits in Yahoo. Gave up. Logged onto the library's Web site and searched some databases there. PsycINFO turned up lots of promising stuff. Chose several citations and e-mailed full records to myself to check out later. Readers' Guide Abstracts also had articles, and some were available as full text. Printed out three of the best ones. Need to start taking notes on them. Will go to the library tomorrow to find PsycINFO sources.

Excerpt from Chandra Johnson's research log

31f How do I determine the purpose and audience for my research paper?

To decide whether your paper will have an informative purpose or a persuasive purpose, see what your research question asks. If the answer to it involves giving facts, information, and explanation, your purpose is to inform. For example, "How have computers changed over time?" calls for INFORMATIVE WRITING. Conversely, if the answer involves offering an educated opinion based on contrasting views and supporting evidence, your purpose is to persuade. For example, "How are computers responsible for postindustrial society and economy?" calls for PERSUASIVE WRITING.

You may find that your purpose shifts during your research process, as Chandra Johnson's did (see 34e). As you work, balance the need to remain open-minded with the need to decide on your purpose before you get too far along.

AUDIENCES for research papers vary. In some situations, only your instructor will read your paper (1d.4). Sometimes your audience starts with your peers, the other students in your class. Next, it moves on to a general public audience or to specialists on your topic, with your instructor as one among many readers. Your sense of these other readers' expertise in your topic can guide your decisions about content, level of detail, and DICTION.

31g What practical steps can help me work efficiently?

To conduct your research with greatest efficiency, you need to do some footwork before you start researching. First, gather the equipment listed in Box 129 so that it's organized and ready for use. Second, become familiar with your library's layout and resources (32c). Third, be sure to become skilled and comfortable with searching topics online, if you're not already (32c).

Gathering supplies for research

Box 129 offers a list of supplies that many students use. Adapt the list to your needs.

BOX 129   SUMMARY

Equipment needed for research

1. A copy of your assignment.
2. This handbook, especially Part Five, or access to the Internet so that you can read the book online. With its guidelines at hand, work efficiently as you evaluate sources, document your sources, and correctly handle other tasks that come up.
3. Your research log (31e).
4. Index cards for taking notes (unless you use a laptop). If you use different colours of index cards, you might colour code the different categories of information you find. Also, you might use one size for bibliography cards and the other for content note cards. Another coding strategy is to use pens of different ink colours or self-sticking dots of various colours.
5. Coins (or cash or a debit card) for copy machines or printers.
6. Empty floppy disks or CDs (or memory keys) for downloading material—but make sure your library allows downloading to disk.
7. If you use index cards and other paper, a small stapler, paper clips, and rubber bands.
8. A separate book bag to carry books you check out from the library. (Librarians joke about researchers with wheelbarrows. You might need a backpack.)

Learning how the library is organized

When you learn how your college or university library is organized, your research efficiency increases. Though almost all libraries in Canada and the United States are organized around the same principles for grouping information, layouts of library buildings differ considerably. Your time is well spent if you visit the library for the sole purpose of figuring out what's located where, so that you'll feel comfortable and confident when you work there.

Some academic libraries provide class tours for specific courses; some offer individual training sessions; and most offer informative, free flyers to help students learn the library layout and the resources available to students. Box 130 provides a checklist for familiarizing yourself with your library.

BOX 130 CHECKLIST

Touring a library

1. Where is the general reference collection? (You can't check out reference books, so when you need to use them, build extra time into your schedule to spend at the library.)

2. Where is the special reference collection? (Same rules apply as for general reference books.)

3. How does the library's catalogue work?

4. What periodical indexes or databases does your library have? (These are lists of articles in journals and magazines, grouped by subject areas.)

5. How and where are the library's collections of journals and magazines stored? Most libraries place periodicals published in the past year in open areas, while older periodicals are on microfiche, CDs, or online. Become adept at using whatever system is in place at your library.

6. Are the book and journal stacks open (fully accessible shelves) or closed (request each item by filling out a form to hand to library personnel)? If the latter, become familiar with the required procedures not only for asking for a book or journal but also for picking it up when it's ready.

7. What, if anything, is stored on microfilm or microfiche? If you think you'll use that material, take the time to learn how to use the machines. (I find that each library's machines work differently enough to stump me at first.)

8. Does the library have special collections, such as local historical works or the writings of notable persons?

9. Does the library give you access to the Internet? If not, find out if this service is available elsewhere on campus—for example, in a student centre or computer lab. When at home or in a residence hall, can you access the library's computerized systems?

Deciding how to use the computer

Today, computers allow you to carry out research quite differently than students did only a few years ago. How you use the computer is largely a matter of personal preference. Some students use a computer only for finding sources and for DRAFTING the paper itself. These students do the rest of their research steps "by hand" on index cards and sheets of paper: keeping their research log (31e), compiling their WORKING BIBLIOGRAPHY (31i), taking content notes (31j), and so forth.

Other students carry out their entire research process on computer. They set up folders for every phase of their project. To accumulate print sources for their working bibliography, these students download them onto a disk or a laptop computer—always carefully recording the origin of the source in the documentation style they've selected (31h). They type their research log, working bibliography, and content notes directly into computer files. Finally, they draft and revise their papers on computer, often using the "Track Changes" feature, or its equivalent, on their word-processing program to keep track of their revisions.

Experiment to find which method works best for you in each research situation. No right or wrong way to use the new technologies exists. Do what feels most comfortable to you.

Arranging field research, if appropriate and necessary

Field research is primary research that involves going into real-life situations to observe, survey, or interview. The majority of undergraduate research projects don't require field research. However, if your project does, you need to organize that experience well in advance (32i).

31h What documentation style should I use?

Ask your instructor which DOCUMENTATION STYLE you're required to use for your research paper: MLA (Chapter 34)? APA (Chapter 35)? Another (Chapter 36)? As you compile your WORKING BIBLIOGRAPHY (31i), be sure to record all the documentation elements the required style demands. Documentation styles vary in their details, and you don't want to have to track down a source again merely to get documentation facts you didn't write down on your first pass.

31i What is a working bibliography?

A **working bibliography** emerges from your search for and evaluation of sources. It's your preliminary list of potentially useful sources for each research project. This list, which is an essential part of your research process, remains fluid in the early stage of your search for sources.

Think of compiling a working bibliography as a survey process. You want to find out what is available on a particular subject before you commit to extensive reading and notetaking. To do this, set aside more than one span of hours to search on a given subject.

As you compile a working bibliography, evaluate the sources you are considering using. Never waste your time looking at unsound or irrelevant sources. First, your sources need to pertain to your topic and RESEARCH QUESTION. Second and more important, they need to be authoritative and reliable. Unfortunately, a tremendous amount of bad information exists in print and, especially, online. Expect to add and drop sources as you refine your research question and locate other sources. Be sure to consult the guidelines in 32j for evaluating sources.

Box 131 lists some of the information you need to include in your working bibliography. You can record your working bibliography on

---

BOX 131   SUMMARY

Formatting bibliography information on each source

- For a library source, write the *call number* in the upper left corner, being careful to copy it exactly. If you conduct research at more than one library, also note the library where you found that source.

- For magazines and journals, write the exact title of the periodical and article, the date of the issue, the volume and issue numbers, and the page numbers on which the article appears.

- For an online source, write the URL (uniform resource locator) address in the upper left corner of the card, being careful to copy it exactly. Also, record any date related to the source: most recent update, date originally made available, and so forth. Most important, write down the date on which you are accessing the material and the date you are downloading the material. If you take notes directly from the screen, use the date you are taking notes. This information is required in *all* documentation styles.

- If you actually look at the source, write two key messages to yourself on the back of the card: (a) the reason the source seems useful at the moment, and (b) the results of your evaluation of the source (32j). Here are typical content notes students have written on their working bibliography cards:

  - "One of the most credible authors about my subject."
  - "Book is old, but has useful background information and definitions."
  - "Article published only two months ago in scholarly journal and answers my research question perfectly!"
  - "This Web page has pertinent information, but I must check whether the author is really an authority on the subject."

note cards or on a computer. Note cards have the advantage of being easy to sift through when you're adding and discarding sources. Also, you can carry them with you to the library when you do library research. Their best use is at the end of your writing process, when you can easily sort and alphabetize cards for the final list of sources you used. Keeping your working bibliography on the computer has the advantage of allowing you to alphabetize and organize it, which can save you time as you complete your WORKS CITED (MLA style) or REFERENCES (APA style) list of sources. The computer also allows you to delete or rearrange sources easily. Whichever method you choose, write only one source per card or clearly separate one entry from another in your computer document.

When you come across a source that seems to have potential for your project, write a bibliography card for it immediately, while the source is in front of you. Doing this helps you evaluate the sources by seeing if expert names, book title, or article title repeat, thus suggesting that you've found a good source. Include all the information you would eventually need to fulfil the requirements of the DOCUMENTATION STYLE your instructor specifies. Record it exactly as it would appear in your finished paper. Spending a few extra moments at this stage can save endless hours of work and frustration later on. If you find that a source is not useful, keep your working bibliography card anyway, and note why you rejected it. What seems useless now may become useful when you revise.

The two working bibliography cards shown here, one of which has a content note on the back, are for two sources Chandra Johnson found when she was doing the research for her paper (shown in 34e.2).

BF 311 .D33 1999

Damasio, Antonio.
The Feeling of What Happens:
Body and Emotion in the
Making of Consciousness

New York: Harcourt Brace, 1999.

Bibliography card: Book

http://www-formal.stanford.edu/jmc/
whatisai/whatisai.html

McCarthy, John
"What Is Artificial Intelligence?"

Access date: 10/14/2003
Date published on Web: 3/29/2003

Bibliography card: Online source

McCarthy's a computer science prof at Stanford U.
An expert source. Web site has lots of basic info.

Content note on the back of the McCarthy bibliography card.

As a rough estimate, your working bibliography needs to be about twice as long as the list of sources you end up using.

Don't be discouraged if your search goes slowly at first. As your knowledge of the topic grows, and your searching skills improve, you'll find yourself narrowing your search and becoming increasingly productive.

31j How do I take content notes?

Content notes record information and ideas from your sources that relate specifically to your topic. You start taking content notes when you think your preliminary search has produced enough sources in your WORKING BIBLIOGRAPHY that relate to your RESEARCH QUESTION. Always try to sort major information from minor information about the topic. This will help you when you organize ideas for DRAFTING. Also, write down whatever understanding you've gained from your reading of the source as it directly relates to your paper.

You can make content notes either in a computer file or on index cards. If you're using the computer, leave plenty of space between notes, and keep careful track of what ideas came from each source. One strategy is to open a new file for each source. Later, after you've taken notes on many of your sources, you can determine what subtopics are important for your paper. You can then open a new file for each topic and use the "Cut" and "Paste" functions to gather notes from all of your sources under each topic.

If you're making content notes on index cards, put a heading on each card that gives a precise link to one of your bibliography items. As with bibliography cards, always include in your content notes the source's title, the page numbers from which you're taking notes, and whatever other information ties your notes to a specific source. Never put notes from more than one source on the same index card. If your notes on a source require more than one index card, number the cards sequentially (that is, when you need two cards, write "1 of 2" on the first card and "2 of 2" on the second card). If you take notes about more than one idea or topic from the same source, start a new card for each.

Keeping track of the kind of note you are taking will help you avoid PLAGIARISM. You might use the code *Q* for quotation, *P* for paraphrase, and *S* for summary. Or you might use a different font (on computer) or ink colour (on index cards) for QUOTATIONS, PARAPHRASES, and SUMMARIES. (Every precaution you take by coding your content notes helps you avoid the risk of plagiarism; see Chapter 33.) Also, you'll progress more quickly if, on the spot, you compose your SYNTHESIS of the material—that is, if you write down connections between the new source and other sources you have found or your personal knowledge of a subject.

Shown below are two content notes written by Chandra Johnson, the student whose research and writing process comprise the case study in this chapter and the narrative and commentary in Chapter 34. The full title of the book by Antonio Damasio is *The Feeling of What Happens: Body and Emotion in the Making of Consciousness*. Johnson put full information about this source in her working bibliography. She kept her notes on index cards. With each note, she used a shortened form of the title, listed the related page numbers, and recorded whether the information was a quotation, paraphrase, or summary.

Some instructors require students to submit photocopies of all sources they consult for research. Photocopying an article or downloading an online source can also save you time as you draft your research paper. Having a copy of articles, book chapters, or Web pages in your research file gives you access to each item in full. Also, photocopies allow you to check for accuracy and prevent your misquoting, or plagiarizing from, the source. If you use photocopies, always be sure to write the same bibliography information and content notes as you would if you did not have the photocopies. Remember to label each photocopied or downloaded source with the author's name, the source, and other identifying information. (It's easy, but wrong, to think that if you have a photocopy, you don't need all crucial bibliographic and content information.) It's also a good idea to underline (on your own copy) the section that caught your attention and to write alongside it why it looks useful. The more detailed you are, the more helpful your comments will be as you narrow your working bibliography and as you draft your paper.

> *Damasio. The Feeling*
> *p. 39*
>
> *Summary:*
> *Many scientists and philosophers think emotion interferes with intelligence (Damasio disagrees)*

Summary note card

> *Damasio. The Feeling*
> *p. 41*
>
> *Quotation:*
> *"emotion is integral to the process of reasoning and decision making"*

Quotation note card

31k How do I draft a thesis statement for a research paper?

Drafting a THESIS STATEMENT for a research paper marks the transition from the research process to the writing process. A thesis statement in a research paper is like the thesis statement in any essay: It sets out the central theme, which you need to sustain throughout the paper (see section 2q, especially Box 12, and section 6c). As with any piece of writing, your research paper must fulfil the promise of its thesis statement.

You might begin thinking of the preliminary thesis statement for your paper at some middle point in the research process, although it's perfectly acceptable to wait until you've completely finished researching. Consider converting your RESEARCH QUESTION into a preliminary thesis statement, worded as a DECLARATIVE SENTENCE, not as a question. Remember that a good thesis statement makes an assertion that conveys your point of view about your topic and foreshadows the content of your paper (again, see Box 12 in 2q). And not least, remember that your research paper needs to support your thesis statement. Ask yourself whether the material you've gathered from sources can effectively give support. If not, revise your thesis statement, conduct further research, or do both.

Case Study

Chandra Johnson (whose research paper appears in Chapter 34) revised her preliminary thesis statement twice before she felt that it expressed the point she wanted to make. Johnson also took the key step of checking that she would be able to support it sufficiently with sources throughout her paper.

FIRST PRELIMINARY THESIS STATEMENT

Artificial intelligence is a complicated problem. [Johnson realized that this draft was much too general for her paper and didn't prepare readers for her specific focus on computers.]

NEXT PRELIMINARY THESIS STATEMENT

Determining whether a computer is "intelligent" is an unsolved problem. [Johnson liked this thesis better but rejected it because it still described a very broad topic, and she wanted to concentrate specifically on the role of emotion in intelligence.]

FINAL THESIS STATEMENT

An unsolved problem is whether computers need emotion for scientists to consider them intelligent. [Johnson felt this got closer to her message; she then checked it to make sure it also satisfied the criteria for a thesis statement listed in Box 12 in 2q.]

As you revise your thesis statement, keep your eye on the research question that guided your research process so that you can point, in general terms, to the question's answer. Here are examples of subjects narrowed to topics, focused into research questions, and then cast as thesis statements.

SUBJECT	*rain forests*
TOPIC	The economic exploitation of rain forests
RESEARCH QUESTION	Is sustainable development of rain forests feasible?
INFORMATIVE THESIS STATEMENT	Market incentives have been integrated into rain forest conservation regimes.
PERSUASIVE THESIS STATEMENT	Conventional definitions of profit and loss are inadequate measures of the value of irreplaceable resources such as rain forests.
SUBJECT	*nonverbal communication*
TOPIC	Personal space
RESEARCH QUESTION	How do standards for personal space differ among cultures?
INFORMATIVE THESIS STATEMENT	Everyone has expectations concerning the use of personal space, but accepted distances for that space are determined by each person's culture.
PERSUASIVE THESIS STATEMENT	To prevent intercultural misunderstandings, people must be aware of cultural differences in standards for personal space.
SUBJECT	*smoking*
TOPIC	Curing nicotine addiction
RESEARCH QUESTION	What are new approaches to curing nicotine addiction?
INFORMATIVE THESIS STATEMENT	Some approaches to curing nicotine addiction are themselves addictive.
PERSUASIVE THESIS STATEMENT	Because some methods of curing addiction are themselves addictive, doctors should prescribe them with caution.

31I How do I outline a research paper?

Some instructors require an OUTLINE of your research paper, either before you hand in the paper or along with the paper. In such cases, your instructor probably expects you to be working from an outline as you write your drafts. Your research log often comes in handy when you group your ideas, especially for a first draft of your paper—and as you make an *informal outline* for it. An outline can serve as a guide as you plan and write your paper. For directions on composing a *formal outline,* see section 2r, which shows you how to head your outline with the paper's thesis statement and explains your choices in using either a *topic outline* or a *sentence outline.* To see a topic outline of Chandra Johnson's research paper, turn to section 34e.2.

31m How do I draft and revise a research paper?

The processes of DRAFTING and REVISING a research paper are much like those of drafting and revising any other piece of writing (Chapters 2 and 3), but more is demanded. You need to demonstrate that you've followed the research steps discussed in this chapter; you've used SOURCES correctly, employing QUOTATIONS, PARAPHRASES, and SUMMARIES without PLAGIARISM (Chapter 33); you've moved beyond summary to SYNTHESIS of your various sources; and you've used DOCUMENTATION correctly (Chapters 34 through 36). To fulfil these special demands, allow ample time for drafting, thinking, revising, reflecting, and completing your paper.

Expect to write a number of drafts of your research paper. Successive drafts help you master the information you've learned and add it authoritatively to the knowledge you already had about the topic. In the first draft, organize the broad categories of your paper. Many research writers move material around within a category or from one category to another. That happens because the act of writing gives you new insights and helps you make fresh connections. A *first draft* is a rough draft. It is a prelude to revising and polishing. Box 132 suggests some ways to write your first draft.

Second drafts (and subsequent versions) emerge from reading your first (or a later) draft critically and then revising. If possible, distance yourself from your material by taking a break for a few days (or at least for a few hours, if you're pressed for time). Then, reread your draft, looking for ways to improve it—something that's hard to do unless you've taken time off between readings. You might ask friends or classmates to read the draft and react. Also, now is the time to begin thinking about the DOCUMENT DESIGN you want for your paper (see Chapter 37).

One key to revising any research paper is to carefully examine the **evidence** you have included. Evidence consists of facts, statistics, expert studies and opinions, examples, and stories. As a reader, you expect writers to provide solid evidence to back up their claims and conclusions. Similarly, when you write, your readers expect evidence that clearly supports your claims and conclusions. Identify each of the points you have made in your paper; these will include your thesis and all of your subpoints. Then ask the following questions (5g):

■ **Is the evidence sufficient?** Sufficient evidence isn't thin or trivial. As a rule, the more evidence, the more convincing the argument is to readers.

■ **Is the evidence representative?** Representative evidence is customary and normal, not based on exceptions.

BOX 132   SUMMARY

Suggestions for drafting a research paper

- Some researchers work with their notes in front of them. They use the organized piles they've made to group material into categories. They spread out each pile and work according to the subcategories of information that have emerged in the course of their research, proceeding deliberately from one pile to the next. This process takes time, but they are assured of a first draft that includes much of the results of their research.

- Some researchers review all their information and then set it aside to write a *partial first draft*. This involves a quickly written first attempt at getting the material under control. This method can help you get a broad view of the material. The second step is to go back and write a *complete first draft*, with research notes at hand. When you combine the two drafts, the pieces begin to fall into place as you move material, add what's been left out, correct information, and insert in-text references.

- Some researchers write their first draft almost as if FREEWRITING (2g), writing without stopping, just getting the words down on paper. Afterward, or whenever they get a sense of how to proceed, they slow down and use their notes.

- Some researchers, when working on computer, use the "Cut" and "Paste" functions to move around the parts of their paper. (If you do this, be sure to save a copy of each draft and partial draft—even random pages—you've written so that you can refer to earlier versions later. You never know when something you've discarded can become useful again.)

- Some researchers like the physical act of working with a printout (or photocopy) of their first draft. They literally cut up the paper to move paragraphs and sentences, a kind of "unpacking" of their thinking. If a new and more readable order suggests itself, these researchers tape the paper together in its new form.

- **Is the evidence relevant?** Relevant evidence relates directly to your claim. It illustrates your reasons straightforwardly and never introduces unrelated material.

- **Is the evidence accurate?** Accurate evidence is correct, complete, and up-to-date. It comes from a reliable SOURCE (32a, 32j). Equally important, you present it honestly, without distorting or misrepresenting the issue.

- **Is the evidence reasonable?** Reasonable, qualified evidence never makes extreme claims. It is logically sound (5j).

As you work, pay attention to any uneasy feelings you have that hint at the need to rethink or rework your material. Experienced writers know that writing is really *rewriting*. Research papers are among the most demanding composing assignments, and most writers revise several times. Once you've produced a *final draft*, you're ready to EDIT (3d), format (Chapter 37), and PROOFREAD (3e) your work. Check for correct grammar, punctuation, capitalization, and spelling. (No amount of careful research and good writing can make up for an incorrectly presented, sloppy, error-laden document.)

Consult Box 17 in section 3c to remind yourself of the general principles of revising, and consult the revision checklist in Box 133 to verify that you've remained aware of all aspects of research writing.

BOX 133　CHECKLIST

Revision checklist for a research paper

If the answer to a question is no, you need to revise. The section numbers in parentheses tell you where to find useful information.

1. Does your introductory paragraph lead effectively into the material? (4b)
2. Have you met the basic requirements for a written thesis statement? (2q and 31k)
3. Does your thesis statement allude to, or directly address, the research question upon which you based your research? (31c and 31k)
4. Does the content of your paper address your research question(s)? (31c and 31e)
5. Have you discussed the topic of each paragraph fully, using RENNS? (4f)
6. Do you stay on the topic of each paragraph? (4f)
7. Have you included appropriate and effective evidence? (4f and 31m)
8. Have you deleted irrelevant or insignificant information from your material? (4d)
9. Do your ideas follow sensibly and logically within each paragraph and from one paragraph to the next? (4g)
10. Have you used quotations, paraphrases, and summaries well? (31j)
11. Have you integrated your source material well without plagiarizing? (Chapter 33)
12. Are the formats for your parenthetical citations correct? (Chapters 34–36) Does each tie into an item in your WORKS CITED (MLA style) list of sources at the end of your paper?

→

Revision checklist for a research paper (*continued*)

13. Does the concluding paragraph end your paper effectively? (4k)
14. Does the paper exactly match the format you've been assigned to follow in terms of margins, spacing, title, name-and-page number headings, and so on? (Chapter 37)

To see one example of the research writing process in action, turn to Chandra Johnson's MLA-style research paper in section 34e. There you'll see the final draft of an MLA-style research paper; a narrative of decisions that the student made during her research process; and commentary that gives you insight into specific aspects of her paper.

For an APA-style research paper, turn to Samuel Fung's APA-style research paper in section 35h. There you'll see the final draft of the paper and a narrative of the decisions that the student made during his research process. For an APA-style science report, see section 40h.1.

Chapter 32

Finding and Evaluating Sources

32a What is a source?

A **source** is any form of information that provides ideas, examples, information, or evidence. For a research paper, sources can be books, articles, Web pages, Internet files, CD-ROMs, videos, lectures, and other types of communication. Sources can also be interviews, surveys, or direct observations, such as when you attend a performance or visit a museum. Sources differ greatly in terms of how accurate and reliable they are. To be able to use sources responsibly for your research, you need to judge each source's trustworthiness and quality. This chapter explains how to locate and then evaluate sources.

A source is either *primary* or *secondary*. A **primary source** is original work such as firsthand reports of experiments, observations, or other research projects; field research you carry out yourself; and documents like letters, diaries, novels, poems, short stories, autobiographies, and journals. When you use a primary source, no one comes between you and the material.

A **secondary source** reports, describes, comments on, or analyzes someone else's work. This information comes to you secondhand. That is, someone other than the primary source relays the information, adding a layer between you and the original material. This does not mean that secondary sources are inferior to primary sources. Scholars and other experts are excellent secondary sources. However, you need to evaluate secondary sources carefully to make sure that what's being relayed to you isn't distorted or biased in the process. Turn to 32j for detailed guidelines for evaluating sources.

32b What is a search strategy?

A **search strategy** is an organized procedure for locating and assembling information for your research. You find this information in two places: on the Internet and in the library. Developing a strategy for your search is crucial. An effective, successful search strategy results from your working systematically and thoroughly to find material that helps to answer your RESEARCH QUESTION. A good search strategy helps you structure your research work so that you don't mistake activity for productivity.

No two research processes are exactly alike. Be guided by your personal needs as you adapt the search strategies I explain. Most of all, know that no search strategy is as tidy as I describe here. Following are three frequently used designs.

The **expert method** is useful when you know your specific topic. Begin by reading articles or books by an expert in the field. Of course, this means that you have to know who the experts are, and sometimes that's difficult. Talk with people who are generally knowledgeable about your topic, learn what you can from them, and ask them to refer you to work by experts on the topic. Alternatively or in addition, INTERVIEW an expert, either in person, on the phone, or through e-mail. Turn to 32i for detailed advice about conducting effective interviews.

The **chaining method** is useful when you know your general topic and need to narrow it to a more specific, manageable topic. Start with reference books and bibliographies from current articles or Web sites. These references will lead you to additional sources. Keep up the chain, watching closely for sources that are mentioned frequently. The frequency is usually evidence that the sources are probably expert and well respected. As you work, your general topic usually begins to group and divide itself into subtopics, one of which might serve as the topic of your research paper. If such division and grouping doesn't emerge for you, take a break of a few hours so that you can reconsider the material with fresh eyes.

The **layering method** is useful when you need to find your own topic. You layer information by first consulting general sources and then finding ones that are more specific. You try to relate the information you gather to other scholarly sources in the same subject area. Chandra Johnson, the student whose research paper appears in 34e, started with the layering method and soon combined it with chaining.

You, too, may find yourself switching or combining methods. This is perfectly acceptable. "Flexibility with focus" is the guiding principle for experienced researchers. Complete your search as soon as possible after you get the assignment. Discovering early in the process what sources are available allows you time to find those that are harder to locate; to use interlibrary loan if an item isn't available in your library or online; to wait for someone to return checked-out books you need; or to schedule interviews, arrange visits, or conduct surveys.

32c How do I find sources?

Start your search strategy by consulting library and online sources on your topic. To do this, you need to figure out the keywords (32c.4) and subject categories that can lead you to useful material.

The **library** building is where generations of students have traditionally gone to do their research. Today, the **Internet,** which includes the World Wide Web and additional files, greatly expands the ways you can access information. At the library, you find books, periodicals, and lists of sources in catalogues, indexes, and databases. While many academic libraries offer home pages to give you remote access to their holdings via Internet connections, the library building itself continues to be a vital place for all research. One key advantage of going to the library is your chance to consult with librarians. They trained for their profession by learning how to advise students and other researchers about using library resources to greatest advantage. Never hesitate to ask questions about how to proceed or where to find a resource.

Catalogues list sources—usually books—that the library owns (see 32d). **Indexes** list articles in periodicals; each index covers a specific topic area (see 32e). Catalogues and indexes exist mainly in electronic format; less commonly, some catalogues and indexes are still in print format. **Databases** always exist electronically (see 32c.1). They consist of one or more indexes and contain extensive lists of articles, reports, and books. You can access and search electronic catalogues, indexes, and databases from computers in the library or by connecting to the library online. You can also subscribe to databases, but this can be expensive. At most colleges and universities, your tuition pays for access to online library resources, so take advantage of them.

If you're accessing a database by connecting to the library online, you need to use a **browser,** a software program that gives you access to the Web and the search engines located there. Netscape Navigator® and Microsoft Internet Explorer™ are the two most frequently used browsers.

32c.1 Using databases

Each entry in a database contains bibliographic information, including a title, author, date of publication, and publisher (in the case of books or reports) or periodical (in the case of articles). The entry might also provide an abstract, or summary, of the material. Once you locate an entry that seems promising, you might need to read a print copy of the source. Some databases provide the full texts of the articles they cite. Other databases allow you to purchase full copies of the sources you find. If you're on a tight budget, try to purchase only what looks truly useful. You can request materials that are not in your library through interlibrary loan (32g).

Sources that you identify through scholarly databases are almost always more reliable and appropriate than sources you find through simply browsing the World Wide Web. Some scholarly research is available from World Wide Web sites, while other research resides at Internet sites not necessarily part of the Web. The reliability of scholarly databases stems from their origins: Only experts and professionals who recognize works of merit compile them.

The best way to access a database at your school's library is to visit the library's Web site. The home page of an academic library shows the resources available through that Web site. More might be available at the library building itself. Sections 32d and 32e explain how to use the catalogue to find books and periodicals (newspapers, magazines, and journals). Most academic libraries subscribe to one or more database services, such as EBSCO, FirstSearch, and IBIS. Because the institution pays for these services, you don't have to, but you'll need an ID or password to use them. Commonly, your student number serves as your ID, but check with a librarian to see what's required at your school.

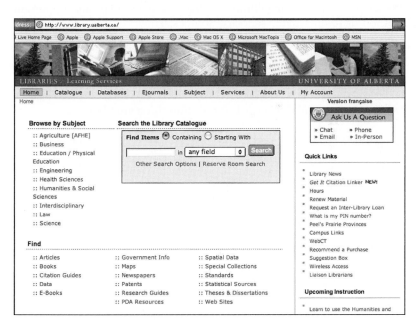

Home page of a university library

EXERCISE 32-1

Working either individually or as part of a group, access your library's Web site. You may do this either by going to the library itself or by connecting to the library online. List all of the types of information available. In particular, list the indexes and databases you can search and the subject areas each one covers. Note whether any of the databases have full-text versions of articles. Note if the library's Web site has any online "help" features or "search suggestions."

32c.2 Searching the World Wide Web

The **World Wide Web** is organized around pages (called *Web pages*) that are linked together electronically. A group of pages that an individual or organization has created and linked together is called a **Web site.** The main page in a Web site (called the *home page*) acts as a table of contents. Although the Web contains billions of pages, including a great many books and periodical articles, only a fraction of these scholarly and literary sources are available on the Web without subscribing or paying a fee. Therefore, searching library databases remains your most important method of finding many scholarly sources. However, the principles for searching the World Wide Web are much like those for searching databases (32c.1). You start with a broad subject and narrow it to arrive at a suitable topic for an academic research paper.

Once you use a browser to get on the Web, you can search for sites by using a SEARCH ENGINE (32c.3) or by typing an address (called a **URL,** for Universal Resource Locator) into the search box.

◎ **ALERT:** When you read, write, or type a URL in your own writing, the Modern Language Association (MLA) tells you to surround it with angle brackets. For example, <http://www.pearsoned.ca/troyka> is the URL for my publisher's Web site about my books, including this handbook. The brackets separate a URL from sentence punctuation so that no one mistakes it as part of the URL. However, never use angle brackets when you type a URL in the locator box at the top of your computer screen. ◎

32c.3 Using search engines

Search engines are programs designed to hunt the World Wide Web and Internet files for sources on specific topics that you identify by using keywords. When you use a search engine, you generally can access materials in one of two ways: through keyword searches (32c.4) and through subject directories (32c.5). Box 134 lists some commonly used search engines. Shown below it is the directory page of the Canadian version of Google, a search engine.

BOX 134   SUMMARY

Addresses for some search engines

AltaVista	\<http://altavista.com\>
Excite	\<http://www.excite.com\>
Lycos	\<http://www.lycos.ca\>
Yahoo!	\<http://ca.yahoo.com\>
Ask Jeeves	\<http://www.ask.com\>
Google	\<http://www.google.ca\>
Metacrawler	\<http://www.metacrawler.com\>
Dogpile	\<http://www.dogpile.com\>
HotBot	\<http://www.hotbot.com\>
AlltheWeb	\<http://www.alltheweb.com\>

Directory page of Google.ca, showing search categories

EXERCISE 32-2

Use at least three different search engines to search online for the same topic. List the different results for each search engine, and also note the strengths and weaknesses of each. (Pay attention to usefulness, ease of use, and so on.) Write a brief report on your findings. You may wish to try this exercise with a second topic before drawing your conclusions.

32c.4 Using keywords

When searching for sources online or in library databases, **keywords,** also called *descriptors* or *identifiers,* are your lifeline to success. Keywords are the main words in a source's title or the words that the author or editor has identified as central to that source. Without keywords, you'd have no way to access sources listed in online or electronic database book catalogues and periodical indexes. Similarly, to find information on the World Wide Web or on the Internet, keywords are essential. Because Web search engines, such as Yahoo, often look for any occurrence of a word in the title or body of a page, you need to take particular care with keyword searches on the Web.

When you use keywords to search for Web sources, chances are you'll come up with a large or even overwhelming number of sources. Much of what turns up won't be relevant to your topic. As a result, you need to figure out which items on the list might be useful. Whenever possible, narrow your list of keywords by using BOOLEAN EXPRESSIONS. Your other alternative is to use a "try and see" approach. Whichever approach you use, always keep a record of poor and good keywords for your TOPIC in your research log so that you'll remember which keywords do and do not work well for you on each topic. This process might seem tedious at times, but don't get discouraged. If you're stumped, try asking a friend who's experienced with online searches or a research librarian for help.

As you become more adept at using keywords, your searches will become more directed and less time-consuming. The two main ways to make keyword searches more efficient are using guided searches and using Boolean expressions.

Using guided searches

Using **guided searches** means that you search a database or search engine by answering prompts provided, usually by filling in a form on the screen. Guided searches often allow you to select a range of dates of publication (for example, after 2002 or between 1990 and 1995) and to specify only a certain language or a certain format (such as books). Shown next is an example of a search for sources that have *artificial intelligence* in their titles, that use *computers* as another keyword, but that are not about *robots.*

Guided keyword search

Using Boolean expressions

Using **Boolean expressions** means that you search a database or search engine by using keyword combinations that narrow and refine your search. To combine keywords, you use the words *AND, OR, NOT,* and *NEAR* or the symbols that represent those words. Boolean expressions, generally placed between keywords, instruct the search engine to list only those Web sites in which your keywords appear in certain combinations and to ignore others. Other commands similarly help you go directly to the sources you most need.

Box 135 explains ways to search with keywords more effectively, using the subject of artificial intelligence as an example. Simply typing the words *intelligence computers emotions* would yield pages that include any of these words—and not necessarily in that order. Imagine

491

BOX 135   SUMMARY

Refining keyword searches

AND or the + ("plus") symbol: Narrows the focus of your search to pages that contain both keywords. If you want to find information on the role of emotions in artificial intelligence, try the expression *artificial AND intelligence AND emotions.* Some search engines, such as Google.com, don't require the word *AND* between terms because they assume that two or more terms are always connected by *AND.* When in doubt, definitely use *AND.*

NOT or the – ("minus") symbol: Narrows a search by excluding texts containing the specified word or phrase. If you want to eliminate robots from your search, type *artificial AND intelligence AND emotions NOT robots.*

OR: Expands a search's boundaries by including more than one keyword. If you want to expand your search to include sources about artificial intelligence in either computers or robots, try the expression *artificial AND intelligence AND emotions AND computers OR robots.* You'll get pages mentioning artificial intelligence and emotions only if they mention computers or robots.

NEAR: Indicates that the keywords may be found close or next to each other. However, depending on the search engine, *NEAR* produces hits that are found only in the same sentence or on the same Web site.

( ): These are parentheses that group two or more expressions together. For example, *(artificial intelligence AND emotions) AND (Turing Test OR Chinese Room)* would find documents about artificial intelligence and emotions along with either the Turing Test or the Chinese Room Test. (Chandra Johnson's research paper in section 34e.2 explains that these are two tests for judging whether people can regard a computer as "intelligent.")

" ": These are quotation marks that direct a search engine to match your exact word order on a Web page. For example, a search for *"robots that think"* will find pages that contain the exact phrase *robots that think.* However, it won't return pages with the phrase *thinking robots.* Also, if you search for *James Joyce* without using quotation marks, most engines will return all pages containing the words *James* and *Joyce* anywhere in the document; however, a search using *"James Joyce"* brings you closer to finding Web sites about the Irish writer.

→

Refining keyword searches (*continued*)

*: The asterisk functions as a wildcard in some search engines. It allows you to look for sites by listing only the first few letters of a keyword. This approach, known as a *truncated search,* is helpful when a term comes in varying forms. For example, a Yahoo search for *cogni** would turn up directory entries for both *cognitive* and *cognition.* You can also direct the search engine to look for variants of a keyword by using the wildcard symbol * in place of either the word ending or some of the letters in the word. For example, a truncated search for *wom*n* would return hits for *woman* and *women.* Please note that not all search engines allow wildcarding; Google.ca, for example, does not. A few search engines use specialized symbols such as *?* or *:* instead of the * for wildcarding.

the staggeringly long list of pages you'd get for the word *computers* alone, and then almost triple that number when you include the two other seemingly unrelated words in your list. In contrast, note the huge amount of weeding out that the Boolean expressions allow.

The examples in Box 135 are not all-inclusive. Always review the database's or search engine's own search tips, as engines differ in how they handle expressions and formats. For example, some search engines are "case sensitive," which means that they look for keywords exactly as you type them, including capitals and lowercase letters. To be sure, check the "Help" box or the "Search Tips" feature of any database or search engine you use. For virtually all search engines, a "Help" button or link appears on the search engine's home page.

To conduct a keyword search, type a word or group of words in the search box on the opening page of the search engine, and click on the "Search" or "Enter" button. The engine scans for your word(s) in Web pages, and then lists sites that contain them. Because the Web has billions of pages, a search on even a moderately common topic may produce thousands of **hits**—sites listed or visited in a search. Not every hit will be what you are looking for. If a search engine finds thousands of hits for your keyword, do not give up. Instead, try more specific keywords, use a guided or "advanced" search feature, or use the strategies listed in Box 135 for refining a keyword search.

EXERCISE 32-3

Use a search engine of your choice to search for sources on "artificial intelligence." For each option below, record how many hits occur.

1. Enter the word *artificial.*
2. Enter the word *intelligence.*
3. Enter the phrase *artificial AND intelligence.*
4. Enter the phrase *"artificial intelligence"* (in quotation marks).
5. Enter the search phrase *"artificial intelligence" computers emotions.*
6. Explore adding other words to your search phrase or using Boolean expressions (Box 135).
7. Repeat this exercise by searching for another topic that interests you.

32c.5 Using subject directories

Subject directories included on most search engines' home pages provide a good alternative to keyword searches. These directories are lists of topics (Education, Computing, Entertainment, and so on) or resources and services (Shopping, Travel, and so on), with links to Web sites on those topics and resources. Most search engines' home pages have one or more subject directories.

Clicking on a general category within a subject directory will take you to lists of increasingly specific categories. Eventually, you will get a list of Web pages on the most specific subtopic you select. These search engines also allow you to click on a category and enter keywords for a search. For example, suppose that you are searching for information on *artificial intelligence.* You would first go to the general directory. There you would find the category *computer science,* and within *computer science* you would find a link to *artificial intelligence,* a page that lists several additional categories and a large number of sources.

Several subject directories exist independently of search engines (see Box 134 in 32c.3). Box 136 lists the Internet addresses of some directories. One useful directory is the *Librarians' Index to the Internet* (*LII*). To use the *Librarians' Index,* type its URL, <http://lii.org>, in the browser's search box. The first screen you see is the lii.org home page. You'll see a number of broad topic areas, and when you click on one of them, you'll see a number of subtopics. As you refine your search, you'll eventually come to specific pages. One advantage of the *Librarians' Index* is that professional librarians have gathered the pages.

Click on "Computer Science"

Click on "Artificial Intelligence"

Sources on "Artificial Intelligence"

Subject directory search for "artificial intelligence"

BOX 136 SUMMARY

Addresses for subject directories

Educators' Reference Desk (contains ERIC)	< http://www.eduref.org>
Canadian Information by Subject	< http://www.collectionscanada.ca/ caninfo/ecaninfo.htm>
Infomine	< http://infomine.ucr.edu>
Internet Public Library	< http://www.ipl.org>
Librarians' Index to the Internet	< http://lii.org>
Library of Congress	< http://lcweb.loc.gov>
Search Canada	< http://www.searchcanada.ca>
UBC Library Subject Guides	< http://www.library.ubc.ca/ home/subjects>
U of T Internet Resources, by Subject	< http://www.utoronto.ca/ subjects.html>
Refdesk.com	< http://www.refdesk.com>

Box 137 summarizes the information in this section by providing some general guidelines for using search engines and directories with keywords.

BOX 137 SUMMARY

Tips on using search engines and directories

■ Use keyword searches only when you have a very specific, narrow topic with unique keywords. If you enter a general topic in most search engines, you will be overwhelmed with thousands of returns. If this happens, switch to a subject directory or see if using additional keywords or Boolean expressions sufficiently restricts the number of hits.

■ Most search engines attempt to search as much of the Web as possible. But because the World Wide Web is vast and unorganized, different search engines will give different results for the same search. Try using more than one search engine, or use a **metasearch engine,** one which searches several search engines at once (such as Dogpile.com), or Google.com, which searches a ranked index of billions of URLs.

■ Always check the "Help" screen for the search engine you use. As with the rest of the Web, search engines add or change features frequently.

→

> ## Tips on using search engines and directories (*continued*)
>
> ■ Specify that the search engine list results by "ranking." If you do not, the search results will be returned in random order, and the most important source may be last.
>
> ■ If possible, limit the date range. For example, you can often ask to see only pages that were updated in the past six months or one year.
>
> ■ When you find a useful site, go to the toolbar at the top of the screen and click on "Bookmark" (or "Favorites") and then click on "Add." Doing so allows you to return to a good source easily by opening "Bookmarks" or "Favorites" and double-clicking on the address.
>
> ■ Use the "History" or "Go" function to track the sites you visit, in case you want to revisit one you previously thought was not helpful. You can also move a site from "History" to "Bookmark."

32d How do I find books?

A library's **book catalogue,** which lists its holdings (its entire collection), exists as a computer database in almost every modern library. You can find a book by searching by **author,** by **title,** by **subject,** and by KEYWORD. When you search the book catalogue, some computer programs ask which of these four categories you would like to search. For instance, try searching the University of Alberta Libraries online.

Suppose you want to find a book by Naomi Klein, but you don't know its title. You can search the online catalogue for books by this author. Click on "Author" below the catalogue search window on the computer screen. In the catalogue search window, you type in "klein, naomi." (Usually you enter the last name first, but check to see how your library's system works.) If the library owns any books by Naomi Klein, the catalogue will show you their titles and other information. Among the books you might find is *No Logo: Taking Aim at the Brand Bullies* (Toronto: Knopf Canada, 2000). Or suppose you know this title, and want to see if the library owns the book. Click on "Title" (which is the default choice) below the catalogue search window and type in "no logo." Usually you do not need to include the full title or words like *the* or *a.*

Often you don't know either an author's name or a book's title. Instead, you have a research topic and need to find sources. In this case you need to search by subject, using the terms listed in the *Library of Congress Subject Headings* (*LCSH*) or another subject directory. The *LCSH* is a multivolume catalogue available in the reference section of your library. It lists only subject headings, organized from most general to most narrow. If you are researching a Canadian topic, consult the National Library of Canada's *Canadian Subject Headings* (*CSH*) at < http://www.collectionscanada.ca/csh/index_e.html>. Suppose you are researching the topic "brand name products—public opinion." If you enter that term in the space for subject searches, *No Logo: Taking Aim at the Brand Bullies* by Naomi Klein will be listed—if your library owns that book. Finally, you may wish to search by keyword. You could find Klein's book using the keywords "brand name," "logo," and so on.

An entry in the library's book catalogue contains a great deal of useful information: a book's title, author, publisher, date and place of publication, and length, along with its location in the library. A full record catalogue entry (a complete set of information about the source rather than a brief listing that may have only author, title, and call number) lists additional subjects covered in that book. The list of additional subjects can provide valuable clues for further searching.

Some libraries allow you to print out this information, send it to your e-mail account, or download it to a disk. Whether you choose one of these options or copy the information yourself directly into your WORKING BIBLIOGRAPHY, it is crucial to record the **call number** exactly as it appears, with all numbers, letters, and decimal points. The call number tells where the book is located in the library's stacks (storage shelves). If you're researching in a library with *open stacks* (that is, you can go where books are shelved), the call number leads you to the area in the library where all books on the same subject can be found. Simply looking at what's on the shelves may yield useful sources. Keep in mind that in browsing the stacks, however, you're missing sources that other students likely have checked out or that are "on hold" at the library's reserve desk. The book catalogue generally will contain information about whether a book is checked out or on reserve.

A call number is especially crucial in a library or special collection with *closed stacks* (that is, a library where you fill in a call slip, hand it in at the call desk, and wait for the book to arrive). Such libraries don't permit you to browse the stacks, so you have to rely entirely on the book catalogue. If you fill in the wrong number or an incomplete number, your wait will be in vain.

32e How do I find periodicals?

Periodicals are magazines and journals published at set intervals during the year. To use periodicals efficiently, consult indexes to periodicals. These indexes allow you to search by subject and author. Most exist as online databases, which are updated frequently. Some indexes are published on CD-ROMs, and a few are published only in print.

Using indexes

Your library's home page generally provides different ways to access various indexes. One example is shown in the university library home page that appeared earlier in this chapter. Users who choose one of the subject areas under "Browse by Subject" will access an alphabetical list of databases and other resources in that area, classified by topic, format, and medium. Choosing one of the categories under "Find" on the same home page directs users to sources classified as articles, books, and so forth. It's important to choose the right index for your search, because the wrong index may miss some of the best sources for your paper. The following paragraphs and boxes describe the contents of commonly used indexes.

Most indexes exist in electronic format. However, to use them you need a paid subscription. Fortunately, your library likely subscribes to several of the indexes that you'll need, and you can access them through the library's Web site. The URL for accessing each index online will vary from one college or university to the next.

General indexes to periodicals list articles in journals, magazines, and newspapers. Large libraries have many general indexes. Find out how to log on by consulting the librarian. Among them are these:

■ *The Readers' Guide to Periodical Literature* (online at *Readers' Guide Abstracts*) is the best-known index, though its uses are limited for postsecondary-level research because it doesn't include scholarly journals. Some libraries still have the print volumes. This index includes over two hundred magazines and journals for general readers. Nevertheless, you can try it to find topics, get a broad overview, and narrow a subject. Chandra Johnson used this guide in the initial stages of her student research paper, shown in 34e.2.

■ *Periodical Abstracts* indexes general and academic journals in business, current affairs, psychology, religion, and many other areas.

■ *NewsBank* covers over four hundred U.S. newspapers. It has full-text coverage from 1993 on. NewsBank also offers reproductions of articles from 1980 to 1992, but they are stored on microfiche, not online, in some libraries.

For research in Canadian periodicals, see *A Bibliography of Canadian Bibliographies, A Guide to Basic Reference Materials for Canadian Libraries, Canadian Newspaper Index,* and *Canadian Periodical Index.* Major newspapers have online archives that include articles from recent years, and sometimes from decades long past.

Specialized indexes are more appropriate than general indexes for most postsecondary-level research. Specialized indexes list articles in journals published by and for expert, academic, or professional readers. Many specialized indexes include the abstract, or summary, that is

BOX 138   SUMMARY

Examples of specialized indexes

Art Abstracts
Business Abstracts
Education Full Text
General Science Abstracts
Humanities Index
*MLA International Bibliography of Books and Articles in the Modern
   Languages and Literatures*
Music Index Online
PsycINFO
Social Sciences Abstracts

printed at the beginning of each scholarly article. Box 138 provides examples of specialized indexes.

You search periodical indexes by using KEYWORDS. Shown here are three screens from a keyword search of PsycINFO for *artificial intelligence*. Chandra Johnson, whose research paper appears in section 34e.2, consulted this source in her research.

Locating the articles themselves

Periodical indexes help you locate the titles of specific articles on your topic. Once you have the listing, though, how do you get your hands on the article itself? Sometimes you can find an online version of the article. Frequently, however, you need to find a paper copy of the periodical.

To do this, you begin by checking what periodicals your school's library lists in its online catalogues. This list might be in the library's catalogue, or the list might be available separately; ask how your library lists periodicals. In either case, search for the periodical name you want, not for the article's author or title. If your library subscribes to that periodical, you use its call number to find its location in the library. You then need to find the specific article you want by looking for the issue in which the article you're looking for is printed.

Few libraries subscribe to all the periodicals listed in specialized indexes. Although you may not be able to locate every periodical and article you find listed in the indexes, the interlibrary loan system (generally free of charge) or document delivery (generally at a small cost to the student) allows you to request that your library get it from another library (32g).

Keyword search

Partial search result

One article selected
from database

**Three screens from a search of the PsycINFO database for sources on
"artificial intelligence"**

32f How do I use reference works?

Reference works include encyclopedias, almanacs, yearbooks, fact books, atlases, dictionaries, biographical reference works, and bibliographies. Some references are *general,* providing information on a vast number of subjects, but without any depth. Others are *specialized,* providing information on selected topics, often for more expert or professional audiences.

32f.1 General reference works

Reference works are the starting point for many researchers—but they're no more than a starting point. **General reference works** contain basic information and are therefore insufficient for academic research. Still, because they can give you an overall picture, they're one of the best places to find useful KEYWORDS for subject headings and online catalogue searches. In addition, general reference works are excellent sources for finding examples and verifying facts. Most widely used reference works are available in electronic versions, either on CD-ROMs or, more commonly, online. Check your library's Web site to see if the reference work you want is available online through a subscription or licence the library has purchased. Alternatively, you can search the Web by entering the work's name to see if it is available there. (For example, *Encyclopaedia Britannica* is at <http://www.britannica.com>.) Be aware that often you have to pay a fee for works you don't access through the library.

General encyclopedias

Articles in multivolume general encyclopedias, such as the *Encyclopaedia Britannica*, summarize information on a wide variety of subjects. The articles can give you helpful background information and the names of major figures and experts in the field, and many end with a brief bibliography of major works on the subject. General encyclopedias aren't the place to look for information on recent events or current research, although sometimes they cover a field's ongoing controversies up until the date that the reference was published.

The Canadian Encyclopedia and *Colombo's Canadian References*, an encyclopedic dictionary, are important sources of information on Canadian topics.

To locate information in an encyclopedia, start with the index volume. (If you are using an online version, type the keywords into the search screen.) An index volume gives you the volume number or letter and the page numbers for your topic. The letters *bib* at the end of an index entry mean that the article contains a bibliography, which makes the entry especially worth checking for the additional sources it can lead you to. If you can't find what you are looking for, try alternative subject headings or KEYWORDS.

Almanacs, yearbooks, fact books

Almanacs, yearbooks, and fact books are huge compilations of facts in many subject areas. They're often available both in print and online. They're excellent for verifying information from other sources and, in some cases, for finding supporting facts and figures on the subject you're investigating. *The Canadian Global Almanac* and *The World Almanac and Book of Facts* present capsule accounts of a year's events along with data on government, politics, economics, science and technology, sports, and many other topics. *Facts on File,* which is indexed online by LexisNexis®, covers world events in a weekly digest and an annual one-volume yearbook.

Sources of Canadian information include *Canada Year Book, Canadian Almanac and Directory,* and *Canadian News Facts.* The annual *Statistical Abstract of the United States,* the international *Demographic Yearbook,* and the *United Nations Statistical Yearbook* carry a wealth of data.

Atlases and gazetteers

Atlases contain maps of our planet's continents, seas, and skies. Gazetteers provide comprehensive geographical information on topography, climates, populations, migrations, natural resources, crops, and so on. Examples include *The Atlas of Canada, Canada Gazetteer Atlas,* the *Times Atlas of the World,* and *The Columbia Gazetteer of the World.*

Dictionaries

Dictionaries define words and terms. In addition to general dictionaries, specialized dictionaries exist in many academic disciplines to define words and phrases specific to a field (21e).

Biographical reference works

Biographical reference books give brief factual information about famous people—their accomplishments along with pertinent events and dates in their lives. Biographical references include the *Who's Who* series (including *Canadian Who's Who*), *The Dictionary of Canadian Biography,* and many others. Specialized biographical references in various fields are also available.

Bibliographies

Bibliographies list books, articles, documents, films, and other resources and provide publication information so that you can find those sources. Some bibliographies are comprehensive and list sources on a wide range of topics. Others list only sources on a particular subject. Specialized bibliographies can be very helpful in your research process. Annotated or critical bibliographies describe and evaluate the works that they list. These resources are increasingly available online but require you either to access them through a library's paid subscription service or to pay a fee each time you use them.

32f.2 Specialized reference works

Specialized reference works, which provide more authoritative and specific information than general reference works, are usually appropriate for postsecondary-level research. They can be a valuable introduction to the controversies and KEYWORDS in a subject area. In particular, finding author's names in such books can help you begin to accumulate a list of credible authors.

Here are a few examples of specialized references:

Encyclopedia of Banking and Finance
Handbook of Modern Marketing
New Grove Dictionary of Music and Musicians
Oxford Companion to Art
Dictionary of Canadian Biography
An Encyclopedia of World History
New Cambridge Modern History
A Dictionary of Literary Terms
Oxford Companion to Canadian Literature
Encyclopedia of Philosophy
Encyclopedia of Religion
Political Science Bibliographies
Political Handbook and Atlas of the World
The Canadian Annual Review of Politics and Public Affairs
Encyclopedia of Chemistry
Encyclopedia of the Biological Sciences
Encyclopedia of Psychology
International Encyclopedia of Film
Oxford Companion to the Theatre

Hundreds of highly specific one-volume works are not listed here. Check what specialized reference books your library has available that might help you in your search.

32g What if my library doesn't have a source I need?

Almost no library owns every book on every topic or subscribes to every periodical. However, many libraries are connected electronically to other libraries' catalogues, giving you access to additional holdings. The Canadian Library Gateway, a project of Library and Archives Canada <http://www.collectionscanada.ca/index_e.html>, coordinates an interlibrary loan system linking the catalogues of university and other large libraries throughout the country. The Internet gives you access to the catalogues of many large libraries worldwide. Librarians can request materials from other libraries—including articles you have found in a periodical index—through interlibrary loan, which is generally free of charge. Alternatively, your school may have a different document delivery system (generally at some cost to you).

32h How do I find government documents?

Canadian government publications are available in astounding variety. You can find information on laws, regulations, populations, weather patterns, agriculture, national parks, education, and health, and many other topics.

A federal government Web site known as the Canada Site <http://www.canada.gc.ca/> is an excellent starting point for online research into current Canadian government publications. It provides direct access to federal departments, boards, and agencies and their publications, as well as to public records, including parliamentary debates and hearings, and to databases. You can also follow its links to provincial and territorial government sites. Statistics Canada <http://www.statcan.ca/> collects and analyzes a wide range of data.

32i What is field research?

Field research is primary research in that it involves going into real-life situations to observe, survey, interview, or be part of some activity first-hand. A field researcher might, for example, go to a factory, a lecture, a daycare centre, or a mall—anywhere that people are engaged in their everyday activities. A field researcher might also conduct interviews of experts and other identified individuals. Because field research yields original data, you can consider it a PRIMARY SOURCE.

Conducting field research takes advance planning. Be sure to allow time to gather the data you want, ANALYZE it, and then SYNTHESIZE it with other sources and with your own knowledge and experience. In general, the activity of field research makes selective notetaking difficult. Therefore, go over your notes right after your research session, while your memory is fresh, and highlight major categories of information. Also, fill in any details you might not have written down. What doesn't seem useful one day might become important later.

Field research many times involves events that can't be revisited. Therefore, record as much information as possible during your research and decide afterward what information you can use. If conditions make taking notes impossible (for example, a dark performance hall), the instant you have an opportunity, find a quiet place and write down notes as fully as you can.

DOCUMENTATION is as important for field research as it is for all other research. Interviews and some performances involve another person's words, concepts, and insights. To document correctly, use the guidelines in Chapter 33 for documenting quotations, paraphrases, and summaries. If you include your own work (creating an original questionnaire, for example), say that it's yours in your paper and list it, as you would any source, in the WORKS CITED (MLA style) or REFERENCES (APA style) at the end of your paper.

Observing and surveying

To observe effectively, you must avoid injecting yourself into the situation. You should try to remain objective so that you can see things clearly. A report from someone with a bias in one direction or another makes the material useless. For observations of behaviour (for example, the audience at a sporting event or elementary school children at play during recess), you can take notes during the activity. Permission to videotape instead of taking notes is hard to get because of privacy concerns.

If you intend to go to an event such as a concert or a play, buy your tickets immediately and be ready with alternative dates if you can't get your first choice. Similarly, if you intend to visit a museum, go as soon as possible so that you can return as needed.

If you want to survey a group of people on an issue, allow time to write, reflect on, and revise a questionnaire. Provide time to test the questionnaire on a few people and revise ineffective or ambiguous questions. For detailed information on the mechanics of creating a questionnaire, see Box 173 in 40a.

Interviewing an expert

An expert can offer valuable information, a new point of view, and first-hand facts, statistics, and examples. Probably the best place to start is with the faculty at your college or university. Your teachers are also scholars and researchers who have expertise in many areas. They may suggest good print and online sources, as well as other experts to contact. Indeed, your family and friends might qualify as experts, if they have been involved in any way with an issue you are researching.

Make every attempt to conduct interviews in person so that you can observe body language and facial expressions as you talk. However, if distance is a problem, you can conduct interviews over the phone or online.

To interview someone in a large corporation or an institution (an insurance company or a hospital, for example), your best approach is to contact the public relations office or customer service department. Professional organizations often have special staff to respond to researchers. Also, public officials are sometimes available for interviews, and many government offices have full-time representatives to provide information to the public.

Perhaps even more than for other kinds of field research, you definitely need to plan far ahead for interviews. It takes time to set up an appointment so that you can fit your research needs into other people's schedules. Part of planning is having a solid knowledge of your topic—you don't want to waste others' time or try their patience by asking for information you should have gathered before the interview. Don't expect your interview to substitute for research you should do yourself.

Although you might not always be granted the interviews you seek, you can assume that many people remember their own experiences doing academic research and will be willing to help. Box 139 provides specific suggestions for interviewing an expert.

BOX 139   CHECKLIST

 Taking notes during interviews

- Rehearse asking your questions without reading them (perhaps highlight key terms). Looking your interviewee in the eye as you ask questions is invaluable for establishing ease and trust. If you are interviewing on the telephone, be organized and precise.
- Create a shortcut symbol or letter for key terms you expect to hear during the interview. This cuts down on the time needed to look away from the interviewee.
- Take careful notes, listening especially for key names, books, or other print or online sources.
- Avoid using a tiny notebook or small sheets of paper. Standard-size paper (8½ by 11 inches) allows you sufficient room to write without having to turn pages often.
- Bring extra pens (in case one runs out of ink) or pencils (in case one breaks).
- Never depend on tape recording an interview. People have become very reluctant to permit anyone to record them. If you want to ask permission in advance when you schedule the interview, or if you want to ask in person when you arrive for the interview, never imply that recording is essential to you or the research. (Indeed, increasingly reports have reached instructors that when tape recording is mentioned, the interviewee cancels the appointment on the spot.)
- If conditions make notetaking impossible, write detailed notes as soon afterward as you possibly can. In all cases, go over and fill in your notes while your memory is fresh so you can highlight major categories of information.

32j   How do I evaluate sources?

Finding a source is only part of your effort. Your next step is to evaluate the quality of each source you find. First, decide whether the information in the source relates to your topic in more than a vague, general sense. Ask how a source might help you answer your research question (31c). Finally, using the criteria in Box 140, evaluate each source with a cold, critical eye.

BOX 140   SUMMARY

Evaluating sources

1. **Is the source authoritative?** Generally, encyclopedias, textbooks, and academic journals are authoritative. Books published by university presses and by publishers that specialize in scholarly books are also trustworthy. Material published in newspapers, in general-readership magazines, and by large commercial publishers may be reliable, but you want to apply the other criteria in this list with special care, cross-checking names and facts whenever possible. If the same information appears in different sources, it is likely to be reliable. Web sites maintained by professional organizations are often authoritative.

2. **Is the author an expert?** Biographical material in the article or book may tell you if the author is an expert on the topic. Look up the author's expertise in a biographical dictionary. Alternatively, enter the author's name in an Internet search engine. Look to see if the author has a degree in this field and whether he or she is affiliated with a reliable institution. Also, if an author is often cited by professionals in the field and published in journals, he or she is probably considered an expert.

3. **Is the source current?** Check the publication date. Research is ongoing in most fields, and information is often modified or replaced by new findings. Check databases and online subject directories to see if newer sources are available.

4. **Does the source support its information sufficiently?** Are its assertions or claims supported with sufficient evidence? If the author expresses a point of view but offers little evidence to back up that position or resorts to logical fallacies, reject the source. Use wise judgment, and don't take chances.

5. **Is the author's tone balanced?** Use your critical thinking skills when you evaluate a source (see Chapter 5). If the TONE is unbiased and the reasoning is logical, the source is probably useful.

The unregulated nature of the Web creates special responsibilities for online researchers. You need to evaluate Web sources particularly carefully for two reasons. First, since anyone can post anything on the Web, some sources you find may very well be plagiarized. Second, many sources on the Web have been written by individuals posing as experts and giving false or misleading information.

You are always accountable for the sources you choose. The criteria in Box 140 can help you separate the sources you want to look at more closely from those not likely to be reputable. Most sites also contain material that will help you assess their credibility, such as a bibliography, links to the author or editor, or a description of the sponsoring organization. Discard sites that do not contain such verifying information, however useful they may seem. To err on the side of caution is far better than to use a corrupt source.

An important question to ask about any Web site is why the information exists and why it was put on the Internet. Be sure to question the motives of the site's author, especially if you are being asked to take a specific action. Box 141 summarizes the questions to ask about online sites.

BOX 141   SUMMARY

 Judging the reliability of an online site

Reliable sites are

- **From educational, not-for-profit, or government organizations.** One sign is an Internet address ending in *.edu, .ac, .org, .gc,* or *.gov.* However, if any of these organizations fail to list their sources, don't use them. After all, many colleges and universities now host student Web sites, whose addresses end identically to the school's address.

- **From expert authors.** Experts have degrees or credentials in their field that you can check. See if their names appear in other reliable sources, in bibliographies on your topic, or in reference books in an academic library. Check whether the site's author gives an e-mail address for questions or comments.

- **From reliable print sources.** Online versions of major newspapers, magazines, journals, and other publications that are produced by the publisher are just as reliable as the print versions.

- **Well supported with evidence and presented in a balanced, unbiased fashion.**

- **Current or recently updated.**

Questionable sites are

- **From commercial organizations advertising a product (*.com*); Web sites that are advertisements or personal pages; junk mail.** These sites may or may not list sources. If they fail to, don't use them. If they do, check that the sources are legitimate, not a front for the commercial enterprise.

- **From anonymous authors or authors without identifiable credentials.** Chat rooms, Usenet, discussion groups, bulletin boards, and similar networks are questionable because they don't give credentials or other qualifying information.

→

> ## Judging the reliability of an online site (*continued*)
>
> ■ **Supported by or composed of second-hand excerpts and quotations.** Materials that appear on a site that is not the official site of the publisher may be edited in a biased or misleading manner. Such sources may be incomplete and inaccurate.
> ■ **Unsupported or biased.** These sites carry declarations and assertions that have little or no supporting evidence.
> ■ **Old** or from a Web site that hasn't been updated in a year or more.

Most sites also contain material that will help you assess their credibility, such as a bibliography or links to the author or editor. Sites that do not contain such verifying information should be discarded, however useful they may seem. It is far better to err on the side of caution than to use a plagiarized source. Box 142 gives you details on applying these general guidelines to individual online sources.

BOX 142   SUMMARY

Evaluating each online source

Evaluating Authority

1. Is an author named? Are credentials listed for the author? (Look for an academic degree, an e-mail address at an academic or other institution, a credentials page, a list of publications. The last part of an e-mail address can be informative: *.edu* indicates a U.S. educational site; *.gc* and *.gov* indicate government sites; and *.com* indicates a commercial or business site.) Be careful: Many colleges and universities now host student Web sites with addresses containing the same endings as regular academic sites.
2. Is the author recognized as an authority in reputable print sources? Is the author cited in any bibliographies found in print sources?
3. Do you recognize the author as an authority from other research on your topic? Is the site cross-referenced to other credible and authoritative sites?

→

Evaluating each online source (*continued*)

Evaluating Reliability

4. Do you detect from the language or layout of information either bias or an unbalanced presentation?

5. Ask, Why does the information exist? Who gains from it? Why was it written? Why was it put on the Internet?

6. Are you asked to take action of any kind? If yes, don't use the source unless you're sure the site isn't trying to manipulate you toward its bias. For example, the World Wildlife Fund can ask for contributions and still maintain a Web site that contains reliable information. Conversely, a hate group can't be trusted to be objective.

7. Is the material outdated? Is the date recent, or was the last update recent?

8. Does the author give an e-mail address for questions or comments?

Evaluating Value

9. Is the information well supported with evidence? Or do the authors express points of view without backing up their position with solid evidence?

10. Remember to read online sources using reflective reading (5c and 5d) and reasoning (5a and 5b). Is the TONE unbiased (5c.2 and 21g) and the reasoning logical (5i and 5j)?

Chapter 33

Using Sources and Avoiding Plagiarism

33a How do I use sources well?

Now's the time to turn from researching to writing your research paper. When you use SOURCES well, your chances of writing a successful research paper increase greatly. In your work so far, you've built a solid foundation by choosing a research-suitable TOPIC, one that's neither too general nor too narrow (31b); formulating a RESEARCH QUESTION (31c); establishing a search strategy for finding sources to answer that question (32b); locating sources that apply to your particular treatment of the topic (32c–32h); writing a WORKING BIBLIOGRAPHY of what you've found (31i); evaluating each source carefully to make sure it's reliable and trustworthy (32j); and taking CONTENT NOTES on the sources that have passed your careful evaluation (31j).

Now you're ready to use CRITICAL THINKING to pull together a SYNTHESIS of your sources combined with your own thinking about the topic. To synthesize well, you think through the information gathered from your sources by

- Mastering the information from each source
- Finding relationships among the sources' information
- Adding your own thinking to the mix

Your written synthesis is your research paper. To write effectively, you organize your paper around a logical sequence based on the main points in your synthesis. Further, you support each main point and important subpoint with specific ideas or words drawn from your sources to show that your claims originate with authorities on your topic.

As you marshal your support, keep the RENNS formula, discussed in 4f, in mind: Be specific by using **R**easons, **E**xamples, **N**ames, **N**umbers, and the five **S**enses. Also, if your PURPOSE is persuasive rather than informative, remember to present opposing viewpoints evenhandedly and then refute them reasonably (6k).

A successful research paper relies on your drawing from your sources. You integrate suitable material into your paper by using QUOTA-

TIONS (33h), PARAPHRASES (33i), and SUMMARIES (33j), while always being sure to avoid PLAGIARISM. Your SOURCE-BASED WRITING needs to be

- Accurate
- Effective
- Honest (the only way to avoid plagiarism)

The final step in using sources well is to use correct documentation (Chapters 34–36). **Documentation** means making two types of entries in your research paper each time you draw upon a source for support:

1. Writing a parenthetical citation for each quotation, paraphrase, and summary you take from sources (for examples in MLA STYLE, see section 34c).
2. Composing a WORKS CITED list, MLA's name for a BIBLIOGRAPHY for the end of your paper. This list needs to include full bibliographic information on each source from which you have quoted, paraphrased, and summarized in your paper (for examples in MLA style, see 34d).

Today's bibliographies differ from those of the past. The prefix *biblio-* means "book," so traditionally, the bibliographic information referred to a book's title, author, publisher, and place and year of publication. Now that the age of the Internet, CD-ROMs, and other technologies is here, researchers include in their bibliographies all the sources they've used not only in print but also from the various technologies.

A **documentation style** refers to a specific system for providing information on sources used in a research paper. Documentation styles vary among the disciplines. This handbook presents five documentation styles in Chapters 34–36, as shown in Box 143.

BOX 143　　SUMMARY

Where to find the MLA, APA, CM, CSE, and COS information you need

MLA Style: Chapter 34

- MLA parenthetical citations: 34b–34c
- Guidelines for compiling an MLA-style Works Cited list (Box 151): 34d
- Directory of MLA Works Cited list models: 34d.1
- Content or other notes with MLA parenthetical documentation: 34d.2

APA Style: Chapter 35

- APA in-text citations: 35b–35c
- Guidelines for compiling an APA-style References list (Box 152): 35f
- Directory of APA References list models: 35f
- Abstracts and content notes: 35d–35e

→

> **Where to find the MLA, APA, CM, CSE, and COS information you need** (*continued*)
>
> **CM Style: Chapter 36**
> - Guidelines for compiling CM-style bibliographic notes (Box 153): 36a
> - Directory of CM-style bibliographic note models: 36b
>
> **CSE Style: Chapter 36**
> - Guidelines for compiling a CSE-style Cited References list (Box 154): 36c
> - Directory of CSE-style list of references models: 36d
>
> **COS: Chapter 36**
> - COS parenthetical citations: 36e
> - Differences between print and online publication in COS bibliographic notes: 36e
> - Guidelines for compiling a COS Works Cited list (Box 155): 36f

33b What is plagiarism?

To **plagiarize** is to present another person's words or ideas as if they were your own. Plagiarism, like stealing, is a form of academic dishonesty or cheating. Because it's a serious offence, plagiarism can be grounds for a failing grade or expulsion from a college or university.

33c How do I avoid plagiarism?

Here's how to avoid plagiarism. First, understand that researchers use sources carefully by honestly and suitably QUOTING (33h), PARAPHRASING (33i), and SUMMARIZING (33j) their ideas and words—a popular memory device for this is **Use QPS.** Second, become comfortable with the concept of DOCUMENTATION, which you need to use each time you quote, paraphrase, and summarize your sources. Box 144 describes the main strategies you can use to avoid plagiarism.

Box 145 lists major types of plagiarism, all of which you can avoid by following the advice in Box 144.

Never assume that your instructor can't detect plagiarism. Instructors have keen eyes for writing styles different from the ones students generally produce and from your own style in particular. In addition, instructors can access Web sites that electronically check your submit-

BOX 144   SUMMARY

Strategies for avoiding plagiarism

- Use DOCUMENTATION to acknowledge your use of the ideas or phrasings of others, taken from the sources you've compiled on your topic.
- Become thoroughly familiar with the documentation style that your instructor tells you to use for your research paper (Chapters 34–36). To work efficiently, make a master list of the information required to document all sources that you quote, paraphrase, or summarize according to your required documentation style.
- Write down absolutely all the documentation facts that you'll need for your paper, keeping careful records as you search for sources. Otherwise, you'll waste much time trying to retrace your steps to get a documentation detail you missed.
- Use a consistent system for taking CONTENT NOTES. Perhaps use different colours of ink or another coding system to keep these three uses of sources separate:
    1. Quotations from a source (require documentation)
    2. Material paraphrased or summarized from a source (requires documentation)
    3. Thoughts of your own triggered by what you've read or experienced in life (no documentation required), making sure to maintain the distinction between your own thinking and the ideas that come directly from a source
- Write clear, perhaps oversize, quotation marks when you're directly quoting a passage. Make them so distinct that you can't miss seeing them later.
- Consult with your instructor if you're unsure about any phase of the documentation process.

ted work against all material available online. Further, Internet sites such as <http://www.turnitin.com> allow instructors to check your writing against hundreds of thousands of papers offered for free or for sale on the World Wide Web and the Internet. (Also, that site adds your paper to its huge database of student papers so that no one can plagiarize your work.) Moreover, when instructors receive papers that they suspect contain plagiarized passages, they can check with other professors to see whether a student paper looks familiar.

Another important way to avoid plagiarism is to dive willingly into any interim tasks your instructors build into their research assignments. These tasks can help you enormously as you conduct your research and

BOX 145   SUMMARY

Types of plagiarism

You're plagiarizing if you do any of the following:

- Buy a paper from an Internet site, another student or writer, or any other source
- Turn in any paper that someone else has written, whether it was given to you, you downloaded it from the Internet, or you copied it from any other source
- Change selected parts of an existing paper, and claim the paper as your own
- Combine the ideas from many sources and claim that they're your own thoughts
- Use general or specific ideas from a source without using full and correct documentation telling where you got the ideas
- Copy or paste into your paper any KEY TERMS, PHRASES, sentences, or longer passages from another source without using documentation to tell precisely where the material came from
- Neglect to put quotation marks around words (or indent long passages) that you quote directly from a source, even if you document the source (28a–e)

write your paper. For example, many instructors today set interim deadlines such as a date for handing in a WORKING BIBLIOGRAPHY (31i), a list of all documentation details for sources you've located in your search but haven't yet evaluated for their value and reliability. Another possible assignment is to prepare an **annotated bibliography,** which includes all documentation information and a brief summary or commentary on each source that you've evaluated (32j) as trustworthy and useful for your research paper. Further, some instructors want to read and coach you about how to improve one or more of your research paper drafts. In some cases, they might want to look over your research log (31e), content notes (31j), and/or photocopies of your sources.

33d How do I work with the Internet to avoid plagiarism?

The Internet can both greatly help researchers and create potential new problems. One problem is that the Internet allows anyone to say anything, so many Internet sources lack reliability and aren't legitimate for research purposes (32j). The second problem is that students might plagiarize more readily from Internet sources.

For example, you might be tempted to download a completed research paper from the Internet. *Don't.* That's intellectual dishonesty, which can get you into real trouble not only with your instructor but also with the college or university you attend. Or you might be tempted to borrow wording from what you wrongly consider an "obscure" Internet source. *Don't.* Not only is this intellectual dishonesty, but instructors will easily detect it (33c). Box 146 provides guidelines for avoiding plagiarism of Internet sources.

BOX 146   SUMMARY

Guidelines for avoiding plagiarizing from the Internet

- Never cut and paste directly into your paper from online sources. You can too easily lose track of what language is your own and what material came from a source. You'll need to document each item.

- Keep downloaded or printed Internet sources in computer files that are separate from your draft, whether you intend to draw upon the sources as quotations, summaries, or paraphrases. Be extremely careful about how you manage those copies. Whenever you know the exact place where you think an item would fit in your paper, record that location very clearly (use another colour or a distinct font), but never paste it in.

- Make sure that you write every detail of information that identifies the source and is called for in the documentation style you need to use.

- If you're taking CONTENT NOTES (31j) in a computer file, copy or paste material onto a blank page if you intend to use it as a direct quotation from a printed or downloaded source. Make certain to place quotation marks around the quoted material and to include proper documentation. Do this at the moment you copy or paste the quotation. If you put off documenting until later, you may forget to do it or get it wrong. Also, in a different font or colour, type your reason for thinking the quotation might be useful.

- SUMMARIZE or PARAPHRASE materials *before* you include them in your paper. If for the sake of convenience you've printed or downloaded Internet sources into separate files, never copy directly from those files into your paper. On the spot, summarize or paraphrase the sources.

- QUOTE carefully if you decide you must quote a passage directly from a source. Make sure to use quotation marks; perhaps signal with a different font or colour that you have quoted.

→

> ### Guidelines for avoiding plagiarizing from the Internet
> (*continued*)
>
> - Keep all documentation information together as you work with each source. Then, at the very moment you put a quotation, paraphrase, or summary in your paper, enter all documentation information in a parenthetical citation and in your bibliography. Never put this off until later, because the details might slip your mind, you might forget to do the documentation entirely, or you might get it wrong as you try to reconstruct your thinking.
> - If you think that you may have plagiarized by mistake, check your work against papers and files on the Internet. Try typing one or two sentences—always putting them in quotation marks—into the search window at Google. You might also submit your work to one of the for-profit plagiarism-detection services. These for-profit services charge you money for their work, and they also keep a copy of your paper in their databases.

33e What don't I have to document?

You don't have to document common knowledge or your own thinking. **Common knowledge** is information that most educated people know, although they may need to remind themselves of certain facts by looking up information in a reference book. For example, here are a few facts of common knowledge that you don't need to document.

- Newfoundland entered Confederation in 1949.
- Mercury is the planet closest to the sun.
- Normal human body temperature is 37°C.
- All the oceans on our planet contain salt water.

Sometimes, of course, a research paper doesn't contain common knowledge. For example, Chandra Johnson, whose research paper appears in Chapter 34, had only very general common knowledge about the broad topic of artificial intelligence. She had even less knowledge of her narrowed topic, "emotions and artificial intelligence." Johnson's research paper includes some of her common knowledge. For example, she had seen the movie *A.I. Artificial Intelligence* and knew its plot, and she also knew about the *Star Trek* television series and the character of Mr. Spock. However, most of her paper consists of ideas and information that she quotes, paraphrases, and summarizes from sources.

A very important component of a research paper that doesn't need documentation is **your own thinking,** which is based on what you've learned as you built on what you already knew about your topic. It consists of your ANALYSIS, SYNTHESIS, and interpretation of new material as you read or observe it. You don't have to document your own thinking. Your own thinking helps you formulate a THESIS STATEMENT and organize your research paper by composing TOPIC SENTENCES that carry along your presentation of information. For example, suppose that you're drawing on an article about the connections between emotions and logic in people. While reading the article, you come to a personal conclusion that computers can't have emotions. This idea is not stated anywhere in the article you are reading or in any other source you use. Obviously, you need to cite the ideas from the article that led to your conclusion, but you don't need to cite your own thinking. On the other hand, if you find a source that states this very idea, you must cite it.

33f What must I document?

You must document everything that you learn from a source. This includes ideas as well as specific language. Expressing the ideas of others in your own words doesn't release you from the obligation to tell exactly where you got those ideas—you need to use complete, correct documentation. Here's an example in action:

SOURCE

Searle, John R. "I Married a Computer." Rev. of *The Age of Spiritual Machines,* by Ray Kurzweil. *New York Review of Books* 8 Apr. 1999: 34+. [This source information is arranged in MLA documentation style.]

ORIGINAL (SEARLE'S EXACT WORDS)

We are now in the midst of a technological revolution that is full of surprises. No one thirty years ago was aware that one day household computers would become as common as dishwashers. And those of us who used the old Arpanet of twenty years ago had no idea that it would evolve into the Internet. [This appears on page 37 of the source.]

PLAGIARISM EXAMPLE (UNDERLINED WORDS ARE PLAGIARIZED)

The current technological revolution is surprising. Thirty years ago, no one expected computers to be as common today as air conditioners. What once was the Arpanet has evolved into the Internet, and no one expected that.

Even though the student changed some wording in the example above, the ideas aren't original to that student. To avoid plagiarism, the student is required to document the source.

CORRECT EXAMPLE (USING QUOTATION, PARAPHRASE, AND DOCUMENTATION)
John Searle states that we live in a technologically amazing time of change in which computers have "become as common as dishwashers" (37). Twenty years ago, no one could have predicted the Arpanet would become the Internet (37). [This citation is arranged in MLA documentation style.]

The writer of the example above has used Searle's ideas properly through a combination of quotation and paraphrase and documentation. She correctly quotes the phrase "become as common as dishwashers." She paraphrases the statement "We are now in the midst of a technological revolution that is full of surprises," rephrasing it as "we live in a technologically amazing time of change." She also paraphrases the sentence "And those of us who used the old Arpanet of twenty years ago had no idea that it would evolve into the Internet" as "Twenty years ago, no one could have predicted the Arpanet would become the Internet." Finally, she gives the author's name in one sentence and twice includes parenthetical citations, which would lead the reader to find the source on the WORKS CITED page. Sections 33g through 33j explain exactly how to use sources effectively and document correctly.

33g How can I effectively integrate sources into my writing?

Integrating sources means blending information and ideas from others with your own writing. Before trying to integrate sources into your writing, you need to have ANALYZED and then SYNTHESIZED the material. Analysis requires you to break ideas down into their component parts so that you can think them through separately. The best time to do this is while you're reading your sources and taking CONTENT NOTES. Synthesis requires you to make connections among different ideas, seeking relationships and connections that tie them together.

33h How can I use quotations effectively?

A **quotation** is the exact words of a source enclosed in quotation marks. You face conflicting demands when you use quotations in your writing. Although quotations provide support, you can lose coherence in your paper if you use too many quotations. If more than a quarter of your paper consists of quotations, you've probably written what some people call a "cut and paste special"—merely stringing together a bunch of quotations. Doing so gives your readers—including instructors—the impression that you've not bothered to develop your own thinking and are letting other people do your talking.

In addition to avoiding too many quotations, you also want to avoid using quotations that are too long. Readers tend to skip over long quotations and lose the drift of the paper. Also, your instructor might assume that you just didn't take the time required to PARAPHRASE or SUMMARIZE the material. Generally, summaries and paraphrases are more effective for reconstructing someone else's argument. If you do need to quote a long passage, make absolutely sure every word in the quotation counts. Edit out irrelevant parts, using ellipsis points to indicate deleted material (29d and 33h.1). Box 147 provides guidelines for using quotations. Sections 33h.1 and 33h.2 give examples of acceptable and unacceptable quotations.

BOX 147   SUMMARY

 Guidelines for using quotations

1. Use quotations from authorities on your subject to support or refute what you write in your paper.
2. Never use a quotation to present your THESIS STATEMENT or TOPIC SENTENCES.
3. Select quotations that fit your message. Choose a quotation only in these cases:
   - Its language is particularly appropriate or distinctive.
   - Its idea is particularly hard to paraphrase accurately.
   - The authority of the source is especially important to support your thesis or main point.
   - The source's words are open to interpretation.
4. Never compose more than a quarter of your paper from quotations. Instead, rely on paraphrase (33i) and summary (33j).
5. Quote accurately. Always check each quotation against the original source—and then recheck it.
6. Integrate quotations smoothly into your writing.
7. Avoid PLAGIARISM (33b–33d).
8. Enter all DOCUMENTATION precisely and carefully.

33h.1 Making quotations fit smoothly with your sentences

When you quote sources, the greatest risk you take is that you'll end up with incoherent, choppy sentences. On the level of the sentence, you can avoid this problem by making the words you quote fit smoothly with three aspects of the rest of your sentence: grammar, style, and logic. Based on the source material that follows, examine these examples.

SOURCE

Goleman, Daniel. *Emotional Intelligence.* New York: Bantam, 1995. 9.
[This source information is arranged in MLA documentation style.]

ORIGINAL (GOLEMAN'S EXACT WORDS)

These two minds, the emotional and the rational, operate in tight harmony for the most part, intertwining their very different ways of knowing to guide us through the world.

INCOHERENT GRAMMAR PROBLEM

Goleman explains how the emotional and rational minds "intertwining their very different ways of knowing to guide us through the world" (9). [Corrected: Goleman explains the process of emotional and rational minds "intertwining their very different ways of knowing to guide us through the world" (9).]

INCOHERENT STYLE PROBLEM

Goleman explains how the "two minds"--here he is referring to "the emotional and rational"--work together while "intertwining their very different ways of knowing," leading to the following result: "guiding us through the world" (9). [Corrected: Goleman explains how the emotional and rational minds work together by "intertwining their very different ways of knowing to guide us through the world" (9).]

INCOHERENT LOGIC PROBLEM

Goleman explains how the emotional and rational minds work together by "their very different ways of knowing to guide us through the world" (9). [Corrected: Coleman explains how the emotional and rational minds work together by combining "their very different ways of knowing to guide us through the world" (9).]

CORRECT USE OF THE QUOTATION

Goleman explains how the emotional and rational minds work together by "intertwining their very different ways of knowing to guide us through the world" (9). [This citation is arranged in MLA documentation style.]

After writing sentences that contain quotations, read the material aloud and listen to whether the language flows smoothly and gracefully. Perhaps you need to add a word or two placed in brackets (29c) within the quotation so that its wording coheres with the rest of your sentence. Make sure your bracketed additions don't distort the meaning of the quotation. For example, the following quotation comes from the same page of the source quoted above. The bracketed material explains what *these minds* refer to in the original quotation—this helps the reader understand what was clear in the context of the original source but isn't clear when quoted in isolation.

ORIGINAL (GOLEMAN'S EXACT WORDS)

In many or most moments, these minds are exquisitely coordinated; feelings are essential to thought, thought to feeling.

QUOTATION WITH EXPLANATORY BRACKETS

"In many or most moments, these minds [emotional and rational] are exquisitely coordinated; feelings are essential to thought, thought to feeling" (Goleman 9). [This citation is arranged in MLA documentation style.]

Another way to create a smooth integration of a quotation in your sentence is to delete some words, always using an ellipsis where the deletion occurs. You also might delete any part of the quotation that interferes with conciseness and the focus you intend in your sentence. When you use an ellipsis, make sure that the remaining words accurately reflect the source's meaning and that your sentence structure still flows smoothly. The original of the following quotation appears on page 522.

QUOTATION WITH ELLIPSIS

Goleman contends that, generally, "these two minds, the emotional and the rational, operate in tight harmony . . . to guide us through the world" (9). [This citation is arranged in MLA documentation style.]

In the example above, the words "for the most part, intertwining their very different ways of knowing" have been deleted from the original material so that the quotation is more concise and focused.

33h.2 Using quotations to enhance meaning

Perhaps the biggest complaint instructors have about student research papers is that sometimes quotations are simply stuck in, for no apparent reason. Whenever you place words between quotation marks, they take on special significance for your message as well as your language. Without context-setting information in the paper, the reader can't know exactly what logic leads the writer to use a particular quotation.

Furthermore, always make sure your readers know who said each group of quoted words. Otherwise, you've used a *disembodied quotation* (some instructors call them "ghost quotations"). Although quotation marks set off someone else's words, they need explanation and context, or they'll tell the reader nothing about who is being quoted and why. This reflects poorly on the clarity of your writing.

SOURCE

Wright, Karen. "Times of Our Lives." *Scientific American* Sept. 2002: 58–66. [This source information is arranged in MLA documentation style.]

ORIGINAL (WRIGHT'S EXACT WORDS)

In human bodies, biological clocks keep track of seconds, minutes, days, months and years.

INCORRECT (DISEMBODIED QUOTATION)

The human body has many subconscious processes. People don't have to make their hearts beat or remind themselves to breathe. "In human bodies, biological clocks keep track of seconds, minutes, days, months and years" (Wright 66).

CORRECT

The human body has many subconscious processes. People don't have to make their hearts beat or remind themselves to breathe. However, other processes are less obvious and perhaps more surprising. Karen Wright observes, for example, "In human bodies, biological clocks keep track of seconds, minutes, days, months and years" (66).

Rarely can a quotation begin a paragraph effectively. Start your paragraph by relying on your TOPIC SENTENCE, based on your own thinking. Then, you can fit in a relevant quotation somewhere in the paragraph, if it supports or extends what you have said.

Another strategy for working quotations smoothly into your paper is to integrate the name(s) of the author(s), the source title, or other information into your paper. You can prepare your reader for a quotation using one of these methods:

- Mention in your sentence directly before or after the quotation the name(s) of the author(s) you're quoting.
- Mention in your sentence the title of the work you're quoting from.
- Give additional authority to your material. If the author of a source is a noteworthy figure, you gain credibility when you refer to his or her credentials.
- Mention the name(s) of the author(s), with or without the name of the source and any author credentials, along with your personal introductory lead-in to the material.

Here are examples of the methods listed above. They use author names and source titles effectively.

SOURCE

Gardner, Howard. *The Disciplined Mind: What All Students Should Understand.* New York: Simon & Schuster, 1999. 72. [This source information is arranged in MLA documentation style.]

ORIGINAL (GARDNER'S EXACT WORDS)

While we all possess all of the intelligences, perhaps no two persons—not even identical twins—exhibit them in the same combination of strengths.

INTEGRATING AUTHOR'S NAME WITH QUOTATION

Howard Gardner explains, "While we all possess all of the intelligences, perhaps no two persons--not even identical twins--exhibit them in the same combination of strengths" (72). [This citation is arranged in MLA documentation style.]

INTEGRATING AUTHOR'S NAME AND SOURCE TITLE

Howard Gardner explains in *The Disciplined Mind: What All Students Should Understand:* "While we all possess all of the intelligences, perhaps no two persons--not even identical twins--exhibit them in the same combination of strengths" (72). [This citation is arranged in MLA documentation style.]

INTEGRATING AUTHOR'S NAME, CREDENTIALS, AND SOURCE TITLE

Howard Gardner, a psychologist and the author of fifteen books on the human mind, states in *The Disciplined Mind: What All Students Should Understand,* "While we all possess all of the intelligences, perhaps no two persons--not even identical twins--exhibit them in the same combination of strengths" (72). [This citation is arranged in MLA documentation style.]

INTEGRATING AUTHOR'S NAME WITH YOUR OWN THINKING AS INTRODUCTORY ANALYSIS

The psychologist Howard Gardner claims that humans possess eight intelligences, but he notes: "While we all possess all of the intelligences, perhaps no two persons--not even identical twins--exhibit them in the same combination of strengths" (72). [This citation is arranged in MLA documentation style.]

You can also integrate a quotation into your own writing by interrupting the quotation with your own words. If you insert your own words *within* the quotation, you are required to put those words between brackets, as with the word "eight" in the following example:

"While we all possess all of the [eight] intelligences," Howard Gardner explains, "perhaps no two persons--not even identical twins--exhibit them in the same combination of strengths" (72). [This citation is arranged in MLA documentation style.]

👁 **ALERT:** After using an author's full name in the first reference, you can decide to use only the author's last name in subsequent references. This holds unless another source has that same last name. 👁

EXERCISE 33-1

Read the original material, a passage taken from page 96 of *Misconceiving Canada: The Struggle for National Unity* by Kenneth McRoberts (Toronto: Oxford UP, 1997). Then, evaluate the passages that show unacceptable uses of quotations, either individually or with your peer-response group. Describe the problems, and then revise each passage. End the quotations with this MLA parenthetical reference: (McRoberts 96).

ORIGINAL

During the 1980s, the three Prairie provinces were all forced to confront the issue of official bilingualism, in light of Supreme Court decisions upholding their obligations under nineteenth-century statutes. In each case, there was clear resistance among anglophones to official status for French.

In the case of Manitoba, the resulting conflict was especially acrimonious. In 1979 the Supreme Court ruled that the province was still bound by the Manitoba Act, 1870 and that all laws passed since 1890 were unconstitutional since they had not been enacted in both official languages. The Manitoba government began translating all its statutes into French, but by 1982 it became concerned that the translation was not proceeding fast enough and began to fear that all its laws might soon be declared unconstitutional.

UNACCEPTABLE USES OF QUOTATIONS

1. The Supreme Court ruled that the Prairie provinces were bound by their nineteenth-century legal obligations. "In each case, there was a clear resistance among anglophones to official status for French" (McRoberts 96).

2. With regard to Manitoba, "the Supreme Court ruled that all laws passed since 1890 were unconstitutional since they had not been enacted in both official languages" (McRoberts 96).

3. By 1982, while translating Manitoba's laws into French, the realization "that the translation was not proceeding fast enough and began

to fear that all its laws might soon be declared unconstitutional" (McRoberts 96).

4. The 1870 Manitoba Act required the province to enact both French and English versions of its legislation. However, "since they had not been enacted in both official languages" (McRoberts 96), the Supreme Court found that Manitoba had violated the Constitution.

5. As a result of the Supreme Court decision, Manitoba began to translate all its laws, although "in 1982 it became concerned that the French translation was not proceeding fast enough" (McRoberts 96).

EXERCISE 33-2

Working individually or with your peer-response group, do the following:

1. For a paper analyzing modern conceptions of place and identity, write a three- to four-sentence passage that includes your own words and a quotation from this paragraph, taken from pages 267–68 of Mark Kingwell's *Marginalia* (Toronto: Penguin, 1999). After the quoted words, use this parenthetical reference: (Kingwell 267–68).

   ORIGINAL

   I have been away from home a lot lately, travelling from city to city across this country and south of the border. Last Sunday I had breakfast with my wife in Boston, lunch with a friend in Toronto, and dinner with a colleague in Ottawa. I started writing this essay in Montreal, worked on it in Vancouver, Edmonton, and Calgary, fiddled with the first few paragraphs in Winnipeg, fleshed out some other parts in upstate New York, and then finished it in Toronto. Covering all those miles, trundling in and out of departure lounges, and putting in hours in rental cars, gives you an appreciation for the vastness and variety of Canada: The way cool kids are cool differently in Quebec than on the West Coast. The way provincial politics dominates Edmonton in a way it doesn't in Winnipeg. The way Vancouver has, like Paris, apparently cornered the regional market on beautiful people. The way the smog and driving habits get worse every year in Toronto.

2. For a paper arguing that writers of children's books should not impose their own views on their readers, quote from the Landsberg paragraph in Exercise 33-6 (section 33j). Be sure to include in your quotation some of the strengths that Landsberg sees in the novel she is discussing, in addition to one or more of its weaknesses. The paragraph appears on page 109 of Landsberg's book.

3. Write a two- to four-sentence passage that includes your own words and a quotation from a source you're currently using for a paper assigned in one of your courses. If you have no such assignment,

choose any material suitable for a college-level or university-level research paper. Your instructor might request a photocopy of the material from which you're quoting, so make a copy to have on hand.

33i How can I write good paraphrases?

A **paraphrase** precisely restates in your own words and your own writing style the written or spoken words of someone else. Select for paraphrase only the passages that carry ideas you need to reproduce in detail. Because paraphrasing calls for a very close approximation of a source, avoid trying to paraphrase a whole chapter—or even a whole page; use SUMMARY instead. Expect to write a number of drafts of your paraphrases, each time getting closer to effectively rewording and revising the writing style so that you avoid PLAGIARISM. Box 148 provides guidelines for writing paraphrases.

BOX 148   SUMMARY

Guidelines for writing paraphrases

1. Decide to paraphrase authorities on your subject to support or dispute what you write in your paper.
2. Never use a paraphrase to present your thesis statement or topic sentences.
3. Say what the source says, but no more.
4. Reproduce the source's sequence of ideas and emphases.
5. Use your own words and writing style to restate the material. If some technical words in the original have no or awkward synonyms, you may quote the original's words—but do so very sparingly. For example, you can use the terms *enacted in both official languages* if you're paraphrasing the original source by Kenneth McRoberts in Exercise 33-1.
6. Never distort the source's meaning as you reword and change the writing style.
7. Expect your material to be as long as, and often longer than, the original.
8. Integrate your paraphrases smoothly into your writing.
9. Avoid plagiarism (33b–33d).
10. Enter all DOCUMENTATION precisely and carefully.

Here's an example of an unacceptable paraphrase and an acceptable one.

SOURCE

Goleman, Daniel. *Emotional Intelligence*. New York: Bantam, 1995. 9.
[This source information is arranged in MLA documentation style.]

ORIGINAL

These two minds, the emotional and the rational, operate in tight harmony for the most part, intertwining their very different ways of knowing to guide us through the world. Ordinarily there is a balance between emotional and rational minds, with emotion feeding into and informing the operations of the rational mind, and the rational mind refining and sometimes vetoing the inputs of the emotions. Still, the emotional and rational minds are semi-independent faculties, each, as we shall see, reflecting the operation of distinct, but interconnected circuitry of the brain.

In many or most moments, these minds are exquisitely coordinated; feelings are essential to thought, thought to feeling. But when passions surge, the balance tips: it is the emotional mind that captures the upper hand, swamping the rational mind.

UNACCEPTABLE PARAPHRASE (UNDERLINED WORDS ARE PLAGIARIZED)

The emotional and the rational parts of our mind operate in tight harmony for the most part as they help us make our way through our lives. Usually the two minds are balanced, with emotion feeding into and informing the operations of the rational mind, and the rational mind refining and sometimes overruling what the emotions desire. Still, the emotional and rational minds are semi-independent faculties, for as research shows, although they function separately, they are linked in the brain.

Most of the time our two minds work together, with feelings necessary for thinking and thinking necessary for feeling. Nevertheless, if strong emotions develop, it is the emotional mind that captures the upper hand, swamping the rational mind (Goleman 9).

ACCEPTABLE PARAPHRASE

According to Goleman, the emotional and rational parts of our mind work together to help us make our way through our lives. Usually, the two minds have equal input. The emotional mind provides information to the logical mind, and the logical mind processes the data and sometimes overrules emotional desires. Nevertheless, while the two minds show a biological connection in the brain, each can assert some independence.

> Most of the time our two minds work together, with feelings necessary for thinking and thinking necessary for feeling. Still, if strong emotions develop, passions overrule logical thinking (9). [This citation is arranged in MLA documentation style.]

The first attempt to paraphrase is not acceptable. The writer simply changed a few words. What remains is plagiarized because the passage keeps most of the original's language, has the same sentence structure as the original, and uses no quotation marks. The documentation is correct, but its accuracy doesn't make up for the unacceptable paraphrasing. The second paraphrase is acceptable. It captures the meaning of the original in the student's own words.

EXERCISE 33-3

Working individually or with your peer-response group, read the original material, a paragraph from *Uniforms: Why We Are What We Wear,* by Paul Fussell (Boston: Houghton, 2002): 49. Then, read the unacceptable paraphrase, and point out each example of plagiarism. Finally, write your own paraphrase, starting it with a phrase naming Fussell and ending it with this parenthetical reference: (49).

ORIGINAL

Until around 1963, part of the routine for Levi's wearers was shrinking the trousers to fit, and the best way to do that was to put them on wet and let them dry on your body. This gave the wearer the impression that he or she was actually creating the garment, or at least emphasizing one's precious individuality, and that conviction did nothing to oppose the illusion of uniqueness precious to all American young people.

UNACCEPTABLE PARAPHRASE

Paul Fussell says that until around 1963 Levi's wearers used to shrink new trousers to fit. The best way to do that was to put them on wet and let them dry while wearing them. Doing this created the impression that wearers were actually creating the garment or emphasizing their precious individuality. It reinforced the illusion of uniqueness precious to all American teens (49).

EXERCISE 33-4

Working individually or with your peer-response group, do the following:

1. For a paper on the place of censorship in the coverage of military conflicts, paraphrase the following paragraph from *Regarding the Pain of Others* by Susan Sontag (New York: Farrar, 2003): 65. Start with words mentioning Sontag, and end with this parenthetical reference: (65).

ORIGINAL

There had always been censorship, but for a long time it remained desultory, at the pleasure of generals and heads of state. The first organized ban on press photography at the front came during the First World War; both the German and French high commands allowed only a few selected military photographers near the fighting. (Censorship of the press by the British General Staff was less inflexible.) And it took another fifty years, and the relaxation of censorship with the first televised war coverage, to understand what impact shocking photographs could have on the domestic public. During the Vietnam era, war photography became, normatively, a criticism of war. This was bound to have consequences: Mainstream media are not in the business of making people feel queasy about the struggles for which they are being mobilized, much less of disseminating propaganda against waging war.

2. In one of your sources for a current research assignment, locate a paragraph that is at least 150 words in length and write a paraphrase of it. If you have no such assignment, choose any material suitable for a college-level or university-level paper. Your instructor may request that you submit a photocopy of the original material, so make a copy to have on hand.

33j How can I write good summaries?

A **summary** differs from a PARAPHRASE (33i) in one important way: A paraphrase restates the original material completely, but a summary provides only the main point of the original source. A summary is much shorter than a paraphrase. Summarizing is the technique you will probably use most frequently in writing your research papers, both for taking notes and for integrating what you have learned from sources into your own writing.

As you summarize, you trace a line of thought. This involves omitting less central ideas and sometimes transposing certain points into an order more suited to summary. In summarizing a longer original—say, ten pages or more—you may find it helpful first to divide the original into subsections and summarize each. Then, group your subsection summaries and use them as the basis for further condensing the material into a final summary. You are likely to have to revise a summary more than once. Always make sure that a summary accurately reflects the source and its emphases.

When you're summarizing a source in your CONTENT NOTES, take care not to be tempted to include your personal interpretation along with something the author says. Similarly, never include in your summary your own judgment about the point made in the source. Your own opinions and ideas, although they have value, don't belong in a summary. Instead, jot them down immediately when they come to mind, but separate them clearly from your summary. Write your notes so that when you go back to them you can be sure to distinguish your opinions or ideas from your summary. Highlight your personal writing with a screen of yellow or some other colour, or use an entirely different font for it. Box 149 provides guidelines for writing good summaries.

BOX 149   SUMMARY

Guidelines for writing summaries

1. Use summaries from authorities on your subject to support or dispute what you write in your paper.
2. Identify the main points your want to summarize, and condense them using your own words without losing the meaning of the original source.
3. Never use a summary to present your THESIS STATEMENT or TOPIC SENTENCES.
4. Keep your summary short.
5. Integrate your summaries smoothly into your writing.
6. Avoid PLAGIARISM (33b–33d).
7. Enter all DOCUMENTATION precisely and carefully.

Here's an example of an unacceptable summary and an acceptable one.

SOURCE

Frye, Northrop. *Anatomy of Criticism*. 1957. Princeton: Princeton UP, 1973. 99. [This source information is arranged in MLA documentation style.]

ORIGINAL

The repetition of certain common images of physical nature like the sea or the forest in a large number of poems cannot in itself be called even "coincidence," which is the name we give to a piece of design when we cannot find a use for it. But it does indicate a certain unity in the nature that poetry imitates, and in the communicating activity of which poetry forms part. Because of the larger communicative context of education, it is possible for a story about the sea to be archetypal, to make a profound imaginative impact, on a reader who has never been out of Saskatchewan. And when pastoral images are deliberately employed in *Lycidas,* for instance, merely because they are conventional, we can see that the convention of the pastoral makes us assimilate these images to other parts of literary experience.

UNACCEPTABLE SUMMARY

The fact that common images of physical nature like the sea or the forest are repeated in many poems is not in itself coincidence. It indicates the unity of the natural world, which poetry imitates, and unity in poetry's aspect as a communicating activity. For example, a story about the sea can be archetypal and therefore able to impact readers who have never been out of Saskatchewan. A pastoral work assimilates its images to other parts of the literary experience.

ACCEPTABLE SUMMARY

Frye simply sees the repetition of images from nature in poetry as a result of the unity of nature--but more important, he argues that this repetition reveals the unity of literature as a form of communication. Thus he sees particular natural images, such as the sea or the pastoral landscape, as archetypes that connect to other elements in the literary experience (99). [This citation is arranged in MLA documentation style.]

The unacceptable summary above has several major problems: It doesn't isolate the main point. It plagiarizes by taking much of its language directly from the source. Examples of plagiarized language include all the underlined phrases. The acceptable summary concisely isolates the main point, puts the source into the writer's own words, calls attention to the author by including his name in the summary, and remains objective throughout.

EXERCISE 33-5

Working individually or with your peer-response group, read the original material from *No Logo: Taking Aim at the Brand Bullies* by Naomi Klein (Toronto: Knopf, 2000): 195–96. Then, read the unacceptable summary. Point out each example of plagiarism. Finally, write your own summary, starting it with a phrase mentioning Klein and ending it with this parenthetical reference: (195–96).

ORIGINAL

Many brand-name multinationals, as we have seen, are in the process of transcending the need to identify with their earthbound products. They dream instead about their brands' deep inner meanings—the way they capture the spirit of individuality, athleticism, wilderness or community. In this context of strut over stuff, marketing departments charged with the managing of brand identities have begun to see their work as something that occurs not in conjunction with factory production but in direct competition with it. "Products are made in the factory," says Walter Landor, president of the Landor branding agency, "but brands are made in the mind." Peter Schweitzer, president of the advertising giant J. Walter Thompson, reiterates the same thought: "The difference between products and brands is fundamental. A product is something that is made in a factory; a brand is something that is bought by a customer." Savvy ad agencies have all moved away from the idea that they are flogging a product made by someone else, and have come to think of themselves instead as brand factories, hammering out what is of true value: the idea, the lifestyle, the attitude. Brand builders are the new primary producers in our so-called knowledge economy.

UNACCEPTABLE, PLAGIARIZED SUMMARY

According to Naomi Klein, many multinational corporations are transcending the need to identify with their products. Instead, they think of the inner meanings of their brands and how they represent individuality, athleticism, and other attributes. Marketing departments today see branding as competing with factory production: The brand is an idea and what a customer buys, while the product is manufactured in a factory. Advertisers no longer think that they are selling products made by someone else. Instead, they consider themselves brand factories, creating the real value in the form of ideas, lifestyles, and attitudes (195–96).

EXERCISE 33-6

Working individually or with your peer-response group, do the following:

1. For a paper examining the author's point of view in Canadian children's literature, summarize this paragraph from *Michele Landsberg's Guide to Children's Books* (Toronto: Penguin, 1985): 109. Start your summary with a mention of the author, and end with this parenthetical reference: (Landsberg 109).

ORIGINAL

One-sidedness is a sore (and fatal) temptation for a novelist, to which too many of Canada's accomplished storywriters have succumbed—particularly, alas, those of dissenting views. Perhaps they have been provoked by the national complacency that smothers critics of the status quo like a monstrous clammy blanc mange. Silver Donald Cameron's novel, *The Baitchopper,* about a Nova Scotia fishermen's strike, has a memorable title, an exciting climactic scene at sea in a storm, and some fine salty local language. Unfortunately, it is weakened by a black-and-white finality about heroic proletarian strikers versus the smug establishment. I would share Cameron's conclusions about the rights and wrongs of the strike and about the base self-interest of those who opposed it, but the writer's fixed viewpoint robs his young characters of the opportunity to come to these conclusions for themselves. Ironically, the drama of that inner struggle would have been far more effective in making the point.

2. Write a summary of your paraphrase of the Sontag material in Exercise 33-4. Use the parenthetical reference given there.

3. Write a summary of a passage from a source you're currently using for a paper assigned in one of your courses. If you have no such assignment, choose any material suitable for a college-level or university-level research paper. Your instructor might request a photocopy of the material you're summarizing, so make a copy to have on hand.

33k Which verbs can help me weave source material into my sentences?

The verbs listed in Box 150 can help you work quotations, paraphrases, and summaries smoothly into your writing. Some of these verbs imply your position toward the source material (for example, *argue, complain, concede, deny, grant, insist,* and *reveal*). Other verbs imply a more neutral stance (for example, *comment, describe, explain, note, say,* and *write*). For many examples of effective use of such verbs, see the student research papers presented in sections 34e.2, 35h.2, and 39g.3.

BOX 150   SUMMARY

Verbs useful for integrating quotations, paraphrases, and summaries

acknowledges	confirms	endeavours to
agrees	connects	establishes
analyzes	considers	estimates
argues	contends	explains
asks	contradicts	expresses
asserts	contrasts	finds
balances	declares	focuses on
begins	demonstrates	grants
believes	denies	illuminates
claims	describes	illustrates
comments	develops	implies
compares	discusses	indicates
complains	distinguishes	informs
concedes	between/among	insists
concludes	emphasizes	introduces

→

Verbs useful for integrating quotations, paraphrases, and summaries (*continued*)

maintains	proves	shows
means	questions	signals
negates	recognizes	specifies
notes	recommends	speculates
notices	refutes	states
observes	rejects	suggests
offers	remarks	supports
organizes	reports	supposes
points out	reveals	thinks
prepares	says	wishes
promises	sees	writes

Chapter 34

MLA Documentation with Case Study

34a What is MLA style?

The Modern Language Association (MLA) sponsors the **MLA style,** a DOCUMENTATION system widely used in English courses and many of the humanities. MLA style involves two equally important features that need to appear in research papers.

First, MLA style calls for you to acknowledge your SOURCES within the text of your research papers by using **parenthetical documentation.** Section 34b explains how parenthetical documentation works, and section 34c shows nineteen models of parenthetical documentation, each of which shows you a different type of source.

Second, MLA style calls for you to list complete bibliographic information about each source that you've mentioned in your parenthetical references. This bibliographic list, titled **Works Cited,** needs to appear on a separate page at the end of your research paper. It includes only the sources you've actually used in your research paper, not any you've consulted but haven't used. Section 34d gives instructions for composing your Works Cited pages, followed by seventy models, each based on a different kind of source (book, article, Web site, etc.) that you might use in your research papers.

For examples of research papers that use MLA-style parenthetical documentation and Works Cited lists, see sections 34e.2 and 39g.3. As you read these papers, notice how the two requirements for crediting sources work together so that readers can learn the precise origin of the material that is QUOTED, PARAPHRASED, and SUMMARIZED. If you need more information than I cover in this chapter, consult the *MLA Handbook for Writers of Research Papers* (6th edition, 2003) by Joseph Gibaldi.

34b What is MLA parenthetical documentation?

MLA-style **parenthetical documentation,** also called either *parenthetical references* or *in-text citations*, is the method required to place SOURCE information in parentheses within the sentences of your research papers. This information, given each time that you QUOTE, SUMMARIZE, or PARAPHRASE specific parts of sources in your paper, signals readers that your material draws on scholarship about your TOPIC.

In parenthetical references, an author's name (or, if none, a shortened title of the work) identifies the source, and the exact page number tells where readers can locate the original material. For readability and good writing technique, always try to introduce names of authors and titles of sources in your own sentences. Then, you need only put into parentheses the page number where you found the material. When possible, position a parenthetical reference at the end of the quotation, summary, or paraphrase it refers to—preferably at the end of a sentence, unless that would place it too far from the source's material. When you place the parenthetical reference at the end of a sentence, put it before the sentence-ending period. The one exception to this rule concerns quotations that you set off block style (MLA requires that quotations longer than four typed lines be handled this way), where you put the parenthetical reference after the period.

34c What are MLA guidelines for parenthetical documentation?

This section shows examples of how to handle parenthetical documentation in the body of your research papers. The following directory corresponds to the numbered examples that follow it. Remember, try to integrate authors' names and titles of SOURCES into your sentences whenever possible (34b).

Directory—MLA Parenthetical Citations

1. Paraphrased or Summarized Source—MLA
2. Source of a Short Quotation—MLA
3. Source of a Long Quotation (and Format of Quotation)—MLA
4. One Author—MLA
5. Two or Three Authors—MLA
6. More Than Three Authors—MLA
7. More Than One Source by an Author—MLA
8. Two or More Authors with the Same Last Name—MLA
9. Group or Corporate Author—MLA
10. Work Listed by Title—MLA
11. Multivolume Work—MLA
12. Material from a Novel, Play, or Poem—MLA
13. Work in an Anthology or Other Collection—MLA
14. Indirect Source—MLA

1. Citing a Paraphrased or Summarized Source—MLA

According to Brent Staples, IQ tests give scientists little insight into intelligence (293). [Author name cited in text; page number cited in parentheses.]

In "The IQ Cult," the journalist Brent Staples states that IQ tests give scientists little insight into intelligence (293). [Title of source, author name, and author credentials cited in text; page number cited in parentheses.]

IQ tests give scientists little insight into intelligence (Staples 293). [Author name and page number cited in parentheses.]

2. Citing the Source of a Short Quotation—MLA

Given that "thoughts, emotions, imagination and predispositions occur concurrently . . . [and] interact with other brain processes" (Caine and Caine 66), it is easy to understand why "whatever [intelligence] might be, paper and pencil tests aren't the tenth of it" (Staples 293).

O'Connor asks, "What actually happened in Walkerton?" (2).

3. Citing the Source of a Long Quotation (and Formatting the Quotation)—MLA

A long quotation in MLA style consists of more than four typed lines. It is set off block style, indented one inch (about 2.5 cm) or ten spaces from the left margin. Never put quotation marks around a set-off quotation, because the indentation and block style communicate that the material is quoted. At the end of an indented quotation, place the parenthetical reference after the end punctuation mark.

Gray and Viens explain how, by tapping into a student's highly developed spatial-mechanical intelligence, one teacher can bolster a student's poor writing skills:

> The teacher asked that during "journal time" Jacob create a tool dictionary to be used as a resource in the mechanical learning center. After several entries in which he drew and described tools and other materials, Jacob confidently moved on to writing about other things of import to him, such as his brothers and a recent birthday party. Rather than shy away from all things linguistic--he previously had refused any task requiring a pencil--Jacob became invested in journal writing. (23-24)

4. Citing One Author—MLA

Give an author's name as it appears on the source: for a book, on the title page; for an article, directly below the title or at the end of the article. Many nonprint sources also name an author; for CDs, tapes, and software, for example, check the printed sleeve or cover. For an online source, identify the author exactly as identified online.

> One test asks four-year-olds to choose between one marshmallow now or two marshmallows later (Gibbs 60).

5. Citing Two or Three Authors—MLA

Give the names in the same order as in the source. Spell out *and*. For three authors, use commas to separate the authors' names.

> As children get older, they begin to express several different kinds of intelligence (Todd and Taylor 23).

> Another measure of emotional intelligence is the success of inter- and intrapersonal relationships (Voigt, Dees, and Prigoff 14).

6. Citing More Than Three Authors—MLA

If your source has more than three authors, you can name them all or use the first author's name only, followed by *et al.*, either in a parenthetical reference or in your sentence. In MLA citations, do not underline or italicize *et al.* No period follows *et*, but do use a period after *al.*

> Emotional security varies depending on the circumstances of the social interaction (Carter et al. 158).

ALERT: The abbreviation *et al.* stands for "and others"; when an author's name followed by *et al.* is a subject, use a plural verb.

> Carter et al. have found that emotional security varies depending on the circumstances of the social interaction (158).

7. Citing More Than One Source by an Author—MLA

When you use two or more sources by an author, include the relevant title in each citation. In parenthetical citations, use a shortened version of the title. For example, in a paper using as sources two of Howard Gardner's works, *Frames of Mind: The Theory of Multiple Intelligences* and "Reflections on Multiple Intelligences: Myths and Messages," use *Frames* and "Reflections" in the parenthetical citations. Shorten the titles as much as you can without making them ambiguous to readers, and start them with the word by which you alphabetize the work in the WORKS CITED. Separate the author's name and the title with a comma, but do not use punctuation between the title and the page number. When you incorporate the title into your own sentences, you can omit a subtitle, but never shorten the main title.

> Although it seems straightforward to think of multiple intelligences as
> multiple approaches to learning (Gardner, <u>Frames</u> 60-61), an intelligence
> is not a learning style (Gardner, "Reflections" 202-03).

8. Citing Two or More Authors with the Same Last Name—MLA

Use each author's first initial and full last name in each parenthetical citation. This is the only instance in MLA style where you use an initial in a parenthetical reference. If both authors have the same first initial, use the full name in all instances.

> According to Anne Cates, psychologists can predict how empathetic an
> adult will be from his or her behaviour at age two (41), but other re-
> searchers disagree (T. Cates 171).

9. Citing a Work with a Group or Corporate Author—MLA

When a corporation or other group is named as the author of a source you want to cite, use the corporate name just as you would an individual's name.

> In a five-year study, the Canadian Institute of Child Health reported that
> these tests are usually unreliable (11).

> A five-year study shows that these tests are usually unreliable (Canadian
> Institute of Child Health 11).

10. Citing a Work Listed by Title—MLA

If no author is named, use the title in citations. In your own sentences, use the full main title and omit a subtitle, if any. For parenthetical citations, shorten the title as much as possible (making sure that the shortened version refers unambiguously to the correct source), and always make the first word the one by which you alphabetize it in your Works Cited list. "Are You a Day or Night Person?" is the full title of the article in the following citation.

> The "morning lark" and "night owl" connotations are typically used to
> categorize the human extremes ("Are You" 11).

MLA

11. Citing a Multivolume Work—MLA

When you cite more than one volume of a multivolume work, include the relevant volume number in each citation. (In the Works Cited list, include the multivolume work once and give the total number of volumes; see item 9 in the Works Cited examples in 34d.1.) Give the volume number first, followed by a colon and one space, followed by the page number(s).

> By 1900, the Amazon forest dwellers had been exposed to these viruses (Rand 3: 202).

> Rand believes that forest dwellers in Borneo escaped illness from retroviruses until the 1960s (4: 518-19).

12. Citing Material from a Novel, Play, or Poem—MLA

When you cite material from literary works, providing the part, chapter, act, scene, canto, stanza, or line numbers usually helps readers locate what you are referring to more than do page numbers alone, especially because literary works frequently appear in different editions. Unless your instructor tells you not to, use arabic numerals for these references, even if the literary work uses roman numerals (except for lowercase roman numerals used for pages of a preface or other front matter in a book).

For novels that use them, give part and/or chapter numbers after page numbers. Use a semicolon after the page number but a comma to separate a part from a chapter.

> Flannery O'Connor describes one character in The Violent Bear It Away as "divided in two--a violent and a rational self" (139; pt. 2, ch. 6).

For plays that use them, give act, scene, and line numbers. Use periods between these numbers.

> In Hamlet, we find the most quoted of Shakespeare's lines, Hamlet's soliloquy beginning "To be, or not to be: that is the question" (3.1.56).

For poems and plays that use them, give canto, stanza, and/or line numbers. Use periods between these numbers. Because the typed or typeset abbreviation for *line* (*l.*, plural *ll.*) can be misread as the numeral 1, the *MLA Handbook* advises beginning your first reference to lines with the word *line* (or *lines*). After the first citation, omit the word and give only the numbers.

> In "To Autumn," Keats's most melancholy image occurs in the lines "Then in a wailful choir the small gnats mourn / Among the river swallows" (3.27-28).

13. Citing a Work in an Anthology or Other Collection—MLA

You may want to cite a work you have read in a book that contains many works by various authors and that was compiled or edited by someone other than the person you are citing. For example, suppose you want to cite "Several Things" by Martha Collins, which you have read in a literature text edited by Pamela Annas and Robert Rosen. Use Martha Collins's name and the title of her work in the sentence, and give the page numbers in a parenthetical citation.

> In "Several Things," Martha Collins enumerates what could take place in the lines of her poem: "Plums could appear, on a pewter plate / A dead red hare, hung by one foot. / A vase of flowers. Three shallots" (2-4).

14. Citing an Indirect Source—MLA

When you want to quote words that you found quoted in someone else's work, put the name of the person whose words you are quoting into your own sentence. Give the work where you found the quotation either in your sentence or in a parenthetical citation beginning with *qtd. in.*

> Pierre Trudeau makes a notably populist statement: "The ordinary person can be appealed to through common sense. Beyond the effects of technology. My grandfather, for instance, was not especially literate but he was able to reason choices out" (qtd. in Powe 126).

> Powe quotes Pierre Trudeau as having made a notably populist statement: "The ordinary person can be appealed to through common sense. Beyond the effects of technology. My grandfather, for instance, was not especially literate but he was able to reason choices out" (126).

15. Citing Two or More Sources in One Reference—MLA

If more than one source has contributed to an idea, opinion, or fact in your paper, cite them all. In a parenthetical citation, separate each block of information with a semicolon followed by one space.

> Once researchers agreed that multiple intelligences existed, their next step was to try to measure or define them (West 17; Arturi 477; Gibbs 68).

Because long parenthetical citations can disturb the flow of your paper, you might want to use an endnote or footnote for citing multiple sources; see 34d.2, page 567.

16. Citing an Entire Work—MLA

References to an entire work usually fit best into your own sentences.

> In Frames of Mind, Gardner proposes a revolutionary expansion of our understanding of human intelligence.

17. Citing an Electronic Source with a Name or Title and Page Numbers—MLA

The principles that govern parenthetical references for electronic sources are exactly the same as the ones that apply to books, articles, letters, interviews, or any other source you get information from on paper or in person.

When an electronically accessed source identifies its author, use the author's name for parenthetical references. If an electronic source does not name its author, use its title for parenthetical references and for the first block of information in that source's Works Cited entry. (See item 10 in this section for an example of a work cited by its title.) When an electronic source has page numbers, use them exactly as you would the page numbers of a print source.

18. Citing an Electronic Source with Paragraph or Screen Numbers—MLA

When an electronic source has numbered paragraphs or screens (instead of page numbers), use them for parenthetical references, with two differences: (1) Use a comma followed by one space after the name (or title); and (2) use the abbreviation *par.* for a reference to one paragraph or *pars.* for a reference to more than one paragraph, followed by the number(s) of the paragraph(s) you are citing.

> Artists seem to be haunted by the fear that psychoanalysis might destroy creativity while it reconstructs personality (Francis, pars. 22-25).

19. Citing an Electronic Source Without Page or Paragraph Numbers—MLA

Many online sources do not number pages or paragraphs. Simply refer to those works in their entirety. Here are two examples referring to "What Is Artificial Intelligence?" by John McCarthy, a Web site without page numbers or paragraph numbers. While either citation is acceptable, try to include the name of the author in your sentence.

> The science of artificial intelligence includes efforts beyond trying to simulate human intelligence (McCarthy).

> John McCarthy notes that the science of artificial intelligence includes efforts beyond trying to simulate human intelligence.

34d How do I compile an MLA-style Works Cited list?

In MLA style, **Works Cited** pages give complete bibliographic information for each source used in research papers. This Works Cited list includes only the sources from which you QUOTE or PARAPHRASE or SUMMARIZE. Never include sources that you have consulted but do not refer to in the paper. Box 151 gives general information about a Works Cited list, and the rest of this chapter provides models of specific kinds of Works Cited entries.

BOX 151   SUMMARY

 ## Guidelines for an MLA-style Works Cited list

■ **TITLE**

Works Cited

■ **PLACEMENT OF LIST**

Start a new page numbered sequentially with the rest of the paper, after the Notes page(s), if any.

■ **CONTENTS AND FORMAT**

Include all sources quoted from, paraphrased, or summarized in your paper. Start each entry on a new line and at the regular left margin. If the entry uses more than one line, indent the second and all other lines one-half inch (about 1.25 cm) or five spaces from the left margin. Double-space all lines.

■ **SPACING AFTER PUNCTUATION**

The *MLA Handbook* explains that computer type fonts have influenced many users of MLA style to leave one space rather than two spaces after punctuation at the ends of sentences. The *MLA Handbook* uses one space but says that it is perfectly acceptable to use two unless your instructor asks you to do otherwise. Always put only one space after a comma, a colon, or a semicolon.

■ **ARRANGEMENT OF ENTRIES**

Alphabetize by author's last name. If no author is named, alphabetize by the title's first significant word (not *A*, *An*, or *The*).

■ **AUTHORS' NAMES**

Use first names and middle names or middle initials, if any, as given in the source. Do not reduce to initials any name that is given in full. For one author or the first-named author in multiauthor works, give the last name first. Use the word *and* with two or more authors. List multiple authors in the order given in the source. Use a comma between the first author's last and first names and after each complete author name except the last. After the last author's name, use a period: Fein, Ethel Andrea, Bert Griggs, and Delaware Rogash.

Include *Jr., Sr., II, III*, but do not include other titles and degrees before or after a name. For example, an entry for a work by Edward Meep III, M.D., and Sir Feeney Bolton would start like this: Meep, Edward, III, and Feeney Bolton.

→

Guidelines for an MLA-style Works Cited list (*continued*)

■ **CAPITALIZATION OF TITLES**

Capitalize all major words and the first and last words of all titles and subtitles.

■ **SPECIAL TREATMENT OF TITLES**

Use quotation marks around titles of shorter works (poems, short stories, essays, articles). Underline titles of longer works (books, names of newspapers or journals containing cited articles).

For underlining, <u>use an unbroken line like this</u> (unless you use software that underlines only with a <u>broken</u> <u>line</u> <u>like</u> <u>this</u>). The MLA Web site states that although computers can create italic type, underlined roman type may be more exact in student papers. Check which style your instructor prefers.

When a book title includes the title of another work that is usually underlined (as with a novel, play, or long poem), the preferred MLA style is not to underline the incorporated title: <u>Decoding</u> Jane Eyre. For a second style MLA accepts, see item 20 in 34d.1.

If the incorporated title is usually enclosed in quotation marks (as with a short story or short poem), keep the quotation marks and underline the complete title of the book, including the final punctuation. This is the only case in which final punctuation is underlined in MLA style: <u>Theme and Form in "I Shall Laugh Purely."</u>

Drop *A*, *An*, or *The* as the first word of a periodical title.

■ **PLACE OF PUBLICATION**

If several cities are listed for the place of publication, give only the first. If a Canadian or U.S. city name alone would be ambiguous, also give the province's or state's two-letter postal abbreviation (see Box 122 in 30k). For an unfamiliar city outside Canada and the United States, include an abbreviated country name.

■ **PUBLISHER**

Use shortened names as long as they are clear: *Pearson* for *Pearson Education, Simon* for *Simon & Schuster.* For university presses, use the capital letters *U* and *P* (without periods): Oxford UP; U of Chicago P.

■ **PUBLICATION MONTH ABBREVIATIONS**

Abbreviate all publication months except *May, June,* and *July.* Use the first few letters followed by a period (*Sept., Dec.*). See Box 121 in 30j.

→

Guidelines for an MLA-style Works Cited list (*continued*)

■ **PARAGRAPH AND SCREEN NUMBERS IN ELECTRONIC SOURCES**

Some electronic sources number paragraphs or screens instead of pages, although most electronic sources include no such information. If paragraphs are numbered, at the end of the publication information give the total number of paragraphs followed by the abbreviation *pars.*: 77 pars. If screens are numbered, give the total number of screens as the final information in the entry. If the source does not number paragraphs or screens, include whatever identifying information is provided.

■ **PAGE RANGES**

Give the page range—the starting page number and the ending page number, connected by a hyphen—of any paginated electronic source and any paginated print source that is part of a longer work (for example, a chapter in a book, an article in a journal). A range indicates that the cited work is on those pages and all pages in between. If that is not the case, use the style shown next for discontinuous pages. In either case, use numerals only, without the word *page* or *pages* or the abbreviation *p.* or *pp.*

Use the full second number through 99. Above that, use only the last two digits for the second number unless it would be unclear: *103–04* and *113–14* are clear, but *567–602* requires full numbers.

■ **DISCONTINUOUS PAGES**

Use the starting page number or range followed by a plus sign (+): 32+, 65-69+.

■ **WORKS CITED ENTRIES: BOOKS**

Citations for books have three main parts: author, title, and publication information (place of publication, publisher, and date of publication).

| | BOOK | PUBLICATION |
| AUTHOR | TITLE | INFORMATION |

Dudek, Louis. Collected Poetry. Montreal: Delta, 1971.

■ **WORKS CITED ENTRIES: PRINT ARTICLES**

Citations for periodical articles contain three major parts: author, title of article, and publication information (usually periodical title, volume number, year of publication, and page range).

| | ARTICLE |
| AUTHOR | TITLE |

Malinowitz, Harriet. "Business, Pleasure, and the Personal Essay."

→

MLA

Guidelines for an MLA-style Works Cited list (*continued*)

```
        JOURNAL      PUBLICATION
         TITLE       INFORMATION
     ┌──────────┐┌──────────────┐
      College English 65 (2003): 305-22.
```

```
                  ARTICLE      MAGAZINE    PUBLICATION
     AUTHOR       TITLE         TITLE      INFORMATION
  ┌──────────┐┌─────────────────┐┌─────┐┌─────────────────┐
   Brewer, Bruce. "Underneath Alaska." Sierra Mar.-Apr. 2003: 34-39+.
```

■ **WORKS CITED ENTRIES: PORTABLE ELECTRONIC SOURCES**

Publications on CD-ROM, diskettes, tape, and so on should include as much of the following as is available: author, title of publication, original print version (if relevant), editor or compiler (if relevant), publication medium, place of publication, name of publisher, date of publication. Here is an entry for an article from a CD-ROM encyclopedia:

```
     AUTHOR        ARTICLE TITLE              CD-ROM TITLE
  ┌──────────┐┌──────────────────┐┌──────────────────────────┐
   Regan, Robert. "Poe, Edgar Allan." Academic American Encyclopedia.
```

```
    ELECTRONIC              CD-ROM
    PUBLICATION           PUBLICATION
      MEDIUM              INFORMATION
  ┌──────────┐┌───────────────────────────┐
   CD-ROM. Danbury, CT: Grolier Electronic, 1993.
```

■ **WORKS CITED ENTRIES: SOURCES FROM THE INTERNET**

To document sources reached by entering a URL or Internet address (including World Wide Web, FTP, and Gopher sites), list as much of the following information as you can find: author, title, publication information about a print version (if there is one), publication information about the online source, the date you accessed the material, and the URL (electronic address). For these sources, the URL is required in the Works Cited entry, enclosed in angle brackets <like these>, after the access date and before the period at the end of the entry. Here is an entry for an article in a scientific news magazine that appears on the Web:

```
     AUTHOR                      ARTICLE TITLE
  ┌──────────┐┌────────────────────────────────────────────
   Lewis, Ricki. "Chronobiology Researchers Say Their Field's Time
```

→

Guidelines for an MLA-style Works Cited list (*continued*)

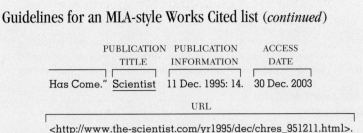

	PUBLICATION TITLE	PUBLICATION INFORMATION	ACCESS DATE
Has Come."	Scientist	11 Dec. 1995: 14.	30 Dec. 2003

URL

<http://www.the-scientist.com/yr1995/dec/chres_951211.html>.

■ **WORKS CITED ENTRIES: SOURCES ACCESSED THROUGH A LIBRARY OR PERSONAL SUBSCRIPTION SERVICE**

Library systems typically subscribe to online services such as EBSCO, InfoTrac, FirstSearch, and so on, and you may access information from them. Individuals may personally subscribe to online services such as AOL Canada. Citations for electronic sources from either type of service generally contain at least six or seven major parts: author, title of work, information about print version (if any), name of database (underlined), name of vendor or computer service, name of library (if accessed through a library service), access date, and URL if it's available and not too long to include. If the specific URL is too long to be usable, give the site's main URL, followed by the word *Path*, a colon, and the link(s) you clicked through to reach the document. Separate multiple links with semicolons. Here is an entry for a journal article accessed through a library service; it also has a print version.

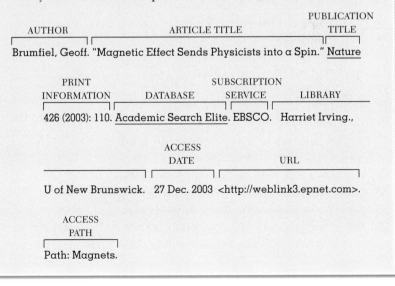

	AUTHOR	ARTICLE TITLE	PUBLICATION TITLE
	Brumfiel, Geoff.	"Magnetic Effect Sends Physicists into a Spin."	Nature

	PRINT INFORMATION	DATABASE	SUBSCRIPTION SERVICE	LIBRARY
	426 (2003): 110.	Academic Search Elite.	EBSCO.	Harriet Irving.,

	ACCESS DATE	URL
U of New Brunswick.	27 Dec. 2003	<http://weblink3.epnet.com>.

ACCESS PATH
Path: Magnets.

34d.1 Following MLA guidelines for specific sources in a Works Cited list

The directory below corresponds to the numbered examples that follow it. Not every possible documentation model is shown here. You may find that you have to combine features of models to document a particular source.

Directory—MLA Style

PRINT SOURCES

1. Book by One Author—MLA
2. Book by Two or Three Authors—MLA
3. Book by More Than Three Authors—MLA
4. Two or More Works by the Same Author(s)—MLA
5. Book by a Group or Corporate Author—MLA
6. Book with No Author Named—MLA
7. Book with an Author and an Editor—MLA
8. Translation—MLA
9. Work in Several Volumes or Parts—MLA
10. One Selection from an Anthology or an Edited Book—MLA
11. More Than One Selection from the Same Anthology or Edited Book—MLA
12. Signed Article in a Reference Book—MLA
13. Unsigned Article in a Reference Book—MLA
14. Second or Later Edition—MLA
15. Anthology or Edited Book—MLA
16. Introduction, Preface, Foreword, or Afterword—MLA
17. Unpublished Dissertation or Essay—MLA
18. Reprint of an Older Book—MLA
19. Book in a Series—MLA
20. Book with a Title Within a Title—MLA
21. Government Publication—MLA
22. Published Proceedings of a Conference—MLA
23. Signed Article from a Daily Newspaper—MLA
24. Editorial, Letter to the Editor, or Review—MLA
25. Unsigned Article from a Daily Newspaper—MLA
26. Signed Article from a Weekly or Biweekly Periodical—MLA
27. Signed Article from a Monthly or Bimonthly Periodical—MLA
28. Article from a Collection of Reprinted Articles—MLA
29. Article from a Looseleaf Collection of Reprinted Articles—MLA
30. Article from a Journal with Continuous Pagination—MLA

31. Article from a Journal That Pages Each Issue Separately—MLA
32. Abstract from a Collection of Abstracts—MLA
33. Published and Unpublished Letters—MLA
34. Microfiche Collection of Articles—MLA
35. Map or Chart—MLA

NONPRINT SOURCES

36. Interview—MLA
37. Lecture, Speech, or Address—MLA
38. Film, Videotape, or DVD—MLA
39. Musical Recording—MLA
40. Live Performance—MLA
41. Work of Art, Photograph, or Musical Composition—MLA
42. Radio or Television Program—MLA
43. Advertisement—MLA

PORTABLE ELECTRONIC SOURCES

44. CD-ROM Database: Abstract with a Print Version—MLA
45. CD-ROM: Article from a Periodical with a Print Version—MLA
46. CD-ROM: Selection from a Book with a Print Version—MLA
47. CD-ROM: Material with No Print Version—MLA
48. Work in More Than One Publication Medium—MLA

SOURCES FROM LIBRARY OR PERSONAL SUBSCRIPTION SERVICES

49. Library Subscription Service: Abstract with a Print Version—MLA
50. Personal Subscription Service: Material with No Print Version—MLA
51. Personal Subscription Service Accessed with a Keyword: Article from a Periodical with a Print Version—MLA
52. Personal Subscription Service Showing a Path—MLA
53. Library Subscription Service: Article—MLA

SOURCES FROM INTERNET SITES

54. Online Book—MLA
55. Online Book in a Scholarly Project—MLA
56. Online Government-Published Book—MLA
57. Article in an Online Periodical—MLA
58. Professional Home Page—MLA
59. Personal Home Page—MLA
60. Government or Institutional Web Site—MLA
61. Academic Department Home Page—MLA

62. URL Access: Poem—MLA
63. URL Access: Work of Art—MLA
64. URL Access: Interview—MLA
65. URL Access: Film or Film Clip—MLA
66. URL Access: Cartoon—MLA
67. URL Access: TV or Radio Program—MLA

OTHER ONLINE SOURCES

68. Online Posting—MLA
69. Synchronous Communication (MOO, MUD, IRC)—MLA
70. E-Mail Message—MLA

PRINT SOURCES

1. Book by One Author—MLA

Trudeau, Pierre E. Federalism and the French Canadians. Toronto: Macmillan,
1968.

2. Book by Two or Three Authors—MLA

Doob, Anthony, and Carla Cesaroni. Responding to Youth Crime in Canada.
Toronto: U of Toronto P, 2004.

Scardamalia, Marlene, Carl Bereiter, and Bryant Fillion. Writing for Results: A
Sourcebook of Consequential Composing Activities. Toronto: OISE, 1981.

3. Book by More Than Three Authors—MLA

Moore, Mark H., et al. Dangerous Offenders: The Elusive Target of Justice.
Cambridge: Harvard UP, 1984.

Give only the first author's name, followed by a comma and the phrase
et al. ("and others"). Otherwise, you must list all authors.

4. Two or More Works by the Same Author(s)—MLA

Atwood, Margaret. The Handmaid's Tale. Toronto: McClelland, 1985.

---. Survival. Toronto: Anansi, 1972.

---. True Stories. Toronto: Oxford UP, 1981.

Give author name(s) in the first entry only. In the second and subsequent entries, use three hyphens and a period to stand for exactly the
same name(s). If the person served as editor or translator, put a comma
and the appropriate abbreviation (*ed.* or *trans.*) following the three
hyphens. Arrange the works in alphabetical (not chronological) order
according to book title, ignoring labels such as *ed.* or *trans.*

MLA

5. Book by a Group or Corporate Author—MLA

American Psychological Association. Publication Manual of the American
Psychological Association. 5th ed. Washington: APA, 2001.

Investors Group. Starting Out: Smart Strategies for Your 20s & 30s. Toronto:
Stoddart, 1998.

Cite the full name of the corporate author first, omitting a beginning *A,
An,* or *The.* When a corporate author is also the publisher, use a shortened form of the corporate name at the publisher position.

6. Book with No Author Named—MLA

The Chicago Manual of Style. 15th ed. Chicago: U of Chicago P, 2003.

If there is no author's name on the title page, begin the citation with the
title. Alphabetize the entry according to the title's first significant word
(*Chicago,* not *The*).

7. Book with an Author and an Editor—MLA

If your paper refers to the work of the book's author, put the author's
name first; if your paper refers to the work of the editor, put the editor's
name first.

Trudeau, Pierre Elliott. The Essential Trudeau. Ed. Ron Graham. Toronto: M&S,
1998.

Graham, Ron, ed. The Essential Trudeau. By Pierre Elliott Trudeau. Toronto:
M&S, 1998.

8. Translation—MLA

Tremblay, Michel. A Thing of Beauty. Trans. Sheila Fischman. Vancouver:
Talon, 1998.

9. Work in Several Volumes or Parts—MLA

Chrisley, Ronald, ed. Artificial Intelligence: Critical Concepts. Vol. 1. London:
Routledge, 2000. 4 vols.

If you are citing only one volume, put the volume number before the
publication information. If you wish, you can give the total number of
volumes at the end of the entry. MLA recommends using arabic numerals, even if the source uses roman numerals (*Vol. 6* for *Vol. VI*).

10. One Selection from an Anthology or an Edited Book—MLA

Morrisseau, Norval. "The Indian That Became a Thunderbird." Canadian
Short Fiction: From Myth to Modern. Ed. W. H. New. Scarborough, ON:
Prentice, 1986. 26-29.

MLA

Give the author and title of the selection first and then the full title of the anthology. Information about the editor starts with *Ed.* (for "Edited by"), so do not use *Eds.* when there is more than one editor. Give the name(s) of the editor(s) in normal order rather than reversing first and last names. The sample papers in section 39g provide further examples of documenting selections from anthologies.

11. More Than One Selection from the Same Anthology or Edited Book—MLA

Gilbert, Sandra M., and Susan Gubar, eds. The Norton Anthology of Literature by Women. New York: Norton, 1985.

Kingston, Maxine Hong. "No Name Woman." Gilbert and Gubar 2337-47.

Welty, Eudora. "The Petrified Man." Gilbert and Gubar 2322-32.

If you cite more than one selection from the same anthology, you can list the anthology as a separate entry with all the publication information. Also, list each selection from the anthology by author and title of the selection, but give only the name(s) of the editor(s) of the anthology and the page number(s) for each selection. Here, *ed.* stands for "editor," so use *eds.* when more than one editor is named. List selections separately in alphabetical order by author's last name.

12. Signed Article in a Reference Book—MLA

Shadbolt, Doris. "Carr, Emily." The Canadian Encyclopedia. 2nd ed. Edmonton: Hurtig, 1988.

If the articles in the book are alphabetically arranged, omit volume and page numbers. If the reference book is frequently revised, give only the edition and year of publication.

13. Unsigned Article in a Reference Book—MLA

"Ireland." The New Encyclopaedia Britannica: Macropaedia. 15th ed. 2002.

If you are citing a widely used reference work, do not give full publication information. Instead, give only the edition and year of publication.

14. Second or Later Edition—MLA

Buckley, Joanne, and David Gates. Put It in Writing. 2nd ed. Scarborough, ON: Prentice, 1995.

If a book is not a first edition, the edition number appears on the title page. Place the abbreviated information (*2nd ed., 3rd ed.,* etc.) between the title and the publication information. Give only the latest copyright date for the edition you are using.

15. Anthology or Edited Book—MLA

New, W. H., ed. <u>Canadian Short Fiction: From Myth to Modern</u>. Scarborough,
ON: Prentice, 1986.

Here, *ed.* stands for "editor," so use *eds.* when more than one editor is named; also see items 10 and 11 in this section.

16. Introduction, Preface, Foreword, or Afterword—MLA

Allmand, Warren. Foreword. <u>The Life and Death of Anna Mae Aquash</u>. By
Johanna Brand. Toronto: Lorimer, 1993. v-ix.

Give first the name of the writer of the part you are citing, then the name of the cited part, capitalized but not underlined or in quotation marks. After the book title, write *By* and the book author's full name, if different from the writer of the cited material. If the writer of the cited material is the same as the book author, include only the last name after *By*. Following the publication information, give inclusive page numbers for the cited part, using roman or arabic numerals as the source does. When the introduction, preface, foreword, or afterword has a title (as below), include it in quotation marks before the name of the cited part.

Fox-Genovese, Elizabeth. "Mothers and Daughters: The Ties That Bind."
Foreword. <u>Southern Mothers</u>. Ed. Nagueyalti Warren and Sally Wolff.
Baton Rouge: Louisiana State UP, 1999. iv-xviii.

17. Unpublished Dissertation or Essay—MLA

Byers, Michele. " 'Buffy the Vampire Slayer': The Insurgence of Television as a
Performance Text." Diss. U of Toronto, 2000.

State the author's name first, then the title in quotation marks (not underlined), then a descriptive label (such as *Diss.* or *Unpublished essay*), followed by the degree-granting institution (for dissertations), and, finally, the date.

18. Reprint of an Older Book—MLA

Lampman, Archibald. <u>Lyrics of Earth</u>. 1895. Ottawa: Tecumseh, 1978.

Republishing information can be found on the copyright page. Give the date of the original version before the publication information for the version you are citing.

19. Book in a Series—MLA

Courchene, Thomas J. <u>In Praise of Renewed Federalism</u>. The Canada Round.
Toronto: C. D. Howe Institute, 1991.

20. Book with a Title Within a Title—MLA

The MLA recognizes two distinct styles for handling normally independent titles when they appear within an underlined title. In the MLA's preferred style, the embedded title should not be underlined or set within quotation marks.

Lumiansky, Robert M., and Herschel Baker, eds. <u>Critical Approaches to Six Major English Works</u>: Beowulf <u>Through</u> Paradise Lost. Philadelphia: U of Pennsylvania P, 1968.

However, the MLA now accepts a second style for handling such embedded titles. In the alternative form, the normally independent titles should be set within quotation marks, and both the titles and the quotation marks should be underlined.

Lumiansky, Robert M., and Herschel Baker, eds. <u>Critical Approaches to Six Major English Works: "Beowulf" Through "Paradise Lost."</u> Philadelphia: U of Pennsylvania P, 1968.

Use whichever style your instructor prefers.

21. Government Publication—MLA

Canada. Indian and Northern Affairs Canada. <u>The Inuit</u>. Ottawa: Supply and Services Canada, 1986.

Canada. Royal Commission on Bilingualism and Biculturalism. <u>Preliminary Report</u>. Ottawa: Queen's Printer, 1965.

For most government publications, use the name of the government (such as Canada) as the first information unit. If no author is named, give the name of the branch of government or the government agency next (such as Department of Finance or Task Force on Program Review).

22. Published Proceedings of a Conference—MLA

Smith, Donald B., ed. <u>Forging a New Relationship: Proceedings of the Conference on the Report of the Royal Commission on Aboriginal Peoples</u>. 31 Jan.-2 Feb. 1997. Montreal: McGill Institute for the Study of Canada, 1997.

23. Signed Article from a Daily Newspaper—MLA

Church, Elizabeth. "Vacancy Rates Rise for First Time in Decade." <u>Globe and Mail</u> 27 Nov. 2002: B1+.

Omit *A*, *An*, or *The* as the first word in a newspaper title. Give the day, month, and year of the issue (and the edition, if applicable). If sections are designated, give the section letter as well as the page number. If an article runs on nonconsecutive pages, give the starting page number followed by a plus sign (for example, *23+* for an article that starts on page 23 and continues on page 42).

24. Editorial, Letter to the Editor, or Review—MLA

"A Black Mark on Local Government." Editorial. London Free Press 27 July
    1994: B8.

Hurka, John. Letter. Calgary Sun 5 July 1994: A18.

Toews, Wendy. "Politics of the Mind." Rev. of They Say You're Crazy: How the
    World's Most Powerful Psychiatrists Decide Who's Normal by Paula J.
    Caplan. Winnipeg Free Press 26 Aug. 1995: C3.

25. Unsigned Article from a Daily Newspaper—MLA

"Private Water May Violate Constitution." Ottawa Citizen 27 Nov. 2002: A1.

"Judge Bars Public from CNR Building in Interim Order." Beacon Herald [Strat-
    ford, ON] 24 July 2004: A1.

If the city of publication is not part of the title, put it in square brackets after the title, not underlined.

26. Signed Article from a Weekly or Biweekly Periodical—MLA

Wood, Chris. "Storm Clouds over Quebec." Maclean's 6 Nov. 1989: 16-17.

As with a newspaper source, an unsigned article in a weekly or biweekly periodical has as its first item the title of the article.

27. Signed Article from a Monthly or Bimonthly Periodical—MLA

O'Malley, Sean. "Make-It-Happen Kinda Dreamer: Theatre Director Diane
    Dupuy Is Nobody's Puppet." Chatelaine Aug. 1994: 36-39+.

An unsigned article in a monthly or bimonthly periodical has as its first item the title of the article.

28. Article from a Collection of Reprinted Articles—MLA

Brumberg, Abraham. "Russia After Perestroika." New York Review of Books
    27 June 1991: 53-62. Rpt. in Russian and Soviet History. Ed. Alexander
    Dallin. Vol. 14 of The Gorbachev Era. New York: Garland, 1992. 300-20.

29. Article from a Looseleaf Collection of Reprinted Articles—MLA

Hayden, Thomas. "The Age of Robots." US News and World Report 23 Apr.

2001, 44+. Applied Science 2002. Ed. Eleanor Goldstein. Boca Raton, FL:

SIRS, 2002. Art. 66.

Give the citation for the original publication first, followed by the citation for the collection.

30. Article from a Journal with Continuous Pagination—MLA

Tyson, Phyllis. "The Psychology of Women." Journal of the American

Psychoanalytic Association 46 (1998): 361-64.

If the first issue of a journal with continuous pagination ends on page 228, the second issue starts with page 229. Give only the volume number before the year. Use arabic numerals for all numbers.

31. Article from a Journal That Pages Each Issue Separately—MLA

Adler-Kassner, Linda, and Heidi Estrem. "Rethinking Research Writing: Public

Litaracy in the Composition Classroom." WPA: Writing Program

Administration 26.3 (2003): 119-31.

When each issue begins with page 1, give both the volume number (*26*) and the issue number (*3*), separated by a period.

32. Abstract from a Collection of Abstracts—MLA

To cite an abstract, first give information for the full work: the author's name, the title of the article, and publication information about the full article. If a reader could not know that the cited material is an abstract, write the word *Abstract*, not underlined, followed by a period. Give publication information about the collection of abstracts. For abstracts identified by item numbers rather than page numbers, use the word *item* before the item number.

Markus, Hazel R., and Shinobu Kitayamo. "Culture and the Self: Implications

for Cognition, Emotion, and Motivation." Psychological Review 88 (1991):

224-53. Psychological Abstracts 78 (1991): item 23878.

33. Published and Unpublished Letters—MLA

Brown, Theodore. Letter to the author. 7 Dec. 2002.

Sand, George. Letter to her mother. 31 May 1831. Letters Home: Celebrated

Authors Write to Their Mothers. Ed. Reid Sherline. New York: Timkin,

1993. 17-20.

MLA

34. Microfiche Collection of Articles—MLA

Wenzell, Ron. "Businesses Prepare for a More Diverse Work Force." St. Louis Post
Dispatch 3 Feb. 1990: 17. NewsBank: Employment 27 (1990): fiche 2, grid
D12.

35. Map or Chart—MLA

Russia and Post-Soviet Republics. Map. Moscow: Mapping Production Association, 1992.

NONPRINT SOURCES

36. Interview—MLA

Friedman, Randi. Telephone interview. 30 June 2003.

For a face-to-face interview, use *Personal interview* in place of *Telephone interview.* For a published interview, give the name of the interviewed person first, identify the source as an interview, and then give
details as for any published source: title; author, preceded by the word
By; and publication details. For a URL-accessed interview, see item 64
in this section.

37. Lecture, Speech, or Address—MLA

Barlow, Maude. Address. League of Canadian Poets. Toronto. 25 May 1991.

38. Film, Videotape, or DVD—MLA

Calendar. Screenplay by Atom Egoyan. Dir. Atom Egoyan. Prod. Ego
Filmarts/ZDF. Perf. Atom Egoyan and Arsinée Khanjian. 1993. DVD.
Alliance Atlantis, 2001.

Shakespeare in Love. Screenplay by Marc Norman and Tom Stoppard. Dir.
John Madden. Prod. David Parfitt, Donna Gigliotti, Harvey Weinstein,
Edward Zwick, and Marc Norman. Perf. Gwyneth Paltrow, Joseph
Fiennes, and Judi Dench. DVD. Miramax, 2003.

Give the title first, and include the director, the distributor, and the year.
For older films subsequently released on videocassette, DVD, or laser
disc, provide the original release date of the movie before the type of
medium. Other information (writer, producer, major actors) is optional
but helpful. Put first names first.

39. Recording—MLA

Cohen, Leonard. "Tower of Song." I'm Your Man. Sony, 1988.

Smetana, Bedrich. My Country. Cond. Karel Ancerl. Czech Philharmonic Orch.
LP. Vanguard, 1975.

Put first the name most relevant to what you discuss in your paper (performer, conductor, the work performed, etc.). Include the recording's title, the medium for any recording other than a CD (e.g., *LP, Audiocassette*), name of the issuer (e.g., *Vanguard*), and the year.

40. Live Performance—MLA

The Merchant of Venice. By William Shakespeare. Dir. Richard Monette. Perf.
    Lucy Peacock and Paul Soles. Festival Theatre, Stratford, ON. 8 May 2001.

41. Work of Art, Photograph, or Musical Composition—MLA

Pratt, Christopher. Shop on an Island. London Regional Art Gallery, London, ON.

Schubert, Franz. Symphony no. 8 in B minor.

Schubert, Franz. Unfinished Symphony.

Do not underline or put in quotation marks music identified only by form, number, and key, but do underline any work that has a title, such as an opera, a ballet, or a named symphony.

42. Radio or Television Program—MLA

"Episode One." The Forsyte Saga. By John Galsworthy. Adapt. Stephen
    Mallatratt and Jan McVerry. Prod. Sita Williams. Masterpiece Theatre.
    PBS. WGBH, Boston. 6 Oct. 2002.

"Mountie and Soul." Due South. Perf. Paul Gross and David Marciano. CTV.
    CFTO, Toronto. 26 Oct. 1997.

Include at least the title of the program (underlined), the network, the local station and its city, and the date(s) of the broadcast. For a series, also supply the title of the specific episode (in quotation marks) before the title of the program (underlined) and the title of the series (neither underlined nor in quotation marks), as in the first example above, where *The Forsyte Saga* is a program in the series Masterpiece Theatre.

43. Advertisement—MLA

WestJet Airlines. Advertisement. CTV. 24 June 2004.

Rogers Digital Cable. Advertisement. Maclean's 2 Aug. 2004: 81.

PORTABLE ELECTRONIC SOURCES
44. CD-ROM Database: Abstract with a Print Version—MLA

Markus, Hazel R., and Shinobu Kitayamo. "Culture and the Self: Implications
    for Cognition, Emotion, and Motivation." Psychological Abstracts 78
    (1991): item 23878. PsycLIT. CD-ROM. SilverPlatter. Sept. 1991.

MLA

All the information through *item 23878* is for the print version of this source. The volume number is 78, and the abstract's number is 23878. All the information from *PsycLIT* to the end of the entry is for the electronic version of the source. *PsycLIT* is the name of the CD-ROM database, and *SilverPlatter* is the name of the producer of the CD-ROM. The CD-ROM was issued in September 1991.

45. CD-ROM: Article from a Periodical with a Print Version—MLA

"The Price Is Right." Time 20 Jan. 1992: 38. Time Man of the Year. CD-ROM.

Compact. 1993.

Information for the print version ends with the article's page number, 38. The title of the CD-ROM is *Time Man of the Year*, its producer is the publisher Compact, and its copyright year is 1993. Both the title of the print publication and the title of the CD-ROM are underlined.

46. CD-ROM: Selection from a Book with a Print Version—MLA

"Prehistoric Humans: Earliest Homo sapiens." The Guinness Book of Records

1994. London: Guinness, 1994. The Guinness Multimedia Disk of Records.

CD-ROM. Version 2.0. Danbury, CT: Grolier Electronic, 1994.

Version 2.0 signals that this CD-ROM is updated periodically; the producer changes version numbers rather than give update dates.

47. CD-ROM: Material with No Print Version—MLA

"Artificial Intelligence." Encarta 2003. CD-ROM. Redmond, WA: Microsoft, 2003.

Encarta 2003 is a CD-ROM encyclopedia with no print version. "Artificial Intelligence" is the title of an article in *Encarta 2003*.

48. Work in More Than One Publication Medium—MLA

Clarke, David James. Novell's CNE Study Guide. Book. Network Support

Encyclopedia. CD-ROM. Alameda, CA: Sybex, 1994.

This book and CD-ROM come together. Each has its own title, but the publication information—*Alameda, CA: Sybex, 1994*—applies to both.

SOURCES FROM LIBRARY OR PERSONAL SUBSCRIPTION SERVICES

Online sources fall into two categories: (1) those you access through a library online service, such as EBSCO or FirstSearch, or a personal service, such as AOL Canada; and (2) those you access by browsing the Internet or entering a specific URL (Internet address). For source material reached through an online service, give the name of the service, and if you used a keyword for your search, give it after the access date.

561

MLA

49. Library Subscription Service: Abstract with a Print Version—MLA

Markus, Hazel R., and Shinobu Kitayamo. "Culture and the Self: Implications
    for Cognition, Emotion, and Motivation." Psychological Abstracts 78
    (1991). PsycINFO. Ovid. Harriet Irving Lib., U of New Brunswick. 10 Apr.
    2003 <http://gateway1.ovid.com/ovidweb.cgi>.

This entry is for the same abstract from *Psychological Abstracts* shown
in item 44, but here it is accessed from an online database (*PsycINFO*)
by means of an online service (*Ovid*). This entry notes *PsycINFO*, the
name of the online database, whereas item 44 notes *PsycLIT,* the name
of the CD-ROM database; and it notes *Ovid,* the service through which
PsycINFO was accessed, whereas item 44 notes the CD-ROM producer, *SilverPlatter.* The name of the library shows where the source
was accessed, and *10 Apr. 2003* is the date that the abstract was
accessed. The entry ends with the specific URL used.

50. Personal Subscription Service: Material with No Print Version—MLA

"Microsoft Licenses OSM Technology from Henter-Joyce." WinNews Electronic
    Newsletter 1 May 1995. CompuServe. 15 May 1995.

Many personal subscription services do not provide a separate URL for
individual materials they offer.

**51. Personal Subscription Service Accessed with a Keyword: Article from a
Periodical with a Print Version—MLA**

Wynne, Clive D. L. "'Willy' Didn't Yearn to Be Free." New York Times 27 Dec.
    2003: Op-ed page. New York Times Online. America Online. 29 Dec. 2003.
    Keyword: nytimes.

Information applying to the print version of this article in the *New York
Times* ends with *Op-ed page,* and information about the online version
starts with the title of the database, *New York Times Online. America
Online* is the service through which the database was accessed, and
29 Dec. 2003 is the access date. The keyword *nytimes* was used to access
New York Times Online, as noted after the access date.

52. Personal Subscription Service Showing a Path—MLA

When you access a source by choosing a series of keywords, menus, or
topics, end the entry with the "path" of words you used. Use semicolons
between items in the path, and put a period at the end.

Futrelle, David. "A Smashing Success." Money.com 23 Dec. 1999. America
    Online. 26 Dec. 1999. Path: Personal Finance; Business News; Business
    Publications; Money.com.

53. Library Subscription Service: Article—MLA

For an article accessed through a library's online service, first give information about the source. Then list the name of the online database (underlined), the name of the online service through which it was accessed, the name of the library, and the access date. Give the URL of the online service's home page, if you know it, after the access date. Enclose the URL in angle brackets (< >), and put a period after the closing bracket.

Dutton, Gail. "Greener Pigs." Popular Science Nov. 1999: 38-39. ProQuest
  Periodical Abstracts Plus Text. ProQuest Direct. Public Lib., Moncton.
  7 Dec. 2003 <http://proquest.umi.com>.

SOURCES FROM INTERNET SITES

This section shows models for online sources accessed through an Internet browser, such as Web sites, FTP and Gopher sites, e-mail discussion lists, forums, and similar groups, and other online sources. For such sources, provide as much of the following information as you can.

1. The author's name, if given.
2. In quotation marks, the title of a short work (Web page, brief document, essay, article, message, and so on); or, underlined, the title of a book.
3. The name of an editor, translator, or compiler, if any, with an abbreviation such as *Ed.*, *Trans.*, or *Comp.* before the name.
4. Publication information for any print version, if it exists.
5. The underlined title of the Internet site (scholarly project, database, online periodical, professional or personal Web site). If the site has no title, describe it: for example, *Home page.*
6. The date of electronic publication (including a version number, if any) or posting, or the most recent update.
7. The name of a sponsoring organization, if any.
8. The date you accessed the material.
9. The URL in angle brackets (< >), with a period after the closing bracket. If the URL is too long or complicated, simply use the URL of the site's search page or of a subscription service, followed by *Keyword* or *Path,* and the links you followed. In MLA style, if the whole URL doesn't fit on one line, divide it only after a slash—*not* after a period.

54. Online Book—MLA

Eaton, Arthur W. Acadian Legends and Lyrics. London and New York: White &
  Allen, 1889. Early Canadiana Online. 16 Feb. 2000. 25 May 2004
  <http://www.canadiana.org/cgi-bin/ECO/mtq?doc=09066>.

MLA

55. Online Book in a Scholarly Project—MLA

Herodotus. The History of Herodotus. Trans. George Rawlinson. Internet
    Classics Archive. Ed. Daniel C. Stevenson. 11 Jan. 1998. Massachusetts
    Institute of Technology. 15 May 2003 <http://classics.mit.edu/Herodotus/
    history.html>.

56. Online Government-Published Books—MLA

Canada. Health Canada. Assessment of Mercury Exposure and Risks from
    Dental Amalgam. By G. Mark Richardson. 18 Aug. 1995. 23 Feb. 2004
    <http://dsp-psd.pwgsc.gc.ca/Collection/H46-1-36-1995E.pdf>.

Canada. Office of the Commissioner of Official Languages. Linguistic Duality
    in Commercial Advertising and Sponsorships. Sep. 2003. 15 Mar. 2004
    <http://dsp-psd.pwgsc.gc.ca/Collection/SF31-68-2003E.pdf>.

For government publications that name no author, start with the name
of the government or government body, and then name the government
agency. For a government text, the title is followed by the writer of the
publication, if available.

57. Article in an Online Periodical—MLA

Ignatieff, Michael. "The Man Who Was Right." Rev. of Reflections on a Ravaged
    Century, by Robert Conquest. New York Review of Books 23 Mar. 2000. 5
    June 2004 <http://nybooks.com/nyrev/WWWarchdisplay.cgi?20000323035R>.

Gold, David. "Ulysses: A Case Study in the Problems of Hypertextualization of
    Complex Documents." Computers, Writing, Rhetoric and Literature 3.1
    (1997): 37 pars. 4 Dec. 2003 <http://www.cwrl.utexas.edu/~cwrl/v3nl/
    dgold/title.htm>.

Keegan, Paul. "Culture Quake." Mother Jones Nov.-Dec. 1999. 6 Feb. 2003
    <http://www.mojones.com/mother_jones/ND99/quake.html>.

Lewis, Ricki. "Chronobiology Researchers Say Their Field's Time Has Come."
    Scientist 11 Dec. 1995: 14. 30 Dec. 2003 <http://www.the-scientist.com/
    yr1995/dec/chres_951211.html>.

Pacienza, Angela. "Cities Could Become Treeless Wastelands." Winnipeg
    Free Press Online Edition 11 June 2001. 9 July 2004 <http://
    www.winnipegfreepress.com/news/canadaworld/273409436518713.html>

58. Professional Home Page—MLA

<u>Mountain Culture</u>. 2003. Banff Centre. 22 Nov. 2003 <http://www.banffcentre.ca/
    mountainculture/>.

This is the home page of an institute based at the Banff Centre. Note that the page title is underlined, but the name of the sponsoring organization (*Banff Centre*) is not.

59. Personal Home Page—MLA

Hesse, Doug. Home page. 15 Nov. 2003. 22 Dec. 2003 <http://www.ilstu.edu/
    ~ddhesse>.

For home pages, include as much of the following information as you can find:

1. If available, the name of the person who created or set up the home page. If first and last names are given, reverse the order of the first author's name.
2. The title, underlined. If there is no title, add the description *Home page*, not underlined, followed by a period.
3. For a professional home page, the name of the professional (not commercial) sponsoring organization.
4. If available, the date the page was last published or updated, followed by a period.
5. The date you accessed the material.
6. The URL in angle brackets (< >), with a period after the closing bracket.

60. Government or Institutional Web Site—MLA

<u>Adult Learners</u>. 2003. Newfoundland and Labrador Department of Education.
    22 Nov. 2003 <http://www.gov.nf.ca/edu/adult/adult.htm>.

61. Academic Department Home Page—MLA

English. Dept. home page. Simon Fraser U. Burnaby. 26 Feb. 2003
    <http://www2.sfu.ca/english>.

62. URL Access: Poem—MLA

Nelligan, Émile. "Automne." <u>Émile Nelligan et son oeuvre</u>. Montreal, 1925.
    <u>Canadian Poetry Archive</u>. 2 Jan. 2002. National Library of Canada.
    22 Nov. 2004 <http://www.nlc_bnc.ca/canvers_bin/
    entry?entry_nbr=754&l=0&page_rows=10&clctn_nbr=1>.

63. URL Access: Work of Art—MLA

Anghik, Abraham. <u>Kittigazuit–1918</u>. 2000. Winnipeg Art Gallery. 18 Nov. 2004
    <http://www.wag.mb.ca/collection/recentacquisition.html>.

64. URL Access: Interview—MLA

Plaxco, Jim. Interview. <u>Planetary Studies Foundation</u>. Oct. 1992. 5 Dec. 2004
    <http://www.planets.org/>.

65. URL Access: Film or Film Clip—MLA

Columbus, Chris, dir. <u>Harry Potter and the Sorcerer's Stone</u>. Trailer. Warner
    Brothers, 2001. 5 Dec. 2003 <http://www.hollywood.com/>.

66. URL Access: Cartoon—MLA

Harris, Sidney. "We have lots of information technology." Cartoon. <u>New Yorker</u>.
    27 May 2002. 26 Aug. 2003 <http://www.cartoonbank.com>.

67. URL Access: TV or Radio Program—MLA

Walsh, Mary. "<u>Regeneration</u> Trilogy by Pat Barker." <u>Open Book</u>. CBC. 29 Sept.
    2002. 15 Nov. 2004 <http://cbc.ca/openbook/episode8.html>.

OTHER ONLINE SOURCES

68. Online Posting—MLA

Woodbury, Chuck. "Free RV Campgrounds." Online posting. 4 Dec. 1999. The
    RV Home Page Bulletin Board. 21 Dec. 1999 <http://www.rvhome.com/
    wwwboard/messages/4598.html>.

Be cautious about using online postings as sources. Some postings contain cutting-edge information from experts, but some contain trash. Unfortunately, you have no way to know whether people online are who they claim to be. To cite an online message, give the author name (if any), the title of the message in quotation marks, and then *Online posting.* Give the date of the posting and the name of the bulletin board, if any. Then give the access date and, in angle brackets, the URL.

69. Synchronous Communication (MOO, MUD, IRC)—MLA

Bleck, Bradley. Online discussion of "Virtual First Year Composition: Distance
    Education, the Internet, and the World Wide Web." 8 June 1997. DaMOO.
    27 July 2004 <http://lrc.csun.edu/DaMOO/cw/brad.html>.

Give the name of the speaker, a title for the event (*"Virtual First Year Composition: Distance Education, the Internet, and the World Wide Web"*), the forum (*DaMOO*), event or posting date, access date, and URL.

MLA

70. E-Mail Message—MLA

Thompson, Jim. "Bob Martin's Opinions." E-mail to June Cain. 11 Nov. 2003.

Start with the name of the person who wrote the e-mail message. Give the title or subject line in quotation marks. Then describe the source (*E-mail*) and identify the recipient. End with the date.

34d.2 Using content or bibliographic notes in MLA style

In MLA style, footnotes or endnotes serve two specific purposes: (1) You can use them for content (ideas and information) that does not fit into your paper but is still worth relating; and (2) you can use them for bibliographic information that would intrude if you were to include it in your text. Place a note number at the end of a sentence, if possible. Put it after any punctuation mark except the dash. Do not put any space before a note number, and put one space after it. Raise the note number a little above the line of words (called a *superscript* number in word-processing programs), as shown in the following examples.

TEXT OF PAPER

Ronald Wright's <u>Stolen Continents</u> surprises us by telling the story of the European conquest of North and South America "through Indian eyes."[1]

CONTENT NOTE—MLA

[1] Wright, who was born and educated in England, brings an outsider's point of view to his adopted country, Canada. This may explain his willingness to examine the post-conquest history of the First Nations from a new and disturbing perspective.

TEXT OF PAPER

Barbara Randolph believes that enthusiasm is contagious (65).[1] Many psychologists have found that panic, fear, and rage spread more quickly in crowds than positive emotions do, however.

BIBLIOGRAPHIC NOTE—MLA

[1] Others who agree with Randolph include Thurman 21, 84, 155; Kelley 421-25; and Brookes 65-76.

34e A student's MLA-style research paper

34e.1 Researching and writing the paper

Case Study

Chandra Johnson was given this assignment for a research paper:
Write a research paper on the general subject of new technologies. The
paper should be 1800 to 2000 words long and should be based on a variety of sources. The final paper is due in six weeks. Interim deadlines for
parts of the work will be announced. To complete this assignment, you
need to engage in three interrelated processes: conducting research,
understanding the results of that research, and writing a paper based on
the first two processes. Consult the *Simon & Schuster Handbook for
Writers,* Fourth Canadian Edition, especially Chapters 32 and 33, which
give practical, step-by-step guidance on what this assignment entails.

Chandra Johnson was eager to plan her research schedule so that she
could budget her time and not end up in a panic because of time pressure. She knew from experience that she would likely have the most
trouble in the first stages of her research process, as she narrowed her
topic and began to look for useful sources. She resolved to face the challenge calmly and patiently.

The general topic assigned was "technology." Johnson realized that
she had to take many steps to narrow it to a TOPIC suitable for a research
paper (31b). Collecting possible subject headings and topic key words
was her first step. Because she was working in her room and had a connection to the Internet, she first connected to the Google subject directory. While she didn't find a heading there for "technology," she did find
ones for "computers" and "science." Clicking on the "science" category,
Johnson found a link to "technology." When she looked at the headings
under "technology," the topic "artificial intelligence" caught her attention. Ever since she had seen the movie *A.I. Artificial Intelligence,* she
had been fascinated by the possibility that people might someday be
able to make machines that act like humans. She browsed several links
under "artificial intelligence" and jotted ideas in her research log. However, she soon became confused by all the available options. Johnson
decided to proceed more systematically through library resources.

When she was next on campus, she went to the library to check its
online catalogue. Johnson decided that finding some general books on the
subject of artificial intelligence would help her get a sense of this complicated topic. She entered the phrase as a keyword search and learned it

was a Library of Congress subject heading, which meant she was on a helpful track. Furthermore, her library owned several recent books on the topic. She chose a few that looked promising. Johnson copied information about them, including their call numbers, onto some note cards she'd brought for her working bibliography, then e-mailed the full citations to herself as a backup. She noticed that the call numbers were mostly around Q335 but that others began with BD or BF. She found that the latter call numbers were from the philosophy and psychology sections of the library.

To limit her search—and because she knew this field was changing rapidly—she decided to focus on books written in the past ten years. Although the most promising volume was checked out, another current book, *Arguing A.I.: The Battle for Twenty-First-Century Science*, was almost as promising. From the book's cover, Johnson saw that its author, Sam Williams, was a freelance writer and not an expert, so she knew she'd have to check his ideas. However, because the book discussed several important figures in artificial intelligence, including John McCarthy and Ray Kurzweil, it pointed to some expert sources that she later consulted for her paper, including various Web resources.

At this point, Johnson was still feeling overwhelmed. Clearly, there was a vast amount of information available on artificial intelligence, and she would need to narrow her search. One breakthrough came as she explored ideas in her research log. As a broad draft RESEARCH QUESTION, she asked, "What is artificial intelligence?" only to realize that there was an even more basic question: "What is intelligence?"

Johnson looked up "intelligence" in the *Columbia Encyclopedia,* a general reference book she was familiar with from high school. A concept developed by Howard Gardner of Harvard University captured her interest. Gardner states that human intelligence actually consists of eight different kinds of intelligence, not just IQ (for "intelligence quotient"). She wrote down Gardner's name as a possible authority (see Box 131 in 31i) and was delighted to find several books by him in her library's catalogue. One of them, *Frames of Mind,* became a source on her topic. Further reading in the area of multiple intelligences stirred her interest in emotional intelligence. Books by Daniel Goleman and Antonio Damasio seemed particularly valuable, and after checking the authors' credentials, she added the book titles to her bibliography cards (31i). Eventually her reading led her to narrow her topic and develop her research question, "Do computers need emotions for scientists to consider them intelligent?" The flowchart on the next page illustrates Johnson's process of narrowing her topic.

To find out if there were more current resources focusing specifically on the role of emotions in creating artificial intelligence, Johnson checked online databases. Her university library uses EBSCO, First-Search, and IBIS online services, each with links to scholarly full-text databases and online journals. In addition, because Johnson was still try-

Flowchart of Chandra Johnson's narrowing process

ing to learn the issues, she consulted *Readers' Guide Abstracts*, which led her to several popular articles. Through EBSCO, she clicked on "Academic Search Elite" and discovered several sources by combining "artificial intelligence" and "emotions" as her search terms. However, she wanted to make certain she was finding the best sources. From her experience with finding books, she knew that artificial intelligence sources existed in both computer sciences and psychology, so she asked a reference librarian what databases she should search. He recommended Computer Database and PsycInfo.

The search of these databases produced the articles by Allen, Bates, Kurzweil, and others that Johnson ultimately used. She also identified more than two dozen citations that she ultimately did not include in the paper. Many of these did not focus specifically enough on the role of emotions in artificial intelligence, some repeated sources she already had, some were too basic, and some were written at such a high technical level that she knew she didn't have the time or expertise to figure them out.

Finally, Johnson decided to see if there were important current sources available on the World Wide Web. She typed "artificial intelligence" into the Google search engine and was delighted (and a little lucky) that the first match that appeared was the home page of the American Association for Artificial Intelligence <http://aaai.org>. She also found an online searchable "Bibliography for Artificial Intelligence." This last source led her to John McCarthy's Web site. As she knew from the book by Williams, McCarthy was a computer science professor at Stanford University and one of the founders of the field of artificial intelligence, which confirmed that his Web site would be credible.

As Johnson conducted her research, she didn't know where to stand on the issue. Many scientists believed that emotions were an important part of artificial intelligence, and many others did not. Of the scientists who believed that emotions were important, some of them thought it impossible to program a computer or robot to experience them, while others considered emotions within reach. Johnson herself was skeptical. However, she intentionally sought sources that took different sides on the debate. She took content notes on her computer, opening a new file for each source and taking care to distinguish direct quotations from her own summaries, paraphrases, and interpretations.

After taking notes, Johnson was ready to DRAFT her research paper. Thinking about her PURPOSE, she first concluded that she should persuade her readers to take a specific position about the role of emotions in artificial intelligence. However, as she completed her outline and first and second drafts, she realized that the topic was too complicated for her to argue for a specific position. Johnson altered her purpose to informing readers about the various issues surrounding emotions and artificial intelligence. Her goal was to make readers see her paper as a thoughtful attempt to explain the issues. As Johnson wrote, she used her note files carefully to make sure she always knew when she was quoting a source and when she was summarizing. She made sure to put in the correct PARENTHETICAL DOCUMENTATION (34c) for each source. She also kept a WORKING BIBLIOGRAPHY (31i) so that she would be ready to list each one of the sources in her WORKS CITED list (34d) at the end of her paper. By the time Johnson came to the final draft of her research paper, she decided to drop a few sources because they repeated what others whom she considered better authorities had said.

Johnson struggled with her concluding paragraph. She had to synthesize complicated material in a fairly limited space. Here's an early draft of her concluding paragraph, which you can compare to the one in her final draft in 34e.2.

The importance of emotions in creating artificial intelligence may

be a matter of definition. For some, like the American Association for

Artificial Intelligence, artificial intelligence already surrounds us in cars,

in computers, in something as simple as postal machines that can sort handwritten postcards. We just fail to recognize it. For others, the true measure of artificial intelligence is consciousness. John Searle argues that just because a computer can *simulate* consciousness does not mean that it *has* consciousness (37). According to this reasoning, a machine that accurately detects and produces emotions may be smarter than a machine that cannot. However, we cannot say it is conscious, and so we cannot say it is intelligent in the same ways that humans are intelligent.

34e.2 Analyzing the research paper

MLA style doesn't call for a title page for research papers. Many instructors, however, require a title page. Inquire as to your instructor's preference. If you're asked to use a title page, follow the format on the facing page.

If you follow MLA style by not using a title page, use the headings shown on the first page of the sample research paper (see page 576). Follow precisely the format instructions shown there.

If you use a title page, never assign it a page number. Use the arabic numeral 1, without *page* or *p.*, for the first page of the actual paper. Put your last name followed by a space and the page number in the upper right corner, one-half inch (about 1.25 cm) below the top edge of the page. (Many writers take advantage of the word-processing function that inserts page numbers and last name as a header, updating automatically.) Then type the paper's title, centring it on the page, one-half inch (1.25 cm) below the name-number heading. Continue numbering pages sequentially through to the last page of your WORKS CITED list. Use one-inch (2.5-cm) margins on all sides of the sheet of paper.

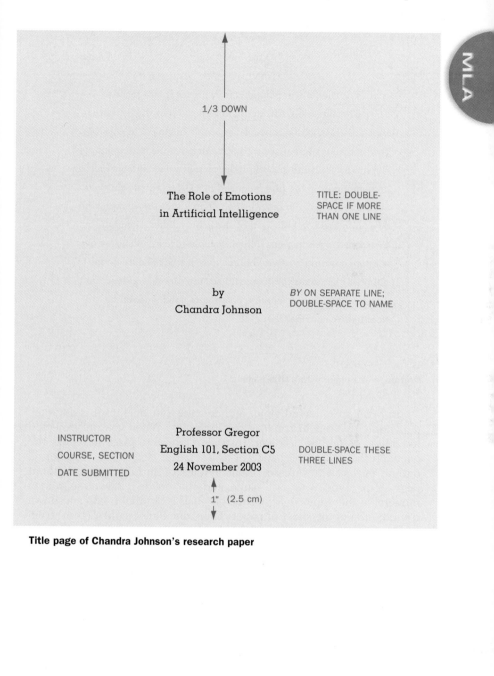

1/3 DOWN

The Role of Emotions
in Artificial Intelligence

TITLE: DOUBLE-
SPACE IF MORE
THAN ONE LINE

by
Chandra Johnson

BY ON SEPARATE LINE;
DOUBLE-SPACE TO NAME

INSTRUCTOR
COURSE, SECTION
DATE SUBMITTED

Professor Gregor
English 101, Section C5
24 November 2003

DOUBLE-SPACE THESE
THREE LINES

1" (2.5 cm)

Title page of Chandra Johnson's research paper

1" (2.5 cm)

¹/₂" (1.25 cm)

Johnson 1

The Role of Emotions in Artificial Intelligence

DOUBLE-SPACE   The movie A.I. Artificial Intelligence portrays a future in which distinguishing robots from people is almost impossible. The robots look human and can produce actions that appear to be human. Still, one important distinction exists: Robots lack true emotions. In the film, released in 2001, scientists create an experimental robotic boy who can deeply love the woman who owns him and can believe that she is his mother. Computer scientists, psychologists, and philosophers today disagree over whether creating artificial beings like this boy should be the ultimate goal of research in artificial intelligence. Indeed, an unsolved problem is whether computers need emotion for scientists to consider them intelligent.

First page of a paper with a title page

In MLA style, including an outline with your final draft is optional, depending on your instructor's requirements. When you are expected to include an outline, ask your instructor where to place it: before the paper, at the end of the paper, or as a separate document. Number all outline pages in lowercase roman numerals starting with *i*, without *page* or *p*. Type your last name and the needed lowercase roman numeral in the upper right corner, one-half inch (about 1.25 cm) down from the top of the sheet of paper. Then, one inch (about 2.5 cm) from the top, centre the word *Outline*. As shown in the sample outline on the facing page, place your thesis statement one double space below *Outline*. Underline only the words *Thesis statement*. Switch to arabic numerals for numbering the pages of the paper itself.

Johnson's instructor required that an outline be submitted with the final draft of her research paper. Johnson chose to use a topic outline, not a sentence outline (see 2r). Either type is acceptable in MLA style, though many instructors prefer a sentence outline because it communicates more information than a topic outline does. Follow the format of the outline shown here: Even if your instructor doesn't require you to submit an outline, you might find that developing one helps clarify your thoughts and ensure that you've covered your TOPIC fully. Examining a paper's "skeleton" helps you focus on the overall shape and organization of your research paper—and it may reveal gaps in your paper's development that you need to fill in.

1" (2.5 cm)

¹/₂" (1.25 cm)

Johnson i

Outline ◄─────── DOUBLE-SPACE

I. Introduction
   A. Example from the movie A.I.
   B. Thesis statement: An unsolved problem is whether computers need emotions for scientists to consider them intelligent.

II. Definitions of intelligence
   A. General definitions
   B. Artificial intelligence (AI)
      1. Qualities of AI
      2. Scientists' opinions of how close we are to AI
      3. Turing test
      4. Chess room argument

III. Types of intelligence
   A. Gardner's eight intelligences
   B. Emotional intelligence
      1. Goleman's research
      2. Damasio's research

IV. Emotions and artificial intelligence
   A. Believers' and doubters' positions on emotions
   B. The role of recognizing and conveying emotions
      1. Children's learning
      2. Applying Disney's techniques to robots

V. Conclusion
   A. The remaining controversy
   B. No emotions in computers any time soon

Outline for Chandra Johnson's research paper

MLA

Put identifying information in upper left corner; double-space.

Centre title one double space below identifying information.

Start first line of paper one double space below title.

In MLA style, put author and page number in parentheses when author is not named in the sentence.

Use ½-inch (1.25-cm) top margin, 1-inch (2.5-cm) bottom and side margins; double-space throughout.

Johnson 1

Chandra Johnson

Professor Gregor

English 101, Section C5

24 November 2003

The Role of Emotions in Artificial Intelligence

The movie <u>A.I. Artificial Intelligence</u> portrays a future in which distinguishing robots from people is almost impossible. The robots look human and can produce actions that appear to be human. Still, one important distinction exists: Robots lack true emotions. In the film, released in 2001, scientists create an experimental robotic boy who can deeply love the woman who owns him and can believe that she is his mother. Computer scientists, psychologists, and philosophers today disagree over whether creating artificial beings like this boy should be the ultimate goal of research in artificial intelligence. Indeed, an unsolved problem is whether computers need emotion for scientists to consider them intelligent.

Defining human intelligence is a major focus of cognitive science, a broad field that studies the mind (Pfeifer and Scheier 5). Members of this field include psychologists, linguists, and computer scientists, among others. Cognitive scientists agree that human intelligence includes several broad abilities. These consist of the abilities to think abstractly, to learn, to adapt to new situations in life, and to profit from experience (7). Intelligence calls for more than the ability to recall information or perform set routines. It involves using past knowledge, intuition, creativity, and experience in new, unfamiliar situations, and learning from them. It also requires using

→

1

2

3

4

5

6

(Proportions shown in this paper are adjusted to fit space limitations of this book. Follow actual dimensions discussed in this book and your instructor's directions.)

MLA

Commentary

1. **Computer tip.** Following MLA style, Johnson used her name and the page number as a running header throughout the paper. She used the "header" command in her word-processing program to insert the proper information on each page automatically.

2. **Introductory strategy.** Johnson attracts the reader's interest by referring to a recent popular movie. From that specific example, she moves to introducing the topic more broadly. Because the movie *A.I.* gave her the idea for her paper topic, the introduction came fairly easily to her.

3. **Thesis.** The last sentence of Johnson's introductory paragraph is her THESIS STATEMENT. In it she tries to prepare readers for the main message of the paper.

4. **PROCESS NOTE:** Paragraph 2 begins to define intelligence. In an early draft, Johnson started writing about scientists' attempts to create artificial intelligence in robots. Later she decided that it made more sense to talk generally about intelligence in humans and then discuss computers and robots.

5. **Summarizing a source.** For much of her initial definition of intelligence, Johnson drew on a scholarly book. She decided to summarize concepts from that book rather than paraphrase or quote them. Note that she took care to include page citations.

6. **PROCESS NOTE:** Johnson revised the sentences from "These consist" through "It also requires" many times. In her first draft, she put all the characteristics of intelligence into one long sentence. She saw immediately that she needed to break the characteristics into small chunks. She set about figuring out which characteristics would go together logically. She then wrote several versions of her shorter sentences, trying to vary lengths and use a variety of words to make the writing more interesting. After she turned in her final draft, however, she discovered that she had repeated "intuition" and "creativity" (see beginning of page 2 of the paper). She wished she had seen that slip earlier.

Johnson 2

intuition and creativity (10). For example, when college student
Joshua Vrana, who worked part-time in a store, was asked to
develop a Web site for the store, he created it from his knowledge of Web design, the store, and its customers. In so doing, he
drew creatively upon his knowledge and experience, thereby
using all aspects of human intelligence.

Cognitive scientists disagree on a definition of artificial
intelligence. At one extreme, some scientists regard it as the
ability of a machine to perform every intelligent act that a
human can perform. Table 1 lists some of those acts. This is a
very high standard. At the other extreme, scientists define
artificial intelligence as the ability to perform even a small act
that requires human intelligence. For example, the American
Association for Artificial Intelligence believes that artificial
intelligence already exists in devices as simple as postal
machines that can sort handwritten postcards. This is a very
low standard.

7

8

9

10

Table 1

11

Some Qualities of Artificial Intelligence

Category	Examples
Problem solving	Using informed search methods to solve problems; game playing
Logical behaviour	Planning for practical action; acting appropriately for a given situation
Knowledge and reasoning	Using memory; dealing with uncertainty; reasoning using probability; making simple and complex decisions

(continued)

➔

578

Commentary

7. **Example from experience.** Johnson decided that the point about intuition and creativity would be clearer if she gave an example. She remembered a conversation with her friend Joshua Vrana about a project he had completed at his job, and she realized that it would illustrate the point effectively.

8. **Elaborating a key issue from the thesis.** Johnson's topic sentence in this paragraph signals the reader that she is about to explain the disagreement between scientists over the proper measure of artificial intelligence. By starting one sentence with "At one extreme" and another sentence with "At the other extreme," she hoped to contrast and clarify the two positions. She had to write several drafts to state the distinctions clearly and concisely.

9. **Reference to a table.** Although she did not want to interrupt her paragraph, Johnson felt her readers would benefit from a reference to Table 1, which would soon follow.

10. **Example.** To provide support for her claim, Johnson included the example from the American Association for Artificial Intelligence.

11. **Table.** Johnson faced a length restriction in this paper, but she needed to present a good deal of information. She decided the most effective way to summarize much of that information would be to include a table. Developing the table also helped her to clarify the ideas it contained.

   As she formatted her paper's final draft, Johnson discovered that the table would not fit on one page. She had two choices: (1) put the table (and any other tables she might create) into an appendix to be placed before her Works Cited list; (2) divide the table between two pages so that it would fall exactly where she wanted her readers to see it. She chose the second option after checking with her instructor.

Johnson 3

Table 1   *(continued)*

Some Qualities of Artificial Intelligence

Category	Examples
Learning	Learning from observations and experience
Communicating, perceiving, and acting	Using language with people; becoming aware of surroundings through the senses; interacting with the environment

Table source note appears in MLA style.

Source: Adapted from Rolf Pfeifer and Christian Scheier,

"Topics in Classical AI," in <u>Understanding Intelligence</u>

(Cambridge, MA: MIT P, 2000) 46.

While the dream of creating robots with human 12

intelligence has existed for almost a century, scientists disagree

In MLA style, put author and page number in parentheses when author is not named in text.

on how close we have come to realizing that dream. Perhaps the

most famous example occurred when computer engineers

developed IBM's Deep Blue computer, which beat chess

grandmaster Garry Kasparov in 1997 (Hayden 46). However,

Murray Campbell, one of Deep Blue's creators, has conceded

No page number is cited when a document is only one page.

that the computer "did not exhibit human qualities and

therefore was not 'intelligent' " (qtd. in Stix). Some computer 13

scientists take a much different position. For example, Hans

Square brackets show words added or changed to make a quotation flow.

Moravec believes that "robot computers [will] achieve human 14

intelligence . . . around 2040" (qtd. in Minerd 9). Ray Kurzweil is 15

even more optimistic in that he believes that Moravec's

prediction will come true as early as 2029 and that by the end of

the twenty-first century, machine-based intelligences will

rightfully claim to be human (21).

→

MLA

Commentary

12. **PROCESS NOTE:** Johnson revised this paragraph several times because it covers several different opinions (note the number of sources cited in a relatively short space). The example of Deep Blue illustrates efforts to create intelligent computers. The quotation from one of Deep Blue's creators was particularly effective because he takes a position opposite the one we might expect.

13. **Key transition within a paragraph.** Because she was summarizing two very different positions in this paragraph, Johnson needed a strong sentence to signal a contrast between scientists who doubt the possibility of artificial intelligence and those who think we are close to achieving it. In an early draft she had divided this material into two paragraphs, but she later decided it would work better as a single paragraph.

14. **Modified quotation.** To make the quotation from Moravec fit the flow of the sentence, Johnson had to add the word *will*. She enclosed the word in square brackets to signal that it was not part of the original quotation. (The original source was written in the hypothetical future and simply said that "computers achieve human intelligence.") Johnson also omitted some words from the source, indicating the omission with an ellipsis.

15. **PROCESS NOTE:** Johnson encountered several references to the work of Ray Kurzweil. Because many of his claims seemed extreme, she was skeptical about whether he was a credible source. However, she found that other respected authors frequently cited him, even if it was only to criticize his ideas. She concluded that Kurzweil offered a perspective that she should represent in her paper.

Johnson 4

The Turing test, developed in 1950 by the British

mathematician Alan Turing, is one commonly accepted measure

of artificial intelligence (McCarthy). A researcher sits in one

room, another person in a second room, and a computer in a

third room. The researcher does not know which room contains

the person and which holds the computer. Communicating only

through a keyboard and screen, the researcher asks the same

questions of both the person and the machine. If the researcher

cannot tell which responses come from the machine, the

computer passes the test.

However, some people dispute the Turing test. The

prominent philosopher John Searle argues that the appearance

of proper answers does not prove the existence of intelligence.

He offers "the chess room argument":

> Imagine that a man who does not know how to play
>
> chess is locked inside a room, and there he is given
>
> a set of, to him, meaningless symbols. Unknown to
>
> him, these represent positions on a chessboard. He
>
> looks up in a book what he is supposed to do, and he
>
> passes back more meaningless symbols. We can
>
> suppose that if the rule book . . . is skillfully written,
>
> he will win chess games. People outside the room
>
> will say, "This man understands chess, and in fact
>
> he is a good chess player because he wins." They
>
> will be totally mistaken. The man understands
>
> nothing of chess, he is just a computer. (qtd. in
>
> Allen 30)

The disagreements about defining artificial intelligence

result partly from how complicated the idea of human

World Wide Web source has no page numbers.

16

Use block indent of 1 inch (2.5 cm) or ten spaces for a quotation longer than four typed lines.

The ellipsis indicates words omitted from a quotation.

In MLA style, parenthetical information follows the period in a block quotation.

17

18

→

Commentary

16. **Example of summary.** Johnson compressed a lengthy description of the Turing test into a brief summary. **PROCESS NOTE:** The first time that Johnson wrote about the Turing test, she needed three full paragraphs to present all the information. She was determined to revise and condense it. She deleted sentences, which she kept in a separate document, in case she wanted to reinstate some information. She ended up with a "nutshell" version in her final draft.

17. **Block-indented quotation.** Johnson was unable to produce a satisfactory summary or paraphrase of Searle's "chess room argument." She decided instead to quote the entire passage. Because the passage was longer than four typed lines, Johnson needed to indent it. She reviewed the MLA guidelines for the format of block quotations and the exact position of the parenthetical citation.

18. **PROCESS NOTE:** Johnson found that Searle's "chess room argument" is actually a variation on his more famous "Chinese room argument," in which the man in the room is simply passing back Chinese symbols without knowing what they mean. She read several essays about Searle's work in John Preston and Mark Bishop, eds., *Views into the Chinese Room: New Essays on Searle and Artificial Intelligence* (Oxford: Oxford UP, 2002). She took notes and wrote summaries. However, Johnson eventually realized that this material was taking her away from the thesis of her paper. Although she had invested many hours, she dropped this work from her paper.

intelligence has become. Between 1980 and 1996, Howard
Gardner, a well-respected researcher in psychology
at Harvard University, defined seven distinctive categories
of human intelligence. Those categories are linguistic,   19
mathematical, spatial, kinesthetic, musical, interpersonal,
and intrapersonal intelligence (Goleman 38). In 1996, Gardner
added an eighth intelligence: naturalistic. He calls this
eight-item list of abilities "multiple intelligences." Gardner   20
believes that every person is born possessing a combination
of all eight intelligences (qtd. in Hoerr).

Daniel Goleman, another highly regarded researcher   21
in psychology, groups the concepts of intrapersonal and
interpersonal intelligence under the label "emotional
intelligence." Goleman says that emotional intelligence
involves more than having traditional feelings of anger,
sadness, fear, enjoyment, love, surprise, disgust, or shame

In MLA style,   (289-90). It determines how well people do in life (28). A study   22
put only page
number(s) in   of high school valedictorians, for example, shows that they
parentheses
when author is frequently have less successful careers than classmates who
named in text. excel at interpersonal or emotional skills (35). Goleman assigns

Quotation   five aspects to emotional intelligence: "knowing one's
marks around
phrases show   emotions," "managing emotions," "motivating oneself,"
they appeared
separately in   "handling relationships," and "recognizing emotions in others"
the source.
(43). The last of these is crucial in the context of artificial
intelligence because it determines how people respond to other
people and, in turn, how the other people respond back.

The neurologist Antonio Damasio explains that scientists   23
and philosophers historically dismissed the significance of

→

Commentary

19. **PROCESS NOTE:** In her first draft, Johnson wrote two or three sentences about each of the eight types of human intelligence. Later she decided that writing so much about the topic would draw attention away from the main topic of her paper, artificial intelligence. In a second draft she simply listed the eight types of intelligence, leaving extra space for emotional intelligence, the most important type for the purpose of her paper. Although she was frustrated at having to omit so much of her work from the final draft, she realized that her paper was stronger as a result.

20. **Expert source.** When Johnson first began reading about intelligence, she came across the name Howard Gardner in several sources. When she realized that Gardner is a leading expert on multiple intelligences, she knew she could depend on the quality of his work.

21. **Elaborating a key point.** Since emotion is a key concept in her paper, Johnson discusses it at some length in this paragraph. Early in her search process, she had used the keywords "emotions" and "intelligence" to search her library's book catalogue. Goleman's book came up through that search; so did the book by Pfeifer and Scheier, which refers extensively to Goleman's work.

22. **Example.** To illustrate the point that success in life does not depend only on verbal and quantitative intelligence, the kinds of intelligence typically associated with schools, Johnson gave the example of some high school valedictorians.

23. **Introduction to paraphrase.** Johnson includes the information that Damasio is a neurologist when she paraphrases his work. Because she was drawing on the work of experts from so many fields, she thought this identifying information would help her readers.

34e MLA DOCUMENTATION WITH CASE STUDY

emotions (38). Traditionally, they associated logic and reason with intelligence. Early scientists and philosophers believed emotion belonged to the body, not the mind (39).

The character of Mr. Spock in the original Star Trek television series represents this belief. Incapable of emotion, Spock is flawlessly logical. Certainly, everyone would agree that he is intelligent.

However, Damasio would be unconvinced by the claim that Spock is intelligent--and not just because Spock is a Vulcan. Damasio conducted numerous experiments with people who lost various emotions through brain injuries. These people otherwise seemed to possess all their reasoning and logical abilities, but they had trouble making logical decisions. The experiments led Damasio to conclude that "emotion is integral to the process of reasoning and decision making" (41). He tells of a patient, David, who suffered a disease that destroyed parts of his brain and left him unable to learn any new fact, to recognize any new person, or to remember recent events or people he had just met. Damasio and his colleagues performed an experiment in which one person treated David rudely and another person treated him well for a period of five days. Although David could not remember details of how these people treated him, he behaved differently in the presence of the two people. Clearly, he had learned on an emotional level, which made him respond sensibly (43-47).

The strongest believers in artificial intelligence mostly downplay the role of emotions, maintaining that only logic and reason define intelligence. Others give a qualified yes to "the provocative question whether robots will in fact need to have

24

25

26

27

Introductory phrase smoothly leads into direct quotation.

Paragraph summarizes several pages of source material, as parenthetical citation shows.

586

MLA

Commentary

24. **Example from popular culture.** Johnson hesitated to give Mr. Spock as an example of intelligence without emotion. The original *Star Trek* series is nearly four decades old, and she worried that the reference might be dated. However, she decided that Mr. Spock was enough a part of popular culture that even people who weren't directly familiar with the show would understand the reference. She checked with several friends just to be sure.

25. **Evaluating a source.** The central issue of Johnson's paper is whether emotion is a necessary part of intelligence. In two sources she found early in her research, she had seen references to Antonio Damasio's work, and she wondered if it would help her to make connections between emotions and reasoning. It did, so she drew heavily on Damasio's book in this section. First, however, she checked his credentials. When she discovered that he was an award-winning researcher and head of the neurological sciences department at a major medical school, she was satisfied that he was a reliable source.

26. **PROCESS NOTE:** Without the story of Damasio's patient David, Johnson knew that this paragraph was extremely thin. However, the story took five pages in the original source. To write a summary of those pages, Johnson kept drafting and cutting until she achieved the length she wanted. She then asked a student friend to read her summary and then the five original pages to make sure she had summarized the story fairly and accurately.

27. **PROCESS NOTE:** In the course of her research, Johnson encountered many different opinions on both the achievability of artificial intelligence and the role of emotions in intelligence. She found it very difficult to synthesize all this material in a manner that read smoothly. Finally, she recognized that believers in and doubters of the possibility of artificial intelligence differed in the importance they assigned to emotions. This discovery gave her a way to organize this paragraph.

emotions, similar to the way humans have emotions" (Pfeifer and
Scheier 642). Doubters, however, point to emotions, feelings, and
intuition as the main barriers to artificial intelligence. The
ability to write fiction, for example, depends on feelings that
computers can never experience. One skeptic even asserts that
computers have "inner lives on a par with rocks" (Bringsjord 33).   28
Programmers design computer programs to be efficient and to sort
problems into separate steps, ignoring everything that is not part
of those steps. In contrast, part of being human is getting bored,
angry, or off the subject. John Searle believes that cognitive   29
scientists make a terrible mistake when they imagine that the
brain works the same way that computers do (qtd. in Allen 30).

    Recognizing that the brain does not function through logic
alone, some researchers are now studying how humans learn
and are trying to incorporate their discoveries into computers. For
example, children learn mainly by interacting in social situations
with others. Emotions play a large role in those situations

Cite part of
title when
source lists ("Sociable" 1). As an illustration, a baby learns that smiling   30
no author.
causes adults to pay more attention to her, so she smiles a lot. In
contrast, a two-year-old learns to recognize when someone is
angry and to avoid that person. A child's growth in emotional
intelligence would be hard to build into a computer. Nonetheless,
Donald Norman and his colleagues believe that understanding
how emotions combine with cognition in humans is vital to
developing computer systems that can function by themselves (38).
In fact, scientists at Vanderbilt University have built robots that
recognize some basic human emotions (Johnson).

    Programming robots so that they can express as well as   31
sense emotions is important because people's abilities to convey

→

Commentary

28. **Colourful quotation.** Bringsjord's statement that computers have "inner lives on a par with rocks" is not a particularly important or well-reasoned assertion. However, Johnson thought it added colour to her paper and helped to make her point, so she included it here.

29. **PROCESS NOTE:** At one point in her second draft, Johnson had included all of the observations from Searle in one place (see page 4 of the research paper). However, she decided that using the reference here to close off the paragraph about emotions was a powerful strategy, so she moved this material when she wrote her final draft.

30. **Popular-press source.** Here Johnson's information comes from a popular source, the newspaper *USA Today*. She realized that in comparison to the many scholarly sources cited in her paper, this one might seem insignificant. However, other things she had read convinced her that the position given in the article was accurate. Because she planned to include the example of Kismet, a robot described in the article, later in her paper, she decided to keep the reference to *USA Today* here. Note that no author was listed for the article, so in her parenthetical citation Johnson referred instead to the first word of the article's title.

31. **PROCESS NOTE:** Johnson's research made clear that there are two main challenges in creating emotional intelligence in computers: getting computers to recognize emotions and getting them to convey emotions. She revised this topic sentence more than any other in her paper so that it would effectively signal those challenges.

Johnson 8

emotions affect the responses that they get from others. To try to learn how inanimate objects suggest emotions, scientists have studied some unlikely sources. One group of researchers analyzed how Disney animators created "the illusion of life" by seeming to give cartoon characters emotions (Bates 122). Using Disney techniques, scientists created computer "creatures" that seemed to display emotions in response to simple situations (123). Further work led to robots that appeared more humanlike. For example, scientists gave a robot named Kismet appealing, childlike features. Kismet's "features, behavior, and 'emotions' " seem to allow the robot to "interact with humans in an intuitive natural way" ("Sociable" 1). Nevertheless, creating the appearance of emotions is much different from creating the existence of emotions.

Do computers need emotions for scientists to consider them intelligent? This question remains unanswered and controversial. As Sam Williams notes, "The current tension over artificial intelligence is a reflection of our own society's tension over the future and what it holds" (xvi). Computers can indeed do some things that resemble a few kinds of intelligence that humans possess, and that is enough to satisfy some scientists. However, Gardner, Goleman, Damasio, Pfeifer and Scheier, and others regard emotions as a crucial part of human intelligence. At present, computers lack anything like the kinds of emotions found in human beings, and scholars like John Searle doubt that computers will ever have them. Clearly, robots like the little boy in A.I. exist only in movies. The possibility of creating real robots similar to him remains only in the very distant future, if at all.

Put quotation marks around even short phrases or key terms taken directly from a source and give source at end of sentence.

Concluding paragraph summarizes paper.

32

33

34

35

36

→

Commentary

32. **Using a technical source.** The article by Bates, from a scientific journal, was fairly difficult to understand. Johnson focused on the theories, findings, and implications of the article rather than on the methodologies, which were harder to follow. This was the oldest source that Johnson consulted for her paper. However, as the reference to the robot Kismet (later in the paragraph) makes clear, the Bates study is still pertinent to current research.

33. **Research question.** Johnson's research question appears at the start of her last paragraph. Often, the research question doesn't directly appear at all in a paper, but Johnson thought it would be a good way to signal her conclusion.

34. **PROCESS NOTE:** Johnson liked the quotation from Sam Williams and tried several places to fit it in her paper. In the first draft, for example, she put it in the opening paragraph. Eventually she decided it helped summarize the deep controversy in her topic, so she moved it to the concluding paragraph.

35. **Summary of positions.** Johnson summarizes both positions on the question to show that she has weighed her evidence. By choosing to summarize Searle's argument last, she shows that she agrees more with his position, that emotions are an important part of artificial intelligence, than with the position of the others.

36. **Forceful conclusion.** In her last two sentences, Johnson returned to the movie example she used at the beginning of her paper. She thought this put a pleasing frame around the paper and made it seem complete.

MLA

Works Cited 37

In MLA style,
the list of
sources, called
Works Cited,
begins a
new page.
Double-space
throughout.

List sources in
alphabetical
order.

Divide a URL
only after a
slash.

Allen, Frederick E. "The Myth of Artificial Intelligence."

American Heritage Feb.-Mar. 2001: 28-30.

American Association for Artificial Intelligence. "The AI Effect." 38

13 Sept. 2003 <http://aaai.org>.

Bates, Joseph. "The Role of Emotion in Believable Agents."

Communications of the ACM 37.7 (1994): 122-25.

Bringsjord, Selmer. "Just Imagine: What Computers Can't Do."

Education Digest Feb. 2001: 31-33.

Damasio, Antonio. The Feeling of What Happens: Body and

Emotion in the Making of Consciousness. New York:

Harcourt, 1999.

Gardner, Howard. Frames of Mind: The Theory of Multiple

Intelligences. New York: Basic, 1994.

Goleman, Daniel. Emotional Intelligence. New York: Bantam,

1995.

Hayden, Thomas. "The Age of Robots." US News and World

Report 23 Apr. 2001: 44-50.

Hoerr, Thomas. "The Naturalistic Intelligence." Building

Tool Room. 20 Sept. 2003 <http://www.newhorizons.org/ 39

strategies/mi/hoerr1.htm>.

Johnson, R. Colin. "Robots Taught to Be Sensitive to Human

Emotions." Electronic Engineering Times 13 Jan. 2003: 43.

Kurzweil, Ray. "Spiritual Machines: The Merging of Man and

Machine." Futurist Nov. 1999: 16-21.

McCarthy, John. "What Is Artificial Intelligence?" 29 Mar. 2003.

16 Sept. 2003 <http://www-formal.stanford.edu/jmc/

whatisai.html>.

➜

Commentary

37. **Search strategy.** Johnson developed a working bibliography that was nearly three times as long as the list of sources she finally used. Initially, she went online to see what sources she could find on the Internet. However, she was overwhelmed by the number of references to "artificial intelligence." After some effort, she identified a few key sources. Library resources were more useful. The library's book catalogue revealed many useful volumes, and the databases she searched turned up both scholarly and popular sources. PsycINFO and Computer Database were the two most useful databases.

38. **Credible Internet source.** Johnson checked that this professional organization of scientists and professors would be a reliable source of information.

39. **Computer tip.** Including a long and complicated URL in a Works Cited page is often tricky. Copying the URL from the browser window and pasting it directly into the Works Cited page reduces the chance of error. Be sure to divide a URL only after a slash, the rule in MLA style.

Johnson 10

Minerd, Jeff. "Robots: Our Evolutionary Heirs?" <u>Futurist</u>
Feb. 1999: 8-9.

Norman, Donald A., Andrew Ortony, and Daniel M. Russell.
"Affect and Machine Design: Lessons for the Development
of Autonomous Machines." <u>IBM Systems Journal</u> 42.2 (2003):
38-45. <u>Computer Database</u>. InfoTrac. Cape Breton Regional
Lib. System, NS. 14 Sept. 2003 <http://
www.infotrac.galegroup.com>.

Pfeifer, Rolf, and Christian Scheier. <u>Understanding Intelligence</u>.
Cambridge, MA: MIT P 2000.

"'Sociable Machine' Interacts with Humans," <u>USA Today</u> June
2001: 1-2. <u>General Reference Center</u>. InfoTrac. Cape Breton
Regional Lib. System, NS. 14 Sept. 2003. <http://
www.infotrac.galegroup.com>.

Stix, Gary. "2001: A Scorecard." <u>Scientific American</u> Jan. 2001: 36.

Williams, Sam. Arguing A.I.: The Battle for Twenty-First-
Century Science. New York: AtRandom.com Books, 2002.

Single quotation marks inside double quotation marks indicate words that were in quotation marks in the source.

40

41

Commentary

40. **Full text online.** Although this source initially appeared in an issue of *USA Today* and old issues were not stocked at her university library, Johnson found a complete copy of the article online, through a database in the library. Because she used the online version, she cited its source.

41. **Proofreading the Works Cited page.** In proofreading her paper, Johnson made sure this list contained all the works she cited in her paper—and only those works.

Chapter 35

APA Documentation with Case Study

35a What is APA style?

The American Psychological Association (APA) sponsors the **APA style,** a DOCUMENTATION system widely used in the social sciences. APA style involves two equally important features that need to appear in research papers.

First, APA style calls for you to acknowledge your SOURCES within the text of your research papers by using **in-text citations** in parentheses. Section 35b explains how APA in-text citations work, and section 35c shows fifteen models of such parenthetical reference citations, each of which gives you an example of a different type of source.

Second, APA style calls for you to list complete bibliographic information about each source that you've mentioned in your parenthetical references. This bibliographic list, titled **References,** needs to begin on a separate page at the end of your research paper. It includes only the sources you've actually used in your research paper, not any you've consulted but haven't used. Section 35f gives instructions for composing your References pages, followed by fifty-one models, each based on a different kind of source (book, article, Web site, etc.) that you might use in your research papers.

For an example of a research paper that uses APA-style in-text citations in parentheses and a References list, see section 35h. As you read the paper, notice how the two requirements for crediting sources work together so that readers can learn the precise origin of the material that is quoted, paraphrased, and summarized.

35b What are APA parenthetical in-text citations?

The APA-STYLE DOCUMENTATION guidelines here follow the recommendations of the *Publication Manual of the American Psychological Association* (5th edition, 2001), which is the most current print edition. The

URL for APA's general Web site is <http://www.apa.org>; it answers some basic style questions and mostly refers you to the *Publication Manual*. However, APA has set up a special free Web site devoted exclusively to **electronic sources** (APA's term for online sources, CD-ROMs, etc.). APA provides this because electronic sources are still evolving rapidly and therefore tend to change. Anyone with Internet access can use the site at <http://www.apastyle.org/elecref.html>. It offers links to selected specific examples of citations of electronic sources, some of which aren't covered in the APA *Publication Manual;* unusually direct, practical FAQs; and other useful material. For example, as this book goes to press, this special APA Web site gives examples of Internet articles based on a print source; articles in an Internet-only journal; articles in an Internet-only newsletter; a stand-alone document with no author identified and no date given; a document available on a university program or department Web site; and an electronic copy of a journal article written by three to five authors and retrieved from a database. Best of all, you can sign up for free notices sent to your e-mail address whenever APA posts an update to this site.

APA style requires parenthetical IN-TEXT CITATIONS that identify a SOURCE by the author's name (if no author is given, use a shortened version of the title) and the copyright year. For readability and a good writing style, you can often incorporate the name, and sometimes the year, into your sentence. Otherwise, place this information in parentheses, located as close as possible to the material you QUOTE, PARAPHRASE, or SUMMARIZE. Your goal is to tell readers precisely where they can find the original material.

The APA *Publication Manual* recommends that if you refer to a work more than once in a paragraph, you give the author's name and the publication date at the first mention and then give only the name after that. (Exception: If you're citing two or more works by the same author, or if two or more of your sources have the same name, each separate citation must include the date to identify which work you're citing.)

APA style requires page numbers for direct quotations and recommends them for paraphrases and summaries. However, some instructors expect you to give page references for paraphrases and summaries, so find out your instructor's preference to avoid any problems in properly crediting your sources.

Put page numbers in parentheses, using the abbreviation *p.* before a single page number and *pp.* when the material you're citing falls on more than one page. For a direct quotation from an electronic source that numbers paragraphs, give the paragraph number (or numbers). Handle paragraph numbers as you do page numbers, but use *para.* or ¶ (the symbol for paragraph) rather than *p.* or *pp.* If no paragraph numbers appear in the source, look for other ways to identify the location, such as sections introduced by main headings.

35c What are APA guidelines for in-text citations?

The directory below corresponds to the numbered examples that follow it. The examples show how to cite various kinds of sources in the body of your research paper. Remember, though, that you often can introduce source names, including titles when necessary, and sometimes even publication years, in your own sentences rather than in the parenthetical IN-TEXT CITATIONS.

Directory—APA In-Text Citations

1. Paraphrased or Summarized Source—APA
2. Source of a Short Quotation—APA
3. Source of a Long Quotation (and Format of Quotation)—APA
4. One Author—APA
5. Two Authors—APA
6. Three, Four, or Five Authors—APA
7. Six or More Authors—APA
8. Author(s) with Two or More Works in the Same Year—APA
9. Two or More Authors with the Same Last Name—APA
10. Group or Corporate Author—APA
11. Work Listed by Title—APA
12. Two or More Sources in One Reference—APA
13. Personal Communication, Including E-Mail and Other Nonretrievable Sources—APA
14. Citing an Online Source
15. Source Lines for Graphics and Table Data—APA

1. Citing a Paraphrased or Summarized Source—APA

People from the Mediterranean prefer an elbow-to-shoulder distance from each other (Morris, 1977). [Author name and date cited in parentheses.]

Desmond Morris (1977) notes that people from the Mediterranean prefer an elbow-to-shoulder distance from each other. [Author name cited in text; date cited in parentheses.]

2. Citing the Source of a Short Quotation—APA

A recent report of reductions in SAD-related "depression in 87 percent of patients" (Binkley, 1990, p. 203) reverses the findings of earlier studies.

[Author name, date, and page reference cited in parentheses immediately following the quotation.]

Binkley (1990) reports reductions in SAD-related "depression in 87 percent of patients" (p. 203). [Author name followed by the date in parentheses incorporated into the words introducing the quotation; page number in parentheses immediately following the quotation.]

3. Citing the Source of a Long Quotation (and Formatting the Quotation)—APA

Incorporate a direct quotation of fewer than forty words into your own sentence and enclose it in quotation marks. Place the parenthetical in-text citation after the closing quotation mark and, if the quotation falls at the end of the sentence, before the sentence-ending punctuation. When you use a quotation longer than forty words, set it off in block style indented one-half inch (about 1.25 cm) or five to seven spaces from the left margin. Never enclose a set-off quotation in quotation marks, because the placement in block style carries the message that the material is quoted. Place the parenthetical reference citation one space after the end punctuation of the last quoted sentence.

DISPLAYED QUOTATION (FORTY OR MORE WORDS)

Jet lag, with its characteristic fatigue and irregular sleep patterns, is a common problem among those who travel great distances by jet airplane to different time zones:

> Jet lag syndrome is the inability of the internal body rhythm to rapidly resynchronize after sudden shifts in the timing. For a variety of reasons, the system attempts to maintain stability and resist temporal change. Consequently, complete adjustment can often be delayed for several days--sometimes for a week--after arrival at one's destination. (Bonner, 1991, p. 72)

4. Citing One Author—APA

> One of his questions is, "What actually happened in Walkerton?" (O'Connor, 2002, p. 2).

In a parenthetical reference in APA style, a comma and a space separate a name from a year and a year from a page reference. (Examples 1 through 3 above also show citations of works by one author.)

5. Citing Two Authors—APA

If a work has two authors, give both names in each citation.

> One report describes 2123 occurrences (Krait & Cooper, 1994).

> The results that Krait and Cooper (1994) report would not support the conclusions Davis and Sherman (1992) draw in their review of the literature.

When you write a parenthetical in-text citation naming two or more authors, use an ampersand (&) between the final two names. If you work the authors' names into your own sentence, write out the word *and* instead.

6. Citing Three, Four, or Five Authors—APA

For three, four, or five authors, use all the authors' last names in the first reference. In all subsequent references, use only the first author's last name followed by *et al.* (meaning "and others").

FIRST REFERENCE

In one anthology, 35% of the selections had not been anthologized before (Elliott, Kerber, Litz, & Martin, 1992).

SUBSEQUENT REFERENCE

Elliott et al. (1992) include 17 authors whose work has never been anthologized.

7. Citing Six or More Authors—APA

For six or more authors, name the first author followed by *et al.* in all in-text references, including the first. (See section 35f, model 3, for the correct References format.)

8. Citing Author(s) with Two or More Works in the Same Year—APA

If you use more than one source written in the same year by the same author(s), alphabetize the works by their titles for the References list, and assign letters in alphabetical order to the years—(1996a), (1996b), (1996c). Use the year-letter combination in parenthetical references. Note that if two or more such works are listed in the same citation, the years appear in alphabetical order.

Most recently, Jones (1996c) draws new conclusions from the results of 17 sets of experiments (Jones, 1996a, 1996b).

9. Citing Two or More Authors with the Same Last Name—APA

Include first initials for every in-text citation of authors who share a last name. Use the initials appearing in the References list. (In the second example, a parenthetical citation, the name order is alphabetical, as explained in item 12.)

R. A. Smith (1997) and C. Smith (1989) both confirm these results.

These results have been confirmed independently (C. Smith, 1989; R. A. Smith, 1997).

10. Citing a Work with a Group or Corporate Author—APA

If you use a source in which the "author" is a corporation, agency, or group, an in-text reference gives that name as author. Use the full name in each citation, unless an abbreviated version of the name is likely to be familiar to your audience. In that case, use the full name and give its abbreviation at the first citation; then use the abbreviation for subsequent citations.

FIRST REFERENCE

After 1949 the federal government took over responsibility for most public housing projects (Canada Mortgage and Housing Corporation [CMHC], 1990).

SUBSEQUENT REFERENCE

The cost of retrofitting older designs was substantial (CMHC, 1990).

11. Citing a Work Listed by Title—APA

If no author is named, use a shortened form of the title for in-text citations. Ignoring *A, An,* or *The,* make the first word the one by which you alphabetize the title in your References. The following example refers to an article fully titled "Are You a Day or Night Person?"

Scientists group people as "larks" or "owls" on the basis of whether individuals are more efficient in the morning or at night ("Are You," 1989).

12. Citing Two or More Sources in One Reference—APA

If more than one source has contributed to an idea or opinion in your paper, cite the sources alphabetically by author in one set of parentheses; separate each block of information with a semicolon followed by one space.

Conceptions of personal space vary among cultures (Morris, 1977; Worchel & Cooper, 1983).

13. Citing a Personal Communication, Including E-Mail and Other Nonretrievable Sources—APA

Telephone calls, personal letters, interviews, and e-mail messages are "personal communications" that your readers cannot access or retrieve. Acknowledge personal communications in parenthetical references, but never include them in your References list at the end of your research paper.

Recalling his first summer at camp, one person said, "The proximity of 12 other kids made me--an only child with older, quiet parents--frantic for eight weeks" (A. Weiss, personal communication, January 12, 2003).

14. Citing an Online Source—APA

When you quote, paraphrase, or summarize an online source that is available to others, cite the author (if any) or title and the date as you would for a print source, and include the work in your References list. To help readers locate a specific part of an online source that does not provide page numbers, use the paragraph number preceded by the abbreviation *para.* If you cannot decipher the page or the paragraph number, cite the heading and the number of the paragraph following it.

> (Anderson, 2003, para. 14)

> (Migueis, 2002, Introduction, para. 1)

For a brief reference to an entire online source, just give the URL in parentheses. Do not include the source in your References list.

> A different approach to regional ecology can be found on the Banff Centre's Mountain Culture home page (http://www.banffcentre.ca/mountainculture/).

15. Providing Source Lines for Graphics and Table Data—APA

If you use a graphic from another source or create a table using data from another source, give a note in the text at the bottom of the table or graphic crediting the original author and the copyright holder. Here are examples of two source lines, one for a graphic from an article, the other for a graphic from a book. Note that in APA-style source lines, unlike APA-style References entries (see 35f), the titles of journal articles and book chapters are enclosed in quotation marks, and the titles of all works (articles, chapters, and books) are capitalized according to the same rules as for journal titles: capitalize the first and last words of both the title and any subtitle, all nouns and adjectives, and any other words four or more letters long.

GRAPHIC FROM AN ARTICLE——APA

Note. The data in columns 1 and 2 are from "Bridge Over Troubled Waters? Connecting Research and Pedagogy in Composition and Business/Technical Communication," by J. Allen, 1992, *Technical Communication Quarterly, 1* (4), p. 9. Copyright 1992 by the Association of Teachers of Technical Writing. Adapted with permission of the author.

GRAPHIC FROM A BOOK——APA

Note. From *Additive Alert: A Guide to Food Additives for the Canadian Consumer* (p. 28), by Linda R. Pim, 1979, Toronto: Doubleday. Copyright 1979 by Pollution Probe Foundation. Reprinted with permission.

35d What are APA guidelines for writing an abstract?

As the APA *Publication Manual* explains, "an abstract is a brief, comprehensive summary" (p. 12) of a longer piece of writing. APA recommends that an abstract should be limited in length to a maximum of about 120 words. Your instructor may require that you include an abstract at the start of a paper; if you're not sure, ask. Make the abstract accurate, objective, and exact. You may be familiar with effective abstracts, for many disciplines have online abstracts of longer sources. See 35g for guidelines on formatting an Abstract page. Here is an abstract prepared for the research paper on biological clocks that appears in 35h.2.

> Circadian rhythms, which greatly affect human lives, often suffer disruptions in technological societies, resulting in such disorders as jet lag syndrome and seasonal affective disorder (SAD). With growing scientific awareness of both natural circadian cycles and the effects of disturbances of these cycles, individuals are learning to control some negative effects.

35e What are APA guidelines for content notes?

Content notes in APA-style papers add relevant information that cannot be worked effectively into a text discussion. Use consecutive arabic numerals for note numbers, both within your paper and on the Notes page(s), which follow the last text page of your paper. See 35g for instructions on formatting the Notes page. With your instructor's permission, you may format content notes as footnotes instead. (The APA *Publication Manual* doesn't show this option because its instructions reflect the needs of the scholarly journals that publish academic papers. When submitted for typesetting, a paper should have only endnotes.)

35f What are APA guidelines for a References list?

The REFERENCES list at the end of your research paper provides complete bibliographic information for readers who may want to access the sources you draw upon for your paper.

Include in a References list all the sources you QUOTE, PARAPHRASE, or SUMMARIZE in your paper so that readers can find the same sources with reasonable effort. Never include in your References list any source that's not generally available to others (see item 13 in 35c).

General format guidelines are presented in Box 152. The directory that follows the box corresponds to the numbered examples in this section. Not all documentation models are shown here. You may have to combine features of models to document a particular source.

BOX 152   SUMMARY

Guidelines for an APA-style References list

■ **TITLE**

References

■ **PLACEMENT OF LIST**

Start a new page numbered sequentially with the rest of the paper, after the Notes page(s), if any.

■ **CONTENTS AND FORMAT**

Include all quoted, paraphrased, or summarized sources in your paper that are not personal communications, unless your instructor tells you to include all the references you have consulted, not just those you have to credit. Start each entry on a new line, and double-space all lines. Use a *hanging indent* style: The first line of each entry begins flush left at the margin, and all other lines are indented. The hanging indent makes source names and dates prominent. Type the first line of each entry full width, and indent subsequent lines one-half inch (about 1.25 cm). The easiest way to do this is through the word processor's ruler bar.

Shuter, R. (1977). A field study of nonverbal communication in Germany, Italy, and the United States. *Communication Monographs, 44,* 298-305.

■ **SPACING AFTER PUNCTUATION**

The APA *Publication Manual* calls for one space after punctuation marks, including within displayed quotations (see 35c, item 3).

■ **ARRANGEMENT OF ENTRIES**

Alphabetize by the author's last name. If no author is named, alphabetize by the first significant word (not *A, An,* or *The*) in the title of the work.

■ **AUTHORS' NAMES**

Use last names, first initials, and middle initials, if any. Reverse the order for all authors' names, and use an ampersand (&) between the second-to-last and last authors: Mills, J. F., & Holahan, R. H.

→

Guidelines for an APA-style References list (*continued*)

Give names in the order in which they appear on the work (on the title page of a book; usually under the title of an article or other printed work). Use a comma between the first author's last name and first initial and after each complete name except the last. The period after the last author's initial(s) ends this part of the entry. Name the first six authors of a source; substitute *et al.* (not italicized) for the rest.

■ **DATES**

Date information follows the name information and is enclosed in parentheses. Place a period followed by one space after the closing parenthesis.

For books, articles in journals that have volume numbers, and many other print and nonprint sources, the year of publication or production is the date to use. For articles from most magazines and newspapers, use the year followed by a comma and then the exact date that appears on the issue. Individual entries in 35f show how much information to give for various sources.

■ **CAPITALIZATION OF TITLES**

For book, article, and chapter titles, capitalize the first word, the first word after a colon between a title and subtitle, and any proper nouns. For names of journals and proceedings of meetings, capitalize the first and last words, all nouns and adjectives, and any other words four or more letters long.

■ **SPECIAL TREATMENT OF TITLES**

Use no special treatment for titles of shorter works (poems, short stories, essays, articles). Italicize titles of longer works (books, names of newspapers or journals). Underlining can be used in place of italic type if italic typeface is unavailable. Draw an unbroken line that includes end punctuation.

Do not drop *A*, *An*, or *The* from the titles of periodicals (such as newspapers, magazines, and journals).

■ **PLACE OF PUBLICATION**

For U.S. publishers, give the city and add the state (use the two-letter postal abbreviations listed in most dictionaries and in Box 122 in 30k) for all U.S. cities except Baltimore, Boston, Chicago, Los Angeles, New York, Philadelphia, and San Francisco. Canadian students and writers publishing in Canada normally use the two-letter postal

→

Guidelines for an APA-style References list (*continued*)

abbreviations for Canadian provinces (omitting them for such major cities as Montreal and the provincial capitals, as long as the city name alone is not ambiguous) as well as for U.S. states. For publishers in other countries, give city and country spelled out; no country name is needed with major world capital cities. However, if the province, state, or country is part of the publisher's name, omit it after the name of the city.

■ **PUBLISHERS**

Use a shortened version of the publisher's name except for an association, corporation, or university press. Drop *Co., Inc., Publishers,* and the like, but retain *Books* or *Press.*

■ **PUBLICATION MONTH ABBREVIATIONS**

Do not abbreviate publication months.

■ **PAGE NUMBERS**

Use all digits, omitting none. *Only* for references to parts of books or material in newspapers, use *p.* and *pp.* before page numbers. List all discontinuous pages, with numbers separated by commas: pp. 32, 44-45, 47-49, 53.

■ **REFERENCES ENTRIES: BOOKS**

Citations for books have four main parts: author, date, title, and publication information (place of publication and publisher).

AUTHOR   DATE   TITLE   PUBLICATION INFORMATION

Dudek, L. (1971). *Collected poetry.* Montreal: Delta.

■ **REFERENCES ENTRIES: ARTICLES**

Citations for periodical articles contain four major parts: author, date, title of article, and publication information (usually, the periodical title, volume number, and page numbers).

AUTHOR   DATE   ARTICLE TITLE

Herxheimer, A., & Waterhouse, J. (2003). The prevention and treatment

                                        VOLUME   PAGE
                    PERIODICAL TITLE   NUMBER   NUMBER(S)

of jet lag. *British Medical Journal,*   326,   296-297.

→

Guidelines for an APA-style References list (*continued*)

■ **REFERENCES ENTRIES: ELECTRONIC AND ONLINE SOURCES**

Styles for documenting electronic and online sources continue to evolve. The 2001 APA *Publication Manual* (pp. 268–281) and the APA Web page <http://www.apastyle.org/elecref.html> are the best sources for up-to-date advice on these formats. Here are two examples of entries. The first is for an abstract on CD-ROM, a searchable "aggregated database" (i.e., a compilation of resources grouped for directed or simplified access). You are not required to document how you accessed the database—via portable CD-ROM, on a library server, or via a supplier Web site—but a "retrieval statement" that accurately names the source (in this case, the database) and lists the date of retrieval is required. (If you include an item or accession number, place it in parentheses.)

          AUTHOR   DATE   ARTICLE TITLE

Markus, H. R., & Kitayamo, S. (1991). Culture and the self:

Implications for cognition, emotion, and motivation.

        JOURNAL TITLE AND
    PUBLICATION INFORMATION   RETRIEVAL INFORMATION

Psychological Abstracts, 78. Retrieved October 2, 2003, from

PsycINFO database (Item 1991-23978-001).

The second example is for an article in a magazine on the World Wide Web. The retrieval statement gives the access date and the URL, which "names" the source.

AUTHOR   DATE   ARTICLE TITLE

Lewis, R. (1995, December 11). Chronobiology researchers say their field's

          PUBLICATION   RETRIEVAL
           TITLE   INFORMATION

time has come. *The Scientist*. Retrieved December 27, 2003,

from http://www.the-scientist.com/yr1995/dec/chres_951211.html

Notice that the only punctuation in the URL is part of the address. Do not add a period after a URL. In APA style, if a URL is too long to fit on one line, it can be split *after* a slash or *before* a period.

Directory—APA Style

APA

PRINT SOURCES

1. Book by One Author—APA

Trudeau, P. E. (1968). *Federalism and the French Canadians*. Toronto: Macmillan Canada.

Use the hanging indent style: the first line of an entry is flush to the left margin and all other lines are indented one-half inch (1.25 cm).

2. Book by Two Authors—APA

Doob, A., & Cesaroni, C. (2004). *Responding to youth crime in Canada*. Toronto: University of Toronto Press.

3. Book by Three or More Authors—APA

Scardamalia, M., Bereiter, C., & Fillion, B. (1981). *Writing for results: A source-book of consequential composing activities*. Toronto: OISE Press.

For a book by three to six authors, include all the authors' names. For a book by more than six authors, use only the first six names followed by *et al.*

4. Two or More Books by the Same Author(s)—APA

Atwood, M. (1972). *Survival*. Toronto: Anansi.

Atwood, M. (1981). *True stories*. Toronto: Oxford University Press.

Atwood, M. (1985.) *The handmaid's tale*. Toronto: McClelland & Stewart.

References by the same author are arranged chronologically, with the earlier date of publication listed first.

5. Book by a Group or Corporate Author—APA

American Psychological Association. (2001). *Publication manual of the American Psychological Association* (5th ed.). Washington, DC: Author.

Investors Group. (1998). *Starting out: Smart strategies for your 20s & 30s.* Toronto: Stoddart.

Cite the full name of the corporate author first. If the author is also the publisher, use the word *Author* as the name of the publisher.

6. Book with No Author Named—APA

The Chicago manual of style (15th ed.). (2003). Chicago: University of Chicago Press.

Alphabetize the entry according to the first significant word in the title (*Chicago*, not *The*).

7. Book with an Author and an Editor—APA

Trudeau, P. E. (1998). *The Essential Trudeau* (R. Graham, Ed.). Toronto: M&S.

8. Translation—APA

Tremblay, M. (1998). *A thing of beauty* (S. Fischman, Trans.). Vancouver: Talon.

9. Work in Several Volumes or Parts—APA

Chrisley, R. (Ed.). (2000). *Artificial intelligence: Critical concepts* (Vols. 1-4). London: Routledge.

10. One Selection from an Anthology or an Edited Book—APA

Morrisseau, N. (1986). The Indian that became a thunderbird. In W. H. New (Ed.), *Canadian short fiction: From myth to modern* (pp. 26-29). Scarborough, ON: Prentice Hall.

Give the author of the selection first. The word *In* introduces the larger work from which the selection is taken.

11. Selection from a Work Already Listed in References—APA

Gilbert, S. M., & Gubar, S. (Eds.). (1985). *The Norton anthology of literature by women.* New York: Norton.

Kingston, M. H. (1985). No name woman. In S. M. Gilbert & S. Gubar (Eds.), *The Norton anthology of literature by women* (pp. 2337-2347). New York: Norton.

Provide full information for the already-cited anthology (first example), along with information about the individual selection. Put entries in alphabetical order.

12. Signed Article in a Reference Book—APA

Shadbolt, D. (1988). Emily Carr. In *The Canadian encyclopedia* (2nd ed.) (Vol. 1,
    p. 366). Edmonton: Hurtig.

Use *In* to introduce the larger work from which the selection is taken.

13. Unsigned Article in a Reference Book—APA

Ireland. (2002). In *The new encyclopaedia Britannica: Macropaedia* (Vol. 21,
    pp. 997-1018). Chicago: Encyclopaedia Britannica.

14. Second or Later Edition—APA

Buckley, J., & Gates, D. (1995). *Put it in writing* (2nd ed.). Scarborough, ON:
    Prentice Hall.

When a book is not the first edition, the edition number appears on the
title page. In your entry, use the publication year of the edition you consulted, and show the edition number followed by *ed.* in parentheses
after the title.

15. Anthology or Edited Book—APA

New, W. H. (Ed.). (1986). *Canadian short fiction: From myth to modern.*
    Scarborough, ON: Prentice Hall.

16. Introduction, Preface, Foreword, or Afterword—APA

Allmand, W. (1993). Foreword. In J. Brand, *The life and death of Anna Mae
    Aquash.* Toronto: Lorimer.

If you're citing an introduction, preface, foreword, or afterword, give its
author's name first. After the year, give the name of the part cited. If the
writer of the material you are citing is not the author of the book, use
the word *In* and the author's name before the title of the book.

17. Unpublished Dissertation or Essay—APA

Byers, M. (2000). Buffy the vampire slayer: *The insurgence of television
    as a performance text.* Unpublished doctoral dissertation, University
    of Toronto.

Never italicize a title within an already-italicized title, even though it
would appear in italic typeface if it were by itself.

18. Reprint of an Older Book—APA

Lampman, A. (1978). *Lyrics of earth.* Ottawa: Tecumseh Press. (Original work
    published 1895)

Republishing information appears on the copyright page.

19. Book in a Series—APA

Give the title of the book, but not of the whole series.

Courchene, T. J. (1991). *In praise of renewed federalism.* Toronto: C. D. Howe Institute.

20. Book with a Title Within a Title—APA

Lumiansky, R. M., & Baker, H. (Eds.). (1968). *Critical approaches to six major English works:* Beowulf *through* Paradise lost. Philadelphia: University of Pennsylvania Press.

21. Government Publication—APA

Indian and Northern Affairs Canada. (1986). *The Inuit.* Ottawa: Supply and Services Canada.

Royal Commission on Bilingualism and Biculturalism. (1965). *Preliminary report.* Ottawa: Queen's Printer.

Use the complete name of a government agency as author when no specific person is named.

22. Published Proceedings of a Conference—APA

Smith, D. B. (Ed.). (1997). *Forging a new relationship: Proceedings of the conference on the Report of the Royal Commission on Aboriginal Peoples.* Montreal: McGill Institute for the Study of Canada.

23. Signed Article from a Daily Newspaper—APA

Church, E. (2002, November 27). Vacancy rates rise for first time in decade. *The Globe and Mail,* pp. B1, B5.

24. Editorial, Letter to the Editor, or Review—APA

A black mark on local government. (1994, July 27). [Editorial]. *The London Free Press,* p. B8.

Hurka J. (1994, July 5). [Letter to the editor]. *The Calgary Sun,* p. A18.

Toews, W. (1995, August 26). Politics of the mind. [Review of the book *They say you're crazy: How the world's most powerful psychiatrists decide who's normal*]. *Winnipeg Free Press,* p. C3.

25. Unsigned Article from a Daily Newspaper—APA

Private water may violate Constitution. (2002, November 27). *The Ottawa Citizen,* pp. A1, A7.

26. Signed Article from a Weekly or Biweekly Periodical—APA

Wood, C. (1989, November 6). Storm clouds over Quebec. *Maclean's*, 16-17.

Use the abbreviation *p.* (or *pp.* for more than one page) for newspapers. Do not use this abbreviation for magazines or journals. Give year, month, and day-date for a periodical published every week or every two weeks. As with a newspaper source, an unsigned article in a weekly or biweekly periodical has as its first item the title of the article.

27. Signed Article from a Monthly or Bimonthly Periodical—APA

O'Malley, S. (1994, August). Make-it-happen kinda dreamer: Theatre director
Diane Dupuy is nobody's puppet. *Chatelaine*, 36-39, 90.

Give the year and month(s) for a periodical published every month or every other month. An unsigned article in a monthly or bimonthly periodical has as its first item the title of the article.

28. Article from a Looseleaf Collection of Reprinted Articles—APA

Hayden, T. (2002). The age of robots. In E. Goldstein (Ed.), *Applied Science 2002*.
SIRS 2002, Article 66. (Reprinted from *U.S. News & World Report*,
pp. 44–51, 2001, April 23).

29. Article from a Journal with Continuous Pagination—APA

Tyson, P. (1998). The psychology of women. *Journal of the American
Psychoanalytic Association, 46*, 361-364.

Give only the volume number after the journal title, and italicize the volume number.

30. Article from a Journal That Pages Each Issue Separately—APA

Adler-Kassner, L., & Estrem, H. (2003). Rethinking research writing: Public
literacy in the composition classroom. *WPA: Writing Program
Administration, 26*(3), 119-131.

Give the volume number, italicized with the journal title. Give the issue number in parentheses; do not italicize it. Leave no space between the italicized volume number and the opening parenthesis that follows it.

31. Published and Unpublished Letters—APA

Sand, G. (1993). Letter to her mother. In Reid Sherline (Ed.), *Letters home:
Celebrated authors write to their mothers* (pp. 17-20). New York: Timkin.

In the APA system, unpublished letters are considered personal communication inaccessible to general readers, so they do not appear in the References list. Personal communications do not provide recoverable data and so are cited only in the body of the paper (see model 33).

32. Map or Chart—APA

Russia and post-Soviet republics [Map]. (1992). Moscow: Mapping Production
Association.

33. Interview—APA

In APA style, a personal interview is considered personal correspondence
and is not included in the References list. Cite the interview in the text
with a parenthetical notation saying that it is a personal communication.

Randi Friedman (personal communication, June 30, 2003) endorses this view.

34. Lecture, Speech, or Address—APA

Barlow, M. (1991, May 25). Address. Speech presented to the League of Canadian
Poets, Toronto.

35. Film, Videotape, or DVD—APA

Ego Filmarts/ZDF (Producer), & Egoyan, A. (Director). (1993). *Calendar* [Film].

Ego Filmarts/ZDF (Producer), & Egoyan, A. (Director). (1993). *Calendar*
[Videocassette].

Madden, J. (Director), Parfitt, D., Gigliotti, D., Weinstein, H., Zwick, E.,
& Norman, M. (Producers). (2003). *Shakespeare in love* [DVD]. (Original
movie released 1998)

36. Musical Recording—APA

Cohen, L. (Performer). (1988). Tower of song. On *I'm your man* [CD]. Toronto:
Sony Music Canada.

Smetana, B. (1975). *My country* [With K. Ancerl conducting the Czech
Philharmonic Orchestra]. [Record]. London: Vanguard Records.

37. Live Performance—APA

Shakespeare, W. (Author), Monette, R. (Director), Peacock, L., & Soles, P.
(Performers). (2001, May 8). *The merchant of Venice* [Live performance].
Stratford, ON: Festival Theatre.

38. Work of Art, Photograph, or Musical Composition—APA

Pratt, C. *Shop on an island* [Artwork]. London, ON: London Regional Art Gallery.

McMillan, D. (2001). *Village grave, Commemoration Day, April, 1995.* [Photo-
graph]. Winnipeg: Winnipeg Art Gallery.

Schubert, Franz. *Unfinished symphony* [Musical composition].

39. Radio or Television Program—APA

Walsh, M. (Interviewer). (2002, September 29). Regeneration Trilogy *by Pat*
     Barker [Television series episode]. In Salter Street Films (Producer),
     Open book. Toronto: CBC.

If you're citing a television series produced by and seen on only one station, cite the station's call letters.

40. Information Services—APA

Davies, S. (2002). *School choice by default?: Understanding the growing de-*
     mand for private tutoring in Canada (Report No. NALL-WP-65). Toronto:
     Research Network on New Approaches to Lifelong Learning, Ontario
     Institute for Studies in Education of the University of Toronto. (ERIC Doc-
     umentation Reproduction Service No. ED479073)

ELECTRONIC AND ONLINE SOURCES

Information from online sources that your readers cannot readily
retrieve for themselves—many e-mail messages and discussion list
communications, for example—should be treated as personal communications (see model 33). Never include them in your References list. If
you have a scholarly reason to cite a message from a newsgroup, forum,
or electronic mailing list that is available in an electronic archive, then
document an author name; the exact date of the posting; the subject
line or "thread" (do not italicize it) followed by an identifier in square
brackets—[Msg 23]; and a "Message posted to" statement that lists the
URL of the message or of the archive. Following is an example:

Hesse, D. (2003, August 1). Research on large class size [Msg 192]. Message
     posted to http://lists.asu.edu/archives/wpa-1.html

The APA system for documenting electronic and online sources in a References list has been evolving. At the time of this writing, the guidelines
in the 2001 APA *Publication Manual* remain most current. In general,
APA recommends giving author, title, and publication information as for
a print source. This information is followed by a "retrieval statement"
that gives the date you accessed the material and leads the reader as
directly as possible to your source.

   In contrast to MLA style, APA style doesn't require you to use angle
brackets around URLs in retrieval statements. Also, APA allows you to
break a URL either after a slash or before a period.

41. Article from an Encyclopedia on CD-ROM—APA

Artificial intelligence. (2003). *Encarta 2003*. Retrieved December 10, 2003, from
     Encarta database.

The retrieval statement gives the retrieval date in full and the name of
the database. The entry ends with a period.

42. Computer Software—APA

Transparent Language Presentation Program (Version 2.0 for Windows)
[Computer software]. (1994). Hollis, NH: Transparent Language.

Provide an author name, if available. Standard software and program languages do not need to be listed in References. Provide the name and, in parentheses, the version number in the text.

43. Book Retrieved from a Database on the Web—APA

Eaton, A. W. (1889). *Acadian legends and lyrics*. London: White & Allen.
Retrieved May 25, 2004, from Early Canadiana Online database:
http://www.canadiana.org/cgi-bin/ECO/mtq?doc=09066

The first information is for the printed version of *Acadian Legends and Lyrics*. The retrieval statement gives the access date, the name of the database, and the URL of the specific work. In APA style, References entries that conclude with a URL do not end with a period.

44. Article from a Periodical on the Web—APA

Lewis, Ricki. (1995, December 11). Chronobiology researchers say their field's time has come. *The Scientist*, 14. Retrieved December 30, 2003, from http://www.the-scientist.com/yr1995/dec/chrono_951211.html

45. Electronic Copy of a Journal Article Retrieved from a Database—APA

Archibald, W. P. (1996). Small expectations and great adjustments: How Hamilton workers most often experienced the Great Depression. *Canadian Journal of Sociology, 21*, 359-402. Retrieved February 23, 2003, from Expanded Academic Index database.

In contrast to MLA style, APA style requires only that you identify the database. You don't need to name either the online service through which you accessed it or the library where you used the online service. You also don't need to give a URL.

46. Personal or Professional Site on the Web—APA

Hesse, D. (2003, November). Home page. Retrieved December 22, 2003, from http://www.ilstu.edu/~ddhesse

Williams, R. W. (2002, November). Neurogenetics at UT Health Science Center. Retrieved November 11, 2002, from http://nervenet.org

47. File Transfer Protocol (FTP), Telnet, or Gopher Site—APA

Taine, H. A. (2001, April). *The French Revolution* (Vol. 2). Retrieved October 21, 2002, from ftp://ibiblio.org/pub/docs/books/gutenberg

After the retrieval data, supply the FTP, telnet, or gopher search path.

48. Synchronous Communication (MOO, MUD, IRC)—APA

Give the name of the speaker, a title for the event, the date of the event or posting, the access date, and the URL.

Bleck, B. (1997, June 8). Online discussion of *Virtual first year composition: Distance education, the Internet and the World Wide Web*. Retrieved July 27, 2004, from http://lrc.csun.edu/DaMOO/cw/brad.html

49. Web Discussion Forum—APA

Higa, S. (2002, June 26). A potential bookmark [Msg. 483]. Message posted to http://groups.yahoo.com/group/Modern_Era/messages/483

50. LISTSERV (Electronic Mailing List)—APA

Caruso, T. (2002, June 30). CFP: Flannery O'Connor and feminism. Message posted to Calls for Papers electronic mailing list, archived at http://www.english.upenn.edu/CFP/archive/American/0421.html

51. Newsgroup—APA

Boyle, F. (2002, October 11). Cemi field theory: The hard problem made easy [Msg 1]. Message posted to news://sci.psychology.consciousness

35g What are APA format guidelines for research papers?

Ask whether your instructor has instructions for preparing a final draft. If not, you can use the APA guidelines here.

General instructions—APA

Use 8½-by-11-inch (standard size) white bond paper. The APA *Publication Manual* recommends double-spacing for a final manuscript of a student research paper. Set at least a one-inch (about 2.5-cm) margin on the left (slightly more if you submit your paper in a binder) and leave no less than one inch on the right and at the bottom.

Leave one-half inch (about 1.25 cm) from the top edge of the paper to the title-and-page-number line, described on the next page. Leave another one-half inch (or one inch from the top edge of the paper) before the next line on the page, whether that is a heading (such as "Abstract" or "Notes") or a line of your paper.

👁 **ALERT:** Most word-processing programs set the top and bottom margins at one inch (2.5 cm) as their default. Also, they generally set the "header" function at a default of one-half inch (1.25 cm). Therefore, formatting the margins for your paper is probably less troublesome than it might seem. You simply need to check the default settings. 👁

617

Use indents of one-half inch (1.25 cm) for the first line of all paragraphs, except in an abstract, the first line of which is not indented. Do not justify the right margin. Indent footnotes one-half inch (1.25 cm).

Order of parts—APA

Number all pages consecutively. Use this order for the parts of your paper:

1. Title page
2. Abstract (if required)
3. Body of the paper
4. Notes, if any
5. References
6. Appendixes, if any
7. Attachments, if any (questionnaires, data sheets, or other material your instructor asks you to include)

Title-and-page-number line for all pages—APA

Use a title-and-page-number line on all pages of your paper. Leaving a margin of one-half inch (about 1.25 cm) from the top edge of the paper, type the title (use a shortened version if necessary), leave a five-character space, and then type the page number. End the title-and-page-number line one inch (about 2.5 cm) from the right edge of the paper. Ask whether your instructor wants you to include your last name in this title-and-page-number line. The "header" tool in a word-processing program will help you create the title-and-page-number line easily.

Title page—APA

Use a separate title page. On it, begin with the title-and-page-number line described above, using the numeral 1 for this first page. Then, centre the complete title vertically and horizontally on the page. Use two or more double-spaced lines if the title is long. Do not italicize (or underline) the title or enclose it in quotation marks. On the next line, centre your name, and below that centre the course title and section, your instructor's name, and the date, each on its own line.

⊚ **ALERTS:** (1) Use the guidelines here for capitalizing the title of your own paper, the titles of sections within your paper, and any titles you mention in the body of your paper. (*Note:* See Box 152 in 35f for guidelines on the capitalization of titles in a References list, since different rules apply.) (2) Use a capital letter for the first and last words of your title and for the first and last words of a subtitle, if any. Start every noun, pronoun, verb, adverb, and adjective with a capital letter. Capitalize each main word in a hyphenated compound word (two or more words used together to express one idea): *Father-in-Law, Self-Consciousness*. Capitalize the word after a colon or a dash.

(3) Do not capitalize an article (*a, an, the*) unless one of the preceding capitalization rules applies to it. Do not capitalize prepositions and conjunctions unless they are four or more letters long. Do not capitalize the word *to* used in an infinitive. ◉

Abstract—APA

See 35d for advice about what to include in an abstract of your paper. Type the abstract on a separate page, using the numeral 2 in the title-and-page-number line. Centre the word *Abstract* one inch (about 2.5 cm) from the top of the paper. Do not italicize (or underline) it or enclose it in quotation marks. Double-space below this title, and then start your abstract, double-spacing it. Do not indent the first line.

Set-off quotations—APA

Set off (display in block form) quotations of forty words or more. Double-space to start a new line for the quoted words, indenting each line of the (double-spaced) quotation one-half inch (about 1.25 cm) or five to seven spaces from the left margin. Do not enclose the quoted words in quotation marks.

If you are quoting part of a paragraph or one complete paragraph, do not indent the first line more than one-half inch. But if you quote two or more paragraphs, indent the first line of the second and subsequent paragraphs one inch (about 2.5 cm).

When the quotation is finished, leave one space after the sentence-ending punctuation, and then give the parenthetical citation. Begin a new line to resume your own words.

Notes—APA

Whenever you use a content note in your paper (35e), try to arrange your sentence so that the note number falls at the end. The ideal place for a note number is after the sentence-ending punctuation. Use an arabic numeral raised slightly above the line of words (called a *superscript* number in word-processing programs) and immediately after the final punctuation mark.

See 35e for whether to use footnotes or endnotes. If you use endnotes, put them on a separate page after the last text page of your paper and before your References list. Use a title-and-page-number line. Then, centre the word *Notes* one inch (about 2.5 cm) from the top of the paper. Do not italicize (or underline) it or put it in quotation marks.

On the next line, indent one-half inch (about 1.25 cm) and begin the note. Start with the superscript note number, and then add the words of your note, leaving no space between the note number and the note's first word. If the note is more than one typed line, do not indent any line after the first. Double-space throughout.

References list—APA

Start a new page for your References list immediately after the end of the body of your paper and after any Notes page(s). Use a title-and-page-number line. Drop down one inch (about 2.5 cm) from the top of the paper, and centre the word *References*. Do not italicize (or underline) it or put it in quotation marks. Double-space below it. Start the first line of each entry at the left margin, and indent any subsequent lines one-half inch (about 1.25 cm) from the left margin. Use this "hanging indent" style unless your instructor prefers a different one. Double-space within each entry and between entries.

35h A student's APA-style research paper

The final section of this chapter presents a student research paper prepared to conform to the style of the American Psychological Association (APA). I discuss the researching, planning, drafting, and revising processes of the student, Samuel Fung, and show the final draft of the paper, including its abstract.

Case Study

Samuel Fung was given this assignment for a research paper in a course called Introduction to Psychology: Write a research paper of 1800 to 2000 words about an unconscious process in humans. For guidance, refer to the *Simon & Schuster Handbook for Writers,* Fourth Canadian Edition, Chapters 32 and 33. Use the documentation style of the American Psychological Association (APA) explained in Chapter 35. Your topic and working bibliography are due in two weeks. An early draft of your paper is due two weeks later (try to get it close to what you hope will be your last draft, so that comments from me and from your peers can concretely help you write an excellent final draft). Your final draft is due one week after your early draft is returned to you with comments.

35h.1 Researching and writing the paper

After Samuel Fung had read his assignment, he started PLANNING by listing various unconscious processes in humans so that he could pick the one most interesting to him. Referring to his class notes and the textbook from his psychology course, he found these topics: "sleep," "dreams," "insomnia," "biological clocks," "daydreams," "hypnosis," and "meditation." He favoured the topic "biological clocks" because of his experiences with jet lag whenever he travelled between his home in Vancouver and his grandparents' home in Hong Kong.

Fung then checked to see whether he could find enough sources useful for research on "biological clocks." From his home computer, he went to his university's Web site and found the university library's home page. He was pleased to find that the online book catalogue listed several appropriate books that had not been checked out. The online databases provided the entire text of hundreds of journal, magazine, and newspaper articles. Using the Yahoo search engine, he found even more sources. During his search, he tried a variety of terms, such as "biological clocks" and "jet lag," which he thought of himself, and "circadian rhythms" and "chronobiology," which he found in articles. Skimming through the online articles, he printed those he thought he could use. Then, he went to his university library to check out several books and to review some other materials that were available only in the library.

So that he could compile a WORKING BIBLIOGRAPHY, Fung began to read and take content notes. The working bibliography that he submitted consisted of twenty-six SOURCES, though he had reviewed and rejected about twelve others (he knew that this represented real progress for him). Fung did not intend to use all twenty-six sources in his paper, but he wanted them available as he wrote his early drafts. Not surprisingly, his instructor urged him to reduce the list once DRAFTING began; otherwise, Fung would risk writing too little about too much. He redoubled his efforts to read even more critically to evaluate his sources (see 5c.3, 5d, and 32j) and weed out material. He narrowed his list to nineteen sources, took detailed notes on each, and began to group his material into emerging subtopics.

Fung had entire books about biological clocks, so he realized that he would need to narrow the TOPIC sufficiently to shape a THESIS STATEMENT. The narrowing process worried him because he had been told in other courses that his topics for research papers were too broad. He was determined this time to avoid that problem.

To start drafting his paper, Fung spread his note cards around him for easy reference, but he felt somewhat overwhelmed by the amount of information at hand, and he wrote only a few sentences. To break through, he decided to type a DISCOVERY DRAFT to see what he had absorbed from his reading and notetaking. That very rough draft became his vehicle for many things, including creating an effective thesis statement, inserting source information according to APA documentation style, and checking the logical arrangement of his material.

Revising for Fung started with his thesis statement, a process that helped him further narrow his focus. He began with "Biological clocks are fascinating," which expressed his feelings but said nothing of substance. His next version served him well as he revised his discovery draft into a true first draft: "Biological clocks, our unconscious timekeepers, affect our lives in many ways, including compatibility in marriage, family life, jet travel, work schedules, illnesses, medical treatments, and space exploration." That version proved to Fung that he was covering too much for an 1800- to 2000-word research paper, and he wanted to drop some material. He decided first to inform his readers about the phenomenon of biological clocks and then to discuss the effects of those clocks on people's alertness in the morning and later in the day, on travellers on jet airplanes, and on workers' performance. For his final draft, Fung used this more focused thesis statement: "Biological clocks, also known as circadian cycles, are a significant feature of human design that greatly affects people personally and professionally."

Fung used a word-processing program that has a template for an APA-style document. Although this provided the overall format, he had to attend very closely to the details of correct parenthetical IN-TEXT CITATIONS (see 35b and 35c) within his paper and a correct REFERENCES list (see 35f and 35g) at the end. Because Fung had used MLA DOCUMENTATION STYLE in other courses, he made sure not to confuse the two styles. For example, he saw that APA-style parenthetical citations include the year of publication (whereas MLA-style citations do not). For format and style details of the References list at the end of his paper, he found Box 152 in section 35f especially helpful.

As Fung checked the logical arrangement of his material, he realized that because he had dropped some aspects of biological clocks when he finally narrowed his topic sufficiently, he needed a little more depth about the aspects that he was retaining. A few hours at the computer led him to what he needed, including examples about baseball players and emergency-room physicians. Fung learned from his research experiences the difference between researching a topic too broadly (and therefore gathering too many sources for the assignment) and researching a few aspects of a topic in depth by focusing on selected sources. His final draft, which appears on the following pages, draws on nineteen sources, a number that is down considerably from the twenty-six with which he started.

Fung's title page and abstract page are shown here. For guidelines on writing an abstract, see 35d. For instructions on formatting each part of an APA-style paper, see 35g.

35h.2 Analyzing the research paper

In APA style, position the title-and-page-number line ½ inch (about 1.25 cm) from the top of the paper.

In APA style, centre the following information in the middle of the page: title, your name, course title and section, the professor's name, and the date; use double-spacing.

½" (1.25 cm)

Biological Clocks   1   1" (2.5 cm)

Biological Clocks:

The Body's Internal Timepieces

Samuel Fung

Introduction to Psychology 115, Section P1

Professor Robert Schmitt

November 17, 2003

APA-style title page

1" (2.5 cm)

½" (1.25 cm)

Biological Clocks   2   1" (2.5 cm)

Abstract

Circadian rhythms, which greatly affect human lives, often suffer disruptions in technological societies, resulting in such disorders as jet lag syndrome and seasonal affective disorder (SAD). With growing scientific awareness of both natural circadian cycles and the effects of disturbances of these cycles, people are learning to control some negative effects.

DOUBLE-SPACE

APA style requires that an abstract be placed on a separate page.

1" (2.5 cm)

APA-style abstract page

623

APA

APA STYLE: Use 1-inch (about 2.5-cm) margins; double-space throughout

Biological Clocks:

The Body's Internal Timepieces

INTRODUCTION: Gets reader's attention

Life in modern technological societies is built around timepieces. People set clocks on radios, microwave ovens, VCRs, and many more devices. Elementary and high school students respond to bells that start and end the school day as well as dividing it into blocks of time. While carefully managing the minutes and hours each day, individuals are often forced by styles of family and work life to violate another kind of time: their body's time. Biological clocks, also known as circadian cycles, are a significant feature of human design that greatly affects people personally and professionally.

THESIS STATEMENT: Gives paper's focus

FIRST HEADING

The Body's Natural Cycles

PARAGRAPH 2: First body paragraph gives background information

The term *circadian*, which is Latin for "about a day," describes the rhythms of people's internal biological clocks. Circadian cycles are in tune with external time cycles such as the 24-hour period of the earth's daily rotation as signalled by the rising and setting of the sun. In fact, according to William Schwartz, professor of neurobiology and a researcher in the field of chronobiology (the study of circadian rhythm), "All such biological clocks are adaptations to life on a rotating world" (as cited in Lewis, 1995, p. 14). Usually, humans set their biological clocks by seeing these cycles of daylight and darkness. Studies conducted in caves or similar environments that allow researchers to control light and darkness have shown that most people create cycles slightly over 24 hours when they are not exposed to natural cycles of day and night (Czeisler et al., 1999). Human perception of the external day-night cycle affects the production and release of a brain hormone, melatonin, which

Statement by Schwartz is in article by Lewis

Author name(s) and year in parentheses when not included in text

→

(Proportions shown in this paper are adjusted to fit space limitations of this book. Follow actual dimensions discussed in this book and your instructor's directions.)

Biological Clocks   4

is important in initiating and regulating the sleep-wake cycle, as Alfred Lewy and other scientists at the U.S. National Institutes of Health have found (Winfree, 1987).

Each individual's lifestyle reflects that person's own circadian cycle. Scientists group people as "larks" or "owls" on the basis of whether individuals are more efficient in the morning or at night. The idea behind the labels is that "in nature certain animals are diurnal, active during the light period; others are nocturnal, active at night. The 'morning lark' and the 'night owl' connotations typically are used to categorize the human extremes" ("Are You," 1989, p. 11).

Disruptions of Natural Cycles

"Larks" who must stay up late at night and "owls" who must awaken early in the morning experience mild versions of "jet lag," the disturbance from which travellers often suffer when they cross several time zones. Jet lag, which is characterized by fatigue and irregular sleep patterns, results from disruption of circadian rhythms:

> Jet lag syndrome is the inability of the internal body rhythm to rapidly resynchronize after sudden shifts in the timing. For a variety of reasons, the system attempts to maintain stability and resist temporal change. Consequently, complete adjustment can often be delayed for several days--sometimes for a week--after arrival at one's destination. (Bonner, 1991, p. 72)

According to Richard Coleman (1986), "the number, rate, and direction of time-zone changes are the critical factors in determining the extent and degree of jet lag symptoms" (p. 67).

In APA style, header has shortened title and page number

No page numbers in parenthetical citations for paraphrases and summaries

PARAGRAPH 3: Defines larks and owls

APA

Partial title used because source does not give an author

SECOND HEADING

PARAGRAPH 4: Applies terms to jet lag

In APA style, block-indented paragraph for quotations over 40 words indents ½ inch (about 1.25 cm) or five to seven spaces from left

Quotations require page number with p., or pp. for more than one page

→

In general, eastbound travellers find it harder than westbound travellers to adjust.

PARAGRAPH 5:
Additional
specific
support for
final sentence
of previous
paragraph

Statistics
illustrate
example

Proof of this theory can be found in professional baseball. Three researchers analyzed win-loss records to discover whether jet lag affected baseball players' performance (Recht, Lew, & Schwartz, 1995). The study focused on the records of eastern and western teams over a period of 3 years. If a visiting team did not have to travel through any time zones, it lost 54% of the time. If the visiting team had travelled from west to east, it lost 56.2% of the time. But if the vistors had travelled from east to west, they lost only 37.1% of the time.

PARAGRAPH 6:
New example
describes
problem as it
affects another
group, shift
workers

Specific details
illustrate
example

Another group that suffers greatly from biological-clock disruptions consists of people whose livelihoods depend on erratic schedules. This situation affects 20 to 30 million U.S. workers whose work schedules differ from the usual morning starting time and afternoon or early evening ending time (Weiss, 1989). Sue Binkley (1990) reports that Charles Czeisler, director of the Center for Circadian and Sleep Disorders at Brigham and Women's Hospital in Boston, found that 27% of the U.S. workforce does shift work. Shift work can mean, for example, working from 7:00 a.m. to 3:00 p.m. for 6 weeks, from 3:00 p.m. to 11:00 p.m. for 6 weeks, and from 11:00 p.m. to 7:00 a.m. for 6 weeks. Shift workers are at greater risk for heart disease, stomach disorders, insomnia, mood disorders, and infertility (Latta & Van Cauter, 2003). In a 1989 report to the American Association for the Advancement of Science, Czeisler states that "police officers, [medical] interns, and

→

Biological Clocks 6

many others who work nights perform poorly and are involved in more on-the-job accidents than their daytime counterparts" (as cited in Binkley, 1990, p. 26).

Other researchers confirm that safety is at risk during late-shift hours. In a study of 28 medical interns observed during late-night shifts over a 1-year period, 25% admitted to falling asleep while talking on the phone, and 34% had had at least one accident or near-accident during that period (Weiss, 1989). Investigations into the *Challenger* space shuttle explosion and the nuclear-reactor disasters at Three Mile Island and Chernobyl reveal critical errors made by people undergoing the combined stresses of lack of sleep and unusual work schedules (Toufexis, 1989).

PARAGRAPH 7: Additional specific support

Emergency-room physicians experience these two stresses all the time. A U.S. professional group, the American College of Emergency Physicians (ACEP), after investigating circadian rhythms and shift work, drafted a formal policy statement, approved by ACEP's board of directors in 1994. The policy calls for "shifts . . . consistent with circadian principles" to prevent burnout and keep emergency physicians from changing their medical specialty as well as enabling them to provide the best care for patients (Thomas, 1996).

PARAGRAPH 8: One group's response to information on biological clocks

Ellipsis indicates that words have been omitted within a direct quotation

If jet lag and circadian disruptions caused by shift work are obvious ways to upset a biological clock, a less obvious disruption is increasingly recognized as a medical problem: the condition known as seasonal affective disorder (SAD). Table 1 lists some of the major symptoms of SAD.

PARAGRAPH 9: Applies problem to a medical condition

→

627

Biological Clocks   7

Table 1

Table title *Common Symptoms of Seasonal Affective Disorder (SAD)*

Sadness	Later waking
Anxiety	Increased sleep time
Decreased physical activity	Interrupted, unrefreshing sleep
Irritability	Daytime drowsiness
Increased appetite	Decreased sexual drive
Craving for carbohydrates	Menstrual problems
Weight gain	Work problems
Earlier onset of sleep	Interpersonal problems

Note. From *The Clockwork Sparrow* (p. 204), by S. Binkley, 1990, Englewood Cliffs, NJ: Prentice Hall. Copyright 1990 by Prentice Hall. Reprinted with permission.*

Ways to Help People Affected by Cycle Disruptions

SAD appears to be related to the short daylight (photoperiod) of winter in the temperate zones of the northern and southern hemispheres. Michael Terman, a clinical psychologist at a leading psychiatric institute in the northeastern United States, has studied SAD patients for many years. He has observed their inability to function at home or at work from fall to spring (Caldwell, 1999). Research by Kelly Rohan, Sandra Sigmon, and Diana Dorhofer (2003) suggests that negative thought patterns and reduced activity enjoyment also correlate with SAD. The phenomenon of SAD not only illustrates the important role of circadian rhythms, but also dramatically proves that an understanding of circadian principles can help scientists improve the lives of people who experience disruptions of their biological clocks. Binkley (1990) claims

⟶

*For professional publications, the APA *Publication Manual* recommends that tables appear on separate pages at the end of your paper. Determine your instructor's preference.

Biological Clocks   8

that exposure to bright light for periods of up to 2 hours a day during the short-photoperiod days of winter reduces SAD-related "depression in 87 percent of patients . . . within a few days; relapses followed" when light treatment ended (pp. 203-204). The treatment works because specific cells in the retina of the eye transmit information to "two clusters of 10,000 nerve cells in the hypothalamus of the brain" that control the body's biological clock (Wright, 2002, p. 60).

Specific method for reducing SAD

Lengthening a person's exposure to bright light can also help combat the effects of jet lag and shift work. Specific suggestions for using light to help reset a jet traveller's biological clock include trying to sleep when it gets dark at your destination and "being outdoors as much as possible during the afternoon" (Herxheimer & Waterhouse, 2003, p. 297). Night-shift workers should stay in the dark during the day and can benefit from exposure to strong bright light at work (Boivin & James, 2002).

PARAGRAPH 11: Applies solution from previous paragraph to other problems discussed in paper

More substantial changes may be required to help some people affected by disruptions of their biological clocks. Susan Black (2000) summarizes research that shows most adolescents' biological clocks are set so that they cannot fall asleep until after 10:30 p.m. Since they need a little more than 9 hours of sleep per night, the customary school starting time of 7:30-8:30 a.m. comes too early. Adolescents may be able to reset their circadian clocks by going to sleep 15 minutes earlier-- including on weekends--over a gradual period of several weeks. Conversely, schools may need to consider later starting times.

PARAGRAPH 12: Continues solution

Establishing work schedules more sensitive to biological clocks can increase workers' sense of well-being and reduce certain safety hazards. A group of police officers in Philadelphia

PARAGRAPH 13: Specific system for reducing time-shift problems

→

629

In APA style, separate two or more sources in a single in-text citation with semicolons

APA

were studied while on modified shift schedules (Locitzer, 1989; Toufexis, 1989). The officers changed between day shifts and night shifts less frequently than they had on former shift schedules. Also, they rotated forward rather than backward in time, and they worked 4 rather than 6 consecutive days. The officers reported 40% fewer patrol car accidents and decreased use of drugs or alcohol to get to sleep. Overall, the police officers preferred the modified shift schedules. Charles Czeisler, who conducted the study, summarizes the importance of these results: "When schedules are introduced that take into account the properties of the human circadian system, subjective estimates of work schedule satisfaction and health improve, personnel turnover decreases, and work productivity increases" (as cited in Locitzer, 1989, p. 66).

Conclusion

CONCLUSION: Points to future

Scientists like Charles Czeisler are guiding individuals to live harmoniously with their biological clocks. The growing awareness of the negative effects of shift work and travel across time zones has led to significant advances in reducing problems caused by disruptions of people's natural cycles. The use of light to manipulate the body's sense of time has also helped. As more of us realize how circadian rhythms can affect our lifestyles, we might learn to control our biological clocks instead of our biological clocks controlling us.

→

Biological Clocks   10

References

Are you a day or night person? (1989, March 4). *USA Today*, p. 11.

Binkley, S. (1990). *The clockwork sparrow*. Englewood Cliffs, NJ: Prentice Hall.

Black, S. (2000, December). A wake-up call on high-school starting times. *Education Digest, 6*, 33-38. Retrieved September 7, 2003, from Academic Search Elite database.

Boivin, D. B., & James, F. O. (2002). Circadian adjustment to night-shift work by judicious light and darkness exposure. *Journal of Biological Rhythms, 17*, 556-567.

Bonner, P. (1991, July). Travel rhythms. *Sky Magazine*, 72-73, 76-77.

Caldwell, M. (1999, July). Mind over time. *Discover, 20*, 52. Retrieved September 8, 2003, from General Reference Gold database (Article A55030836).

Coleman, R. (1986). *Wide awake at 3:00 a.m.: By choice or by chance?* New York: Freeman.

Czeisler, C., Duffy, J. F., Shanahan, T. L., Brown, E. N., Mitchell, J. F., Rimmer, D. W., et al. (1999, June 25). Stability, precision, and near-24-hour period of the human circadian pacemaker. *Science, 284*, 2177-2181.

Herxheimer, A., & Waterhouse, J. (2003). The prevention and treatment of jet lag. *BMJ: British Medical Journal, 326*, 296-297.

Latta, F., & Van Cauter, E. (2003). Sleep and biological clocks. In M. Gallagher and R. J. Nelson (Eds.), *Handbook of Psychology: Vol. 3: Biological Psychology* (pp. 355-375). New York: Wiley.

Lewis, R. (1995, December 24). Chronobiology researchers say their field's time has come. *The Scientist, 9*, 14. Retrieved September 6, 2003, from http://www.the-scientist.com/yr1995/dec/chres_951211.html

Begin References on new page

Double-space throughout

List References in alphabetical order

See page 604 for advice about formatting an APA-style References list using a "hanging indent" style

→

Biological Clocks   11

Locitzer, K. (1989, July/August). Are you out of sync with each other? *Psychology Today, 23,* 66.

Source is a letter appearing in *Nature* publication

Recht, L., Lew, R., & Schwartz, W. (1995, October 19). Baseball teams beaten by jet lag [Letter]. *Nature, 377,* 583.

Rohan, K. J., Sigmon, S. T., & Dorhofer, D. M. (2003). Cognitive-behavioral factors in seasonal affective disorder. *Journal of Consulting and Clinical Psychology, 71,* 22-30.

Thomas, H. A. (2003). Circadian rhythms and shift work. ACEP Online. Retrieved September 28, 2003, from http://www.acep.org/1,509,0.html

Toufexis, A. (1989, June 5). The times of your life. *Time, 133,* 66-67.

Weiss, R. (1989, January 21). Safety gets short shrift on long night shift. *Science News, 135,* 37.

Winfree, A. (1987). *The timing of biological clocks.* New York: Freeman.

Wright, K. (2002, September). Times of our lives. *Scientific American, 287,* 58-64. Retrieved September 12, 2003, from Academic Search Elite database.

Chapter 36

CM, CSE, and COS Documentation

This chapter presents three more systems of documentation (in addition to MLA STYLE in Chapter 34 and APA STYLE in Chapter 35). The first two are the styles of the University of Chicago Press (CM) and the Council of Science Editors (CSE). Additionally, some instructors require Columbia Online Style (COS) to document electronic sources, although with the very recent publication of manuals updated for electronic sources (for all but CSE style), COS is often no longer necessary as a separate style.

CM-STYLE DOCUMENTATION

The University of Chicago Press endorses two styles of documentation. One is an author-date style similar to the APA style of IN-TEXT CITATIONS and a list of sources usually called WORKS CITED or REFERENCES.

The other CM style uses a bibliographic note system that consists of footnotes or endnotes and a Bibliography that lists all sources used in a research paper. I present this style here because it's often used in such humanities courses as art, music, history, philosophy, and sometimes English.

36a How does the bibliographic note system work in CM style?

The *Chicago Manual* (CM) **bibliographic note system** gives information about each source in two places: in a **footnote** or an **endnote** and, if required, in a **Bibliography** that begins on a separate page at the end of a research paper.

When using footnotes or endnotes, the first time a source is named, you can choose either to give full bibliographic information or—but only if you have a Bibliography at the end of your research paper—to use shortened information that includes the last name(s) of the author(s) and the key words in the work's title. When a source is named again, you can give less information in the later endnote or footnote.

633

In CM style, place your notes either before the Bibliography at the end of a paper (endnotes) or at the foot of the page on which you refer to a source (footnotes). Microsoft Word and most other word-processing programs offer built-in ways to use footnotes and endnotes. In Word, for example, the "Insert" menu contains a command for footnotes; selecting the footnotes command also provides an option for endnotes. For more detailed explanations, use the "Help" menu in your software. Following is an example of how text and footnotes work together in CM style. Below that is a sample from a research paper showing text and full bibliographic endnotes.

TEXT

Trudeau also makes this point.[3]

FOOTNOTE (ON SAME PAGE)

3. Pierre E. Trudeau, *Federalism and the French Canadians* (Toronto: Macmillan Canada, 1968), 25.

TEXT

Perhaps the most famous attempt to create artificial intelligence occurred when computer engineers developed IBM's Deep Blue computer, which beat chess grandmaster Garry Kasparov in 1997.[11] However, Murray Campbell, one of Deep Blue's creators, has conceded that the computer "did not exhibit human qualities and therefore was not 'intelligent.'"[12] Some computer scientists take a much different position. For example, Hans Moravec believes that "robot computers [will] achieve human intelligence . . . around 2040."[13]

ENDNOTES (BEFORE BIBLIOGRAPHY AT END OF PAPER)

11. Thomas Hayden, "The Age of Robots," *U.S. News and World Report*, April 23, 2001, 46.

12. Gary Stix, "2001: A Scorecard," *Scientific American*, January 2001, 36.

13. Jeff Minerd, "Robots: Our Evolutionary Heirs?" *Futurist*, February 1999, 9.

CM-style text and bibliographic notes

CM style requires a separate Bibliography only if abbreviated footnotes or endnotes are used. The alphabetical Bibliography list (similar to the Works Cited list in MLA style or the References list in APA style) is sequenced by authors' last names, and it belongs on a separate page at the end of a research paper. A perfect match between the information in endnotes or footnotes and the Bibliography is required.

Box 153 provides guidelines for compiling CM-style bibliographic notes. The directory and examples in 36b show how to prepare notes according to CM style.

BOX 153   SUMMARY

Guidelines for compiling CM-style bibliographic notes

■ **TITLE AND PLACEMENT**

- Use the title Notes if you're using endnotes. Start them on a separate page, numbered sequentially with the rest of your paper, after your last text page and before your bibliography. If you're using footnotes, place them at the bottom of the page on which the source needs to be credited. Never use a label, such as *Footnotes*, above the footnote(s) at the bottom of the page. Also, never use a line to divide the footnote(s) from the text.

- Use Bibliography for your list of sources on a separate page at the end of your research paper.

■ **FORMAT FOR ENDNOTES AND FOOTNOTES**

- Include an endnote or a footnote every time you use a source.

- Number notes sequentially throughout your paper whether you're using endnotes or footnotes.

- Use superscript (raised) arabic numerals for the footnote or endnote numbers in your paper. Position note numbers after any punctuation mark except the dash, preferably at the end of a sentence if the note number is no more than several words from the source material.

- Never use raised numbers in the endnote or footnote itself. Place the number followed by a period on the same line as the content of the note. (Some word-processing programs override this same-line rule in CM style, so you might need to adapt to those demands. If this happens, use a consistent style throughout your paper—and be sure to get your instructor's permission to deviate from standard CM style before you hand in the final draft of a research paper.)

- Place footnotes at the bottom of the page on which you've used the material that calls for crediting your source.

- Place endnotes at the end of your paper, before the Bibliography, on a separate page titled Notes. Centre the word *Notes*, neither underlined nor in quotation marks, an inch (about 2.5 cm) from the top of the page, and double-space after it. For the notes themselves, single-space both within each note

→

Guidelines for compiling CM-style bibliographic notes
(*continued*)

and between notes. Indent each note's first line three-tenths of an inch (0.3″ tab), which equals about three characters or 0.75 centimetres, but place subsequent lines flush left at the margin.

■ **SPACING AFTER PUNCTUATION**

A single space, not two spaces, follows all punctuation, including the period.

■ **AUTHORS' NAMES**

- In endnotes and footnotes, give the name in standard (first name first) order, with names and initials as given in the original source. Use the word *and* before the last author's name if your source has two or three authors. If your source has more than three authors, follow the guidelines for model 3 in 36b.

- In the Bibliography, invert the name (last name, first name) that comes first in a list of two or more authors (see model 2 in 36b). If your source has two to ten authors, give all the authors' names. If your source has eleven or more authors, list only the first seven and use *et al.* for the rest.

■ **CAPITALIZATION OF SOURCE TITLES**

Capitalize the first word, the last word, and all major words.

■ **SPECIAL TREATMENT OF TITLES**

- Use italics for titles of long works, and use quotation marks around the titles of shorter works. However, if italics aren't available in your word-processing program, you can use underlining.

- Omit *A, An,* and *The* from the titles of newspapers and other periodicals. For an unfamiliar newspaper title, list the city (and the province or state, in parentheses, where useful for clarity): *London (ON) Free Press,* for example. You can use postal abbreviations for provinces and states, though some instructors might prefer the older abbreviated forms (e.g., *Alta.* for *Alberta; Fla.* for *Florida; Ont.* for *Ontario*).

■ **PUBLICATION INFORMATION**

Enclose publication information in parentheses in numbered bibliographic notes—but not in a separate Bibliography section

→

Guidelines for compiling CM-style bibliographic notes (*continued*)

(see also 36b, models 1 and 2). Use a colon and one space after the city of publication. Give complete publishers' names or abbreviate them according to standard abbreviations in *Books in Print,* available in the reference section of most libraries. Omit *Co., Inc.,* and the like. Spell out *University* (never use *U* alone) and *Press* (never use *P* alone). Do not abbreviate publication months.

■ **PAGE NUMBERS**
- For inclusive page numbers, give the full second number for 2 through 99. For 100 and beyond, give the full second number only if a shortened version would be ambiguous: 202-6, 243-47, 300-304 .
- List all discontinuous page numbers; see the model at "First Endnote or Footnote: Book," toward the end of this box.
- Use a comma to separate parenthetical publication information from the page numbers that follow it. Use the abbreviations *p.* and *pp.* with page numbers only for material from newspapers, for material from journals that do not use volume numbers, and to avoid ambiguity.

■ **CONTENT NOTES**
Try to avoid using content notes. If you must use them, use footnotes, not endnotes, with symbols rather than numbers: an asterisk (*) for the first note on that page and a dagger (†) for a second note on that page.

■ **FIRST BIBLIOGRAPHIC ENDNOTE OR FOOTNOTE: BOOK**
For books, include the author, title, publication information, and, when applicable, the page numbers of the material you used.

1. Eudora Welty, *One Writer's Beginnings* (Cambridge: Harvard University Press, 1984), 25-26, 30, 43-51, 208.

■ **FIRST BIBLIOGRAPHIC ENDNOTE OR FOOTNOTE: ARTICLE**
For articles, include the author, article title, journal title, volume number, year, and page numbers.

1. D. D. Cochran, W. Daniel Hale, and Christine P. Hissam, "Personal Space Requirements in Indoor versus Outdoor Locations," *Journal of Psychology* 117 (1984): 132-33.

→

Guidelines for compiling CM-style bibliographic notes (*continued*)

■ **SECOND MENTION IN BIBLIOGRAPHIC ENDNOTES OR FOOTNOTES**
Whether you give full or shortened, bibliographic information in the endnote or footnote accompanying your first use of each source, subsequent citations of the same source can be brief. Include the author name(s), the title of the work, and a page reference. For example, a second citation of the Welty book in the example above might be:

> 14. Welty, *One Writer's Beginnings*, 46.

If the title has more than four words, give a shortened version that contains the key words. See model 4 in 36b for additional guidelines.

36b What are CM-style guidelines for bibliographic notes?

The directory below corresponds to the sample bibliographic note forms that follow it. In a few cases, I give sample Bibliography forms as well. If you need a model that is not here, consult *The Chicago Manual of Style* (15th edition, 2003), which gives footnote, endnote, and Bibliography forms for a multitude of sources.

Directory—CM Style for Footnotes and Endnotes

1. Book by One Author—CM
2. Book by Two or Three Authors—CM
3. Book by More Than Three Authors—CM
4. Multiple Citations of a Single Source—CM
5. Book by a Group or Corporate Author—CM
6. Book with No Author Named—CM
7. Book with an Author and an Editor—CM
8. Translation—CM
9. Work in Several Volumes or Parts—CM
10. One Selection from an Anthology or an Edited Book—CM
11. More Than One Selection from an Anthology or an Edited Book—CM
12. Signed Article in a Reference Book—CM
13. Unsigned Article in a Reference Book—CM
14. Second or Later Edition—CM
15. Anthology or Edited Book—CM

16. Introduction, Preface, Foreword, or Afterword—CM
17. Unpublished Dissertation or Essay—CM
18. Reprint of an Older Book—CM
19. Book in a Series—CM
20. Book with a Title Within a Title—CM
21. Government Publication—CM
22. Published Proceedings of a Conference—CM
23. Signed Article from a Daily Newspaper—CM
24. Editorial, Letter to the Editor, or Review—CM
25. Unsigned Article from a Daily Newspaper—CM
26. Signed Article from a Weekly or Biweekly Magazine or Newspaper—CM
27. Signed Article from a Monthly or Bimonthly Periodical—CM
28. Article from a Collection of Reprinted Articles—CM
29. Article from a Journal with Continuous Pagination—CM
30. Article from a Journal That Pages Each Issue Separately—CM
31. Personal Interview—CM
32. Published and Unpublished Letters—CM
33. Film, Videotape, or DVD—CM
34. Musical Recording—CM
35. Computer Software—CM
36. ERIC Information Service—CM
37. Secondary Source—CM

ELECTRONIC SOURCES
38. Source from a CD-ROM—CM
39. Online Book—CM
40. Article from a Periodical Available Only Online—CM
41. Article Accessed Through a Database—CM
42. Source from an Internet Site—CM
43. Electronic Mailing List—CM
44. E-Mail Message—CM

1. Book by One Author—CM

Footnote or Endnote

1. Pierre E. Trudeau, *Federalism and the French Canadians* (Toronto: Macmillan Canada, 1968).

Bibliography

Trudeau, Pierre E. *Federalism and the French Canadians*. Toronto: Macmillan Canada, 1968.

The bibliographic format is the reverse of the note or endnote format, in which first lines indent. In a Bibliography entry, the first line is placed flush left to the margin and the second and other lines are indented three-tenths of an inch (0.3″ tab), or about 0.75 centimetres. Notice also where periods replace commas and parentheses are dropped.

Typically, notes and endnotes end with page references, as shown in Box 153.

2. Book by Two or Three Authors—CM

Footnote or Endnote

1. Anthony Doob and Carla Cesaroni. *Responding to Youth Crime in Canada* (Toronto: University of Toronto Press, 2004).

2. Marlene Scardamalia, Carl Bereiter, and Bryant Fillion, *Writing for Results: A Sourcebook of Consequential Composing Activities* (Toronto: OISE Press, 1981).

Bibliography

Scardamalia, Marlene, Carl Bereiter, and Bryant Fillion. *Writing for Results: A Sourcebook of Consequential Composing Activities*. Toronto: OISE Press, 1981.

In a Bibliography entry, invert only the name of the first author listed.

3. Book by More Than Three Authors—CM

1. Mark H. Moore et al., *Dangerous Offenders: The Elusive Target of Justice* (Cambridge, MA: Harvard University Press, 1984).

Give the name of the author listed first on the title page, and then put either *et al.* or *and others,* using no punctuation after the author's name.

4. Multiple Citations of a Single Source—CM

For subsequent references to a work you've already named, give the last name of the author, the title of the work, and the page number, all separated by commas. Shorten the title if it is longer than four words. This example shows the form for a subsequent reference to the work fully described in model 1.

1. Trudeau, *Federalism*, 25.

If you cite two or more authors with the same last name, include first names or initials in each note.

2. Pierre Trudeau, *Federalism*, 25.

3. Garry Trudeau, *Revolt*, 128.

If you cite the same source as the source immediately preceding, you may use *Ibid.* (Latin *ibidem*, "in the same place"), followed by a comma and the page number, instead of repeating the author's name and the title.

> 4. Ibid., 152.

5. Book by a Group or Corporate Author—CM

> 1. American Psychological Association, *Publication Manual of the American Psychological Association*, 5th ed. (Washington, DC: American Psychological Association, 2001).

> 2. Investors Group, *Starting Out: Smart Strategies for Your 20s & 30s* (Toronto: Stoddart Publishing, 1998).

If a work issued by an organization has no author listed on the title page, give the name of the organization as the author of the work. The organization may also be the publisher of the work.

6. Book with No Author Named—CM

> 1. *The Chicago Manual of Style*, 15th ed. (Chicago: University of Chicago Press, 2003).

Begin the citation with the name of the book.

7. Book with an Author and an Editor—CM

> 1. Pierre Elliott Trudeau, *The Essential Trudeau*, ed. Ron Graham (Toronto: M&S, 1998).

In this position, the abbreviation *ed.* stands for "edited by," not "editor." Therefore, *ed.* is correct whether a work has one or more than one editor. (Also see model 10.)

8. Translation—CM

> 1. Michel Tremblay, *A Thing of Beauty*, trans. Sheila Fischman (Vancouver: Talon, 1998).

The abbreviation *trans.* stands for "translated by," not "translator."

9. Work in Several Volumes or Parts—CM

The two notes below show ways to give bibliographic information for a specific place in one volume of a multivolume work. Use whichever you prefer, staying consistent throughout a paper. If you are writing about the volume as a whole (as opposed to citing specific pages), end the note with the publication information.

> 1. Ernest Jones, *The Last Phase*, vol. 3 of *The Life and Work of Sigmund Freud* (New York: Basic Books, 1957), 97.

> 1. Ernest Jones, *The Life and Work of Sigmund Freud*, vol. 3, *The Last Phase* (New York: Basic Books, 1957), 97.

If you're citing an entire work in two or more volumes, use the form shown below.

> 2. John Herman Randall, Jr., *The Career of Philosophy*, 2 vols. (New York: Columbia University Press, 1962).

10. One Selection from an Anthology or an Edited Book—CM

> 1. Norval Morrisseau, "The Indian That Became a Thunderbird," in *Canadian Short Fiction: From Myth to Modern*, ed. W. H. New (Scarborough, ON: Prentice Hall, 1986), 26-29.

Give page numbers for the cited selection.

11. More Than One Selection from an Anthology or an Edited Book—CM

If you cite more than one selection from the same anthology or edited book, give complete bibliographic information in each citation, following the format shown in model 10.

12. Signed Article in a Reference Book—CM

> 1. Doris Shadbolt, "Carr, Emily," in *The Canadian Encyclopedia*, 2nd ed. (Edmonton: Hurtig, 1988), 366.

13. Unsigned Article in a Reference Book—CM

> 1. *Encyclopaedia Britannica*, 15th ed., s.v. "Ireland."

The abbreviation *s.v.* stands for *sub verbo*, meaning "under the word." Capitalize the heading of the entry only if it is a proper noun. Omit publication information except for the edition number.

14. Second or Later Edition—CM

> 1. Joanne Buckley and David Gates, *Put It in Writing*, 2nd ed. (Scarborough, ON: Prentice Hall, 1995).

Here the abbreviation *ed.* stands for "edition." Give the copyright date for the edition you are citing.

15. Anthology or Edited Book—CM

> 1. W. H. New, ed., *Canadian Short Fiction: From Myth to Modern* (Scarborough, ON: Prentice Hall, 1986).

Here the abbreviation *ed.* stands for "editor." For a source with two or more editors, use the plural *eds.*

16. Introduction, Preface, Foreword, or Afterword—CM

> 1. Warren Allmand, foreword to *The Life and Death of Anna Mae Aquash*, by Johanna Brand (Toronto: Lorimer, 1993).

CM

If the author of the book is different from the author of the cited part, give the name of the book's author after the title of the book.

17. Unpublished Dissertation or Essay—CM

1. Michele Byers, " 'Buffy the Vampire Slayer': The Insurgence of Television as a Performance Text" (PhD diss., University of Toronto, 2000), 23-24.

List the author's name first, then the title in quotation marks (not italicized), a descriptive label (such as *PhD diss.*, or *master's thesis*), the degree-granting institution, the date, and finally the page number(s) you are citing.

1. Claire J. Kramsch, "Context and Culture Online" (paper presented at the annual meeting of the Modern Language Association, New Orleans, December 2001).

To cite a paper read at a meeting, give the name of the meeting in parentheses, along with the location and the date.

18. Reprint of an Older Book—CM

1. Archibald Lampman, *Lyrics of Earth* (1895; repr., Ottawa: Tecumseh Press, 1978).

Republishing information is located on the copyright page. List the original date of publication first, followed by the publication information for the reprint.

19. Book in a Series—CM

1. Thomas J. Courchene, *In Praise of Renewed Federalism*, The Canada Round (Toronto: C. D. Howe Institute, 1991).

If the series numbers its volumes and the volume number is not part of the title, include the volume number after the series title. Separate the volume number from the series title with a comma.

20. Book with a Title Within a Title—CM

1. Aljean Harmetz, *The Making of "The Wizard of Oz"* (New York: Hyperion, 1998).

If the name of a work that is usually italicized appears in an already-italicized title, add quotation marks around it. If the name of a work that is usually in quotation marks appears within an italicized title, keep it in quotation marks and italicize it.

CM

21. Government Publication—CM

1. Indian and Northern Affairs Canada, *The Inuit* (Ottawa: Supply and Services Canada, 1986).

If a government department, bureau, agency, or committee produces a document, cite that group as the author.

22. Published Proceedings of a Conference—CM

1. Ovide Mercredi, "The Future Is Our Collective Rights as Distinct Peoples," in *Forging a New Relationship: Proceedings of the Conference on the Report of the Royal Commission on Aboriginal Peoples*, ed. Donald B. Smith, 55-80 (Montreal: McGill Institute for the Study of Canada, 1997).

Treat a selection from published conference proceedings as you would a chapter in a book.

23. Signed Article from a Daily Newspaper—CM

1. James Christie, "Award Bittersweet for Hockey Women," *Globe and Mail*, sec. D, March 26, 1998.

Because many newspapers print more than one edition a day and reposition the same articles on different pages, CM style recommends that you omit page numbers from note entries. When applicable, identify the specific edition (such as *national edition* or *final edition*); make this the last information in the entry, preceded by a comma. For a paper that specifies sections, use *sec.* before the section's letter or number or use *section* after a section's name (such as *Weekend section*). If a paper gives column titles, you may use the title (not italicized or in quotation marks) in addition to or in place of the article title. Separate all items with commas.

24. Editorial, Letter to the Editor, or Review—CM

1. "A Black Mark on Local Government," editorial, *London Free Press*, sec. B, July 27, 1994.

2. John Hurka, letter to the editor, *Calgary Sun*, sec. A, July 5, 1994.

3. Wendy Toews, "Politics of the Mind," review of *They Say You're Crazy: How the World's Most Powerful Psychiatrists Decide Who's Normal* by Paula J. Caplan, *Winnipeg Free Press*, sec. C, August 26, 1995.

Before page numbers, use a comma for popular magazines and a colon for journals.

25. Unsigned Article from a Daily Newspaper—CM

1. "Private Water May Violate Constitution," *Ottawa Citizen*, sec. A, November 27, 2002.

26. Signed Article from a Weekly or Biweekly Magazine or Newspaper—CM

1. Chris Wood, "Storm Clouds over Quebec," *Maclean's*, November 6, 1989, 16-17.

For general-readership weekly and biweekly magazines and newspapers, give the month, day, and year of publication. Separate page numbers from the year with a comma. As with a newspaper source, an unsigned article in a weekly or biweekly periodical has as its first item the title of the article.

27. Signed Article from a Monthly or Bimonthly Periodical—CM

1. John Tyler Bonner, "The Evolution of Evolution," *Natural History*, April 1999, 20-21.

For general-readership monthly and bimonthly magazines, give the month and year of publication. Separate page numbers from the year with a comma. An unsigned article in a monthly or bimonthly periodical has as its first item the title of the article.

28. Article from a Collection of Reprinted Articles—CM

1. Thomas Hayden, "The Age of Robots," *Applied Science*, Social Issues Resources Series (Boca Raton, FL: Social Issues Resources, 2002).

Cite only the publication actually consulted, not the original source. If you use a Bibliography, cite the article's location in both the reprint collection you consulted and the publication where the article first appeared.

29. Article from a Journal with Continuous Pagination—CM

1. Phyllis Tyson, "The Psychology of Women," *Journal of the American Psychoanalytic Association* 46 (1997): 361-64.

30. Article from a Journal That Pages Each Issue Separately—CM

1. Linda Adler-Kassner and Heidi Estrem, "Rethinking Research Writing: Public Literacy in the Composition Classroom," *WPA: Writing Program Administration* 26, no. 3 (2003): 119-31.

The issue number of a journal is required only if each issue of the journal starts with page 1. In this example, the volume number is 26 and the issue number, abbreviated as *no.*, is 3.

31. Personal Interview—CM

1. Randi Friedman, interview by author, September 30, 2003, Winnipeg, Manitoba.

For an unpublished interview, give the name of the interviewee and the interviewer, the date of the interview, and the location of the interview.

32. Published and Unpublished Letters—CM

1. George Sand to her mother, May 31, 1831, in *Letters Home: Celebrated Authors Write to Their Mothers*, ed. Reid Sherline (New York: Timkin, 1993), 17-20.

2. Theodore Brown, letter to author, December 7, 2002.

For an unpublished letter, give the name of the author, the name of the recipient, and the date the letter was written.

33. Film, Videotape, or DVD—CM

1. Atom Egoyan, *Calendar*, VHS (Canada/Armenia/Germany: Ego Filmarts/ZDF, 1993).

2. Atom Egoyan, *Calendar*, DVD (1993; Toronto: Alliance Atlantis, 2001).

3. Marc Norman and Tom Stoppard, *Shakespeare in Love*, DVD (1998; New York: Miramax Films/Universal Pictures, 2003).

In these examples, the first information gives the authors of the screenplay. If the point of a note were about the director or the producers, then the title would appear first and the abbreviations *dir.* and/or *prod.* ("directed by," "produced by") would follow a comma after the title along with the relevant names.

34. Musical Recording—CM

1. Leonard Cohen, "Tower of Song," on *I'm Your Man*, Sony CK 44191.

2. Bedrich Smetana, *My Country*, Czech Philharmonic, Karel Ancerl, Vanguard SV-9/10.

Bedrich Smetana is the composer and Karel Ancerl is the conductor.

35. Computer Software—CM

1. Dreamweaver Ver. MX, Macromedia, San Francisco, CA.

Place the version or release number, abbreviated *Ver.* or *Rel.*, directly after the name of the software. Then list the company that owns the rights to the software, followed by that company's location.

36. ERIC Information Service—CM

1. Hunter M. Breland, *Assessing Writing Skills* (New York: College Entrance Examination Board, 1987), ERIC, ED 286920.

ERIC stands for *Educational Resources Information Center.*

37. Secondary Source—CM

1. Mary Wollstonecraft, *A Vindication of the Rights of Woman* (1792), 90, quoted in Caroline Shrodes, Harry Finestone, and Michael Shugrue, *The Conscious Reader*, 4th ed. (New York: Macmillan, 1988), 282.

When you quote one person's words, having found them in another person's work, give information as fully as you can about both sources. Note 1 shows the form you use when the point of your citation is Mary Wollstonecraft's words. If your point is what Shrodes, Finestone, and Shugrue have to say about Wollstonecraft's words, handle the information as in note 2.

> 2. Caroline Shrodes, Harry Finestone, and Michael Shugrue, *The Conscious Reader*, 4th ed. (New York: Macmillan, 1988), 282, quoting Mary Wollstonecraft, *A Vindication of the Rights of Woman* (1792), 90.

ELECTRONIC SOURCES

If there is a print version of the source (as in model 41), provide information about that source. Also include information about how to find the electronic version. Unlike some other documentation styles (such as MLA), CM style does not generally recommend including "access dates," nor does it include angle brackets around URLs. Following are examples in CM style of a few common types of electronic sources. For additional types, consult *The Chicago Manual of Style*.

38. Source from a CD-ROM—CM

If you're citing a portion of a CD-ROM, include the author (if named) and title of that portion, then the title of the CD-ROM, the publisher, and the date. The following example omits the author's name.

> 1. "Artificial Intelligence," *Encarta 2003*, CD-ROM (Microsoft, 2003).

39. Online Book—CM

Include the author's name, the title, and access information—in this case, the name of the organization that sponsors the site, and the URL.

> Arthur W. Eaton, *Acadian Legends and Lyrics* (Canadian Institute for Historical Microreproductions, 1889), http://www.canadiana.org/cgi-bin/ECO/mtq?doc=09066.

40. Article from a Periodical Available Only Online—CM

Include the author, title of the article, title of the publication, volume and issue number (if given), publication date, and URL.

> 1. Veronica Austen, "Writing Spaces: Performances of the Word," *Kairos* 8, no. 1 (2003), http://english.ttu.edu/kairos/8.1/binder2.html?coverweb/austen/austen.html.

41. Article Accessed Through a Database—CM

Begin with the information for the article's original print version: author(s), article title, publication title, and other data as required by the type of print publication (see models 23 through 30). Then give the URL of the database through which you accessed the article. CM style

CM

recommends that you include an access date when citing information retrieved through a database. Insert the access date in parentheses after the URL, followed by a period.

1. Gail Dutton, "Greener Pigs," *Popular Science*, November 1999, 38-39, http://proquest.umi.com (accessed September 2, 2003).

2. Hazel Rose Markus and Shinobu Kitayama, "Culture and the Self: Implications for Cognition, Emotion, and Motivation," *Psychological Review* 98 (1991): 224-53, http://web2.infotrac.galegroup.com/itw/infomark (accessed November 17, 2003).

42. Source from an Internet Site—CM

Provide the author's name, the title of the Web page, the title or owner of the site, and the URL. When no specific author is listed, you may use the owner of the site as the author, as in the following example. Include an access date if your source is likely to be updated frequently, as is often the case with Internet sites.

1. American Association for Artificial Intelligence, "AI Overview," American Association for Artificial Intelligence, http://www.aaai.org/AITopics/html/overview.html (accessed December 22, 2003).

43. Electronic Mailing List—CM

1. T. Caruso, e-mail to Calls for Papers mailing list, June 30, 2002, http://www.english.upenn.edu/CFP/archive/American/0421.html.

44. E-mail Message—CM

1. Jim Thompson, e-mail message to author, November 11, 2003.

USING AND CITING GRAPHICS—**CM**

Place the credit line for a table or illustration from another source next to the reproduced material. (If you intend to publish your paper, you must receive permission to reprint copyrighted material from a source.) Spell out the terms *map*, *plate*, and *table*, but abbreviate *figure* as *fig*.

Reprinted by permission from Linda R. Pim, *Additive Alert: A Guide to Food Additives for the Canadian Consumer* (Toronto: Doubleday, 1979), 28, fig. 2. Copyright 1979 by Pollution Probe Foundation.

CSE-STYLE DOCUMENTATION

In its 1994 style manual, *Scientific Style and Format* (6th edition), the Council of Science Editors (CSE) endorses two documentation systems widely used in mathematics and the physical and life sciences. (Note that before 2000, the organization was called the Council of Biology Editors; that earlier name appears on the group's 1994 style manual.) At the time of this writing, the CSE is preparing a revised seventh edition of *Scientific Style and Format.* For up-to-date information, see <http://councilscienceeditors.org>.

36c What should I know about CSE-style documentation?

The first system endorsed by the CSE uses name-year parenthetical citations in the text of a paper, together with an alphabetically arranged Cited References (or References) list that gives full bibliographic information for each source. This kind of IN-TEXT CITATION system tied to a required BIBLIOGRAPHY is similar to both MLA style (Chapter 34) and APA style (Chapter 35).

The second CSE system marks citations in the text of a paper with numbers that correlate with a numerically arranged Cited References list. This chapter covers the numbered reference system, sometimes referred to as a *citation-sequence system.* Here's the way it works:

1. The first time you cite each source in your paper, assign it an arabic number in sequence, starting with 1.

2. Mark each subsequent reference to that source with the assigned number.

3. Use superscript (raised) numbers for source citations in your sentences, although numbers in parentheses are also acceptable.

4. Don't use footnotes or endnotes to credit your sources. Use only a Cited References list, and number each entry in the order of its appearance in your paper, starting with 1. Place the number, followed by a period, on the same line as the content of the citation. Never list sources alphabetically. Never underline or use italics for titles of works.

Here's an example of a sentence that includes in-text citations and the corresponding cited references.

IN-TEXT CITATIONS

Sybesma[1] insists that this behaviour occurs periodically, but Crowder[2] claims never to have observed it.

CITED REFERENCES

1. Sybesma C. An introduction to biophysics. New York: Academic Pr; 1977. 648 p.

2. Crowder W. Seashore life between the tides. New York: Dodd, Mead; 1931. New York: Dover Reprint; 1975. 372 p.

Thereafter, throughout your paper, follow each citation of Sybesma's *An Introduction to Biophysics* by a superscript 1 and each citation of Crowder's *Seashore Life* by a superscript 2.

When you're citing more than one reference—for example, a new source and the previous three sources as well as a source from your first page—list each source number, followed by a comma with no space. Use a hyphen to show the range of numbers in a continuous sequence, and put all the numbers in superscript: [2,5-7,8]

Box 154 gives guidelines for compiling a Cited References list.

BOX 154   SUMMARY

Guidelines for compiling a CSE-style Cited References list

■ **TITLE**

Cited References or References

■ **PLACEMENT OF LIST**

Begin the list on a separate page at the end of the research paper. Number the page sequentially with the rest of the paper.

■ **CONTENT AND FORMAT OF CITED REFERENCES**

Include all sources that you QUOTE, PARAPHRASE, or SUMMARIZE in your paper. Centre the title about one inch (2.5 cm) from the top of the page. Start each entry on a new line. Put the number, followed by a period and a space, at the regular left margin. If an entry takes more than one line, use a "hanging indent" for the second and all other lines. Single-space each entry, and double-space between entries.

■ **SPACING AFTER PUNCTUATION**

CSE style specifies no space after the date, issue number, or volume number of a periodical, as shown in the models in section 36d.

■ **ARRANGEMENT OF ENTRIES**

Sequence and number the entries in the precise order you first use them in the body of your paper.

■ **AUTHORS' NAMES**

Reverse the order of each author's name, giving the last name first. For book citations, you can give first names or use only the initials of first and (when available) middle names; for journal citations, use only initials. Don't use a period or a space between first and middle initials. Use a comma to separate the names of multiple authors identified by initials; however, if you use full first names, use a semicolon. Don't use *and* or *&* with authors' names. Place a period after the last author's name.

→

Guidelines for compiling a CSE-style Cited References list
(*continued*)

■ **TREATMENT OF TITLES**

- Never underline or italicize titles or enclose them in quotation marks.
- Capitalize a title's first word and any proper nouns. Don't capitalize the first word of a subtitle unless it's a proper noun.
- Capitalize the titles of academic journals. If the title of a periodical is one word, give it in full; otherwise, abbreviate the title according to recommendations established by the *American National Standard for Abbreviations of Titles of Periodicals.*
- Capitalize a newspaper title's major words, giving the full title but omitting a beginning *A, An,* or *The.*

■ **PLACE OF PUBLICATION**

Use a colon after the city of publication. If the city name could be ambiguous, add in parentheses the provincial or state postal abbreviation (see Box 122 in section 30k): Springfield (VA). If the location of a city outside North America will be unfamiliar to readers, add in parentheses the country name, abbreviating it according to International Organization for Standarization (ISO) standards. For example, *Nijmegen (NLD)* refers to a city in the Netherlands. ISO abbreviations can be accessed at <http://www.iso.org/iso/en/ prods-services/iso3166ma/02iso-3166-code-lists/list-en1.htm>.

■ **PUBLISHER**

Give the name of the publisher, without periods after initials, and use a semicolon after the publisher's name. Omit any beginning *The* or ending term such as *Co., Inc., Ltd.,* or *Press.* However, for a university press, abbreviate *University* and *Press* as *Univ* and *Pr* without periods.

■ **PUBLICATION MONTH ABBREVIATIONS**

Abbreviate all month names to their first three letters, but do not add a period.

■ **INCLUSIVE PAGE NUMBERS**

Shorten the second number as much as possible, making sure that the number isn't ambiguous. For example, use *233–4* for *233 to 234,* and *233–44* for *233 to 244;* but use *233–304,* not *233–04.* Where *p* is used, do not follow it with a period unless it is the last item in the entry.

→

651

Guidelines for compiling a CSE-style Cited References list
(*continued*)

■ **DISCONTINUOUS PAGE NUMBERS**

List all discontinuous pages, shortening inclusive page numbers and separating successive numbers or ranges with a comma: *54–7, 60–6.*

■ **TOTAL PAGE NUMBERS**

When citing an entire book, for the last information unit give the total number of book pages, followed by the abbreviation *p* and a period.

■ **CITED REFERENCES ENTRIES: BOOKS**

Citations for books usually have four main parts: author(s), title, publication information, and pages (either total pages when citing an entire work or inclusive pages when citing part of a book). Each unit of information ends with a period.

1. Stacy RW, Williams DT, Worden RE, McMorris RO. Essentials of biological and medical sciences. New York: McGraw-Hill; 1955. 727 p.

■ **CITED REFERENCES ENTRIES: ARTICLES**

Citations for articles usually have three main parts: author(s), article title, and journal name and publication information, with each section followed by a period. Abbreviate a journal's name only if doing so is standard in your scientific discipline. For example, *Exp Neurol* is the abbreviated form of *Experimental Neurology.* In the example below, the volume number is 184, and the issue number, in parentheses, is 1. Notice the lack of space after the semicolon, before and after the parentheses, and after the colon.

1. Ginis I, Rao MS. Toward cell replacement therapy: promises and caveats. Exp Neurol 2003;184(1):61-77.

36d What are CSE guidelines for specific sources in a list of references?

The directory below corresponds to the sample references that follow it. If you need a model not included in this book, consult *Scientific Style and Format,* Sixth Edition (1994). If you're looking for examples for citing electronic and online sources, consult a recent issue of a journal in the discipline in which you are writing.

Directory—CSE Style

1. Book by One Author—CSE
2. Book by More Than One Author—CSE
3. Book by a Group or Corporate Author—CSE
4. Anthology or Edited Book—CSE
5. Selection from an Anthology or Edited Book—CSE
6. Translation—CSE
7. Reprint of an Older Book—CSE
8. All Volumes of a Multivolume Work—CSE
9. Unpublished Dissertation or Thesis—CSE
10. Selection from Published Conference Proceedings—CSE
11. Signed Newspaper Article—CSE
12. Unsigned Newspaper Article—CSE
13. Article from a Journal with Continuous Pagination—CSE
14. Article from a Journal That Pages Each Issue Separately—CSE
15. Journal Article on Discontinuous Pages—CSE
16. Article with Author Affiliation—CSE
17. Entire Issue of a Journal—CSE
18. Article with No Identifiable Author—CSE
19. Map—CSE
20. Unpublished Letter—CSE
21. Videorecording—CSE
22. Slide Set—CSE
23. Electronic Sources—CSE

1. Book by One Author—CSE

1. Hawking SW. Black holes and baby universes and other essays. New York: Bantam Books; 1993. 320 p.

Use one space but no punctuation between an author's last name and the initial of the first name. Do not put punctuation or a space between first and middle initials (*Hawking SW*). Do, however, use the hyphen in a hyphenated first and middle name (see model 2, where *Gille J-C* represents *Jean-Claude Gille*).

2. Book by More Than One Author—CSE

1. Wegzyn S, Gille J-C, Vidal P. Developmental systems: at the crossroads of system theory, computer science, and genetic engineering. New York: Springer; 1990. 595 p.

3. Book by a Group or Corporate Author—CSE

1. Canadian Institute of Child Health. Family-centred maternity and newborn care. Ottawa: CICH; 1980. 178 p.

4. Anthology or Edited Book—CSE

1. Heerman B, Hummel S, editors. Ancient DNA: recovery and analysis of genetic material from paleontological, archeological, museum, medical, and forensic specimens. New York: Springer; 1994. 1020 p.

5. Selection from an Anthology or Edited Book—CSE

1. Basov NG, Feoktistov LP, Senatsky YV. Laser driver for inertial confinement fusion. In: Bureckner KA, editor. Research trends in physics: inertial confinement fusion. New York: American Institute of Physics; 1992. p 24-37.

6. Translation—CSE

1. Magris C. A different sea. Spurr MS, translator. London: Harvill; 1993. 194 p. Translation of: Un altro mare.

7. Reprint of an Older Book—CSE

1. Carson R. The sea around us. New York: Oxford Univ Pr; 1951. New York: Limited Editions Club Reprint; 1980. 220 p.

8. All Volumes of a Multivolume Work—CSE

1. Crane FL, Moore DJ, Low HE, editors. Oxidoreduction at the plasma membrane: relation to growth and transport. Boca Raton (FL): Chemical Rubber Company; 1991. 2 vol.

9. Unpublished Dissertation or Thesis—CSE

1. Baykul MC. Using ballistic electron emission microscopy to investigate the metal-vacuum interface [dissertation]. Orem (UT): Polytechnic Univ; 1993. 111 p. Available from: UMI Dissertation Express, http://tls.il.proquest.com/hp/Products/DisExpress.html, Document 9332714.

10. Selection from Published Conference Proceedings—CSE

1. Tsang CP, Bellgard MI. Sequence generation using a network of Boltzmann machines. In: Tsang CP, editor. Proceedings of the 4th Australian Joint Conference on Artificial Intelligence; 1990 Nov 8-11; Perth, AUS. Singapore: World Scientific; 1990. p 224-33.

11. Signed Newspaper Article—CSE

1. Christie J. Award bittersweet for hockey women. Globe and Mail 2003 Mar 26:sect D:1.

Sect stands for *Section*. Note that there is no space between the date and the section or between the section and the page number(s).

12. Unsigned Newspaper Article—CSE

1. [Anonymous]. Arctic drilling study. Globe and Mail 1995 Sep 2;sect D:8.

13. Article from a Journal with Continuous Pagination—CSE

1. Lomas J, Woods J, Veenstra G. Devolving authority for health care in Canada's provinces: 1. an introduction to the issues. CMAJ 1997;156:371-7.

Give only the volume number (*156* here), not an issue number, before the page numbers. Note that there is no space between the year and the volume or the volume and the page number(s).

14. Article from a Journal That Pages Each Issue Separately—CSE

1. Driver D. Doctor turnout high in Saskatchewan health board vote. Med Post 1995 Nov 7;31(40):53.

Give both the volume number and the issue number (here, *31* is the volume number and *40* is the issue number). Also include the month and (where given) day of publication.

15. Journal Article on Discontinuous Pages—CSE

1. Richards FM. The protein folding problem. Sci Am 1991;246(1):54-7, 60-6.

16. Article with Author Affiliation—CSE

1. DeMoll E, Auffenberg T (Department of Microbiology, University of Kentucky). Purine metabolism in *Methanococcus vannielii*. J Bacteriol 1993;175:5754-61.

17. Entire Issue of a Journal—CSE

1. Whales in a modern world: a symposium held in London, November 1988. Mamm Rev 1990 Jan;20(9).

The date of the symposium, November 1988, is part of the title of this issue.

18. Article with No Identifiable Author—CSE

1. [Anonymous]. Cruelty to animals linked to murders of humans. AWI Q 1993 Aug;42(3):16.

19. Map—CSE

1. Russia and post-Soviet republics [political map]. Moscow: Mapping Production Association; 1992. Conical equidistant projection; 100×120 cm; colour, scale 1:8 000 000.

20. Unpublished Letter—CSE

1. Darwin C. [Letter to Mr. Clerke, 1861]. Located at: University of Iowa Library, Iowa City, IA.

21. Videorecording—CSE

1. The discovery of the pulsar: the ultimate ignorance [videocassette]. London: BBC; 1983. 1 cassette: 48 min, sound, colour.

22. Slide Set—CSE

1. Human parasitology [slides]. Chicago: American Society of Clinical Pathologists; 1990. Colour. Accompanied by: 1 guide.

23. Electronic Sources—CSE

Because the CSE style book was published in 1994, its instructions for citing electronic sources are minimal. In 2003, the CSE Web site noted that forthcoming revised guidelines would follow the U.S. *National Library of Medicine Recommended Formats for Bibliographic Citation* and referred users to this Web site: <www.nlm.nih.gov/pubs/formats/internet.pdf>.

In general, the CSE style book advises that you cite electronic sources by starting with a statement of the type of document, and then provide the information you would give for a print version. Next, supply specific information that can help a reader locate the electronic source. End with your access date for online sources or the date of the update that you used for a CD-ROM database.

COS DOCUMENTATION

The development of electronic and Internet sources in the 1990s created a gap in existing documentation systems. *The Columbia Guide to Online Style* (COS) by Janice R. Walker and Todd Taylor Taylor (1998) filled that gap, and some instructors continue to recommend COS. Since the late 1990s, however, MLA, APA, and other systems have incorporated considerably more detailed information about electronic documentation styles. Now that COS tends to be used less frequently, this chapter outlines only its basic elements. If your instructor requires you to use COS, consult Columbia University Press's Web site for more specific guidelines: <www.columbia.edu/cu/cup/cgos/idx_basic.html>

36e How do I cite sources in the body of a paper using COS?

COS uses many of the same citation elements that are present in predominantly print documentation styles such as MLA and APA. However, COS includes new format elements unique to electronic publications. COS for the humanities is similar to MLA style, while COS for the sciences shares elements of APA style. Be sure to find out from your instructor which documentation style to use.

For print publications, in-text or PARENTHETICAL REFERENCES include elements such as the author's last name and the page number of any directly quoted material. Many electronic sources lack such elements, and COS allows for these differences. If the author's name is unknown, refer to the source by its title. Since pages in most electronic sources are not numbered, page references may be irrelevant. Commonly, COS parenthetical citations use only the author's name for humanities style and the author's name and date of publication for scientific style.

👁 **ALERT:** If page numbers, sections, or other navigational aids are available, include them at the end of the parenthetical citation, preceded by a comma. 👁

Here are examples of in-text citations using COS guidelines for the humanities and for the sciences.

Humanities style

According to the survey, over 80% of the students waited until the night before an exam to begin studying (Jani).

When the author's name is included in the sentence, no parenthetical citation is necessary. If you cite more than one work by the same author, refer to each by its title.

Scientific style

The research proved conclusively that individuals deprived of sleep were as dangerous as those driving under the influence of drugs or alcohol (Rezik, 2000).

If the publication date is unavailable, use the date of access (in day-month-year format).

36f How do I create COS bibliographic citations?

Box 155 gives guidelines for a COS Works Cited list. The labelled screen on the next page identifies elements mentioned in Box 155. For more specific COS guidelines for sources in a Works Cited list, consult the Columbia University Press Web site, cited opposite.

URL   Source title   Publication date

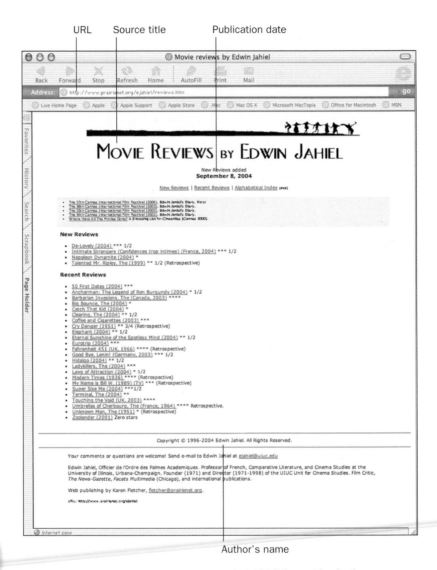

Author's name

Web page showing elements to be included in COS bibliographic citations

BOX 155   SUMMARY

Guidelines for a COS Works Cited list

■ **TITLE**

Works Cited

■ **PLACEMENT OF LIST**

- If you are producing a print document, begin the Works Cited list on a new page, numbered sequentially with the rest of the paper. *Works Cited* should be centred, one inch (about 2.5 cm) below the top of the page, in upper- and lowercase letters. The title should not be enclosed in quotation marks or be boldfaced, italicized, or underlined.

- If your document is a hypertext publication, you may use a separate file and a link to this page in the table of contents.

■ **CONTENT AND FORMAT**

See MLA guidelines in Box 151 in 34d.

■ **ARRANGEMENT OF ENTRIES**

See MLA guidelines in Box 151 in 34d.

■ **AUTHORS' NAMES**

Finding the author of a source may not be simple. Often, online writers use an alias. List your source by these alternative names when they are the only ones you find. If no author name or alias can be identified, cite the source by its title.

In the humanities style, give the author's full last name and first and middle names (if available). In the scientific style, give the author's full last name and first and middle initials (if applicable). List any additional authors by first name (humanities) or first initial (scientific), followed by the full last name.

■ **CAPITALIZATION AND SPECIAL TREATMENT OF TITLES**

Use italics rather than underlining for the titles of complete works. Since hypertext links are underlined online, an underlined title may confuse your readers.

In the humanities style, enclose titles of articles or excerpts from longer works in quotation marks, and capitalize all major words. In the scientific style, do not distinguish titles of articles or excerpts of longer works in any way, and capitalize only the first word of the title and proper nouns. (If a title is not available, use the file name.)

→

COS

Guidelines for a COS Works Cited list (*continued*)

■ **PLACE OF PUBLICATION, PUBLISHER, AND ELECTRONIC ADDRESS**

With electronic sources available in fixed formats, such as software and certain electronic publications, a publisher and city are usually listed and should be cited.

In online publishing, the city of publication and publisher are often not relevant to Web sites and other electronic sources that are not in fixed formats. In those cases, provide the URL (uniform resource locator), which is a source's entire electronic address. For URLs that exceed a line, follow MLA style: Break only after slashes, and do not insert your own hyphens.

■ **VERSION OR FILE NUMBER**

When applicable, provide the specific file number or version of a program in your reference.

■ **DOCUMENT PUBLICATION DATE OR LAST REVISION DATE**

Include a page's publication date or the date of its last revision, unless it is identical to the access date. For the humanities style, abbreviate all names of months longer than three letters to their first three letters, followed by a period. Give the date in a year-month-day format with a comma after the year. Enclose the date in parentheses, followed by a period. For the scientific style, do not abbreviate names of months. Give the date in a day-month-year format, and do not enclose it in parentheses.

■ **DATE OF ACCESS**

With the constant updates of online material, readers may have a difficult time finding the same content in a source you cite. Always provide the date of access for an online source, because it specifies the version of the page you have cited. For both the humanities and the scientific styles, abbreviate names of months to three letters, followed by a period. Give the date in a day-month-year format enclosed in parentheses, followed by a period.

■ **NAVIGATION POINTS**

On the World Wide Web, a single "page" may be quite long. When available, list any helpful navigational aids, such as paragraph numbers, sections, or parts, in your citation. Keep in mind that often these aids are not available.

→

Guidelines for a COS Works Cited list (*continued*)

- **BIBLIOGRAPHIC CITATION: HUMANITIES**

  Follow this form as closely as possible in your citations:

  Author's Last Name, First Name. "Title of Document." *Title of Complete Work* [if applicable]. Version or File Number [if applicable]. Document date or date of last revision [if known and if different from access date]. Protocol and address, access path or directories (date of access).

- **BIBLIOGRAPHIC CITATION: SCIENCES**

  Follow this form as closely as possible in your citations:

  Author's Last Name, Initial(s). (Date of document [if known and if different from date accessed]). Title of document. *Title of complete work* [if applicable]. Version or File number [if applicable]. (Edition or revision [if applicable]). Protocol and address, access path or directories (date of access or date of message).

Chapter 37

Effective Document Design

PRINT

37a | What is document design?

Document design refers to the visual appearance of a print document (how it looks), as opposed to the content of the document (what it says). Of course, design and content are closely related. The process of document design includes everything from setting margins and headings to choosing and placing graphics to determining the use of colour.

Document design is important for several reasons, not least because first impressions count. As soon as readers see your document, they form an opinion about you and your project. A well-designed document shows that you respect your readers and have spent time formatting your work so that it's attractive and readable. Making a good first impression influences readers to respond positively to your message.

Some document design is standardized and therefore gives you few options. As explained in Chapters 34, 35, and 36, the formatting of discipline-related styles such as those of the Modern Language Association (MLA), the American Psychological Association (APA), and *The Chicago Manual of Style* (CM) needs to conform to the guidelines that these professional organizations require, especially for formatting research papers. In addition, you need to format letters, memos, and e-mail messages according to customary patterns (41a–41e). Most word-processing programs have templates and "wizards" that provide many standard formats for such documents.

Other documents allow more leeway for your design creativity. Flyers, brochures, manuals, and certain kinds of reports give you considerable room for originality. You don't have to be a design expert to produce well-designed documents. With modest tools and knowledge, you can produce simple yet effective documents. Box 156 lists types of software that you can use for document design.

BOX 156   SUMMARY

Computer programs used in designing documents

Word-Processing Software

Most word-processing programs, such as Microsoft Word and Corel WordPerfect, have features that allow you to vary the format of your document and create charts, graphs, and tables. Word-processing programs are sufficient for formatting most basic documents in ACADEMIC WRITING, BUSINESS WRITING, and public writing. In fact, such programs can do things once possible only with more complicated page layout software.

Page Layout Software

Page layout software—for example, Adobe PageMaker and Microsoft Publisher—makes precise control of the elements of your document, such as text and graphic placement, possible. Though these programs take time to learn, they help you produce effective advanced documents such as newsletters, brochures, and other formats you might use in writing for the public (Chapter 41).

Graphic Design Software

Graphic design software—for example, Macromedia FreeHand and Adobe Photoshop—allows you to create and edit graphics, pictures, and other forms of art. You can then save these files in formats that are compatible with word-processing and page layout software to insert into your written document.

37b   What are basic principles of design?

The basic principles of design—whether for a chair, a car, a painting, or a written document—are *unity, variety, balance,* and *emphasis.* Box 157 describes these principles for effectively communicating your message in a document.

BOX 157   SUMMARY

Principles of document design

- **Unity** results from repetition and consistency. Ask: Do all elements in my document—such as fonts and colours—work together visually?
- **Variety** comes from a logical, appropriate break from unity that adds interest. Ask: Have I introduced design elements, where appropriate, that break up monotony—such as inserting headings in academic papers that add to clarity or on-the-topic illustrations that add to content?

→

> ### Principles of document design (*continued*)
>
> - **Balance** refers to a sense of harmony or equilibrium. Ask: Are the parts of my document in proportion to each other?
> - **Emphasis** directs the eye to what is most important. Ask: Does my document design draw attention to what is most important?

37c What is page layout?

Layout is the arrangement of text and visuals on a page, which makes the document a kind of spatial composition. You use layout to reinforce the organizational plan of your writing. For example, when you begin a new paragraph of an essay, you start a new line and indent from the left margin. When using block style for a business letter, you add a space between paragraphs. In each case, your layout decision indicates that you are moving to a new idea. The Web site available with this book <http://www.pearsoned.ca/troyka> contains links to Web sites that provide help with page layout.

37c.1 Positioning text and visuals

If you're using both text and visuals in a document, arrange them so that they balance and complement each other. Unless the style you're using dictates otherwise, don't put all text or all visuals on one page. Experiment with ideas for layout by creating mock-up pages on a computer or by sketching possibilities by hand. Group related items together. If you're writing a survey questionnaire, for example, you might number and name each category, and then use a lettered or bulleted list for the questions. You also may choose to indent the lettered lists. Such a visual grouping of like items makes the information more immediately understandable to your reader. Box 158 gives tips on page layout and positioning text and visuals.

BOX 158 SUMMARY

Page layout: Positioning text and visuals

- Consider the size of visuals in placing them so that they don't cluster at the top or the bottom of a page. That is, avoid creating a page that's top-heavy or bottom-heavy.
- Avoid splitting a chart or table between one page and the next. If possible, the entire chart or table should fit on a single page.

→

Page layout: Positioning text and visuals (*continued*)

- Try working with layout by dividing a sheet of paper into sections. Divide it in half (either horizontally or vertically), then divide it into fourths or eighths (depending on the amount of text and the size of your visuals).

- Use the "Table" feature of your word-processing program to position text and visuals exactly where you want them. Turn off the grid lines when you are done so that the printed copy shows only the text and visuals.

- Use the "Print Preview" feature to show you what the printed version will look like. This helps you revise before completing your final document.

- Print out hard copies of various layouts and look at them from different distances. Ask others to look at your layouts and tell you what they like best and least about them.

- Consider grouping all the visuals in an appendix if putting your graphics exactly where you want them is too difficult to work out. (Such a case is an exception to the rule that tells you to avoid placing either all visuals or all text on one page.)

37c.2 Using white space

White space, the part of your document that is blank, is as important as all other elements of design. White space allows readers to read your document more easily and to absorb information in chunks rather than in one big block. White space also indicates breaks between ideas and thereby focuses attention on the key features of your document.

Traditionally, ACADEMIC WRITING includes relatively little white space, except occasionally between sections of a document. (Double spacing in academic writing, however, gives instructors and peers space to write comments.) BUSINESS WRITING usually calls for single-spaced lines, with an added line of white space between paragraphs. Flyers, brochures, posters, reports, and other documents tend to make extensive and varied use of white space because they rely heavily on graphical elements such as illustrations, different fonts and colours, bulleted lists, and so on.

37c.3 Justifying and indenting

When you make your text lines even either in length or in relation to the left or right margin, you're **justifying** them. There are four kinds of justification, or ways to line up text lines on margins: left, right, centred, and full, as shown in the following examples.

> **Left justified** text (text aligns on the left)

> **Right justified** text (text aligns on the right)

> **Centre justified** text (text aligns in the centre)

> **Full justified** text (both left and right justified to full length, or measure, of the line of type)

Most documents are left justified, including those for ACADEMIC WRITING and BUSINESS WRITING. This means that the right ends of the lines are unjustified, or *ragged*. Such a setup helps avoid end-of-line hyphens for broken words (see 29g), which are correct but distracting to the reader. (Most lines in textbooks are full justified, so you'll see many hyphens.)

Use centre, right, and full justification in designing announcements, advertising, and similar public writing, as design elements that attract attention (see Chapter 41). Such documents also often include features such as wrapping text around boxes, pictures, or objects.

When you move text toward the right margin, you are *indenting*. Essays and research papers usually call for indenting the first line in paragraphs. The standard indent is one-half inch, or about 1.25 cm. (See the indenting formats of student research papers in MLA style in 34e and in APA style in 35h.) Business writing requires paragraphs in block style, which calls for no indent of first lines and single spacing within paragraphs, with double spacing between paragraphs. Never mix these two styles of indenting. Box 159 lists helpful tips on using justification and indentation.

BOX 159   SUMMARY

Tips on justifying and indenting

- Use the ruler line in your word-processing program to control the indentation of text instead of using the space bar or tab keys. The top arrow of the bar sets the paragraph indentation, while the bottom arrow sets the indentation for everything else in the paragraph.

  Alternatively, use the "Increase Indent" and "Decrease Indent" functions on your computer to control the indentation of text. This ensures that the indents stay constant in relation to the rest of the document, even if you change the type size or font (37d.2) of the text.

- Use indents to indicate subsections of a document—except in academic writing. For example, in a brochure, you might left justify headings and then indent the subsequent text.

- Indent bulleted and numbered lists (37d.3) to make them stand out.

37c.4 Setting margins and borders

Margins are the boundaries of a page, which means the white space or blank areas at the top, bottom, and sides of a paper or screen. Essays and research papers call for one inch, or about 2.5 cm, of space on all sides. BUSINESS WRITING also usually uses that size of margin.

Borders around text serve to set off information, as in a table or chart. A sales brochure, for example, might "box in"—enclose in four borders, or *rules*—testimonials from satisfied customers, or a newsletter might set off upcoming events in a special box. A single rule (a simple straight line, horizontal or vertical) can emphasize breaks between major sections of a long report. Box 160 contains a list of guidelines for how to use margins and borders effectively.

BOX 160   SUMMARY

Tips for using margins and borders

- **Narrow margins** allow you to fit more information on a page but also decrease the amount of white space available. This can make a page appear cluttered, dense, and difficult to read.
- **Wide margins** allow less information on a page. Avoid wide margins for ACADEMIC WRITING; they make your document look thin and lacking in content.
- **Borders** can be made of thin lines of repeated small graphic elements (such as asterisks). Simplicity is the key: Getting too fancy can be distracting.
- **Colour** should be used sparingly in borders. Stick to darker colours (blue, black, or red) and avoid heavy (thick) rules that distract from the content.

37d How do I format text?

To format text, you need to decide which typeface you'll use. A **typeface** is a particular style of type, such as Verdana or Century. A **font** is a specific kind of typeface, such as Verdana italics or Century bold. You also have to decide how you'll present headings and how you'll highlight important material.

37d.1 Writing headings

Think of headings as headlines in your document. Headings clarify the document's organization and tell your readers what to expect in each section. Longer documents, including this handbook, use headings to break content into chunks that are easier to digest and understand.

Keep your headings brief and informative so that your readers can use them as cues. Also, write in PARALLEL structure and use consistent capitalization. Box 161 presents common types of headings, with examples showing parallel structure. Box 162 offers additional help on writing and formatting headings.

BOX 161   SUMMARY

Common types of headings

- **NOUN PHRASES can cover a variety of topics.**
  Federal Government Responsibilities
  Provincial Government Responsibilities
  Municipal Government Finances
- **Questions can evoke reader interest.**
  Can the Federal Government Overrule Provincial Laws?
  Who Mediates Between Ottawa and the Provinces?
  What Is the "Notwithstanding Clause"?
- **GERUNDS and -*ing* phrases can explain instructions or solve problems.**
  Submitting the Federal Budget
  Debating the Federal Budget
  Approving the Federal Budget
- **Imperative sentences can give advice or directions.**
  Identify a Problem
  Consult Interest Groups
  Introduce a Bill in Parliament

BOX 162   SUMMARY

Guidelines for writing and formatting headings

- **Create headings in larger type than the type size in the body of your text.** You can use the same or a contrasting typeface, as long as it coordinates visually and is easy to read.
- **Use parallel structure in writing headings.** Always start your listed items with the same part of speech. For example, the items in this box all start with VERBS. In longer documents, you can vary the form of the heading at different levels. For example, you might make all first-level heads questions and all second-level heads noun phrases. Any combination is acceptable, as long as you are consistent throughout your document.

→

> ## Guidelines for writing and formatting headings (*continued*)
>
> ■ **Change the format for headings of different levels.** Changing the format for different levels of headings creates a clear outline for the reader. You can do this in various ways: You can centre heads or left justify them; you can vary the typeface by using boldface, italics, or underlining; or you can use various combinations of capitals and lowercase letters (37d.2 and 37d.3). Always be consistent in the style you use within each document.
>
> | | |
> |---|---|
> | Level one heading (most important) | **First-Level Head** |
> | Level two heading | Second-Level Head |
> | Level three heading | *Third-level head* |

37d.2 Choosing type fonts and sizes

Fonts are specific typefaces. Most computer programs come with a variety of fonts, and you can download more from the Internet. Be sure to consult your instructor or a style manual for your discipline before you format your paper. Fonts are divided into two major categories: *serif* and *sans serif*. Serif fonts have little extensions at the top and bottom of each letter, and sans serif fonts do not. Generally, serif fonts are easier to read for extended periods of time, while sans serif fonts are effective when reserved for shorter documents or for headings.

SERIF FONTS	**SANS SERIF FONTS**
Times New Roman 12 pt	Arial 12 pt
Garamond 12 pt	Helvetica Neue 12 pt
Palatino Linotype 12 pt	Optima 12 pt

Examples of serif and sans serif fonts

Display fonts are excellent for special effects, so use them sparingly and reserve them for appropriate occasions such as invitations, announcements, printed programs, and so on.

Old English Text MT	Braggadocio
Broadway	*Monotype Corsiva*

Examples of display fonts

Fonts come in different sizes (heights) that are measured in "points." Most word-processing programs have font sizes ranging from 6 points, which is tiny, to 72 points, which is about 1.5 cm.

For most ACADEMIC WRITING, select fonts that range from 10 to 12 points for body text and from 14 to 18 points for headings. Since different font faces and sizes take up different amounts of room on a line and on a page, some instructors specify a specific typeface and size to ensure that students produce a certain amount of text per page. See Box 163 for guidelines to follow in using fonts.

BOX 163 SUMMARY

Guidelines for using type fonts

- **Choose readable fonts.** Serif fonts are more comfortable to read for long periods of time. Therefore, body text is usually in a serif font. For body text in work you submit, a serif font such as Times New Roman is appropriate. Sans serif fonts are easier to read from a distance and are good choices for headings and posters.

- **Pick different font sizes for headings.** Varying sizes helps distinguish headings from body text. It also helps readers see different levels of headings; see Box 162.

- **Avoid fancy typefaces for essays and research papers.** Many instructors consider elaborate fonts too distracting.

- **Notice the difference between how a font appears on a screen and on a printed document.** If you're designing a document to appear on a computer screen, choose fonts that are screen-friendly. If you're making a print document, choose a print-friendly font.

37d.3 Highlighting

Highlighting draws attention to key words or elements of a document. You can highlight in various ways, but the one guideline that applies in all cases is this: *Use moderation.* For example, putting headings in bold is a good way to set them off, but emphasis is lost if too many words are in bold. Using different fonts and type sizes is one way of highlighting. This section looks at three other ways: (1) boldface, italics, and underlining; (2) bulleted and numbered lists; and (3) colour.

Boldface, italics, and underlining

Italics and underlining—they mean the same thing—have special functions in writing (for example, to indicate titles of certain works; see 30f), but they're also useful for emphasis and for headings. **Boldface** is reserved for heavy emphasis.

Bulleted and numbered lists

You can use bulleted and numbered lists when you discuss a series of items or steps in a complicated process or when you want to summarize key points or guidelines. A bulleted list identifies items with small dots or squares. Lists provide your reader with a way to think of the whole idea you are communicating. For this reason, they work particularly well as summaries. In ACADEMIC WRITING, use such lists sparingly, if at all. Complete sentences and explanations are better.

Colour

Adding colour to a document can change it dramatically. Take time, however, to think about your reasons for adding colour to a specific project. How does colour suit the genre of your document? How will it help you accomplish your purpose? What expectations does your audience have about the use of colour? Academic writing rarely calls for colour. On the other hand, brochures, advertising materials, posters, mass-mail sales letters, and letters soliciting donations all rely on colour and varying fonts to add appeal to their message. Use colour for variety and emphasis, but never overuse it.

37e How should I incorporate visuals?

Visuals, also called *graphics,* can enhance document design when used appropriately. A visual can condense, compare, and display information more effectively than words, but only if its content is suitable. A graph showing how sales increased over a period of time, for example, makes the point more quickly and clearly than an explanation. A photo or drawing can illustrate or reinforce a point you want to make.

Most word-processing programs offer help for formatting and placing visuals. When produced on a colour printer, charts, diagrams, and other graphics can look quite dramatic. However, resist any temptation to use visuals simply for the sake of using visuals. They should enhance your writing, not replace it. The Web site for this book, <http://www.pearsoned.ca/troyka>, contains links to Web sites on using visuals.

37e.1 Using charts and graphs

Business and scientific reports rely heavily on charts and graphs, and so do some research papers. They are compact ways to present large amounts of information.

Bar graphs compare values, such as the numbers of students following different programs at a college, as shown in the following graph.

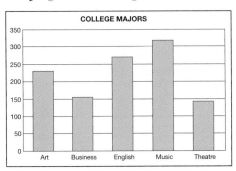

Line graphs indicate changes over time. For example, advertising revenue is shown over an eight-month period in the following graph.

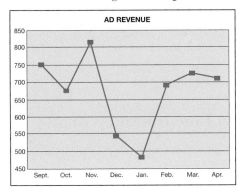

Pie charts show the relationship of each part to a whole, such as a typical budget for an undergraduate student, as shown in the following chart.

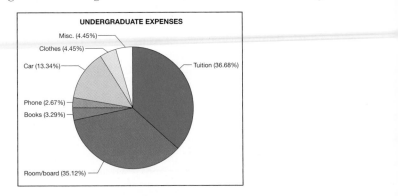

37e.2 Using other types of visuals

Time lines display events over time, such as the progress of historical events or a manufacturing process.

Diagrams show the parts of a whole, as in the following diagram of the human brain.

Tables present data in list form, as shown in the MLA-style research paper in 34e, the APA-style research paper in 35h, and below.

Table 1 Total Number of Computer Lab Users by Semester		
Semester	Number of Users	Percentage (%) of Student Population
Spring 2004	2321	25.8
Summer 2004	592	6.6
Fall 2004	3425	38.1

Clip art refers to pictures, sketches, and other graphics available on some word-processing programs. It can also be downloaded from the Internet. Though clip art is rarely, if ever, appropriate in ACADEMIC WRITING and BUSINESS WRITING, it can add interest to flyers, posters, newsletters, and brochures designed for certain audiences. The Web site for this book, <www.pearsoned.ca/troyka>, contains links to several clip art sources. Here are samples of clip art.

Photographs can be downloaded from a digital camera or scanned from printed photos, books, and articles into a computer. Web sites exist that contain thousands of photographs available free or for a minimal charge. (See the Web site for this book for examples.) Once a photograph is in your computer, you can place it in your document, usually with an "Insert" or "Import" command. A modest software program like Microsoft Photo Editor or a powerful program like Adobe Photoshop can help you adjust a photograph by cropping it (trimming the top, bottom, or sides), rotating it, or even modifying colours.

When you use a photograph, always be sure to give credit to the SOURCE so you don't PLAGIARIZE the material. You may even need to secure written permission from the source to use the photo, so check the copyright information that accompanies the picture. Copyright and perhaps other images may require permission to crop or modify in any other way.

Box 164 offers guidelines and additional help in using visuals in your documents.

BOX 164   SUMMARY

Guidelines for using visuals

- **Design all visuals to be simple and uncluttered.** They should be clearly labelled, as needed, and easy to read.

- **Never use unnecessary visuals.** Putting cute clip art on the pages of your writing won't make your reader think your work is well done. However, including a chart that summarizes your findings might.

- **Number figures and tables, if more than one, and number them sequentially.** If possible, choose only one term in a relatively short piece of writing: *Table 1, Table 2;* or *Figure 1, Figure 2,* and so forth).

- **Never overwhelm your text with visual elements.** If the visuals you want to use are much larger than the text, consider putting them on separate pages or in an appendix.

- **Credit your source if a visual isn't your own.** Always avoid plagiarism by crediting your source using DOCUMENTATION. If your source includes a statement or symbol that says it's copyrighted, you need written permission to use any part of it in your work. Check for this information in a print source by looking for a copyright notice (often at the beginning or end of the document) or a credits list. For a Web page, look at the top or bottom of the document.)

WEB

37f What should I know about writing for the Web?

The WORLD WIDE WEB, known popularly as *the Web,* consists of millions of locations on the Internet. These locations, called *Web sites,* are made up of one or a series of **Web pages.** Web pages can inform, entertain, and persuade through text, images, colour, and often sound and video. If you want to create your own Web page, or a class assignment or group project requires one, this chapter will help you get started. (If you are interested in creating a blog, or Web log, see 41h.)

Print documents communicate in a *linear* fashion: You begin at page one and proceed to the last page, moving in a straight line. A Web document, on the other hand, is *nonlinear:* Web pages are created in ways that allow readers to jump from page to page (or to other linked material, such as movies or sound) in whatever order they wish. Web documents, as a result, provide readers with exceptional flexibility. This affects how you design a Web page because you need to consider not only how each page looks but also how each page relates to the other pages you've created on your Web site.

Almost all Web sites have a *home page,* a page that introduces the site and provides links to the other pages that the site contains. The home page functions like a table of contents in print or, perhaps better, the entryway to a public building. You want the people who visit your home page to find it appealing, with clear directions for how they can navigate your site, or move from page to page. Most guidelines and principles that contribute to good design in printed documents apply equally to Web design. Basic design questions apply: Why create a Web page? Who will view your Web page? What features will you include on your Web page to appeal to those readers? As you make these decisions, you want to rely on the basic design principles of unity, variety, balance, and emphasis discussed in 37b. Early in your planning process, look at some Web sites that seem similar to what you have in mind.

37g How do I plan a Web site?

Planning a Web site involves two main decisions: (1) What will be the different pages within the site, and how will users navigate between them? (2) What will be the design of each page within the site? (See 37c.) Creating a Web site is a process very much like writing a paper. You generate ideas and plan; draft and revise; edit and proofread.

Begin by determining all the pages your site might contain and whether pages should be grouped into *categories:* groups of pages all on the same topic. For example, if you wanted to include a page for each event that a club has sponsored, you could use the category "Special Events." People using the club's home page might click on a "Special Events" link that then directs them to pages for individual events.

To generate a list of categories, you might use the planning techniques of BRAINSTORMING, FREEWRITING, and CLUSTERING discussed in Chapter 2. Once you have a complete list, decide whether you can group any of the pages together; too many links from your home page can be overwhelming, but too few can make for overly long or complicated pages in your Web site. Then draft a map of your Web site to show how all the pages fit together. Below is a possible map of a club's Web site.

Web site map

Web design is similar to print design, but users look at your document on a computer screen instead of on separate sheets of paper. This means that your Web site should load quickly on viewers' screens, be easy to read and navigate, and provide the right amount of information for your intended audience. Research shows that people viewing a Web page tend to expect a single screen full of information at a time and don't like to scroll down to read a lengthy document. One main exception is when they're reading a full-text article online that they've located through a database.

The distinction between a Web *site* and a Web *page* is important. The site is the larger category. A site may consist of a single page or of many connected pages. As a rule, if your site is to contain a good deal of information, you will need to create several different pages.

Once you've drafted a map of your Web site, you begin designing and creating your individual Web pages. Generally, all the pages within a site need to have the same basic design and similar navigation features. That way your Web site will look unified, and users will have an easier and more pleasant experience.

37h **How do I create a Web page?**

Create a Web page, first, by planning its general appearance. Make decisions about the placement of texts and graphics, the use of colour and white space, and what you want to emphasize. Here's some general advice about designing Web pages.

1. **Choose an appropriate title.** Make sure your page has a title that tells readers exactly what they'll find there.

2. **Keep backgrounds and texts simple.** Dark text on a plain light background is easiest to read, with white being the preferred background, even by expert Web designers. Sans serif fonts (37d.2) tend to be easier to read on computer screens than serif fonts, in contrast to print documents. Multiple typefaces, sizes, and colours, multiple images and graphics, and busy backgrounds are difficult to bring together effectively if you lack design training. Professional Web designers tend these days to strive for a clean, uncluttered look.

3. **Use images to attract attention to important elements of your page and to please the reader.** Readers will tend to look first at pictures and graphics on a page, so make sure to choose—and position—them to reinforce your page's content.

4. **Unify the pages in your site.** If your Web site has multiple pages, make each of them share some features, perhaps the same basic layout, font, colour scheme, and header or navigation bar. A navigation bar is a set of links that appears on every page within a site and that allows users to get back to the site's home page and to locate major parts of the site.

Generally, the bottom of the home page includes the date the page is updated, or added to, along with the name of the page's creator or a contact person who can answer questions, perhaps including an e-mail address for that person. See Box 165 for questions to ask yourself about the special aspects of planning Web site layout.

BOX 165   SUMMARY

 Questions for designing a Web page

Navigation

How do I want my readers to move through the content on the page? How do I arrange information so that it's clear and easy to read? How will my readers navigate between different pages on my site? Do I provide my readers with links back to my home page and to the other content?

→

Questions for designing a Web page (*continued*)

Grouping Content

How do I arrange content on my page? How will I group related elements? How can I use headings and subheadings to help group content? Are blocks of text short? Should I arrange some elements in lists?

Emphasizing Content

How can I make the title of my page stand out? How will I draw attention to the most important material? Can I use colour, sound, or animation to enhance, not detract from, the text?

Placement of Images

Where will I put images on my page? How will I arrange images so that they don't distract from the other content on the page?

Choosing Backgrounds

What background will support my content most effectively? Can my text be read easily against the background? Would a single colour or a pattern be better?

Establishing Links

Are my links obvious to a reader, or are they buried in text? Will my site provide links to the other pages in my site? What other reputable sites might interest my readers?

37h.1 Using HTML editors

Web sites are written in a computer program language. The original language format is called **HTML,** for **H**ypertext **M**arkup **L**anguage. Originally, people designing Web pages had to know HTML commands and type each of them into the Web page they were creating.

Producing Web pages became much easier with the development of programs called *HTML editors.* HTML editors generate "tags," or codes, for you much in the same way that word-processing programs generate boldface type or other formatting. The most common HTML editors are Netscape Composer, Microsoft FrontPage, and Macromedia Dreamweaver.

HTML editor programs employ *WYSIWYG* (what you see is what you get, pronounced "whizzy-wig") coding. The advantage of WYSIWYG programming is that as you work, you "see" the page you are creating rather than just the words and codes you type. You create your page by typing in text and inserting images and other content, and then the WYSIWYG editor generates the needed codes for you.

The most important codes are those for links. In most programs you create a link by first highlighting the words you want to serve as the link and then by providing the URL, or Web address, of the page you want users to see when they click on the link.

For links to tutorials and advice, connect to the Web site for this handbook, <http://www.pearsoned.ca/troyka>.

37h.2 Using images

Web pages that you create can include many different kinds of graphics. For example, small icons such as coloured balls can be used to mark off a list of items, the way bullets are used in print documents. You can also use photographs imported from a digital camera or inserted using a scanner. Graphic design programs allow you to create your own graphics. Some WYSIWYG editors come with clip art and images. You can also download photographic images and other graphics from the Internet. The Web site for this handbook, <http://www.pearsoned.ca/troyka>, contains links to several useful sites.

As in print documents, images on Web pages are effective only if they help communicate the message you want to deliver. Simply dropping in an image in a random spot is more distracting than helpful. Try to find graphics that provide a consistent look. Also, consider whether the images you're using are appropriate for your audience.

Keep in mind that graphics, especially photographs, require lots of digital storage space, which means they can take a long time to download. Therefore, use only the images that enhance your page. You also want to optimize images for the Web, which means using a feature in programs like Adobe Photoshop or Macromedia Fireworks to reduce the size of an image file to allow it to load faster. Images in a Web page exist as separate files, which means that even when you cut and paste an image into a Web page, the HTML editor is including a link to the separate file that contains the image.

37h.3 Using tables and frames

Tables and frames are devices that allow you to use HTML editors to place text and images accurately. A table divides the screen into a grid of spaces. You can then change the size of different rows, columns, or cells in the table in order to place blocks of text, images, links, and so on exactly where you want them. As with print documents, you can use the table feature to arrange text and images (see Box 158 on pages 664–665).

Optionally, you may choose to create frames on your Web site. A frame is a part of a Web page that functions independently of the other parts of the page. A common use of frames is for menus of links. When a user clicks on a link, its contents appear in a new frame or box on the page, while the original frame remains unchanged.

37i How do I display my Web page?

Having created a Web page, you're ready to display it on the World Wide Web. To do this, you need two things: First, you need space on a Web server, a centralized computer that is always online and that is primarily dedicated to storing and making available Web pages. Second, you need the ability to load all of your files to that server, including the page(s) you have made and any associated graphics that you have included.

Finding space on the Web

You can create HTML files (using a WYSIWYG or not) either online or offline, but you'll need to upload them to a Web server for the files to be visible on the Web. In other words, you need a host. If you have a commercial Internet service provider (ISP), such as AOL Canada, Telus, Sympatico, and others, you may be able to use it to post your Web page. Your college or university may offer Web space to its students, so check with your computing service office. Some services on the Internet offer free Web space as well as help in building Web pages. Try Yahoo! GeoCities at <http://ca.geocities.yahoo.com/home/>. Note that if you use "free" Web space, the provider may insert advertising on your page.

You will also need some kind of File Transfer Protocol (FTP) program to upload the HTML files to your Web server. The host of your space should be able to advise you on the best way to upload files and which FTP program to use.

Using nontext files

If you've used graphics, pictures, icons, or sound on your Web page, you'll also need to upload those files to the Web server where your page is now located. Otherwise, they can't be accessed by Web browsers, the programs viewers use to access your site.

Be careful to save the files with the correct extensions. Picture files normally have *.jpg* or *.gif* extensions, and sound files normally have *.wav*, *.mp3*, or *.mid* extensions. If your files don't have the correct extensions, the Web browser will not be able to process them.

Editing your page

Before you publish your Web page (that is, before you upload it to a server), edit and proofread it as carefully as you would a print document. Some WYSIWYG editors allow you to preview a Web page in a Web browser, but most likely you'll have to upload your site to the Web server where it will be hosted. The key difference between editing a Web page and editing a print document is that you also need to check that all the parts of your page are working properly. Use the checklist in Box 166.

BOX 166   SUMMARY

 Editing checklist for a Web site

- **Are any images broken?** Broken images show up as small grey icons instead of the pictures you want. The usual cause of broken images is mistyping the file name or failing to upload the image to the server along with the your Web page.

- **Do all the links work?** For each link to a page on your own site, be sure a file with that exact name exists on the server. For example, if you're linked to a page called *essay.html* from your home page, make sure there's a file called *essay.html* on the server. Mistyped or mislabelled files can cause broken links.

- **Does your site work on different browsers and computers?** Your site needs to look the same on different browsers and different computers. If it doesn't, you may want to revise your HTML. Using default settings for font, text size, and colour ensures that your page is compatible with most browsers.

- **Is the Web site highly readable?** As with print documents, the most important part of designing your Web page is making it easy to read. Ask friends and other students to give you feedback about your page before you publish it.

Publishing your page

Posting a Web page is a form of publishing. Like all original writings, your Web site is automatically copyrighted. If you want to make this clear to users (to discourage plagiarism, for example) include a copyright notice by typing the word *copyright,* the copyright symbol (©), the year of publication, and your name. If you want feedback, include your e-mail address. If you use material from SOURCES, credit them completely by using DOCUMENTATION. Always ask for permission to use someone else's work on your Web site. Plagiarism is plagiarism (Chapter 33), whether the medium is print or electronic.

37j   How do I maintain my Web site?

Be sure to maintain your Web site by checking and updating. The Internet is always changing, and if your page contains links to other sites, you need to make sure your links still work. You may also want to add new information, new links, or features. Always put a date at the bottom of your page to let visitors know when you last updated the site. Keep in mind that viewers tend to be wary of pages that haven't been updated recently. They perceive that the information may be old or unreliable or that the author doesn't care.

Part Six

Writing Across the Curriculum—and Beyond

Visit the Troyka Web site at
http://www.pearsoned.ca/troyka for

- an additional chapter on oral presentations
- more details on targeted résumés
- chapter exercises
- other resources, including an e-book version of this text

Chapter 38

Comparing the Disciplines

38a How do the disciplines compare?

The humanities, the social sciences, and the natural sciences all have their own perspectives on the world. Each of the disciplines also has its own customary primary sources, analytic strategies, and writing styles. To understand some of the differences among the disciplines, consider these three quite different paragraphs about a mountain.

HUMANITIES

The mountain stands above all that surrounds it. Giant timbers—part of a collage of evergreen and deciduous trees—conceal the expansive mountain's slope, where cattle once grazed. At the base of the mountain, a cool stream flows over rocks of all sizes, colours, and shapes. Next to the outer bank of the stream stands a shingled farmhouse, desolate, yet suggesting its active past. Unfortunately, the peaceful scene is interrupted by billboards and chairlifts, landmarks of a modern, fast-paced life.

SOCIAL SCIENCES

Among the favourite pastimes of Canadian city dwellers is the "return to nature." Many outdoor enthusiasts hope to enjoy a scenic trip to the mountains, only to be disappointed. They know they have arrived at the mountain that they have travelled hundreds of kilometres to see because huge billboards are directing them to its base. As they look up the mountain, dozens of people are riding over the treetops in a chairlift, littering the slope with paper cups and food wrappers. At the base of the mountain stands the inevitable refreshment stand, found at virtually all Canadian tourist attractions. Land developers consider such commercialization a way to preserve and utilize natural resources, but environmentalists are appalled.

NATURAL SCIENCES

The mountain rises approximately 2100 metres above sea level. The underlying rock is igneous, of volcanic origin, composed primarily of granites and feldspars. Three distinct biological communities are present on the mountain. The community at the top of the mountain is alpine, dominated by very short grasses and forbs. At middle altitudes, the community is a typical northern boreal coniferous forest community, and at the base and lower altitudes, deciduous forest is the dominant community. This community has, however, been highly affected by agricultural development along the river at its base and by recreational development.

These examples illustrate that each discipline has its own perspective and emphasis. The paragraph written for the humanities describes the mountain from the individual perspective of the writer—a perspective both personal and yet representative of a general human response. The paragraph written for the social sciences focuses on the behaviour of people as a group. The paragraph written for the natural sciences reports observations of natural phenomena.

As you study and write in each of the academic disciplines, you experience alternative ways of thinking. As you come to know the habits of mind that characterize each discipline, you develop specialized vocabularies to participate in its conversations. As the range of your perspectives grows, you gain lifelong access to the major benefits of a postsecondary education: the abilities to think through alternative points of view, to make connections among different sources and types of knowledge, and to make fully informed decisions. Indeed, you discover that no matter what differences exist among the academic disciplines, all subject areas interconnect and overlap. Box 167 describes the similarities and differences among the academic disciplines. Box 168 summarizes the strategies that are important in all academic writing situations, regardless of the discipline.

BOX 167   SUMMARY

Comparing the disciplines

Humanities (history, languages, literature, philosophy, art, music, theatre, and so on)

Types of assignments: reviews, essays, response statements, analyses; original works such as stories, poems, autobiographies, creative nonfiction

Primary sources: literary works, manuscripts, paintings and sculptures, historical documents, films, plays

Secondary sources: reviews, journal articles, research papers, books

Usual documentation styles: MLA, CM

→

Comparing the disciplines (*continued*)

Social sciences (psychology, sociology, anthropology, education, and so on)

> *Types of assignments:* research reports, case studies, reviews of the literature, analyses
>
> *Primary sources:* surveys, interviews, direct observations, tests and measures
>
> *Secondary sources:* journal articles, scholarly books, literature reviews
>
> *Usual documentation style:* APA

Natural sciences (biology, chemistry, physics, mathematics, and so on)

> *Types of assignments:* lab reports, research proposals and reports, science reviews
>
> *Primary sources:* experiments, field notes and direct observations, measurements
>
> *Secondary sources:* journal articles, research papers, books
>
> *Usual documentation styles:* Vary by discipline, but often CSE

BOX 168   SUMMARY

Strategies important in all academic writing situations

1. Consider your PURPOSE,* AUDIENCE, and TONE (Chapter 1).
2. Use the WRITING PROCESS to PLAN, SHAPE, DRAFT, REVISE, EDIT, and PROOFREAD (Chapters 2–3).
3. Develop a thesis (Chapters 2–3).
4. Arrange and organize your ideas (Chapter 2).
5. Use supporting EVIDENCE (Chapters 2–4).
6. Develop paragraphs thoroughly (Chapter 4).
7. Critically read, think, synthesize, and write (Chapter 5).
8. Avoid confusing SUMMARY with SYNTHESIS (Chapter 5).
9. Reason well; use good logic (Chapter 5).
10. Write effective sentences (Chapters 16–19).

* Find the definition of all words in small capital letters (such as PURPOSE) in the Terms Glossary at the back of this book directly before the Index.

→

> ## Strategies important in all academic writing situations
> (*continued*)
>
> 11. Argue well (Chapter 6).
> 12. Choose words well (Chapters 19–21).
> 13. Use correct grammar (Chapters 7–15).
> 14. Spell correctly (Chapter 22).
> 15. Use correct punctuation and mechanics (Chapters 23–30).

Consider the following examples of how various different disciplines can interconnect.

- In a humanities class, you might read *Lives of a Cell,* a collection of essays about science and nature written by the noted physician and author Lewis Thomas. As you consider the literary style of the writer, you also think deeply about biology and other sciences.

- In a philosophy class exploring the concept of infinity, you might read selections from *A Brief History of Time* by the astronomer Stephen Hawking.

- In an art history class discussing the Italian Renaissance, you might read social and political histories to understand how artists at the time earned a living and how that influenced their choice of subject matter.

- In an education course, you might read court decisions and laws to understand how and why schools must meet the needs of people with disabilities.

38b What are primary research and secondary research in the disciplines?

PRIMARY SOURCES offer you firsthand exposure to information, providing the exciting experience of discovering material on your own. But research methods differ among the disciplines when primary sources are used.

In the humanities, existing documents are primary sources; the task of the researcher is to analyze and interpret these primary sources. Typical primary source material for humanities research could be a poem by Dylan Thomas, the floor plans of Egyptian pyramids, or the early drafts of musical scores. A humanities class assignment might invite you to create primary sources yourself. For example, in a studio art class, you paint, draw, or sculpt. In a music composition class, you create pieces of music.

In the social and natural sciences, primary research entails either designing and undertaking experiments that measure the effect of some specific action or making careful direct observations of natural or social phenomena. The task of the researcher in the social and natural sciences is to conduct experiments or observations or to read the firsthand reports of experiments and studies by the people who conducted them. The researcher then has to analyze and explain what those reports and studies mean or why they're significant.

SECONDARY SOURCES—articles and books that draw on primary sources—are important but are not firsthand reports. In the humanities, secondary sources offer analysis and interpretation in that the author of a secondary source steps between you and the primary source. In the social and natural sciences, secondary sources SUMMARIZE, then SYNTHE-SIZE findings, and draw parallels that offer new insights.

38c How do I use documentation in the disciplines?

Writers use DOCUMENTATION to give credit to the sources they have used. A writer who neglects to credit a source is guilty of PLAGIARISM, a serious offence that can lead to negative academic consequences (33b). DOCUMENTATION STYLES differ among the disciplines.

In the humanities, most fields use the documentation style of the Modern Language Association (MLA), as explained and illustrated in Chapter 34. The student research paper in Chapter 34 and the student literary analysis in Chapter 39 use MLA documentation style. CM (*Chicago Manual*) style is sometimes used in the humanities, as explained and illustrated in Chapter 36. In the social sciences, most fields use the documentation style of the American Psychological Association (APA), as explained and illustrated in Chapter 35. The student research paper in Chapter 35 uses APA documentation style. (Research writing in the social sciences is also discussed in the first half of Chapter 40.) In the natural sciences, documentation styles vary widely, although the Council of Science Editors (CSE) style is frequently used (see Chapter 36). Ask each of your science and technology instructors about the particular documentation style required for his or her assignments.

Chapter 39

Writing About Literature and the Humanities

39a What are the humanities?

The humanities consist of a set of disciplines that seek to represent and understand human experience, art, thought, and values. These disciplines include literature, languages, philosophy, and sometimes history, which is often grouped with the social sciences, however. The fine arts (music, art, dance, theatre, and creative writing) may either be grouped with the humanities or given their own independent classification.

39b What forms of inquiry do I use to write about the humanities?

Inquiry calls for thinking beyond the obvious by intelligently questioning, investigating, and examining a subject. Because the humanities cover an impressively broad range of knowledge, writing in the various disciplines involves several forms of intellectual inquiry. These include responses, narratives, interpretations, critiques, and analysis of works or objects or ideas. In practice, many writing assignments in the humanities require you to combine these activities, but I present each of them individually here for ease of reference.

SYNTHESIS plays a major role in the habits of mind involved in inquiry. Synthesis relates several texts, ideas, or pieces of information to one another. For example, you might read several accounts of the origins of the Quebec independence movement and then write a synthesis that explains what caused the movement's rise. Or you might read several philosophers' definitions of morality and then write a synthesis of the components of a moral life. Unsynthesized ideas and information are like separate spools of thread, neatly lined up, possibly coordinated but not integrated. Synthesized ideas and information are threads woven into a tapestry—a new whole that shows relationships.

Responses in the humanities

In a response, you give your personal reaction to a work, supported by explanations of your reasoning. For example, what do you think of

689

Hamlet? Do you agree with Peter Singer's philosophical arguments against using animals in scientific experiments? Some instructors want you to justify your response with references to a text, while other instructors do not. Clarify what your instructor wants before you begin.

Narrative in the humanities

When you write a NARRATIVE, you construct a coherent story out of separate facts or events. Historians, for example, assemble public records, diaries and journals, news events, laws, incidents, and related materials to create a chronological version of what happened. Similarly, biographers take isolated events in people's pasts, interviews with the people themselves if possible, interviews of those who know or knew the people, letters written to or from the people, and related SOURCES to form a coherent story of their subjects' lives.

Interpretation in the humanities

An interpretation explains the meaning or significance of a particular text, event, or work of art. For example, what does Plato's *Republic* suggest about the nature of a good society? What message does Picasso's painting *Guernica* convey about the nature of war? What does it suggest when authorities in some countries try to censor the Internet? Your reply isn't right or wrong; rather, you present your point of view and explain your reasoning.

Critique in the humanities

In a critique (also called a CRITICAL RESPONSE or a review), you present judgments about a particular work, supported by your underlying reasoning. For example, movie, book, music, and art reviews present a writer's carefully reasoned, well-supported opinion of a work. Critical responses and reviews may focus on the literary form, or genre, of a work (for example, "How does this poem work within the conventions of a sonnet?" or "How genuine is the emotion portrayed in Expressionist painting?"). Responses or reviews may focus on a work's accuracy, logic, or conclusions ("Does this history of the development of rap music contain a local bias?"). Finally, responses or reviews may analyze a work's relations to other works ("How does the Broadway version of *The Producers* compare to the earlier film version?") or a work's similarities to and differences from the "real" world ("To what extent does *Everybody Loves Raymond* accurately portray middle-class family life?").

Analysis in the humanities

When you engage in analysis, you examine material by breaking it into its component parts and discovering how the parts interrelate. You examine and explain texts, events, objects, or documents by identifying and discussing important elements in them. These elements can include formal matters (how the work is put together) or the ideas, assumptions, and evidence they include. The humanities use a number of *analytic frame-*

works, or systematic ways of investigating a work. Box 169 summarizes some common analytic frameworks used most notably in literary analysis. Nearly all writing in the humanities depends on analysis to some extent.

BOX 169   SUMMARY

Selected analytic frameworks used in the humanities

Cultural/New Historical

Explores how social, economic, and other cultural forces influence the development of ideas, texts, art, laws, customs, and so on. Also explores how individual texts or events provide broader understanding of the times in which they were written or occurred or of today's world.

Deconstructionist

Assumes that the meaning of any given text is not stable or "in" the work. Rather, meaning always depends on contexts and the interests of those in power. The goal of deconstruction is to produce multiple possible meanings of a work, usually in order to undermine traditional interpretations.

Feminist

Focuses on how women are presented and treated, concentrating especially on power relations between men and women.

Formalist

Centres on matters of structure, form, and traditional literary devices (plot, rhythm, images, symbolism, DICTION; see Box 171 in 39e).

Marxist

Proceeds from the assumption that the most important forces in human experience are economic and material ones. Focuses on power differences between economic classes and the effects of those differences.

Reader-Response

Emphasizes how the individual reader determines meaning. The reader's personal history, values, experiences, relationships, and prior reading life all contribute to how he or she interprets a particular work or event.

39c   What is literature?

Literature includes fiction (novels and short stories); drama (plays, scripts, and some films); poetry (poems and lyrics); as well as nonfiction with artistic qualities (memoirs, personal essays, and the like). Since ancient times, literature has represented human experiences, entertained, and enlarged readers' perspectives on themselves, others, diverse cultures, and different ways of living.

By writing about literature, you shape and refine the insights that result from your reading. Writing about reading helps you move to a deeper understanding of other people and of ideas, times, and places. Writing about literature facilitates your investigations of how authors use language to stir the imaginations, emotions, and intellects of their readers. And, of course, writing allows you to share your own reading experiences and insights with other readers.

39d What reading skills help me interpret literature?

In academic work, although you may initially read a work for sheer enjoyment, during further readings you need to attend more closely to various elements in the text. Many readers are surprised to discover that CRITICAL READING enhances their enjoyment of the text.

Critical reading means reading systematically, closely, and actively (5d). Above all, it means asking questions: What does the work mean? Why has the author made particular choices in plot, characterization, and word choice? What other works influenced the author? How do readers react to the work?

Sometimes instructors ask students to answer questions that deal with material on a literal level: that is, to tell exactly what is said on the page. If a question asks what happens in the plot or what a passage is saying, you need to answer with a SUMMARY or PARAPHRASE of the work. If a question asks about the historical context of a work, or asks for biographical or situational information about the author, you likely need to do some research and then report exactly what you find.

More often, assignments call for making INFERENCES, which I discuss in detail in section 5c. Making inferences means reading "between" the lines to figure out what is implied but not stated. This reading skill is especially crucial for reading literature because literature tends to "show" rather than to "tell." It depicts events, characters, conversations, and settings, but the author doesn't say precisely what the work means. For example, your instructor might ask you to discuss why a character does something for which the author provides no explicit reason; to explain the effect of images in a poem; to investigate how a work depicts the roles of women, men, and/or children; or to explore the author's stance on a social issue. In such papers you're not only analyzing the literary text but also examining your own experiences and beliefs.

To read a literary work closely, and then to write about it, you look for details or passages that relate to each other. In so doing, you can form a TOPIC or THESIS STATEMENT for writing about the text. As you read, mark up the text by selectively underlining or highlighting passages, by writing notes, comments, or questions in the margin, or by taking notes separately on paper or on a computer. If you use the third method, be sure to note exactly what part of the text you're referring to.

39e What forms of inquiry do I use to write about literature?

Several different types of inquiry are used for writing about literature. They include all types discussed in 39b, with the following adaptations.

Personal response to literature

In a personal response you explain your reaction to a work of literature or some aspect of it. As with all effective papers about literature, you explain your response through discussions of specific passages or elements from the text. You might write about whether you enjoyed reading the work—and why. You might discuss whether situations in the work are similar to your personal experience, and why such observations are worth the reader's consideration. You might explain whether you agree with the author's point of view (Box 171)—and why. You might answer a question or explore a problem that the work raised for you—for example, how you reacted when a likeable character broke the law.

Interpretation of literature

Most works of literature are open to more than one interpretation. Your task, then, is not to discover the single right answer. Instead, you determine a possible interpretation and provide an argument that supports it. The questions in Box 170 can help you write an effective interpretation paper.

BOX 170 SUMMARY

Questions for a literary interpretation paper

1. What is the central theme of the work?
2. How do particular parts of the work relate to the central theme of the work?
3. What do patterns, if they exist in various elements of the work, mean?
4. What meaning does the author create through the elements listed in Box 171?
5. Why does the work end as it does?

Formal analysis of literature

A formal analysis explains how elements of a literary work function to create meaning or effect. The term "formal analysis" refers to analysis of *formal elements* that make up a work of literature, such as the plot structure of a novel or the rhythm of a poem. Box 171 describes many of these formal elements. Your instructor may ask you to concentrate on just one formal element (for example, "How does the point of view in the story affect its meaning?") or to discuss how a writer develops a theme through several elements (for example, "How do setting, imagery, and symbolism reveal the author's viewpoint?").

BOX 171   SUMMARY

Major elements of formal analysis in literary works

PLOT	Events and their sequence
THEME	Central idea or message
STRUCTURE	Organization and relationship of parts to each other and to the whole
CHARACTERIZATION	Traits, thoughts, and actions of the characters
SETTING	Time and place of the action
POINT OF VIEW	Perspective or position from which the material is presented—by a narrator, a main character, another character, or an external observer
STYLE	Words and sentence structures chosen to present the material
IMAGERY	Pictures created by the words through similes, figurative language, and other devices
TONE	Author's attitude toward the subject of the work—and sometimes toward the reader—expressed through choice of words, imagery, and point of view
FIGURE OF SPEECH	Unusual use or combination of words, as in metaphor and simile, for enhanced vividness or effect
SYMBOLISM	Meaning beneath the surface of the words and images
RHYTHM	Beat, metre
RHYME	Repetition of similar sounds for their auditory effect

To prepare to write your formal analysis, read the work thoroughly, looking for patterns and repetitions. Write notes as you read to help you form insights about these patterns and repetitions. For example, if you need to analyze a character, pay attention to everything that character says or does, everything that other characters say about him or her, and any descriptions of the character.

Cultural analysis of literature

A cultural analysis relates the literary work to broader historical, social, cultural, and political situations. Instructors might ask you to explain how events or prevailing attitudes influence the writing of a work or the way readers understand it. For example, "How do personal identity and ethnic discrimination intersect in Joy Kogawa's novel *Obasan*?" or "How do differences between the institution of marriage in the early nineteenth century and today affect readers' interpretations of *Pride and Prejudice*?" Box 172 lists some common focuses for cultural analysis.

BOX 172   SUMMARY

Major topics for cultural analysis

GENDER	How does a work portray women or men and define—or challenge—their respective roles in society?
CLASS	How does a work portray relationships among the upper, middle, and lower economic classes? How do characters' actions or perspectives result from their wealth and power—or the lack thereof?
RACE AND ETHNICITY	How does a work portray the influences of race and ethnicity on the characters' actions, status, and values?
HISTORY	How does a work reflect—or challenge—past events and values in a society?
AUTOBIOGRAPHY	How might the writer's experiences have influenced this particular work? Similarly, how might the times in which the writer lives or lived have affected his or her work?
GENRE	How is the work similar to, or different from, other works of its type, often—but not always—those written at the same general time? Literature's genres include fiction and memoirs, plays, and poems, and their subclassifications.

39f What special rules apply to writing about literature?

When you write about literature, certain special elements come into play.

39f.1 Using first and third person appropriately

Many instructors require students to use the FIRST PERSON (*I, we, our*) only when writing about their personal point of view in evaluations; they want students to use the THIRD PERSON (*he, she, it, they*) and to comment impersonally, without referring to themselves, for all other content. These rules are becoming less rigid, but be sure to ask about your instructor's requirements.

39f.2 Using present and past tense correctly

Always use the PRESENT TENSE when you describe or discuss a literary work or any of its elements: *Constance's adventures in Cyprus and Verona—the settings of the Shakespearean tragedies—**are** framed by two brief scenes set in her campus office.* The present tense is also correct for discussing what the author has done in a specific work: *By transforming Desdemona into a warrior, MacDonald **is playing** upon an imaginary implication of Desdemona's taste for Othello's gory tales and of her wish to accompany Othello to the battlefield in Cyprus.*

If you are discussing events that take place before the action of a literary work has begun, a PAST-TENSE VERB is correct: *But her own career **has come*** [before the action starts] *to a dead end.* Also use past tenses, as appropriate, to discuss historical events or biographical information: *MacDonald's play opens with an epigraph taken from the psychologist Carl Gustav Jung, who **theorized** that our unconscious combines archetypal characters found in myth and literature: the Fool, the Hero, and so on.*

39f.3 Using primary and secondary sources

Some assignments call for only your own ideas about the literary work that is the subject of your essay. In such cases, you are dealing only with a PRIMARY SOURCE. In writing about literature, a primary source is the original creative work (a poem, play, story, novel, memoir, diary). Other assignments require you additionally to use SECONDARY SOURCES, which consist of interpretations of literary works. As with all source-based writing, you need to DOCUMENT primary sources and secondary sources so that readers never mistake someone else's ideas for yours. Otherwise, you're PLAGIARIZING, which is a serious academic offence (for a complete discussion, see Chapter 33).

Most literature instructors require students to use the DOCUMENTATION STYLE of the Modern Language Association (MLA), described in Chapter 34. However, some instructors prefer APA style (Chapter 35) or CM or CSE style (Chapter 36), so check with your instructor before you begin to conduct your research.

Secondary sources include books, articles, and Web sites in which experts discuss some aspect of the literary text or other material related to your topic. You might use secondary sources to support your own ideas, perhaps by drawing upon the ideas of a scholar who agrees with you or debating the ideas of a scholar who disagrees with you. Or, if you think that you have a new or different interpretation, you might summarize, analyze, or critique what others have written, in order to provide a framework for your own analysis. You can locate secondary sources by

Cuneo

Work Cited

Poe, Edgar Allan. "The Tell-Tale Heart." Anthology of American Literature. Vol. 1. Ed. George McMichael, Frederick Crewes, J. C. Levenson, Leo Marx, and David E. Smith. Upper Saddle River: Prentice, 1997. 767-70.

39g.2 Student essay analyzing character in a drama

The following essay examines *Goodnight Desdemona (Good Morning Juliet)* by Ann-Marie MacDonald, a playwright, novelist, and actor. MacDonald won the Governor General's Award for Drama for this comic play in 1990. Although the play's protagonist is apparently on a quest for the key to a strange manuscript that could unlock a literary mystery, her search takes her into the unexplored territory of her own personality. MacDonald shifts playfully among scenes, characters, and scripts, tantalizing us with clues to the play's deeper mystery. The student's paper examines how MacDonald uses the framework of the quest to "take apart" elements in two Shakespearean tragedies and in the process allow the main character to construct her own fully developed personality.

Brook 1

Simon Brook

Professor Boland

Drama 250

12 April 2004

The Construction of the Protagonist in

Goodnight Desdemona (Good Morning Juliet)

On the surface, Ann-Marie MacDonald's comedy Goodnight Desdemona (Good Morning Juliet) is the story of an imaginary literary puzzle. Constance, a talented but ineffectual academic, believes that the two Shakespearean tragedies Othello and Romeo and Juliet were

→

---

using the research process discussed in Chapters 31 and 32. A particularly important resource for research about literature is the *MLA International Bibliography*, which is the most comprehensive index to literary scholarship (Box 138 in section 32e).

39g Sample student essays

This section includes three student essays of literary analysis. Two do not use SECONDARY SOURCES (39g.1 and 39g.2) and one does use them (39g.3). All three essays use MLA STYLE DOCUMENTATION.

39g.1 Student essay interpreting a plot element in a short story

The student essay in this section interprets a plot element in Edgar Allan Poe's story "The Tell-Tale Heart."

Edgar Allan Poe was an important American journalist, poet, and fiction writer born in 1809. In his short, dramatic life, Poe gambled, drank, lived in terrible poverty, saw his young wife die of tuberculosis, and died himself under mysterious circumstances at age forty. He also created the detective story and wrote brilliant, often bizarre short stories that still stimulate readers' imaginations.

When the student Valerie Cuneo read Poe's "The Tell-Tale Heart," first published in 1843, she was fascinated by one of the plot elements: the sound of a beating heart that compels the narrator of the story to commit a murder and then to confess it to the police. In her paper shown below, Cuneo discusses her interpretation of the source of the heartbeat.

Cuneo 1

Valerie Cuneo

Professor Aaron

English 10B

2 February 2004

The Sound of a Murderous Heart

In Edgar Allan Poe's short story "The Tell-Tale Heart," several interpretations are possible concerning the source of the beating heart that causes the narrator-murderer to reveal himself to the police. The noise could simply be a product of the narrator's obviously deranged mind. Or perhaps the murder victim's spirit lingers, heart beating, to exact revenge upon the narrator. Although either of these interpretations is possible, most of the

→

evidence in the story suggests that the inescapable beating heart that haunts the narrator is his own.

The interpretation that the heartbeat stems from some kind of auditory hallucination is flawed. The narrator is clearly insane--his killing a kind old man because of an "Evil Eye" demonstrates this--and his psychotic behaviour is more than sufficient cause for readers to question his truthfulness. Even so, nowhere else in the story does the narrator imagine things that do not exist. Nor is it likely that he would intentionally attempt to mislead us since the narrative is a confessional monologue through which he tries to explain and justify his actions. He himself describes his "disease" as a heightening of his senses, not of his imagination. Moreover, his highly detailed account of the events surrounding the murder seems to support this claim. Near the end of the story, he refutes the notion that he is inventing the sound in his mind when he says, "I found that the noise was not within my ears" (792). Although the narrator's reliability is questionable, there seems to be no reason to doubt this particular observation.

Interpreting the heartbeat as the victim's ghostly retaliation against the narrator also presents difficulties. Perhaps most important, when the narrator first hears the heart, the old man is still alive. The structure of the story also argues against the retaliation interpretation. Poe uses the first-person point of view to give readers immediate access to the narrator's strange thought processes, a choice that suggests the story is a form of psychological study. If "The Tell-Tale Heart" were truly a ghost story, it would probably be told in the third person, and it would more fully develop the character of the old man and explore his relationship with the narrator. If the heartbeat that torments the narrator is his own, however, these inconsistencies are avoided.

The strongest evidence that the tell-tale heart is really the narrator's is the timing of the heartbeat. Although it is the driving force behind the entire story, the narrator hears the beating heart only twice. In both of these instances, he is under immense physical and psychological stress--times when his own heart would be

pounding. The narrator first hears the heartbeat with the shock of realizing that he has accidentally awakened his intended victim:

> Meantime the hellish tattoo of the heart increased. It grew quicker and quicker, and louder every instant. The old man's terror must have been extreme! It grew louder, I say, louder every moment!--do you mark me well? I have told you that I am nervous: so I am. And now at the dead hour of the night, amid the dreadful silence of that old house, so strange a noise as this excited me to uncontrollable terror. (791)

As the narrator's anxiety increases, so does the volume and frequency of the sound, an event easily explained if the heartbeat is his own. Also, the sound of the heart persists even after the old man is dead, fading slowly into the background, as the murderer's own heartbeat would after his short, violent struggle with the old man. This reasoning can also explain why the narrator did not hear the heart on any of the seven previous nights when he looked into the old man's bedchamber. Because the old man slept and the "Evil Eye" was closed, no action was necessary (according to the narrator-murderer's twisted logic), and, therefore, he did not experience the rush of adrenaline that set his heart pounding on the fatal eighth visit.

The heart also follows a predictable pattern at the end of the story when the police officers come to investigate a neighbour's report of the dying old man's scream. In this encounter, the narrator's initial calm slowly gives way to irritation and fear. As he becomes increasingly agitated, he begins to hear the heart again. The narrator clearly identifies it as the same sound he heard previously, as shown by the almost word-for-word repetition of the language he uses to describe it, calling it "a low, dull, quick sound--much such a sound as a watch makes when enveloped in cotton" [Poe's emphasis] (792). As the narrator-murderer focuses his attention on the sound, which ultimately overrides all else, his panic escalates until, ironically, he is betrayed by the very senses that he boasted about at the start of the story.

originally written as comedies by an unknown author. By deciphering a mysterious manuscript, Constance hopes to find the original texts of the two plays and the identity of their author. MacDonald does not show us Constance's literary labours, however. Instead, most of the play is a dream sequence in which Constance becomes a character in the two Shakespearean tragedies. Only at the play's end do we learn that Constance's true search is not a literary quest at all: The dream sequence is a descent into Constance's unconscious, and her literary puzzle is a metaphor for her quest for herself.

Constance's adventures in Cyprus and Verona--the settings of the Shakespearean tragedies--are framed by two brief scenes set in her campus office. There we see her as a comical figure, timid and socially awkward; her nickname, we discover later on, is "Mouse." Constance's talents are exploited by the suave Professor Claude Night, with whom she is hopelessly in love, and who has built a successful career by plagiarizing Constance's work. But her own career has come to a dead end.

Her colleagues ridicule her bizarre theory about the two Shakespearean tragedies. From her observation that the tragic outcomes of the two plays turn on "flimsy mistakes--a lost hanky, a delayed wedding announcement" (21), Constance reasons that Shakespeare (as plagiarist) eliminated the role of a fool from each play. This "Wise Fool" would have been the unknown author's agent in concocting and then correcting the "mistakes" in the original comic versions of Othello and Romeo and Juliet. By confronting the characters and situations in the plays, Constance believes, the Wise Fool would have engineered happy endings for them.

No sooner does Constance set this part of her thesis down on paper than Professor Night arrives to collect the latest scholarly pieces she has ghostwritten for him. He casually announces that he is eloping with one of his students and is taking the post at Oxford University that Constance has coveted. She takes it all quietly, as usual.

Betrayed in love and blocked in her career, Constance has reached the lowest point in her life. She imagines herself falling into a decline and dying pathetically. In her vision she is awarded a posthumous doctorate; a chastened Claude Night lays roses daily on her

→

grave. Rousing herself from this hallucination, Constance immediately begins to discard the paraphernalia of her trivial and unsatisfying identity, tossing keepsakes into the wastebasket. When a few pages of the mysterious manuscript fall into the trash as well, the inscription on its cover catches her eye:

> You who possess the eyes to see
> this strange and wondrous alchemy,
> where words transform to vision'ry,
> where one plus two makes one, not three;
> open this book if you agree
> to be illusion's refuge,
> and of return no guarantee--
> unless you find your true identity.
> And discover who the Author be. (28-29)

Sent on her search with these words, Constance falls into her own wastebasket and directly into the action of Othello.

Constance enters Shakespeare's plots at two crucial moments: just as the jealous Othello is about to murder his innocent wife, Desdemona, in Cyprus, and at the moment when family hatreds in Verona lead Romeo to fight Juliet's cousin in the duel that sets in motion the lovers' downfall. Constance struggles to set things right between the characters while she hunts unsuccessfully for the key to the original manuscript of the two plays. A comedy of errors and incongruities is the result.

As Constance stumbles through Othello and then Romeo and Juliet, we witness odds and ends of famous Shakespearean speeches and scenes. MacDonald's playing on stage reality and our reality is reminiscent of Tom Stoppard's absurdist version of Hamlet in Rosencrantz and Guildenstern Are Dead. When Constance hears gunfire at the siege of Cyprus, she wonders, "They can't use real blood, can they?" (37) She is an incongruous visitor, knowing more about the characters and their circumstances than they believe possible, intruding on their lives, demolishing Shakespeare's plots, answering Shakespearean speeches in colourless Canadian English. (At one point she remembers how she ought to be speaking as a character in an Elizabethan play and starts counting iambic pentameter on her fingers.)

By interfering in their plots, Constance inadvertently transforms the
two plays into the comedies she believes they were intended to be.
She saves Desdemona by revealing the trap that Iago had set to make
Othello murderously jealous.

> CONSTANCE   . . . I've preempted the Wise Fool!
>
>   He must be here somewhere--I'll track
>
>   him down and reinstate him in the
>
>   text . . . (38)

She cannot find her fool, however. Constance barely escapes
with her life from Othello, falling suddenly into Romeo and Juliet,
where she stops Romeo's fateful duel.

Revisiting these two plays with Constance forces us to reimagine
their two heroines. As Constance suspected, in the "pre-Shakespearean"
comic versions of their plays (that is, the plays as MacDonald shows
them), Desdemona and Juliet are not innocent, helpless, doomed victims. Rather, Constance finds Desdemona to be a warlike woman who
advises her:

> If thou wouldst know thyself an Amazon,
>
> acquire a taste for blood. (36-37)

In Shakespeare's Othello, the Venetian general has wooed
Desdemona with stories of military victories in exotic lands. By transforming Desdemona into a warrior, MacDonald is playing upon an
imaginary implication of Desdemona's taste for Othello's gory tales
and of her wish to accompany Othello to the battlefields in Cyprus.

The teenaged characters Constance meets in Verona really are
teenagers--randy, brawling, and rather shallow. In MacDonald's version of her story, Juliet is independent and sexually adventurous. A
piece of quasi-Shakespearean stage nonsense has Constance imper-
sonating a man, and Romeo a woman; both Romeo and Juliet become
infatuated with Constance/Constantine. A flustered Constance
exclaims at the insistent Juliet:

> Heavenly days, what's come over you?!
>
> You're supposed to be all innocence. (69)

Desdemona and Juliet, as transformed by MacDonald, represent
possible models for Constance as an autonomous twentieth-century
woman.

$\longrightarrow$

Brook 5

Meanwhile, MacDonald has been dropping hints at the progress of Constance's quest.

CONSTANCE	. . . I have to find the Author first; or else the Fool to lead me to the bard.
JULIET	Author? Fool?
CONSTANCE	And Self. It is my quest, and means more to me than love or death. (71)

These hints are for the audience, but not for Constance. Bound up in the pursuit of her thesis, she follows false trails and misconstrues the message contained in the introduction to the manuscript: "where one plus two makes one, not three. . . ." She does not yet recognize that these words bid her to reconstruct her one-dimensional personality by reassembling the neglected parts of her "self," and that this is her true quest.

Earlier on, in her office, Constance had tossed the signs of her mouse-like identity into her wastebasket. Now she is inspired by the two not-quite-Shakespearean heroines. Desdemona, who knows the scholarly Constance as "the pedant," adds another dimension to Constance's personality by dubbing her an Amazon and inciting her to admit her hatred for her betrayer, Professor Night. Thinking of her own betrayer, Constance nearly kills the traitorous Iago in a swordfight.

I saw a flash of red before my eyes.

I felt a rush of power through my veins.

I tasted iron blood inside my mouth.

I loved it! (50)

Then, in Verona, Constance begins to reclaim her sexual and passionate side. Constance had earlier admitted to only a delayed adolescent crush on Claude Night--now Juliet coaxes her to proclaim that she once truly loved him. Juliet and Romeo nearly succeeded in drawing Constance into their romantic escapades. Finally, Desdemona and Juliet confront each other and stage a tug-of-war over Constance, who refuses to surrender completely to the obsessions of either one. In an instant, Constance realizes who the Wise Fool is. She is the Fool. And the Author.

In following her supposed scholarly quest, Constance has deconstructed Shakespeare's two plays, helped us to reimagine Desdemona and Juliet, and constructed her own identity. The Amazon ➡

in Desdemona and the sexual being in Juliet combine, in proper measure, with the pedant. The end of Constance's search is the integration of her personality followed by a symbolic rebirth--all three women have their birthday on the day the play ends. MacDonald's play opens with an epigraph taken from the psychologist Carl Gustav Jung, who theorized that our unconscious combines archetypal characters found in myth and literature: the Fool, the Hero, and so on. Hints scattered throughout the play seem to point to this idea of the self and its construction. Other hints, as we have seen, lead to the interpretation of Constance's quest as a quest for herself. Her dreamed adventures in Cyprus and Verona, therefore, may be seen as a healing journey into her unconscious. As Constance learns to act as an autonomous and complete personality, it becomes clear that she is the Author of the tale by the same token that she has become the author of her own life.

Works Cited

MacDonald, Ann-Marie. Goodnight Desdemona (Good Morning Juliet). Toronto: Playwrights Canada, 1997.

Stoppard, Tom. Rosencrantz and Guildenstern Are Dead. New York: Grove, 1968.

39g.3 Student MLA-style research paper analyzing a poem

The following essay is a literary analysis of a poem. It uses SECONDARY SOURCES. E. J. Pratt, a major figure in Canadian poetry, was born in 1882 in Western Bay, Newfoundland. Pratt's narrative poetry attempts to mythologize Canadian history, a subject he takes up in *Towards the Last Spike*, for which he won his third Governor General's Award. In this paper, the student discusses Pratt's reconciliation of epic tradition and modern Canadian historical events. (Note that the title of a long poem is given in italics, not in quotation marks.)

David Gates
Professor Baum
English 304
14 March 2004

Towards the Last Spike: A Canadian Epic?

In a review of Towards the Last Spike that appeared in the University of Toronto Quarterly, Northrop Frye made this comment: "The poem is in the epic tradition, without any of the advantages of epic to sustain it" (270). Pratt took a subject that was "epic" in scope and size, and created instead the "verse panorama," as he called it in its lengthy subtitle. It can be argued that Canadian poets lack the poetic tradition that would turn their history into epic poetry. Pratt comes close to the epic in Towards the Last Spike, but through his choice of dramatic technique, he has, in effect, originated a style of narrative poetry that works against the ultimately unifying vision of the epic. The poem anthologizes the past in a series of vignettes linked by historical "progress reports." This structure enables Pratt to achieve variety and contrast without distorting the remainder of the poem; the work ultimately has the cumulative effect of richness and a textured quality. At the same time, the fragmentation of the narrative mirrors the political divisiveness and lack of national unity that the poem portrays, finally subverting Pratt's epic aim.

In keeping with his panoramic vision, Pratt sets up a complex web of themes through the course of the poem. The poem has two protagonists, mankind and nature. Not only do these two contend with each other, but man also quarrels with man, and natural elements are in conflict with each other as well. The two protagonists are equated as "two fortresses: the mind, the rock" (65). The conflicts take place in two different worlds, each carefully characterized by Pratt: the political realm of Macdonald and the natural one of the nameless Canadian workers and the landscape--the "Laurentian monster."

The poem is as much a reflection of how politicians operate as it is an account of the building of the railroad. In his political sections, Pratt illustrates

→

> . . . the battle of ideas and metaphors
> And kindred images called by the same name
> Like brothers who with temperamental blood
> Went to it with their fists. (51)

This political struggle is waged between the imaginative, emotional man represented by Macdonald and Van Horne, and the cerebral, practical man typified by Blake and Mackenzie. The characterization is not as simple as this opposition would imply, however, for Macdonald in his own way is as calculating as Blake. One of Pratt's major accomplishments in this poem is the credible portrait of the political consciousness in action. Pratt describes Macdonald's political awareness at length in the section entitled "The Gathering" and shows the politician at work concocting his platform:

> He could make use of that--just what he needed
> A Western version of the Arctic daring,
> Romance and realism, a double dose. (43)

Pratt continually emphasizes the power of metaphors and words in the political context. Macdonald recognizes the potency of Blake's phrase "To build a Road over that sea of mountains" (53), with its implication that the task is impossible. This idea frightens Macdonald more than the rest of Blake's massive rhetoric, for

> This carried more than argument. It was
> A flash of fire which might with proper kindling
> Consume its way into the public mind. (53)

The theme of control runs as a corollary to Pratt's concept of words and metaphors. Macdonald is able to gain control in the House of Commons through his vision and his use of words, while Blake, "the homicidal master of the opiates," loses his audience and therefore his support through boredom (53). Van Horne is shown to be a master of control to rival Macdonald, since he is able to manage both the resources of nature and the inventions of man:

> . . . Electricity
> And rock, one novel to the coiling hand,
> The other frozen in the lap of Age,
> Were playthings for the boy, work for the man. (57)

→

Macdonald and Van Horne also share the passion of the vision-ary man; symbolically, each spends a sleepless night gazing at the stars and at the landscape. Blake, in ironic comparison, needs help to see the country around him:

> Though with his natural eyes
> Up to this time he had not sighted mountains
> He was an expert with the telescope. (52)

At the same time Pratt undercuts the vision of Macdonald because it originates in liquor, "his medicine":

> A blessed sleep fell like a dew upon him,
> And soon, in trance, drenched in conciliation,
> He hiccupped gently--"Now let S-S-Stephen come!" (76)

Pratt's ability and craftsmanship as a poet are reflected clearly in the poem. He uses various patterns of images to draw the poem together: The metaphor of music is one example of this technique and further elaboration of the drive to control. The image is first applied to the vision of the railroad:

> The airs had long been mastered like old songs
> The feet could tap to in the galleries.
> But would they tap to a new rhapsody,
> Whose ear could be assured of absolute pitch
> To catch this kind of music in the West? (49)

Political language is equated with music as well, so that the battle between Blake and Macdonald is not just of rival visions, but also of rival musical expressions:

> Blake had returned to the attack and given
> Sir John the ague with another phrase
> As round and as melodious as the first:
> "The Country's wealth, its millions after millions
> Squandered--LOST IN THE GORGES OF THE FRASER":
> A beautiful but ruinous piece of music
> That could only be droned with drums and fifes. (65)

Pratt also uses the image of the orchestra as a description of the Conservatives in defeat, with Macdonald shown as the "old conduc-tor off the podium" (50). The metaphor returns to conclude the

→

poem effectively, as the completion of the railroad becomes the new
beginning for the young nation: "Merely the tuning-up!" (80). The
image is appropriate in this context, for it implies that the railroad
has finally organized Canada into a new harmony. The tone rises in
the last section to a pitch of excitement and optimism in its celebration of the achievement. Occasionally, like Macdonald, Pratt uses a
phrase that provides a striking visual image for the reader. An example of this occurs in his treatment of Blake, in the expression
"Rumours he heard had gangrened into facts" (46).

The elemental conflict between humans and the landscape is
contrasted with the sophisticated battle of political visions. The landscape is splendidly characterized by Pratt as a primeval reptile whose
primary weapon is its immense size:

> Whose tail had covered Labrador and swished
> Atlantic tides, whose body coiled itself
> Around the Hudson Bay, then curled up north
> Through Manitoba and Saskatchewan
> To Great Slave Lake. In continental reach
> The neck went past the Great Bear Lake until
> Its head was hidden in the Arctic Seas. (61)

Traditionally, the epic hero battles the monster to defend or reach his
home; here, however, the homeland is the monster. The characterization of home as alien or "other" makes identification with the land in
the interests of a national vision impossible and undercuts the poet's
epic ambition. In addition, Pratt points to the apparently indissoluble
link between terror and beauty in the Canadian scene:

> They needed miles to render up their beauty
> As if the gods in high aesthetic moments
> Resenting the profanity of touch
> Chiselled this sculpture for the eye alone. (64)

Here Pratt would seem to be anticipating the ambivalent relationship
to the natural world, at once home and enemy, illustrated in the work of
later writers like Margaret Atwood in The Journals of Susanna Moodie
or Charles Lillard and Barry McKinnon in their "Bushed" poems.

→

The landscape is a living thing that wrestles not only with man, but with itself as well. The conflict exists on many levels at one time:

> The men were fighting foes which had themselves
> Waged elemental civil wars and still
> Were hammering one another at this moment. (65)

Although the men are ultimately successful in the combat, and the poem is, in part, a celebration of the triumph of human will over nature, Pratt, in concluding his poem, chooses to focus on the landscape rather than on his "hero." The "Laurentian monster" endures and has the ability to adapt to the new conditions that humans have imposed on it:

> . . . To drown
> The traffic chorus, she must blend the sound
> With those inaugural, narcotic notes
> Of storm and thunder which would send her back
> Deeper than ever in Laurentian sleep. (80)

Pratt makes certain, though, that the reader is aware of the cost of the railroad in terms of human life and strength. His interlude "Ring, Ring the Bells" underlines this by illustrating the process of metamorphosis that changes men into landscape.

The title Towards the Last Spike emphasizes not the final event, but rather the movement toward the climax. This is reflected in the anticlimactic treatment of the driving of the last spike, which undercuts the epic and heroic quality of the previous events. Pratt creates a realistically human scene. Donald Smith does not drive the spike home with one superhuman or legendary blow: He fumbles it.

The poem is uneven in quality, and Pratt can be amazingly trite in some of his images. The following part of his description of Van Horne can be cited as an example of Pratt's verse at its most overworked:

> Here he could clap the future on the shoulder
> And order Fate about as his lieutenant
> For he would take no nonsense from a thing
> Called Destiny--the stars had to be with him. (57)

→

710

These are understandable flaws in a work of this range, and Pratt is for the most part successful in bringing his immense work and all its characters vividly to life. He can write convincingly as an observer of Canadian nature or as a political cartoonist in his depiction of British Columbia as "the Lady" wavering between the respective lures of Macdonald and the Americans. Pratt's modern awareness of discords and divisions admits irony into the poem and diminishes its epic world view. His diversity becomes in itself an impediment to the realization of epic coherence. The question that the poem, with its contradictory impulses, asks is whether epic form and feeling can be sustained in the twentieth century.

Towards the Last Spike is epic in proportions and in its universal theme, but it lacks the conventions and formulaic devices that characterize the earlier epic style. It moves toward the epic vision just as the country moves toward national unity with the creation of the railroad, but the conflicts that are still unresolved prohibit anything beyond a momentary glimpse of a binding national identity, one of the prerequisites of epic vision. Towards the Last Spike is unique in Canadian poetry, for it is a compendium of our historical experience, and as such, it becomes almost by default our Canadian "epic."

Works Cited

Frye, Northrop. "Poetry." University of Toronto Quarterly 22 (1953): 270-73.

Pratt, E. J. Towards the Last Spike. 1952. Poets Between the Wars. Ed. M. T. Wilson. Toronto: McClelland, 1967.

Chapter 40

Writing in the Social Sciences and Natural Sciences

SOCIAL SCIENCES

40a How do I gather information in the social sciences?

The social sciences focus on the behaviour of people as individuals and in groups. The social science field includes disciplines such as economics, education, geography, political science, psychology, and sociology. At some colleges and universities, history is included in the social sciences; at others, it's part of the humanities.

The social sciences use several methods of inquiry. These include observations, interviews, questionnaires, and experiments. Some of these methods lead to *quantitative research,* which analyzes statistics and other numerical data, and other methods lead to *qualitative research,* which relies on careful descriptions and interpretations.

Observation is a common method for inquiry in the social sciences. To make observations, use whatever tools or equipment you might need: a laptop or notebook, sketching materials, tape recorders, cameras. As you observe, take complete and accurate notes. In a report of your observations, tell what tools or equipment you used, because your method might have influenced what you saw (for example, your taking photographs may make people act differently than they would otherwise).

Interviews are useful for gathering people's opinions and impressions of events. If you interview, remember that interviews are not always a completely reliable way to gather factual information, because people's memories are not precise and people's first impulse is to present themselves in the best light. If your only source of facts is interviews, try to interview as many people as possible so that you can cross-check the information. See Box 139, in section 32i, on taking notes during interviews.

👁 **ALERTS:** (1) If you use abbreviations to speed your notetaking, be sure to write down what they stand for so that you'll be able to understand them later when you write up your observations. (2) Before you interview anyone, master any equipment you might need to use so that mechanical problems do not intrude on the interview process (32i).

Questionnaires systematically gather information from a number of individuals using a pen-and-paper or Internet-based survey. To write questions for a questionnaire, use the guidelines in Box 173. When you administer a questionnaire, be sure to survey enough people so that you do not reach conclusions based on too small a sample of responses.

BOX 173   SUMMARY

Guidelines for writing questions for a questionnaire

1. Define what you want to find out and then write questions that will elicit the information you seek.
2. Phrase questions so that they are easy to understand.
3. Use appropriate language (21b) and avoid artificial language (21h–21m).
4. Be aware that how you phrase your questions will determine whether the answers that you get truly reflect what people are thinking. Make sure that your choice of words does not imply what you want to hear.
5. Avoid questions that invite one-word answers about complex matters that call for a range of responses.
6. Test a draft of the questionnaire on a small group of people. If any question is misinterpreted or hard to understand, revise and retest it.

Experiments are also sometimes used in the social sciences. For example, if you want to learn how people react in a particular situation, you can set up that situation artificially and bring individuals into it to observe their behaviour. People who take part in such experiments are usually called "subjects."

With all methods of inquiry in the social sciences, you need to be *ethical.* This means that you're required to treat subjects fairly and honestly. In addition, you aren't allowed to treat them in ways that could cause them harm in body, mind, or reputation. In fact, it is standard now for professional social scientists to seek explicit written permission from their subjects, and panels of authority often review research proposals to make sure the studies are ethical.

40b How can I understand writing purposes and practices in the social sciences?

The purpose of much writing in the social sciences is explanatory. Writers try to explain both what a behaviour is and why it happens. SUMMARY and SYNTHESIS (5e) are important fundamental strategies for explanatory writing in the social sciences.

ANALYSIS (4i and 5b) helps social scientists write about problems and their solutions. For example, an economist writing about financial troubles in a major automobile company might start by breaking the situation into parts: analyzing the costs of production, the selling prices of cars, and the costs of doing business. Next, the economist might show how these parts relate to the financial health of the whole company. Finally, the economist might suggest how specific changes would help solve the company's financial problems.

Social scientists often also use ANALOGY (4i) to make unfamiliar ideas clear. For example, sociologists may talk of the "culture shock" that some people feel when they enter a new society. The sociologists might compare this shock to the reaction of someone suddenly being moved hundreds of years into the future or the past.

Social scientists are particularly careful to define their KEY TERMS when they write, especially when they discuss complex social issues. For example, if you are writing a paper on substance abuse in the medical profession, you must first define what you mean by the terms *substance abuse* and *medical profession.* Does *substance* mean alcohol and drugs or only drugs? What defines *abuse,* and how do you measure it? By *medical profession,* do you mean nurses and doctors or only doctors? Without defining such terms, you confuse readers or lead them to wrong conclusions.

In courses in the social sciences, your goal is usually to be a neutral observer, so most of the time you need to use the THIRD PERSON (*he, she, it, one, they*) and comment impersonally on the data. Using the FIRST PERSON (*I, we, our*) is acceptable only when you write about your own reactions and experiences. Some writing in the social sciences overuses the PASSIVE VOICE (8o and 8p); style manuals for the social sciences recommend using the ACTIVE VOICE whenever possible.

40c How can I use documentation style in the social sciences?

If you use SOURCES when writing about the social sciences, you must credit these sources by using DOCUMENTATION. The most commonly used DOCUMENTATION STYLE in the social sciences is that of the American Psychological Association (APA). APA documentation style uses PARENTHETICAL REFERENCES in the body of a paper and a REFERENCES list at the end of a paper. APA documentation style is described in detail in Chapter 35. You can also find a sample student research paper using APA documentation style in section 35h.

Chicago Manual (CM) documentation style is sometimes used in the social sciences. The CM BIBLIOGRAPHIC NOTE style is described in detail in Chapter 36.

40d How can I write different types of papers in the social sciences?

Case studies and research papers are the two major types of papers written in the social sciences.

40d.1 Writing case studies in the social sciences

A case study is an intensive study of one group or individual. If you write a case study, describe situations as a *neutral observer*. Refrain from interpreting them unless your assignment says that you can add your interpretation after your report. Also, always differentiate between fact and opinion (5c.2). For example, you may observe nursing home patients lying on their sides in bed, facing the door. Describe exactly what you see: If you interpret or read into this observation that patients are lonely and watching the door for visitors, you could be wrong. Perhaps because medicines are injected in the right hip, patients are more comfortable lying on their left side, which just happens to put them in a position facing the door. Such work requires FIELD RESEARCH (32i).

A case study is usually presented in a relatively fixed format, but the specific parts and their order vary. Most case studies contain the following components: (1) basic identifying information about the individual or group; (2) a history of the individual or group; (3) observations of the individual's or group's behaviour; and (4) conclusions and, perhaps, recommendations as a result of the observations.

40d.2 Writing research papers in the social sciences

RESEARCH WRITING in the social sciences can be based on your FIELD RESEARCH (40d.1 on case studies; 40a on interviews, questionnaires, or data analysis). Papers that primarily explain your own original research based on primary sources are sometimes called *research reports*. More often, social science research requires undergraduate students to consult SECONDARY SOURCES (see Chapters 31 and 32, especially 32e on using periodicals and 32f on using specialized reference works). These sources are usually articles and books that report, summarize, and otherwise discuss the findings of other people's research. You can find a sample of a student research paper using secondary sources, written for an introductory psychology course, in Chapter 35.

NATURAL SCIENCES

40e How do I gather information in the natural sciences?

The natural sciences include disciplines such as astronomy, biology, chemistry, geology, and physics. Scientists form and test hypotheses, which are assumptions made in order to prove their logical soundness and consequences in the real world. They do this to explain CAUSE AND EFFECT (5h) as systematically and objectively as possible.

The scientific method, commonly used in the sciences to make discoveries, is a procedure for gathering information related to a specific hypothesis. The scientific method is the cornerstone of all inquiry in the sciences. Box 174 gives guidelines for using the scientific method.

BOX 174   SUMMARY

Guidelines for using the scientific method

1. Formulate a tentative explanation—known as a *hypothesis*—for a scientific phenomenon. Be as specific as possible.
2. Read and summarize previously published information related to your hypothesis.
3. Plan and outline a method of investigation to uncover the information needed to test your hypothesis.
4. Experiment, following exactly the investigative procedures you have outlined.
5. Observe closely the results of the experiment, and write notes carefully.
6. Analyze the results. If they prove the hypothesis to be false, rework the investigation and begin again (to double-check your results). If the results confirm the hypothesis, say so.
7. Write a report of your research. At the end, you can suggest additional hypotheses that might be investigated.

40f What are writing purposes and practices in the natural sciences?

Because scientists usually write to inform their AUDIENCE about factual information, SUMMARY and SYNTHESIS are important fundamental writing techniques (5e).

Exactness is extremely important in scientific writing. Readers expect precise descriptions of procedures and findings, free of personal biases. Scientists expect to be able to *replicate*—repeat step by step—the experiment or process the researcher carried out and obtain the same outcome.

Completeness is as important as exactness in scientific writing. Without complete information, a reader may misunderstand the writer's message and reach a wrong conclusion. For example, a researcher investigating how plants grow in different types of soil needs to report these facts: an analysis of each soil type, the amount of daylight exposure for each plant, the soil's moisture content, the type and amount of fertilizer used, and all other related facts. By including all this information, the researcher tells the reader how the conclusion was founded in the experiment or analysis. Further, inclusion of this information allows a critical reader to determine which variables are significant and which do not affect the result.

Because science writing depends largely on objective observation rather than subjective comments, scientists generally avoid using the FIRST PERSON (*I, we, our*) in their writing. The sciences generally focus on the experiment rather than on the person doing the experimenting.

When writing for the sciences, you are often expected to follow fixed formats, which are designed to summarize a project and present its results efficiently. In your report, organize the information to achieve clarity and precision. Writers in the sciences sometimes use charts, graphs, tables, diagrams, and other illustrations to present material. Illustrations in many cases can explain complex material more clearly than words can.

40g How do I use documentation style in the natural sciences?

If you use SECONDARY SOURCES when you write about the sciences, you are required to credit your sources by using DOCUMENTATION. DOCUMENTATION STYLES in the various sciences differ somewhat. Ask your instructor which style to use.

The Council of Science Editors (CSE) has compiled style and documentation guidelines for the life sciences, the physical sciences, and mathematics. CSE documentation guidelines are described in sections 36c and 36d.

40h How do I write different types of papers in the natural sciences?

Two major types of papers in the sciences are *reports* and *reviews*.

40h.1 Writing science reports

Science reports tell about observations and experiments; such reports are sometimes called *laboratory reports* when they describe laboratory experiments. Formal reports feature the eight elements identified in

717

Box 175. Less formal reports, which are sometimes assigned in introductory courses, might not include an abstract or a review of the literature. Ask your instructor which sections to include in your report.

BOX 175   SUMMARY

Parts of a science report

1. **Title.** This is a precise description of what your report is about. Your instructor may require a *title page* that lists the title, your name, the course name and section, your instructor's name, and the date. If so, there is no recommended format in CSE style; generally, students use APA format (35g) or their instructor's.

2. **Abstract.** This is a short overview of the report. Readers may review this to decide whether or not your research is of interest to them.

3. **Introduction.** This section states the purpose behind your research and presents the hypothesis. Any needed background information and a review of the literature appear here.

4. **Methods and Materials.** This section describes the equipment, materials, and procedures used.

5. **Results.** This section provides the information obtained from your efforts. Charts, graphs, and photographs help present the data in a way that is easy for readers to grasp.

6. **Discussion.** This section presents your interpretation and evaluation of the results. Did your efforts support your hypothesis? If not, can you suggest why not? Use concrete evidence in discussing your results.

7. **Conclusion.** This section lists conclusions about the hypothesis and the outcomes of your efforts, with particular attention given to any theoretical implications that can be drawn from your work. Be specific in suggesting further research.

8. **Cited References.** This list presents references cited in the review of the literature, if any. Its format conforms to the requirements of the documentation style in the particular science that is your subject.

Sample student science report

The sample science report here is by a student in an intermediate course in biology. Like this sample, your typed report would be likely to follow APA format for margins, page numbering, and title page. The text and references would follow CSE-style recommendations.

Adam Furman

Biology 201, Lab

Professor Joshua Mann

November 13, 2003

Title of report ⟶ The Effectiveness of Common Antibiotics

Title of sub-section ⟶ Introduction

Abstract omitted in this sample

The purpose of this experiment was to test the effectiveness of antibiotics against two common bacteria.

Antibiotics are substances that inhibit life processes of bacteria. There are two types of antibiotics. One interferes with cell wall synthesis, causing death. The other disrupts protein synthesis, thus preventing replication.

Escherichia coli is a gram-negative bacterium. It is found in the colon of many mammals, including humans. Commonly, it contaminates beef and chicken products. Staphylococcus epidermidis is a gram-positive bacterium found naturally on the skin. This bacterium is often the cause of infected burns and cuts. Both bacteria were used in this experiment.

It is hypothesized that five chemical antibiotics will be effective against both bacteria. Also hypothesized is that two natural antimicrobials, echinacea and garlic, would not work very well.

Methods and Materials

Using aseptic techniques, two petri dishes were inoculated. Staphylococcus epidermidis was used on one dish and Escherichia coli on the second dish. A sterile paper disc was saturated with Streptomycin. The disc was placed on one of the dishes. The process was repeated for the other dish. Both dishes were marked with identification and location of the paper discs. Each of the following was also saturated on paper discs and placed into its own zone on both dishes: sterile water (control), Ampicillin, Erythromycin, Chloramphenicol, Tetracycline, Gentamycin, echinacea, and garlic.

The dishes were incubated overnight at room temperature. The zone of inhibition of growth in centimetres was measured and recorded.

➡

Effectiveness 2

Results

Streptomycin, a protein synthesis disrupter, worked effectively to prevent growth of the S. epidermidis and the E. coli. Tetracycline inhibited the reproduction of the S. epidermidis and the E. coli. Ampicillin, a common bactericide, worked better on the S. epidermidis than on the E. coli, because the S. epidermidis is gram positive and the E. coli is gram negative. Gentamycin effectively prevented the growth of E. coli. Erythromycin and Chloramphenicol behaved similarly to the Ampicillin.

The antibiotics behaved as expected in regard to effectiveness against gram-positive and gram-negative bacteria. As hypothesized, the echinacea inhibited growth only slightly, indicating that it probably would not function as an antibiotic. The garlic had a zone of inhibition greater than expected for a non-antibiotic. Zero centimetres of inhibition from the sterile water control demonstrates that there was no contamination of the experiment.

Discussion section omitted in this sample

Conclusion

The results imply that the Ampicillin would be an effective treatment against S. epidermidis infection and Gentamycin would prove effective in treating an infection of E. coli.

As with any experiment, it would be wise to repeat the tests again to check for accuracy. Other antibiotics could be tested against a larger range of bacteria for broader results.

No Cited References needed in this type of science report

40h.2 Writing science reviews

A science review is a paper discussing published information on a scientific topic or issue. The purpose of the review is SUMMARY: to assemble for readers all the current knowledge about the topic or issue. Sometimes, the purpose of a science review is SYNTHESIS: to suggest a new interpretation of the old material. Reinterpretation combines the older views with new and more complete or more compelling information. In such reviews, the writer must present evidence to persuade readers that the new interpretation is valid.

If you're required to write a science review, you want to (1) choose a very limited scientific issue currently being researched; (2) use information that is current—the more recently published the articles, books, and journals you consult, the better; (3) accurately PARAPHRASE (33i) and SUMMARIZE (33j) material; and (4) DOCUMENT your sources (Chapters 34–36). If your review runs longer than two or three pages, you might want to use headings to help your reader understand the organization and idea progression of your paper. See Chapters 32 and 33 for advice on finding and using sources.

Chapter 41

Business and Public Writing

Business and public writing start where writing in all other disciplines does, with thinking about your PURPOSE and your AUDIENCE. This chapter explains how to write typical business correspondence—letters, memos, résumés, job application letters, and e-mail messages. The second part of this chapter discusses types of public writing, writing intended for members of your community, for readers in general, or for public officials. Box 176 gives you general guidelines for business and public writing.

BOX 176   SUMMARY

Guidelines for business and public writing

- Consider your audience's needs and expectations.
- Have a clear purpose.
- Put essential information first.
- Make your points concisely, clearly, and directly.
- Use conventional business formats.

BUSINESS WRITING

41a How do I write and format a business letter?

Business letters give information, build goodwill, or establish a foundation for discussions or transactions. Experts in business and government agree that the letters likely to get results are short, simple, direct, and human. Following is the most useful advice for writing business letters:

- Address the person by name.
- Tell what your letter is about in the first paragraph.

- Be honest, clear, and specific.
- Use correct EDITED CANADIAN ENGLISH.
- Be positive and natural.
- Edit ruthlessly.

Keep the following points in mind when writing a business letter:

- **Format:** Select block style (in which all lines begin at the left margin) or modified block style (lines for inside address and body begin at left margin; heading, closing, and signature begin about halfway across the page).

- **Paper:** Use only $8^{1}/_{2}$-by-11-inch paper. The most acceptable colours are white or very light beige. (Business letters from other countries are often on other sizes of paper. Still, write back on North American standard-size paper.)

- **Letterhead:** When writing from a company, use its official letterhead. If you're writing on your own behalf, use or create your own letterhead on your computer. Centre your full name, address, and phone number (and any e-mail address you use for business) at the top of the page. Use a larger size font than for the content of the letter. Avoid any font that's fancy or loud.

- **Name of recipient:** Be as specific as possible. An exact name (or at least a specific category of people) tells readers you have taken the time to do some research. If you use a category, place the key word first: For example, use "Billing Department," not "Department of Billing." Avoid using "To Whom It May Concern," which implies you didn't do the necessary research and expect the person who receives the letter to do the work of figuring out the specific recipient. Such letters are often ignored.

- **Spacing:** Use single spacing within paragraphs and double spacing between paragraphs.

- **Content:** Write using CONCISE and clear language. Open by explaining immediately your purpose for writing. Check that your information is accurate and includes all relevant facts. Never repeat yourself. Use as evenhanded a TONE as possible; you can express disappointment or make a complaint without resorting to inflammatory language. A reasonable approach always gets the best results.

- **Tone:** Use a medium LEVEL OF FORMALITY in word choice and style.

- **Final copy:** Proofread carefully. Your neat, error-free letter reflects well on you and your company or organization. Also, your reader is more likely to read it because you took the time to show the importance of your message and your respect for your reader.

In a business letter, always use GENDER-NEUTRAL LANGUAGE in the salutation (the opening "To" or "Dear"). If you don't know the specific person to whom you need to address your letter, take the steps listed in Box 177; see also 21g.

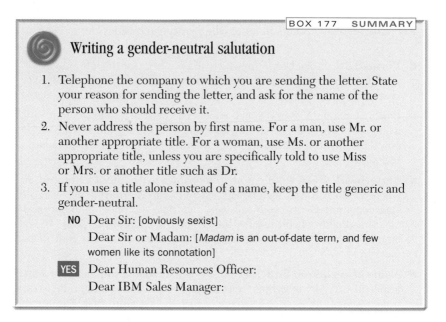

BOX 177   SUMMARY

Writing a gender-neutral salutation

1. Telephone the company to which you are sending the letter. State your reason for sending the letter, and ask for the name of the person who should receive it.

2. Never address the person by first name. For a man, use Mr. or another appropriate title. For a woman, use Ms. or another appropriate title, unless you are specifically told to use Miss or Mrs. or another title such as Dr.

3. If you use a title alone instead of a name, keep the title generic and gender-neutral.

  NO Dear Sir: [obviously sexist]

  Dear Sir or Madam: [*Madam* is an out-of-date term, and few women like its connotation]

  YES Dear Human Resources Officer:

  Dear IBM Sales Manager:

The sample envelope and sample business letter that follow are models of typical formats you can use.

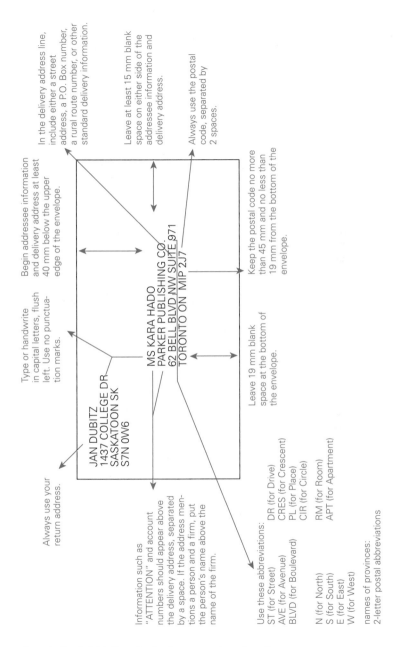

In the delivery address line, include either a street address, a P.O. Box number, a rural route number, or other standard delivery information.

Leave at least 15 mm blank space on either side of the addressee information and delivery address.

Always use the postal code, separated by 2 spaces.

Begin addressee information and delivery address at least 40 mm below the upper edge of the envelope.

Type or handwrite in capital letters, flush left. Use no punctuation marks.

Keep the postal code no more than 45 mm and no less than 19 mm from the bottom of the envelope.

Always use your return address.

Leave 19 mm blank space at the bottom of the envelope.

JAN DUBITZ
1437 COLLEGE DR
SASKATOON SK
S7N 0W6

MS KARA HADO
PARKER PUBLISHING CO.
62 BELL BLVD NW SUITE 971
TORONTO ON MIP 2J7

Information such as "ATTENTION" and account numbers should appear above the delivery address, separated by a space. If the address mentions a person and a firm, put the person's name above the name of the firm.

Use these abbreviations:
ST (for Street)   DR (for Drive)
AVE (for Avenue)   CRES (for Crescent)
BLVD (for Boulevard)   PL (for Place)
                       CIR (for Circle)

N (for North)   RM (for Room)
S (for South)   APT (for Apartment)
E (for East)
W (for West)

names of provinces:
2-letter postal abbreviations

Canada Post guidelines for business envelope format

725

Jan Dubitz
1437 College Dr.
Saskatoon SK S7N 0W6
(306) 555-3723
jdubitz@dubitz.ca

September 14, 2003

▲

4 lines

▼

Ms. Kara Hado
Parker Publishing Company
62 Bell Blvd. NW
Suite 971
Toronto ON M1P 2J7

Dear Ms. Hado:

▲

2 lines

▼

SALUTATION: Use an appropriate title (*Mr., Ms., Dr., Professor*) and the person's name. If you do not know the name, use a title (*Dean of Students, Human Resources Coordinator*). Add a colon at the end of the salutation.

Since our telephone conversation of September 8, I have decided to accept your offer of an internship at Parker Publishing. I am pleased at the interest you took in my course work and my student journalism portfolio, and grateful at having been chosen. My program adviser assures me that I will gain much valuable experience at Parker.

I look forward to meeting you in person this coming October 15.

Sincerely,

CLOSING: Capitalize only the first word (*Yours truly, Sincerely yours*) and follow with a comma.

4 lines

Jan Dubitz

Jan Dubitz

SIGNATURE: If you have a title, type it underneath your name. Sign letter in space above your name.

cc: V. Mehta, Adviser, Student Internships

OTHER: Use *cc:* to indicate that you have sent any courtesy copies. Use *Enc:* or *Enclosure:* if you include material *with* your letter.

Sample business letter

41b How do I write a memo?

Many business memos are sent through e-mail, although some are printed and circulated on paper. Be specific, not general, in your "subject" line. Prefer "Results of Evaluation" over "Update." Readers need to determine quickly the importance of a memo by reading the headings, especially the "subject" line. A memo from a supervisor asking for sales figures will receive prompt attention, whereas a memo from the office manager about new forms for ordering supplies will probably not receive a careful reading until the time comes to order more supplies.

The AUDIENCE for a memo, sent through e-mail or on paper, is usually "local." For example, in the workplace, local audiences can be senior management, other levels of supervisors or managers, people at your level, all employees, or customers. Non-local audiences can be people who share interests (religious, political, or leisure-time groups) or causes (environment, education, health care). Be as specific as possible in naming your memo's audience on the "to" line.

The PURPOSE of memos, whether sent through e-mail or on paper, is to give new information; to SUMMARIZE, clarify, or SYNTHESIZE known information; to put information officially on the record; to make a request or suggestion; or to record recent activities and outcomes. Most word-processing software provides formats for paper memos. All e-mail services provide an on-screen format for entering headings. For example, in versions of Microsoft Word™, you can click FILE>NEW>MEMO. Select the style you want—"Professional" is a good choice for workplace use. A memo has the following parts:

- **Headings**

TO:	[Your audience, named as specifically as possible]
FROM:	[Your name]
DATE:	[Month, day, and year you're writing]
SUBJECT:	[Memo's topic, specifically and concisely stated]

- **Contents**

  Introductory paragraph: State the memo's purpose and give needed background information.

  Body paragraph(s): State the point of the memo and why it's worth the recipient's time to read it. Or, as the sample memo on page 728 shows, give the data required.

  Conclusion: End with a one- or two-sentence summary or, when appropriate, with a specific recommendation. If the memo is short, like the sample memo, end either with a sentence of instructions or a thank-you message.

TO: English Teaching Assistants
FROM: Professor Thomas Nevers, Director,
          First-Year Composition
DATE: December 1, 2003
SUBJECT: New Computer Programs

Several new writing programs will be installed in the English computer labs. Training sessions are scheduled during the week before classes begin next semester.

Tuesday, January 6	9:00-11:00 a.m.
Wednesday, January 7	1:00-3:00 p.m.
Thursday, January 8	8:30-10:30 a.m.
Friday, January 9	1:30-3:30 p.m.

Please stop by my office by December 12 to sign up for one of the two-hour workshops.

Sample memo

Before sending your memo, proofread it to eliminate grammar and spelling errors, to check the accuracy of the content, and to make sure it's clearly and concisely stated. Perhaps ask others to review it before you send it out.

One or at most two pages is the expected length of a memo. If you need more pages, you're writing a report (see 41f and sample memo).

41c How do I create a résumé?

A **résumé** details your employment experience, education, and other accomplishments for a potential employer. Because your résumé will be compared with those of numerous other applicants, take time to make a favourable impression. Format your résumé so that it's easy to read, and include only information relevant to the position available. A worksheet to help you think through what to say, and not say, in a résumé appears on pages 731–32.

Use the guidelines below for writing a résumé; also, examine the sample on page 730. A guide to writing a targeted résumé is found on page 733. A helpful Web site for writing résumés is <http://www1.umn.edu/ohr/ecep/resume/>.

- Use the Résumé Worksheet to draft your résumé.
- Adjust the emphasis in your résumé to fit your purpose: For a job as a computer programmer, you need to emphasize different facts about yourself than what you'd offer when applying to be a retail salesperson.
- Fit all information on one page (or two at the most—but one-pagers usually appeal to employers more) by stressing what will interest your potential employer. If you must use a second page, put the most important information on the first page.
- Put the most recent item first in each category.
- Use clear headings to separate blocks of information.
- Write telegram-style under the headings. Start with verb phrases, not with the word *I*, and omit *a, an, the*. Write, for example, "Created new computer program to organize company's spreadsheets," not "*I* created *a* new computer program to organize *the* company's spreadsheets."
- Don't pad entries with irrelevant information or wordy writing.
- *Never* lie.
- Include references or state that you can provide them "upon request" (and have them ready to go).
- Print your résumé on high-quality white or very light beige paper.
- *ESL writers:* For a job in Canada or the United States, never include personal information that may be expected in other countries. For example, don't state your age, marital status, or religion.

Margaret Lorentino
1338 Sunflower Lane
Halifax, NS N3J 3J6
(902) 555-3756
mlor94@home.ca

OBJECTIVE:	Seeking a full/part-time position as a medical transcriptionist to utilize my medical, computer, and office skills
EDUCATION:	Certificate in Medical Transcription Nova Scotia Community College, Institute of Technology, Halifax, NS, December 2004 Bachelor of Science Dalhousie University, Halifax, NS, May 2003
EMPLOYMENT:	Dalhousie University, January 2001–Present Lab Assistant and Computer Skills Teacher RTD Real Estate, Halifax, August 1995–August 1996 Receptionist, Accounting Assistant Atlantic Mutual Life, Dartmouth, NS, May 1994–July 1995 Sales Assistant Reliable Personnel, Summerside, PE, May 1993–May 1994 Temporary Employment Manager

SKILLS: Computer
- Experienced with Microsoft Office 2003
- Type 60 wpm
- Have experience with Lotus, Excel, and Access
- Teach basic computer skills in first-year college English classes

Organizational
- Girl Scout leader, soccer coach, summer camp counsellor
- Trained employees in data entry and accounting principles
- Managed a temporary workforce of 20–30 employees

REFERENCES: Available upon request

Sample résumé

RÉSUMÉ WORKSHEET

Photocopy and fill in this résumé worksheet to help you create your own résumé.

(Name) _____

(Address) _____

(City, Province, Postal Code) _____

(Home Telephone) _____

(Work Telephone) _____

(Fax Number, if applicable) _____

(E-mail Address) _____

Position Desired or Career Objective _____
_____
_____

[Include below only if relevant and meaningful; add more lines in a category, as necessary.]

Education (most recent education first)

1. (Degree or Certificate) _____ (Dates) _____
   (Institution) _____
   (Major or Area of Concentration) _____

2. (Degree or Certificate) _____ (Dates) _____
   (Institution) _____
   (Major or Area of Concentration) _____

Experience (most recent experience first)

1. (Job Title) _____ (Dates) _____
   (Employer) _____
   (Responsibilities and Accomplishments) _____
   _____
   _____

2. (Job Title) _____ (Dates) _____
   (Employer) _____
   (Responsibilities and Accomplishments) _____
   _____
   _____

→

Licence or Certification, if any (nursing, accounting, massage therapy, etc.)

1. (Licence) _____ (Dates) _____
   (Issuing Agency) _____

2. (Licence) _____ (Dates) _____
   (Issuing Agency) _____

Related Experience

(Description) _____ (Dates) _____
(Organization or Company) _____
(Duties/Accomplishments) _____

Honours/Awards, if any

_____
_____
_____

Publications/Presentations, if any

_____ (Dates) _____
_____ (Dates) _____

Activities/Interests (clubs, organizations, volunteer work)

_____
_____
_____

Special Abilities, Skills, Knowledge (languages, computer, travel)

_____
_____
_____

References (personal, professional)

_____
_____
_____

Targeting Your Résumé

A résumé targeted to the specific company and the specific position you are applying for makes its reader think, "We should talk to this person. This candidate looks like someone who would be an asset to our business."

What is an "asset to the business"? Employers look for evidence of your attitude, work ethic, and "trainability"—your ability to help the company meet its goals and to fit into its corporate culture.

The first step in identifying what a particular company is looking for in an employee is to "decode" the job advertisement that led you to that company:

- Circle the terms (usually adjectives and adverbs) that describe the type of person the company is seeking.
- Underline terms that describe the specific skills required for the position.

Use the same or similar terms in your résumé and the job application letter that accompanies it to demonstrate your knowledge of the company and your "fit" with its corporate culture.

Supplement what you discover in the job advertisement by visiting the company's Web site to learn more about its products or services and to look at its mission statement and the terminology it uses. With the information you gather, you can "crack the code" and identify what that company considers essential in a successful applicant.

The Web site for this book, <http://www.pearsoned.ca/troyka>, has more information about targeted résumés.

41d How do I compose a job application letter?

A job application letter always needs to accompany your résumé. Avoid simply repeating what is already in the résumé. Instead, acquaint yourself with available descriptions of the position and its responsibilities, and connect the company's expectations to your experience. Stress how your background has prepared you for this position. Follow the guidelines below for writing your letter; also, examine the sample job application letter.

- Use one page only.
- Use the same name, content, and format guidelines you use for a business letter (41a).
- Open by identifying the position you want to apply for.
- Address the letter to a specific person. If you can't find out a name, use a title (such as "Human Resources Coordinator"). Avoid using "To Whom It May Concern" (41a) because it tells employers you've made only a minimal effort.
- Think of your letter as a polite sales pitch about you. Don't be shy, but don't exaggerate what you can do for the company if you get the job.
- Explain how your background will meet the requirements of the job at this workplace in particular.
- Stress your qualifications for the specific position for which you're applying.
- If the job will be your first, give your key attributes—keeping them relevant and true—such as that you're punctual, self-disciplined, a "team player," eager to learn, and ready to work hard for the company.
- State when you're available for an interview and also how you can be reached easily by mail and telephone (and cell phone, if you have one).
- Edit and proofread carefully. Even one misspelled word can hurt your chances.

The sample letter that follows is by Margaret Lorentino, a mother with young children, who seeks a position that would allow her to work at home. She is responding to a newspaper ad for a medical transcription position. The format is modified block style.

Margaret Lorentino
1338 Sunflower Lane
Halifax, NS B3J 3J6

December 1, 2004

Ms. Arlene Chang
Employment Coordinator
Rockford Medical Centre
820 Cornwallis Rd.
Halifax, NS B5A 2C2

Dear Ms. Chang:

I had a chance to talk with you last spring about your company at the Medical Professions Job Fair. I am very interested in the medical transcription position that I noticed in the *Register Star* on November 29.

I will be completing my Certificate in Medical Transcription at the end of December. I have taken courses in medical transcription, medical office procedures, and keyboarding, as well as numerous computer courses. I have a bachelor's degree in general science from Dalhousie University. I believe that this background would help me in this position.

The enclosed résumé will give you the details of my experience and qualifications. I think that my experience and education make a great combination for this position. I am available for an interview at your convenience. My home phone number is (902) 555-3756, and my e-mail address is mlor94@home.ca.

Sincerely yours,

Margaret Lorentino

Margaret Lorentino

Sample job application letter

41e What are guidelines for writing e-mail?

Today, a great deal of business and other communication is conducted by e-mail. Business and professional e-mails differ from casual, every-day e-mails and instant messages that you send to friends and family. An e-mail resembles a business memo, but it is relayed in electronic form. Follow the guidelines below for writing a business e-mail.

- Write a specific, not general, topic in the Subject box. Unless you do this, you won't capture your reader's attention. After all, attention spans when reading e-mail can be quite short, especially for business people who get dozens of e-mails a day and therefore tend to skim the screen.
- Use block style by single-spacing within paragraphs and double-spacing between paragraphs.
- Never write in all capital letters or all lowercase letters. Not only are they hard (and annoying) to read, but all capital letters are considered "flam-ing," the written equivalent of shouting. This is poor, even insulting, "netiquette," the word for etiquette online.
- Use bulleted or numbered lists when itemizing.
- Keep your message brief and your paragraphs short. Reading from the screen is harder on the eyes than reading a print document.
- Be cautious about what you say in business e-mail. After all, the recipient can forward to others without your permission, even though this practice is considered unethical and rude. And, of course, never give personal information to strangers, and never give credit information on a non-secure site.
- Forward an e-mail message *only* if you have asked the original sender for permission.
- Check your e-mail and any attachments to make sure your message is clear, your TONE is appropriate, and your spelling, grammar, and punctu-ation are correct.
- Use emoticons only if you are sure the reader appreciates them. :-) Some people do not. :-(
- Never make personal attacks on others, share jokes that would offend some groups of people, or gossip in a business e-mail.
- Never "spam" (send unsolicited, or "junk," mail).

When you want to include in your e-mail a separate document, such as a business report, a proposal, or the like, compose it in a word-processing program and then attach the document to an e-mail message using the "Attachments" function of your e-mail service. Attached docu-ments look better than copied and pasted documents because they maintain the original formatting (margins, spacing, italics). One word of caution: If an attached file is large, alert your recipient to its size so that the person can decide whether to download it—and ask whether they'd prefer to receive the document by fax or in the mail.

In the sample e-mail below, a reporter is writing to MP3 users on a listserv (Internet discussion group) for the first time.

E-mail to listserv of MP3 users

PUBLIC WRITING

In addition to ACADEMIC WRITING and BUSINESS WRITING, you may also find occasion to do *public writing*—writing addressed either to members of your community, the community as a whole, or public officials. Some public writing is also known as *civic writing* because you're communicating as a citizen in order to affect actions or beliefs in a democratic society.

Examples of writing for the public include letters to the editor of a newspaper or magazine, to your member of Parliament, and to a group you either belong to or want to address. You might write a newspaper article to publicize a local theatre group, a brochure to draw new members into a service organization, a proposal to the municipal council for building a park at the site of a disused warehouse, or an e-mail to your MPP or MLA inquiring about his or her position on hospital funding.

Writing for the Internet is perhaps the broadest form of public writing, in the sense that anything you post there is available for anyone to read—anyone, that is, with access to the Internet. On the Internet, you might post book reviews on a bookseller's Web site or a message about an upcoming concert to a newsgroup. You might create a Web site for an organization, a social cause, or a special interest group and share information and ideas through your site. You might keep a Web log, or blog (see 41h). Although the Internet provides easy access to broad publics, access does not guarantee attention. The best Web site in the world has little impact if no one visits it.

In all of these examples—and you can add many more of your own—you are generally writing for an AUDIENCE that you do not know personally. You are also discussing subjects that you think affect others, not just you alone. For these reasons, public writing requires that you take special care in analyzing your audience, being honest, and establishing your credibility.

"Establishing credibility" means convincing your readers that they need or want to listen to you. You do this by being accurate and honest and by explaining your connection with the reader(s). What do you have in common with your readers? How does your experience make you a reputable source—or, have you done research to become a knowledgeable source? Can you name other authorities who agree with your perspective? Readers can discern fake information quite quickly.

For example, if you are writing a letter to the editor of your local newspaper, you will gain credibility if you begin, "As a resident of Green County for twelve years," and then go on to give your opinion. By establishing yourself first as a member of your audience's community, you convey that you have a sincere and long-standing interest in the welfare of that community. Or suppose you are writing to ask for your MP's support for a new wildlife refuge. You might present your argument on the basis of your research into the benefits and drawbacks of setting aside the land. In this way, you make yourself credible by demonstrating that you understand the complexities of the issue.

Sections 41f, 41g, and 41h describe three common types of public writing for civic purposes: reports, letters to the editor or political representatives, and other types.

41f How do I write reports for the public?

Reports for the public vary in length, format, and content. An "action brief" from a political organization might consist of a few pages detailing recent developments on an issue of concern. A "technology update" from a local association of people with a shared, specialized hobby might contain news of technological advances, along with critical reviews and, perhaps, information on where to purchase each item. An "impact study" may explain the effect that a proposed development will have on the local environment or economy.

Write your material in an evenhanded TONE so that your credibility is supported by your fairness. If you want to criticize something, be sure your argument is well reasoned and supported—and that it lacks BIAS or malice toward any person(s) or specific idea(s). This doesn't means that your writing needs to be limp. Indeed, you can choose writing that's spirited, enthusiastic, and even stirring.

To write a public report, follow the guidelines in Box 178.

BOX 178　　SUMMARY

Writing a public report

■ Decide how far to go in your report. Will you only inform, or will you also analyze the information you present? Or—going one step further—will you make a recommendation based on the information and your analysis?

■ State your findings in an objective tone. Though you may later bring in your opinion by interpreting the data or recommending a course of action, your credibility depends on your first reporting accurately.

■ A formal report usually follows the organization listed below. Depending on the purpose of your report, however, you might combine or expand any of the sections.

- **Introduction:** Explains the purpose of the report, describes the problem studied, and often describes or outlines the organization of the entire report.
- **Methods:** Describes how the data were gathered.
- **Results:** Presents the findings of the report.
- **Discussion:** States the implications of your findings.
- **Conclusion:** Makes recommendations or simply summarizes the findings.

The following page shows the executive summary to a report on climate changes in the Great Lakes region. An executive summary is a brief overview sometimes included before a lengthy report. The report was produced by the Union of Concerned Scientists and the Ecological Society of America. The entire work, which contains the elements described in Box 178, was published online and as a 105-page booklet.

Executive Summary

T he Great Lakes region of the United States and Canada is a land of striking glacial legacies: spectacular lakes, vast wetlands, fertile southern soils, and rugged northern terrain forested in spruce and fir. It is also home to 60 million people whose actions can profoundly affect the region's ecological bounty and the life-sustaining benefits it provides. Now that the world is entering a period of unusually rapid climate change, driven largely by human activities that release heat-trapping greenhouse gases into the atmosphere, the responsibility for safeguarding our natural heritage is becoming urgent.

Growing evidence suggests that the climate of the Great Lakes is already changing:
- Winters are getting shorter.
- Annual average temperatures are growing warmer.
- The duration of lake ice cover is decreasing as air and water temperatures rise.
- Heavy rainstorms are becoming more common.

This report examines these trends in detail and discusses the likelihood that they will continue into the future. The consequences of these climatic changes will magnify the impacts of ongoing human disturbances that fragment or transform landscapes, pollute air and water, and disrupt natural ecosystems and the vital goods and services they provide. *Confronting Climate Change in the Great Lakes Region* explores the potential consequences of climate change, good and bad, for the character, economy, and environment of the Great Lakes region during the coming century. It also examines actions that can be take now to help forestall many of the most severe consequences of climate change for North America's heartland.

CONFRONTING CLIMATE CHANGE IN THE GREAT LAKES REGION
Union of Concerned Scientists • The Ecological Society of America

Executive Summary of a public report

41g How do I write letters to my community or its representatives?

Letters to your community include letters to the editors of newspapers and magazines, statements of position for a local or national newsletter, and material you self-publish (37j). Such letters allow you to participate in a discussion with a community of peers. When writing in response to a particular piece of writing in the same publication, always begin by referring precisely to what you are responding to, using title, section, and date, if possible.

In the following example, a citizen argues for preserving a city park in its present form.

To the Editor:

Re "Parking Plan Threatens Green Space" (news article, May. 14):

For well over a century, Claremont Park has provided a welcome oasis in downtown Exeter. Office workers eat lunches there, school children play there on the way home, and evening concerts and other events unite the community.

It is very shortsighted, then, that the City Council now considers converting a third of the park into additional parking.

I acknowledge that parking downtown has gotten difficult. As the manager of a small shop, I know that our customers sometimes have trouble finding a parking place. However, the park itself is one of the reasons our downtown has become more popular in the past decade. Ironically, destroying the park's attractive green space will reduce the need for more parking, by hurting business.

A better solution is for the city to purchase the vacant property at the corner of Queen and Elm streets and build a multi-storey garage. No doubt this option is more expensive than using the park. However, I'm sure most residents would prefer to leave future generations a legacy of trees, grass, and inviting benches rather than a debt of sterile concrete.

John C. Bradway
Exeter, May 17, 2003

Many letters to the editor propose solutions to a community problem. These letters aim to persuade other readers that a problem exists and that a particular solution is not only feasible but also the most advantageous of all the possible alternatives. Keep the following guidelines in mind when writing to propose a solution:

■ Explain briefly the specific problem you are attempting to solve.

■ Tell how your solution will solve all elements of the problem.

■ Address briefly the possible objections or alternatives to your proposed solution.

■ State why your solution offers the most advantages of all the alternatives.

Letters to civic and political leaders can influence their opinions and actions. You might write in reaction to a proposed law or course of action, to object to an existing law or situation, or to thank or compliment the person for action taken. State your purpose at the outset; be concise; and end by clearly stating what action you request so that a response, if given, can be to the point.

41h What other types of public writing exist?

In addition to the writing that they do for business, civic, or academic purposes, many people write simply to express themselves or to entertain others. The most obvious examples are fiction, poetry, plays, film scripts, and, at another level, instant messages or postings to an Internet discussion group. In addition, many people write for or produce newsletters or Web sites related to their hobbies or special interests. The Internet has made publication to very broad publics not only instantaneous but also cost free, giving writers the capability of sharing words, graphic designs, and images.

One form of public writing that has exploded in popularity in recent years is the Web log, or *blog* (the last letter of We*b* plus *log*). Blogs are online journals that writers update on a fairly regular basis, usually daily. Some writers focus their blogs on a single topic or a narrow range of topics. Others record the events of their lives, as in a diary—that is, a diary open for all the world to see and read.

Special software allows bloggers (as the authors are known) to create blogs. As with a Web site, writers need access to a server to publish their work. Many Internet providers (such as Yahoo! and AOL) support blogs. Additionally, there are Web sites such as blogger, <http://new.blogger.com>, that not only maintain your blog but also allow you to read the blogs of thousands of other people.

Chapter 42

Writing Under Pressure

The demands of writing under pressure can sometimes seem overwhelming, but if you break the challenge into small, sequential steps and then focus on each step in turn, you can succeed. When you write under the pressure of time constraints, you are expected to write as completely and clearly as possible. If you tend to freeze under pressure, force yourself to take slow, deep breaths or to use a relaxation technique such as counting backward from ten. When you turn to the task, remember to break the whole into parts so that the process is easier to work through.

Writing answers for essay tests is one of the most important writing tasks that you face in your postsecondary education. Common in all disciplines, including the natural sciences, essay tests demand that you recall information and also put assorted pieces of that information into contexts that lead to GENERALIZATIONS you can support. Essay tests give you the chance to SYNTHESIZE and apply your knowledge, helping your instructor determine what you've learned.

42a How do I prepare for essay exams?

Begin preparing for exams well before the day of the test itself. Attend class diligently and take good notes. Just as important, be an active reader, annotating your textbook and putting concepts into your own words. Reading and writing are closely connected, but there is no substitute for actually doing some writing yourself.

Perhaps the best preparation comes from writing practice exams. Doing this will give you experience in writing under pressure about course material. Your instructors may offer questions they used in previous years, or they may provide a number of questions to guide your studying. Alternatively, you and your classmates may generate your own exam questions. Use cue words and key terms drawn from your course material to help develop potential questions. Finally, ask each instructor if books or notes are allowed in the exam. Some exams are "open book," meaning that you can use your books or notes; most, however, are closed book.

42b What are cue words and key terms?

Most essay questions contain a *cue word*, a word of direction that tells what the content of your answer is expected to emphasize. Knowing the major cue words and their meanings can increase your ability to plan efficiently and write effectively. Be guided by the list of cue words and sample essay test questions in Box 179.

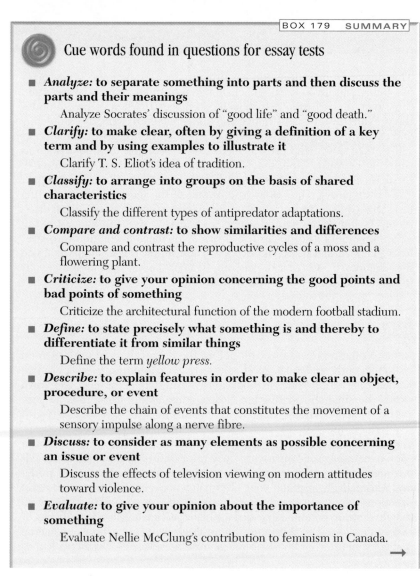

BOX 179 SUMMARY

Cue words found in questions for essay tests

- *Analyze:* **to separate something into parts and then discuss the parts and their meanings**
    Analyze Socrates' discussion of "good life" and "good death."
- *Clarify:* **to make clear, often by giving a definition of a key term and by using examples to illustrate it**
    Clarify T. S. Eliot's idea of tradition.
- *Classify:* **to arrange into groups on the basis of shared characteristics**
    Classify the different types of antipredator adaptations.
- *Compare and contrast:* **to show similarities and differences**
    Compare and contrast the reproductive cycles of a moss and a flowering plant.
- *Criticize:* **to give your opinion concerning the good points and bad points of something**
    Criticize the architectural function of the modern football stadium.
- *Define:* **to state precisely what something is and thereby to differentiate it from similar things**
    Define the term *yellow press.*
- *Describe:* **to explain features in order to make clear an object, procedure, or event**
    Describe the chain of events that constitutes the movement of a sensory impulse along a nerve fibre.
- *Discuss:* **to consider as many elements as possible concerning an issue or event**
    Discuss the effects of television viewing on modern attitudes toward violence.
- *Evaluate:* **to give your opinion about the importance of something**
    Evaluate Nellie McClung's contribution to feminism in Canada.

→

Cue words found in questions for essay tests (*continued*)

- **Explain: to make clear or intelligible something that needs to be understood or interpreted**

  Explain how the amount of carbon dioxide in the blood regulates rates of heartbeat and breathing.

- **Illustrate: to give examples of something**

  Illustrate the use of symbolism in Richard Wright's novel *Native Son*.

- **Interpret: to explain the meaning of something**

  Give your interpretation of Michael Ondaatje's poem "The Cinnamon Peeler."

- **Justify: to show or prove that something is valid or correct**

  Justify the existence of labour unions in a postindustrial economy.

- **Prove: to present evidence that cannot be refuted logically or with other evidence**

  Prove that smoking is a major cause of lung cancer.

- **Relate: to show the connections between two or more things**

  Relate increases in specific crimes in the period 1932–1933 to the prevailing economic conditions.

- **Review: to evaluate or summarize something critically**

  Review the structural arrangements in proteins to explain the meaning of the term *polypeptide*.

- **Show: to point out or demonstrate something**

  Show what effects pesticides have on the production of wheat.

- **Summarize: to identify the major points of something**

  Summarize the major benefits of compulsory education.

- **Support: to argue in favour of something**

  Support the position that the destruction of rain forests is endangering the planet.

Each essay question also has one or more *key terms* that tell you the information, topics, and ideas you are to write about. For example, in the question "Criticize the architectural function of the modern football stadium," the cue word is *criticize* and the key terms are *architectural function* and *football stadium*. To answer the question successfully, you need first to define the term *architectural function,* then to describe the typical modern football stadium (mentioning major variations when important), and then to discuss how well the typical modern football stadium fits your definition of architectural function.

42c How do I write effective responses to essay test questions?

An effective response to an essay test question is complete and logically organized. Here are two answers to the question "Classify the different types of antipredator adaptations." The first one is successful; the second is not. The sentences are numbered for your reference, and they are explained in the text.

ANSWER 1— YES

(1) Although many antipredator adaptations have evolved in the animal kingdom, all can be classified into four major categories according to the prey's response to the predator. (2) The first category is hiding techniques. (3) These techniques include cryptic coloration and behaviour in which the prey assumes characteristics of an inanimate object or part of a plant. (4) The second category is early enemy detection. (5) The prey responds to alarm signals from like prey or other kinds of prey before the enemy can get too close. (6) Evasion of the pursuing predator is the third category. (7) Prey that move erratically or in a compact group are displaying this technique. (8) The fourth category is active repulsion of the predator. (9) The prey kills, injures, or sickens the predator, establishing that it represents danger to the predator.

ANSWER 2—NO

(1) Antipredator adaptations are the development of the capabilities to reduce the risk of attack from a predator with minimal change in the life-supporting activities of the prey. (2) There are many different types of antipredator adaptations. (3) One type is camouflage, hiding from the predator by cryptic coloration or imitation of plant parts. (4) An example of this type of antipredator adaptation is the praying mantis. (5) A second type is the defence used by monarch butterflies, a chemical protection that makes some birds ill after eating the butterfly. (6) This protection may injure the bird by causing it to vomit, and it can educate the bird against eating other butterflies. (7) Detection and evasion are also antipredator adaptations.

Below, an explanation is given of what happens, sentence by sentence, in the two answers to the question about antipredator adaptations.

SENTENCE	ANSWER 1: YES	ANSWER 2: NO
1	Sets up classification system and gives number of categories based on key term	Defines key term

2	Names first category	Throwaway sentence—accomplishes nothing
3	Defines first category	Names and defines first category
4	Names second category	Gives an example for first category
5	Defines second category	Gives an example for second (unnamed) category
6	Names third category	Continues to explain example
7	Defines third category	Names two categories
8	Names fourth category	
9	Defines fourth category	

Answer 1 sets about immediately answering the question by introducing a classification system, as called for by the cue word *classify*. Answer 2, by contrast, defines the key term, a waste of time on a test that will be read by an audience of specialists. Answer 1 is tightly organized, easy to follow, and to the point. Answer 2 rambles, never names the four categories, and says more around the subject than on it.

42d What strategies can I use when writing under pressure?

If you use specific *strategies* when writing under pressure, you can be more comfortable and your writing will likely be more effective. As you use the strategies listed in Box 180, remember that your purpose in answering questions is to show what you know in a clear, direct, and well-organized way. When you're studying for an essay exam, write out one-sentence summaries of major areas of information. This technique helps fix the ideas in your mind, and a summary sentence may become a thesis sentence for an essay answer.

The more you use the strategies in the box and adapt them to your personal needs, the better you'll use them to your advantage. Practise them by making up questions that might be on your test and timing yourself as you write the answers. Doing this offers you another benefit: If you study by anticipating possible questions and writing out the answers, you'll be very well prepared if one or two of them show up on the test.

BOX 180   SUMMARY

Strategies for writing essay tests

1. Do not start writing immediately.

2. If the test has two or more questions, read them all at the start. Determine whether you're supposed to answer all the questions. Doing this gives you a sense of how to budget your time, either by dividing it equally or by allotting more time for some questions than for others. If you have a choice of questions, select those about which you know the most and that you can write about most completely within the time limit.

3. Analyze each question that you answer by underlining the *cue words* and *key terms* (see 42b) to determine exactly what the question asks.

4. Use the writing process as much as possible within the constraints of the time limit. Try to allot time to plan and revise. For a one-hour test on one question, take about ten minutes to jot down preliminary ideas about content and organization, and save ten minutes to reread, revise, and edit your answer. If you're pressed suddenly for time—but try to avoid this—consider skipping a question that you can't answer well or a question that counts less toward your total score. If you feel blocked, try FREEWRITING (2g) to get your hand and your thoughts moving.

5. Support any GENERALIZATIONS with specifics (see 4f about using the RENNS TEST for being specific).

6. Beware of going off the topic. Respond to the cue words and key terms in the question, and do not try to reshape the question to conform to what you might prefer to write about. Remember, your reader expects a clear line of presentation and reasoning that answers the stated question.

EXERCISE 42-1

Look back at an essay that you have written under time pressure. Read it over and decide whether you would change the content of your answer or the strategies you used as you were writing under pressure. List these specific strategies, and if you think they were useful, add them to Box 180.

Chapter 43

Oral Presentations

Preparing an oral presentation and writing an essay involve some of the same processes. In each, you determine your PURPOSE, analyze your AUDIENCE, and work to deliver a clear, controlling idea. This chapter will help you move from written to oral delivery and show you how to use what you know about writing to prepare effective oral presentations. You will also learn about the special considerations that apply to speaking, instead of writing, your thoughts.

PREPARING AN ORAL PRESENTATION

43a How do I determine my purpose and topic?

Just as writing purposes change from one situation to the next, so do speaking purposes. You might address students living in your dorm to *inform* them about a film club you are starting on Monday nights. You might try to *persuade* the history department or the registrar to transfer credits from a class you took overseas. The toast you give at a friend's wedding is meant, in part, to *entertain* the wedding guests.

In the academic setting, to inform and to persuade are the most common purposes: To *inform* is to help your audience understand something; to *persuade* is to influence the attitudes and behaviours of your audience.

With a general purpose in mind, you are ready to think about your TOPIC. Sometimes your topic will be assigned, but if not, follow these guidelines: Select a topic that you care about and that your audience will care about also. Choose one that you either already know about or that you can learn about in the time you have to prepare. Be sure you can do justice to your topic within the time constraints of the presentation itself.

Now, narrow your topic to the one main point you want to make, and state the specific purpose of your speech. Write your specific purpose as an INFINITIVE PHRASE: *to inform about . . . , to convince that . . . , to show how . . . , to explain why. . . .* Use specific terms and precise language.

How do I adapt my speech's message to my audience?

To determine how best to approach your TOPIC, consider your AUDIENCE and adapt your message accordingly. Begin by asking yourself these questions: How much does my audience already know about this topic? What terms and concepts will they not know? What information must I provide as a foundation for my message? Does my audience have a particular bias toward my topic that I need to consider?

Based on your responses to these questions, you will probably find that your audience falls into one of three categories: *uninformed, informed,* or *mixed.* Box 181 offers help in adapting your message to each type of audience.

BOX 181   SUMMARY

Adapting oral presentations to the audience

Uninformed Audience

Limit the number of new ideas you present. Use visual aids to establish the basics, avoiding technical terms as much as possible. Define new terms and concepts. Repeat key ideas and use vivid examples.

Informed Audience

Don't waste their time with the basics, but introduce new ideas and concepts. From the beginning, reassure them that you will be covering new ground.

Mixed Audience

Start with simple concepts and move toward more complex ones. In the introduction, acknowledge the presence of the more informed members of the audience and explain that you are only reviewing the basics so that everyone can build from the same knowledge base.

Adapting your presentation to the general needs and expectations of your audience does not mean catering to their views and saying only what they might want to hear. It means rather that you need to consider their knowledge of your topic and their interest in it. You can then make your message understandable and relevant by using appropriate language and examples.

43c How do I formulate my speech's working thesis?

As with the THESIS STATEMENT of an essay, the working thesis for an oral presentation makes clear the main idea and the speaker's PURPOSE. It also reflects the speaker's AUDIENCE analysis in its content (neither too sophisticated nor too simple) and its language (the word choice is at the right level). In addition, a working thesis is a practical preparation step because it helps you stay on your topic, and it introduces and connects the key concepts of your presentation.

Box 182 demonstrates how a student speaking on infertility worked from a general purpose and topic to arrive at a specific purpose and working thesis.

BOX 182   SUMMARY

Formulating a working thesis for a speech

GENERAL PURPOSE	To inform
TOPIC	"Infertility"
SPECIFIC PURPOSE	To explain medical advancements in the treatment of infertility
WORKING THESIS	Infertility is becoming a thing of the past for many couples thanks to medical procedures such as donor insemination, in vitro fertilization, and egg harvesting.

43d How do I organize my oral presentation?

When you have compiled the information you will use in your oral presentation, develop an organizational outline. An organizational outline shows the three-part structure of an oral presentation—introduction, body, conclusion—and lists major points (as lettered headings) with two to three supporting points (as numbered subheadings). Use sentences for your main points to sharpen your thinking as you DRAFT. Box 183 presents a typical organizational outline.

BOX 183 SUMMARY

Organizational outline for an oral presentation

Title

General purpose:
Topic:
Specific purpose:
Thesis statement:

Introduction

A. _____

B. _____

(transition)

Supporting material

A. _____

    1._____

    2._____

(transition)

B. _____

    1. _____

    2. _____

(transition)

C. _____

    1. _____

    2. _____

(transition)

Conclusion

A. _____

B. _____

C. _____

Introduction

The members of an audience waiting to hear a speaker have three questions in mind: Who are you? What are you going to talk about? Why should I listen? They are good questions, and you want to respond to them in the introduction to your talk. Here are some suggestions:

- Grab your audience's attention with a question, a quotation, a fascinating statistic or fact, an anecdote, background information, or a compliment. Whether someone introduces you or not, tell your audience what qualifies you to speak on your particular subject.
- Explain briefly the organization of your talk. This gives your audience a road map so that they know where you are starting, where you are going, and what they can look forward to as you speak.

Supporting material

Though much of the advice given for oral presentations applies to written communication as well, audiences for oral presentations generally need some special help from the speaker. When you are reading an article and lose sight of the main point, you can turn back a few paragraphs and reread. But when you are listening to a speech and your mind wanders, you cannot ask the speaker to go back and repeat.

As a speaker, you can employ strategies to keep listeners interested and aware of your purpose and where you are. Below are some suggestions.

- Give signals to show where you are on the road map. Use *first, second,* and *third* appropriately. Show CAUSE AND EFFECT with words such as *subsequently, therefore,* and *furthermore.* If you are telling a story, use signpost terms such as *before, then,* and *next.*
- Define unfamiliar terms and give vivid examples to help the audience understand new ideas and concepts.
- Comment on your own material. Tell the audience what is significant, memorable, or relevant—and why.
- Repeat key ideas. If you do so sparingly, you can emphasize the importance of the idea and help the audience remember it.
- Provide internal summaries. Every so often, take a moment to resume what you have covered as reassurance for both yourself and your audience.

Conclusion

In the conclusion of a speech, an audience looks for a sense of closure. Here are some ways to conclude your presentation.

- Signal the end with verbal cues ("In conclusion") and nonverbal cues (facial expressions, gestures).
- Offer a fresh restatement of your main message—but do not introduce new ideas.
- Use a dramatic clincher statement, cite a memorable quotation, or issue a challenge.

- When you say "Finally," make sure you mean it. In other words, do not conclude more than once.

43d.1 Researching my speech

Doing research for an oral presentation requires the same kind of planning as doing research for written documents. To keep yourself calm and focused, divide the preparation into manageable tasks, according to a realistic time line (31d). Set small goals and stick to your calendar in order to give yourself enough time to research, organize, and practise your presentation (43i). Review Chapters 31–33 for help on finding and evaluating sources, taking notes, planning a research strategy, and documenting sources. An oral presentation won't have a WORKS CITED or REFERENCES page to be read out, but your instructor might ask you to turn in such a typed list before or after you give your presentation.

43d.2 Drafting my speech

Most of the preparation involved in an oral presentation is written work. Writing helps you take four important steps in your preparation: (1) to organize your thoughts; (2) to distance yourself from the ideas and remain objective; (3) to pay attention to words and language; and (4) to polish for clarity and impact.

When drafting your speech, it may help you to review Chapters 20–22 on usage and the impact and correct form of words. In particular, see section 21b for a discussion of a medium LEVEL OF FORMALITY in language, which is an appropriate level for most public speaking. Careful DICTION (21e) will make your speech both easy to listen to and memorable. Box 184 presents some tips on language that apply specifically to oral presentations.

BOX 184   SUMMARY

Using language effectively in oral presentations

- **Recognize the power of precise words.**
  "Never in the field of human conflict was so much owed by so many to so few."
  —Winston Churchill

  Substitute "history" for *the field of human conflict* and note the diminished effect.
- **Take care not to offend.** If you see the slightest chance that a word, phrase, or example could offend your audience, don't use it. Such material distracts your listeners and detracts from your message. It also suggests that you're insensitive to the impact of SLANTED LANGUAGE (21h). Avoid SEXIST PRONOUNS and NOUNS (10s and 21g).

$\rightarrow$

Using language effectively in oral presentations (*continued*)

- **Use guide phrases.** Words such as *now, first, my next point,* and so on help listeners follow the organization of your presentation.
- **Use the active voice.** The ACTIVE VOICE is generally desirable in writing (8o), but it is crucial in oral presentations. Listeners can more easily grasp your point if you state the subject at the beginning of a sentence. Consider the following two sentences:

  A challenge to the country's fiscal health is posed by rising medical costs. [passive]

  Rising medical costs pose a challenge to the country's fiscal health. [active]

43e How do I present a speech collaboratively?

At some point, you might be asked to present an oral report as part of a group. As with collaborative projects of any sort, special considerations apply.

- Make sure, when choosing a topic, that most members of the group are familiar with the subject. All members of the group are required to be able to contribute in some way.
- Find out whether all members of the group are required to speak for an equal amount of time. If so, agree on firm time limits for each person, so that everyone can participate in the delivery. If there is no such requirement, students who enjoy public speaking can take more responsibility for delivery, while others do more of the preparatory work or contribute in other ways.
- Lay out clearly what each member's responsibilities are in preparing the presentation. Try to define roles that complement one another; otherwise, you may end up with overlap in one area and no coverage in another.
- Allow enough time for practice. Though each member can practise on his or her own part alone, schedule practice sessions for the entire presentation as a group. This will help you (a) work on transitions, (b) make sure the order of presenters is effective, and (c) time the length of the presentation.

DELIVERING AN ORAL PRESENTATION

When you create a document to be read privately, you not only consider the information you present, you also think about DOCUMENT DESIGN— the "how" of presentation for written documents (Chapter 37). When preparing an oral presentation, you also must consider how—not just what—you present. In oral presentations, the "how" is called *delivery*.

43f How do I choose an oral presentation style?

Presentation style is the way you deliver your speech: You may memorize it, read it, or speak *extemporaneously*—that is, without a text. (An extemporaneous speech can be created on the spur of the moment or carefully prepared, but it is delivered free of text, possibly using notes but never reading from them word by word.)

Memorized speeches often sound unnatural, and there is no safety net if you forget a word or sentence. Fortunately, memorization is not necessary in most academic and professional speaking situations.

Reading a presentation often bores listeners, and it can create an uncomfortable barrier between you and your audience. If you must read your speech, remember to make frequent eye contact with the audience, vary your tone of voice, and use appropriate gestures.

Presenting extemporaneously is usually your best choice. You are well prepared, and you have an outline or index cards to keep you focused. A presentation outline, which isn't the same as an organizational outline (43d), lists the major points you want to make, but the language you use to develop these points is "of the moment." The outline or index cards will need to include the names of any sources so that you can correctly cite their contributions to your speech. Box 185 gives specific help in preparing the two main types of presentation aids. Choose whichever feels more comfortable to you.

BOX 185 SUMMARY

Preparing oral presentation aids

For a presentation outline, follow the same style as the organizational outline (Box 183 in 43d) with these changes:

Using Sheets of Paper

- Type the outline in a large font so that you can glance at it easily without holding the pages close to your face.
- Number or label in large handwriting the sequence of your pages so that you don't lose your place.
- Clearly label or separate the introduction, supporting material, and conclusion. Perhaps use different fonts or colours for each section.
- Try to enter only key words and phrases as cues to what you want to say. Otherwise, you can end up keying in a word-for-word script of your presentation.
- Highlight key points you cannot afford to skip—small sticky notes can help as long as they don't cover your words.
- Write in visual cues to remind you to pause, use a visual, emphasize a point by gesture and/or voice, and so on. →

Preparing oral presentation aids (*continued*)

■ Use only one side of each sheet of paper so that you avoid flipping pages over, which can look like shuffling paper aimlessly.

Using Index Cards

■ Follow the advice above for using separate sheets of paper.

■ Choose a suitable size of index card—not too small.

■ Use only one side of each card.

■ Use only one index card per major point. For minor points, use another card that you number in relation to the card with the main point.

■ Use various colours of pen on white cards or different card colours to separate the introduction, supporting material, and conclusion of your speech.

43g How do I vary my voice and use nonverbal communication in my speech?

Your voice is the focus of the presentation, so be aware of it and project. If you are unsure of your volume, it is fine to ask the audience if they can hear you. Articulate—speak slowly and deliberately—but not so slowly that there is no rhythm or pace to the speech. Change the tone of your voice for emphasis and clarity. Insert planned pauses. In general, try to sound like yourself, but in an intensified version. Remember that if you are using a microphone, you do not need to raise your voice.

Eye contact is the most important nonverbal communication tool. Try to make eye contact with your audience immediately. If you have to walk up to a podium, do not begin speaking before you are standing squarely behind the podium, looking directly at the audience. Eye contact communicates confidence.

Your body language can either add to or detract from your overall message. Use appropriate facial expressions to mirror the emotions of your message. Gestures, if not overdone, contribute to your message by adding emphasis. The best gestures appear natural rather than forced or timed. If you are unsure of where to place your hands, rest them on the podium—and try not to fidget. Body movements need to be kept to a minimum and used in pace with the speech. Step forward or backward to indicate transitions, but avoid rocking from side to side. And, of course, dress appropriately for your audience and the type of event.

43h How do I incorporate multimedia into my oral presentation?

Multimedia elements such as visual aids, sound, and video can make ideas clear, understandable, and engaging, but they can never take the place of a well-prepared speech. They add interest to an already interesting topic. They reinforce key ideas by providing illustrations or concrete images for the audience, and if done well, they can make long explanations unnecessary and add to your credibility.

43h.1 Using traditional visual aids

For all the suggestions in this list, remember one overriding principle: Always make text or graphics large enough to be easily read.

- **Posters.** Posters can dramatize a point, often with colour or images. Make sure the poster is large enough for everyone in your audience to see it.
- **Dry-erase boards.** These boards are preferable to chalkboards because their colours are visually appealing. Use them to emphasize an occasional technical word or to do a rough sketch when illustrating a process.
- **Transparencies.** Transparencies used with an overhead projector combine the advantages of posters and dry-erase boards. You can prepare transparencies in advance and then write on them for emphasis.
- **Handouts.** Handouts are preferable to other visual aids when the topic calls for a longer text or when you want to give your audience something to take home. Short and simple handouts work best during a presentation; save longer and more detailed ones for the end, if possible. If you distribute handouts during the speech, wait until everyone has one before you begin (or resume) speaking, and do not distribute a handout until you are ready to discuss it. Always include DOCUMENTATION information for your SOURCE on the handout, if it's other than your own writing or graphic (see Chapters 34–36 for specific guidelines for using various DOCUMENTATION STYLES). Using handouts has the advantage of your not having to rely on other technologies, which might be missing or broken.
- **Slides.** The development of digital technologies such as PowerPoint has made photographic slides less common. However, if you use them, make sure before your speech that the slides are in the proper order and correctly placed (upright) in the machine.

43h.2 Using electronic media

Computer technologies have opened a new range of possibilities for supplementing oral presentations. Generally, ask your instructor if it's permissible to use electronic media, and make sure you have the needed equipment. However, never rely too much on these aids, and make sure that they enhance your presentation rather than detract from it. Especially problematic is your spending so much time developing multimedia materials that you don't concentrate on actually writing your presentation.

PowerPoint slides

PowerPoint, the most widely used presentation software, is a computer program that can create and project digital slides. (Some other presentation software programs are Aldus Persuasion, Compel, and WordPerfect Presentations.) PowerPoint slides consist of words, images, or combinations of both, and they can sometimes include sound or movies. To create and project digital slides you need a computer with a PowerPoint program or similar software; an LCD projector connected to your computer; and a screen.

The principles of document and Web page design apply to PowerPoint and other presentation software. You want each slide to have unity, variety, balance, and emphasis (37b). Most important, you don't want to present so much information on each slide that your audience pays more attention to reading it than to listening to you or, worse, feels insulted that you are going over material they can clearly figure out for themselves. The major complaint people make about PowerPoint presentations concerns speakers who simply read large amounts of text from slides. If you do that, your audience will quickly—and rightfully—become bored.

An effective PowerPoint slide is clearly titled and well balanced, presenting all text concisely and in logical order. Graphics should be informative as well as attractive, to capture attention. Everything on the slide should be large and clear enough for the audience to see easily.

Sound and video clips

A brief sound file (for example, a poet's reading or a politician's speech) or a video clip (an excerpt from a news story or footage you have shot) can occasionally help you illustrate a point during your presentation. These clips can be as simple as a CD or a DVD or as complicated as *.wav* or Quicktime files on a computer. However, if you use any of them, be sure to follow three important principles. First, keep sound and video clips brief. Second, make sure they're vital to your presentation. Third, be absolutely sure the clips greatly enhance your presentation. Otherwise, they can diminish the impact of your message by causing the audience to wonder why, except for the show of it, you've used the clips. Media should enhance your presentation, not substitute for it. Omit anything that doesn't directly relate to your thesis and purpose.

43h.3 Planning for multimedia

Nothing is more frustrating to you or annoying to your audience than serious technical problems. You need to make sure all of your visual aids and multimedia will work well—and you need a backup plan. Rehearse carefully and often with the technology you need so that your use of the technology is seamless during your presentation.

If you are making a PowerPoint presentation, you need to double-check the in-place computer system before you begin. Hooking your computer up to an LCD projector can be tricky, so make sure you practise with the actual equipment before your presentation. If possible, bring your own laptop in case the software or a specific computer is not compatible with the disk that contains your slides. Presentation software can be very impressive, but you should consider it only an enhancement. Your information—spoken with clarity and authority—is the main attraction.

Arrive early to double-check that any technology you're planning to use is available and working, even if you've practised with it beforehand. Learn how to turn on computers, video players, and projectors. Learn how to raise or lower the screen, if you're using one, and how to dim the lights. Box 186 offers tips on using visuals.

BOX 186   SUMMARY

Tips for using visuals in oral presentations

- Make visuals large enough for the entire audience to see.
- Use simple layouts or drawings, nothing cluttered or overly complicated.
- Practise with the visuals you plan to use.
- Keep your focus on the audience, not the visual aid.
- Let the visuals enhance your speech, not distract your audience from your message.
- Never overwhelm your audience and your message by using too many visuals.
- Proofread your written visuals as carefully as you would the final draft of an essay or research paper.
- Whenever possible, arrive early to check the equipment.

43i   What can I do to practise for my oral presentation?

Good delivery requires practice. In preparing to speak, figure in enough time for at least four complete run-throughs of your entire presentation, using visuals if you have them. When you practise, keep the following in mind:

- Practise conveying ideas rather than particular words so that your tone does not become stilted.
- Time yourself and cut or expand material accordingly.

- Practise in front of a mirror or videotape yourself. As you watch yourself, notice your gestures. Do you look natural? Do you make nervous movements that you were not aware of as you spoke?
- Practise in front of a friend. Ask for constructive feedback by posing these questions: What was my main point? Did the points flow? Did any information seem to come from out of nowhere or not fit in with the information around it? Did I sound natural? Did I look natural? How did the visuals add to my message?

If you suffer from stage fright—as almost everyone does—remember that the better prepared and rehearsed you are, the less frightened you will be. Keep in mind that your aim is to communicate, not perform. Box 187 suggests ways to overcome physical signs of anxiety.

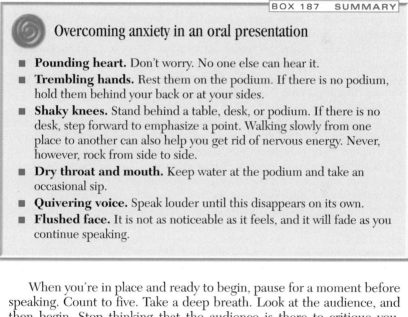

BOX 187   SUMMARY

Overcoming anxiety in an oral presentation

- **Pounding heart.** Don't worry. No one else can hear it.
- **Trembling hands.** Rest them on the podium. If there is no podium, hold them behind your back or at your sides.
- **Shaky knees.** Stand behind a table, desk, or podium. If there is no desk, step forward to emphasize a point. Walking slowly from one place to another can also help you get rid of nervous energy. Never, however, rock from side to side.
- **Dry throat and mouth.** Keep water at the podium and take an occasional sip.
- **Quivering voice.** Speak louder until this disappears on its own.
- **Flushed face.** It is not as noticeable as it feels, and it will fade as you continue speaking.

When you're in place and ready to begin, pause for a moment before speaking. Count to five. Take a deep breath. Look at the audience, and then begin. Stop thinking that the audience is there to critique you. Instead, concentrate on delivering your message so that you appear sincere and confident.

PREFACE FOR ESL STUDENTS

If you ever worry about your English writing, you have much in common with me and with many college and university students. The good news is that errors you make demonstrate the reliable truth that you are moving normally through the unavoidable, necessary stages of second-language development. Unfortunately, there are no shortcuts. The process is like learning to play a musical instrument. Few people learn to play fluently without making lots of errors.

What can you do to progress as quickly as possible from one writing stage to another? I recommend that you start by bringing to mind what school writing is like in your first language. Specifically, recall how ideas are presented in your written native language, especially when information is explained or a topic requires a logical argument.

Most college and university writing in Canada is very direct in tone and straightforward in structure. In a typical essay or research paper, the reader expects to find a THESIS STATEMENT that clearly states the central message of the entire piece of writing. Usually, the thesis statement falls in the first paragraph, or in a longer piece, perhaps in the second paragraph. Then, each paragraph that follows relates in content directly to the essay's thesis statement. Also, each paragraph begins with a TOPIC SENTENCE that contains the main point of the paragraph, and the rest of the paragraph supports the point made in the topic sentence. This support consists of RENNS (4f) that provide specific details. The final paragraph brings the piece of writing to a logical conclusion.

Writing structures typical of your first language most likely differ from those in this country. Always honour your culture's writing traditions and structures, for they reflect the richness of your heritage. At the same time, try to adapt and to practise the academic writing style characteristic of English-speaking Canada. Later, some instructors might encourage you to practise other, more subtle English writing styles that allow greater liberty in organization and expression.

Distinctive variations in school writing styles among people of different cultures and language groups have interested researchers for the past thirty years. Such research is ongoing, so scholars hesitate to generalize. Even so, interesting differences have been observed. Many Spanish-speaking students feel that English-language school writing in North America lacks grace because writers do not include any wide-ranging background material: in fact, writing teachers here usually say that such broad introductory material is wordy or not really relevant to the central message. Japanese school writing customarily begins with references to nature. In some African nations, a ceremonial, formal opening is expected as an expression of respect for the reader. As a person, I greatly enjoy discovering the rich variations in the writing traditions of the many cultures of the world. As a college teacher, however, my responsibility is to explain the expectations in this culture.

If you were in my class, I would say "Welcome!" and then ask you to teach me about writing in your first language. Using that knowledge, I would respectfully teach you the approach to writing that is used here so that I could do my best to help you succeed in a North American academic program.

Lynn Quitman Troyka

Part Seven

Writing When English Is a Second Language

Visit the Troyka Web site at
http://www.pearsoned.ca/troyka for

- additional grammar practice
- chapter exercises
- other resources, including an e-book version of this text

Chapter 44

Singulars and Plurals

44a What are count and noncount nouns?

Count nouns name items that can be counted: *a radio* or *radios, a street* or *streets, an idea* or *ideas, a fingernail* or *fingernails.* Count nouns can be SINGULAR or PLURAL.

Noncount nouns name things that are thought of as a whole and not split into separate, countable parts: *rice, knowledge, traffic.* There are two important rules to remember about noncount nouns: (1) They are never preceded by *a* or *an,* and (2) they are never plural. Box 188 lists eleven categories of uncountable items, giving examples in each category.

BOX 188   SUMMARY

Uncountable items

GROUPS OF SIMILAR ITEMS	clothing, equipment, furniture, jewellery, junk, luggage, mail, money, stuff, traffic, vocabulary
ABSTRACTIONS	advice, equality, fun, health, ignorance, information, knowledge, news, peace, pollution, respect
LIQUIDS	blood, coffee, gasoline, water
GASES	air, helium, oxygen, smog, smoke, steam
MATERIALS	aluminum, cloth, cotton, ice, wood
FOOD	beef, bread, butter, macaroni, meat, pork
PARTICLES OR GRAINS	dirt, dust, hair, rice, salt, wheat
SPORTS, GAMES, ACTIVITIES	chess, homework, housework, reading, sailing, soccer
LANGUAGES	Arabic, Chinese, Japanese, Spanish
FIELDS OF STUDY OF STUDY	biology, computer science, history, literature, math
EVENTS IN NATURE	electricity, heat, humidity, moonlight, rain, snow, sunshine, thunder, weather

Some nouns can be countable or uncountable, depending on their meaning in a sentence. Most of these nouns name things that can be meant either individually or as "wholes" made up of individual parts.

COUNT You have **a hair** on your sleeve. [In this sentence, *hair* is meant as an individual, countable item.]

NONCOUNT Kioko has black **hair.** [In this sentence, all the strands of *hair* are referred to as a whole.]

COUNT **The rains** were late last year. [In this sentence, *rains* is meant as individual, countable occurrences of rain.]

NONCOUNT **The rain** is soaking the garden. [In this sentence, all the droplets of *rain* are referred to as a whole, similarly to Box 188's particles.]

When you are editing your writing (see Chapter 3), be sure that you have not added a plural *-s* to any noncount nouns, for they are always singular in form.

👁 **ALERT:** Be sure to use a singular verb with any noncount noun that functions as a SUBJECT in a CLAUSE. 👁

To check whether a noun is count or noncount, look it up in a dictionary that makes the distinction. For example, the *Dictionary of American English* (Heinle & Heinle) indicates count nouns with [C] and noncount nouns with [U] (for "uncountable"). Nouns that have both count and noncount meanings are marked [C;U].

44b How do I use determiners with singular and plural nouns?

Determiners, also called *expressions of quantity,* are used to tell how much or how many with reference to NOUNS. Other names for determiners include *limiting adjectives, noun markers,* and ARTICLES. (For information about articles—the words *a, an,* and *the*—see Chapter 45.)

Choosing the right determiner with a noun can depend on whether the noun is NONCOUNT or COUNT (see 44a). For count nouns, you must also decide whether the noun is singular or plural. Box 189 lists many determiners and the kinds of nouns that they can accompany.

BOX 189   SUMMARY

Determiners to use with count and noncount nouns

Group 1: Determiners for Singular Count Nouns

With every **singular count noun,** always use one of the determiners listed in Group 1.

a, an, the	**a house**	**an egg**	**the car**
one, any, some, *every, each, either,* *neither, another,* *the other*	**any house**	**each egg**	**another car**
my, our, your, his, *her, its, their,* nouns with *'s* or *s'*	**your house**	**its egg**	**Connie's car**
this, that	**this house**	**that egg**	**this car**
one, no, the first, *the second,* etc.	**one house**	**no egg**	**the fifth car**

Group 2: Determiners for Plural Count Nouns

All the determiners listed in Group 2 can be used with **plural count nouns.** Plural count nouns can also be used without determiners, as discussed in section 45b.

the	**the bicycles**	**the rooms**	**the ideas**
some, any, both, *many, more, most,* *few, fewer, the* *fewest, a lot of,* *a number of, other,* *several, all, all the*	**some bicycles**	**many rooms**	**all ideas**
my, our, your, his, *her, its, their,* nouns with *'s* or *s'*	**our bicycles**	**her rooms**	**students' ideas**
these, those	**these bicycles**	**those rooms**	**these ideas**
no, two, three, etc.; *the first, the second,* *the third,* etc.	**no bicycles**	**four rooms**	**the first ideas**

Group 3: Determiners for Noncount Nouns

All the determiners listed in Group 3 can be used with **noncount nouns** (always singular). Noncount nouns can also be used without determiners, as discussed in section 45b.

→

Determiners to use with count and noncount nouns (*continued*)

the	the rice	the rain	the pride
some, any, much, more, most, other, the other, little, less, the least, enough, all, all the, a lot of	enough rice	a lot of rain	more pride
my, our, your, his, her, its, their, nouns with '*s* or *s*'	their rice	India's rain	your pride
this, that	this rice	that rain	this pride
no, the first, the second, the third, etc.	no rice	the first rain	no pride

👁 **ALERT:** The phrases *a few* and *a little* convey the meaning "some": *I have **a few** rare books* means "I have *some* rare books." *They are worth **a little** money* means "They are worth *some* money."

Without the word *a*, the words *few* and *little* convey the meaning "almost none": *I have **few** [or very few] books* means "I have *almost no* books." *They are worth **little** money* means "They are worth *almost no* money." 👁

44c How do I use *one of*, nouns as adjectives, and *states* in names or titles?

One of *constructions*

One of constructions include *one of the* and a NOUN or *one of* followed by an ADJECTIVE-noun combination (*one of my hats, one of those ideas*). Always use a plural noun as the OBJECT when you use *one of the* with a noun or *one of* with an adjective-noun combination.

> **NO**   *One of the **reason** to live here is the beach.*
> **YES** *One of the **reasons** to live here is the beach.*

> **NO**   *One of her best **friend** has moved away.*
> **YES** *One of her best **friends** has moved away.*

The VERB in these constructions is always singular because it agrees with the singular *one*, not with the plural noun: ***One** of the most important inventions of the twentieth century **is** [not are] television.*

For advice about verb forms that go with *one of the . . . who* constructions, see section 10l.

Nouns used as adjectives

ADJECTIVES in English do not have plural forms. When you use an adjective with a PLURAL NOUN, make the noun plural but not the adjective: *the **green** [not greens] leaves.* Be especially careful when you use a word as a MODIFIER that can also function as a noun.

> The bird's wingspan is 25 centimetres. [*Centimetres* is functioning as a noun.]
> The bird has a 25-centimetre wingspan. [*Centimetre* is functioning as a modifier.]

Do not add -*s* (or -*es*) to the adjective even when it is modifying a plural noun or pronoun.

> **NO** Many **Canadians** students are basketball fans.
> **YES** Many **Canadian** students are basketball fans.

Names or titles that include the word states

States is a plural word. However, names such as *United States* or *Organization of American States* refer to singular things—one country and one organization, even though made up of many states. When *states* is part of a name or title referring to one thing, the name is a SINGULAR NOUN and therefore requires a SINGULAR VERB.

> **NO** The **United States have** a large entertainment industry.
> **NO** The **United State has** a large entertainment industry.
> **YES** The **United States has** a large entertainment industry.

How do I use nouns with irregular plurals?

Some English nouns have irregularly spelled plurals. In addition to those discussed in section 22c, here are others that often cause difficulties.

Plurals of foreign nouns and other irregular nouns

Whenever you are unsure whether a noun is plural, look it up in a dictionary. If no plural is given for a singular noun, add -*s* to form the plural.

Many nouns from other languages that are used unchanged in English have only one plural. If two plurals are listed in the dictionary, look carefully for differences in meaning. Some words, for example, keep the plural form from the original language for scientific usage and have another, English-form plural for nonscientific contexts: *formula, formulae, formulas; appendix, appendices, appendixes; index, indices, indexes; medium, media, mediums; cactus, cacti, cactuses; fungus, fungi, funguses.*

Words from Latin that end in *-is* in their singular form become plural by substituting *-es: parenthesis, parentheses; thesis, theses; oasis, oases.*

Other words

Medical terms for diseases involving an inflammation end in *-itis: tonsillitis, appendicitis.* They are always singular.

The word *news*, although it ends in *s*, is always singular: *The **news is** encouraging.* The words *people, police,* and *clergy* are always plural even though they do not end in *s: The **police are** prepared.*

EXERCISE 44-1

Consulting all sections of this chapter, select the correct choice from the words in parentheses and write it in the blank.

> EXAMPLE Statistics Canada has been monitoring Canadians' (spending, spendings) <u>spending</u> in the postindustrial economy.

1. As people's (spendings, spending) _____ power increases, they devote a changing proportion of their (wealth, wealths)_____ to different categories of purchases.
2. The necessities of life—food, clothing, and shelter—took up more than half of (Canadian, Canadians) _____ consumers' spending in 1961, but today they take up only 40 percent.
3. Anyone who looks will see instantly that this is not because Canadians eat less (food, foods) _____ than in 1961 or that (much, many) _____ people are paying less rent than before.
4. Some may argue that we wear worse (clothings, clothing) _____ than in 1961, but those people are not referring to the number of shirts hanging in our closets or to the (qualities, quality) _____ of the fabrics; they are criticizing our taste.
5. One of the main (reason, reasons) _____ for the change in our spending is the simple fact that we now have more (moneys, money) _____ and therefore we have more opportunity to spend on luxuries, especially (consumer, consumers) _____ electronics and entertainment.

EXERCISE 44-2

Consulting all sections of this chapter, select the correct choice from the words in parentheses and write it in the blank.

> EXAMPLE A work that the British mathematician George Boole published in 1847 has had remarkable (influence, influences) <u>influence</u>.

(1) George Boole had the (inspiration, inspirations) _____ to link mathematical notation to the rules of human (thought, thoughts) _____ (2) He noticed that nearly every (statement, statements)_____ can be expressed in a kind of algebra with the three logical operators AND, OR, and NOT. (3) After Boole's death, (much, many) _____ philosophers adopted similar systems to analyze (argument, arguments) _____ as either true or false. (4) In 1938, an engineering student named Claude Shannon wrote one of the most important master's (thesis, theses) _____ ever. (5) Shannon realized that when the categories *true* and *false* are stated as *on* and *off,* Boolean algebra can be used to run the (switching, switchings) _____ processes of electronic circuits. (6) This discovery has had several important (application, applications) _____, especially in computers. (7) Today, one of the (way, ways) _____ in which we are reminded of Boole is when we perform a "Boolean search" on the Web: This means that we refine the search topic using Boole's logical operators AND, OR, and NOT.

Chapter 45

Articles

45a How do I use *a*, *an*, or *the* with singular count nouns?

The words *a* and *an* are called **indefinite articles.** The word *the* is the **definite article.** Articles are one type of DETERMINER. (For more on determiners, see section 7f; for other determiners, see Box 189 in section 44b.) Articles signal that a NOUN will follow and that any MODIFIERS between the article and the noun refer to that noun.

a chair	**the** computer
a brown chair	**the** teacher's computer
a cold, metal chair	**the** lightning-fast computer

Every time you use a singular count noun, a COMMON NOUN that names one countable item, the noun requires some kind of determiner; see Group 1 in Box 189 (in 44b) for a list. To choose between *a* or *an* and *the*, you need to determine whether the noun is **specific** or **nonspecific.** A noun is considered specific when anyone who reads your writing can understand exactly and specifically to what item the noun is referring. If a noun refers to any of a number of identical items, it is nonspecific.

For nonspecific singular count nouns, use *a* (or *an*). When a singular noun is specific, use *the* or some other determiner. Box 190 can help you decide when a singular count noun is specific and therefore requires *the*.

👁 **ALERT:** Use *an* before words that begin with a vowel sound. Use *a* before words that begin with a consonant sound. Go by the sound, not the spelling. For example, words that begin with *h* or *u* can have either a vowel or a consonant sound. Make the choice based on the sound of the first word after the article, even if that word is not the noun.

an idea	**a g**ood idea
an umbrella	**a u**seless umbrella
an honour	**a h**istory book 👁

771

One common exception affects Rule 3 in Box 190. A noun may still require *a* (or *an*) after the first use if more information is added between the article and the noun: *I bought **a sweater** today. It was **a** (not *the*) **red sweater.** (Your audience has been introduced to *a sweater* but not *a red sweater,* so *red sweater* is not yet specific in this context and cannot take *the.*) Other information may make the noun specific so that *the* is correct. For example, *It was **the red sweater that I saw in the store yesterday*** uses *the* because the *that* CLAUSE makes specific which red sweater is meant.

BOX 190   SUMMARY

When a singular count noun is specific and requires *the*

- **Rule 1: A noun is specific and requires *the* when it names something unique or generally and unambiguously known.**

  The sun has risen above **the horizon.** [Because there is only one *sun* and only one *horizon*, these nouns are specific in the context of this sentence.]

- **Rule 2: A noun is specific and requires *the* when it names something used in a representative or abstract sense.**

  I would like to know who chose **the unicorn** to be **the symbolic** animal on Canada's coat of arms. [Because *unicorn* and *symbolic animal* are representative references rather than references to a particular unicorn or animal, they are specific nouns in the context of this sentence.]

- **Rule 3: A noun is specific and requires *the* when it names something defined elsewhere in the same sentence or in an earlier sentence.**

  The ship *St. Roch* was the first vessel to navigate the Northwest Passage in both directions. [The name *St. Roch* denotes a specific ship.]

  The carpet in my bedroom is new. [*In my bedroom* defines exactly which carpet is meant, so *carpet* is a specific noun in this context.]

  I have **a computer** in my office. **The computer** is often broken. [*Computer* is not specific in the first sentence, so it uses *a*. In the second sentence, *computer* has been made specific by the first sentence, so it uses *the*.]

- **Rule 4: A noun is specific and requires *the* when it names something that can be inferred from the context.**

  Monday, I had to call **the technician** to fix my computer again. [*A technician* would be any of a number of individuals; *the technician* implies the same person has been called before, and so it is specific in this context.]

45b How do I use articles with plural nouns and with noncount nouns?

With plural nouns and NONCOUNT NOUNS, you must decide whether to use *the* or to use no article at all. (For guidelines about using DETERMINERS other than articles with nouns, see Box 189 in 44b.) What you learned in 45a about NONSPECIFIC and SPECIFIC NOUNS can help you choose between using *the* or using no article. Box 190 in 45a explains when a singular count noun's meaning is specific and calls for *the*. Plural nouns and noncount nouns with specific meanings usually use *the* in the same circumstances. However, a plural noun or a noncount noun with a general or nonspecific meaning usually does not use *the*.

> Geraldo grows **flowers** but not **vegetables** in his garden. He is thinking about planting **corn** sometime. [three nonspecific nouns]

Plural nouns

A plural noun's meaning may be specific because it is widely known.

> **The oceans** are being damaged by pollution. [Because there is only one possible meaning for *oceans*—the oceans on the Earth—it is correct to use *the*. This example is related to Rule 1 in Box 190.]

A plural noun's meaning may also be made specific by a word, PHRASE, or CLAUSE in the same sentence.

> Geraldo sold **the daisies from last year's garden** to the florist. [Because the phrase *from last year's garden* makes *daisies* specific, *the* is correct. This example is related to Rule 3 in Box 190.]

A plural noun's meaning usually becomes specific by its use in an earlier sentence.

> Geraldo planted **tulips** this year. **The tulips** will bloom in May. [*Tulips* is used in a general sense in the first sentence, without *the*. Because the first sentence makes *tulips* specific, *the tulips* is correct in the second sentence. This example is related to Rule 3 in Box 190.]

A plural noun's meaning may be made specific by the context.

> Geraldo fertilized **the bulbs** when he planted them last October. [In the context of the sentences about tulips, *bulbs* is understood as a synonym for *tulips,* which makes it specific and calls for *the*. This example is related to Rule 4 in Box 190.]

Noncount nouns

Noncount nouns are always singular in form (see 44a). Like plural nouns, noncount nouns use either *the* or no article. When a noncount noun's meaning is specific, use *the* before it. If its meaning is general or nonspecific, do not use *the*.

Kalinda served us **rice.** She flavoured **the rice** with curry. [*Rice* is a noncount noun. By the second sentence, *rice* has become specific, so *the* is used. This example is related to Rule 3 in Box 190.]

Kalinda served us **the rice that she had flavoured with curry.** [*Rice* is a noncount noun. *Rice* is made specific by the clause *that she had flavoured with curry*, so *the* is used. This example is related to Rule 3 in Box 190.]

Generalizations with plural or noncount nouns

Rule 2 in Box 190 tells you to use *the* with singular count nouns that carry general meaning. With GENERALIZATIONS using plural or noncount nouns, omit *the*.

> NO **The tulips** are **the flowers** that grow from **the bulbs.**
>
> YES **Tulips** are **flowers** that grow from **bulbs.**

> NO **The dogs** require more care than **the cats** do.
>
> YES **Dogs** require more care than **cats** do.

45c How do I use *the* with proper nouns and with gerunds?

Proper nouns

PROPER NOUNS name specific people, places, or things (see 7b). Most proper nouns do not require ARTICLES: *We visited **Lake Rossignol** with **Asha** and **Larry**.* As shown in Box 191, however, certain types of proper nouns do require *the*.

BOX 191   SUMMARY

Proper nouns that use *the*

- **Nouns with the pattern *the* . . . *of* . . .**

  the Dominion **of** Canada   **the** eleventh **of** November

  the Republic **of** Mexico   **the** University **of** Paris

- **Plural proper nouns**

  the United Arab Emirates

  the Johnsons

  the Rocky Mountains [*but* Mount Fuji]

  the Vancouver Canucks

  the Falkland Islands [*but* Baffin Island]

  the Great Lakes [*but* Lake Superior]

  →

> **Proper nouns that use *the*** (*continued*)
>
> - **Collective proper nouns (nouns that name a group)**
>   **the** Modern Language Association
>   **the** Society of Friends
> - **Some (but not all) geographical features and regions**
>   **the** Amazon   **the** Gobi Desert   **the** Indian Ocean
>   **the** Beauce, **the** Gaspé [Quebec]
> - **A few countries and cities**
>   **the** Congo   **the** Sudan   **the** Netherlands
>   **The** Pas   **the** Hague   **the** Czech Republic

Gerunds

GERUNDS are PRESENT PARTICIPLES (the *-ing* form of VERBS) used as nouns: ***Skating*** *is challenging*. Gerunds are usually not preceded by *the*.

> NO **The constructing** new bridges is necessary to improve traffic flow.
>
> YES **Constructing** new bridges is necessary to improve traffic flow.

Use *the* before a gerund when two conditions are met: (1) The gerund is used in a specific sense (see 45a), and (2) the gerund does not have a DIRECT OBJECT.

> NO **The designing fabric** is a fine art. [*Fabric* is a direct object of *designing*, so *the* should not be used.]
>
> YES **Designing** fabric is a fine art. [*Designing* is a gerund, so *the* is not used.]
>
> YES **The designing of** fabric is a fine art. [*The* is used because *fabric* is the object of the preposition *of* and *designing* is meant in a specific sense.]

EXERCISE 45-1

Consulting all sections of this chapter, select the correct article from the words in parentheses and write it in the blank.

EXAMPLE   Be forewarned: (A, An, The) <u>The</u> camera as we know it may soon be obsolete.

1. At (a, an, the) _____ dawn of (a, an, the) _____ twenty-first century comes (a, an, the) _____ invention so advanced that it may rid (a, an, the) _____ industrialized world of every camera that has come before it.

2. (A, An, The) _____ digital camera, which allows photos to appear on (a, an, the) _____ computer monitor, takes up virtual space, not physical space.

3. As (a, an, the) _____ result, if you see (a, an, the) _____ bad photo on (a, an, the) _____ screen, you can simply erase (a, an, the) _____ poor photo to make room for (a, an, the) _____ new one.

4. With this new technology, (a, an, the) _____ aunt can e-mail photos to her niece or nephew, or she can post photos to (a, an, the) _____ Web page.

5. Digital cameras allow people to alter (a, an, the) _____ appearance of people or things, which, according to many critics, is (a, an, the) _____ chief disadvantage of (a, an, the) _____ digital camera.

EXERCISE 45-2

Consulting all sections of this chapter, decide which of the words in parentheses is correct and write it in the blank. If no article is needed, leave the blank empty.

EXAMPLE If you are (a, an, the) a student from (a, an, the) a foreign country, what can you do to learn about (a, an, the) the Canadian way of life?

1. Some people say that (a, an, the) _____ best thing (a, an, the) _____ newcomer can do to discover (a, an, the) _____ new culture is to watch (a, an, the) _____ local television programs.

2. (A, An, The) _____ entertainment that Canadians like to watch on television reveals much about (a, an, the) _____ culture in this country.

3. News and public affairs are also important, which is why it is (a, an, the) _____ good idea to subscribe to (a, an, the) _____ newspaper or (a, an, the) _____ magazine.

4. (A, An, The) _____ student who wants to learn more about Canada may also consider finding (a, an, the) _____ activities to do outside (a, an, the) _____ walls of (a, an, the) _____ campus—tutoring or volunteering, perhaps.

5. Finally, (a, an, the) _____ excellent way to soak up (a, an, the) _____ culture is to live with (a, an, the) _____ local family, as long as (a, an, the) _____ family involves (a, an, the) _____ student in its activities.

Chapter 46

Word Order

46a How do I understand standard and inverted word order in sentences?

In **standard word order,** the most common pattern for DECLARATIVE SENTENCES in English, the SUBJECT comes before the VERB. (To understand these concepts more fully, review sections 7l through 7p.)

SUBJECT   VERB

That book   was heavy.

With **inverted word order,** the MAIN VERB or an AUXILIARY VERB comes before the subject. The most common use of inverted word order in English is in forming DIRECT QUESTIONS. Questions that can be answered with a yes or no begin with a form of *be* used as a main verb, with an auxiliary verb (*be, do, have*), or with a MODAL AUXILIARY (*can, should, will,* and others; see Chapter 49).

Questions that can be answered with a yes or no

MAIN VERB   SUBJECT

Was   that book heavy?

AUXILIARY VERB   SUBJECT   MAIN VERB

Have   you   heard the noise?

MODAL AUXILIARY VERB   SUBJECT   MAIN VERB

Can   you   lift the book?

To form a yes-or-no question with a verb other than *be* as the main verb and when there is no auxiliary or modal as part of a VERB PHRASE, use the appropriate form of the auxiliary verb *do*.

A question that begins with a question-forming word like *why, when, where,* or *how* cannot be answered with a yes or no: **Why** *did the book fall?* Some kind of information must be provided to answer such a question; the answer cannot be simply yes or no because the question is not "*Did* the book fall?" Information on *why* it fell is needed: for example, *It was too heavy for me.*

Information questions: Inverted order

Most information questions follow the same rules of inverted word order as yes-or-no questions.

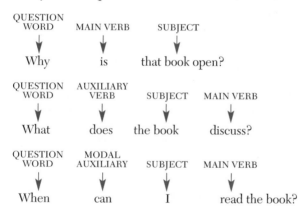

Information questions: Standard order

When *who* or *what* functions as the subject in a question, use standard word order.

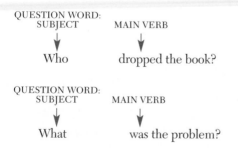

👁 **ALERT:** When a question has more than one auxiliary verb, put the subject after the first auxiliary verb.

FIRST AUXILIARY	SUBJECT	SECOND AUXILIARY	MAIN VERB
↓	↓	↓	↓
Would	you	have	replaced the book? 👁

The same rules apply to emphatic exclamations: ***Was*** *that book heavy!* ***Did*** *she enjoy that book!*

Negatives

When you use negatives such *as never, hardly ever, seldom, rarely, not only,* or *nor* to start a CLAUSE, use inverted order. These sentence pairs show the differences, first in standard order and then in inverted order.

I have never seen a more exciting movie. [standard order]
Never have I seen a more exciting movie. [inverted order]

She is not only a talented artist **but also** an excellent musician.
Not only is she a talented artist, **but she is also** an excellent musician.

I didn't like the book, and **my husband didn't either.**
I didn't like the book, and **neither did my husband.**

👁 **ALERTS:** (1) With INDIRECT QUESTIONS, use standard word order.

NO	She asked **how did I drop** the book.
YES	She asked **how I dropped** the book.

(2) Word order deliberately inverted can be effective, when used sparingly, to create emphasis in a sentence that is neither a question nor an exclamation (also see 19e). 👁

46b How can I understand the placement of adjectives?

ADJECTIVES modify—describe or limit—NOUNS, PRONOUNS, and word groups that function as nouns (see 7f). In English, an adjective comes directly before the noun it describes. However, when more than one adjective describes the same noun, several sequences may be possible. Box 192 shows the most common order for positioning several adjectives.

BOX 192 SUMMARY

Word order for more than one adjective

1. **Determiners, if any:** *a, an, the, my, your, this, that, these, those,* and so on

2. **Expressions of order, including ordinal numbers, if any:** *first, second, third, next, last, final,* and so on

3. **Expressions of quantity, including cardinal (counting) numbers, if any:** *one, two, few, each, every, some,* and so on

4. **Adjectives of judgment or opinion, if any:** *pretty, happy, ugly, sad, interesting, boring,* and so on

5. **Adjectives of size or shape, if any:** *big, small, short, round, square,* and so on

6. **Adjectives of age or condition, if any:** *new, young, broken, dirty, shiny,* and so on

7. **Adjectives of colour, if any:** *red, green, blue,* and so on

8. **Adjectives that can also be used as nouns, if any:** *French, Protestant, metal, cotton,* and so on

9. **The noun**

1	2	3	4	5	6	7	8	9
a		few		tiny		red		ants
the	last	six					Thai	carvings
my			fine		old		oak	table

How can I understand the placement of adverbs?

ADVERBS modify—describe or limit—VERBS, ADJECTIVES, other adverbs, or entire sentences (see 7g). Adverbs may be positioned first, in the middle, or last in CLAUSES. Box 193 summarizes adverb types, what they tell about the words they modify, and where each type can be placed.

👁 **ALERT:** Do not let an adverb separate a verb from its DIRECT OBJECT or INDIRECT OBJECT. 👁

BOX 193   SUMMARY

Types of adverbs and where to position them

ADVERBS OF MANNER	■ describe *how* something is done	Nick **carefully** groomed the dog.
	■ are usually in middle or last position	Nick groomed the dog **carefully.**
ADVERBS OF TIME	■ describe *when* or *how long* about an event	**First,** he shampooed the dog.
	■ are usually in first or last position	He shampooed the dog **first.**
	■ include *just, still, already,* and similar adverbs, which are usually in middle position	He had **already** brushed the dog's coat.
ADVERBS OF FREQUENCY	■ describe *how often* an event takes place	Nick has **never** been bitten by a dog.
	■ are usually in middle position	
	■ are in first position when they modify an entire sentence (see "Sentence adverbs" below)	**Occasionally,** he is scratched while shampooing a cat.
ADVERBS OF DEGREE OR EMPHASIS	■ describe *how much* or *to what extent* about other modifiers	Nick is **extremely** calm around animals. [*Extremely* modifies *calm.*]
	■ are directly before the word they modify	
	■ include *only,* which is easy to misplace (see 14a)	
SENTENCE ADVERBS	■ modify the entire sentence rather than just one word or a few words	**Incredibly,** he was once asked to groom a rat.
	■ include transitional words and expressions (see 4g.1), as well as such expressions as *maybe, probably, possibly, fortunately, unfortunately,* and *incredibly*	
	■ are in first position	

EXERCISE 46-1

Consulting all sections of this chapter, find and correct any errors in word order.

1. For two hundred years almost, the North Pacific humpback whales have returned to the tropical waters of Hawaii.
2. Why they are returning to these particular waters year after year?
3. The humpbacks do not accidentally arrive in Hawaiian waters; they are precise extremely in searching for this specific location, where they gather to complete their breeding rituals.
4. The whales first to arrive are sighted sometime in late November, after completing a 5000-kilometre journey from the coast of British Columbia.
5. The humpbacks last to migrate to Hawaii arrive by December late or January early.

EXERCISE 46-2

Consulting all sections of this chapter, find and correct any errors in word order.

1. A beautiful few flowers began to bloom in my garden this week.
2. A neighbour asked me, "You did grow all these yourself?"
3. "Yes," I replied, "the roses are my favourite husband's, but the tulips are my favourite."
4. My neighbour, who extremely was impressed with my gardening efforts, decided to grow some flowers of her own.
5. Weeks later, as I strolled by her house, I saw her planting happily seeds from her favourite type of plant—petunias.

Chapter 47

Prepositions

Prepositions function with other words in PREPOSITIONAL PHRASES (7o). Prepositional phrases usually indicate *where* (direction or location), *how* (by what means or in what way), or *when* (at what time or how long) about the words they modify.

This chapter can help you with several uses of prepositions, which function in combination with other words in ways that are often idiomatic—that is, peculiar to the language. The meaning of an IDIOM differs from the literal meaning of each individual word. For example, the word *break* usually refers to shattering, but the sentence *Yao-Ming* **broke into** *a smile* means that a smile appeared on Yao-Ming's face. Knowing which preposition to use in a specific context takes much experience in reading, listening to, and speaking the language. A dictionary like the *Dictionary of American English* (Heinle & Heinle) or the *Oxford Advanced Learner's Dictionary* can be especially helpful when you need to find the correct preposition to use in cases not covered by this chapter. Section 47a lists many common prepositions. Section 47b discusses prepositions with some expressions of time and place. Section 47c discusses combinations of verbs and prepositions called PHRASAL VERBS. Section 47d discusses prepostions with PAST PARTICIPLES. Section 47e discusses common expressions using prepositions.

47a How can I recognize prepositions?

Box 194 lists many common prepositions.

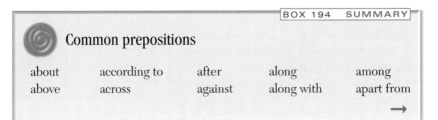

BOX 194 SUMMARY

Common prepositions

about	according to	after	along	among
above	across	against	along with	apart from

→

Common prepositions (*continued*)

around	by	in back of	on	till
as	by means of	in case of	onto	to
as for	concerning	in front of	on top of	toward
at	despite	in place of	out	under
because of	down	inside	out of	underneath
before	during	in spite of	outside	unlike
behind	except	instead of	over	until
below	except for	into	past	up
beneath	excepting	like	regarding	upon
beside	for	near	round	up to
between	from	next	since	with
beyond	in	of	through	within
but	in addition to	off	throughout	without

47b How do I use prepositions with expressions of time and place?

Box 195 shows how to use the prepositions *in, at,* and *on* to deliver some common kinds of information about time and place. The box, however, does not cover every preposition that indicates time or place, nor does it cover all uses of *in, at,* and *on.* Also, the box does not include expressions that operate outside the general rules. (Both these sentences are correct: *You ride **in** the car* and *You ride **on** the bus.*)

BOX 195   SUMMARY

Using *in, at,* and *on* to show time and place

Time

- ***in* a year or a month** (*during* is also correct but less common)
  in 1995   **in** May
- ***in* a period of time**
  in a few months (seconds, days, years)
- ***in* a period of the day**
  in the morning (afternoon, evening)
  in the daytime (morning, evening) *but* **at** night

→

Using *in, at,* and *on* to show time and place (*continued*)

- ■ *at* **a specific time or period of time**
  at noon   **at** 2:00   **at** dawn   **at** nightfall
  at takeoff (the time a plane leaves)
  at breakfast (the time a specific meal takes place)

- ■ *on* **a specific day**
  on Friday   **on** my birthday

Place

- ■ *in* **a location surrounded by something else**
  in Alberta   **in** the kitchen
  in Utah   **in** the apartment
  in downtown Bombay   **in** the bathtub

- ■ *at* **a specific location**
  at your house   **at** the bank
  at the corner of Maple Avenue and King Street

- ■ *on* **a surface**
  on page 20
  on the second floor *but* **in** the attic *or* **in** the basement
  on Wellington Street
  on the mezzanine
  on the highway

47c How do I use prepositions in phrasal verbs?

Phrasal verbs, also called *two-word verbs* and *three-word verbs,* are VERBS that combine with PREPOSITIONS to deliver their meaning. In some phrasal verbs, the verb and the preposition should not be separated by other words: ***Look at** the moon* [not ***Look** the moon **at**]*. In **separable phrasal verbs,** other words in the sentence can separate the verb and the preposition without interfering with meaning: *I **threw away** my homework* is as correct as *I **threw** my homework **away**.*

On the next page is a list of some common phrasal verbs. The ones that cannot be separated are marked with an asterisk (*).

SELECTED PHRASAL VERBS

ask out	get along with*	look into*
break down	get back	look out for*
bring about	get off*(as an	look over
call back	INTRANSITIVE)	make up
call up	go over*	run across*
drop off	hand in	speak to*
figure out	keep up with*	speak with*
fill out	leave out	throw away
fill up	look after*	throw out
find out	look around*	turn down

Position a PRONOUN OBJECT between the words of a separable phrasal verb: *I threw **it** away.* Also, you can position an object PHRASE of several words between the parts of a separable phrasal verb: *I threw **my research paper** away.* However, when the object is a CLAUSE, do not let it separate the parts of the phrasal verb: *I threw away **all the papers that I wrote last year.***

Many phrasal verbs are informal and are used more in speaking than in writing. For ACADEMIC WRITING, a more formal verb is usually more appropriate than a phrasal verb. In a research paper, for example, *propose* or *suggest* might be a better choice than *come up with.* For academic writing, acceptable phrasal verbs include *believe in, benefit from, concentrate on, consist of, depend on, dream of* (or *dream about*), *insist on, participate in, prepare for,* and *stare at.* None of these phrasal verbs can be separated.

EXERCISE 47-1

Consulting the preceding sections of this chapter and using the list of phrasal verbs in 47c, write a one- or two-paragraph description of a typical day at work or school in which you use at least five phrasal verbs. After checking a dictionary, revise your writing, substituting for the phrasal verbs any more formal verbs that might be more appropriate for academic writing.

47d How do I use prepositions with past participles?

PAST PARTICIPLES are verb forms that function as ADJECTIVES (48f). Past participles end in either *-ed* or *-d*, or in an equivalent irregular form (8d). When past participles follow the LINKING VERB *be,* it is easy to confuse them with PASSIVE verbs (8n), which have the same endings. Passive verbs describe actions. Past participles, because they act as adjectives, modify NOUNS and PRONOUNS and often describe situations and conditions. Passive verbs follow the pattern *be* + past participle + *by: The child* **was frightened by** *a snake.* An expression containing a past participle, however, can use either *be* or another linking verb, and it can be followed by either *by* or a different preposition.

- The child **seemed frightened by** snakes.
- The child **is frightened of** all snakes.

Here is a list of expressions containing past participles and the prepositions that often follow them. Look in a dictionary for others. (See 48b on using GERUNDS after some of these expressions.)

SELECTED PAST PARTICIPLE PHRASES + PREPOSITIONS

be accustomed to	be interested in
be acquainted with	be known for
be composed of	be located in
be concerned/worried about	be made of (*or* from)
be disappointed with (*or* in someone)	be married to
be discriminated against	be pleased/satisfied with
be divorced from	be prepared for
be excited about	be tired of (*or* from)
be finished/done with	

47e How do I use prepositions in expressions?

In many common expressions, different PREPOSITIONS convey great differences in meaning. For example, four prepositions can be used with the verb *agree* to create five different meanings.

agree to means "to give consent": *I cannot* **agree to** *my buying you a new car.*

agree about means "to arrive at a satisfactory understanding": *We certainly* **agree about** *your needing a car.*

agree on means "to concur": *You and the seller must* **agree on** *a price for the car.*

agree with means "to have the same opinion": *I* **agree with** *you that you need a car.*

agree with also means "to be suitable or healthful": *The idea of having such a major expense does not* **agree with** *me.*

You can find entire books filled with English expressions that include prepositions. The list on the next page shows a few that you're likely to use often.

SELECTED EXPRESSIONS WITH PREPOSITIONS

ability in	different from	involved with [*someone*]
access to	faith in	knowledge of
accustomed to	familiar with	made of
afraid of	famous for	married to
angry with *or* at	frightened by	opposed to
authority on	happy with	patient with
aware of	in charge of	proud of
based on	independent of	reason for
capable of	in favour of	related to
certain of	influence on *or* over	suspicious of
confidence in	interested in	time for
dependent on	involved in [*something*]	tired of

Chapter 48

Gerunds, Infinitives, and Participles

PARTICIPLES are verb forms (see 8b). A verb's *-ing* form is its PRESENT PARTICIPLE. The *-ed* form of a regular verb is its PAST PARTICIPLE; IRREGULAR VERBS form their past participles in various ways (for example, *bend, bent; eat, eaten; think, thought*—for a complete list, see Box 60 in section 8d). Participles can function as ADJECTIVES (*a **smiling** face, a **closed** book*).

A verb's *-ing* form can also function as a NOUN (***Sneezing** spreads colds*), which is called a GERUND. Another verb form, the INFINITIVE, can also function as a noun. An infinitive is a verb's SIMPLE or base FORM, usually preceded by the word *to* (*We want everyone **to smile***). Verb forms—participles, gerunds, and infinitives—functioning as nouns or MODIFIERS are called VERBALS, as explained in section 7e.

This chapter can help you make the right choices among verbals. Section 48a discusses gerunds and infinitives used as subjects. Section 48b discusses verbs that are followed by gerunds, not infinitives. Section 48c discusses verbs that are followed by infinitives, not gerunds. Section 48d discusses meaning changes that depend on whether certain verbs are followed by a gerund or by an infinitive. Section 48e explains that meaning does not change for certain sense verbs no matter whether they are followed by a gerund or an infinitive. Section 48f discusses differences in meaning between the present participle form and the past participle form of some modifiers.

48a How can I use gerunds and infinitives as subjects?

Gerunds are used more commonly than infinitives as subjects. Sometimes, however, either is acceptable.

> **Choosing** the right health club is important.
> **To choose** the right health club is important.

👁 **ALERT:** When a gerund or an infinitive is used alone as a subject, it is SINGULAR and requires a singular verb. When two or more gerunds or infinitives create a COMPOUND SUBJECT, they require a plural verb. (See 7l and 10e.) 👁

48b When do I use a gerund, not an infinitive, as an object?

Some VERBS must be followed by GERUNDS used as DIRECT OBJECTS. Other verbs must be followed by INFINITIVES. Still other verbs can be followed by either a gerund or an infinitive. (A few verbs change meaning depending on whether they are followed by a gerund or an infinitive; see 48d.) Box 196 lists common verbs that must be followed by gerunds, not infinitives.

Yuri **considered** *calling* [not *to call*] the mayor.
He **was having trouble** *getting* [not *to get*] a parking permit.
Yuri's boss **recommended** *taking* [not *to take*] an interpreter to the permit agency.

BOX 196   SUMMARY

Verbs and expressions that must be followed by gerunds

acknowledge	detest	mind
admit	discuss	object to
advise	dislike	postpone
anticipate	dream about	practise
appreciate	enjoy	put off
avoid	escape	quit
cannot bear	evade	recall
cannot help	favour	recommend
cannot resist	finish	regret
complain about	give up	resent
consider	have trouble	resist
consist of	imagine	risk
contemplate	include	suggest
deter from	insist on	talk about
delay	keep (on)	tolerate
deny	mention	understand

Gerund after go

The word *go* is usually followed by an infinitive: *We can* **go to see** [not *go seeing*] *a movie tonight*. Sometimes, however, *go* is followed by a gerund in phrases such as *go swimming, go fishing, go shopping*, and *go driving: I will* **go shopping** [not *go to shop*] *after work*.

Gerund after be + complement + preposition

Many common expressions use a form of the verb *be* plus a COMPLE-MENT plus a PREPOSITION. In such expressions, use a gerund, not an infinitive, after the preposition. Here is a list of some of the most frequently used expressions in this pattern.

SELECTED EXPRESSIONS USING *BE* + COMPLEMENT + PREPOSITION

be (get) accustomed to	be interested in
be angry about	be prepared for
be bored with	be responsible for
be capable of	be tired of (*or* from)
be committed to	be (get) used to
be excited about	be worried about

We **are excited about** *voting* [not *to vote*] in the next election.
They were **interested in** *hearing* [not *to hear*] the candidates' debate.

👁 **ALERT:** Always use a gerund, not an infinitive, as the object of a preposition. Be especially careful when the word *to* is functioning as a preposition in a PHRASAL VERB (see 47c): *We are committed* **to changing** [not *to change*] *the rules.* 👁

48c When do I use an infinitive, not a gerund, as an object?

Box 197 lists selected common verbs and expressions that must be followed by INFINITIVES, not GERUNDS, as OBJECTS.

She **wanted** *to go* [not *wanted going*] to the lecture.
Only three people **decided** *to question* [not *decided questioning*] the speaker.

Infinitive after be + complement

Gerunds are common in constructions that use a form of the verb *be* plus a COMPLEMENT and a PREPOSITION (see 48b). However, use an infinitive, not a gerund, when *be* plus a complement is not followed by a preposition.

We **are eager** *to go* [not *going*] camping.
I **am ready** *to sleep* [not *sleeping*] in a tent.

BOX 197   SUMMARY

Verbs and expressions that must be followed by infinitives

afford	decide	know how	refuse
agree	decline	learn	require
aim	demand	like	seem
appear	deserve	manage	struggle
arrange	do not care	mean	tend
ask	expect	need	threaten
attempt	fail	offer	volunteer
beg	force	plan	vote
cannot afford	give permission	prefer	wait
care	hesitate	prepare	want
claim	hope	pretend	would like
consent	intend	promise	

Infinitive to indicate purpose

Use an infinitive in expressions that indicate purpose: *I read a book **to learn** more about Mayan culture.* This sentence means "I read a book for the purpose of learning more about Mayan culture." *To learn* delivers the idea of purpose more concisely (see Chapter 16) than expressions such as *so that I can* or *in order to.*

Infinitive with the first, the last, the one

Use an infinitive after the expressions *the first, the last,* and *the one: Nina is the first **to arrive** [not arriving] and the last **to leave** [not leaving] every day. She's always the one **to do** the most.*

Unmarked infinitives

Infinitives used without the word *to* are called **unmarked infinitives,** or sometimes *bare infinitives.* An unmarked infinitive may be hard to recognize because it is not preceded by *to.* Some common verbs followed by unmarked infinitives are *feel, have, hear, let, listen to, look at, make* (meaning "compel"), *notice, see,* and *watch.*

> Please let me **take** [not to take] you to lunch. [unmarked infinitive]
> I want **to take** you to lunch. [marked infinitive]
>
> I can have Kara **drive** [not to drive] us. [unmarked infinitive]
> I will ask Kara **to drive** us. [marked infinitive]

The verb *help* can be followed by a marked or an unmarked infinitive. Either is correct: *Help me **put** [or **to put**] this box in the car.*

ALERT: Be careful to use parallel structure (see Chapter 18) correctly when you use two or more gerunds or infinitives after verbs. If two or more verbal objects follow one verb, put the verbals into the same form.

> NO   We went **sailing** and **to scuba dive.**
> YES   We went **sailing** and **scuba diving.**

> NO   We heard the wind **blow** and the waves **crashing.**
> YES   We heard the wind **blow** and the waves **crash.**
> YES   We heard the wind **blowing** and the waves **crashing.**

Conversely, if you are using verbal objects with COMPOUND PREDICATES, be sure to use the kind of verbal that each verb requires.

> NO   We enjoyed **scuba diving** but do not plan **sailing** again.
>   [*Enjoyed* requires a gerund object, and *plan* requires an infinitive object; see Boxes 196 and 197 in this chapter.]
> YES   We enjoyed **scuba diving** but do not plan **to sail** again.

48d How does meaning change when certain verbs are followed by a gerund or an infinitive?

With stop

The VERB *stop* followed by a GERUND means "finish, quit." *Stop* followed by an INFINITIVE means "interrupt one activity to begin another."

We **stopped *eating.*** [We finished our meal.]
We **stopped *to eat.*** [We stopped another activity, such as driving, in order to eat.]

With remember *and* forget

The verb *remember* followed by an infinitive means "not to forget to do something": *I must **remember to talk** with Isa. Remember* followed by a gerund means "recall a memory": *I **remember talking** in my sleep last night.*

The verb *forget* followed by an infinitive means "fail to do something": *If you **forget to put** a stamp on that letter, it will be returned. Forget* followed by a gerund means "do something and not recall it": *I **forget having put** the stamps in the refrigerator.*

With try

The verb *try* followed by an infinitive means "make an effort": *I **tried to find** your jacket.* Followed by a gerund, *try* means "experiment with": *I **tried jogging** but found it too difficult.*

48e # Why is the meaning unchanged whether a gerund or an infinitive follows sense verbs?

Sense VERBS include words such as *see, notice, hear, observe, watch, feel, listen to,* and *look at.* The meaning of these verbs is usually not affected by whether a GERUND or an INFINITIVE follows as the OBJECT. *I **saw** the water **rise*** and *I **saw** the water **rising*** both have the same meaning.

EXERCISE 48-1

Write the correct form of the verbal object (either a gerund or an infinitive) for each verb in parentheses. For help, consult 48b through 48e.

EXAMPLE   On some campuses, it seems as if nearly every student wants (find) <u>to find</u> a better apartment or dormitory room.

1. Often, students become as anxious over (find) _____ a suitable apartment as they do over (write) _____ a final exam.
2. In many places, senior undergraduates and graduate students tend (avoid) _____ dormitories.
3. Some students consider (live) _____ off campus a sign of maturity and independence.
4. Others just seem (need) _____ the extra physical and mental space.
5. In later life, people who were able (share) _____ a big, roomy house with school friends often remember the experience fondly.
6. We rarely see students (come) _____ up with an ideal solution, though, if they have left their search to the last minute.
7. The idea is to plan ahead and actively try (find) _____ a place that suits you; otherwise, you may be forced to try (sleep) _____ on your friend's couch for a few weeks.
8. The housing problem at one large Ontario university became known after a student acknowledged (live) _____ hidden in a campus stairwell.
9. (Explain) _____ this situation was a huge embarrassment for university officials, even after social workers attempted (blame) _____ this student's predicament on personal problems.

48f # How do I choose between *-ing* and *-ed* forms for adjectives?

Deciding whether to use the *-ing* form (PRESENT PARTICIPLE) or the *-ed* form (PAST PARTICIPLE of a regular VERB) as an ADJECTIVE in a specific sentence can be difficult. For example, *I am **amused*** and *I am **amusing*** are both correct in English, but their meanings are very different. To make the right choice, decide whether the modified NOUN or PRONOUN is causing or experiencing what the participle describes.

Use a present participle (*-ing*) to modify a noun or pronoun that is the agent or the cause of the action.

Micah described your **interesting** plan. [The noun *plan* causes what its modifier describes—interest; so *interesting* is correct.]

I find your plan **exciting.** [The noun *plan* causes what its modifier describes—excitement; so *exciting* is correct.]

Use a past participle (*-ed* in regular verbs) to modify a noun or pronoun that experiences or receives whatever the modifier describes.

An **interested** committee wants to hear your plan. [The noun *committee* experiences what its modifier describes—interest; so *interested* is correct.]

Excited by your plan, they called a board meeting. [The pronoun *they* experiences what its modifier describes—excitement; so *excited* is correct.]

Here are frequently used participles that convey very different meanings, depending on whether the *-ed* or the *-ing* form is used.

amused, amusing	frightened, frightening
annoyed, annoying	insulted, insulting
appalled, appalling	offended, offending
bored, boring	overwhelmed, overwhelming
confused, confusing	pleased, pleasing
depressed, depressing	reassured, reassuring
disgusted, disgusting	satisfied, satisfying
fascinated, fascinating	shocked, shocking

EXERCISE 48-2

Choose the correct participle from each pair in parentheses. For help, consult 48f.

EXAMPLE   It can be a (satisfied, satisfying) <u>satisfying</u> experience to learn about the lives of artists.

1. The artist Frida Kahlo led an (interested, interesting) _____ life.

2. When Kahlo was eighteen, (horrified, horrifying) _____ observers saw her (injured, injuring) _____ in a streetcar accident.

3. A (disappointed, disappointing) _____ Kahlo had to abandon her plan to study medicine.

4. Instead, she began to create paintings filled with (disturbed, disturbing) _____ images.

5. Some art critics consider Kahlo's paintings to be (fascinated, fascinating) _____ works of art, though many people find them (overwhelmed, overwhelming) _____.

EXERCISE 48-3

Choose the correct participle from each pair in parentheses. For help, consult 48f.

EXAMPLE   Learning about the career of a favourite actor is always an (interested, interesting) <u>interesting</u> exercise.

1. Jim Carrey is an actor/comedian with a (fascinated, fascinating) _____ history.
2. (Raised, Raising) _____ by his parents in southern Ontario, Carrey grew up in one of the most media-rich areas in North America.
3. Biographies of Carrey reveal the (surprised, surprising) _____ news that this bright and talented student dropped out of school in grade ten.
4. After relocating to Los Angeles in the 1980s, a (disappointed, disappointing) _____ Carrey discovered the difficulties of acting after his first (cancelled, cancelling) _____ TV series left him briefly out of work.
5. Carrey's career skyrocketed with his (amused, amusing) _____ appearances on *In Living Color,* a TV show that led to numerous box office hits: *Ace Ventura: Pet Detective, The Mask, The Truman Show,* and others.

EXERCISE 48-4

Choose the correct participle from each pair in parentheses. For help, consult 48f.

EXAMPLE   Studying popular myths that turn out to be false can be a (fascinated, fascinating) <u>fascinating</u> experience.

1. While doing research for a paper about birds, I discovered some (interested, interesting) _____ information about ostriches.
2. I encountered an (unsettled, unsettling) _____ passage in a book, which said that ostriches do not, in fact, stick their heads into the sand for protection when they feel fear.
3. This myth about (frightened, frightening) _____ ostriches began among the ancient Arabs and has since been passed on by many reputable writers.
4. In reality, an ostrich does not have to do something as useless as bury its head in the sand when a predator approaches, because a (hunted, hunting) _____ ostrich can reach speeds of nearly 55 kilometres an hour and can thus outrun most other animals.
5. A (threatened, threatening) _____ ostrich can also kick its way out of many dangerous situations with its powerful legs, and, at a height of well over two metres, it presents itself as a (frightened, frightening) _____ opponent.

Chapter 49

Modal Auxiliary Verbs

AUXILIARY VERBS are known as *helping verbs* because adding an auxiliary verb to a MAIN VERB helps the main verb convey additional information (see 8e). For example, the auxiliary verb *do* is important in turning sentences into questions. *You have to sleep* becomes a question when *do* is added: *Do you have to sleep?* The most common auxiliary verbs are forms of *be, have,* and *do.* Boxes 62 and 63 in section 8e list the forms of these three verbs.

MODAL AUXILIARY VERBS are one type of auxiliary verb. They include *can, could, may, might, should, had better, must, will, would,* and others discussed in this chapter. Modals differ from *be, have,* and *do* used as auxiliary verbs in the specific ways discussed in Box 198.

This chapter can help you use modals to convey shades of meaning. Section 49a discusses using modals to convey ability, necessity, advisability, possibility, and probability. Section 49b discusses using modals to convey preferences, plans or obligations, and past habits. Section 49c introduces modals in the PASSIVE VOICE.

BOX 198   SUMMARY

Modals and their differences from other auxiliary verbs

- Modals in the present future are always followed by the SIMPLE FORM of a main verb: *I **might go** tomorrow.*
- One-word modals have no *-s* ending in the THIRD-PERSON SINGULAR: *She **could** go with me; he **could** go with me; they **could** go with me.* (The two-word modal *have to* changes form to agree with its subject: *I **have to** leave; she **has to** leave.*) Auxiliary verbs other than modals usually change form for third-person singular: *I **do** want to go; he **does** want to go.*
- Some modals change form in the past. Others (*should, would, must,* which convey probability, and *ought to*) use *have* + a PAST PARTICIPLE. *I **can do** it* becomes *I **could do** it* in PAST-TENSE CLAUSES about ability. *I **could do** it* becomes *I **could have done** it* in clauses about possibility.

→

> **Modals and their differences from other auxiliary verbs**
> (*continued*)
>
> ■ Modals convey meaning about ability, necessity, advisability,
> possibility, and other conditions: For example, *I can go* means
> "I am able to go." Modals do not describe actual occurrences.

49a How do I convey ability, necessity, advisability, possibility, and probability with modals?

Conveying ability

The modal *can* conveys ability now (in the present), and *could* conveys
ability before (in the past). These words deliver the meaning "able to."
For the future, use *will be able to.*

> We **can** work late tonight. [*Can* conveys present ability.]
>
> I **could** work late last night, too. [*Could* conveys past ability.]
>
> I **will be able to** work late next Monday. [*Will be able* is the future tense;
> *will* here is not a modal.]

Adding *not* between a modal and the MAIN VERB makes the CLAUSE
negative: We **cannot** work late tonight; **I could not** work late last night;
I **will not be able to** work late next Monday.

👁 **ALERT:** You will often see negative forms of modals turned into
CONTRACTIONS: *can't, couldn't, won't, wouldn't,* and others. Because
contractions are considered informal usage by some instructors, you will
never be wrong if you avoid them in ACADEMIC WRITING, except when
you are reproducing spoken words. 👁

Conveying necessity

The modals *must* and *have to* convey a need to do something. Both *must*
and *have to* are followed by the simple form of the main verb. In the
present tense, *have to* changes form to agree with its subject.

> You **must** leave before midnight.
>
> She **has to** leave when I leave.

In the past tense, *must* is never used to express necessity. Instead,
use *had to.*

> PRESENT TENSE   We **must** study today. We **have to** study today.
>
> PAST TENSE   We **had to** [not *must*] take a test yesterday.

The negative forms of *must* and *have to* also have different meanings. *Must not* conveys that something is forbidden; *do not have to* conveys that something is not necessary.

> You **must not** sit there. [Sitting there is forbidden.]
> You **do not have to** sit there. [Sitting there is not necessary.]

Conveying advisability or the notion of a good idea

The modals *should* and *ought to* express the idea that doing the action of the main verb is advisable or is a good idea.

> You **should** go to class tomorrow morning.

In the past tense, *should* and *ought to* convey regret or knowing something through hindsight. They mean that good advice was not taken.

> You **should have** gone to class yesterday.
> I **ought to have** called my sister yesterday.

The modal *had better* delivers the meaning of good advice or warning or threat. It does not change form for tense.

> You **had better** see the doctor before your cough gets worse.

Need to is often used to express strong advice, too. Its past-tense form is *needed to*.

> You **need to** take better care of yourself. You **needed to** listen.

Conveying possibility

The modals *may, might,* and *could* can be used to convey an idea of possibility or likelihood.

> We **may** become hungry before long.
> We **could** eat lunch at the diner next door.

For the past-tense form, use *may, might,* and *could,* followed by *have* and the past participle of the main verb.

> I **could have studied** German in high school, but I studied Spanish instead.

Conveying probability

In addition to conveying the idea of necessity, the modal *must* can also convey probability or likelihood. It means that a well-informed guess is being made.

Marisa **must** be a talented actress. She has been chosen to play the lead role in the school play.

When *must* conveys probability, the past tense is *must have* plus the past participle of the main verb.

I did not see Boris at the party; he **must have left** early.

EXERCISE 49-1

Fill in each blank with the past-tense modal auxiliary that expresses the meaning given in parentheses. For help, consult 49a.

EXAMPLE   I (advisability) <u>should have</u> gone straight to the doctor the instant I felt a cold coming on.

1. Since I (necessity, no choice) _____ work late this past Monday, I could not get to the doctor's office before it closed.
2. I (advisability) _____ gone to bed after dinner, but I stayed awake for a while instead.
3. Even after I finally got into bed, I (ability) _____ not relax.
4. I (making a guess) _____ not _____ heard the alarm the next morning, because I overslept nearly two hours.
5. When I finally arrived at work, my boss came into my office and said, "Julie, you (necessity) _____ stayed home and rested if you are sick."

EXERCISE 49-2

Fill in each blank with the past-tense modal auxiliary that expresses the meaning given in parentheses. For help, consult 49a.

EXAMPLE   We (advisability) <u>had better</u> finish that research we were planning to do before reading week.

1. I think you (advisability) _____ looked at the latest report from Statistics Canada on consumer spending patterns.
2. Given your specialization in economics, you (probability) _____ find those reports essential to your research.
3. You (making a guess) _____ not _____ been thinking when you let your online subscription to *Perspectives on Labour and Income* expire, then.
4. If I had looked at that issue before my midterms, I (ability) _____ aced the question on economic structures and population change.
5. I'd take more pleasure in reading about how little of their spending Canadians now (necessity) _____ devote to the necessities of life, though, if I (ability) _____ find a decent part-time job.

49b How do I convey preferences, plans, and past habits with modals?

Conveying preferences

The modal *would rather* expresses a preference. *Would rather,* the PRESENT TENSE, is used with the SIMPLE FORM of the MAIN VERB, and *would rather have,* the PAST TENSE, is used with the PAST PARTICIPLE of the main verb.

> We **would rather see** a comedy than a mystery.
> Carlos **would rather have stayed** home last night.

Conveying plan or obligation

A form of *be* followed by *supposed to* and the simple form of a main verb delivers a meaning of something planned or of an obligation.

> I **was supposed to meet** them at the bus stop.

Conveying past habit

The modals *used to* and *would* express the idea that something happened repeatedly in the past.

> I **used to** hate going to the dentist.
> I **would** dread every single visit.

👁 **ALERT:** Both *used to* and *would* can be used to express repeated actions in the past, but *would* cannot be used for a situation that lasted for a period of time in the past.

> NO   I **would** live in Corner Brook.
> YES   I **used to** live in Corner Brook. 👁

49c How can I recognize modals in the passive voice?

Modals use the ACTIVE VOICE, as shown in sections 49a and 49b. In the active voice, the subject does the action expressed in the MAIN VERB (see 8n and 8o).

Modals can also use the PASSIVE VOICE (8p). In the passive voice, the doer of the main verb's action is either unexpressed or is expressed as an OBJECT in a PREPOSITIONAL PHRASE starting with the word *by*.

> PASSIVE   The waterfront **can be seen** from my window.
> ACTIVE   **I can see** the waterfront from my window.

> PASSIVE   The tax form **must be signed** by the person who fills it out.
> ACTIVE   The person who fills out the tax form **must sign** it.

EXERCISE 49-3

Select the correct choice from the words in parentheses and write it in the blank. For help, consult 49a through 49c.

> **EXAMPLE** I (should, should have) <u>should have</u> taken kayaking lessons my first summer in British Columbia.

1. I (would, used to) _____ live far from the ocean and the mountains.
2. In those days I (can, could) _____ only dream of kayaking down the coast where the Rocky Mountains meet the Pacific.
3. Sometimes I think I (must be come, must have come) _____ to the world's most beautiful landscape.
4. My move to the West Coast (should not have been, should not have) _____ put off for so long.
5. If you have a dream, you (cannot, should not) _____ leave it unfulfilled.

EXERCISE 49-4

Select the correct choice from the words in parentheses and write it in the blank. For help, consult 49a through 49c.

> **EXAMPLE** We (must have, must) <u>must</u> study this afternoon.

1. I have heard that Natasha (should not, cannot) _____ go skiing with us because she has a research paper due.
2. Juan (would have, would have been) _____ granted a fellowship if he had completed his course work.
3. You (ought not have, ought not to have) _____ arrived while the meeting was still in progress.
4. Louise (must be, must have been) _____ sick to miss the party last week.
5. Had I not found a roommate, I (might not have, might not have been) _____ able to afford the rent on my apartment.

Terms Glossary

This glossary defines important terms used in this handbook, including the ones that are printed in small capital letters. Many of these glossary entries end with parenthetical references to the handbook section(s) or chapter(s) where the specific term is fully discussed.

absolute phrase A phrase containing a subject and a participle that modifies an entire sentence. (7o)

■ **The semester** [subject] **being** [present participle of *be*] **over,** the campus looks deserted.

abstract noun A noun that names something not knowable through the five senses: *idea, respect.* (7b)

academic writing Writing you do for college or university classes, usually intended to inform or to persuade. (1c)

action verbs Strong verbs that increase the impact of your language and reduce wordiness. *Weak verbs,* such as *be* or *have,* increase wordiness. (16e)

active voice An attribute of verbs showing that the action or condition expressed in the verb is done by the subject, in contrast with the *passive voice,* which conveys that the action or condition of the verb is done to the subject. (8n, 8o)

adjective A word that describes or limits (modifies) a noun, a pronoun, or a word group functioning as a noun: *silly, three.* (7f, Chapter 11)

adjective clause A dependent clause, also known as a *relative clause.* An adjective clause modifies a preceding noun or pronoun and begins with a relative word (such as *who, which, that,* or *where*) that relates the clause to the noun or pronoun it modifies. Also see *clause.* (7p)

adverb A word that describes or limits (modifies) verbs, adjectives, other adverbs, phrases, or clauses: *loudly, very, nevertheless, there.* (7g, Chapter 11)

adverb clause A dependent clause beginning with a subordinating conjunction that establishes the relationship in meaning between the adverb clause and its independent clause. An adverb clause modifies the independent clause's verb or the entire independent clause. Also see *clause, conjunction.* (7p)

agreement The required match of number and person between a subject and verb or a pronoun and antecedent. A pronoun that expresses gender must match its antecedent in gender also. (Chapter 10)

analogy An explanation of the unfamiliar in terms of the familiar. Unlike a simile, an analogy does not use *like* or *as* in making the comparison. Analogy is a rhetorical strategy for developing paragraphs. (4i, 21d, 40b)

analysis A process of critical thinking that divides a whole into its component parts in order to understand how the parts interrelate. Sometimes called *division,* analysis is a rhetorical strategy for developing paragraphs. (4i, 5b, 39e, 40b)

antecedent The noun or pronoun to which a pronoun refers. (9l–9s, 10o–10t)

APA style See *documentation style.*

appeals to reason Tools a writer uses to persuade the reader that the reasoning in an argument is sound and effective; there are three types—logical, emotional, and ethical appeals. (6i)

appositive A word or group of words that renames a preceding noun or noun phrase: *my favourite month,* **October.** (7n)

argument A rhetorical attempt to persuade others to agree with a position about a topic open to debate. (1b, Chapter 6)

articles Also called *determiners* or *noun markers,* articles are the words *a, an,* and *the. A* and *an* are indefinite articles, and *the* is a definite article; also see *determiner.* (7f, Chapter 45)

assertion A statement. In a thesis statement, an assertion expresses a point of view about a topic; in an argument, an assertion states the position you want to argue. (2q, 6c)

audience The readers to whom a piece of writing is directed; the three types include *general audience, peer audience,* and *specialist audience.* (1d)

auxiliary verb Also known as a *helping verb,* an auxiliary verb is a form of *be, do, have, can, may, will,* or certain other verbs that combines with a main verb to help it express tense, mood, and voice. Also see *modal auxiliary verb.* (8e)

balanced sentence A sentence composed of two parallel structures, usually two independent clauses, that present contrasting content. (18b)

base form See *simple form.*

bias In writing, a distortion or inaccuracy caused by a dislike or hatred of individuals, groups of people, or ideas. (5c2)

bibliographic notes In a note system of documentation, a *footnote* or *endnote* gives the bibliographic information the first time a source is cited. (33f, 34d.2, Chapter 36)

bibliography A list of sources used or consulted for research writing. (Chapters 34, 35, and 36)

body paragraphs Paragraphs that provide the substance of your message in a sequence that makes sense. (4c)

Boolean expressions In a search engine, symbols or words such as And, Or, and Not that let you create keyword combinations that narrow and refine your search. (2l, 32c.4)

brainstorming Listing all ideas that come to mind on a topic and then grouping the ideas by patterns that emerge. (2h)

bureaucratic language Sometimes called *bureaucratese;* language that is overblown or overly complex. (21m)

business writing Writing designed for business, including letters, memos, résumés, job application letters, and e-mail messages. (1e, Chapter 41)

case The form of a noun or pronoun in a specific context that shows whether it is functioning as a subject, an object, or a possessive. In modern English, nouns change form in the possessive case only (*city* = form for subjective and objective cases; *city's* = possessive-case form). Also see *pronoun case.* (9a–9k)

cause and effect The relationship between outcomes (effects) and the reasons for them (causes). Cause-and-effect analysis is a rhetorical strategy for developing paragraphs. (4i, 5h–5j)

chronological order Also called *time order,* an arrangement of information according to time sequence; an organizing strategy for sentences, paragraphs, and longer pieces of writing. (4h)

citation Information that identifies a source quoted, paraphrased, summarized, or referred to in a piece of writing; *in-text citations* appear within sentences or as *parenthetical references.* Also see *documentation.* (Chapters 33 and 34)

classical argument An argument with a six-part structure consisting of introduction, thesis statement, background, evidence and reasoning, response to opposing views, and conclusion. (6f)

classification A rhetorical strategy for paragraph development that organizes information by grouping items according to underlying shared characteristics. (4i)

clause A group of words containing a subject and a predicate. A clause that delivers full meaning is called an *independent* (or *main*) *clause.* A clause that lacks full meaning by itself is called a *dependent* (or *subordinate*) *clause.* Also see *adjective clause, adverb clause, nonrestrictive element, noun clause, restrictive element.* (7p)

cliché An overused, worn-out phrase that has lost its capacity to communicate effectively: *smooth as silk, ripe old age.* (21h, 21j)

climactic order Sometimes called *emphatic order,* an arrangement of ideas or other information from least to most important. (4h, 6f)

clustering See *mapping.*

coherence The clear progression from one idea to another using transitional expressions, pronouns, selective repetition, or parallelism to make connections between ideas. (3c.4, 4g)

collaborative writing Students working together to write a paper. (1d, 3f)

collective noun A noun that names a group of people or things: *family, committee.* Also see *noncount noun.* (7b, 10j, 10t)

colloquial language Casual or conversational language. Also see *slang.* (21h)

comma fault See *comma splice.*

comma splice The error that occurs when only a comma connects two independent clauses; also called a *comma fault.* (Chapter 13)

common noun A noun that names a general group, place, person, or thing: *dog, house.* (7b)

comparative form The form of a descriptive adjective or adverb that shows a different degree of intensity between two things: *bluer, less blue; more easily, less easily.* Also see *positive form, superlative form.* (11e)

comparison and contrast A rhetorical strategy for organizing and developing paragraphs by discussing similarities (*comparison*) and differences (*contrast*). It has two patterns: *point-by-point* and *block organization.* (4i)

complement An element after a verb that completes the predicate, such as a direct object after an action verb or a noun or adjective after a linking verb. Also see *object complement, predicate adjective, predicate nominative, subject complement.* (7n)

complete predicate See *predicate.*

complete subject See *subject.*

complex sentence See *sentence types.*

compound-complex sentence See *sentence types.*

compound construction A group of nouns or pronouns connected with a coordinating conjunction. (9d)

compound noun See *subject.*

compound predicate See *predicate.*

compound sentence See *coordinate sentence, sentence types.*

compound subject See *subject.* (7l, 10e)

compound word Two or more words placed together to express one concept. (22g)

conciseness An attribute of writing that is direct and to the point. (Chapter 16)

concrete noun A noun naming something that can be seen, touched, heard, smelled, or tasted: *smoke, sidewalk.* (7b)

conjunction A word that connects or otherwise establishes a relationship between two or more words, phrases, or clauses. Also see *coordinating conjunction, correlative conjunction, subordinating conjunction.* (7i)

conjunctive adverb An adverb, such as *therefore* or *meanwhile,* that communicates a logical connection in meaning. (7g)

connotation Associations and emotional overtones implied by a word that go beyond the word's dictionary definition. (21e.2)

contraction A word where an apostrophe takes the place of one or more omitted letters. (27d)

coordinate adjectives Two or more adjectives of equal weight that modify a noun. (24e)

coordinate sentence Independent clauses joined by either a semicolon or a comma with coordinating conjunction showing their relationship; also called a *compound sentence.* Also see *coordination.* (17b)

coordinating conjunction A conjunction that joins two or more grammatically equivalent structures: *and, or, for, nor, but, so, yet.* (7i, 13c.3, 17b, 17c)

coordination The use of grammatically equivalent forms to show a balance or sequence of ideas. (17a–17d, 17i)

correlative conjunction A pair of words that joins equivalent grammatical structures, including *both . . . and, either . . . or, neither . . . nor, not only . . . but* (or *but also*). (7i)

count noun A noun that names an item or items that can be counted: *radios, streets, ideas, fingernails.* (7b, 44a, 44b, 45a, 45b)

critical reading A parallel process to *critical thinking.* (5d, 39d)

critical response Formally, an essay summarizing a source's central point or main idea. It includes a *transitional statement* that bridges this summary and the writer's synthesized reactions in response. (5f)

critical thinking A form of thinking where you take control of your conscious thought processes with the aim of making an evaluation. (5a, 5b, 31b, 32j)

cumulative adjectives Adjectives that build meaning from word to word: *distinctive musical style.* (24e)

cumulative sentence The most common sentence structure, with the subject and verb followed by modifiers; also called a *loose sentence.* (19f)

dangling modifier A modifier that attaches its meaning illogically, either because it is closer to another noun or pronoun than to its true subject or because its true subject is not expressed in the sentence. (14d)

declarative sentence A sentence that makes a statement: *Skydiving is exciting.* Also see *exclamatory sentence, imperative sentence, interrogative sentence.* (7k)

deduction, deductive reasoning The process of reasoning from general claims to a specific instance. (5i)

definite article See *articles.*

definition A rhetorical strategy in which you define or give the meaning of words or ideas. Includes *extended definition.* (4i)

demonstrative pronoun A pronoun that points out the antecedent: *this, these; that, those.* (7c, 7f)

denotation The dictionary definition of a word. (21e.1)

dependent clause A clause that cannot stand alone as an independent grammatical unit. Also see *adjective clause, adverb clause, noun clause.* (7p, 12b)

description A rhetorical strategy that appeals to a reader's senses—sight, sound, smell, taste, and touch. (4i)

descriptive adjective An adjective that names the condition or properties of the noun it modifies and (except for a very few, such as *dead* and *unique*) has comparative and superlative forms: *flat, flatter, flattest.*

descriptive adverb An adverb that names the condition or properties of whatever it modifies and that has comparative and superlative forms: *happily, more happily, most happily.* (7g)

determiner A word or word group, traditionally identified as an adjective, that limits a noun by telling how much or how many about it. Also called *expression of quantity, limiting adjective,* or *noun marker.* (7f, 44b, Chapter 45)

diction Word choice. (21e)

direct address Words naming a person or group being spoken to. Written words of direct address are set off by commas. (24g)

■ The answer, **my friends,** lies with you. Go with them, **Gene.**

direct discourse In writing, words that repeat speech or conversation exactly and so are enclosed in quotation marks. (15e, 24h, 28b)

direct object A noun or pronoun or group of words functioning as a noun that receives the action (completes the meaning) of a transitive verb. (7m)

direct question A sentence that asks a question and ends with a question mark: *Are you going?* (23a, 23c)

direct quotation See *quotation.*

discovery draft A first draft developed from focused freewriting. (2g, 3a)

documentation The acknowledgment of someone else's words and ideas used in any piece of writing by giving full and accurate information about the person whose words were used and where those words were found. For example, for a print source, documentation usually includes names of all authors, title of the source, place and date of publication, and related information. (33e–33k, Chapters 34–36)

documentation style A system for providing information about the source of words, information, and ideas quoted, paraphrased, or summarized from a source. Documentation styles discussed in this handbook are MLA, APA, CM, CSE, and COS. (31h, 33f, Chapters 34–36)

document design A term for the placement of tables, graphs, and other illustrations in printed and online material. (Chapter 37)

double negative A nonstandard negation using two negative modifiers rather than one. (11c)

drafting A part of the writing process in which writers compose ideas in sentences and paragraphs. *Drafts* are versions—*first* or *rough, revised,* and *final*—of one piece of writing. (3a)

edited Canadian English English language usage that conforms to established rules of grammar, sentence structure, punctuation, and spelling in Canada; a variety of *standard English*. (21c)

editing A part of the writing process in which writers check the technical correctness of grammar, spelling, punctuation, and mechanics. (3d)

elliptical construction The deliberate omission of one or more words in order to achieve conciseness in a sentence. (7p, 15h, 16d.3)

essential element See *restrictive element*.

euphemism Language that attempts to blunt certain realities by speaking of them in "nice" or "tactful" words. (21l)

evaluate A step in the critical thinking process where you judge the quality of the material you are assessing. (5b, 5c.3, 5g)

evidence Facts, data, examples, and opinions of others used to support assertions and conclusions. Also see *sources*. (5g)

exclamatory sentence A sentence beginning with *What* or *How* that expresses strong feeling: *What a ridiculous statement!* (7k)

expletive The phrase *there is (are), there was (were), it is,* or *it was* at the beginning of a clause, changing structure and postponing the subject:

- **It is** Mars that we hope to reach. [Compare: *We hope to reach Mars*]. (9n, 16c)

expository writing See *informative writing*.

expressive writing Writing that reflects your personal thoughts and feelings. (1c.1)

faulty parallelism Grammatically incorrect writing that results from non-matching grammatical forms. (18e)

faulty predication A grammatically illogical combination of subject and predicate. (15g)

field research Primary research that involves going into real-life situations to observe, survey, interview, or be part of some activity. (32i, 40d.1)

figurative language Words that make connections and comparisons and draw on one image to explain another and enhance meaning. (21d)

finite verb A verb form that shows tense, mood, voice, person, and number while expressing an action, occurrence, or state of being.

first person See *person.*

focused freewriting A technique that may start with a set topic or may build on one sentence taken from earlier freewriting. (2g)

freewriting Writing nonstop for a period of time to generate ideas by free association of thoughts. Also see *discovery draft.* (2g)

fused sentence See *run-on sentence.*

future perfect progressive tense The form of the future perfect tense that describes an action or condition ongoing until some specific future time: *I will have been talking.* (8j)

future perfect tense The tense indicating that an action will have been completed or a condition will have ended by a specified point in the future: *I will have talked.* (8i)

future progressive tense The form of the future tense showing that a future action will continue for some time: *I will be talking.* (8j)

future tense The form of a verb, made with the simple form and either *shall* or *will,* expressing an action yet to be taken or a condition not yet experienced: *I will talk.* (8g)

gender The classification of words as masculine, feminine, or neutral. (10s, 21g)

gender-free language See *gender-neutral language.*

gender-neutral language Also called *gender-free language* or *nonsexist language,* it uses terms that do not unnecessarily say whether a person is male or female, as with *police officer* instead of *policeman.* (10s, 21g)

generalization A broad statement without details. (1c.3)

gerund A present participle functioning as a noun: ***Walking*** *is good exercise.* Also see *verbal.* (7e, 45c, Chapter 48)

helping verb See *auxiliary verb.*

homonyms Words spelled differently that sound alike: *to, too, two.* (22f)

hyperbole See *overstatement.*

idiom A word, phrase, or other construction that typically has a different meaning from its literal meaning:

- He lost his head. She hit the ceiling. (Chapter 47)

illogical predication See *faulty predication.*

imperative mood The mood that expresses commands and direct requests, using the simple form of the verb and often implying but not expressing the subject, *you: Go.* (8l)

imperative sentence A sentence that gives a command: *Go to the corner to buy me a newspaper.* (7k, 12b.3)

incubation The prewriting technique of giving ideas time to develop. (2m)

indefinite article See *articles, determiner.*

indefinite pronoun A pronoun, such as *all, anyone, each,* and *others,* that refers to a nonspecific person or thing. (7c, 7f, 10i)

independent clause A clause that can stand alone as an independent grammatical unit. (7p)

indicative mood The mood of verbs used for statements about real things or highly likely ones:

- I think Grace is arriving today. (8l, 15d)

indirect discourse Reported speech or conversation that does not use the exact structure of the original and so is not enclosed in quotation marks. (15e, 24h)

indirect object A noun or pronoun or group of words functioning as a noun that tells to whom or for whom the action expressed by a transitive verb was done. (7m)

indirect question A sentence that reports a question and ends with a period:

- I asked if you are leaving. (23a, 23c, 46a)

indirect quotation See *quotation.*

induction The reasoning process of arriving at general principles from particular facts or instances. (5i)

inductive reasoning A form of reasoning that moves from particular facts or instances to general principles. (5i)

inference What a reader or listener understands to be implied but not stated. (5c.2)

infinitive A verbal made of the simple form of a verb and usually, but not always, *to* that functions as a noun, adjective, or adverb. Infinitives without the word *to* are called *unmarked* (or *bare*) *infinitives.* (7e, 8k, Chapter 48)

infinitive phrase An infinitive, with its modifiers and object, that functions as a noun, adjective, or adverb. Also see *verbal phrase.* (7e)

informal language Word choice that creates a tone appropriate for casual writing or speaking. (1e, 21h)

informative writing Writing that gives information and, when necessary, explains it; also known as *expository writing.* (1c.2)

intensive pronoun A pronoun that ends in *-self* and that emphasizes its antecedent. Also called *reflexive pronoun:*

■ Vida **himself** argued against it. (7c)

interjection An emotion-conveying word that is treated as a sentence, starting with a capital letter and ending with an exclamation point or a period: *Oh! Ouch!* (7j, 24c)

interrogative pronoun A pronoun, such as *whose* or *what,* that implies a question:

■ **Who** called? (7c, 12b.1)

interrogative sentence A sentence that asks a direct question:

■ Did you see that? (7k)

in-text citation Source information placed in parentheses within the body of a research paper. Also see *citation, parenthetical reference.* (34b, 35b)

intransitive verb A verb that does not take a direct object. (8f)

invention techniques Ways of gathering ideas for writing. Also see *planning.* (2g–2m)

inverted word order In contrast to standard order, the main verb or an auxiliary verb comes before the subject in inverted word order. Most questions and some exclamations use inverted word order. (10h, 19f, Chapter 46)

irony Words used to imply the opposite of their usual meaning. (21d)

irregular verb A verb that forms the past tense and past participle in some way other than by adding *-ed* or *-d.* (8d)

jargon A particular field's or group's specialized vocabulary that a general reader is unlikely to understand. (21k)

key terms In an essay, the words central to its topic and its message. (6e)

keywords The main words in a source's title or the words that the author or editor has identified as central to that source. Use keywords in searching for sources online or in library databases. (32c.4)

levels of formality Word choices and sentence structures reflecting various degrees of formality of language. A formal level is used for ceremonial and other occasions when stylistic flourishes are appropriate. A medium level, neither too formal nor too casual, is acceptable for most academic writing. (21b)

levels of generality Degrees of generality used to group or organize information or ideas as you write, as when moving from the most general to the most specific. (2o)

limiting adjective See *determiner.*

linking verb A main verb that links a subject with a subject complement that renames or describes the subject. Linking verbs, sometimes
called *copulative verbs,* convey a state of being, relate to the senses, or
indicate a condition. (8a, 8c)

logical fallacies Flaws in reasoning that lead to illogical statements. (5j)

main clause See *independent clause.*

main verb A verb that expresses action, occurrence, or state of being
and that shows mood, tense, voice, number, and person. (8b)

mapping An invention technique based on thinking about a topic and
its increasingly specific subdivisions; also known as *clustering* or
webbing. (2j)

mechanics Conventions governing matters such as the use of capital
letters, italics, abbreviations, and numbers. (Chapter 30)

metaphor A comparison implying similarity between two things. A
metaphor does not use words such as *like* or *as,* which are used in a simile and which make a comparison explicit: *a mop of hair* (compare the
simile *hair like a mop*). (21d)

misplaced modifier Describing or limiting words that are wrongly positioned in a sentence so that their message is either illogical or relates
to the wrong word or words. Also see *squinting modifier.* (14a)

mixed construction A sentence that unintentionally changes from one
grammatical structure to another, incompatible one, so that the meaning
is garbled. (15f)

mixed metaphors Incongruously combined images. (21d)

MLA style See *documentation style, parenthetical reference.*

modal auxiliary verb One of a group of nine auxiliary verbs that add
information such as a sense of needing, wanting, or having to do something or a sense of possibility, likelihood, obligation, permission, or ability. (8e, Chapter 49)

modifier, modify A word or group of words functioning as an adjective
or adverb to describe or limit another word or word group. Also see
misplaced modifier. (7n, Chapter 11, 19d)

mood The attribute of verbs showing a speaker's or writer's attitude toward the action. English has three moods: imperative, indicative, and
subjunctive. Also see *imperative mood, indicative mood, subjunctive
mood.* (8l, 8m)

narrative A rhetorical strategy that tells a story; a narrative deals with
what is or what has happened. (4i)

noncount noun A noun that names a thing that cannot be counted: *water, time.* Also see *collective noun.* (7b, Chapters 44 and 45)

nonessential element See *nonrestrictive element.*

nonrestrictive clause See *nonrestrictive element.*

nonrestrictive element A descriptive word, phrase, or dependent clause that provides information not essential to understanding the basic message of the element it modifies and so is set off by commas. Also see *restrictive element.* (24f)

nonsexist language See *gender-neutral language.*

nonspecific noun A noun that refers to any of a number of identical items; it takes the indefinite articles *a, an.* (45a)

nonstandard English Language usage other than what is called *edited English.* (21c)

noun A word that names a person, place, thing, or idea. Nouns function as subjects, objects, or complements. (7b)

noun clause A dependent clause that functions as a subject, object, or complement. (7p)

noun complement See *complement.*

noun determiner See *determiner.*

noun phrase A noun and its modifiers functioning as a subject, object, or complement. (7o)

number The attribute of some words indicating whether they refer to one (*singular*) or more than one (*plural*). (8a, 10b, 15b, Chapter 44)

object A noun, pronoun, or group of words functioning as a noun or pronoun that receives the action of a verb (*direct object*); tells to whom or for whom something is done (*indirect object*); or completes the meaning of a preposition (*object of a preposition*). (7m)

object complement A noun or adjective renaming or describing a direct object after verbs such as *call, consider, name, elect,* and *think:*

■ I call some joggers **fanatics.** (7n)

objective case The case of a noun or pronoun functioning as a direct or indirect object or the object of a preposition or of a verbal. A few pronouns change form to show case (*him, her, whom*). Also see *case.* (Chapter 9)

outline Technique for laying out ideas for writing. An outline can be formal or informal. (2r, 3l)

overstatement Deliberate exaggeration for emphasis; also called *hyperbole.* (21d)

paragraph A group of sentences that work together to develop a unit of thought. They are the structured elements of an essay, which is composed of an *introductory paragraph, body paragraphs,* and a *concluding paragraph.* Also see *shaping.* (2n, Chapter 4)

paragraph arrangement Ordering sentences by specific techniques to communicate a paragraph's message. (4h)

paragraph development Using specific, concrete details (RENNS) to support a generalization in a paragraph; rhetorical strategies or patterns for organizing ideas in paragraphs. (4f, 4i)

parallelism The use of equivalent grammatical forms or matching sentence structures to express equivalent ideas and develop coherence. (4g.4, Chapter 18)

paraphrase A restatement of someone else's ideas in language and sentence structure different from those of the original. (33i)

parenthetical reference Information enclosed in parentheses following quoted, paraphrased, or summarized material to alert readers to the use of material from a specific source. Parenthetical references, also called *in-text citations,* function together with a list of bibliographic information to document the writer's use of sources. Also see *citation.* (34b)

participial phrase A phrase that contains a present participle or a past participle and any modifiers and that functions as an adjective. Also see *verbal phrase.* (7o)

passive construction See *passive voice.*

passive voice The form of a verb in which the subject is acted on; if the subject is mentioned in the sentence, it usually appears as the object of the preposition *by:*

■ **I was frightened by** the thunder. [Compare the active voice: The thunder **frightened me.**]

The passive voice emphasizes the action, in contrast to the *active voice,* which emphasizes the doer of the action. (8n–8p)

past participle The third principal part of a verb, formed in regular verbs, like the past tense, by adding -*d* or -*ed* to the simple form. In irregular verbs, it often differs from the simple form and the past tense: *break, broke, broken.* (7e, 8b, 48f)

past perfect progressive tense The past perfect tense form that describes an ongoing condition in the past that has been ended by something stated in the sentence: *I had been talking.* (8j)

past perfect tense The tense that describes a condition or action that started in the past, continued for a while, and then ended in the past: *I had talked.* (8g, 8i)

past progressive tense The tense that shows the continuing nature of a past action: *I was talking.* (8j)

past subjunctive The simple past tense in the subjunctive mood. (8m)

past tense The tense that tells of an action completed or a condition ended. (8g)

past-tense form The second principal part of a verb, in regular verbs formed by adding *-d* or *-ed* to the simple form. In irregular verbs, the past tense may change in several ways from the simple form. (8b, 8d)

peer-response group A group of students formed to give each other feedback on writing. (1d.1)

perfect infinitive An infinitive form used to state an action that occurs before the action in the main verb. (8k)

perfect tenses The three tenses—the present perfect (*I have talked*), the past perfect (*I had talked*), and the future perfect (*I will have talked*)—that help show complex time relationships. (8g, 8i)

periodic sentence A sentence that begins with modifiers and ends with the independent clause, thus postponing the main idea—and the emphasis—for the end; also called a *climactic sentence*. (19f)

person The attribute of nouns and pronouns showing who or what acts or experiences an action. *First person* is the one speaking (*I, we*); *second person* is the one being spoken to (*you, you*); and *third person* is the person or thing being spoken about (*he, she, it, they*). All nouns are third person. (8a, 10b, 39f.1)

personal pronoun A pronoun that refers to people or things, such as *I, you, them, it.* (7c, 9n)

persuasive writing Writing that seeks to convince the reader about a matter of opinion. It is also known as *argumentative writing.* (1c.3, Chapter 6)

phrasal verb A verb that combines with one or more prepositions to deliver its meaning: *ask out, look into.* (47c)

phrase A group of related words that does not contain both a subject and a predicate and thus cannot stand alone as an independent grammatical unit. A phrase functions as a noun, verb, or modifier. (7o)

plagiarism A writer's presenting another person's words or ideas without giving credit to that person. Documentation systems allow writers to give proper credit to sources in ways recognized by scholarly communities. Plagiarism is a serious offence, a form of intellectual dishonesty that can lead to course failure or expulsion. (1f, 33b, 33c)

planning An early part of the writing process in which writers gather ideas. Along with shaping, planning is sometimes called *prewriting.* (Chapter 2)

plural See *number.*

positive form The form of an adjective or adverb when no comparison is being expressed: *blue, easily.* Also see *comparative form, superlative form.* (11e)

possessive case The case of a noun or pronoun that shows ownership or possession: *my, your, their,* and so on. Also see *case, pronoun case.* (Chapter 9, 27a–27c)

predicate The part of a sentence that contains the verb and tells what the subject is doing or experiencing or what is being done to the subject. A *simple predicate* contains only the main verb and any auxiliary verbs. A *complete predicate* contains the verb, its modifiers, objects, and other related words. A *compound predicate* contains two or more verbs and their objects and modifiers, if any. (7l)

predicate adjective An adjective used as a subject complement:
- That tree is **leafy.** (7n)

predicate nominative A noun or pronoun used as a subject complement:
- That tree is a **maple.** (7n)

prediction A major activity of the *reading process,* in which the reader reasons toward what comes next. (5c)

premises In a deductive argument expressed as a syllogism, statements presenting the conditions of the argument from which the conclusion must follow. (5i)

preposition A word that conveys a relationship, often of space or time, between the noun or pronoun following it and other words in the sentence. The noun or pronoun following a preposition is called its *object.* (7h, Chapter 47)

prepositional phrase A preposition and the word it modifies. Also see *phrase, preposition.* (7h, 7o)

present infinitive Names or describes an activity or occurrence coming together either at the same time or after the time expressed in the main verb. (8k)

present participle A verb's *-ing* form. Used with auxiliary verbs, present participles function as main verbs. Used without auxiliary verbs, present participles function as nouns or adjectives. (7e, 8b, 48f)

present perfect participle A participle form used to state an action that occurs before the action of the main verb. (8k)

present perfect progressive tense The present perfect tense form that describes something ongoing in the past that is likely to continue into the future: *I have been talking.* (8j)

present perfect tense The tense indicating that an action or its effects, begun or perhaps completed in the past, continue into the present: *I had talked.* (8g, 8i)

present progressive tense The present-tense form of the verb that indicates something taking place at the time it is written or spoken about: *I am talking.* (8j)

present subjunctive The simple form of the verb for all persons and numbers in the subjunctive mood. (8m)

present tense The tense that describes what is happening, what is true at the moment, and what is consistently true. It uses the simple form (*I talk*) and the *-s* form in the third-person singular (*he, she, it talks*). (8g, 8h)

prewriting All activities in the writing process before drafting. Also see *planning, shaping.* (2e–2m)

primary sources Firsthand work: write-ups of experiments and observations by the researchers who conducted them; taped accounts, interviews, and newspaper accounts by direct observers; autobiographies, diaries, and journals; expressive works (poems, plays, fiction, essays). Also known as *primary evidence.* Also see *secondary source.* (5g.2, 32a, 32i)

process A rhetorical strategy in writing that reports a sequence of actions by which something is done or made. (4i)

progressive forms Verb forms made in all tenses with the present participle and forms of the verb *be* as an auxiliary. Progressive forms show that an action, occurrence, or state of being is ongoing. (8g, 8j)

pronoun A word that takes the place of a noun and functions in the same ways that nouns do. Types of pronouns are *demonstrative, indefinite, intensive, interrogative, personal, reciprocal, reflexive,* and *relative.* The word (or words) a pronoun replaces is called its *antecedent.* (7c, Chapter 9)

pronoun–antecedent agreement The required match in number and person—and for personal pronouns, gender—between a pronoun and its antecedent. (10o–10t)

pronoun case The way a pronoun changes form to reflect its use as the agent of action (*subjective case*), the thing being acted upon (*objective case*), or the thing showing ownership (*possessive case*). (9a–9k)

pronoun reference The relationship between a pronoun and its antecedent. (9l–9s)

proofreading Reading a final draft to find and correct any spelling or mechanics mistakes, typing errors, or handwriting illegibility; the final step of the writing process. (3e)

proper adjective An adjective formed from a proper noun: *Victorian, American.* (30e)

proper noun A noun that names specific people, places, or things and is always capitalized: *Moose Jaw, Buick.* (7b, 30e, 45c)

purpose The goal or aim of a piece of writing: to express oneself, to provide information, to persuade, or to create a literary work. (1b, 1c)

quotation Repeating or reporting another person's words. *Direct quotation* repeats another's words exactly and encloses them in quotation marks. *Indirect quotation* reports another's words without quotation marks except around any words repeated exactly from the source. Both *direct* and *indirect quotation* require *documentation* of the *source* to avoid *plagiarism.* Also see *direct discourse, indirect discourse.* (Chapter 28, 33h)

readers Readers are the audiences for writing; readers process material they read on the literal, inferential, and evaluative levels. (1b, 5c)

reading process Critical reading that requires the reader to read for *literal meaning,* to draw *inferences,* and to *evaluate.* (5c)

reciprocal pronoun The pronouns *each other* and *one another* referring to individual parts of a plural antecedent:

- We respect **each other.** (7c)

References In many documentation styles, including APA, the title of a list of sources cited in a research paper or other written work. (31h, 31i, 32c, 35f)

reflexive pronoun A pronoun that ends in *-self* and that refers back to its antecedent:

- They claim to support **themselves.** (7c)

regular verb A verb that forms its past tense and past participle by adding *-ed* or *-d* to the simple form. Most English verbs are regular. (8b, 8d)

relative adverb An adverb that introduces an adjective clause:

- The lot **where** I usually park my car was full. (7g)

relative clause See *adjective clause.*

relative pronoun A pronoun, such as *who, which, that, whom,* or *whoever,* that introduces an adjective clause or sometimes a noun clause. (7c)

RENNS test See *paragraph development.* (4f)

research question The controlling question that drives research. (31c)

research writing Also called *source-based writing,* a process in three steps: conducting research, understanding and evaluating the results of the research, and writing the research paper with accurate documentation. (Chapter 31)

restrictive clause See *restrictive element.*

restrictive element A word, phrase, or dependent clause that contains information that is essential for a sentence to deliver its message. Do not set off with commas. (24f)

revising, revision A part of the writing process in which writers evaluate their rough drafts and, based on their assessments, rewrite by adding, cutting, replacing, moving, and often totally recasting material. (3c)

rhetoric The area of discourse that focuses on the arrangement of ideas and choice of words as a reflection of both the writer's purpose and the writer's sense of audience. (Chapter 1, 4i)

rhetorical strategies In writing, various techniques for presenting ideas to deliver a writer's intended message with clarity and impact. Reflecting typical patterns of human thought, rhetorical strategies include arrangements such as chronological and climactic order; stylistic techniques such as parallelism and planned repetition; and patterns for organizing and developing writing such as description and definition. (4i)

Rogerian argument An argument technique adapted from the principles of communication developed by the psychologist Carl Rogers. (6h)

run-on sentence The error of running independent clauses into each other without the required punctuation that marks them as complete units; also called a *fused sentence* or *run-together sentence*. (Chapter 13)

search engine An Internet-specific software program that can look through all files at Internet sites. (32b, 32c.3)

secondary source A source that reports, analyzes, discusses, reviews, or otherwise deals with the work of someone else, as opposed to a primary source, which is someone's original work or firsthand report. A reliable secondary source should be the work of a person with appropriate credentials, should appear in a respected publication or other medium, should be current, and should be well reasoned. (5g.2, 32a, 32i, 38b, 39f.3)

second person See *person.*

sentence See *sentence types.*

sentence fragment A portion of a sentence that is punctuated as though it were a complete sentence. (Chapter 12)

sentence types A grammatical classification of sentences by the kinds of clauses they contain. A *simple sentence* consists of one independent clause. A *complex sentence* contains one independent clause and one or more dependent clauses. A *compound-complex sentence* contains at least two independent clauses and one or more dependent clauses. A *compound* or *coordinate sentence* contains two or more independent clauses joined by a coordinating conjunction. Sentences are also classified by their grammatical function; see *declarative sentence, exclamatory sentence, imperative sentence, interrogative sentence.* (7k, 7q, 17b)

sentence variety Writing sentences of various lengths and structures; see *coordinate sentence, cumulative sentence, periodic sentence, sentence types.* (19a)

sexist language Language that unnecessarily communicates that a person is male or female or that assigns characteristics based on gender. For example, *fireman* implies that only males fight fires; *fire fighter* includes males and females. (10s, 21g)

shaping An early part of the writing process in which writers consider ways to organize their material. Along with planning, shaping is sometimes called *prewriting*. (2n–2r)

shift Within a sentence, an unnecessary abrupt change in *person, number, subject, voice, tense, mood,* or *direct* or *indirect discourse*. (15a–15e)

simile A comparison, using *like* or *as,* of otherwise dissimilar things. (21d)

simple form The form of the verb that shows action, occurrence, or state of being taking place in the present. It is used in the singular for first and second person and in the plural for first, second, and third person. It is also the first principal part of a verb. The simple form is also known as the *dictionary form* or *base form*. (8b)

simple predicate See *predicate.*

simple sentence See *sentence types.*

simple subject See *subject.*

simple tenses The present, past, and future tenses, which divide time into present, past, and future. (8g, 8h)

singular See *number.*

slang A kind of colloquial language, it is coined words and new meanings for existing words, which quickly pass in and out of use; not appropriate for most academic writing. (21a)

slanted language Language that tries to manipulate the reader with distorted facts. (21h)

source-based writing See *research writing.*

sources Books, articles, print or Internet documents, other works, and persons providing credible information. In *research writing,* often called *outside sources.* (1f, Chapters 32 and 33)

spatial order An arrangement of information according to location in space; an organizing strategy for sentences, paragraphs, and longer pieces of writing. (4h)

specific noun A noun understood to be exactly and specifically referred to; uses the definite article *the.* (45a)

split infinitive One or more words coming between the two words of an infinitive. (14b)

squinting modifier A misplaced and unclear modifier that may describe the word that comes before it or the word that follows it. (14a)

standard English See *edited Canadian English.*

standard word order The most common order for words in English sentences: The subject comes before the predicate. Also see *inverted word order.* (19f, Chapter 46)

stereotype A kind of hasty generalization (a *logical fallacy*) in which a sweeping claim is made about all members of a particular ethnic, racial, religious, gender, age, or political group. (5j)

subject The word or group of words in a sentence that acts, is acted upon, or is described by the verb. A *simple subject* includes only the noun or pronoun. A *complete subject* includes the noun or pronoun and all its modifiers. A *compound subject* includes two or more nouns or pronouns and their modifiers. (7l)

subject complement A noun or adjective that follows a linking verb, renaming or describing the subject of the sentence; also called a *predicate nominative.* (7n)

subjective case The case of the noun or pronoun functioning as a subject. Also see *case, pronoun case.* (Chapter 9)

subject–verb agreement The required match between a subject and a verb in expressing number and person. (10b–10n)

subjunctive mood A verb mood that expresses wishes, recommendations, indirect requests, speculations, and conditional statements.

   ■ I wish you **were** here. (8l, 8m)

subordinate clause See *dependent clause.*

subordinating conjunction A conjunction that introduces an adverb clause and expresses a relationship between the idea in it and the idea in the independent clause. (7i, 13c.4, 17f, 17g)

subordination The use of grammatical structures to reflect the relative importance of ideas. A sentence with logically subordinated information expresses the most important information in the independent clause and less important information in dependent clauses or phrases. (17e–17i)

summary A brief version of the main message or central point of a passage or other discourse; a critical thinking activity preceding synthesis. (5e, 33j)

superlative form The form of an adjective or adverb that expresses comparison among three or more things: *bluest, least blue; most easily, least easily.* (11e)

syllogism The structure of a deductive argument expressed in two *premises* and a *conclusion.* The first premise is a generalized assumption or statement of fact. The second premise is a different assumption or statement of fact based on evidence. The conclusion is also a specific instance that follows logically from the premises. (5i)

synonym A word that is very close in meaning to another word: *cold* and *icy*. (21e)

synthesis A component of critical thinking in which material that has been summarized, analyzed, and interpreted is connected to what is already known (one's prior knowledge) or to what has been learned from other authorities. (5b, 5e)

tag question An inverted verb-pronoun combination added to the end of a sentence, creating a question that asks the audience to agree with the assertion in the first part of the sentence. A tag question is set off from the rest of the sentence with a comma:

- You know what a tag question is, **don't you?** (24g)

tense The time at which the action of the verb occurs: the present, the past, or the future. Also see *perfect tenses, simple tenses.* (8g–8k)

tense sequence In sentences that have more than one clause, the accurate matching of verbs to reflect logical time relationships. (8k)

thesis statement A statement of an essay's central theme that makes clear the main idea, the writer's purpose, the focus of the topic, and perhaps the organizational pattern. (2q)

third person See *person.*

tone The writer's attitude toward his or her material and reader, especially as reflected by word choice. (1e, 5c.2, 6j)

topic The subject of discourse. (2d)

topic sentence The sentence that expresses the main idea of a paragraph. A topic sentence may be implied or stated. (4e)

Toulmin model A model that defines the essential parts of an argument as the *claim* (or *main point*), the *support* (or *evidence*), and the *warrants* (or *assumptions behind the main point*). (6g)

transition The connection of one idea to another in discourse. Useful strategies within a paragraph for creating transitions include transitional expressions, parallelism, and the planned repetition of key terms and phrases. In a long piece of writing, a *transitional paragraph* is the bridge between discussion of two separate topics. Also see *critical response.* (4g.1, 4j)

transitional expressions Words and phrases that signal connections among ideas and create coherence. (4g.1)

transitive verb A verb that must be followed by a direct object. (8f)

understatement Figurative language in which the writer uses deliberate restraint for emphasis. (21d)

unity The clear and logical relationship between the main idea of a paragraph and the evidence supporting the main idea. (3c.4, 4d, 4e)

unstated assumptions Premises that are implied but not stated. (5i)

usage A customary way of using language. (Chapter 20)

valid Correctly and rationally derived; applied to a deductive argument whose conclusion follows logically from the premises. Validity applies to the structure of an argument, not its truth. (5i)

verb Any word that shows action or occurrence or describes a state of being. Verbs change form to convey time (*tense*), attitude (*mood*), and role of the subject (*voice*, either *active* or *passive*). Verbs occur in the predicate of a clause and can be in verb phrases, which may consist of a main verb, auxiliary verbs, and modifiers. Verbs can be described as *transitive* or *intransitive,* depending on whether they take a direct object. Also see *voice.* (Chapters 8 and 49)

verbal A verb part functioning as a noun, adjective, or adverb. Verbals include *infinitives, present participles* (functioning as adjectives), *gerunds* (present participles functioning as nouns), and *past participles.* (7e, Chapter 48)

verbal phrase A group of words that contains a verbal (an infinitive, participle, or gerund) and its modifiers. (7o)

verb phrase A main verb, any auxiliary verbs, and any modifiers. (7o)

verb tense Verbs show tense (time) by changing form. English has six verb tenses. (8g)

voice An attribute of verbs showing whether the subject acts (*active voice*) or is acted on (*passive voice*). (8n–8p)

warrants One of three key terms in the *Toulmin model* for argument; refers to implied or inferred assumptions. They are based on *authority, substance,* and *motivation.* (6g)

Web See *World Wide Web.*

webbing See *mapping.*

Web page On the Internet, a file of information. Such a file is not related in length to a printed page, as it may be a paragraph or many screens long. (37h)

wordiness An attribute of writing that is full of empty words and phrases that do not contribute to meaning. The opposite of *conciseness.* (16a)

World Wide Web The *Web,* a user-friendly computer network allowing access to information in the form of text, graphics, and sound on the Internet. (37f–37j)

working bibliography A preliminary list of useful sources in research writing. (31i)

Works Cited In MLA and COS documentation, the title of a list of all sources cited in a research paper or other written work. (34a, 34d)

writer's block The desire to start writing, but not doing so. (3b)

writing process Stages of writing in which a writer gathers and shapes ideas, organizes material, expresses those ideas in a rough draft, evaluates the draft and revises it, edits the writing for technical errors, and proofreads it for typographical accuracy and legibility. The stages often overlap; see *planning, shaping, drafting, revising, editing, proofreading.* (Chapters 1, 2, and 3)

writing situation The beginning of the writing process for each writing assignment as defined by four elements: topic, purpose, audience, special requirement. (2c)

Index

Colloquial language
  avoiding, 356
  defined, 326
Colons, 406–10
  with appositives, 407
  in Bible citations, 408
  in business writing, 408
  capitalization after, 407,
    441–42
  between independent
    clauses, 407–8, 409
  before lists, 406–7
  misuse of, 409
  quotation marks with, 424
  before quotations, 407
  summary of, 406
  with time of day, 408
  between titles and subtitles,
    408
Colour, in document design, 667,
  671
Columbia Online Style (COS)
  documentation style, 656–61
  humanities and scientific
    styles, 657, 661
  in-text citations, 657
  models, 661
  print publications, 657
  Works Cited lists, 659–61
Comma faults. *See* Comma
  splices
Commands
  as complete sentences, 256
  exclamation point with, 374
  as imperative sentences,
    168
  period with, 372
  for variety and emphasis,
    322
Commas, 377–99

with act and scene
  numbers, 394
in addresses, 393, 394
to clarify meaning, 395
with coordinate adjectives,
  385–86, 397
with coordinating
  conjunctions, 378–80,
  396
in correspondence, 393
with dates, 392, 394
with degrees, 393
with direct address, 390
with expressions of
  contrast, 389
with Imperial measures,
  394
with introductory clauses,
  phrases, and words,
  380–82
with items in series,
  382–84, 397
with *Jr., Sr.,* and the like,
  393
misuse of, 396–99
with names, 393
with nonrestrictive
  elements, 386–88
with numbers, 393–94
with page and line
  numbers, 394
with parentheses, 429–30
with parenthetical
  expressions, 389
with province names, 393
with quotation marks, 423
with quoted words, 390–91,
  398
separating elements, 398
serial, 382–84, 397

HOW TO FIND INFORMATION
IN THIS HANDBOOK

You can use your *Simon & Schuster Handbook for Writers* as a reference book, just as you use a dictionary or an encyclopedia. At each step, use one or more suggestions to find the information you want.

Step 1: Use lists to decide where to go.

- Scan the Overview of Contents (on inside front cover).
- Scan the Index at the back of the book for a detailed alphabetical list of all major and minor topics.
- Scan the Part Openers.

Step 2: Locate the number that leads to the information you seek.

- Find a chapter number.
- Find a number-letter combination for a section in a chapter and the question it asks.
- Find a box number.
- Find a page number.

Step 3: Check elements on each page, to confirm where you are in the book.

- Look for the shortened title at the top of each page (left page for chapter title and right page for section title).
- Look for a section's number-letter combination in white inside a green rectangle.
- Look for a box title and number.
- Look for a page number at the bottom of the page.

Step 4: Locate and read the information you need. Use special features, illustrated on the next page, to help you.

- Use cross-references to related key concepts.
- Find the definition for any word printed in small capital letters in the Terms Glossary starting on page 803.
- Use ⊚ **ALERTS** ⊚ and ⊕ **ESL NOTES** ⊕ for pointers about related matters of usage, grammar, punctuation, and writing.

ELEMENTS ON THE PAGES OF THIS HANDBOOK

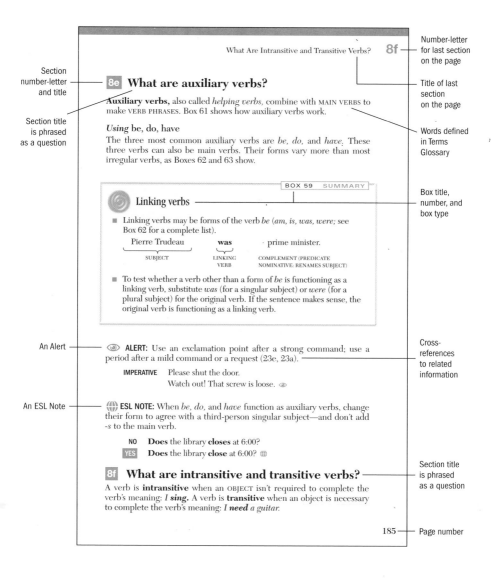

Number-letter for last section on the page

What Are Intransitive and Transitive Verbs? **8f**

Section number-letter and title

8e What are auxiliary verbs?

Title of last section on the page

Auxiliary verbs, also called *helping verbs,* combine with MAIN VERBS to make VERB PHRASES. Box 61 shows how auxiliary verbs work.

Section title is phrased as a question

Using be, do, have
The three most common auxiliary verbs are *be, do,* and *have.* These three verbs can also be main verbs. Their forms vary more than most irregular verbs, as Boxes 62 and 63 show.

Words defined in Terms Glossary

BOX 59   SUMMARY

Linking verbs

Box title, number, and box type

■ Linking verbs may be forms of the verb *be* (*am, is, was, were;* see Box 62 for a complete list).

Pierre Trudeau   **was**   · prime minister.

SUBJECT   LINKING VERB   COMPLEMENT (PREDICATE NOMINATIVE: RENAMES SUBJECT)

■ To test whether a verb other than a form of *be* is functioning as a linking verb, substitute *was* (for a singular subject) or *were* (for a plural subject) for the original verb. If the sentence makes sense, the original verb is functioning as a linking verb.

An Alert

👁 **ALERT:** Use an exclamation point after a strong command; use a period after a mild command or a request (23e, 23a).

IMPERATIVE   Please shut the door.
              Watch out! That screw is loose. 👁

Cross-references to related information

An ESL Note

🌐 **ESL NOTE:** When *be, do,* and *have* function as auxiliary verbs, change their form to agree with a third-person singular subject—and don't add *-s* to the main verb.

NO   **Does** the library **closes** at 6:00?
YES   **Does** the library **close** at 6:00? 🌐

8f What are intransitive and transitive verbs?

Section title is phrased as a question

A verb is **intransitive** when an OBJECT isn't required to complete the verb's meaning: *I sing.* A verb is **transitive** when an object is necessary to complete the verb's meaning: *I need a guitar.*

185